PALS
$1.70

D1648394

ENGLISH PLACE-NAME SOCIETY. VOLUME VIII

GENERAL EDITORS
A. MAWER *and* F. M. STENTON

THE
PLACE-NAMES OF DEVON

PART I

ENGLISH PLACE-NAME SOCIETY

The English Place-Name Society was founded in 1924 to carry out the survey of English place-names and to issue annual volumes to members who subscribe to the work of the Society. The Society has issued the following volumes:

The volumes for the following counties are in an advanced state of preparation: *Berkshire, Cheshire, the City of London.*

All communications with regard to the Society and membership should be addressed to:

THE HON. SECRETARY, English Place-Name Society, University College, Gower Street, London, W.C.1.

DA
645
. A4
1969
v. 8

THE
PLACE-NAMES OF DEVON

By

J. E. B. GOVER, A. MAWER *and*
F. M. STENTON

PART I

CAMBRIDGE
AT THE UNIVERSITY PRESS
1969

Published by the Syndics of the Cambridge University Press
Bentley House, 200 Euston Road, London, N.W.1
American Branch: 32 East 57th Street, New York, N.Y. 10022

Standard Book Number: 521 07158 5

First published 1931
Reissued 1969

First printed in Great Britain
at the University Press, Cambridge
Reprinted in Great Britain
by William Lewis (Printers) Ltd, Cardiff

PREFACE

THIS double volume upon the place-names of Devon owes its inception to Mr J. E. B. Gover and on his shoulders has fallen the main burden of its preparation. To him the volume owes ninety per cent. and more of the material drawn from printed and unprinted sources alike, and to him are due the identifications of the place-names found in that material with those to be found on the present-day O.S. maps. To him is also due the arrangement of all that material in the ordered topographical arrangement familiar to students of the earlier volumes of the Place-name Survey. The task of interpreting that material has been the joint work of Mr Gover and of the editors of the volumes of the Survey, working from the outset in close co-operation with one another.

Soon after Mr Gover started working, he found that Dr Bertil Blomé of Uppsala was working on the place-names of North Devon. When he first heard this he determined to confine himself to South Devon. He placed at Dr Blomé's disposal a considerable amount of material relating to North Devon, which he had found in unprinted Assize and Subsidy Rolls and had himself transcribed at the Public Record Office, and in exchange Dr Blomé placed at his disposal material for the county gathered from certain printed documents, viz. the Calendar of Close Rolls down to the year 1400 and the Calendar of Patent Rolls down to the year 1350. As the work developed it became clear that, for the purposes of the Place-name Survey, work based on any such artificial division of the county was unsatisfactory, and that Devon must be treated as a whole if it was to take its right place in the Survey of English place-names. Mr Gover, therefore, proceeded to supplement his earlier work on the county by an extensive use of other unprinted documents relating to the whole of the county, north and south alike, and made an independent examination of the printed documents named, since with fuller gazetteers, etc., at his disposal, a good deal of material, of which the significance was not previously apparent, now became of importance.

Dr Blomé's book on the *Place-Names of North Devon* was published at Uppsala in 1929 and has naturally been constantly before the authors in their treatment of the names contained in it. It has again and again been helpful to them in dealing with the etymology of difficult names. Wherever such an etymology has been accepted we have endeavoured to record our indebtedness. Blomé's name has not (for reasons of space) been mentioned where the etymologies are such as would have occurred independently to any skilled student of place-names. Where the authors differ from Blomé they have given reasoned grounds for that difference when their early evidence is the same as that used by him. Where, as is often the case, the fuller material at their command compels them to adopt a different interpretation from that given by Blomé, the new interpretation is given without any unneeded attempt on their part to controvert the old one. The part which the new material plays in this respect is interestingly illustrated in the very valuable review by Wallenberg of Blomé's book, which appeared in *Studia Neophilologica* (2, 84 ff.). Again and again Dr Wallenberg suggests a fresh interpretation of Blomé's material which is confirmed by new material now at our disposal. As might be expected with Dr Wallenberg, the number of cases where he suggests a fresh interpretation which is contradicted by the new material are far fewer in number, but there are some such[1].

As has always been the case with the volumes of the Survey, these have been prepared in close and constant consultation with those who live in the county itself and are fully conversant with its history, antiquity, local lore and topography. In Devon our chief channel of communication has been Mrs Rose-Troup, who throughout the preparation of the volumes has been untiring in her efforts to help us. She organised the Place-Name Section of the Devonshire Association as a means of roping in all those who could help us, she has herself answered or obtained answers to innumerable enquiries which we have addressed to her and has placed freely at our disposal her own gleanings from unpublished

---

[1] It may be noted that Dr Blomé omitted most of the names in his area which were to be found only on the 6″ O.S. maps, since these were not available to him during the greater part of the time occupied by his work. Also a certain number of other names, including those of the three parishes of Abbots Bickington, Calverleigh and Kennerleigh, do not appear in his book. The total number of names dealt with by him is about 1400, while the total number of names dealt with in the EPNS volumes (for the corresponding area) is about 3560.

material. To her Devon owes the discovery and we the use of two hitherto unknown Anglo-Saxon charters (*v. infra* 296 *n.*, 603) and, in particular, much new material relating to the history of Exeter and of East Devon. We have also had from her the benefit both at the typescript stage and at the printed proof stage of many criticisms and suggestions. We have not always been able to incorporate those criticisms and suggestions, and Mrs Rose-Troup must not be held in any sense responsible for the volumes as they now appear. We must, however, record our great indebtedness to her and say that the book would have been far fuller of errors alike of fact and interpretation than it now is, had it not been for her watchful care.

Next to Mrs Rose-Troup must be mentioned Mr J. J. Alexander, late headmaster of Tavistock Grammar School. Alike personally, by correspondence, and by criticism and correction of typescript and proof-sheets, he has done us invaluable service, and our volumes, especially in the Hundreds of Lifton, Tavistock, Roborough and Haytor, would be very different from what they now are had he not put his rich store of knowledge at our disposal.

To the late Lt.-Colonel Prowse our debt is a heavy one. His scrupulous accuracy and untiring devotion to scholarly detail made him an ideal helper in the early days of our work on the place-names of Devon. He compiled gazetteers (sheet by sheet and parish by parish) of all names on the 1″ and 6″ O.S. maps. To him we owed the use of the great index of names found in the volumes of the Devon Association (down to 1924), which he had compiled after many years' labour, and much topographical and historical information derived from note-books formerly in his possession and since lent to us.

Others we can but refer to in the alphabetical order of their names:

The Rev. H. G. Baker for extracting the Devon material from Feudal Aids.

Mr C. W. Bracken for the loan of a book of Plymouth Municipal Records and for much valuable topographical information for Plymouth and the adjacent parishes.

The Rev. E. S. Chalk for help with the Tiverton and Bradninch districts.

Mr R. Pearse Chope for much material from local unprinted records for the parish of Hartland and for topographical information and local pronunciations of many place-names in North Devon and particularly for those in the Hundred of Hartland.

Mr R. L. Clowes for permission to transcribe documents at the Duchy of Cornwall Office, London, and for facilitating the work done there.

Mr G. M. Doe for help with the Torrington district.

Mr Anton Fägersten for information about and forms for those Devon parishes formerly included in Dorset.

Mr C. H. Laycock for help with the Dartmoor district.

Miss Lega-Weekes for notes on the manorial history of certain places in the Hundred of Wonford and on certain Exeter street-names.

The Rev. G. H. Melhuish for local pronunciations and topographical notes on places in Ashwater and the adjacent parishes.

Mr B. W. Oliver for help with the Barnstaple district.

Mr H. Tapley-Soper for permission to inspect deeds and other documents at the Exeter City Public Library.

Major F. C. Tyler for completing a gazetteer of all names on the 6″ map for a considerable part of North Devon.

Mr H. R. Watkin for much valuable topographical information regarding places in Haytor and Teignbridge Hundreds and for many local pronunciations.

We are similarly indebted to the Rev. E. G. Cocks and the Rev. L. H. Fenn and several other rectors and vicars for valuable information about local pronunciations.

Thanks are due also to the Dean and Chapter of Exeter Cathedral for permission to transcribe forms from Court Rolls and Rentals in their possession and to the Rev. H. E. Bishop and Mr J. Packman for valuable help and suggestions offered to the transcriber at work there.

To Dr Ritter we are once again indebted for comments upon various difficult problems submitted to him for his consideration.

To Professor Max Förster, who has recently been working on Devon manumissions in the MSS of the Dean and Chapter of Exeter Cathedral, we are indebted for the collation and correction of certain place-name forms and also for his generosity in helping us with comments on certain difficult problems, especially those involving place-names of Celtic origin.

Finally under the head of help received from distinguished foreign students of our place-names we have once again to express our deep indebtedness to Professor Ekwall, who has most generously placed himself at our disposal at various stages in the preparation of the volumes. Our indebtedness to him is shown again and again by explicit mention of his name, but that represents only a small part of our general obligations to him. As the sheets were passing through the press he allowed us to see the proof-sheets of his own *Studies on English Place and Personal Names*. To it we owe many valuable suggestions, some of which we have been able to incorporate in the printed page as it stands; others have had to be relegated to the Addenda and Corrigenda.

We are once again indebted to our President, Professor Tait, for his kindness in reading the proofs and making certain suggestions with regard to historical matters.

To the officers of the Ordnance Survey and to the staff of the Cambridge University Press we are heavily indebted for the care with which the volumes and the accompanying maps have been prepared.

The volumes are a good deal larger than any hitherto produced by the Survey and the number of names treated is very large. The task of securing accuracy and uniformity has been heavier than usual. The editors are desirous to express their thanks to Miss A. M. Armstrong for all that she has done towards the fulfilment of that task.

A. M.
F. M. S.

Easter, 1931.

The preparation of these volumes, and, in particular, the collection of material from unprinted documents has been greatly facilitated by grants received from the British Academy. They are dedicated to the memory of

SIR ISRAEL GOLLANCZ

*the first Secretary of
the Academy*

To his watchful foresight the English Place-Name Society owes a debt which its founders can never forget.

CONTENTS

MAP

INTRODUCTION

THE exact date of the fixing of the boundary between Devon and Dorset and Somerset is not known. On the west the Tamar has always, at least since the time of Aethelstan[1], formed the boundary between Devon and Cornwall throughout its course, except at one point, where a finger of land consisting of the parishes of North Petherwin and Werrington projects several miles into Cornwall. It has been suggested[2] that the reason for the inclusion of this area in Devon is that these two parishes were granted to Tavistock Abbey at its foundation (c. 970), and that the abbot desired to bring the whole monastic endowment within the one county. Already in Domesday Book, these parishes were included in Devon.

On the east the forest of Exmoor in the north, and further south the Blackdown Hills and the old forest of Neroche separate Devon from Somerset. The short dividing line between Devon and Dorset is marked by no natural boundary.

The county is remarkably hilly, including hardly any level ground except for the alluvial tracts by the side of the larger rivers and estuaries. Much of it is very fertile, particularly the old red sandstone area and the South Hams district between the Plym and Dart rivers. The clay area in the north-west has a colder and less productive soil, but, to judge from the great number of settlements with names going back to OE times, it also must have proved attractive to the English settlers. Numerous prehistoric remains suggest that the huge granite mass of Dartmoor extending over nearly 100 square miles was at one time thickly populated. There is, however, no evidence that it was occupied during the Celtic period and it was probably equally unattractive to the English colonists.

The parishes of Devon, like those of Cornwall and West Somerset, consist of hamlets and scattered homesteads, the broken nature of the county being unfavourable to the development of the nucleated villages which Maitland[3] noted were the

---

[1] Crawf 7.   [2] DCo NQ 14, 273; 15, 270.
[3] *Domesday Book and Beyond* 15, cf. also *Antiquity*, 1, 448.

rule in the more open country of the English Midlands. As the overwhelming majority of the names in this county are of English origin, it is hard to believe that the settlements which they denote are, in any appreciable number, Celtic survivals.

Few questions in Early English history are more obscure than the chronology of the English occupation of what is now the county of Devon. The only direct information which we possess comes from three brief entries in the Old English Chronicle and an incidental passage in the eighth-century life of St Boniface (*v. infra* xvii). There is no evidence at all as to the conditions under which the eastern boundary of the shire was fixed, nor, indeed, as to the limits of the British kingdom of *Dumnonia* from which it takes its name[1]. Any attempt to reconstruct the early history of the shire must depend in the main on inference from materials which are singularly vague as to matters of fact.

The English occupation of Devon cannot have begun before the seventh century was well advanced. There are no heathen Saxon burial grounds within the county, nor have any references to Germanic heathenism been noted in its place-names. The local nomenclature of the county, as a whole, is obviously of a later character than that of any district with which the Survey has hitherto dealt. It includes no names ending in *-ingas*, and only one name which suggests derivation from an original ending in *-ingaham*. It contains an unusual number of names in which the first element is that of a person living in the eleventh century. Even among the names of places which were well established by

---

[1] The forms of the name found in the early historians and geographers are Δαμνόνιοι, Δουμνόνιοι (Ptolemy), *Dumnonii* (Solinus), *Damnonia* (Gildas). For further forms *v. s.n.* Exeter *infra* 20. We may also note Δαμνόνιον ἄκρον, probably the Lizard, in Ptolemy. The meaning of *Dumnon(ia)* was formerly thought to be 'deep valleys,' an etymology well suited to the character of the county, but depending entirely upon the modern Welsh form Dyfnaint, *naint* being the plural of Welsh *nant*, 'valley.' This Welsh spelling is certainly a piece of folk-etymology and no certain interpretation of the name can be offered, beyond suggesting that it contains the root *Dumno-*, found in other Old Celtic names such as *Dumnorix*. There was also a tribe called *Damnonii* in South-West Scotland considered by Watson (*History of the Celtic place-names of Scotland* 24) to be of the same origin.

The name of the old inhabitants of Devon is perhaps preserved in Denbury *infra* 523. This would seem to mean 'the burh of the men of Devon,' with reference to the large earthwork here, but the origin of the name and its connexion with that of the county are by no means clear. Possibly at some period in the Saxon advance this strongly fortified post held out for a long time against the invaders.

1086, a considerable number contain compound personal names of a type which is found for the most part in place-names of comparatively late origin (IPN 42), while the number of feminine personal names entering into the place-names of Devon is also suggestive of late settlement. It seems, in fact, that the settlement of the county was a very gradual process, spread over all the centuries between the seventh and the eleventh, and, indeed, continuing into medieval times.

Nevertheless, there can be no doubt that this settlement had gone far by the middle of the ninth century. If the names of the boundary-marks of the land by the river Creedy which Aethelheard gave to bishop Forthred in 739[1] could be regarded as original, they would prove that the Saxons had already carried through an intensive settlement of the surrounding country. But it is safest to regard these boundaries as a tenth-century addition to the text of an earlier charter. and, if this is correct, the first document which gives indisputable evidence for the character of the early local names of Devon will be the charter dated 847 by which king Aethelwulf 'booked' to himself twenty hides *on Homme*[2]. The area cannot be identified with precision but it certainly lay in the south of the county, and the large number of English names which occur in the boundaries prove a long-established occupation of this part of Devon. Earlier than this, a charter issued by King Egbert in 833[3] mentions incidentally that one of three daughters dividing their father's inheritance "withdrew into Domnonia and took her part there in the place called *Derentunehomm*," i.e. Dartington, a phrase which shows the Dart valley to have been in English occupation at least as early as the first part of Egbert's reign. For the north of the county there is less clear evidence, but Galford in Lew Trenchard where the men of Devon and of Cornwall fought probably in 825[4], though only some twelve miles from the Tamar valley, already bore an English name. The settlement which these names imply must have begun long before the end of the eighth century.

On the other hand, unless the chronology of the Old English Chronicle is wholly at fault, the West Saxons cannot have entered Devon for the purpose of settlement before the year 658. In

---

[1] Crawf 1 and 2.   [2] BCS 451.
[3] BCS 410.   [4] ASC *s.a.* 823.

that year, we are told, Cenwalh king of the West Saxons fought
with the Britons *æt Peonnum* and drove them in flight as far as
the Parret[1]. There is no reason to doubt that this battle was
fought in the immediate neighbourhood of Penselwood, on the
borders of Somerset and Wiltshire. The forest of Selwood was
the boundary between the eighth-century dioceses of Winchester
and Sherborne. It is highly probable that it had been the western
boundary of the original Wessex, and that the battle of 658 marks
the beginning of the seventh-century expansion which carried
the West Saxons over Somerset, and ultimately included Devon
within their kingdom. It is at any rate clear that the West Saxon
occupation of Devon must belong to a later time than this, and,
in fact, it is generally assumed that the effect of the battle of
Penselwood was to fix the boundary between Britons and Saxons
at the Parret, leaving the country between the river and the
Devon border to be conquered in the course of unrecorded
fighting in the future.

But this conclusion does not necessarily follow from the
language of the Chronicle. The annalist who recorded that
Cenwalh "drove the Britons in flight as far as the Parret" was
not recording the establishment of a boundary. He was making
a note of a great battle and a long pursuit—a pursuit which
extended over the twenty miles between Penselwood and the
river Parret. There is nothing in the annal to imply that the
Parret was the boundary of the territory which the West Saxons
won as a result of the battle. The limit to which a beaten enemy
is pursued is not necessarily the limit of the victors' advance in
force, and it is perfectly possible that as a result of this battle
the West Saxons moved westward at least as far as the hills along
which the boundary between Devon and Somerset now runs. In
the present state of our knowledge, 658 is the date which seems
most probable for the West Saxon occupation of the Vale of
Taunton and the whole country between the Parret and the
Blackdown Hills.

For more than twenty years there is no record of any fighting
between Britons and Saxons in the south-west. Then, under the
year 682, we are told that king Centwine "drove the Britons in
flight as far as the sea.[2]" A phrase like this leaves almost un-

[1] ASC *s.a.* 658.   [2] ASC *s.a.* 682.

limited room for speculation. The battle of which this is the record must have been fought far to the west of the Parret; it was almost certainly fought in Devon, and the configuration of the country suggests that it took place in the south of the county. Beyond this it is impossible to go, but fortunately we possess a piece of evidence, external to the Chronicle, which shows that the West Saxons had reached Exeter, if not by this very year 682, at any rate before the end of the decade. The first biographer of Wynfrith, better known as Boniface, the evangelist of Western Germany, states that Wynfrith, while still young, was placed with his father's consent in the monastery *quod priscorum nuncupatur vocabulo Adescancastre*, and committed to the charge of its abbot Wulfheard[1]. Whatever interpretation may be given to the annal for 682, this passage shows the West Saxons in possession of Exeter at a date which cannot well be later than 690. It gives ground, moreover, for thinking that they had reached the neighbourhood of the city some time previously, for its context suggests that the monastery to which Wynfrith was sent was not far from his father's home, and to some extent supports the late tradition that he was born at Crediton. However this may be, it seems certain that the English settlement of Devon, at least as far as the Exe valley, was accomplished well before the end of the seventh century.

The conquest of Western Devon belongs to a later period. At the close of the seventh century there was still a British kingdom of Dumnonia. Geraint, its king, was obviously an important person in his day. A famous letter sent to him by Aldhelm, abbot of Malmesbury[2], opens with the address *Domino gloriosissimo occidentalis regni sceptra gubernanti.... Geruntio regi simulque cunctis Dei sacerdotibus per Domnonia conversantibus*; and when all allowance has been made for Aldhelm's expansive style, it is clear that this 'western kingdom' was more than a remote and attenuated British survival. To Aldhelm, who was himself a member of the West Saxon royal house, it was evidently important to bring Geraint and the priests of his kingdom into conformity with continental ecclesiastical usage. We have no direct evidence as to the extent of this kingdom, nor as to the conditions under

---

[1] *Vita Sancti Bonifacii* MGH *Scriptores* ii, 335.
[2] Migne, *Patrologia* lxxxix, 87.

B

which it ceased to exist, but a suggestive entry in the Chronicle under the year 710 states that Ine king of the West Saxons and Nunna his kinsman fought in that year with Geraint king of the Britons[1]. The result of the fighting is not stated, but the association of Ine and Nunna king of the South Saxons shows that the battle was more than a local affair on the West Saxon border, and there seems no later evidence for the existence of an independent Dumnonian kingdom.

Twelve years later, according to an entry in the *Annales Cambriae (s.a. 722)*, a battle was fought at *Hehil apud Cornuenses* in which the Britons were victorious[2]. There is no mention of this event in the Anglo-Saxon Chronicle and the identity of *Hehil* is not certain. If, as has been suggested, it corresponds to the mouth of the Camel in Cornwall (earlier *Hayle, Heyle*, cf. Ekwall RN 192), we must assume that the English had advanced a considerable distance into Cornwall and had there met with a check severe enough to prevent any further progress. Since nearly all the place-names between Hayle and the Poundstock-North Petherwin line (*v. infra* xxi) are British, we must assume, if the battle was fought on the Cornish Hayle, that the Saxons abandoned the intervening country and withdrew to that line. However, there is a place called Hele in Jacobstow near Poundstock and it is just possible that we are to look here for the site of *Hehil* and not so far to the west as the Camel estuary. At any rate it is likely that the Tamar for the next hundred years formed the dividing line between Celt and Saxon, the English settlements to the west of the river dating from a time after the defeat of the combined British and Danish forces by Egbert at Hingston Down[3].

It would therefore seem that the Saxon occupation of Eastern Devon may have begun very soon after the year 658, that the Saxons reached Exeter before the last decade of the seventh century, and that the west and north of the county were opened to them by the battle of 711. In any case, it is clear that they did not reach any part of Devon until the first energy of their invasion had long since spent itself. Under these conditions it is natural to expect a strong British element in the place-names of the

---

[1] ASC *s.a.* 710.   [2] *Y Cymmrodor* 9, 160.
[3] ASC *s.a.* 835.

county and especially in those of the north and west. British
names are in fact to be found in every part of the county but the
proportion of such names does not appreciably increase as the
Cornish border is approached, and the total number of Celtic
names in the county, excluding river-names, is less than one per
cent. of the whole. In general the most remarkable fact brought
out by the present survey is the prevailingly English character
of the local nomenclature of Devon. The British element is much
more evident in the place-names of Dorset or Somerset than in
most parts of Devon. Allowance must, of course, be made for
deficiencies in our information, and for the possibility that in
some cases a Celtic name has been transformed by English
speakers into a pseudo-English form, but allowances of this kind
will not materially affect the impression produced by a survey
of the local nomenclature of the county as a whole. So far as it
goes, the evidence for the English character of this nomenclature
is remarkably consistent. The minor names recorded in Old
English land-books, of which a considerable number relate to
Devon, are no less English than are the names of villages and
hamlets which first appear in medieval Assize and Subsidy Rolls.
And even the local names of Dartmoor, obscure as many of them
are, have as a whole the English character which belongs to the
nomenclature of the county at large.

Some important conclusions are suggested by these facts. It
is clear that the Saxon conquest of Devon cannot be regarded
as the imposition of the rule of an alien minority upon a large
British population. The whole topographical vocabulary of the
region is English. In view of this fact, it is impossible to believe
that the Saxons who settled in Devon were outnumbered by its
indigenous inhabitants, and it becomes necessary to face the
question whether in the eastern half of the county any considerable number of Britons remained in occupation of the land under
its new lords. In this connexion, it is well to ask whether what
is now the county of Devon was supporting any large British
population as late as the second half of the seventh century, when
the Saxon conquest certainly began. It has recently been suggested from the archaeological standpoint[1] that "Devon was
thinly inhabited during the Romano-British period" and that a

---

[1] *Antiquity* 4, 265.

smaller proportion of place-names of Celtic origin should be expected in this county than in the adjacent Dorset. If, moreover, as is highly probable, the Breton kingdom of Domnonia was colonised in the sixth century by migrants from the insular Dumnonia, a large number of the Celtic inhabitants of Devon must have withdrawn from Britain a century and more before the Saxon penetration of the south-west. Every line of evidence, in fact, suggests that in the middle of the seventh century Devon was a sparsely settled Celtic kingdom, and that when once the resistance of its kings had been broken down no considerable native population remained to complicate the life of the new settlers. By the eleventh century that life had created a local nomenclature less varied, indeed, than that of the regions of the earliest English settlements, but having its own distinctive character and extending over every part of the county.

The nomenclature of North and South Devon is in many respects (v. infra 675–6) different. The entire absence of cott-names and the almost entire absence of worthy-names in the south and south-east of the county seems to point to a conquest and occupation of this area by a group of settlers distinct from those in the rest of the county, though not necessarily belonging to a different period. The nomenclature of North and North-west Devon and of North-east Cornwall strongly resembles that of West Somerset, while that of South or at least of South-east Devon has many points in common with that of Dorset. Topographical considerations could not account for the absence or presence of elements such as tun, cot(e) or worþig, and we must believe, therefore, that the north, west, and centre of Devon were occupied mainly by settlers advancing from Somerset, while the south and south-east of the county were reached by men from Dorset with different habits of place-nomenclature.

The rarity of British names in the county in general has already been commented upon (supra xviii–xix). It may further be noted that even among the river- and stream-names the English element is very much more noticeable than in Dorset, Somerset or Wiltshire, though it still remains true that most of the larger rivers bear pre-English names. On this point see further infra 1–18. It should be noted that the Tamar does not mark the boundary between the English and Celtic names as has sometimes been supposed. The parishes on the west side of the Tamar are nearly as English as those on the east side, except for the small area between the Ottery and the Inney, where Cornish place-names predominate right up to the Tamar itself. This area under the name of *Landwiþan* (now *Lawhitton*) was given to the Bishop of Sherborne by King Egbert[1]. If, as is possible, it had been an ecclesiastical estate before the conquest of Cornwall, it may be that the Celtic inhabitants were left undisturbed. Throughout South-east Cornwall English names occur in greater or smaller numbers, but in North-east Cornwall the boundary between English and British names is much more sharply defined, being roughly a line drawn from the end of the projecting finger of land noted above (*supra* xiii) to the sea at Poundstock, west of which English names are few, while east of it Celtic names are either rare or absent. The preponderance of English names on the Bodmin Moors is even more marked than the absence of British ones on Dartmoor.

The few surviving pre-English names rarely, as in Lancashire or Cumberland, fall into particular groups, such as might indicate the late survival of a British-speaking population. In the Hundred of Lifton we find six Celtic names, viz. Breazle, Carley, Dunterton, Kelly, Maindea and Trebick. Of these Carley, Dunterton and Kelly are near the Tamar, the two latter opposite Lawhitton (*v. supra*). The other three are some distance to the east but at no very great distance from each other. Wrixhill near Breazle may contain a British personal name as first element. Apart from this one group the British names are scattered over the county. In the north we find only Charles, Landkey and Trellick, while Countisbury preserves the name of an old British stronghold (*v. infra* 62). Trellick is the only certain British name in the strictest sense in the north-west, though Rosedown in the same parish may contain a Celtic first element[2]. Landkey is a considerable distance to the east. Charles is on the borders of Exmoor. If this place contains the Cornish word *lis*, *les*, 'court, palace,' as suggested *infra* 61, this now insignificant village may once have been a place of considerable importance,

---

[1] Crawf 7.
[2] The etymology of Clovelly is so doubtful that the name is best left out of consideration here.

for *lis* was used especially to designate the residence of a chieftain.

Moving eastwards we find in the centre of the county Crooke, Treable, Trusham, Morchard and Dunchideock. Of these Treable, Trusham and Dunchideock are at no great distance from one another and in the neighbourhood is Marshall, which may contain as first element a British personal name *Moroc*. East of the Exe we have Aunk, Crooke, Duvale, Yawl, Pinn and possibly Poltimore, for Dowrish, Hemyock and Whimple are almost certainly stream-names and need not be taken into account in this connexion. In South and South-west Devon British names are of even rarer occurrence. The only certain example is Penquit in Ermington *infra* 272. It is noteworthy as being a distinctly Cornish form without palatalisation of the *c* and this may indicate a late survival of British-speaking people near here in spite of the absence of other Celtic names in the immediate neighbourhood. Elsewhere in this part we find only Camel's Head, which may possibly contain a stream-name, and the doubtful example of Crowdy in Harberton *infra* 325[1].

Turning to British personal names as found in place-names we find that these are equally rare. This is to be expected, for it is not likely that many British landowners would be left in undisputed possession of their estates. The thoroughness of the English conquest of the south-west may be realised from the fact that even in Cornwall, not excluding the extreme west, nearly all the manors were held in 1066 by men bearing English names. In Devon only some ten certain examples of British personal names as the first elements in place-names have been noted.

The rarity of place-names in *Wal-*, containing OE *Weala*, gen. pl. of *Wealh*, 'stranger, serf, Briton,' is a further interesting

---

[1] A complete list of the Celtic names in the county will be found *infra* 674. It will be seen that among them there are but few compounds of the 'Tre, Pol and Pen' type, so common in Cornwall. The second of these elements is, in fact, not found at all. Only three compounds with *Tre-* (an element which occurs over a thousand times in Cornwall) have been noted. *Pen-* occurs in Penquit and in Penrose, but the latter is geographically in Cornwall since it is situated to the west of the Tamar in North Petherwin. Most other Celtic elements occur but once or twice in Devon names. Further, most of the Celtic names are of a late type, with the defining element last, as in modern Cornish, Welsh and Breton names. Morchard *infra* 380, 408 is an important exception, being a more ancient form of the compound found in Cutmeer (Co) and Coedmawr (Wales).

feature in Devon names. The only certain examples are Walla Brook, Walland, Wallover in Challacombe, the lost *Walford* in Plympton and Walreddon. Wallover in Buckfastleigh is a doubtful case. All these names occur in districts where a Celtic population might have survived late. None except Wallover in Challacombe, which is on the borders of Exmoor, belong to the east of the county. The most interesting example is Walreddon in Whitchurch, only a few miles from the Cornish border. If the explanation given *infra* 248 is correct, there may have existed here a small community of Britons living independently in a free condition. Of the remaining names Walla Brook is on Dartmoor and the name might have reference to Britons who had found their way to this inhospitable district under pressure of the invading Saxons. The two Wallovers, Walland, and *Walford* may have been places where Britons had survived as serfs.

Although few wholly Celtic place-names survive, there are a fairly large number of hybrid compounds consisting of a British place-name to which an OE terminal has been added, e.g. Countisbury, Kentisbury, Mambury, Membury, Crackaway. It is to be noted that most of the examples quoted are compounded with burh and it may be that the places in question were ancient strongholds which successfully resisted the Saxon advance for a sufficiently long period for their native names to become known to the invaders. In a name like Membury the English form may possibly have replaced a British *Caer Maen* or the like. Another fairly common type of hybrid name is represented by place-names such as Mainstone (?), Breadon, Penhill, Rosedown, etc., where we have place-names consisting of two elements of similar or nearly similar meaning, the first British and the second English. Such compounds as these, however, are to be found throughout the country (cf. PN Bk 118 *s.n.* Brill), and no special inference can be drawn from their presence. There is no reason to think that they are more numerous in Devon than elsewhere in proportion to the whole number of names in the county. Examples of an old English terminal having been added to an already existing British compound are of much rarer occurrence. The two chief examples, Dunterton and Breazle, have already been noted.

A few words may here be added on the elements 'combe' and

'tor,' so common in the place-names of the county. Their frequency has often been used by historians as proof of the strong Celtic influence on the nomenclature of the county. There is no real proof, however, that either word is of British origin. The place-names in 'combe' and 'tor' in Cornwall are almost all to be found in the east of the county, and in every case either uncompounded or with an English first element. In true Cornish names they are replaced by *nant* (*nans*), 'valley,' and *carn* or *bre*, 'cairn, rock-pile, hill.' In Brittany neither element is found. In Wales names in *cwm* are, of course, common, but in many instances they are fairly modern formations, while 'tor' names are almost unknown. The only example which has been noted is Tarr in Pembrokeshire, *La Torre* 1325 Ipm, *Torre* 1349 Ipm, and, as this is in the English part of that county, it probably belongs to the group of place-names introduced by the Flemish settlers of the twelfth century.

If the two words 'combe' and 'tor' were borrowed from British sources, they must have been admitted into the language at a very early date, long prior to the conquest of Devon, for both elements occur in other counties. Two examples of 'tor' were noted in Sussex (PN Sx 549) and intensive study may bring to light other examples in the south and south-east of England. The great frequency of 'combe' in Devon and to a less extent in Somerset and Dorset is certainly connected with the innumerable deep valleys in those counties, and similarly the common use of 'tor' in Devon (evidenced at least as early as 956) may have been suggested by the peculiar shape of the Dartmoor heights, each with its crowning rock-pile. The word was probably carried into Cornwall by the English but was never adopted by the Cornish-speaking folk in the west of that county. 'Combe' may have been similarly adopted. It may be noted that it is of somewhat rare occurrence in the land boundaries of those OE charters which relate to Devon.

Passing on to the English element we find here that there are comparatively few names of individual interest. The various second elements with their distribution and meaning will be dealt with in detail *infra* 657 ff. Devon was conquered late and there are not in this county, as there were in Sussex, examples of newly discovered elements of an archaic type, though a few, such as *torr*, *stūt*, *holca* and *spræg* have been rarely met with elsewhere. Certain common words such as hlæw (hlaw), hyrst, falod and eg are absent or nearly absent from the nomenclature of the county. Topographical reasons would in part at least account for the absence of eg. As regards hyrst we must assume that this element had become obsolete as an independent word at an early date in this part of England, for the county is well wooded and the alternative wudu is common, while the frequency of bearu is one of the distinctive features of the nomenclature of the county. We have evidence (*v. infra* 674–87) that certain elements were still in living use at the time of the Conquest. One might mention in particular tun, worþig, leah, cumb, torr, cot(e), all of which were in use to form new compounds in 1086 and some at a much later date. For names in 'hayes,' 'hayne,' see *infra* 129.

A name of particular interest is Galmpton (*infra* 304). This compound is found in various modern forms, four times in Devon and twice in Somerset, but has not hitherto been noted in any other county. The meaning would appear to be 'farm of the *gafol* men,' i.e. men distinguished from their neighbours by the payment of rent, and the fact that the compound is confined to Devon and Somerset suggests that there may have existed in these two counties some particular tenurial custom much rarer in the rest of the country. For such strictly local distribution we may compare the place-name Sevenhampton (PN Wo 35) which is only to be found in certain areas, chiefly in the west and south-west.

The OE personal name element in Devon place-names does not call for much comment. It might have been suspected that names of the dithematic type would be specially common in this part of England. Such, however, is not the case. Simple and compound names occur in about the same proportion as elsewhere and the distribution throughout the county is also fairly regular. An interesting point is the great frequency of certain individual names, of which *Babba*, *Bic(c)a*, *Cada*, *Cola* and *Dod(d)a* are perhaps the best examples. The number of compounds with *Bic(c)a* is remarkable but may be due in part at least to a local popularity of the name, which is also very common in Somerset place-names. Moreover, some compound names are of similarly frequent occurrence; *Lēofwine*, for example, is found five times and *Dunstān* four times. The same repetition of individual personal names is to be noted in Cornwall. There we have the Old British personal name *Gwrgi* (*Wurci*) compounded seven times with 'Tre-,' three times with 'Bod-' and once with 'Car-[1],' while *Dewi* (David) occurs six times in combination with 'Tre[2].' When one takes into account the very large number of ancient place-names in Cornwall, Devon and Somerset, the numbers compounded with the same personal name cannot be regarded as unduly large.

Of feminine personal names recorded as the first element of Devon place-names some fifteen have been noted, the proportion being hardly larger than in other counties. It is interesting to find that two of these are mentioned in Domesday as the holders of the manors of Goodcott (*Godgiefu*) and Lovacott (*Lufu*) respectively (TRE).

Scandinavian influence on the place-names of the county is extremely slight[3]. Lundy Island bears a Norse name but no certain example of a Scandinavian name in the strictest sense can be found on the mainland[4]. This is in striking contrast to the Welsh counties of Pembrokeshire and Glamorgan on the opposite side of the Channel. There not only do nearly all the islands off the coast bear Norse names (e.g. Skokholm, Ramsey, Grassholm) but there is also in such names as Swansea, Fishguard, Haverford, Freystrop, Colby, etc., evidence of a strong Scandinavian settlement on the mainland[5]. That there was no corresponding invasion of Devon or of Cornwall, where, except for the doubtful example of Helford, there is also a complete absence of Scandinavian names, is probably due to the inhospitable character of the coast.

We have in Devon a few examples of Anglo-Scandinavian

[1] The modern form is *-worgey, -worgie*.
[2] Modern forms *Trethewey, Trethevy*.
[3] The initial *sk-* of certain Devon names is not due to Scandinavian influence, *v. infra* xxxv.
[4] Possible examples are, however, the two places called Hope (*infra* 308, 519), both being on the coast in sheltered bays. The ON *hóp*, 'inlet, bay,' occurs as the second element of Lydstep (Pembr), olim *Ludeshop*. It may be noted also that the common Devon suffix *-beer, -bear* has, by some early writers, been derived from the ON *byr, boer* (Sw, D, *by*), 'farm, village,' but there is no justification for this derivation. Apart from all other considerations final inflexional *r* is not thus retained in England.
[5] Cf. *Archaeologia Cambrensis*, Ser. 6, vol. 20, 51 ff.; IPN 80.

personal names, but most of these are probably due to settlers of the time of Canute or later, when Scandinavian names were popular. At any rate it is certain that none date back to the Viking raids of the eighth and ninth centuries. There is one interesting group of place-names with Anglo-Scandinavian personal names as first elements. In the South Hams we find the place-names Grimston, Oldstone and Gripstone all in the immediate neighbourhood of each other. This may be a mere chance, but it is at least possible that these names record a small Scandinavian settlement made during the raids of the early eleventh century. It is noteworthy, however, that no Scandinavian names can be traced in the immediate neighbourhood of those parts which we know to have been ravaged, such as the neighbourhood of Exeter and around the Tamar and Taw estuaries[1].

Norman-French and Feudal influence has left a considerable mark on the place-names of Devon, though place-names of French origin are few. We may note Meshaw *infra* 382, which seems to be a compound of OFr *mal* and *essart*, 'poor clearing,' an uncomplimentary nickname, and Bever *infra* 633 which is near to Newenham Abbey and may have been named by French-speaking inmates of that house. The names Justment, Viza, Purps, Sart, Strayer, which are fairly common, are derived from common legal terms and may have come into existence at any period after the Norman settlement. Nevertheless with the exception of Sart no other examples of these words have been noted in the place-names of other counties of which the survey has been completed or is in course of preparation. The modern *Justment* for *agist(e)ment* is probably due to the initial *a* having been understood as the indefinite article, showing that the term was in popular use, and *sart* for *assart* is perhaps to be explained in the same way.

When we come to consider names of the Feudal type a distinction may be made between those names in which a former owner's name has been added as a separate word, as in Churston Ferrers, Stoke Rivers, etc., and those cases in which it is prefixed as in Rose Ash, Spence Combe, and the like. In the latter the union is much less artificial and the names are felt to be

---

[1] ASC *s.a.* 997 and 1001.

genuine compounds somewhat resembling the type discussed *infra*.

Devon like Dorset and Somerset is remarkable for the very large number of cases in which the name of a medieval holder has been added to an earlier place-name. In IPN 127 it is suggested that one reason for this might be the need of distinguishing the many places of the same name such as Stoke, Combe, Compton, etc., but there are two facts which suggest that this is not necessarily the case. One is that the manorial addition is often added to place-names of which only one example exists in the county, as in Churston Ferrers, and in many cases such as Feniton Malherbe, Knowston Beaupel, the feudal addition has not proved permanent. In the second place, names of this type are almost unknown in Cornwall, where the chances of confusion between names identical in form were almost as great as in Devon.

A special point of interest in the history of the county is the unusually large number of place-names of post-Conquest origin, consisting of an early or late ME personal name or surname compounded with a second element, usually tun[1]. Such compounds have been noted in larger or smaller numbers in all the south-western counties but only in Dorset does the proportion of such names approach that of Devon. The majority of these names probably came into being in the twelfth or thirteenth centuries, but some, such as Murchington, Chubston, *infra* 453, 239, appear to belong to a considerably later date. One cannot always be certain whether these names were given to new holdings carved out of larger estates, or whether they may sometimes have replaced earlier lost place-names, possibly of Celtic origin. It is at any rate certain that some of them arose owing to the need for distinguishing manors originally known simply by the name of the river or stream on the banks of which they stood. An example of this type is Dotton in Colaton *infra* 587, which represents the manor of *Otrit* (from the Otter river) held by one *Dodo* TRE. So also Waringstone in Awliscombe *infra* 609, represents the manor of *Otri* held by *Warin* TRE. This may account in part for the rarity in Devon (with the remarkable exception of Clyst)

---

[1] For a complete list *v. infra* 688.

of strings of parishes deriving their names from the rivers on which they stand, such as we find in the Dorset Tarrants and Winterbornes.

These late compounds are fairly evenly distributed over the county but there is one remarkable cluster to be noted in Witheridge Hundred, where we find Drewstone, Grilstone, Johnstone and Rawstone all in the parish of Bishop's Nympton. These places do not lie along the same stream, but the parish was once well wooded, and these new settlements may represent fresh clearings or intakes from the forest.

The personal names found in these late compounds are as a rule Norman-French or Continental in origin, as in Corstone, Champson, Lovistone, Jurston, Rapson and Rabscott. Less frequent are ordinary ME surnames as in Hearson, Luxton, Brousentor (*Brounstountor*). As one might expect, the former are usually, though not invariably, found in places which became manors, while the latter are in general compounded with names of ordinary tenements or small holdings. Many names in the former group seem to be those of sub-tenancies created out of larger manors.

Finally mention must be made of a group of names peculiar to Devon and the adjacent part of Dorset and Somerset which consist of a personal name and the word *hay, hayes* or *hayne* (v. infra 129). In these names, which are rarely if ever those of manors, *hay*, originally answering to the OE (ge)hæg, 'enclosure,' probably came to have little more than the sense of 'farm' or 'holding,' so that Palmerhayes and Bennettshayes would be the equivalent of Palmer's (Farm) and Bennett's (Farm) in other parts of England. In the same area *hayes* or *hayne* is also added frequently to monosyllabic place-names such as Wood, Coombe, Ford, with little if any change of meaning. This type of name may in some instances undergo as thorough a levelling down as the earliest types of place-name, so that in such names as Pacehayne, Mountshayne, Cottarson, Tolcis, the ultimate origin is completely disguised.

A few words may be added on the material from which the early forms of the place-names which follow have been collected. The OE charters relating to Devon, though fairly numerous, cover only a small part of this vast county, and that chiefly in the south and the south-east[1]. The greater number are fortunately originals and the muniments of the Dean and Chapter of Exeter Cathedral supplied most of them. Of the remainder the majority are, for place-name purposes, satisfactory, only the Ipplepen and Littleham charters showing in their land boundaries the work of a ME scribe.

Old English entries in the Leofric Missal, though of late eleventh-century date, provide excellent spellings of names for which we should otherwise have to rely solely upon DB or later forms. Shebbear *infra* 107 is a case in point. Of later records Assize Rolls are more important in Devon, even than elsewhere, owing to the rarity of twelfth- and early thirteenth-century charters relating to this county. The number of surviving cartularies is not large, and comparatively little has been obtained from these sources. It is unfortunate that the Tavistock cartulary is lost, and that only a fragment survives of the cartulary of Buckfast, a house founded in the late twelfth century. The cartularies of Torre, Canonsleigh and St Nicholas Exeter are well preserved, but none of these houses possessed very extensive properties. Much trouble has been taken in the endeavour to search out records for Dartmoor and the neighbourhood owing to the general interest of this area. Valuable material has been discovered at the Duchy of Cornwall Office and also in the excellent series of Court Rolls and Ministers Accounts at the Public Record Office. But for many of the interesting names of natural features on 'the Moor,' medieval forms are late or wanting, and this applies specially to places outside the royal 'Forest.'

The Domesday forms are on the whole much less corrupt than is the case for Sussex and some other counties with which the Survey has dealt. We have, moreover, for Devon the valuable Exon Domesday which serves as a check upon the forms supplied by the Exchequer Domesday. The identification of the Devon places mentioned in the Survey is not always an easy task owing to the fact that there are so many manors in the county bearing the same name, and there is no grouping of manors under their Hundreds. The identifications made by Reichel in the VCH

---

[1] An attempt has been made to trace the bounds of these charters in notes appended to the parishes with which they are chiefly concerned.

have been accepted in most cases, except on rare occasions when the evidence of later forms has shown them to be improbable.

For a good many names, in particular for those of small farms and tenements, the material is scanty or late. In most cases of this kind it has seemed best to refrain from suggesting any etymology on the basis of late forms alone. The early spellings of such names as Easton in Cheriton, Sutton in Halberton, Sheepsbyre, Sheepstor, Great Tree, Clyst William, show that here as elsewhere etymologies propounded on the basis of the modern form alone are often worse than useless. In all such cases it has, therefore, been considered best to avoid any comment or comparison, and to give merely the early spelling without any attempt at explanation. It may be added that even an etymology based on thirteenth- or fourteenth-century forms cannot always be regarded as certain. Without the DB spelling, for example, the interpretations of Arlington, Worlington, and Werrington would hardly have been decisive. In a few cases names may have already been altered from their original form before the Conquest. It is possible that this process may have occasionally included the changing by folk-etymology of earlier Celtic names into a new and more intelligible form (*v. supra* xix). Folk-etymology has certainly been at work in more modern times. One might mention as cases in point Sheepstor, Sheepsbyre, Eagle Down, Holy Street, Great Tree, Rose Ash, Field Irish, Camel's Head and others. A good many of these are single farms or homesteads where the spelling of the name would depend largely on the taste and fancy of the owner. To this class belong also certain 'phonetically spelt' names such as Thornery, Caute, Lowery, Growen, Villavin and the quaint Coppa Dolla. In other cases the reverse is the case and a spelling entirely incorrect, alike historically and phonetically, has replaced the correct local development on the modern map. Cawsand *infra* 448, may be noted as an example of this.

NOTES ON THE DIALECT OF DEVON AS ILLUSTRATED BY ITS PLACE-NAMES

OE *æ* appears in ME as *a* and in Modern English as [æ] in almost all *Ash*-names as well as in many others, e.g. *Blatchborough*, *Bratton*, though occasionally ME spellings with *e* are found. Rarely we have lengthening of the vowel as in *Arscott*, *Martinhoe*, *Parford*, and in one case, viz. *Speccott*, we have ME and Modern English *e*-forms.

OE *ā* before *w* shows a curious history in Devon. In *Rew* we have a descendant of OE *rǣw*, an unexplained variant of the more common *rāw*. More interesting is the series of names containing OE *crāwe*, 'crow,' which in ME often show spellings *crewe* and the like, side by side with *crawe*, and give modern English forms in *Cray-*, *Cre-*, *Crea-*, *Cree-*, *Crey-*, as in *Craythorne*, *Crealake*, *Crebar*, *Creely*. So similarly with *Peamore*. The line of phonological development is not clear.

OE *ĕa* preserves its diphthongal character in ME later than elsewhere in England, e.g. *Heanton* is frequently spelled *Heanton*, *Hyanton*, *Heyanton*, *Heaunton*, in the thirteenth and fourteenth centuries. Similarly we have *Neatteton* for Netton, *Pearecombe* and *Piarecombe* for Parracombe, *Beasselegh* for Besley, *Trendelbiare* for Trundlebeer and *Vialepitt* for Fallapitt, all from thirteenth- and fourteenth-century documents.

Initial *ĕa* becomes a rising diphthong in ME and Modern English, with initial [j]. The commonest examples are those with *eald* as a first element, e.g. *Yalland*, *Yelland*, *Yoldon*, *Yollacombe*, with ME forms *Yalde-*, *Yealle-*, *Yolde-*, *Yolle-*. We may note also the numerous *Yeo* river-names, besides *Yarner* and *Yarnscombe*.

ēa sometimes becomes *eo* as in *Yeo* and various compounds of *Yeo*.

OE *ĕo* commonly becomes *u* (with occasional variant *o*) in ME. There are comparatively few ME forms in *e*. The *u*-form is fairly often preserved in the modern English name as in *Durdon*, *Muze*, *Pruston* with OE *ēo*, *Buscombe*, *Chorland*, *Sowell* with OE *ĕo*, but in many names the StEng development has taken place, especially where the element is familiar in ordinary speech, as in *Prestacott*, *Hartwell*, *Charlacott*.

c

OE *ī* remains unchanged in the Devon development of *wic* to *week*. So also ME *ī* remains in *Weach* from OE *wice*.

OE *ie* before l+consonant developed regularly to ME [*i*], and spellings with *i* are common from DB onwards, the spellings in ME often having *y*. The *i* is sometimes maintained until the present day, as in *Halwill, Holwill, Will, Wiltown*, but ultimately the StEng form *well* usually replaced it. Apart from these words containing OE **wielle**, we may note OE *Ielf-* for *Ælf-* in *Elmscott* and *Ilfracombe* and possibly in *Ilsington* (cf. Ekwall, *Contribution to the History of OE Dialects* 42 ff.).

OE *ie* in other positions, and occasionally before l+consonant appears as *u, o, a,* in ME. In Modern English it sometimes keeps the south-west dialectal form, as in *Dornaford, Dulford*. More commonly it has been influenced by StEng, as in *Bideford, Birchen, Tytherleigh, Yard*.

ME *ŏ* is commonly unrounded to [a]. The process would seem to belong to the early Modern English period, for no spellings with *a* are found in ME documents. The process is specially common before dentals, as in *Battisford, Dadworthy, Darracott* (earlier *Dodecote*), *Fatherford, Sha(f)tsborough, Statfold*, and labials, as in *Abham, Caffins Heanton, Labdon* and *Rapson*.

Further examples of the **unrounding and fronting of OE *ŭ* to *ĭ*** (already noted in PN Wo xxviii) are to be found in Devon. This is not a dialectal change, but a general sound-development not hitherto noted apart from p.n.'s. It is found before and between dentals and (occasionally) before labials, as in *Bibbear, Didworthy, Dinworthy, Sitcott, Sittycleave* and *Tythecott*.

OE *ȳ* appears in ME most commonly as *i*, occasionally as *e*, and fairly frequently as *u* or *o*. In Modern English the *i* form has almost always prevailed. The only common exception is that OE **hyll** appears seven times as *Rull* on the modern map.

OE **ceald** and **cealf** alike develop modern forms with initial *ch*, as in *Challacombe, Chelfham, Cholash*. There is one exception, viz. *Coldacott*, in which the StEng form has prevailed.

OE **f** (pronounced [v] initially and medially alike) **retains the old voiced pronunciation**, but the *f* spelling frequently remains throughout the ME period, as in *Bradavin, Varracombe,*

Venn, Voaden, Volehouse. This **v** develops to **w** in a few names as in *Coarsewell, Gorwyn, Verwill, Withywind*. The reverse **development of medial** *w* **to** *v* is illustrated in the history of *Belliver, Cadover, Lifton, Meavy, Woodville* (see further Ekwall, RN 282 *s.n.* Meavy). Names like *Cadover* so closely resemble those names in *ford* which show the characteristic Devon pronunciation of final *-ford* as *-ver* (e.g. *Fullaford*, pronounced *Follaver*), that they often appear nowadays with final *-ford*, as in *Honeyford, Tottiford*. There is a curious **development of** final *w* to *v* in *Reeve* and in some late spellings of *Shaugh*, and a further example is to be found in *Shave* Cross (Do), earlier *atte Shawe* (1333 *SR*). Initial **w** becomes **v** in *Vellacott*, and **f** in *Flankwell*.

Initial **w is often lost before a back vowel**, a common dialectal change, as in *Huccaby, Odle, Oatnell*.

OE initial *s* (pronounced [z]) retains the old voiced pronunciation in a few names like *Zeal, Zeaston*, but is always written with an *s* in ME.

OE initial *sc* frequently develops to Modern English [sk]. This is a characteristic Devon feature. It is found whatever the following vowel or consonant may be, as in *Landskerry, Scarhill, Skillaton, Score, Scruell*, and is evenly distributed over the county. The distribution of the names showing this development is such as to make it impossible to suggest that it is due to Scandinavian influence, which might perhaps be suspected in some of the coastal districts. The only example of this development at present noted outside the county is *Skilgate* (So). All the examples of initial *sk* that have been noted are in names of English origin, but it may be observed that initial *sk* is a sound which is always preserved in Cornish and Breton.

ME initial *thr* commonly becomes Modern English *dr* in Devon dialect (cf. Wright, § EDD 313), and this change is illustrated in *Drupe, Drewston* and *Dringwell*. The forms of certain Devon place-names suggest that **interchange of** *d* **and** *th* (or *th* **and** *d*) is a common phenomenon in other positions also. Cf. *Doggaport, Dorsely* and *Tythecott infra* 95, 325, 89.

OE *æt* **coalesces freely with the following definite article** in the dative feminine form *þære* in its ME form *at there*, developing either to *atte* with *r* prefixed to the following word, or to *at* with *tere* (commonly reduced to *tre*) similarly prefixed. The first type, illustrated in the common Devon *Rill* and *Rull* (from hyll), and in *Rashleigh* (for *Ashleigh*), is familiar in other parts of England. The second type, illustrated in *Terleigh*, *Traymill*, *Tredown*, *Trehill*, has not been noted elsewhere, except in the somewhat similar Bedfordshire *Thurleigh* (*v.* PN BedsHu 47 and Addenda li *infra*).

The final *e* (or *a*) of the OE dative singular inflexion is commonly preserved in Devon, both in ME and in Modern English. Cf. *Beara*, *Fludda*, *Forda*, *Wooda*, etc. The inflexional syllable is often spelled -*er* in Modern English, e.g. *Braunder*, *Forder*, or -*or* as in *Tutchenor*. In the ME forms we have *e* or, less commonly, *a*, e.g. *Forda*, (Walter de) *la Pynda*.

Final or medial inflexional *a* sometimes gives ME forms in *ia*, *ya*, *ye*, as in the pers. name *Lovya*, *Lovye*, from OE *Lufa* (*v. s.n. Lovaton infra* 230), and in the form *Piliaknolle* (1333) for *Pennicknold infra* 108. See also forms, and in some cases pers. names, under *Skillaton*, *Scorriton*, *Gitcombe*, *Capton infra* 67, 294, 320, 322.

A medial inflexional syllable usually survives in Devon and is sometimes inserted with no warrant. Examples are as follows: (1) adjectival inflexions: *Fullabrook*, *Grenofen*, *Horralake*, *Langaford*, *Narracott*, *Rightadown*, *Shortacombe*, *Southerley*, (2) genitival plurals: *Knightacott*, *Litchadon*, *Priestaford*, *Rookabeare*, *Yarnacombe*, (3) weak genitive singular: *Babbacombe*, *Baccamoor*, *Brightlycott*, *Vaddicott*, (4) with no warrant: *Downacarey*. These are frequently spelt in ME with *a* rather than the *e* commonly found in other ME dialects.

Weak noun-inflexional forms are very common in Devon place-names, as in *Smemington* and *Smynacott infra* 121, 389, numerous Exeter street-names, and a large number of names like *Buskin*, *Fursdon*, *Hayne*, *Pitton* and *Withen*, in which it is clear we have the weak nominative plural rather than the strong dative plural which has commonly been assumed in explanation of them (cf. *infra* 130).

The weak adjectival inflexion is found in numerous examples of *Heanton* and in three *Newnhams*. Some of the earlier forms of the *Newtons* also show an *n*.

NOTE. One interesting feature of Devon place-nomenclature is the abundance of names formed with a prefixed prepositional phrase. So far, no parallel to these names has been noted elsewhere. The most obvious examples are the numerous cases in which the first element is OE *begeondan*, as in *Indio* from *begeondan ēa*, 'on the far side of the river.' In the modern form the unstressed *be-* has always disappeared, presumably because it was unconsciously treated as a reduced form of *by*, and not as forming part of the place-name itself. Another clear set are those formed with OE *beniþan*, 'below,' the best example being *Neadon* in Manaton which is *Beneadone* as early as DB, and is clearly a case in point, since it appears later as *Bynythedon*; so also *Nethercleave* in Chittlehampton, earlier *Bynytheclyve*. Further examples will be found under **behindan** and **betweonan** in the list of elements *infra* 658. In all alike the *be-* has disappeared from the modern form. These names throw new light on a large group of names which have hitherto been interpreted in a somewhat different way. Names like *Eastwood*, *Northway*, have commonly been interpreted as 'east wood,' 'north way.' The Devon evidence suggests beyond any possibility of ambiguity that in many of these names we have a short form of old compounds *bi eastan wuda*, *bi norþan wege*, 'to the east of the wood,' 'to the north of the way.' Thus we find actual places called *Bysouthebrok*, *Bysouthewhimpel*, in ME documents, and these help us to interpret the very numerous forms like *Bynorthedowne*, *Bisudebrok*, found in personal names. 'Adam *Bynorthedowne*' did not live 'by north down,' but 'by the north of the down,' and so similarly 'Walter *Bisudebrok*' lived 'to the south of the brook.' It should be noted further that this gives a more reasonable explanation of many of the names than has hitherto been possible. There is no church at *Eastchurch* in Crediton, but Walter *Byestechurch* who was living here in 1330 was so called because he lived just to the east of Hittisleigh church in the adjacent parish. *Northway* and *Southway* in Widdecombe are not on different roads, they lie respectively to the north and south of the same road. Similarly with *Norway* and *Southway* in Whitestone.

ABBREVIATIONS

Abbr	*Placitorum Abbreviatio*, 1811.
AC	*Ancient Charters* (Pipe Roll Soc.), 1888.
AD	*Catalogue of Ancient Deeds*. (In progress.)
AD	Unpublished Deeds at the PRO.
Add	Additional MSS in the Brit. Museum.
AddCh	Additional Charters in the Brit. Museum.
AFr	Anglo-French.
AN	Anglo-Norman.
ANG	*Ungedrückte anglo-normannische Geschichtsquellen*, ed. Liebermann, 1879.
AnnMon	*Annales Monastici* (Rolls Series), 5 vols., 1864–9.
AOMB	Augmentation Office, Miscellaneous Books (PRO).
ASC	*Anglo-Saxon Chronicle*.
Ass	Assize Rolls (unpublished) for Devon (PRO), nos. 174–181, 188, 189, 191, 192, 193, 195, 196, 198, and for divers counties rolls for various dates between 1256 and 1418.
Banco	*Placita de Banco* 1327–8 (PRO Lists and Indexes no. 32).
Barum	*The Barnstaple Records*, ed. J. R. Chanter and Thos. Wainwright, 2 vols., 1900.
Bath	*Two Cartularies of Bath Abbey* (Somerset Rec. Soc. 7), 1893.
BCS	Birch, *Cartularium Saxonicum*, 3 vols., 1885–93.
Beds	Bedfordshire.
Berks	Berkshire.
Bk	Buckinghamshire.
Blomé	Blomé, *The Place Names of North Devonshire*, 1929.
BM	*Index to the Charters and Rolls in the British Museum*, 2 vols., 1900–12.
Br	Breton.
Bracton	*Bracton's Note-book*, ed. Maitland, 1887.
BT and Supplt	*An Anglo-Saxon Dictionary* and *Supplement*, ed. Bosworth and Toller, 2 vols., 1898, 1921.
Buckfast	Fragment of the Cartulary of Buckfast Abbey, *v.* Appendix to Bishop Grandisson's Register in Exon *infra* xli.
Buckland	*A Cartulary of Buckland Priory* (Somerset Rec. Soc. 25), 1909.
C	Cambridgeshire.
Cai	*Admissions to Gonville and Caius College*, ed. Venn, 1887.
Camden	*Britannia*, 1586; ed. Gibson, 1695; ed. Gough, 1789.
Canonsleigh	Cartulary of Canonsleigh, Harl 3660.
Cartae Antiquae	Charters in PRO.
Ch	Cheshire.
Ch	*Calendar of Charter Rolls*. (In progress.)
Ch	Charter at P.R.O., Chancery Master's Exhibits. Blunt 21.
ChancP	*Chancery Proceedings in the reign of Elizabeth*, 3 vols., 1827–32.
Chancery Warrants	*Calendar of Chancery Warrants*. (In progress.)
ChR	*Rotuli Chartarum*, 1837.
Chrest	J. Loth, *Chrestomathie bretonne*, 1890.
Cl	*Calendar of Close Rolls*. (In progress.)

Cl	Close Rolls, unprinted (PRO).
ClR	*Rotuli Litterarum Clausarum*, 2 vols., 1833–44.
Co	Cornish, Cornwall.
Coins	*Catalogues of English Coins. Anglo-Saxon Series*, 2 vols., 1887, 1893. *Anglo-Norman Series*, 2 vols., 1916.
Crawf	*The Crawford Charters*, ed. Napier and Stevenson, 1895.
Crossing	W. Crossing, *Guide to Dartmoor*, 1914.
Ct	Court Rolls (unpublished) in BM, PRO, in possession of the Dean and Chapter of Exeter Cathedral, and in private hands.
CtAugm	Court of Augmentations (PRO).
CtRequests	Court of Requests (PRO).
CtWards	Court of Wards (PRO).
Cu	Cumberland.
Cur	*Curia Regis Rolls.* (In progress.)
D	Devon.
D	T. Donne, *Map of the County of Devon*, 1765.
DA	*Transactions of the Devonshire Association.* (In progress.)
Dartmoor	*A short History of the Rights of common upon the Forest of Dartmoor and the Commons of Devon.* Dartmoor Preservation Association, vol. 1. Plymouth 1891.
Db	Derbyshire.
DB	*Domesday Book.* The forms are taken from the Exeter copy (Exon) and may be assumed to be the same as the Exchequer copy (Exch), unless otherwise stated, except that the final *a* of the latinised form in the Exon copy has usually been replaced by the *e* of the Exchequer copy.
DCo NQ	*Devon and Cornwall Notes and Queries.* (In progress.)
Deed	Unpublished deeds in Exeter City Public Library, in possession of the Dean and Chapter of Exeter Cathedral, and in private hands.
Deeds Enrolled	Enrolments of deeds at the PRO.
Depositions	Exchequer Special Commissions and Depositions (PRO).
DKR	*Deputy Keeper's Reports*, vols. 38, 39, 40, 41, 42.
Do	Dorset.
Du	Durham.
Du	Dutch.
Ducange	*Glossarium mediae et infimae Latinitatis*, 10 vols., 1884–7.
DuCo	Documents in the Duchy of Cornwall Office.
Dunsford	Dunsford, *Historical Memoirs of Tiverton*, Exeter, 1790.
Earle	J. Earle, *A Hand-Book to the Land-Charters*, 1888.
ECP	*Early Chancery Proceedings* (PRO Lists and Indexes nos. 12, 16, 20, 29, 38, 48, 50).
EDD	*English Dialect Dictionary.*
EDG	Wright, *English Dialect Grammar*, 1905.
EEW	*The Earliest English Wills.* (Early English Text Society No. 78), 1882.
EHR	*English Historical Review.* (In progress.)
EME	Early Middle English.
EPN	*Chief Elements in English Place-names*, 1923.
Ess	Essex.
Exmoor	*History of the Forest of Exmoor* by E. MacDermot. Taunton, 1911.

Exon	*The Episcopal Registers of the diocese of Exeter*, ed. T. L. Hingston-Randolph, 1886 ff.
FA	*Feudal Aids*, 6 vols., 1899–1920.
Fees	*Book of Fees*, 2 vols., 1922–3.
FF	*Feet of Fines* for Devon (1216–1272), (Devon and Cornwall Record Society), 1912.
FF	Feet of Fines (unpublished) at the PRO.
Fine	*Calendar of Fine Rolls.* (In progress.)
FineR	*Excerpta e rotulis finium*, 2 vols., 1835–6.
Forssner	Forssner, *Continental-Germanic Personal Names in England*, 1916.
Förstemann	Förstemann, *Altdeutsches Namenbuch, Personennamen* (PN), *Ortsnamen* (ON), 2 vols. in 3, 1901–16.
France	*Calendar of Documents preserved in France*, 1899.
F. R.-T.	*ex inf.* Mrs F. Rose-Troup.
FW	Florence of Worcester, *Chronicon ex chronicis*, 2 vols., 1848–9.
G	Greenwood, *Map of Devon*, 1827.
Geld Roll	The Geld Roll of 1084. (From end of Exeter DB.)
Gerv	*Gervasius Cantuariensis* (Rolls Series), 2 vols., 1867–9.
Gl	Gloucestershire.
H	William Harrison, *The Description of Britaine*, 1577. (In Holinshed's *Chronicles*.) Second edition 1586.
Ha	Hampshire.
Harl	Harleian MSS (BM).
He	Herefordshire.
Hellquist	E. Hellquist, *Svensk Etymologisk ordbok*, 1925.
Herts	Hertfordshire.
HMC	*Historical MSS Commission.*
HMC Exeter	*Historical Manuscripts Commission. Report on the records of Exeter*, 1916.
HMC Var	*HMC Reports on Manuscripts in Various Collections*, 8 vols., 1901–23.
Holder	*Alt-celtischer Sprachschatz*, ed. Holder, 1896–1904.
Hu	Huntingdonshire.
IE	Indo-European.
Inq aqd	*Inquisitiones ad quod damnum*, 1803.
InstPRO	Institutions to benefices (PRO).
Ipm	*Calendar of Inquisitions post mortem.* (In progress.)
IpmR	*Inquisitiones post mortem* (Record Commission), 4 vols., 1806–28.
IPN	*Introduction to the Survey of English PN*, 1923.
JAA	*Journal of the British Archaeological Association.* (In progress.)
J. J. A.	*ex inf.* Mr J. J. Alexander.
K	Kent.
KCD	Kemble, *Codex Diplomaticus*, 6 vols., 1839–48.
Kelly	*Directory of Devonshire*, 1902 ed.
KW	Förster, *Keltisches Wortgut*, 1921.
L	Lincolnshire.
La	Lancashire.
Launceston	Cartulary of Launceston Priory (Lambeth Palace Library).
Laws	*Die Gesetze der Angelsächsen*, ed. Liebermann, 3 vols., 1903–16.
Lay	Layamon, *Brut*, 3 vols., 1847.

Lei	Leicestershire.
Leland	John Leland, *Itinerary*, ed. L. T. Smith, 5 vols., 1906–10.
LGer	Low German.
LGS	*Little Guide Series, Devon*, ed. Baring-Gould, 1907.
Lib	*Calendar of Liberate Rolls*. (In progress.)
Lives	G. Oliver, *Lives of the Bishops of Exeter*, 1861–77.
LL	Late Latin.
LN	*Liber Niger Scaccarii*, ed. Hearne, 1774.
LP	*Letters and Papers Foreign and Domestic*. (In progress.)
LRMB	Miscellaneous Books Land Revenue (PRO).
Lysons	*Magna Britannia*, Vol. 6. Devon, 1822.
M	Mudge, *Map of Devon*, 1809.
Macray	*Charters and Documents illustrating the history of… Salisbury*. (Rolls series), ed. W. D. Macray, 1858.
ME	Middle English.
Middendorff	H. Middendorff, *Altenglisches Flurnamenbuch*, 1902.
MidDu	Middle Dutch.
MinAcct	Ministers' Accounts (PRO).
Misc	*Calendar of Inquisitions Miscellaneous*, 2 vols., 1916.
MLG	Middle Low German.
MLR	*Modern Language Review*. (In progress.)
Mo	Monmouth.
ModGer	Modern German.
Montacute	*Bruton and Montacute Cartularies* (Somerset Rec. Soc. 8), 1894.
Moore	T. Moore, *History of Devonshire*, 2 vols., 1829–31.
Moulton	*Palaeography, Genealogy and Topography*. Selections from the collection of H. R. Moulton, 1930.
Mx	Middlesex.
Nb	Northumberland.
NCy	North Country.
NED	New English Dictionary.
Newnham	Cartulary of Newnham Abbey, MS Arundel 17 (BM).
Nf	Norfolk.
NGl	*Notes and Gleanings*, Exeter, 1888–92.
NI	*Nonarum Inquisitiones*, 1807.
NoB	*Namn och Bygd*. (In progress.)
nom. loc.	place-name.
Norw	Norwegian.
NRY	North Riding of Yorkshire.
NSB	J. Loth, *Les noms des saints bretons*, 1910.
Nt	Nottinghamshire.
Nth	Northamptonshire.
O	Oxfordshire.
Obit	Obit-book of the Vicars Choral, Exeter.
ODan	Old Danish.
OE	Old English.
OET	Sweet, *Oldest English Texts* (Early Eng. Text Soc.), 1885.
OFr	Old French.
OGer	Old Germanic.
Ogilby	Ogilby, *Itinerarium Angliae*, 1675.
OHG	Old High German.
Oliver	G. Oliver, *Monasticon Diocesis Exoniensis*, 1846
ON	Old Norse.
ON	Ortsnamen.

Orig	*Originalis Rolls*, 2 vols., 1805–10.
O.S.	Ordnance Survey.
OSax	Old Saxon.
Ottery	AS grant of land at Ottery (*v. infra* 603).
P	*Pipe Rolls*, Record Commission, 3 vols., 1833–44, Pipe Roll Soc. (in progress); *Great Roll of the Pipe* for 26 Henry 3, ed. Cannon, 1918.
(p)	Place-name form derived from personal name.
Pap	*Calendar of Papal Registers*. (In progress.)
Parl Surv	Parliamentary Surveys (PRO).
ParReg	Parish Registers.
ParReg	Parish Registers. (Unpublished.)
Pat	*Calendar of Patent Rolls*. (In progress.)
PatR	*Rotuli Litterarum Patentium*, vol. 1, Part i, 1835.
Pemb Surv	*A Survey of the lands of William First Earl of Pembroke*, Roxburghe Club, 1909.
Peramb	Perambulation of Dartmoor Forest in 1240. (MS at Duchy of Cornwall Office.)
PlymRec	*Calendar of the Plymouth Municipal Records*. (Privately printed.) 1893.
p.n.	place-name.
PN in *-ing*	Ekwall, *Place Names in -ing*, 1923.
Pococke	*Travels of Dr R. Pococke* (Camden Society, N.S. 42, 44), 1888.
Pole	Sir W. Pole, *Collections towards a description of the County of Devon*, 1791.
Polwhele	R. Polwhele, *History of Devonshire*, 3 vols., 1793–1806.
PRO	Public Record Office.
QW	*Placita de Quo Warranto*, 1818.
R	Rutland.
RBE	*Red Book of the Exchequer*, 3 vols., 1896.
Recov	Recovery Rolls (PRO).
Redin	M. Redin, *Uncompounded Personal Names in Old English*, 1915.
Rental	Rentals and Surveys (PRO).
RG	*Chronicle of Robert of Gloucester.* (Rolls Series.) 2 vols., 1887.
RH	*Rotuli Hundredorum*, 2 vols., 1812–18.
Risdon	Tristram Risdon, *Chorographical Description or Survey of the County of Devon*, 1811.
RN	Ekwall, *English River-names*, 1928.
Rowe	S. Rowe, *A Perambulation of the...Forest of Dartmoor*, 1896.
s.a.	sub anno.
Sa	Shropshire.
St Johns	Cartulary of St Johns Priory (*pen*. Dean and Chapter, Exeter Cathedral).
St Mary Magd	Cartulary of St Mary Magdalen, Exeter.
St Nicholas	Cartulary of St Nicholas Priory, Exeter (Cott MS Vit. D. ix).
Saints	*Die Heiligen Englands*, ed. Liebermann, 1889.
Sarum	*Vetus Registrum Sarisberiense.* (Rolls Series.) 2 vols., 1883, 1884.
Saxton	*Map of the County of Devon*, 1577.
Scand	Scandinavian.
SCy	South Country.
Searle	Searle, *Onomasticon Anglo-Saxonicum*, 1897.

Seld	*Selden Society Publications.* (In progress.)
Sf	Suffolk.
Skene	W. F. Skene, *The Four Ancient Books of Wales,* Edinburgh, 1868.
So	Somerset.
Sr	Surrey.
SR	Lay Subsidy Rolls, PRO (unprinted), for various dates between 1286 and 1672.
St	Staffordshire.
Star Chamber	Proceedings in the Court of Star Chamber (PRO).
StEng	Standard English.
StudNP	*Studia Neophilologica.* (In progress.)
SWY	South-west Yorkshire (*v.* EPN viii *s.n.* Goodall).
Sx	Sussex.
TA	Tithe Awards.
Tax	*Taxatio Ecclesiastica.* (Printed as a supplement to Bishop Bronescombe's Register, *v.* Exon *supra* xli.)
Thorndon Hall Charter	See p. 296, n. 1.
Torre	Torre Abbey Cartulary. Exchequer K. R. Misc. Books, vol. 19 (PRO).
Totnes	H. R. Watkin, *The History of Totnes Priory and Medieval Town,* 1914.
TRE	Tempore Regis Edwardi.
TRW	Tempore Regis Willelmi
Var	*Calendar of Chancery Rolls Various,* 1912.
VCH	*Victoria County History of Devon,* vol. 1, 1908.
VE	*Valor Ecclesiasticus,* 6 vols., 1810–34.
Verwijs and Verdam	*Middelnederlandsch Woodenboek* ed. Verwijs and Verdam, 1885–1929.
Vising Mélanges	*Mélanges de philologie offerts à M. Johan Vising,* 1925.
W	Wiltshire.
W	Wales, Welsh.
Wa	Warwickshire.
Wardens	*Wardens Accounts of the parish of Morebath* (DCo NQ Extra volume), 1904.
We	Westmorland.
Wells	*Wells Manuscripts* (HMC, 2 vols., 1907 to 1914).
Westcote	Thomas Westcote, *View of Devonshire in* 1630. Exeter, 1845.
Wills	*Devonshire Wills* (British Rec. Soc. vol. 35).
WillsDo	*Dorset Wills* (British Rec. Soc., vol. 22).
Wm Wo	*Itineraria Symonis Simeonis et Willelmi de Worcestre,* 1778.
Wo	Worcestershire.
Worth	R. N. Worth, *History of Plymouth,* 1871.
Wreyland	*Wreyland Documents,* ed. C. Torr, 1910.
WRY	West Riding of Yorkshire.
WS	West Saxon.
Wt	Isle of Wight.
Y	Yorkshire.
ZEN	Björkman, *Zur Englische Namenkunde,* 1912.
ZONF	*Zeitschrift für Ortsnamenforschung.* (In progress.)

PHONETIC SYMBOLS USED IN TRANSCRIPTION
OF PRONUNCIATIONS OF PLACE-NAMES

p	*p*ay	ʃ	*sh*one	tʃ	*ch*urch	ei	fl*ay*
b	*b*ay	ʒ	a*z*ure	dʒ	*j*udge	ε	Fr. jam*ai*s
t	*t*ea	θ	*th*in	ɑ·	f*a*ther	ε·	*th*ere
d	*d*ay	ð	*th*en	au	c*ow*	i	p*i*t
k	*k*ey	j	*y*ou	a	Ger. m*a*nn	i·	f*ee*l
g	*g*o	χ	lo*ch*	ai	fl*y*	ou	l*ow*
ʍ	*wh*en	h	*h*is	æ	c*a*b	u	g*oo*d
w	*w*in	m	*m*an	ɔ	p*o*t	u·	r*u*le
f	*f*oe	n	*n*o	ɔ·	s*aw*	ʌ	m*u*ch
v	*v*ote	ŋ	si*ng*	oi	*oi*l	ə	*e*v*e*r
s	*s*ay	r	*r*un	e	r*e*d	ə·	b*i*rd
z	*z*one	l	*l*and				

Examples:

Harwich (hæridʒ), Shrewsbury (ʃrouzbəri, ʃru·zbəri),
Beaulieu (bju·li).

NOTES

(1) The names are arranged topographically according to the Hundreds. Within each hundred the parishes are dealt with in alphabetical order, and within each parish the names of primary historical or etymological interest are arranged similarly, but in a large number of the parishes these are followed by one, or two, or even three further groups of names. These groups, so far as they are represented, always appear in the following order: (i) Minor names of topographical origin found largely in the second names of persons mentioned in the Subsidy Rolls and other similar local documents. (ii) Names embodying some family-name of Middle English or Early Modern English origin. (iii) Minor names of obvious origin, or for which we have only very late forms, e.g. all three types are represented under Berrynarbor, p. 27, and Braunton, p. 32. It should be added that in some cases these names now represent comparatively important places and are only 'minor' names from the point of view of the place-name student. The river-, hill- and island-names are dealt with at the beginning of the volume.

(2) After the name of every parish will be found the reference to the sheet and square of the 1-in. O.S. map (Popular Edition) on which it may be found. Thus, BOVEY TRACY 138 F 6.

(3) Where a place-name is found only on the 6-in. O.S. map this is indicated by putting 6″ after it in brackets, e.g. PITLEY (6″).

(4) Place-names now no longer current are marked as 'Lost.' This does not necessarily mean that the site to which the name was once applied is unknown. We are dealing primarily with names and the names are lost. These names are printed in italics when referred to elsewhere in the volume.

(5) The local pronunciation of the place-name is given, wherever it is of interest, in phonetic script within square brackets, e.g. Poughill [pauəl].

(6) In explaining the various place-names summary reference is made to the detailed account of such elements as are found in the *Chief Elements in English Place-names* by printing those elements in Clarendon type, e.g. Holcombe, *v.* holh, cumb.

(7) In the case of all forms for which reference has been made to unprinted authorities, that fact is indicated by printing the reference to the authority in italic instead of ordinary type, e.g. 1296 *Ass* denotes a form derived from a MS authority in contrast to 1316 FA which denotes one taken from a printed text.

(8) Where two dates are given, e.g. 1040 (12th), the first is the date at which the document purports to have been composed, the second is that of the copy which has come down to us.

(9) Where a letter in an early place-name form is placed within brackets, forms with and without that letter are found, e.g. *Lang(e)ford* means that forms *Langford* and *Langeford* are alike found.

(10) All OE words are quoted in their West Saxon form unless otherwise stated.

ADDENDA ET CORRIGENDA

VOL. I, PART I

p. 43, l. 4. For 'Keddleston' read 'Kedleston.'
p. 109, l. 17 from bottom. For 'Sodinton' read 'Sodington.'
p. 119, ll. 15 and 14 from bottom. For 'Blankquets' read 'Blanquettes.'
Index. p. 195, *s.n.* ANDOVER. For 'W' read 'Ha.'
p. 196. For 'BECKBROOK' read 'BEGBROKE.'
p. 196, *s.n.* CAUS. For '114' read '115.'
p. 197. For 'CORSTON' read 'CORSTONE.'
p. 197, *s.n.* DRINKSTONE. For 'St' read 'Sf.'
p. 197, *s.n.* EPPING. For '73' read '173.'
p. 198, *s.n.* GROSMONT. For '114' read '115.'
p. 199, *s.n.* MOLD. For '114' read '115.'
p. 199, *s.n.* PONTEFRACT. For '92, 114' read '93, 115.'
p. 200, *s.n.* SANDFORD ORCAS. For 'D' read 'Do.'
p. 200, *s.n.* SHEAT, SHEET. For '26' read '27.'
p. 200, *s.n.* STOKE DAMARELL. For 'So' read 'D.'
p. 201. Insert 'Towsington (D), 132.'

VOL. I, PART II

p. 21, *s.v.* deop. Delete reference to Debden (Ess).
p. 22, l. 15. For 'Dorton (O)' read 'Dorton (Bk).'
p. 45, *s.v.* leah. Ekwall (*Studies* 96 ff.) has recently pointed out that there are a good many place-names in which the interpretation 'woodland' rather than the later 'clearing' is to be preferred. It is often impossible to be sure which interpretation to give to the term in any particular instance. It would be cumbrous to say 'wood' or 'clearing' in interpreting all leah-names in our volumes. The best compromise in future seems to be to leave the element untranslated.
p. 48, *s.v.* ofer. Delete 'Noverton, Nurton (Wo).'
p. 62, l. 2 from bottom. For 'H' read 'Y.'

VOL. II

p. 7, *s.n.* STOCKING GREEN. Add '*Stokinge* 1200 Cur (p).'
p. 13, *s.n.* EAKLEY. Add '*Yekle* Ch 1439.'
p. 18, *s.n.* CALVERTON. Add '*Cauverton* Cur 1206, Fines 1207.'
p. 27, *s.n.* WOOLSTONE. Add '*Wulfsiestona* 1187 P.'
p. 31, *s.n.* GREAT BRICKHILL. Add '*Magna Brikhelle* 1197 FF.'
p. 31, *s.n.* GT. BRICKHILL. Add '*Magna* in 1205 (Dunst).'
p. 33, l. 3. For 'CHICHELE' read 'CHICHELEY.'
p. 34, *s.n.* NORTH CRAWLEY. Insert 'HURST END. *Hurst* FF 1197, *Herst* Cur 1204.'
p. 42. Insert 'BLACKPIT. *Blakepete* 1198 FF (p).'
p. 53, *s.n.* KINGSBRIDGE. Add '*Kingesbrug* 1227 Cl.'
p. 55. Insert 'STAN MOOR (6"). *Stanmere* 1201, 1205 Cur. *v.* stan, mere.
p. 84, *s.n.* CHELMSCOTT. Add '*Chelmediscot*, 12th Dunst.'
p. 84, *s.n.* LISCOMBE. Add '*Liscumba* 1191 P, *Lichecumbe* 1206 Cur.'
p. 87, *s.n.* ASCOTT. Add '*Estcota* 1187 P.'
p. 87, *s.n.* BURCOTT. Add '*Burcote* 1196 Cur.'
p. 97, *s.n.* SEABROOK. Add '*Sebroc* Cur 1203.'

D

p. 97, *s.n.* SEABROOK. Add to the examples of *Seibroc*, two 12th cent. ones from the Dunstable Cartulary.

p. 115, *s.n.* ARNGROVE. Major Laffan calls attention to forms *Ermegrave*, *Hermegrave* (c. 1230 St Frideswide Cartulary), *Hermgrave* (1230 Ch) which make it clear that this name is not a derivative of OE *earn*, 'eagle.'

p. 118, l. 1. For '*a* to *e*' read '*e* to *a*.'

p. 127, *s.n.* CATSBRAIN. Cf. further Catsbrain Hill in South Stoke (O), 1366 Eynsham Cart. *Catesbrayn.*

p. 145, *s.n.* AYLESBURY. For '871' read '571.'

p. 146, *s.n.* WALTON. Add '*Wauton* P 1195.'

p. 148. Add '*DANCERSEND* probably takes its name from the family of Richard *Daunser* and Thomas *Dauncer* found in the neighbouring parish of Aston Clinton in 1566 and 1587 (ParReg).'

p. 157, *s.n.* BACOMBE. Add '*Baccombe* 1682 ParReg.'

p. 159, *s.n.* ASTON MULLINS. Add '*Eston* Cur 1196.'

p. 166, *s.n.* BEDGROVE. Add '*Babbegrave* P 1190, *Pepegrave* Cur 1205.'

p. 173, *s.n.* LONGWICK. Add '*Longewyk* 1215 ClR.'

p. 176, l. 11. Add comma after 'parishes.'

p. 177, l. 3. Read '*Cada* is on record and may also be inferred.'

p. 177. Insert 'RACKLEY'S FM (6″) in Fingest. *Rachelea* 1194 Cur.'

p. 182, *s.n.* HUGHENDEN. Add '*Hidgingdon* 1700 Chesham ParReg.'

p. 184. Add 'HUNTS HILL may take its name from the family of Samuel *Hunt* (1662 ParReg).'

p. 190, *s.n.* MEDMENHAM. Add '*Medmenham* 1204 Cur.'

p. 192. Saunderton should have been placed in Risborough Hundred after the Risboroughs (p. 174) and not in Desborough Hundred. Cf. map showing Hundreds and Parishes.

p. 207, *s.n.* FASTENDICH. A further example of this term is found in *Fastyngesdych* (1298 Harl Dd 1 8) in the bounds of Finkley bailiwick (Ha). Here it possibly refers to the Devil's Ditch. (*ex inf.* Mr O. G. S. Crawford.)

p. 207. Add 'DOWNLEY. 1684 High Wycombe ParReg *Downley*.'

p. 208. Add 'PLOMERS GREEN is called *Plummer Green* in 1705 (ParReg) and probably takes its name from the family of John *Plomer* and Thomas *Plummer* (ib. 1653, 1671).'

p. 213, *s.n.* ASHLEY GREEN. Add '*Esselega in Cestresham* 1193 P.'

p. 215, *s.n.* BURNHAM. Add '106 J 4.'

p. 217, *s.n.* BROOKEND. Add '*Broc* 1182 P.'

p. 223 top. A parallel to such a river-name as *Isene* is found in *aquam q. vocat. Ysme* (sic) 1278 QW, *Isenwater, Yseneye* c. 1400 *Waltham Cartulary*, apparently an old name for the river Ash (Herts). As the spelling *m* is entirely isolated, all other spellings of Easney itself showing an *n*, the *m* is presumably an error.

p. 225, *s.n.* LATIMER. Add '*Latemus* 1701 ParReg.'

p. 225. Add 'HAZELDEAN FM *Haseldon* 1681 ParReg.'

p. 227, *s.n.* COLESHILL. The pers. name *Col* is on record in DB.

p. 228, *s.n.* DORNEY. Ekwall (RN 129) takes *Dorne* (O) to be a back-formation from Dornford.

p. 231. SEER GREEN is first so called, in the form *Seare Greene* in 1625 (ParReg of Chalfont St Giles).

p. 232, *s.n.* DILEHURST. Tyler's Green in Penn probably takes its name from the family of Johannes *le Tyler*, found in Penn in 1332 (*SR*).

p. 238, *s.n.* BULSTRODE. Add '*Burstwde* 1184 P, *Burestrode* 1193 P.'

p. 238, *s.n.* GERRARD'S CROSS. Cf. Henry *Jarrard* (1556), Elizabeth *Jarret* (1566), in the Parish Register of Chalfont St Peter.

p. 263, *s.n.* Aldridge Grove. For '157' read '151.'

p. 263, *s.n.* Bassetbury. For '205' read '204.'
p. 263, *s.n.* Berry Fm. For '243' read '244.'
p. 264, *s.n.* Bulstrode. Delete '237.'
p. 264, *s.n.* Chalvey. For '244' read '234.'
p. 265, *s.n.* Easton St. Delete '160.'
p. 265, *s.n.* Gerrard's Cross. For '247' read '238.'
p. 266, *s.n.* Lathbury. Delete '249.'
p. 267. Delete 'The Limes, 112, 248.'
p. 267, *s.n.* The Linces. Add '248.'
p. 267, *s.n.* Littlecote. Delete '106.'
p. 267, *s.n.* Littleworth. Insert '106.'
p. 267, *s.n.* Nash Brake. For '61' read '71.'
p. 267, *s.n.* Oak End. For '238' read '239.'
p. 268, *s.n.* Parlaunt. For '242' read '243.'
p. 268, *s.n.* Riding Court. For '234' read '235.'
p. 269, *s.n.* Southlea. For '234' read '235.'
p. 269, *s.n. Spitelbrigge.* For '236' read '237.'
p. 269, *s.n.* Stocken. For '173' read '174.'
p. 269, *s.n.* Wadley. For '235' read '236.'
p. 270, *s.n.* Eton Wick. For '236' read '237.'

VOL. III

p. 4, *s.n.* ICKNIELD WAY. The name *Ikenyldway* was in the 14th cent. applied to an ancient road in Andover, called *Ickland Road* in 1785. 'It led from Waleworth Turnpike Gate by the west side of Waighte croft across the London turnpike-road.' (*ex inf.* Mr O. G. S. Crawford.)

p. 4, *s.n.* ICKNIELD WAY. l. 12 from bottom. For 'towards Marlborough,' read 'along Hackpen.'

p. 27, *s.n.* BLETSOE. Ekwall (*Studies* 5–6) has an interesting discussion of this name and makes a good case for an OE pers. name *Blæccin* as the source of the first element.

p. 47, *s.n.* THURLEIGH. Dr Fowler notes a similar development in a field-name in Southill which, in a 12th cent. document is called indifferently *Refurlang* and *Therefurlange.*

p. 58, *s.n.* HARDWICKE. Add '84 D 13.'

p. 73, *s.n.* DENEL END. Delete the reference to Denshanger (Nth). Ekwall (*Studies* 23 n) points out that this goes back to *dinnes hangra* (BCS 712).

p. 75, *s.n.* KEMPSTON. Insert '84 G 7.'

p. 107, *s.n.* BEESTON. For this name (and other Beestons), Ekwall (*Studies* 55 ff.) makes the interesting suggestion that the first element is a lost OE *bēos* (cognate with MLG *biese*, MDa *bies*), 'bent' or 'coarse grass.' This would suit the forms and avoid an awkward genitival compound.

p. 118, *s.n.* HUSBORNE. *Hess(e)burn* is a common form in the Dunstable Cartulary in 12th cent. documents.

p. 132, *s.n.* STANBRIDGE. For '95 C 5' read '95 E 5.'

p. 160, *s.n.* PULLOXHILL. Add '95 B 8.'

p. 171, *s.n.* HOO. Add '*Hoo* (p) 1200 Cur.'

p. 198, *s.n.* WANSFORD. Mr Norman Dixon notes the form *Welmesford* in one of the Peterborough forgeries (12th cent.) in the ASC *s.a.* 656.

p. 218, l. 2 from foot. For the second 'Db' read 'Sr.'

p. 226, *s.n.* WARBOYS. For '1077 (17th)' read '1077 (14th).'

p. 238, l. 11 from bottom. For 'W' read 'L.'

p. 246, *s.n.* SALOME WOOD. Canon Foster notes two earlier references to the *capella de Sala* (attached to Leighton Church) from the *Registrum*

Antiquissimum of Lincoln, where we have early 13th cent. copies of a charter of 1163.

p. 261, l. 15 from bottom. For 'Wo' read 'Gl.'
p. 261, l. 22. For 'Wo' read 'Gl.'
p. 272, l. 2 from bottom. For 'elation' read 'relation.'
p. 274, l. 6 from bottom. For 'by-names' read '*by*-names.'
p. 307, *s.n.* WYMINGTON. For '243' read '244.'
p. 313. For 'Aketon' read 'Acton.'
p. 314. Delete 'Harleston (Nf), 124.'

VOL. IV

p. xxii, l. 15. For '397' read '398.'

p. 15, *s.n.* TIRLE BROOK. The note on Tirle Mill should be expanded as follows: 'In the Evesham Chronicle (c. 1400) we have mention of a fishpool in Ombersley called *Trylpole*, with certain mills there. One of these mills is called *Tirmill* in 1540 (*MinAcct*) and *Tirle Mill* in 1613 (VCH, III, 464). It appears on the present 6″ map as *Turn Mill*. The forms show that this pool and mill name contains the river-name *Tirle* or *Trill* (RN 409, 418).

p. 21, *s.n.* WORCESTER and p. 1, *s.n.* WYRE. Ekwall (*Studies* 97 ff.) has developed very interestingly the suggested association of *Worcester* and the Forest of *Wyre*. He notes that in BCS 357 we have a grant of thirty hides of land in a district called *Weogorena leage* and that the large area of land lies west of the Severn and north-west of Worcester itself. He suggests that *Weogorenaleag* was the old name for the forest-area which then stretched up to and included what is now called the Forest of *Wyre*, which may itself go back to some such old name as *Weogorenawudu*, later *Worewude* or, alternatively, 'forest of Wyre.'

p. 21, *s.n.* FISH ST. Add '*le Fysshestrett* 1538 *MinAcct*.'

p. 92 top. Add 'Cutmill Fm (O) in Stanton Harcourt, *Cottedmulne* 1278 RH.'

p. 100, *s.n.* PYE MILL. Cf. Pie Mill in Chipping Campden (Gl) 1601 Wills *Pye Mill.*

p. 106, *s.n.* CHURCHILL. Ekwall (*Studies* 33 ff.) has a valuable study of *church*-names in which he shows that one must not too readily assume the equivalence of *church* and the OBrit *cruc*. His article is too long to summarise or discuss here. He rightly points out that points v and viii in the PN Wo article on Churchill are invalid. The first because we have in 1332 (Ch) a reference to a *capella* at Churchfield, the second because *ciric* and not *cirice* was the regular form taken by the word *cirice* in OE compounds of that word.

p. 143, *s.n.* ICCOMB. For '93 F 5' read '93 F 9.'

p. 164, *s.n.* SHIPSTON-ON-STOUR. Add: 'FURZE HILL was formerly called *Cyrichyll* (Heming 347) and appears as *Chirchehulle* in *Chirchehulleweye*, "land by the Fosse" *Underchirchehull* (1320 Pat).' *v.* Ekwall *Studies* 51.

p. 171, *s.n.* RAVENSHILL. For 'Bk 61' read 'Bk 13.'

p. 183, *s.n.* WITLEY. Ekwall (*Studies* 94) suggests that as in Whitehall (O) the *wiht* may refer to the marked recess in Abberley hill in which Great Witley is situated. The hill forms almost a right angle.

p. 190, *s.n.* BRICKLEHAMPTON. For '87 A 1' read '82 H 1.'

p. 214, *s.n.* MILLERS COURT. Already in 1204 (Cur) we have mention of a free tenement in Birtsmorton held by one Emma, the wife of Robertus *Molendinarius*.'

p. 217, *s.n.* PERSHORE. Cf. Persh Fm (Gl), 13th St Peter Gl. *Pers*, 1541 LP *The Persh.*

p. 225, *s.n.* COLLETT'S GREEN. In 1538 (*MinAcct*) John *Colyke* held lands in Powick.

p. 231, *s.n.* YARDLEY. Ekwall (*Studies* 95 ff.) suggests that leah when compounded with *gyrd*, stocc and stæf, denotes woodland suitable respectively for getting yards or spars, heavier timber, and light staves.

p. 232, *s.n.* GREET. Add '*Grete* Cur 1198.'

p. 319, *s.n.* IPPLESBOROUGH. Add '*boscus suis de Yppel in Fekeham* CIR 1215.'

p. 341, *s.n.* GANNOW. We probably have a similar compound of gamen and ac in Gannock (Herts), *Gannok* 1294 *SR* (p), 1348 Cl, 1349 Ipm, *le Gannok* 1335 *St Pauls*, atte *Gannok* 1287 *Ass*, and Ganwick (Mx), *Gannokk* 1479 *Add.*

p. 359, BRIDENBRIDGE. Cf. *Bredenbrugge* (1298 Eynsham Cart.) in the bounds of Shotover Forest (O), and *domus W. atte Bredenebrigg* (1284 *Ass*) in Hurst (Berks).

p. 362, *s.n.* TARDEBIGGE. Mr F. T. S. Houghton, with help from Miss Dickins of Hook Norton (O), has worked out some further points in the boundaries of Tardebigge as given in Heming (362). The *Withi broc* is still known locally as *Withybrook*, a small stream to the north-west of the church. *Gateshoh*, 'goat's-hill' (*v.* hoh), is *Catyshoo* (1485 *Ct*), *Gatesway* (1561 Survey), and is found as *Gatesway* in the Tithe-map at the present day. *Sandwællan* survived as *Sandwel medowe* (1485 *Ct*), *Sandeymeadow* (1691 Rate Bk) which is called *Sandy Mead* in a Court Roll of 1829. Nash in 1645 mentions 'The old gospel Place oake' on Redditch Common which touched the Ipsley-Tardebigge boundary. This must have been identical with the *Cristel Mael ac* of Heming. Heming's *Cloddesleage* and *Cloddeswællan* survive as *Chadesleys* (sic). *Croft* (1485 *Ct*), *Clodesley* (1514 *Ct*), *Cloddisley Felde* (1535 VE), *Clodesley* (1689 *Assessment*). There is also a Cladshill (6"), which is *Clodshill* in a Survey of 1812, so that we have three places within a few miles of one another containing the same pers. name *Clodd*.

p. 418. Delete 'Harpsford (Sr), 75.'

VOL. V

p. 22, *s.n.* TOLLERTON. The form *Toletun* from BCS 1279 is based on Birch's reading, but a further examination of the MS (Harl 55, 4 d) shows that the correct reading is *Ioletun* (that is, Youlton, p. 22); the later copy (Harl 6841, p. 129) also has *ioletun* (*ex inf.* Dr A. H. Smith).

p. 43 *s.n.* MALTON. Ekwall (*Stud NP* 2, 28–31) takes this to be 'Middle farm,' the variant vowels being due to confusion between OE *middel* and the substituted Scandinavian *meðal* which, like Danish *miæthel*, *meaðal*, had developed a form *meaðal* in English. Such an explanation would also fit Melton-on-the-Hill much better than that advanced in the PN volume.

p. 125, l. 12 from bottom. For '*w* especially in the neighbourhood of *r*' read '*r* especially in the neighbourhood of *w*.'

p. 152, l. 1 from bottom. For 'south-east' read 'south-west.'

p. 206, *s.n.* LANDMOTH. An interesting parallel to this name is provided by an unidentified place in Flasby (WRY), *Landemotes*, -*motisgil*(*l*)*am* 1200–16, c. 1320 Furness Cartulary ii, 363, 460, *Landemosegile* 1246 ib. 435. (A.H.S.)

p. 308. Add after HUNDERTHWAITE: 'LAITHKIRK, though not evidenced in early spellings, is an interesting compound of hlaða and kirkja. Mr W. Bell points out that the church is an old barn, in fact it was the tithe barn of this part of the ancient parish of Romaldkirk, out of which the present ecclesiastical parish of Laithkirk has since been carved.'

p. 326, l. 24. For 'Bk 257' read 'BedsHu 293.'

VOL. VI

p. xliii, l. 10. For 'Aldeminster' read 'Alderminster.'

p. xliii, l. 22. For '260' read '261.'

p. 7, l. 12 from bottom. For 'RN 36' read 'RN 362.'

p. 10, *s.n.* RAPE OF CHICHESTER. Add '*Balliva de Cycestrya Ass* 1263, *Rapp' de Cycestr'* RH 1273–4.'

p. 11, *s.n.* CHICHESTER. Ekwall (*Studies* 16) suggests that Chichester may really go back to an OE *Cissesceaster*, with early loss of *s* due partly to dissimilation and partly to assimilation from *Cisse* or *Cissi*, an early pet-form of *Cissa*.

p. 11. CHICHESTER STREET-NAMES. *Parislane* doubtless contains the same first element as Paris Street in Exeter (*v.* 23 *infra*).

p. 12, *s.n.* GREYLINGWELL. The required pers. name is probably on actual record in Godwine *Grelling* (Feudal Book of Abbot Baldwin of Bury, f. 138 *b*, c. 1100).

p. 17, *s.n.* GREVATT'S. Mr P. H. Reaney notes from Essex, Burkitt's Lane and Bargate's Lane Fm in Dedham, 1291 *For Birchette*, Alracks in Gestingthorpe (*Alrette* 14th), Bushett Fm in Great Bardfield, Russets in Chingford (*Rissett* 1222), and numerous field-names, all showing this formation.

p. 29, *s.n.* INHOLMS COPSE. Mr Reaney adds *Innams* in Pattiswick (1289) Ass), *Inham* (Bocking) 1547–8 Pat.

p. 35, l. 15 from bottom. For '245' read '242.'

p. 49, HAT HILL. Cf. High Hat, the name of a cliff in St Lawrence (Wt) 1462 *Ct, la hatte.*

p. 54, THE TRUNDLE. Miss M. S. Holgate notes the pers. name *Ali'* at Trendle in a copy (c. 1500) of an early manor roll of the manor of Slindon in the Cathedral Library at Canterbury. It is possible that this family name gives us an early reference to the Trundle.

p. 59, *s.n.* CHIDHAM. Ekwall (*Studies* 70) suggests that we have here as the first element OE *cēod(e)*, 'bag,' either used metaphorically to describe one or both of the inlets between which Chidham lies, or with a new sense development 'inlet' such as we find in its ON cognate *kióss.* Hence *Cēodanhām*, 'homestead of or at the bay,' or *Cēodahām*, 'homestead of the bays.'

p. 62, *s.n.* BOX and STOCKBRIDGE HUNDRED. Add '*Boxe and Stokkebrugg*' Ass 1263.'

p. 68, *s.n.* WORTH (lost). Mr A. C. Wood notes a later reference *le Worthe* (1537 *MinAcct*).

p. 99, *s.n.* TOPLEIGH. Add '*Toppeleghe* 1280 *Ass* (p).'

p. 101, *s.n.* BLEATHAM. Miss Holgate has supplied us with a reference from Lansdowne MS 873, f. 51 (1324), which shows that the districts named Bleatham and Egdean are not co-terminous, for there we have the phrase *Apud Bletenham in Eggedean.*

p. 109, *s.n.* WOOLAVINGTON. Add '*Wollerton* (1423 *Ancient Petitions*). The corresponding entry in the Patent Rolls is *Wollavynton*.'

p. 114, *s.n.* FISHERSTREET. Mr Straker (Sx NQ 3, 89) notes that in the old maps this is called Jack Fisher Street, suggesting that it was associated with the heron, known in popular speech as 'Jack Fisher.' In the light of this information the suggested association with Will *Fissere* must be withdrawn.

p. 128, top. Delete the reference to BROOKDEAN. The Hon. Lady Maxse points out that this is a modern name given to the house when it was built in 1847. The old house on this little holding is *Holts.*

p. 143, *s.n.* AVISFORD HO. Mr C. T. Aylwin points out to us that the little river at Avisford is locally called the *Ave*. This river-name is almost certainly a back-formation.

p. 144, *s.n.* YAPTON. Miss Holgate gives us an early example of the alternative forms of this name from Archbishop Chichele's Register (1430) par. 1, f. 185 *d. Yapton alias Abynton*.

p. 149, *s.n.* PARBROOK. Miss M. S. Holgate notes a 13th cent. pers. name Wm de *Pathebrok* (Canterbury Cathedral MS E 24, f. 103). It may well be that his family came from *Parbrook* and that this name should be explained as from pæð and broc, 'water-meadow by the path.'

p. 158, *s.n.* WEYHURST FM. Mr Secretan points out that the 'way' here must be not the Horsham-Guildford road, which only dates from 1806, but the lane from Lynwick running past Hornshill Fm and Weyhurst Copse.

p. 158, GRAVATT'S FM. There is a large pond here formed from water which has filled up an earlier hollow made by quarrying stone (*ex inf.* Mr Secretan). This is clearly a derivative of OE *grafan*, 'to cut, quarry.'

p. 166, *s.n.* SILKDEN (lost). The reviewer in the *West Sussex Gazette* points out that SILKDEN, here stated to be lost, still survives as SELDEN FM in Patching, on the borders of Angmering parish. This name is of particular interest, as it gives us the source of the surname of the famous lawyer's family, whose memory is associated with West Tarring.

p. 169, *s.n.* POTLANDS. Mr A. C. Wood notes an earlier reference *Potlondes* (1537 *MinAcct*).

p. 175, l. 1. For '*Chiltancumb*' read '*Ciltancumb*.'

p. 175, l. 2. For '(C)' read '(Ess).'

p. 182, *s.n.* WEST GRINSTEAD HUNDRED. Miss H. M. Cam points out that the quotation from the Assize Roll (which is printed in the *Placita de Quo Waranto*, p. 749, among the pleas from the county of Sussex), refers to an exchange of land whereby the Abbey of Fécamp received lands in Gloucestershire in exchange for Winchelsea and Rye (cf. *Calendar of Charter Rolls* 1, 321–2). The passage in the Hundred Roll refers to the manor of Cheltenham and the Hundred (of that name) with its appurtenance Slaughter in Gloucestershire and the Hundred of Sulmonsbury in the same county. The whole of the paragraph so far as it suggests an alternative name for the Hundred of West Grinstead should therefore be deleted.

p. 197, *s.n.* CISSBURY. Mr E. C. Curwen calls attention to the form *Sissasbury* (sic) in Camden's *Britannia*, and to *Sizbury* in Findon ParReg (1586). The latter form suggests the true local pronunciation which doubtless has been altered under the influence of a late association with the StEng pronunciation of the name Cissa.

p. 208, *s.n.* STUMBLEHOLM FM. Cf. *Ocstumbelden*, 1387 *Walden* (P. H. R.).

p. 209, *s.n.* WYNDHAM HALF-HUNDRED. Delete "In 1279...i.e. Shermanbury." *v. supra*.

p. 217, l. 10, l. 11. For 'FF' and 'FA' read '*For*.' For Chestwood, cf. also *Chesten Wood* in Upchurch (K), 1598 *Arch Cant* 18, 400 (P. H. R.).

Map. Mr Budgen notes that the bounds of the Hundred of Eastbourne are here given as identical with those of the modern Borough of Eastbourne. Historically the Hundred does not include those pieces of Willingdon now included in the Borough, especially the piece that comes down to the shore between Eastbourne and Westham.

VOL. VII

p. 266, *s.n.* HASSOCKS. Cf. *Hassokes* (1207 *FF*), a field-name in Desborough (Nth).

p. 267, *s.n.* FURNACEGREEN SHAW (6"). Mr Straker (Sx NQ 3, 89) notes that this is close by the site of Blackfold Furnace, near Handcross, not at the Cuckfield furnace.

p. 270, *s.n.* WEST HOATHLY. Now pronounced [houðlai] with the usual stressing of the last syllable. The Very Rev. the Dean of Ely tells us that it was formerly pronounced [houdlai].

p. 271, *s.n.* BIRCHGROVE. The modern and wilful substitution of *Birchgrove* for *Bunchgrove* is doubtless due to the desire to replace an apparently absurd name by a picturesque one.

p. 271, l. 14 from bottom. For '*Rookhurst*' read '*Rockhurst*' as on p. 273.

p. 274, WHITESTONE. The Very Rev. the Dean of Ely suggests that the house took its name from the rocks on the side of the lane close by, which broke up into fine white sand.

p. 278, *s.n.* HANDCROSS. Doubtless as suggested by Mr Straker (Sx NQ 3, 89) the modern name records the way in which the *via regia* through the forest here divides, fanwise, into five, like the digits of a hand.

p. 282, *s.n.* THREE BRIDGES. Mr Straker (Sx NQ 3, 89) gives the following further information: 'In the Worth furnace accounts 1546–49, mention is made of the "new makyng of thre bridges upon the wayes between the hamer at Worth and Crawley." In the tithe map of 1842, three narrow bridges, only a few yards apart, are shown, with three separate streams. The railway has altered their courses and one larger bridge now takes their place.'

p. 286, MUDDLESWOOD. Mr W. G. Wallace suggests that this farm-name may perhaps be associated with the family of *Moodell* found in Waldron (1547), or *Muddyll* in Mayfield (1558), cf. Muddles Green, p. 400. The family is not actually on record in the neighbourhood of Newtimber.

p. 314, *s.n.* IRON RIVER. Mr Straker (Sx NQ 3, 89) suggests that this was used for the transport of iron from Sheffield to Lewes.

pp. 327, 335. The correct dates for the formation of Forest Row and Dane-hill parishes are 1847 and 1851 respectively.

p. 336, *s.n.* FURNER'S GREEN. Mr Straker (Sx NQ 3, 90) points out that Thomas *Furnar* may well have worked at the Sheffield furnace near by.

p. 343. Add 'SLUTTS LANE (6″).' It is possible that this lane should be associated with the family of Willelmus at *Slutte*, mentioned in the 13th cent. in a Court Roll of the Archbishop's manor of South Malling (*ex inf.* Miss M. S. Holgate).

p. 350, REEDING's FM. Mr P. H. Reaney notes early forms for Woodridden Fm in Waltham, Redyn's Wood in Theydon Garnon, showing them to be identical with this name, as well as numerous field-names of the same form.

p. 351, *s.n.* WYCH CROSS. An additional form is *Wyggecrouche* (1356 *FM*).

p. 354, CLIFFE HILL. Mr W. G. Wallace calls attention to the variant form '*Mary Akehurst in the Cleft near Lewes*' on a token of 1667, and to the parish-name St Thomas in the Cliffe (1623).

p. 364, l. 12. For '61' read '56.'

p. 366, *s.n.* CHARTNESS FM. For '1609 *Recov*' read '1610 *Recov*.'

p. 374, *s.n.* BAYHAM. For the possibility of a different origin for this name, cf. Wallenberg in *Stud NP* (2, 97).

p. 386, *s.n.* MARLING. So similarly *le Marlynge* in Terlingham (K) in 1362 (Ipm).

p. 408, *s.n.* LONGBRIDGE. The bridge is so called in 1538 (*MinAcct*).

p. 428, *s.n.* CRUMBLES POND. Mr Budgen points out that a letter (1729) of Mr Richard Budgen, who surveyed the Crumbles for Lord Wilmington, speaks of two places with water, one called Willow Crumble, and the other Hogs Crumble, and he suggests that *crymel* here is used of a 'fragment of water' rather than of a 'fragment of land.'

p. 435, *s.n.* DILL. For '88' read '79.'

p. 438, SNAPSON'S DROVE. If these names are connected we have a further example of added initial *s*, cf. *s.n.* Poles Pitch, Vol. VI, p. 190.

p. 439, BOSHIP. Professor Tait calls attention to a passage in Below's *Der Ursprung der deutschen Stadtverfassung* (p. 40) which shows that the equivalent German *burschaft, bauerschaft*, are used as old names for the *dorf* in some districts of Germany, e.g. Saxony and the neighbourhood of Cologne.

p. 443, SHAWPITTE. The Rev. J. B. Johnston suggests with much likelihood that *Sharpettes* is from earlier *Shard-pettes*, 'pits where shards or fragments are found.'

p. 444, *s.n.* PEVENSEY. Delete the reference to Pusey (Berks). Cf. Ekwall, *Studies* 11.

p. 445, YOTHAM. The Rev. J. B. Johnston suggests that the first element in this difficult name is OE *geoht*, 'yoke.' This would agree with the first and last forms. The sense of the compound is obscure. Cf. the equally difficult use of *yoke* in Yokehurst (PN Sx 300).

p. 452, *s.n.* HAMMERDEN. Mr Straker (Sx NQ 3, 90) makes the following note: 'The name does not refer to a power forge as there is no stream of sufficient size, but probably to a considerable bloomery, now mainly overlaid by the building of Ticehurst Road Station.'

p. 465, n. For 'Nettleswell' read 'Netteswell.'

pp. 472, 475, *s.n.* DARWELL. These places are still known locally as [dɑ'vəl]. (*ex inf.* Lt.-Col. Curteis.)

p. 482, *s.n.* WINDMILL HILL. Lt.-Col. Curteis points out that the *Windmill Hill* of the Court Roll of 1587 refers to the house, or rather its predecessor, and its estates now called Windmill Hill Place (6″) in Wartling. The earlier name of the hamlet of Windmill Hill was Posey Green and this should also have been shown as in the Parish of Wartling and not in Herstmonceux.

pp. 480, 481, 484, 494, *s.nn.* CHILSHAM, PEBSHAM, MERSHAM, WORSHAM. Lt.-Col. Curteis notes that all these places should be pronounced with final [səm] and not [ʃəm]. The latter is purely a spelling pronunciation which here as elsewhere is ousting the local one.

p. 492. GRINSES and KEWHURST appear as *Grenes* and *Kewers* in 1538 (*MinAcct*).

p. 499. TELHAM COURT is not the original *Telham*. It is a revival of the old name which was made in order to give an air of antiquity to the estate formerly called *Quarry Hill* (cf. Quarry Wood, p. 500), *ex inf.* Lt.-Col. Curteis.

p. 507, *s.n.* FAIRLIGHT. Mr Norman Dixon calls attention to the mention of Fairlight in the sea-shanty 'Spanish Ladies' in the line 'We sailed then by Beachy, by *Fairlee*, and Dungeness.'

p. 519, *s.n.* MORGAY FM. Mr P. H. Reaney notes possible Essex parallels: *Moriyenesfeld* (Layer), 12th Colch, *Morghynelond* (Langenhoe) 1240 FF, *Morzenescroft* (Brightlingsea), 1300 ColchA, *Morithynelond* (Sandon), 1279 FF. Presumably in all these *n* is an error of transcription for *u*, and we may add *le Moriʒeue gardyn* (1342 AD ii) in Caversham (O) and *Moreʒeue Halle* in Watford (Nth) in 1365 (AD iv). It may well be that this also is the source of the *Moreʒyf* discussed in PN Bk xii, n. 2, and that this latter name is not Celtic at all.

p. 523, *s.n.* DIXTER. Mr J. W. Batterham points out that the original house was probably built between the upper and lower moats, which are still traceable in the grounds. The dic clearly refers to the moats.

p. 560, *s.n.* MENESSE. Cf. also 'a marsh of *La Menesse*' in Worth (K) in 1227 (Ch).

p. 567, *s.n.* BEACHY HEAD. For '426' read '427.'

p. 611. For 'Nettleswell' read 'Netteswell.'

VOL. VIII

p. 23, *s.n.* RACK STREET. Miss Lega-Weekes sends the following note: 'Samuel Izacke's Survey of the City in 1671 mentions "a garden sometime iiij sullons of land...bounded by the street or lane called Tighte Street or Racke Lane on the west." In 1464 it is spelt *Tygherstrete*, and in the plan of the land in question, in the Cartulary of St John's Hospital, *Tey3testrete*. A will of 1327 mentions *Tyghetehaye*, and a deed of 1380 grants "a certain tenement in *Thightestrete* with a *Tyghta* in *Tyghtheghes*," also the reversion of "a place of land in *Tyghteheghes*."'

These forms make it clear that the *Teygle-* form is an error, and establish clearly an element *tyght* appearing not only in the earlier name of the street, but also as an independent word with the characteristic Devon inflexional final syllable. Miss Lega-Weekes points out that this word *tyght(a)* must be an alternative name for the 'racks' or 'frames' which gave rise to the later name of the street. This word is clearly the *tight* sb. 1, recorded in the Oxford Dictionary as an obsolete word. The sense which is recorded there is that of 'pulling' or 'drawing'; there must have been a further sense development whereby the name of the action was transferred to the instrument giving rise to the action.

p. 29, *s.n.* YELLATON. The adj. 'old' (OE eald) is found in Devon frequently compounded with land, but also with cumb, dun, mæd, tun. In contrast to 'new' which denoted land recently taken into cultivation, it probably denoted primarily land which had been long under cultivation, then land worn out by cultivation, and even land which has passed out of cultivation altogether. Cf. *old-land* (EDD) used of ground that has lain untilled a long time, arable land which has been laid down in grass more than two years. It is found compounded with dun (BCS 564), possibly with dæl (BCS 604), with land (BCS 723, a Devon charter), and with slæd (BCS 299).

p. 33, *s.n.* HALSINGER. This and other names like Halsbury, Halsdon, are difficult of interpretation. Theoretically *hals* in the ME forms of these names may go back to either OE *heals*, 'neck,' or to OE *hæsel*, 'hazel,' which is found in modern Devon and Somerset dialect as *halse*. OE *heals*, 'neck of land,' is found in Halse (Nth), DB *Hasou*, Survey *Hausho*, 1247 *Ass Halsho*, and probably also in Halse (So), DB *Halse* and Halse *infra* 360. Topographical conditions allow of it in Halsinger, and in Halsbury, Halsdon *infra* 104, 139, but if *hals(e)* was in use in ME as a dialect form for *hasel*, that word is equally possible. That it could be so used is made almost certain by the forms of Horsewell *infra* 283, 314, Haswell *infra* 304, and Hazelwood *infra* 306, where the second element makes a first element *hæsel* exceedingly likely. Halswell (So), DB *Hasewelle*, 1334 Ch *Halswill*, tends to confirm this, though the DB form is not free from ambiguity. The ME forms in *Hales-* for Halsinger, Halsdon and Halsbury offer difficulties, but they have their parallels in such forms as *Halleswelle* (FA) for Halswell (So). On the whole we are probably right in assuming *hæsel* for Halsinger, but no certainty is possible with regard to Halsdon and Halsbury.

p. 47, *s.n.* LINCOMBE. No certainty is possible with regard to this name or Lincombe in South Brent or Lincombe in Malborough, for the early forms of which *v. infra* 292, 308. It should be noted that except for Lincombe in Ilfracombe there are unfortunately no really early forms. In addition there are examples of Lincombe in Bigbury and in Culmstock for which we have no early forms at all. From the point of view of form the first element is, in order of probability, lin, lind, or hlinc. lin fits exactly, but flax-growing is not likely in this Lincombe or in Lincombe in Sidbury. lind, with early loss of *d* from the cons. group *ndc*, is possible on grounds of phonology and possible on the score of topography. If the first element is hlinc we should expect some ME forms in *Linch(e)*-, but no such forms have been found. If the first element is hlinc, the reference would be presumably to cultivated terraces on the side of the valley. Such are possibly to be found at the Sidbury Lincombe. Lyncombe (So), for which we have an early form *lincumb* (BCS 1009) must be a compound of lin and cumb. It is possible that one or more of the other Lincombes may contain a lost stream-name *Lyn* (OE *hlynn*), identical with the well-known Devon river-name (*infra* 9).

p. 84, l. 4. Add KENWITH CASTLE. This name and the transformation of HUBBASTONE (103 *infra*) from earlier *Wibblestone* (Risdon 1630) are due to the attempt to place here the site of the *arx Cynuit* of Asser (cf. 62 *supra*), and to identify the burial place of the Viking *(H)ubba* who was defeated there. These identifications have no authority (*v.* Asser's *Life of King Alfred*, ed. Stevenson, pp. 262 ff.).

p. 142, *s.n.* HATHERLEIGH. Professor Ekwall notes that Hatherley (Gl) is almost certainly the *Hegherleo* (sic) of KCD 1317. This would agree well with an earlier *hægþornleah* and later *Haiderleie*.

Dr Schram (ZONF 3, 205–6) has pointed out that *hedder* and *hadder* are evidenced in the East Anglian dialect and may be found in Hethersett (Nf). Dr A. H. Smith calls attention to Faweather in Bingley (WRY) with forms *Faghadre* t. Hy 1 Dugd vi 195, *Fauedre* 1150–60 Riev, 1333 Pat, *Faueddre* 1160 Riev, *Fagheder* c. 1230 YD i, 1235 FF, 1333 Riev, *Fahedder* 1276 RH, *Fahedre* 1285 Riev, *Fawedre* 1539 Riev, *Faweather* 1828 Langd. This seems beyond question to be a compound of OE fag, 'variegated,' and the same word, 'heather.' The Norfolk and Yorkshire forms suggest an OE **hæddre*.

p. 148, *s.n.* TREWYN. Mr Alexander informs us that it is pronounced [tru'win]. The accenting of the final syllable may be due to the influence of Cornish names with initial *Tre-*, or it may be an attempt to conform to the common Devon type of name noted under Tredown *infra* 146.

p. 192, *s.n.* BRIMPTS. Mrs Rose-Troup notes that this is a common field-name in Devon.

p. 206, STENG-A-TOR. It is suggested in DA (58, 370) that behind these inconsistent forms we have a Devon word *stinka* or *stenga*, 'marshy,' not yet obsolete. The ground around the tor is always wet.

p. 213, *s.n.* BRENTOR. In the light of the forms with *Brient-* and *Brint-*, Professor Ekwall would now prefer to derive this name from the British word corresponding to Romano-Celtic *Brigantia*, a well-known hill-name.

p. 234, Note. Add VINTRY. This is the name of one of the four original wards into which the town was divided c. 1440, the earliest form being *Vintre* (J. J. A.). This, like the Vintry in London, is from earlier *vinetrie*, 'place where vintners assemble.'

p. 264, *s.n.* THE SOUTH HAMS. Mrs Rose-Troup would prefer to take the *Homme* charter as containing two lines of bounds, both beginning on Dartmoor and both ending in the sea. The one would start at the *miercecumb*, the other from a *þyrelanstan* which is not Thurlestone by the sea but a lost *Thurlestone* on the moor which she places at Glazemeet.

p. 270, *s.n.* FARDEL. Professor Tait calls attention to the use of the term *ferding* (as noted by Ellis, *Introd. to Domesday* i, 157) in Devon and Somerset. This term denoted a quarter of a virgate, and doubtless *feorða dæl* is an alternative expression for this unit. This word goes back to OE *feorðling*, 'fourth part,' and is often found as *ferling* in ME (*v. s.n.* Topsham Bridge 306 *infra*).

p. 285, *s.n.* MARRIDGE. Professor Ekwall suggests that the first element here may be a lost OE *māwe, meaning a 'meadow' or the like, which in *Studies* 72 he takes to be the second element of Dunmow (Ess), which goes back to OE *Dunmawe* 1045 Thorpe 574. This word survives in Devon dialect as *mow* 'meadow', and would explain the forms of Marridge.

NOTE. In these Addenda and Corrigenda we are much indebted to Mr A. C. Wood for notes from various unprinted documents at the Record Office; to the late Major J. de C. Laffan for supplementary Buckinghamshire material; to Mr F. T. S. Houghton for supplementary Worcestershire material and for comparative material from Gloucestershire and Warwickshire; to Miss Holgate for supplementary Sussex material; to Mr P. H. Reaney for various Essex parallels.

DEVON

The earliest reference to the shire is *Defenascir* (ASC Ā *s.a.* 851), later spellings being *Defnascir* (ASC Ā *s.a.* 894, C *s.a.* 977), *Dæfenascir* (ASC E *s.a.* 1017). The men of Devon are spoken of as *Defena* (gen. pl.) in 823 (ASC Ā). See Introd. xiv n. 1.

RIVER-NAMES[1]

Of the 120 river- and stream-names treated here only some 35 can definitely be stated to be of pre-English origin and although among these 35 are to be found most of the large rivers, yet a considerable number of the names of later origin refer to important or at least well-known Devon streams. As pointed out by Ekwall (RN lviii) the river-nomenclature of Devon differs markedly from that of Dorset and Somerset and the number of back-formations both late and early is comparatively large.

ALLER BROOK[2] (Teign) is *Aller water* c. 1550 Leland, *Aller brooke* 1577 H. A back-formation from Aller *infra* 504.

ALPHIN (Exe) is *the Alphin* 1797 Polwhele. A back-formation from Alphington *infra* 422. The older name may have been *Ide* (*v. infra* 497).

AVON

> *to, upon Afene* 847 BCS 451, *afne* 962 Thorndon Hall Charter, *Auene* 1233–8 (14th) Buckfast, 1238 *Ass*, 1240 Exon, 1244, 1281 *Ass*, *Avena* 1354 Dartmoor, *Avenne* 1557 Oliver
> *Owne al. Aven* 1608 Dartmoor, *Awne, Aune, Avon* c. 1550 Leland

The name is of Celtic origin and the meaning is simply 'river,' *v.* Ekwall RN 23.

---

[1] Throughout this section we are greatly indebted to Ekwall RN.
[2] In the case of tributary streams, the name of the main stream is enclosed in brackets after it.

AXE

> *on, of Axan* 1005 (12th) KCD 1301, *Axe* 1244, 1249, 1281 *Ass,*
> *Ax* c. 1550 Leland, 1577 Saxton, *aqua de Axemynstre* 1244
> *Ass*
> *Hausse* 1198 FF

The meaning is simply 'water,' *v.* Ekwall RN 152. It is of Celtic origin and clearly allied to Exe. It may be the *Axium* of the Ravenna Geographer, *v. infra* 10.

BALA BROOK (Avon) is so spelt 1809 M. Ekwall (RN 25) suggests that it may be the same river-name as that found in Ball Mill (PN Wo 141), OE *Bæle* (acc.).

BATHERM (Exe) is *Batham River* 1765 D. Ekwall (RN 27) takes this to be a back-formation from some form *Bæðhǣmatūn,* 'farm of the dwellers by (More)bath,' the source of the p.n. Bampton *infra* 530. This involves many difficulties. Even if we admit that *Bæðhæmatun* might appear in DB as *Badentone* and, except for one form, never show any other trace of the medial consonant, we are still faced with the difficulty that the back-formation *Batham* must on this etymology have been evolved before 1200, as there are no forms after that date which could give rise to it. It is to be noted also that Morebath is not on the Batherm itself but on a nameless tributary of it. Further, More-bath and Bampton are some three miles apart and it is difficult to see why the inhabitants of Bampton should be named after (More)bath. The origin of Batherm must remain undetermined.

BECKA BROOK (Bovey) is *little river Becky* 1797 Polwhele. Probably a back-formation from Beckaford *infra* 483.

BLACKABROOK (Dart) is *Blakebroke* t. Hy 6 *Ct, Blakebrokehed* 1481 *Ct.* 'Dark brook.' The bed of the stream has a dark colour.

BOVEY (Teign) [bʌvi] is *aqua de Boui* 1238 *Ass, Bouy, Bouie* 1577, 1586 H, *the Bovey* c. 1620 Risdon. The name is pre-English and the meaning doubtful. Cf. Ekwall RN 44 and *v.* Bovey Tracy *infra* 466 for other and earlier forms.

BRAY (Mole) is *aqua de Bray* 1249 *Ass, Bray* 1577 Saxton. Ekwall (RN 49) takes this to be an early back-formation from High Bray *infra* 57.

BRIM BROOK (Okement) is *Brembrok* 1346 Dartmoor. Probably 'bramble brook.' *v.* bremel.

CAEN (Taw estuary) is called *Knowle Water* in 1667 (DA 8), and is probably a back formation from Knowle in Braunton *infra* 34. The name seems now to have been transferred to a small tributary of the Caen. The origin of the present name is uncertain, but there is a *Caen* Street in Braunton, and possibly both alike derive their name ultimately from the French town.

CAREY (Tamar) is *aqua de Kari* 1238 *Ass*, *Kary* 13th *Deed*, *Care flu* 1577 Saxton, *the Corewater* 1586 H, *Car* 1612 Drayton. According to Ekwall (RN 71) the root is a British word corresponding to W *caru*, 'to love,' *car*, 'friend,' the meaning being perhaps 'the friendly, pleasant stream.'

CHERRYBROOK (Dart) is *Churybrok(set)* 1347 Dartmoor, *Churebrok* 1452 *MinAcct*. There are many barrows in the neighbourhood and the first element may be OE *cyric* from *cryc*, 'barrow,' cf. cirice (EPN) and Churchill (PN Wo 106). Ekwall (*Studies* 53) would prefer OE *cierr*, 'turn,' with reference to its winding course.

CHOLAKE (Dart) (6″) is *Collake* 1358 Dartmoor, *Callak* 1417 *DuCo*, *Coullake* 1609 *DuCo*. Probably 'cool streamlet,' *v.* col, lacu, with later assimilation to the Devon dialectal form *chol(d)* for *cold*.

CLAW (Tamar) is *little river Claw* c. 1620 Risdon. For a discussion of this name *v.* Clawton *infra* 138.

CLYST (Exe) [klist] is *on, of clyst* 937, 963 BCS 721, 1103, *Clyst* 1281 *Ass*, *aqua de Clist* 1321 Exon. Ekwall (RN 82) derives this from a root **kleu-*, 'to wash,' with a suffix *-st* found also in Test (Ha). The meaning may have been 'clear stream.'

COLY (Axe) [kɔli] is *cullig* 1005 (12th) KCD 1301, *Coley river* c. 1550 Leland, *Coly* 1577 H. Ekwall (RN 91) would connect this with the root of W *cul*, 'narrow.'

CORRIE BROOK (Axe) is *small river...called Cor or Corry* 1797 Polwhele. *v. s.n.* Cory *infra* 160.

COWSICK (Dart) is *Cowlsick Coume* 1612 *DuCo*, *Cowsick Head* 1702 Dartmoor. The forms are too late for any suggestion to be offered.

CREEDY (Exe)

> *on Cridian* 739(11th), Crawf 1, *on, oþ cridian* 930 BCS 1343,
>   *Cridia* 1244 *Ass*
> *Cride* c. 1550 Leland, 1577, 1586 H
> *Creddy* 1612 Drayton

    v. also under Crediton, Creedy, Creedy Bridge *infra* 404–5,
419. Ekwall (RN 104) derives this from a British root meaning
'winding.'

CROOKED OAK (Mole) is *Crooked Ham* or *Crooked Oak* 1750
Recov and must originally have denoted some particular hamm
or tree, its transference to a stream-name being probably quite
recent.

CULM (Exe)

> *on, up, of culum, oð culum lace* 938 BCS 723–4, *Culum* 1238
>   *Ass, Colum* 1281 *Ass*
> *aqua de Culmstok* 1281 *Ass*
> *Culumþ, Culmþ* 1291 (1408) Dartmoor, *Columb* 1577 Saxton,
>   *Columbus* 1586 Camd

This is probably a British word corresponding to W *cwlm*, Co
colm, 'knot, tie,' referring to the numerous twists and loops
which the river makes in its course. *v.* Ekwall RN 109.

CULVERY (Creedy) is called *Culver* by Westcote (1630). It may
be that the modern form is more correct than the 17th century
one and that this is a derivative of OE *culfre*, 'dove, pigeon,' of
the same type as Otter, earlier *Oteri* (*v. infra* 11), from the otter.
This stream is referred to simply as *stream* in the great Crediton
Charter (cf. *Crawford Charters*, p. 51).

DALCH (Taw) is *on, oþ doflisc* 739 (11th) Crawf 1. 'Black or dark
stream,' a compound of Brit. *dubo*, 'black,' and the word for
stream found in Welsh and Irish as *glais*, cf. Ekwall RN 130 ff.
Identical with Dawlish *infra* 5.

DART is *to Dertan, on dertan stream* 10th BCS 1323, *Derte*
1162–5 Totnes, c. 1270 Gerv, 1244 *Ass*, 1249 *Ass*, *Dert* 1360 Cl,
Derta(m) 13th Buckfast, 1240 Dartmoor, *Derthe* 1244 *Ass*,
Dart 1577 Saxton. The root is a British word meaning 'oak,'

hence 'oak-grown stream,' *v.* Ekwall RN 114. Of similar origin are two further examples of Dart in Devon.

DART (Exe) is *Dart river* 1765 D. *v.* Dart Cottages *infra* 560.

LITTLE DART (Taw) is *Darte* 1544 *Augm. Office, Enrolment of Leases* (PRO), *Little Dart* 1765 D. *v.* also Dart Raffe *infra* 398.

DAWLISH WATER is *on doflisc ford* 1044 OS Facs ii, Exeter xii, *water of Doulys* 1284 *Deed, Dawlishwater, Dawlishford al. Dawliford* 1547 *FF.* Cf. Dalch *supra* 4 and Dawlish *infra* 491.

DEAD LAKE (Plym) (6″) is *Dedlakeheadd* 1608 Dartmoor. The meaning may be 'slow, sluggish streamlet,' *v.* lacu.

DEAN BURN (Dart) (6″) is *Deneburne* t. Hy 6 *Ct. v.* burna. It flows past Dean Prior *infra* 298.

DEER (Tamar) is *aqua de Dyraton* 1281 *Ass, Deer river* 1765 D. Probably a back-formation from Derriton *infra* 164.

DERRILL (Tamar) is *Derle river* 1765 D. Probably a back-formation from Derrill *infra* 163.

DRY LAKE (Erme) (6″) is *Drylake* 1608 Dartmoor. *v.* lacu.

ENGLEBOURNE (Dart) is *aquam de Engleburn* 1270 *Ass. v.* Englebourne *infra* 325.

ERME

> *Irym* 1240 Buckfast, *Hyrm* 1281 *Ass, Irm* 1346 Dartmoor, 1355 *DuCo, Irum* 1354 Dartmoor
> *Erme* 1240 Dartmoor, 1280 AD vi, *Erm* 1303 Misc, 1405 Pat *water of Ermyn* 1425 AD ii, *Arme Haven* c. 1550 Leland

Professor Max Förster compares the German river-name *Erms*, earlier *Armisa* (Holder *s.n.*), suggesting that there may have been a British *Armā by the side of *Armissa* (cf. Thames and Tame). Ekwall (RN 150) inclines to the view that it is a back-formation from Ermington *infra* 272.

EXE

> Ἴσκα (var. Ἰσάκα) ποταμοῦ ἐκβολαί c. 150 (13th) Ptolemy
> *Uuisc* c. 1000 Asser
> *to, andlang Eaxan* 739 (11th) BCS 1331, *Eaxa* a. 1118 (12th) FW

E

on, andlang exa, on exan stream 937 (11th) BCS 721, *ut on, andlang exan* 938 (11th) BCS 723, 1044 OS Facs ii, Exeter xii *ad Exam* c. 1180 HMC 4, 54, *Exe* 1238 *Ass et passim, Ex* c. 1550 Leland *watre Desse* c. 1200 Lay, *Esshe* 1281 *Ass* The meaning is simply 'water,' *v.* Ekwall RN 153. *Iska > Esca* by British *ā*-mutation. Asser's form is due to confusion of the British form of the river-name with the Welsh *Usk* and the like.

FISH LAKE (Avon) (6″) is *Fysshlake* 1474 *Ct.* 'Fish streamlet,' *v.* lacu.

GARA RIVER is called *aqua de Slapton* in 1244 (*Ass*) from Slapton *infra* 330. No explanation of Gara can be offered. Cf. however Gara Bridge in Diptford *infra* 300.

THE GESSAGE (6″) and GISSAGE LAKE. These are the names of two streams, the first joining the Yeo near Zeal Monachorum, the second joining the Otter at Honiton. No early forms have been found but it is almost certain that the names are identical with Gussage (Do), explained by Ekwall (RN 187) as a compound of an OE root *gyse meaning 'to gush or break forth' (related to the ON *geysir*, 'hot spring') and OE *sīc*, 'water course.' It may be noted that the Gessage falls 400 feet in about 4½ miles, passing over two waterfalls and turning a mill.

GLAZE BROOK (Avon) is *terra de Glas, Ester-, Westerglas* 13th Oliver, *due Glas, ad caput glas* 1240 Buckfast, *Glase, Glass* 1287, 1297 *Add, waters called Esterglas and Westerglas* 1316 Pat, *Les Glases, Glase Head* 1557 Dartmoor, *Glazebrook* 1827 G. 'Grey stream,' the first element being the British *glas* 'grey, green, blue,' cf. Ekwall RN 175.

GRINDLE BROOK (Clyst—Exe) is *on, anlang Grendel* 963 BCS 1103, *grendelbroc* 13th *St Nicholas.* See also *s.n.* Greendale *infra* 586. Ekwall (RN 186) takes this to be an early example of the transference of a name from a valley to the stream which runs through it. It is difficult to suggest a parallel for such a formation and Ekwall himself has noted the difficulty involved in the uninflected form of the first element. On these grounds and on the additional ground that *dæl* or *del* is otherwise unknown in

Devon p.n.'s, Zachrisson has suggested (*Jespersen Miscellany* 39 ff.) that we may have a derivative of OE *grand*, 'gravel,' and that *grendel* denotes the 'gravelly brook.' This would suit the topography.

HARBOURNE (Dart) is *Hurburn(e)* 1244 *Ass*, 1315 Totnes, *Hurberne* t. Ed 2 Exon, *Hurburnewelne, -willene* 13th Buckfast, *Hareborne* 1577 Saxton, *Hartburn* 1577 H. *v.* burna. The first element may be OE *hēore, hȳre*, 'gentle, mild, pleasant.' Equally possible, and with frequent parallels, is *heort-burna*, 'hart-stream,' with early loss of *t*. See further Harberton *infra* 325, and Ekwall RN 191.

HARTLAKE (Erme) (6″) is *Hurtelake* 1474 *Ct*. 'Hart streamlet,' *v.* lacu.

HEDDON is no doubt a late formation from HEDDON's MOUTH, the name of the cove where the stream enters the sea. This probably derives from the family of *Heddon* found in North Devon (Morthoe, etc.) in the 17th and 18th centuries (Wills).

HEMS (Dart) is *Hemese* 1287, *Hemse* 1467 *Deed. v.* Broadhempston *infra* 509.

HOLY BROOK (Dart) is called *Nordbroc, Northbroke* 13th Buckfast. Probably because north of the Mardle *infra* 9, the next tributary of the Dart.

HURRABROOK (Plym) (6″) is *Horebrok* 1276 *Ass*, *Horingbrok* 1291 (1408) Dartmoor. Probably 'dirty brook,' *v.* horh.

KATE BROOK (Teign) is called *Cranemereslake* 1313 Misc, i.e. 'heron-pool streamlet,' *v.* cran, mere, lacu. Cf. Crammer *infra* 558.

KENN is *Ken* or *Kenton brooke* 1577 H, *Ken flu* 1610 Speed. *v.* also Kenn and Kenton *infra* 498–9. This is a non-English rivername, found also in Kenn (So), DB *Chen(t)*, and in Ken Water (He). The meaning is doubtful. The most probable source is perhaps the Celtic **canto*, 'brilliant, white,' found in W pers. names such as *Morcant* ('Morgan'), cf. Ekwall RN 224.

KESTER BROOK (Lemon) is recorded in the phrase *in aquis de Kersbrooke et lemon* 1634 *Recov*. The relation of the early and

modern forms is obscure. *Kersbrooke* is naturally explained as
'cress brook,' cf. Kerswell *infra* 144, but it is difficult to see
how that could ever have become Kester Brook.

KNATHORN BROOK (Yeo-Taw) is identical with *scipbroc* 974 BCS
1303, 'sheep brook.' The present name is a new formation
from Knathorn *infra* 410.

LEGISLAKE (Plym) (6″) is identical with *Yaddabrok* 1291 (1408)
Dartmoor. '*Ead(d)a*'s brook.' The origin of the present name
is unknown.

LEMON (Teign) is *on lymen stream* 10th BCS 1323, *Limene*,
Limne 1244 *Ass*, *Leman water* c. 1550 Leland, *Lemman* 1559
Deed. The name is a derivative of a Celtic word meaning 'elm'
(OIr *lem*, W *llwyf*). Cf. Ekwall RN 243.

LEW (Torridge) is *aqua de Lyu* 1281 *Ass*, 1370 *Ass*. A British
name; cf. Ekwall RN 253, where it is connected with Welsh *lliw*,
OCo *liu*, 'colour.' The meaning is perhaps 'bright stream.'
A further example is

LEW (Lyd—Tamar), *watercourse called Lywe* 1565 DCo NQ 3.

LILLY BROOK (Tedburn) is *oþ lillan broc* 739 (11th) Crawf 1,
Lilly brooke 1717 *Deed*. '*Lilla*'s brook.'

LIM[1] is *Lim* 774 (12th) BCS 224, *Lym* 938 (14th) BCS 728, *Lyme*
1322 Pat. The name is probably connected with W *llif*, 'flood,'
Gk λειμών, 'wet place,' λίμνη, 'pond.' Cf. Ekwall RN 274 and
Uplyme *infra* 649.

LOMAN (Exe) is *Loman* 1563 *Deed*, 1577 Saxton, *Lomund water*
1577, 1586 H, *Leman flu* 1610 Speed, *Lowman* or *Leman* 1797
Polwhele. For earlier forms of this river see the forms for
Uplowman, Chieflowman *infra* 552, which stand on its banks.
Ekwall (RN 265), taking the *nm* of the DB forms of those names to
be due to faulty attempts to transcribe the river-name, would
carry Loman back to an OE *Leomene*, *Lumene*, a river-name of
Celtic origin found in Lemon *supra*.

---

[1] Rises in Devon but enters the sea at Lyme Regis in Dorset.

LUMBURN (Tavy) is (*the bank of*) *Lambre* t. Hy 2 (15th) Buckland, *the Lamber* 1750 Pococke. *v.* also Lamerton *infra* 185. This stream is called *lamburna* in BCS 1247, where it is used apparently as the name of the present Lamerton *infra* 185. From the 12th century to the 18th a back-formation *Lambre* or *Lambe* from such a ME form for the village as *Lambreton* (DB) was in use. In modern times this has been made to end in the more common *-burn*. As the pasturage here is bad for sheep[1] the etymology may be *lām-burna*, 'loam-stream,' rather than *lamb-burna*.

LYD (Tamar) is *aqua de Lide* 1249 *Ass*, *Lede* 1577 Saxton, *Lidde* 1577, 1586 H. 'Noisy, loud stream,' a common English rivername, *v.* Ekwall RN 273.

LYN is *aquam de Lyn* 1281 *Ass*, *riveret Linne* 1630 Westcote, *Lyne* 1727 DA 38. This is probably the OE *hlynn*, 'torrent.' The stream is short and very rapid. Cf. Ekwall RN 274.

LYNOR (Culm)[2] is *to, andlang linor* 958 (12th) BCS 1027, *Lino* 1173-5 (1329) Ch, *Lynor* c. 1200 (14th) *Canonsleigh*, *Linor* 1408 Dartmoor, *Lunor* 12th (14th) *Canonsleigh*. The name is identical with Lynher (Co). Various etymologies are possible. *v.* Ekwall RN 276. The most likely is that which associates it with a root *lei-*, 'to pour, flow, drip,' found in Welsh *lliant*, OIr *lie*, 'flood.'

MANGA BROOK (Teign) is *Mangersford* 1442 Dartmoor. *Manga* is probably a back-formation from Mangersford, the first element being the OE *mangere*, 'dealer, monger,' possibly here a pers. name.

MARDLE (Dart) is *Myreles, Merylis, Miriles, Mirilisse* 13th Buckfast, *Marles* 1497 *Ct*. The meaning may be 'bramble stream,' from British words corresponding to W *mwyar*, 'blackberries,' or *miaren*, 'bramble,' and *glais*, 'stream.' Cf. Dalch *supra* 4 and Ekwall RN 278.

MEAVY (Plym)

on mæwi 1031 KCD 744
Mewy3 t. Hy 2 Oliver 135, *Mewyhevet* 1281 *Ass*, *Mewy* 1291

---

[1] *Ex inf.* Mr J. J. Alexander.
[2] This is the name of the upper part of the stream. Lower down it is now called Spratford Stream from Spratford Bridge *infra* 550.

(1408) Dartmoor, *Mewe* 1638 DCo NQ 12, 239, *Mew* 1577
HMC 9, 281, *Mewie water* 1614 *Deed*
Meve 1589 HMC 9, 278

In his book on *English River-names* (283), Ekwall suggests,
with a good deal of hesitation, that here we may have a compound of OE *mǣw,* 'sea-gull,' and *īe,* 'river,' as in Otter *infra* 11.
Mr O. G. S. Crawford has recently been collating manuscripts
of the Ravenna Geographer, and notes, with regard to the list of
rivers given there that we have successively *Traxula, Axium,
Mavia, Sarna, Tamaris* (*Mavia* is the reading of the Vatican
and Basle Manuscripts, *Maina* of the Paris Manuscript). It
would seem from the order that as the second and fifth of these
must be taken to refer to the Axe or (less probably) the Exe and
the Tamar, the third is the Meavy which, as a tributary of the
Plym, enters the sea at Plymouth Sound. If so the name must
be pre-English, as Ekwall suspected might possibly be the case.
For the change from *w* to *v* cf. Introd. xxxv.

MERE (Torridge) is *riveret called Meer* in 1630 (Westcote).
v. Marland *infra* 97.

MINCING LAKE (Exe) (6") is *Mynchynlake* 1461 Pat and was so
called because the stream flowed past Polsloe Nunnery, *v.*
myncen. The earlier name was *Wynford* 937 BCS 721, *Womford*
1244 *Ass, Wonford water* t. Jas I *Rental*, which very likely corresponds to W *gwyn,* 'white,' and *ffrwd,* 'stream.' Cf. Ekwall RN
462, and Wonford *infra* 441.

MOLE (Bray) is *Moll* 1553 Pat, *Moule flu* 1577 Saxton, *Moul flud*
1610 Speed. The history of this river-name is bound up with that
of North and South Molton *infra* 344 ff., which stand on it, with
Molland, six miles east of North Molton which stands not on
the Yeo (as suggested by Blomé 72) but on an unnamed tributary of that stream, and with Molland Cross and Higher
Molland, away from any stream in the north of North Molton
parish. The occurrence of an element *Mol-* in the names of three
scattered places linked together by no common feature suggests
that we may here have the same phenomenon as in Hartland and
Hindharton *infra* 71, 74, Kilkhampton and *Kilkhamland* (Co),

Callington and *Calliland* (Co), where we have apparently *land* used of a large area and *tun* of some smaller unit within it. Is it possible that *Mol* is some such name, applied to a large area in the angle between the Bray and the Yeo, possibly bounded by Somerset on the north? If this is correct, we must with Ekwall (RN 295) interpret *Mole* river as a back-formation from Molton.

NADDER BROOK (Exe) is *Adderbrook* 1675 Ogilby. In a *Rental* of 1344 there is mention of Richard *Bynaddre* and in one of 1382 of Richard *atte Nadder*, cf. also the forms for Nadder in Whitestone *infra* 459. The name is probably identical in origin with the *Nadrid* in Nadrid Water *infra*.

NADRID WATER (Taw) is named from Nadrid in North Molton *infra* 344. This is *Naddereheved* 1330 SR (p), i.e. head of the *Naddere*, suggesting that this was the old name of the stream on which Nadrid stands. Cf. also *Naddermede* 1399 Ct nearby. Blomé (73) suggests that the stream was so called from its winding course, suggesting an *adder* (OE *nædre*). Another possibility is that we have the same name as in the Wiltshire Nadder. That goes back to OE *Nodre* and first appears as *Nadder* in 1540.

NARRATOR BROOK (Meavy) (6″) is a modern formation from Narrator in Sheepstor *infra* 240. An earlier name was *Denebrok* 1291 (1408) Dartmoor, *Denbroke* 1622 *Deed*, *v*. denu.

OBROOK (Dart) is *Ocbroke, Ocbrokesfoten* 1240 Buckfast, *Okebrok, Okebrokysfote* 1240 Dartmoor, *Obrokefote* 1525 DuCo, *Wobrooke-foote* 1608 Dartmoor. Perhaps 'oak brook,' though oaks are rare here. The element *fot* in some of the forms probably refers to the 'foot' of the stream, where it joins the Dart.

OKEMENT (Torridge) is *aqua de Okem* 1244 *Ass*, *Okemund* 1281 *Ass*, *Ockment flu* 1577 Saxton. The first element is derived by Bradley (*Furnival Miscellany* 13) and Ekwall (RN 308) from the Celtic *aku*, 'swift,' found in the OWelsh *di-auc*, 'not swift, lazy.' The second syllable is derived by Bradley from a derivative of the root in Welsh *myned*, 'to go,' by Ekwall from an Aryan root *mim*, 'noisy.'

OTTER is *on otrig* 1061 (1227) *Ottery, aqua de Otery* 1244 *Ass*, *Ottery* 1249 *Ass*, *water of Oter* 1540 LP, *Autri* 1577 H. This name and Ottery (Co) are derived by Ekwall (RN 313) from the OE *oter*, 'otter,' and *īe, ī* or *īg* the dative of *ēa*, 'water,' which was generalised for all cases.

PIALL (Yealm) is *Pial, Piall, Pialhavede* 13th *Add.* No explanation of the name can be offered.

PLYM is *Plyme* 1238 FF, *Plime* 1244 *Ass, Plym* 1359 Pat, *Plymma* 1291 (1408) Dartmoor, and is thought by Ekwall (RN 328) to be a very early back-formation from Plympton and Plymstock *infra* 251, 256.

RATTLEBROOK (Tavy) is *Rakylbrokesfote* 1240 Buckfast, *Rakernebrokysfote* 1240 Dartmoor, *Rattylbroke fote* 1539 *Deed.* The first element may be ME *rakel*, 'rash, hasty, impetuous,' *v.* NED *s.v. rackle* and Ekwall RN 334.

RED LAKE (Dart) (6") is *Redlake* 1475 *MinAcct, Radlake* 1555 *MinAcct.*

REDLAKE (Erme) is *La Redelake* 1240 Buckfast, *Rydelake* 1377 *Ct, Redlake* 1479 Dartmoor.

REDLAKE (Tavy) (6") is *wester Redlake* 1608 Dartmoor. All three examples should probably be interpreted as 'red streamlet.' *v.* lacu. The absence of *rud*-forms combined with the known red colour of the stream-bottoms in Dartmoor favours 'red' rather than 'reed.'

SHOBROOKE LAKE (Creedy) is possibly *sceoca broc* 938 BCS 726. For further forms *v.* Shobrooke *infra* 416. The original name was probably *sceoccanbroc*, i.e. 'goblin's brook.'

SID is *aqua de Sideford* 1238 *Ass, Side* c. 1250 Oliver, *(le) Syde* 1284 BM, 1420 *Ct, Sid river* c. 1550 Leland. On the banks of the Sid we have Sidmouth, Sidbury and Sidford, the first two going back to the 11th century, so that it is clear that we have to do with a genuine river-name. Ekwall (RN 364) takes it to be from OE *sīd*, 'wide,' but hesitates about the interpretation, as the stream is not particularly wide. It may, however, as he suggests, have been so called in contrast to some yet narrower stream.

SILVERBRIDGE LAKE (Yealm) is *the Silver, a little clear stream* 1797 Polwhele. Cf. also *Silverbridge* 1641, *Silvercleave* 1726

Deed nearby. For a discussion of this name *v.* Little Silver *infra* 358.

SMALLBROOK (Dart) (6″) is *Smalebrok(e)* 13th Buckfast, 1520 *Recov*, *Smallbrook Foot* 1557 Dartmoor. 'Narrow brook,' *v.* smæl.

SMALL BROOK (Taw) (6″) is *Smalebroke* t. Hy 6 *Ct.*

SMALLHANGER BROOK (Tory Brook) (6″) is referred to as *per aquam de Lobbe* 1356 *Ass*, which must be so named from Lobb Fm on its banks. See further *s.n.* Lobb *infra* 33. The modern name is derived from Smallhanger *infra* 255.

STRANE (Dart) is *Strane head*, *Strane foot* 1808 *DuCo.*

SWINCOMBE RIVER (Dart) is named from Swincombe *infra* 61. The older name (preserved in Sherberton *infra* 197) was *Shir-*, *Shurburnmede* 1355 *DuCo*, *Shirbornefoote* t. Mary, *Sherborne-foote* 1561 *MinAcct.* For 'foot' *v.* Obrook *supra* 11. The name means 'bright stream,' *v.* scir, burna.

TADDIFORD BROOK (Exe) (6″) is probably named from a lost place *Tadieford*, c. 1280–5 HMC Exeter, *Tadyeforde* 1367 *Deed.* 'Toad-frequented ford,' the first element being OE *tādige*, 'toad.'

TALE (Otter) is *on tælen* 1061 (1227) *Ottery*, *Tale* 1238 FF, 1339 *Ass*, *Tala* 1185 (15th) Buckland. Ekwall (RN 388) derives this from OE *getæl*, 'quick, active,' hence 'swift.' It should be noted, however, that the stream is sluggish in character and a different etymology may well have to be sought. There is also Tala Water, a tributary of the Tamar, in Werrington.

TAMAR

  ταμάρου ποταμοῦ ἐκβολαί c. 150 (13th) Ptolemy
  Tamaris c. 650 (13th) Ravenna Geographer
  tamur 980–8 Crawf 7
  into Tamer mūðan 997 E (c. 1200) ASC, *Tamer* 1018 OS Facs
    ii, Exeter ix, 1281 *Ass*
  Tambra c. 1125 WM, *Tambre*, *Tanbre* 1205 Lay, *Taumbre*
    1242 Fees 797

The name is a derivative with an -*ar* suffix of the root *tam* seen in Tame (Wa), Thame (O), Team (Du). The sense is uncertain, *v.* Ekwall RN 389.

TAVY (Tamar) is *Taui* c. 1125 WMP, 1238, 1281 *Ass*, *Tavie* 1291 (1408) Dartmoor, *Tave* c. 1550 Leland. A derivative of the root found in Tamar *supra* 13. *v.* Ekwall RN 393.

TAW

> *Táwmuða* 1068 D (c. 1100) ASC, *Thau(e)* 1198 FF, 1350 Ipm,
> *Tau* 1244 *Ass*, *Taw(e)* 1249 *Ass*, 1314 Ipm, 1479 *FF*
> *Thou* 1249 *Ass*, *Tow(e)* c. 1280 Barum, 1394 Cl, 1398 Pat

The name means 'the silent one' (Ekwall RN 394), and is identical with Tay in Scotland. *v.* Appledore *infra* 102.

TED (Yeo—Creedy) is *on tettan burnan* 739 (11th) Crawf 1. The name is a back-formation from Tedburn *infra* 451.

TEIGN [ti·n]

> *on teng* 739 (11th) Crawf 1, *on tenge muðan* 1044 OS Facs ii,
> Exeter xii
> *Teine* c. 1200 Lay, *Tyng* 1240 Dartmoor, 1577 Saxton, *Teyng*
> 1244 *Ass*, 1249 *Ass*, *Tengne* 1277 *Ass*, *Teygne* 1281 *Ass*

The meaning may have been simply 'stream,' *v.* Ekwall RN 398. Cf. W *taen*, 'sprinkling,' and Lat *stagnum*.

THRUSHEL (Lyd) is *aqua de Frischel*[1] 1244 *Ass*, *Thrushel flu* 1577 Saxton. This is a back-formation from Thrushelton *infra* 210. Interchange of *th* and *f* is fairly common, cf. Fingest PN Bk 176.

TIDDY BROOK (Tavy) (6″) is *Tuddebroke* 1561 *FF*. Possibly '*Tud(d)a*'s brook,' but Tiddy river (Co), *Tudi* 1018 OS Facs ii, Exeter ix, suggests that we may have here an original streamname of pre-English origin. Cf. Ekwall RN 406 and Tidwell, Tidlake *infra* 382, 521, 583.

TORRIDGE

> *on toric stream* 938 (11th) BCS 725
> *Thoriz, Toriz* 1238 *Ass*, *Toryz* 1249 *Ass*, *Thori* 1249 *Ass*
> *Torrygg* 1345 *Ass*, *Torighe* 1391 Cl, *Tor(r)ygg(e)* 1388 IpmR,
> 1389 *FF*, *Toryg* 1398 Exon

---

[1] *Frischel* rather than *Fruschel* (RN 406) is the correct reading.

The name corresponds to modern W *terig*, 'ardent, severe, harsh,' from *torri*, 'to break,' hence 'violent, rough stream' (Ekwall RN 413). Cf. also Tory Brook *infra*.

TORR BROOK (Avon) is called *aqua de Wudleg* 1249 *Ass* from Woodleigh *infra* 312.

TORY BROOK (Plym) is *aqua de Torygg* 13th *Add*, *Torey broke* c. 1550 Leland, *Torrey brooke* 1577 H. *v.* Torridge *supra* 14. The form *Torygg* now brought to light confirms Ekwall's surmise with regard to this name (RN 413).

TRONEY (Crediton Yeo). This name must be a late back-formation from Troney Bridge *infra* 404.

UMBER is called *Humber* by Westcote (1630). This may well be an antiquary's mis-spelling and the probability is that, as suggested by Ekwall (RN 426), it is identical with Umborne *infra*.

UMBORNE (Coly) is *little river Womborne* c. 1620 Risdon, *The Omber or Wombern* 1797 Polwhele. The forms for *Womberford infra* 625 make it clear that Ekwall (RN 427) is right in associating this with the stream-name found in Wimborne (Do), earlier *Winburna* (BCS 114) which Ekwall (RN 460) derives from OE *winn*, 'meadow.' For the phonological development we may compare Swincombe *infra* 61 and Somborne (Ha) which stands on a stream called *Swinburna* (BCS 629). Grundy (*Arch. Journ.* 81, 441) is unnecessarily sceptical about the correctness of this last form.

VENFORD BROOK (Dart) (6″) is *Wenford* 1355 *DuCo, Wendford* 1358 Dartmoor, *Wandeford* 1452 *MinAcct, Wendford lake* 1609 *DuCo.* The forms are not sufficiently early to decide whether this is derived from some lost place *Wendford* or whether the *d* is unoriginal, in which case the name may be British and identical with Wonford (*v. s.n.* Mincing Lake *supra* 10).

VINE WATER (Otter) (6″) is *on Finan* 1061 (1227) *Ottery, Vine* 1797 Polwhele. Ekwall (RN 429) suggests connexion with W *ffin*, 'boundary,' a loan word from Lat *finis.* It here forms the boundary of the parish of Ottery. The same word may be the first element of *on finfos* 960 BCS 1056 (Co), the second being Co *fos*, 'ditch, dike.'

WALDON RIVER (Torridge) is *Waldon river* 1765 D, and takes its name from Waldon *infra* 153. It is perhaps identical with *aqua de Mine* 1281 *Ass*, *v. infra* 18.

WALKHAM (Tavy)

> *aquae de...et de Walkamp* 1291 (1408) Dartmoor, *in aquis de Walkham et Tavy* 1684 *Recov*, *river of Walkham* 1813 *Recov*, *water of Walcomton* 15th *Deed*
> *the Stoure* 1586 H, *the river Store* c. 1620 Risdon, *little river Stour* 1797 Polwhele

Ekwall (RN 430) rightly suggests that this is probably a backformation from the p.n. Walkhampton. The late *Sto(u)re* forms may represent a genuine survival of an earlier *Stour*-name for the river, or they may possibly be late antiquarian inventions.

WALLA BROOK (Dart) iş *Walebrokesheved* 1240 Buckfast, *Wallebrok* 1240 Dartmoor 1384 *Ct*, *Walebrok* 1347 *DuCo*, *Walbrookland* 1379 Dartmoor, *Wallebrokeland* 1417 *MinAcct*. OE *Wēala brōc*, 'stream of the Britons.' *v*. Introd. xxiii.

WALLA BROOK (Avon) (6″) is *Welebroc* 13th Buckfast, *Wester Wellabroke* 1240 Dartmoor, *Willebrok* 1382 Dartmoor, *Welbroklond* Hy 7 *MinAcct*, *Wellebrooke* 1608 Dartmoor. This is probably a compound of *wielle-brōc*, 'brook fed by a spring,' cf. Wellesbourn (Wa), *Welesburna* (BCS 430).

WALLA BROOK (Tavy). This is called *Endlesbrooke* in 1488 (*Rental*), a name which is probably connected with Indescombe (*infra* 218), a farm in the valley. The present name does not appear before 1809 (M) and may have been suggested by the not far distant Dartmoor Walla Brooks.

WALLA BROOK (Teign) is referred to as *Wotesbrokelakesfote* 1240 Dartmoor. *v*. lacu. The first syllable may be a pers. name *Wott*, cf. Waddesdon (PN Bk 137). The modern name appears first as *Walla Brook*, *Wallbrook* 1827 G. For *fote*, cf. Obrook *supra* 11.

WEAVER (Culm—Exe) is *Weure* 1231 *St Nicholas*, *Weuer flu* 1577 Saxton, *Veuer flud* 1610 Speed. This is identical with Weaver (Ch). The meaning is uncertain, *v*. Ekwall RN 443.

WEBBURN (Dart) is *Wedeburne, an Wedeburnan* 10th BCS 1323, *Wedeborna* 13th AD vi, *Webborna* 13th AD v, *Weburne* 1310 *Ass*. The meaning is probably 'raging stream,' the first element being a derivative of OE *wōd*, 'mad.' *v.* Ekwall RN 444.

WOLF (Otter) must be a late back-formation from Wolford in Dunkeswell *infra* 615. There is also WOLF, a tributary of the Lyd, the origin of which is unknown.

WRAY (Teign) is *aque de Wrey* 1478, 1488 Wreyland, *The Wray*, *river Wrey* 1829 Moore. Further forms are supplied by Wray Barton in Moretonhampstead *infra* 484. These suggest that the name may be a compound of OE *wearg*, 'felon' (cf. Whitchurch Down *infra* 248), and *īe*, as in Otter *supra* 11. For such a stream-name with its possible reference to the execution of felons by drowning, cf. Wreigh Burn (RN 473).

YARTY (Axe) is *Jerti* 1238 *Ass*, *Yearte* 1467, 1479 *Ct*, *Yerty* 1511 Oliver, *Yartey* c. 1550 Leland, *Artey* 1577 H. The root according to Ekwall (RN 479) may be a British word *artio*, *-ia*, derived from **arto*, 'bear' (W *arth*). The bear was formerly a British mammal, not becoming extinct till about the 8th century.

YEALM [jæm] is *Yhalam* 1310 Ipm, *Yalme* 1414 Exon, *Yalam* 1466 Pat, *Yaulme* c. 1550 Leland. Ekwall (RN 480) would take this to be from a British adjective allied to Lat. *almus*, 'kind.'

YEO (Creedy) is *on eowan* 739 (11th) Crawf 1, *Iouwe* 1238 *Ass*, *Iou* 1244 *Ass*, *Yew* 1630 Westcote. Possibly 'yew stream,' cf. Zachrisson in NoB 14, 54.

YEO (Dart) is *æscburne, oð æscburnan* 10th BCS 1323, *water called Ayssheborne* 1504 DA 56, *water called Aysheborne* 1553 DA 28, *the Yeo* 1797 Polwhele. The old name meant 'ash stream,' *v.* æsc, burna. Cf. Ashburton *infra* 462.

YEO (Taw at Barnstaple) is *Yeo* 1630 Westcote, 1765 D. *v.* Yeotown in Goodleigh *infra* 44, past which place the stream runs.

YEO (Taw at Lapford) is *river Lovebrook, Lovebroke* 1590 DKR 38, *river called Lovebrook al. Yeo* t. Eliz DA 33, 451. '*Lēofa's* brook.'

There is good reason to believe that the (*on*) *nymed*, *nimed* of BCS 1331, 1332 and the (*on*) *nymed* of BCS 1303 refer to this stream. See further *s.n.* George Nympton *infra* 348.

YEO (Torridge) is *Yeo Rivulet* 1765 D. In all these names except the first the modern Yeo is simply a dialectal form of OE *ēa*, 'water,' which became in Devon *eā*, *ya*, later *yo. v.* Introd. xxxiii.

Among lost river-names of pre-English origin may be noted *aqua de Duuelis* (1249 *Ass*, Black Torrington Hundred) and *aqua de Dowlis* (1249 *Ass*, Shebbear Hundred), both of which are identical in origin with Dalch *supra* 4. Also *aqua de Myrigg* (1281 *Ass*) and *aqua de Mine* (1281 *Ass*, Shebbear Hundred), the latter possibly the present Waldon River *supra* 16. Lost stream-names of English origin generally survive as farm-names. See also *infra* 658-9: *s.v.* broc, burna.

HILL-NAMES

Individual hill-names will be discussed under the parishes in which they occur. The most important hill-ranges are:

BLACKDOWN HILLS. These are referred to as *Blakedoune* 13th *Canonsleigh*, *Blacke Downe* 1566 DA 43. They form the boundary between Devon and Somerset for the greater part of their range.

DARTMOOR is *Dertemora*, *-e* 1181 P, c. 1200 *Torre et passim*, (*forest of*) 1232-9 Ch, (*juxta Ludeford*) 1359 *Ass*, *Dartmore* 1579 Dartmoor, taking its name from the river Dart (*supra* 4), the chief of the many streams which rise within its boundaries.

EXMOOR is *Exemora* t. John (1313) Ch, 1249 *Ass*, *-mor(e)* 1204 Exmoor, 1238 *Ass*, 1275 RH, *Essemore* 1225 Ass (So), *Esshemor* 1238 *Ass*, *Axmore* 1591 Exmoor, taking its name from the river Exe *supra* 5. The actual Forest of Exmoor lies in Somerset, but a large part of the moor lies in Devon.

GREAT HALDON (hill-range)

    (*super montem de*) *Hagheledon* 1281 *Ass*, 1313 Misc, (*hill of*)
        Hagheldon 1301 Ipm, 1306 Lives, 1331 Ipm
    Hayeldoune 1329 Exon

Hauldon 1296 *MinAcct*
Haghenedon 1298 BM
Heweldon 1475 IpmR

The first element would appear to be OE *hagol*, 'hail,' and the hill may have been named from some famous storm, cf. Snowdon *infra* 294, 311.

LITTLE HALDON (hill-range) is *Lytlehaldon al. Letheweldowen* 1564 *Deed, Little Haldon al. Leughwelldoune* 1614 *Recov*, (*al. La Well Doune*) 1692 *Recov*.

ISLANDS

Lundy Island in the Bristol Channel is a part of Devon and is reckoned in Braunton Hundred. Except for Borough Island (*infra* 267) there are no other true islands, though there are numerous rocks or rocky islets which will be noted under the parishes in which they occur, if there is mention of them in early documents.

Lundy Island

LUNDY ISLAND

Lundey, (*til*) *Lundeyar* 1139–48 (14th) Orkneyingasaga
Lundeia 1199 ChR
Londay 1275 RH, 1322 Misc, 1350 Ipm, 1385 *FF*
Lunday 1281, 1322 Ch, 1321 *Ass*, 1333 *FF*, *-dey* 1353 Exon
Lounday 1326 Fine, 1332 Exon, *-dey* 1353 Exon

This is, as has often been suggested in histories and guide-books, from the ON *lundi*, 'puffin,' and ey, 'island.' Puffins are still frequent visitors to the island though they are rarely met with on the mainland.

NAMES OF BAYS, INLETS AND ESTUARIES

Most names of bays and estuaries will, when occurring in early documents, be found under the parishes in which they are situated.

BIGBURY BAY is *Bigberie Baie* 1588 PlymRec from Bigbury *infra* 266.

CATTEWATER. *v. infra* 234, *s.n.* CATTEDOWN.

HAMOAZE [hæm'ouz] is *ryver of Hamose* 1588 PlymRec, *Ham-os*
1594 Norden. This name is now applied to the estuary of th
Tamar between Saltash and Plymouth Sound. It probabl
originally referred to a much smaller area, viz. the creek whic
runs up to Ham manor in Weston *infra* 246. At a later perio
the name must have been extended to the main channel of th
estuary. *Ose* is no doubt for 'ooze' (OE *wāse*, 'mud'), th
creek at low tide consisting of mud-banks. Cf. Wapping (Pl
Mx 90) and Ouse (PN Sx 6).

LAIRA [lɛ·rə] is *le lare, The Lary Poynt* t. Hy 7 DA 10, *Lar*
t. Eliz Worth, *Lary poynte, Steartlary* 1638 *Recov, the Leer*
1643 Worth. This is the name given to the estuary of the Plyr
below Plympton as far as Cattewater. Laira Bridge crosses th
river above Mount Batten. The forms are too late for certaint
but the name may be of Celtic origin, cf. Welsh *llaeru*, 'to ebl
to grow shallow.' Derivation from the ON *leirr*, 'clay,' *leir*
'clayey place,' referring to the mud-banks here, is less likel}
Steartlary must be the old name for Mount Batten, referring t
the point of land here, *v.* steort.

PLYMOUTH SOUND is *the Sounde* 1585 PlymRec. The wor
'sound' in the sense 'channel' is first recorded in the 13t
century and goes back to OE *sund*, 'swimming,' 'place fo
swimming.'

TOR BAY is *Torrebay* 1401 Pat, *Torrebaie, -bay* 1412 Seld 10 an
is named from Torre *infra* 524.

Exeter

Ἴσκα c. 150 (13th) Ptolemy

Isca Dumnoniorum 4th Tabula Peuteringana, (*Dumnuniorun*
3rd (8th) Antonine Itinerary, (*Dumnamorum*) c. 650 (13th
Ravenna Geographer

Adescancastre c. 750 Vita S. Bonifacii, *Escanceaster* 876 .
(c. 890) ASC

Exanceaster 894 Ā (c. 900) ASC, t. Alfred Coins, 938 BCS 72.
-ceastre c. 1000 Asser, 900–25 (c. 1140) Laws, *-cestre* 93
BCS 693, c. 1000 Earle, *-cester* 1067 D (c. 1100) ASC

Eaxanceastre 925–39 Laws, *-ceaster* t. Athelstan, *-cestre* t. Cnut
Coins, *Eaxeancestre* c. 1000 Asser, *Eaxeceaster* 1003 E (1121)
ASC, t. Ethelred 2 Coins

Execeaster 928 (12th) BCS 663, *Exaceaster* 938 BCS 723,
Exceaster t. Cnut Coins, *Ecxeceaster* t. Harold 1 Coins

Execester t. Ed Conf Coins, *excestre* 1050–73 Earle, *Exacestre*
1070 Wells i, 434, *Execestre* 1135 E (12th) ASC, 1196 P

Essecestra 1086 DB (Exon), *Execestre* (Exch)

la cite Dexcestre c. 1200 *Canonsleigh*

Æexechæstre, Axcetre, Exchæstre, Excestre c. 1225 Lay

Essexestr' 1242 Cl, *Eccestre* c. 1300 RG

Excetur 1456, *Excetyr* 1466 Pat, *Excyter* 1523 *SR*

Excestre, Excetour, Exceter 1477 Seld 16, *Excester* 1577
Saxton

Exeter 1547 Wardens, *Exiter* 1549 Som Rec Soc 2, 195

In British times the city was clearly named from the river
alone. Cf. Romano-British *Dano* for Doncaster. Later this was
compounded with **ceaster**.

NOTE[1]. The following are the chief street names. BARBICAN (lost)
is *Barbigan east* 1397 *St Johns*, *the Barbycan* 1562 HMC Exeter and
must have referred to an outer defensive work on the city walls. *v.*
NED *s.v.* BARTHOLOMEW STREET was earlier *Britaynne* c. 1250 *Deed*,
Britayne a. 1355, (*highway called*) 1460 HMC Exeter, *Bretayne street
now called Bartholomew street* 16th Oliver. This street, like Little
Britain in London (*Brettone strete* 1329, *Pety Bryttayne* 1561), may owe
its name to a settlement of Bretons. Cf. the street-name *Petty France*
in Westminster. BONHAY ROAD takes its name from *pasture of the Bonhay*, *Bonhaye mylles* 1577, *feldes named Bonnehay* 1584 HMC Exeter.
The forms are too late for any explanation of the first element to be
possible. For *hay*, *v.* Calenderhay *infra*. BULLHILL STREET is *street
called Bulehulle* 1290 *Deed*, *Bolehillestrete* 1295 Exon, *Bulhylstrete* 1549
HMC Exeter. BUTCHER ROW is *le Bocherew* n.d. HMC Exeter, *Bocher-
rewe* 1443 *Obit*. Both self-explanatory. CALENDERHAY is *Kalenderhaie*
1271 *Deed*, *Kalendarhay* 1469 *Obit*, *Olde Callyanderhay* 1594 *Deed*.
hay is used several times in minor names in Exeter. It is clear that
etymologically it is OE (ge)hæg, 'enclosure,' perhaps used in towns
of a yard or enclosed space or even of a messuage. Cf. the development
of the allied OE *haga*, later *haw*. The *calendar* here was the church-
officer who prepared the calendars of obits. One or more of them
must have lived in this enclosure (F.R.-T.). CARFOIX (lost) is (*the*)
Carfoix 1350 NGl 5, 173, 1419 *St Mary Magd*, 1436 HMC Exeter.

[1] For all points connected with Exeter street-names we are greatly indebted to Mrs Rose-Troup.

F

This was formerly the name for the junction of High Street and North and South Streets. Cf. Carfax in Oxford and in Horsham (PN Sx 225). *v.* NED *s.v.* CATHARINE STREET was earlier *Doddehaystrete* t. Hy 2 Oliver and must take its name from the enclosure called *Doddehey* 1247 (NGl 3, 120), from the pers. name *Dodda*. COOMBE STREET is *Cumstrete* 1256, *Cumbestrete* 1270–82 *Deed*, *Combe Stret* 1320 *Deed* and takes its name from the valley in which it lies called *La Comba* c. 1260 HMC Exeter. COOKSROW (lost) is *the Cookerewe* n.d. HMC Exeter, *Cocrewe, Cokerewe* 1421 Oliver, *the Cokery* 1541 HMC Exeter. Self-explanatory. It extended from the higher corner of South Street to St George's church. CRULDITCH (lost) is *Crulledech* 1295 Exon, *Croldyche, Cruldyche in Southynhay* 1323 HMC Exeter, *Crulledych* 1336 HMC Exeter, 1422 IpmR, *Curlediche* 1545 HMC Exeter. This would seem to be a compound of ME *crull*, 'curly,' and to refer to the course of the dic though its applicability is by no means clear. ST DAVIDS HILL is *montem S. Dauid* 1247 *St Nicholas*, *Seynt Davys Doune* 1494 Ipm and takes its name from the church of St David without the walls, *v. infra* 436. EASTGATE is *porta de Esteyete* 1407 Exon. EGYPT LANE was earlier *Strikinestrete, Strichene, Strikene-* c. 1265 *Rental*, *Stykestret* 1297, *Styckestreete* 1458 HMC Exeter, *Stekeslane* 1399 (ib.). This is 'bullocks' street,' the first element being a ME weak gen. pl. of OE *styrc*, ME *stirk, strik*, 'bullock, heifer.' For such a weak form cf. Smith Street *infra* 24. EWINGS LANE was earlier *Seynt Mari lane* 1453 *Deed*, from the church near by. EXETER CASTLE is *Castellum, Castrum* c. 1265 *Rental*, *Exeter Castell* 1439 FF, *Castrum de Excestre vocatur castellum Rugemond* 1478 Wm Wo, *Rougemont* c. 1590 Shakespeare Ric iii, 4, 2. The Norman castle was built on the red sandstone here. FISH STREET was earlier *Vico S' Martin* 1150–1286 *St Johns*, *Seyntemartynyslane* 1369, *Martynyslane* 1375 *Deed*. It is *Fyssh Street* in 1447. Cf. Fish Street Hill (London), *Fysshestrete-hyll* 1568 Ipm. FRIERNHAY STREET is *Frerenhay* 1288, 1460 HMC Exeter and is identical with *Irlesberi* 1175–99 HMC Exeter, *Jorlesbyri* 1287 Exon. The earlier name suggests a house (*v.* burh) belonging to some pre-Conquest earl or *ealdormann*. The later one takes its rise from the Franciscan house close by. GANDY STREET takes its name from Henry *Gandy*, twice Mayor of Exeter 1661, 1662 (HMC Exeter). An earlier name was *Correstret(e)* t. Hy 2 Oliver, c. 1265 *Rental*, *Currestrete* c. 1190 *St Nicholas*, 14th HMC Exeter, *Corrystrete* 1396 HMC Exeter. No certainty is possible. The first element may be either ME *curre*, 'dog,' or ME *curray*, 'currying of leather,' *v.* NED *s.v.* GOLDSMITH STREET is *Aurifabria* 1291, 1309 Exon, *Goldsmythe-streate* 1606 *Deed*. GUINEA STREET is *Gennestrete* t. Hy 2 Oliver, c. 1320 HMC Exeter, *Gyne strete* 1421 Oliver, *Gennystrete* 1610 Speed. This may possibly be connected with the obscure *ginnel*, earlier *gennel*, used of a narrow passage, sometimes pronounced with stopped *g*. An alternative name was *Peruerectes lane* 1235 *Deed*, *Pervectis, Peruettes lane* 1293 *St Mary Magd*, *Prevates Lane* 13th *Deed*. HIGH STREET is *la graunt ruwe Dexcestre* 13th *Canonsleigh*, *magno vico* 1237, *magna placea, summo vico* 13th, 1359 *St Nicholas, altum vicum* 1401 *Obit, the Queens highe streete* 1583 HMC Exeter. HOLLOWAY STREET was earlier *Carterne strete* 1291 NGl 5, 84, *Carterestrete* 1314 *Deed, Cartrynstrete* 1419 *St Mary Magd, Cartynestrete nowe called Holoway* 1515–18 ECP 4, 570. This is clearly 'carters' street,' with the same ME weak gen. pl. as is found in Smith Street *infra* 24. IDLE LANE is *Idle Lane* 1589 HMC Exeter and may be near the spot called *Ydellond* in 1435 (NGl 4, 188). The meaning was possibly 'vacant, empty, unused land,' cf. Iddlecott *infra* 162. LONGBROOK STREET is *Langbrokestrete* c. 1369 HMC Exeter and takes its name from an old stream called *Langebrok* c. 1250 HMC Exeter, *Langbroke* 1461 Pat. MAGDALEN STREET is *Maudeleynestrete* 1419 HMC Exeter, *Mawdeleynstrete* 1435 NGl 4, 88, from the almshouse of St Mary Magdalen here. ST MARY ARCHES LANE is *in vico Sce. Marie de Arcubus* c. 1260 *St Nicholas, Archelane* n.d., 1499 HMC Exeter, taking its name from the church near by. MILK STREET is *Melkstrete* t. Hy 2 Oliver. Cf. Milk Street (London), *Melecstrate* c. 1125–50 HMC ix, 18. ST NICHOLAS LANE is *Seynt Nicollyslane* (1477 Oliver) from the ancient priory near by. NORTHGATE is *extra portam de North* 1212–23 *St Nicholas, Northyetstret* 13th HMC Exeter. NORTH STREET is *Vicus Borealis* 1302 *St Nicholas*. NORTHERNHAY is *Northynghay* c. 1415, *(diche)* 1562, *Northenghey* 1639 HMC Exeter, cf. Southernhay *infra* 24. PACY STREET (lost) is *Pacystrete, Pastrete* 13th HMC Exeter, *Pacy(e)stret(e)* 1343 NGl 5, 154, 1396 HMC Exeter, *Pacie stret* 1352, 1419 HMC Exeter. In 1343 there is mention also of *Pacyeswyll* (NGl) and in 1419 of *Paci Well* (*St Mary Magd*). These probably contain the common ME pers. name *Pacy*. PANCRAS LANE is *in vico Sci Pancras* c. 1285 *Obit* and takes its name from the church of St Pancras near by. PARIS STREET is *Pary(e)stret(e)* 1422, 1427 DA 14, *Parrysstrete* c. 1560, *Parres, Parys Street* 16th HMC Exeter, *Paryshestreate* 1570 *Deed*. These may contain OFr *pareis* from Latin *paradisus*, 'an enclosure,' cf. *Parislane* (PN Sx 11). PAUL STREET is *Poulestret(e)* 13th *St Nicholas*, 14th HMC Exeter, *Paulestrete* c. 1240 HMC Exeter, *(in) vico S. Pauli* 13th *St Nicholas*, taking its name from the church of St Paul's. PRESTON STREET is *in vico Presbiterorum* Hy 2 *Deed, Prustene strete, Prustestreta* 13th *St Nicholas, Prustestret, Prustonstrete, Prestonestrete* c. 1260 HMC Exeter, *Prustastret* c. 1260 NGl 5, 44, *in vico Sacerdotum* c. 1265 *Rental, Prustenestrete* 1295, *Prustestrete* 1320 Exon, 'Priests' street.' With weak gen. pl. in *-ene*. QUARRY LANE, cf. *Quarry Close under Northernhay* 1672 HMC Exeter. RACK STREET was earlier called *Teyglestrete* n.d. *St Johns, Teyȝtstrete* t. Hy 2 Oliver, *Tythestrete, Tygherstrete* c. 1328 HMC Exeter. It is *Racke Lane* in 1562 (HMC Exeter) and is probably to be associated with a place called *Rackhaye* 1448, *Rekkehay* 1452, *le Rakkehay* 1462 DA 14. The later name contains the word *rack*, 'framework for stretching cloth,' cf. Raxhayes *infra* 608. The earlier name is difficult to explain because of the inconsistency of the forms. If stress is to be laid on the first it may contain the trade-name *tiler*, from OE *teglere*. See Addenda lviii. SHUTBROOK STREET (lost) is *Schutebrokstrete* t. Hy 2 Oliver, *Schitebrokestrete,*

Scheotebrokstrete, Shetebrokestrete n.d. HMC Exeter, *Schytbrookestreate* 1570 *Deed* and takes its name from a former stream called *Schutebroke* t. Hy 2 Oliver, *Schytebroke, Shutebrok* 1370, 1415 NGl 3, 140, *Schytebroke, Shutebrok, Shetbroke* n.d. HMC Exeter. The first element is possibly identical with Shute *infra* 184. SIDWELL STREET is *vico Sancte Sativole* 15th *Obit* and takes its name from the church of St Sidwell's near by, *v. infra* 437. SMITH STREET is *Smythenestrete* t. Hy 2 Oliver, 1264 *Deed, Smithene strete* 13th *St Nicholas, in vico fabrorum* c. 1265 *Rental.* 'Smiths' street,' cf. Smithincott *infra* 538, both showing the weak ME gen. pl. form *smithene*. SOUTHERNHAY is *Beʒuthenehye* 1265 *Deed, Southynghay* 1276 HMC Exeter, *Bysouthynghaye* 1295 Exon, *Bysouthinthehaye* 1318 *Deed, Southernhay* 1634 *Depositions.* This and Northernhay *supra* 23 were enclosures to the south and north respectively of the city walls. Mrs Rose-Troup tells us that these fields had hedges to keep the citizens' cattle from straying and were thus naturally called *hays, v.* (ge)hæg. The somewhat inconsistent early forms make it different to determine the exact interpretation of the first element in these names. SOUTHGATE is *extra portam de Suth* 1212–23 *St Nicholas, Southyetstret* c. 1210 HMC Exeter. SOUTH STREET is *in vico australi* 1253 *St Mary Magd.* STEPCOTE HILL is *Styppecotehyll* c. 1270 HMC Exeter, *Stepcote Hill* 1588 *Deed.* This narrow street goes up a series of steps to this day and the name records that fact. WATERBEER STREET is *Waterberestrete* 1253 *Deed, Waterber Strete* 1327 HMC Exeter. Possibly 'street of the water bearers or carriers.' WESTGATE is (*extra*) *Portam Occidentalem* 1295 Exon, *Westyate* 1377 Cl, (*Exiland al.*) 1479 IpmR.

I. BRAUNTON HUNDRED

Brantone, Branctone, Bractona 1084 Geld Roll
Bramtun 1219 Fees 265, *Branton* 1229 Ch, *Brampton* 1244 Ass, *Braunton* 1303 FA
v. Braunton *infra* 32.

Ashford

ASHFORD 118 F 5

Aiseforda 1086 DB (Exon), *Esforda* (Exch), *Esforde* 1264–9 Exon, *Esseforde* 1311 Exon
Asford(e) 1242 Fees 784, 1264–9 Exon, *Ayshford* 1316 FA, 1356 AD iv

Self-explanatory. The ford can only have been over the Taw estuary.

Barnstaple

BARNSTAPLE 118 G 6

Beardastapol, Barda-, Bardan- 979–1016 Coins, *Beardastapol,*
Beard-, Barda- 1016–1066 Coins, *Beardastapol* 1018 Crawf 4
Barnestaple 1086 DB, 1158 P, *-lia* t. Hy 1 (1316) Ch, *Berne-*
stap(e)le 1236 Cl *et freq* to 1345 Fine, *Barnestaple al.*
Bardestaple 1286 Ipm, *Barnstable* 1421 IpmR
Bardestaple 1107–28 (t. Ed 2) AD vi, c. 1130 France, 1159,
1160 P, *-lia* t. Hy 1 (1316), *-pel* 1219 *Ass*, *Barte-* 1322 Cl
Berdestaple 1155 RBE *et passim* to 1326 Ipm
Bordestaple 1195 FF
Barestapł, Berestapł 1244 *Ass*, *Berstaple* 1302 Cl
Ecclesia Barum 1291 Tax
Barstaple upon the ryver of Severn 1466–84 ECP 1, 365
Barstable 1549 Pat, 1553 *Recov*, (*al. Barnstaple*) 1675 Ogilby,
Bastable 1675 Ogilby

This place must clearly be taken with Barnacott *infra* 69,
both alike containing an OE pers. name **Bearda*, which appears
in DB as *Berda* and is clearly evidenced from such OE p.n.'s as
Bardney (L), *Beardan eu* c. 750 Bede, Bardingley (K), *beardin-*
galeag (BCS 343) and others quoted by Blomé (10). Blomé
notes with Karlström (*OE Compound PN's in -ing*, 149) that we
have apparently three names in which an element *Bearda-* is
compounded with stapol and considers that this is against a pers.
name. He further adduces Beard (Db) in support of a significant
interpretation of the name. We may note, however, (i) that even
a threefold coincidence is not decisive against a pers. name
(cf. Mawer, *Problems of PN Study*, 86–7), (ii) that the word
which lies behind *Beard*, uniformly *Berd(e)* in early forms
(PN Db 55), cannot phonologically explain the OE forms of
Barnstaple, Bardney, Bardingley, (iii) that Barstable (Ess) and
the unidentified field-name *Berdestaple* may contain the word
which lies behind Beard (Db) and not an OE *Beard-* at all, for
all the early forms of these names have *Berde-*, so that they are
by no means certainly identical with Barnstaple in their origin.
Hence, '*Bearda*'s stapol'[1].

[1] Karlström (StudNP 2, 68) suggests that Barnstaple may be from an OE
beardedan stapole, 'the bearded pillar,' so called from some distinctive
decoration of it. The well-attested 10th century forms of the name forbid our

The reference 'Barstaple upon the ryver of Severn' is curious. Barnstaple is on the Taw which joins the Torridge and flows into the Bristol Channel. Possibly ports on or near this sea were regarded as being on the Severn, the estuary of which gradually widens to merge into the Bristol Channel. *Barum*, like *Sarum* for Salisbury, comes from the common medieval Latin abbreviation for Barnstaple (cf. Zachrisson, *Latin Influence* 2), and is still found on old milestones on roads leading to Barnstaple.

NOTE. The following are the chief street names. BARBECAN ROAD is *Barbigan Lane* 1610 Barum. Cf. the Barbican in Exeter *supra* 21. BEAR ST is *Barrestret* 1394. Barum, *Barestret* 1550 AOMB and was so called from its course from the bar (cf. *juxta baram de Berdestaple* 1244 *Ass*) or barrier at the town entrance. Cf. Temple Bar (London) and *bar* NED. BOUTPORT ST is *Bouteporte juxta Barnastapol* 1305 *Ass*, *Bowdeporte* 1445 AD vi, *Bowtport* 1652 Barum. It is clearly OE *būtan porte*, 'outside the town,' from its situation just outside the walls, *v.* port. CASTLE ST is *Castle Lane* 1582 Barum, from the Norman castle of Barnstaple. Cf. also *the Castlehay* 1551 HMC ix. CROCK ST is *Crokstrete* 1482, *Crockstrete* 1585 HMC ix, i.e. a street where pots or 'crocks' were made. GREEN LANE is *Greny Lane* 1440 Barum. HOLLAND ST is *Holond strete* 1482 HMC ix. This must have been where William de *Holonde* was living in 1319 (Barum), *v.* holh, land. JOY ST is *Joy Stret* 1578 Barum, of obscure origin. LITCHDON ST is *Lycheton* 1370, *Lecheton* 1412 HMC ix, *Lychedon* 1550 AOMB and must represent OE *līc-tūn*, 'cemetery.' It was probably by the medieval burying ground of Barnstaple. PAIGES LANE is *Pages Lane* 1513 Barum, probably from a former owner. RACK ST is *Rack hayes* 1549 Barum. Cf. Rack Street *supra* 23. SOUTH ST is *Southyat stret*, i.e. Southgate Street, 1578 Barum. STRAND is *the Kay and Stronde of Barnestaple* 1567 HMC ix, referring to a way along the *strand* of the Taw. VICARAGE ST is *Frogge Lane or Vicaredge Lane* 1570 AD vi. WELLS ST is *Welstret* 1578 Barum, *Willstreet* 1643 *Deed*, *v.* wielle. In early records we have mention also of a *Smythyn stret* 1461, *Smythstret* 1578 Barum, i.e. 'smiths' street,' cf. Smith Street *supra* 24, a *Maydenstret* 1319 Barum, cf. Meddon Street in Bideford *infra* 87, an *Anker Lane* 1582 Barum, and a *Paternoster Rowe* 1652 Barum, with which we may compare Paternoster Row in London.

MAIDENFORD is *Medeneford* 13th AD vi (p), 1242 Fees 772, 1326 Ipm, *Maydeneford* 1244 *Ass* (p), 1249 *Ass*, *Medenford* 1442 IpmR. 'Maidens' ford,' i.e. probably one easily crossed. For

assumption of the contractions involved in this etymology and it leaves entirely unexplained the name Barnacott *infra* 69, which must stand in close relation to Barnstaple.

maiden-names, cf. Medbury (PN BedsHu 71). To the names there quoted add *Maydeneford* (1284 *Ass*) in Garford (Berks), and Maidenhatch (Berks), c. 1180 *Add Maidenhecha* (p). Maidford (Nth) has an early form *Maideneford* (1166 P). From Devon we have a *Maidenpill* (1613), *v.* pyll.

NEWPORT is *Neuport by Barnstaple* 1295 Ch, *Nyweport by Tauton* 1311 *Ass*, *Burgus de Nyuport* 1330 *SR*. *v.* niwe, port. Presumably 'new town' in relation to the older Barnstaple.

BARNSTAPLE BRIDGE is (*juxta*) *pontem Barnastapolie* 1329 Exon. FRANKMARSH is *Franckmarsh* 1687 DKR 40, 413. GORWELL is *Gorwill* 1618 Barum. 'Dirty spring,' *v.* gor, wielle. RUMSAM is *Romysham* 1499 Ipm, *Rumysham* 1518–29 ECP 5, 511, *Rompsham* 1586 Barum, *v.* ham(m). Perhaps containing the same pers. name *Rūm* found in Romsey (Ha), *Rumesige* c. 1000 Saints. SOWDEN was the home of Robert *Bysouthedon* (1333 *SR*). 'South of the hill,' *v.* dun. STICKLEPATH is *Styklepeth* c. 1280 Barum. 'Steep path,' cf. same name *infra* 166. STONEYARD is *Stonar'* 1469 AD iii, *Stonegate al. Stoner* 1694 *Recov*. WAYTOWN is *Waytowne* 1618 Barum. For the *town*, *v. infra* 676. WELLCLOSE (6″) is *a close called Willeclose* 1397 Barum. *v.* wielle.

Berrynarbor

BERRYNARBOR 118 C 6

Hurtesberia 1086 DB, *Hertesberie* 1121 AC
Biri 1167 P, 1261 Exon, *Bery* 1209 FF, 1234 Fees 400, *Bury juxta Ilfredcumbe* 1281 *Ass*
Ber(r)i Neyberd 1281 *Ass*, 1315 Exon, *Bery Nerberd* 1288 *Ass*, *Biry Nerber* 1315 Ipm, *Birinerbert* 1321 *FF*
Birienherberd 1382 Cl, *Byry in Arberd* 1394 *Ass*, *Bury in Erber* 1492 Ipm

v. burh. The family of *Nerebert* is first associated with the place in 1209 (FF). If, as is probable, the DB and 12th cent. forms refer to this place the original name was ' *Heortes burh*,' 'burh of a man named *Heort*.' Cf. Hartland *infra* 71.

ETTIFORD is *Etteford* 12th AD iii (p), 1412 IpmR, *Eteford* c. 1280 Barum, *Hetteford* 1330 SR (p). Possibly '*Et(t)a*'s ford,' as suggested by Blomé (12).

GRATTON PLANTATION (6"). We have here an element which is very common in Devon field-names and occurs also some twenty times on the 6" map as the name of a field, copse, or small holding. It has been found only in late records, e.g. *le Gratton* 1636, *close called Gratton* 1656, *the Gratton* 1700 *Deed*, and it is difficult to say how early the word was in use in the county. The meaning is clearly that given under *gratton, gratten* in EDD, viz. 'stubble, stubble-field,' applied to land after corn, hay or other crops have been removed, on which it is customary to turn sheep, pigs, geese, etc. to feed. Cf. also NED *s.v. gratten.*

HAGGINTON, EAST AND WEST[1]

> *Hagi(n)tona* 1086 DB (Exon), *Haintone* (Exch), *Haginton(a)* 1167 P, (*West-*) 1300 Ipm, (*Est-*) 1326 Ipm, *Hagginton* 1213 FF
> *Akinton* 1197 FF, *Hakynton'* 1242 Fees 784
> *Est Hagyngton* 1316 FA

Probably '*Hæcga*'s farm,' *v.* ingtun. This may, as Blomé (21) suggests, be a pet form for such an OE name as *Heardgār.* See further PN Wo 292 *s.n.* Hagley.

HAMMONDS (6"), HARPER'S MILL (6") and HODGES are probably to be associated with the families of Robert *Hamond* (1330 *SR*), David *Harper* (1544 *SR*) and John *Hodge* (t. Eliz *SR*).

HILL BARTON[2], HOLE, LEE and SLEW (6") were probably the homes of Stephen de *la Hille* (1244 *Ass*), John *atte Hole* (1330 *SR*), Robert de *la Leye* (1244 *Ass*) and William de *la Slo* (1279 *Ass*), *v.* holh, leah. The last is from OE *slōh*, 'slough, mire.'

BERRY DOWN is *Byrydowne* 1450 BM, *v.* burh. BLURRIDGE (6") is *Blowridge* 1747 *FF*, 'exposed, bleak, ridge,' *v.* bla and cf. Blowden *infra* 282. BODSTONE is *Bodeneston* 1270 *Ass*, *Bodeston* 1330 *SR* (p). Perhaps '*Bodwine*'s farm.' BOWDEN is *Bowedon* 1270 *Ass.* 'Curved hill,' *v. infra* 37. BRINSCOTT is *Brunescot(e)* 1228 FF, 1330 *SR* (p), *Brymeskote, Brinnescote* 1270 *Ass.* '*Brȳni*'s cot(e).' COCKHILL is *Kochull* 1330 *SR* (p), *Cok-* 1412 IpmR. 'Cock hill.' HENSTRIDGE is so spelt 1809 M, cf. Hens-

---

[1] West Hagginton is in Ilfracombe.　　[2] *Hull* 1412 IpmR.

tridge *infra* 78. INDICKNOWLE is *Indeknoll* t. Eliz *SR* (p), *Indeknoll al. Indenoll* 1772 *Recov.* 'Beyond the cnoll,' cf. Indicombe *infra* 35. ORCHARD PARK COTTAGE (6") is *Orcharde Parke* 1701 *Recov.* RUGGATON is *Raggaton Park* t. Jas 1 ECP. SMITHSON is *Smytheston* 1314 *Ass* (p), 1330 *SR* (p), *Smethenyston* 1333 *SR* (p). STAPLETON (6") is *Stapeldon* 1197 FF, *-ton* 1604 *Recov*, *v.* stapol, dun. THORNLAND is so spelt 1604 *Recov.* WATERMOUTH is *Watermuth* 1314 *Ass* (p), *Est, West Watermouth* 1529 *Recov*, referring to the spot where the little stream here enters the sea. WHEEL was perhaps *Wille* 1412 IpmR and the home of William *atte Welle* (1333 *SR*). WOOLSCOTT is *Wurfardescote* 1228 FF, *Wlfardescote* 1244 *Ass, Walfardiscote* 1370 *Ass.* '*Wulfheard*'s cot(e).' YELLATON is *Yealleton* 1604 *Recov*, *Yellowton* 1765 D. Probably 'old farm,' *v.* tun and Addenda lviii. YETLAND is *Yeatlonde* 1563 *FF*, *v.* geat.

Bittadon

BITTADON 118 D 6

Bedendona 1086 DB
Betesdenna 1121 AC
Bettenden 1205 FF, *Betedenn* 1219 *Ass*, *-don* 1279 *Ass*
Bittedene 1242 Fees 771 *et freq* to 1384 Exon with variant spelling *Bytte-, -dayn* 1550 *SR, Bitedone* 1259 Exon, *Byttedon* 1346 FA

Probably '*Bitta*'s valley,' *v.* denu. The name is not on record but cf. *bitancnoll* (BCS 594), *bittan cnol* (BCS 1080) and OGer *Bizzo* (Förstemann PN 309).

FROGMORE PLANTATION (6") is *Frogemere* 1589 *Deed.* 'Frog pool,' *v.* mere. NARRACOTT is *Northecote* 1330 *SR* (p), 1340, 1345 *FF.* 'North cot(e),' the usual Devon form of this name, *v.* Introd. xxxiv. UPCOTT is so spelt 1620 *Recov.*

Bratton Fleming

BRATTON FLEMING 118 F 9

Bratona 1086 DB
Bratton(e) 1242 Fees 796 *et passim*
Bretton 1285 Pat

This place, together with Bratton *infra* 173, Bratton in Minehead (So) and Bratton (W), offers difficulties. These uniformly show *Bratt*-forms in ME, except for one *Brett*-form for this Bratton and the other Devon Bratton, and one for Bratton in Minehead, while Bratton (W), first recorded in the 13th cent., shows 4 out of 9 forms with *Brett*-. Blomé (13) and Ekblom (PN W 34) derive these names from OE *brādatūn*, but it is difficult to see how all trace of the *d* and of the medial vowel should have been lost in these names while all other compounds of *brad*- show no such phenomenon. Further, this explanation leaves the *Bret*- forms entirely unexplained. Possibly a ray of light is shed by the form *Brakton* (1335) for the Somerset p.n. This would suggest a compound of OE *bræc*, *brec*, 'strip of uncultivated land,' and tend to confirm the correctness of the form *Bracton* found once for Bratton Clovelly *infra* 173. It would also explain the alternation between *Bratt*- and *Brett*-forms. Owing to the similarity between *c* and *t* in 13th and 14th cent. script, it is difficult to say how far other *Bratt*-forms should really have been read as *Bract*-[1].

Fleming to distinguish from Bratton Clovelly *infra* 173. Baldwin *le Flemeng* held the manor in the 13th cent. (1242 Fees, 1249 *Ass*).

BENTON

> *Bo(n)tintona* 1086 DB, *Bontingden* 1379 IpmR, *Boutingdon* (sic) 1379 Cl
> *Duntingthon* (sic) 1242 Fees 792, *Buntingeton* 1270 *Ass*
> *Botyngdon* 1301 Ipm, 1346 FA, *Bodyngdon* 1316 FA
> *Bunton* 1582 *FF*

'*Bunta's* farm,' *v.* ingtun, cf. also Birchgrove (PN Sx 271) and Bountisborough Hundred (Ha), 1248 *Ass Bontesburg*, 1280 *ib.* *Bontesberegh*.

CHUMHILL is *Chymewell'* 1237 Cl, *Chumewell(e)* 1270 *Ass*, 1329 Exon, *Chimwell* 1630 Westcote. The first element in this name

---

[1] The great Henry de *Bracton* certainly came from one of the Brattons. Round (EHR 31, 586 ff.) gave good reasons for Bratton Fleming. His name is once found as *Braketon* (*v.* Selden, *Dissertatio ad Fletam*, ed. Ogg, p. 14) and this tends to confirm the reading in his *De Legibus* (188 B) where he says that a writ in which *Brachtone* was written for *Bractone* would be invalid. Another text says *Bractone* for *Brattone*, but the evidence of the *k*-forms tends to invalidate this.

is probably the same as that found in *ceommenige* (KCD 940), now Chimney (O), *ceomman bricg* (KCD 652[1]) and *ceomman treow* (BCS 820). All these point to an OE pers. name *Cēomma*, a pet form of such a name as *Cēolmær*. The second element must be **wielle**, 'spring'; the place lies high up on the hillside so that it is not likely even on topographical grounds that we can have any stream-name here, as suggested by Blomé (14). There are springs all along the ridge.

HAXTON is *Haustona* 1086 DB, *Haggeston* 1219 *Ass et freq* to 1379 IpmR, *Hakeston'* 1242 Fees 792, *Hackeston* 1380 IpmR. This name would seem to contain a strong form *Hæcgi* of the weak *Hæcga* found in Hagginton *supra* 28. Cf. also Haxter *infra* 242.

KIPSCOMBE is *Kyppescumb* 1249 *Ass* (p), *Kybbescomb(e)* 1330 *SR* (p), 1359 *Ass*, *Kyppyscombe* 1492 Ipm. The second element is OE cumb. The first is either *Cyppi* as demonstrated for Kipson (PN Sx 71) or *Cybbi* as suggested by Blomé (14). Cf. Eseger *Kyppe*, a juror in Kenton (D) in 1249 (*Ass*).

DOWN, FERNHAM, KNIGHTACOTT, NARRACOTT, SOUTHACOTT, NORTH (6″) and SOUTH THORNE and TOWN FM were probably the homes of Henry de *Doune* (1333 *SR*), William de *Fernham*, Richard de *Knyghtecote*, William de *Northecote*, Robert de *Southecote*, Thomas de *Thorne* (1330 *SR*) and Henry *atte Touneshende* (1333 *SR*), *v.* dun, ham(m), cniht, cot(e), tun. Narracott and Southacott are north and south respectively of Knightacott, while Town Fm is at the south-west end of the village.

BEARA is *Beerah* 1809 M, *v.* bearu. CHELFHAM is *Chelfham* 1238 *Ass et freq* to 1359 Ipm (p), *Chalfhama* 1284 *Ass*, *Cheltheham* (sic) 1504 Ipm. 'Calves' ham(m).' HUNNACOTT is *Honnecot* 1330 *SR*, *Honyecote* 1333 *SR* (p). *v.* Honeychurch *infra* 165. LEWORTHY is *Loveworthi* 1330, *Lyva-* 1333 *SR* (p). '*Lēofa*'s worþig.' RIDGE GATE, cf. *North*, *South Ridge* 1662 DA 8. SPRECOTT is *Sprecote* 1330 *SR* (p), *Spreycot* 1809 M. 'Brushwood cote,' cf. Sprytown *infra* 208.

---

[1] This is not Kim Bridge (Ha) as has been asserted. A series of early forms for Kim Bridge, *Kimbrige* 1202, *Kinebrig* 1218 *FF*, *Kingbrigge*, *Kyngesbrugge* 1271 *Ass*, *Kyngbrigge* 1327 *SR* (p), show that it has no connexion with *ceomman bricg* and topographical difficulties confirm this.

Braunton

BRAUNTON [bra·ntən] 118 F 4

> *Branton(a)* 1086 DB *et freq* to 1242 Fees 782, *Brauntone* 1269
> Exon
> *Brampton(e)* 1157 RBE *et freq* to 1302 BM, *Bramton(a)* 1167,
> 1172 P, 1219 *Ass*, 1229–35 Ch
> *Brompton* 1226 Pat

On the basis of the forms for the town alone one would without hesitation suggest that the name was of the common *Brampton* type from OE *brame-tūn* with the usual confusion between brame and brom and assimilation of *mt* to *nt*. In the Geld Roll forms for the Hundred-name, however, we have forms *Branctone*, *Bractone*. Unless these are purely erroneous they necessitate a new etymology. They have been explained in two ways, (i) by assuming derivation from the saint's name *Branoc* (cf. Branscombe *infra* 620) found in St *Brannock*'s Well in the immediate neighbourhood, but a compound of a saint's name with tun is unparalleled and we should in any case expect it to be in the genitival form, (ii) Blomé (15) suggests an unrecorded river-name *Brannoc* of the same type as that found in Craddock *infra* 538. No certainty is possible, and it may well be that the Geld Roll forms are incorrect.

ASH BARTON is *Essa* 1086 DB, *Esse* 1219 FF, *Asshe Rogus* 1372 *Ass*, *Asshroges juxta Bratton* 1380 IpmR. The identity of *Rogus* is not known. It is probably the same personal name as in Holcombe Rogus *infra* 535.

BEER CHARTER BARTON is *Bera* 1086 DB, 1167 P, *Bara* 1265 Misc, *Bairecharteray* 1288 *Ass*, (*La*) *Beare* 1303 FA, 1367 *FF*, *Bear Chartrie* 1386 Fine. *v.* bearu. The manor was held by Simon de *Chartray* in 1242 (Fees) and by John de *Charteray* in 1288 (*Ass*).

BUCKLAND is *Bochelant* 1086 DB, *Bokelaunde Kayllou* 1301 Ipm, *Parva Boclond* 1303 FA. *v.* bocland. Adam *Cayllo* held the manor in 1303.

FAIRLINCH is *Underfayrlinch* 1324 Cl, *Fairelinche* 1330 SR (p), *Fayrelynch* 1359 *Ass*. '(Below) the fair slope,' *v.* hlinc.

HALSINGER is *Halsangra* 1167 P (p), *-gre* 1238 *Ass*, *Halshangre, Halesangre* 1244 *Ass*. This is clearly a compound of OE *heals,* 'neck' and hangra, 'wood.' The place lies on a neck of high ground. See further Addenda *supra* lviii.

INCLEDON is *Hingledon* 1238 *Ass* (p), *Incledene* 1242 Fees 771, 1244 *Ass* (p), 1330 *SR* (p), *-don* 1333 *SR* (p), *Inkeldene* 1360 *Ass, Inkyldon* 1428 FA, *-denne* 1428 FA (p). No certainty is possible. Professor Ekwall suggests that the first element may be OE *Inghild* (cf. OHG *Inghild*) or *Ingflǣd* (feminine names), with unvoicing of *g* to *c* before *h* or *f*. Dr Ritter suggests OE *Incla,* an *l*-derivative of OE *Inca,* a pet-form of an OE name in *Ing-.*

LOBB is *Loba* 1086 DB, *Lobbe* 1242 Fees 787, *et freq* to *Lobba* 1365 *FF*, *Suthlobbe* 1463 IpmR. The same element occurs in Lobb, Lobhill, Lopwell and Labdon (*v.* Index), in the personal name atte *Lobbe* in Beaminster (Do) in 1333 (*SR*) and possibly in Lobb (PN O 149). It must, as suggested by Blomé (16), be the word *lob* in some topographical sense. EDD gives the meaning 'wide extent or surface,' NED associates it with various Teutonic words denoting 'something heavy, clumsy or loosely pendent.' All these places are situated by steep slopes, Lobb itself being at the bottom of a fairly steep hill above the flat sandy waste known as Braunton Burrows.

LUSCOTT is *Luscote* 1238 *Ass* (p) *et freq* to 1380 Exon, *Lustecote* 1244 *Ass* (p). Blomé (16) suggests that this may be elliptical for earlier *lūsþorncote*, 'cottages by the spindletree.' This may be so, but the occurrence of forms like *lusdun* (BCS 1023), *lusa pull* (BCS 1107), *lusebeorg* (BCS 748) and the curious *lusan þorne* (BCS 473), side by side with *lusðorn* (KCD 612), offers difficulties. The first three of these cannot be elliptical compounds of *lusþorn,* while *lusan* in the last form but one is inexplicable. *lūs,* 'louse' (cf. Wallenberg in StudNP 2, 85), is possible with cot(e), but will hardly suit the other compounds. Professor Ekwall would lay stress on the 1244 form and take the first element to be the same as in Lustleigh *infra* 480.

SAUNTON [sɑˑntən] is *Santon(a)* 1086 DB, 1242 Fees 774, *Saunton* 1304 Ch, 1326 Ipm, *Sampton* 1505 Ipm. 'Farm by the sands,' *v.* tun. These are referred to in the phrase *super sablon de Santon* 1249 *Ass*.

WINSHAM is *Wenneham* 1086 DB, *Winesham* 1244 *Ass* (p), *Wynes-* 1244 *Ass*, 1333 *SR* (p). Probably '*Wine*'s ham(m).'

DOWN HOUSE, NETHERCOTT, NEWTON (6″), PARK FM, UPCOTT and WELL were probably the homes of Thomas de *Doune* (1322 *Ass*), Richard de *Nethercote* (1244 *Ass*), Geoffrey de *Nywton* (1324 Cl), Gregory *atte Parke* (1333 *SR*), John Cotes de *Uppecote* (1322 *Ass*) and Adam le *la Wille* (1322 *Ass*). *v.* dun, cot(e), tun, pearroc, wielle.

BOODE is *Boghewode* 1330, 1333 *SR* (p). 'Curved wood,' *v.* Bowden *infra* 37. BROADEFORD (6″) is *Bradeford* 1281 *Ass.* 'Wide ford.' BRAUNTON BURROWS is *Burgh in Brampton* 1570 *Recov*, *Braunton Boroughes* 1609 *Deed*, referring to the sand hills here, *v. infra s.n.* Northam Burrows 103. CLARKE'S LANE (6″) is to be associated with the family of John *Clerk* (1330 *SR*). FULLABROOK is *Fulebroc* 1167 P, 1244 *Ass* (p), *Foulebrok* 1333 *SR* (p), 1386 *Ass.* 'Dirty brook,' *v.* ful. GREEN LANE (6″). Cf. *Byest-*, *Bywestegreneweye* 1324 Cl. KITTYWELL (6″) is *Kittewell* 1714 *Recov*. KNOWLE is (*la*) *Knolle* 1298 *Ass* (p), 1412 IpmR, *v.* cnoll. LONGLANDS (6″) is *La Longeland* 1324 Cl. MOOR LANE (6″) is *La Morlane* 1324 Cl. PIPPACOTT is *Pippecote* 1311 Exon, 1330, 1333 *SR* (all p), *Puppe-* 1326 Ipm, *Pyppe-* 1356 *Ass.* '*Pippa*'s cot(e).' PITLANDS (6″) is *La Putte* 1324 Cl, *v.* pytt. SCUR FM (6″) was probably the home of John *atte Score* (1330 *SR*). There are really two farms of this name in the village, on the right and left banks of the river. Both are at the foot of steep hills. *v.* Score *infra* 47. SHELLHOOK (6″) is *Chardellhoke Weare* 1609 *Deed*, *Sherleshook al. Shadishook al. Shaddlehook* 1738 *Recov*. It is the name of a pointed sandbank in the Taw estuary, *v.* hoc. SWANPOOL BRIDGE (6″) is *Swanpool* 1700 DA 8.

East Buckland

EAST BUCKLAND 118 G 10

> *Bochelanda* 1086 DB, *Estbokland'* 1242 Fees 772, *Yestbokelond* 1346 FA
>
> *v.* bocland. 'East' to distinguish it from West Buckland *infra* 35. For *Yest-*, *v.* Introd. xxxiii.

BRAYLEY BARTON is *Bredelia* 1086 DB, *Brailega* 1166 RBE (p),

Braylegh 1242 Fees 774, 1326 Ipm, 1333 *SR* (p). 'Clearing by the river Bray' *supra* 2, *v.* leah. The *d* in the DB form is almost certainly an error. Cf. Raleigh *infra* 55.

HUXTABLE gave name to John de *Hokestaple* 1330 *SR*, *v.* hoc, stapol. The name may have referred to some post on the spur of land here.

MIDDLECOTT is *Middelcot* 1228 FF. Why *Middle* is not clear. There is an *Upcott* to the west, but no other *cott*-name to the east.

CROSSBURY[1], UPCOTT[1] and WESTACOTT were probably the homes of Semann *atte Crosse* (1333 *SR*), Roger de *Uppecote* (id.) and John de *Westecote* (1322 *Ass*). *v.* cot(e).

West Buckland

WEST BUCKLAND 118 G 9

Bochelant 1086 DB, *West Boclaunde* 1242 Fees 784

FURZE is *Fersa* 1086 DB and was the home of Roger *atte Forse* (1330 *SR*). *v.* fyrs.

INDICOMBE was the home of John de *Byendecoumbe* (1314 *Ass*), John de *Hyndecomb* (1330 *SR*) and Thomas de *Yundecomb* (1333 *SR*). The first element is one that is common in Devon p.n.'s, *v. infra* 658[2]. In all cases the meaning must be 'beyond' or 'on the other side of' from OE *begeondan, begeonde*. In most cases the places in question were probably named by the people in the nearest village or large settlement. Thus Indicombe is about one mile distant from West Buckland on the slope of a hill above an intervening valley. Indio in Bovey Tracy *infra* 467 would have been so named by the people of Bovey village because it lies on the other side of the Bovey river. See further *supra* xxxvii.

LEARY BARTON is *Lery, Lerrey, Lerey* 1581 *SR*. Since we have also five other farms of this name, viz. Bright's, Buckingham's, Huxtable's, Gould's, Mary's Leary, Leary Cross and a Leary

---

[1] *Crosse, Upcote* 1581 *SR*. bury is apparently a late addition. The 'cross' is East Buckland Cross.

[2] We may note also Indilake in Knowstone and Indiwell in Swimbridge for which no early forms have been found.

Moor, all at no great distance from each other, it is likely that the name originally denoted the stream here, which joins the Taw at Bishop's Tawton. It may possibly be connected with the stream-name noted under Laira *supra* 20.

STOODLEIGH is *Estotleia* 1086 DB (Exon), *Stodlei* (Exch), *Stodelegh'* 1242 Fees 772, *Northstodł* 1244 *Ass*, *Stodlegh* 1330 *SR* (p), 'stud clearing,' *v*. stod, leah.

BUSHTON is *Bysshton* 1314 *Ass* (p), *Bushton* 1632 *Recov*. 'Farm by the bush or bushy place,' *v*. bysc, tun. ELWELL is *Ellewell* 1270 *Ass et freq* to 1423 IpmR with variant spelling -*will*(*e*), *Allewille* 1321 Exon (p), '*Ella*'s spring,' or 'elder-tree spring,' *v*. ellen, wielle and Elwell *infra* 291. GUBBS is to be associated with the family of William *Gubbe* of Charles (1638 Wills). TADDIPORT is *Tydaport* 1765 D. WHITSFORD is *Wyttokesford* 1279 *Ass*, 1281 *Ass* (p), *Whytekesford* 1281 *Ass*, *Whyttokesford* 1298 *Ass*. '*Hwītuc*'s ford,' cf. Whiteoxen *infra* 310. YOLLA-COMBE PLANTATION (6") is *Yoldecomb* 1333 *SR* (p). 'The old combe,' cf. Addenda *supra* lviii.

Combe Martin

COMBE MARTIN 118 C 7

    Comba 1086 DB, *Cumbe* 1198 FF, *Coumb' Martin* 1276 RH

    v. cumb. Robert, the son of *Martin*, held the manor in 1133 (*Lewes Cartulary*).

BUZZACOTT is *Bursecote* 1399 *Ct*, *Bussacott* 1667 *Recov*. Perhaps '*Beorhtsige*'s cot(e).' This pers. name occurs as *Birhsie* in Devon (BCS 1248) and as *Byrhsie* in the Bodmin Manumissions (KCD 981) and possibly as the second element of Trebursey in South Petherwin (Co), *Trebursi* 1229 Oliver 24, 1327 *SR* (p).

HOLDSTONE FM is *Haldestan*(*a*) 1198 FF, 1239 Bracton, *Aldiston* 1379 IpmR. Probably 'sloping stone,' the first element being OE *heald*, 'sloping, inclined.' There are tumuli and stones on the hill here.

TRUCKHAM is *Trocumbe* 1198 FF, *Troccomb* 1330 *SR* (p). The first element may be OE *trog*, 'trough,' in some topographical sense. The place lies in a small semicircular hollow, *v*. cumb.

Cf. Trafford (Ch), *Trosford* DB, *Trochford* c. 1100, *Trocford* c. 1190, *Trohford*, *Trowefordia* late 13th St Werburgh Cartulary.

COMERS and NUTT'S (both 6″) are to be associated with the families of Alice *Comere* (1330 *SR*) and William *Nutte* (t. Eliz *SR*).

BLAKEWELL (6″), BOWHAY LANE (6″), NETHERTON (6″) and VERWILL were perhaps the homes of Robert de *Blakewill* (1330 *SR*), William de *Bogheweye* (ib.), i.e. 'curved way,' *v. s.n.* Bowden *infra*, Richard de *Nithereton* (ib.) and John de *Fairefeld* (1333 *SR*), *v.* blæc, wielle, tun, feld. feld frequently yields final -*vill(e)* in Mod.Eng. Here the development seems to have gone a stage further, cf. Introd. xxxiv–v. The change was helped by the presence of springs at the farm.

CHALLACOMBE is *Chaluecumba* 1167 P (p), -*comb* 1333 *SR* (p), *Chelvecombe* 1339 *Ass.* 'Calves' combe.' COULSWORTHY is *Cowlsworthy* 1809 M. There was a place called *Culeford* in the parish in 1198 (FF) and the two may be associated. Cf. Introd. xxxv. GIRT is *La Grutte* 1198 FF, *Gurt* 1667 *Recov*. This is OE greot, 'gravel.' HANGMAN HILL is so spelt 1792 *Recov*. KNAP DOWN is *Knapdowne* 1667 *Recov*, *v.* cnæpp. NUTCOMBE is *Nodcomb* 1330 *SR* (p), *Notecombe* 1473 *FF*. Perhaps 'nut valley,' *v.* cumb. VELLACOTT LANE (6″) is *Velecote* 1399 *Ct*, *Velacote* 1428 FA (p).

East Down

EAST DOWN 118 D 7

Duna 1086 DB, *Estdoune* 1260 Exon, *Estdone* 1291 Tax

v. dun. 'East' to distinguish from West Down *infra* 39.

ASHELFORD is *Asscheleswurth*, *Asseneswurth* 1244 *Ass* (p), *Aslesworthy*, *Assele(s)worth* 1284 *Ass*, *Aishelford* 1672 *Recov*. '*Æscel's* farm,' *v.* worþ. Cf. Ashling PN Sx 60.

BOWDEN is *Boghedon* 1333 *SR* (p), cf. Bowdon (Ch), DB *Bogadone*. The first element is very common in Devon p.n.'s. It is found seventeen times with dun, thirteen times with wudu and occasionally with bearu, clif, cumb, dic, hyll, mor,

G

weg[1]. It is noteworthy that in every case the second element is some word denoting a natural feature, not a place of habitation, so that we should look for a descriptive term rather than a pers. name as the source of this first element. Bow (*infra* 315) and Bow (Mx, Wo) clearly contain the OE *boga*, 'bow, arch, curve,' probably with reference in each case to an arched bridge. Probably we have this word also in most or all of the above-noted compounds, the meaning being 'curved, well rounded, or arched' according to the significance of the following word. The frequency of the element in Devon place-names need not be surprising to those acquainted with the topography of the county[2]. There are interesting Celtic parallels to the Bowood series of names. In Cornwall we have Stephen Gelly in St Neot, earlier *Stengelly*, Tamsquite in St Tudy, earlier *Stumcoyt* in which we have the Cornish equivalent of Welsh *ystum*, 'bend, curve,' compounded with Cornish *coit* and *celli*, 'wood' or 'grove.' Cf. the similar frequency of byge in Devon p.n.'s as compared with those of other counties. *v. infra* 658–9.

BUGFORD is *Buggeforde* 1630 DCo NQ 3, and is probably identical with the DB manor of *Boewrda* which appears in the 1330 SR in the pers. name *Bogheworthi*. Confusion of final worþig and ford is fairly common. *v.* Introd. xxxv. The etymology of the name of the DB manor is difficult. It may be from the pers. name *Buga*, hence '*Buga*'s enclosure.' Less probably the first element is OE *boga*, 'curve' (*v. supra*), from the situation of the farm in a bend of land. If the DB manor and Bugford are identical, then we have stopping of continuant [g] to [g] as in Wagaford *infra* 171.

CHURCHILL

> *Cercilla* 1086 DB, *Cherchill* 1121 France
> *Chirkehull* 1216 ClR
> *Churchehille* 1242 Fees 782, -*hull(e)* 1284 *Ass*, 1326 Ipm
> *Churechull* 1284 *Ass*, *Churchulle* 1303 FA

[1] In field-names we find other compounds, viz. *Boghewill* (1333), *Boghemulle* (1330), *Boghebrok* (1311), *Bogherewe* (1317), *Boghestanys* (1430).
[2] It has been suggested that some of these names in *Bow-* go back to OE (*on*) *bufan wuda*, 'above the wood' and the like. This may possibly be true of Bowood in Abbotsham and Bude in Plympton, but in all other cases, when we have ME forms in *boghe*, such a solution is not possible and for the vast majority of these names we have such forms.

v. cyric(e). For this hybrid hill-name, *v.* PN Wo 106, and see further Ekwall, *Studies* 42 ff. and Addenda *supra* lii.

NORTHCOTE is *Norcota* 1086 DB, *Northecoth'* 1242 Fees 771, *Northcott* 1631 *Recov.*

VIVEHAM is *Fiffeham* 1244 *Ass* (p), *Vyfham* 1330 *SR* (p), *Visham* 1421, *Vyseham* (sic) 1472 IpmR. This name is difficult. In PN Wo 35 (*s.n.* Sevenhampton) we saw that groups of *seven* homesteads (*v.* ham) might have some legal significance. This name suggests a group of *five*, but how such a group could arise is not clear.

HOLE, OKEWILL, ROOKBEAR and SHORTACOMBE were probably the homes of Richard *atte Hole* (1330 *SR*), *v.* holh, Robert de *Okewill* (1333 *SR*), John de *Rokebeare* (1330 *SR*), i.e. 'rook wood,' *v.* bearu, and Paulin' de *Shortecomb* (1333 *SR*), *v.* cumb.

BECCOT is *Baccote* 1310 *Ass*, 1311 Exon (p), 1330 *SR* (p), *Bakcote* 1333 *SR* (p). '*Bacca*'s cot(e).' HIGHER BROCKHAM (6″) is so spelt 1742 *Recov.* CLIFTON is *Estclyftowne*, *West Clyftowne* 1630 DCo NQ 3, 47, *v.* clif, tun. DUDLAND is *Dodeland'* 1175 P (p), *Dudlands* 1630 DCo NQ 3, 47. Probably '*Dud(d)a*'s land.' FORD (6″) is *la Forde* 1325 *Ass.* HOLWELL is *Holewill(e)* 1244 *Ass*, 1333 *SR* (p), *Holiwill* 1330 *SR* (p). 'Spring in the hollow,' *v.* holh, wielle. INDICOTT is *Indycote* 1499 Ipm. 'Beyond the cot(e),' cf. Indicombe *supra* 35. WHITE'S WOOD (6″) is to be associated with the family of Robert *Whita* (1330 *SR*). WIGMOOR is *Wyggemere* 1292 *Ass*, *Wygemore* 1333 *SR* (p). Probably '*Wicga*'s pool,' *v.* mere.

West Down

WEST DOWN 118 D 5

> *Duna* 1086 DB, *Dunne* (sic) 1216 ClR, *Dune* 1242 Fees 771, *Westdone* 1273 Exon, *-doune* 1288 Exon, *Doune Columbers* 1316 FA

'West' as opposed to East Down *supra* 37. Philip de *Columbariis* held the manor in 1216.

AYLESCOTT

> *Ailesvescota* 1086 DB (Exon), *Eilvescote* (Exch)

Aileuecote 1167 P, *Aylyvecoth*' 1242 Fees 771, *Aylevescote* 1270
Ass
Aylescoth' 1242 Fees 795, *Aylyscote* 1489 Ipm
Al(l)escote 1303, 1346, 1428 FA
Possibly 'the cottage(s) of a man *Eilaf*,' bearing an Anglo-Scandinavian name. *v.* Zachrisson, *Some PN Etymologies* 8.

BRADWELL is *Bradeuilla* 1086 DB (Exon), *-welle* (Exch), *-will*'
1242 Fees 794. 'Broad stream,' *v.* brad, wielle.

BUTTERCOMBE is *Botercumbe* 1286 *Ass*, *-combe* 1345 *Ass* (p).
Compounds in *Butter-* are common in the county, *v.* 659 *infra*.
Elsewhere we have Butterdon (Co), id. 1302 *Ass*, Buttermere
(PN W 45), Butterworth (PN La 55), Butterwick (Herts),
Boturwyk, Boterwik c. 1430 AnnMon, Butterhill (O), *Buterhil*
1320 Ch, *Boterferlang, Boterknolle* 13th (*Canonsleigh*) and *buter-
w(y)elle* KCD 813 (Ess). In Butterwick and Butterworth the
name may refer simply to a farm which provided good butter,
cf. Chiswick (Mx) from ciese. Its exact sense in other names is
less certain. In some cases, e.g. when compounded with bearu,
dun, cumb, leah, mor, it may refer to land which provided good
pasturage. In Butterford *infra* 150 the meaning is less obvious.
Perhaps here and in *buterwyelle* and in Buttermere the word
may have had some reference to the appearance or colour of the
water.

CRACKAWAY is *Crakewey(e)* 1242 Fees 771, 1303 FA, 1326, 1501
Ipm, *Cra(c)kway* 1423 IpmR, 1428 FA. This, as suggested by
Blomé (18), may be a compound of weg and a British word
*krako, denoting 'rock' or the like. Cf. Crake (RN 101) and
Crakelond in Luppitt (1479 Ct), though this last may contain the
pers. name *Krake*, of Anglo-Scandinavian origin, which is found
in the name Henry *Krakya* in 1330 (*SR*).

LITTLE COMFORT is so marked in 1809 (M). Names such as this
and Little Joy, *infra* 474, were probably given either to a particularly barren and unproductive piece of land or possibly in
some cases to a dilapidated or ruined dwelling. Cf. also *Little
Regarded* in Kenwyn (Co), so marked in Martyn's map (1748).

Stowford, West and East[1]

Estaveforda 1086 DB (Exon), *Staveford* (Exch)
Eststaufford, Weststafford 1289 *Ass*
Stouford(e) 1289 *Ass*, 1330 *SR* (p), *Stoford* 1333 *SR* (p)

'Ford marked by staves or posts.' Stowford is a very common name in Devon, *v.* Index. It has at least three possible sources. The first, clearly illustrated in this example, is OE *stæfa-ford*, 'ford of the staves,' i.e. presumably one marked by stakes. Cf. the common Stapleford. There may also in other names have been forms *stæf-ford*, with the nom. sing. of the same word, cf. *Stafwyll* 1449 BM (Devon). The phonological development of such a compound to *Stowford* is difficult but it is certain, and Blomé (18) suggests the line of development along which it may have taken place. The second source is OE *stæþ-ford*. We are familiar with that compound in the modern Stafford (PN St 141), with *stæþ*-forms on OE coins, and DB forms *Stadford, Statford*. *stæþ* means 'shore, bank' in OE and presumably a *stæþ-ford* is one where you definitely go down a bank to the ford. For Stowford *infra* 208 we have DB *Estatforda*, and for Stafford in Dolton we have DB *Stadforda*. Stafford shows the normal development. Stowford, unless the *t* is an error, contains *stæþ*, which must have lost its *þ* by assimilation and then, by a similar process to that noted for *Staveford supra*, become Stowford. The third and probably much the most common source is OE *stānford*. The only *stanford* in a Devon charter surviving on the map is Stafford in Colyton *infra* 623 in KCD 1301, which does once have a form *Stoford* and even *Stouford*, unless that be an error for *Stonford*. Elsewhere we have Stover (Gl), *Stanford* (BCS 887), Stowford near Trowbridge (W), *Stanford* (KCD 658), Stowford by Wishford (W), *Stanford* (BCS 782) and Stolford (So), *Stanford* (BCS 610). Altogether we have noted some thirteen Sto(w)fords and three Staffords in Devon[2]. As a rule it is impossible to be certain about the origin of any particular one, especially as forms *Stauford, Stouford* are ambiguous and may at times be errors of transcription for *Stanford* and *Stonford*. Topographical

---

[1] East Stowford is in Berrynarbor.
[2] For the phonological process cf. Ekwall in the *Klaeber Miscellany*, 21–7.

investigation is not of much service here, as most fords are likely to have a more or less stony bottom.

TRIMSTONE is *Trempelstan* 1238 *Ass*, *Trympeston* 1330 *SR*, *Trimpestone* 1351 Exon (all p). No stone survives here to help in explaining this difficult name. Professor Ekwall suggests that the first element may be a noun *trempel, a derivative of the verb to *tramp*. In that case the compound might denote a stone used as a stile or the like.

GILLARDS, PEARDS and SHUTES FM (all 6") are probably to be associated with the families of Peter *Gaillard* (1333 *SR*), Robert *Peard* (t. Eliz *SR*) and William *Shote* (1333 *SR*).

CHEGLINCH is *Chekelinche* 1330 *SR* (p), *Cheglinge* 1612 *FF*. '*Cēoca*'s hlinc.' DEAN is *Dene* 1216 ClR, 1281 *Ass*, 1326 Ipm, 1345 *FF*, *v.* denu. PINE'S DEAN is perhaps to be associated with the family of Ralph de *Pinu*, who held the neighbouring manor of Bradwell in 1242 (Fees 794). TWITCHEN is *Twichene* 1330 *SR* (p), *Towchyn al. Twychyn* 1650 *Recov*. 'Crossways,' cf. Twitchen *infra* 54, 57. WILLINGCOTT is *Welyngcote* 1312, *Wyvelyngcote* 1313 Exon (p), *Willingcott* 1691 *Recov*. '*Wifel*'s cot(e),' *v.* ing, cf. Willsworthy *infra* 232. YELLOWAYS is *Oldewaye* 1549 Pat. For the modern form *v.* Introd. xxxiii.

Filleigh

FILLEIGH 118 H/J 9

> *Fileleia* 1086 DB *et freq* to 1297 Pat with variant spellings
> *Fyle-, -legh(e)*, *Fillelegh* 1294 *Ass*
> *Fileslee* 1219 *Ass*
> *Fylylegh* 1256 *Ass*, *Fillilegh* 1278 *Ass*, *Philleigh* 1736 Exmoor
> *Felelegh* 1441 IpmR

This is probably OE *filiðlēah*, a compound of *filiðe*, 'hay,' and leah, with early loss of the *th* before *l*. Cf. Fillham *infra* 285.

PROUTWORTHY is *Prowtysburie* 1550 AOMB, *Prowtisbury* 1607 *Recov*, *Prowtworthy* 1692 *Recov* and is to be associated with the family of William *Prouta* (1333 *SR*).

BEER was the home of Walter *atte Beare* (1333 *SR*), *v.* bearu. HEDDON is *Hethdon* 1238 FF. 'Heath hill,' *v.* dun. PAYNES (6")

is to be associated with the family of Richard *Payn* (1333 *SR*).
WINSLADE (6″) is *Wydeslade* 1330 *SR* (p). 'Wide slæd,' or
'withy slæd,' *v.* wiðig.

Georgeham

GEORGEHAM [dʒɔˑdʒˊhæm] 118 E 3

> *Hama* 1086 DB, *Hamme* 1242 Fees 774, (*Sci Georgii*) 1356
> *Ass*, *Over-*, *Netherhamme* 1365 *FF*, *Georgeham* 1535 VE

v. hamm. The dedication of the church is to St George. There
is still a *Higher* Ham just to the north of the village.

NORTH BUCKLAND is *Bochelant* 1086 DB, *Boclaunde Dyn(e)ham*
1301 Ipm, 1561 *Deed*, *v.* bocland. It is north in relation to Buckland in Braunton *supra* 32. The *Dyneham* connexion, presumably a manorial addition, is unknown.

CROYDE, CROYDE HOE, CROYDE BAY

> *Crideholda* 1086 DB, *-ho* 1242 Fees 796, 1261 Exon, 1329
>   Exon, *Cridaho* 1303 FA, *Cridyho* 1308 Exon
> *Cryden-*, *Cridenho* 1307 Oliver 200
> *Credyhogh* 1499 Ipm, *Credye* 1600 *Recov*
> *Cride Bay* 1577 Saxton, *Cride al. Cridehoe* 1670, 1713 *Recov*
> *Croyde* 1765 D

The first element *Cride(n)* is probably the name of the stream
here, and identical with Creedy *supra* 4. Croyde village is on
this stream, while Croyde Hoe is properly the name of the
promontory to the north of Croyde Bay. The modern form
would date from the 17th or 18th century when there was much
confusion between long *i* and *oi*. Cf. Bystock *infra* 600.

DARRACOTT is *Dodecote* 1302 *Ass*, 1330 *SR* (p), *Doddecote* 1501
Ipm, *Dorracott al. Dodecot* 1617 *Deed*. 'Dod(d)a's cot(e).' This
is possibly the *Doda* who held the not far distant manor of
Saunton TRE (DB f. 408).

HOLE is *Hola* 1086 DB, *Hole* 1242 Fees 774, 1402 Exon, *North-*,
South- 1371 Cl. *v.* holh. This place-name is very common in
the county, as indeed its topography would lead us to expect.
In most cases it refers to a small hollow or 'combe' opening out
of some wider valley.

PICKWELL

> *Pediccheswella* 1086 DB (Exon), *Wedicheswelle* (Exch)
> *Pido(c)keswell* 1207 PatR (p), 1230 P, -*ekes*- 1219 *Ass*, *Pideke-will'* 1242 Fees 772, 1249 FF, *Pydikeswyll* 1244 *Ass*, *Pydekewill'* 1303 FA, *Pydikwell* 1326 Ipm, *Pyckewyll al. Pydyckswell* 1560 *Deed*
> *Paddikkeswell* 1285 FA

Ekwall (PN La 62 *s.n.* Pigsden) suggests that in Pickwell we have a pers. name which is a diminutive of OE *Piuda*. That should give us some ME forms in *Pud-*. Perhaps we ought rather therefore to assume a diminutive *Piddic*, of uncertain origin. Hence, '*Piddic*'s spring,' *v.* wielle. The form in the Exchequer DB shows the common confusion of the OE symbols for *þ* and *w*. Cf. Pilton and *Dewdon infra* 54, 527.

COTT (6″) and FORD were probably the homes of John de *Cotes* (1333 *SR*) and Mauger' *atte Forde* (1333 *SR*), *v.* cot(e).

BAGGY POINT is *Bag Poynt* 1577 Saxton. BURVER (6″) is *Burford* 1503 Ipm. It adjoins CROWBERRY for which no early forms have been found, but both names probably referred to the same burh. PUTSBOROUGH is *Pottysburghe* 1313 Exon (p), *Puttesborught* (sic) 1515–18 ECP 5, 73. Probably '*Putt*'s beorg,' this being the strong form of the recorded *Putta*. The name may, however, be of ME origin.

Goodleigh

GOODLEIGH 118 G 7

> *Godelega* 1086 DB *et passim* to 1394 *Ass* with variant spelling -*leg(he)*, (*juxta Barnastapol*) 1314 *Ass*, (*juxta Shirewille*) 1345 *Ass*
> *Godesleg'* 1234 Fees 401
> '*Gōda*'s leah.'

SNAPPER is *La Snappe* 1256 FF, *Snape* 1621 *FF*. This must be the word *snap*, 'boggy land,' discussed under Snaplands (PN Sx 28). Cf. further Snap (W), *Snappe* in 1332 (*SR*). For the final *er*, *v.* Introd. xxxvi.

DEAN and YEOTOWN were the homes of William *atte Dene* (1333

SR), *v.* denu, and Roger *atte Yea* (ib.), i.e. at the water, *v.* Yeo *supra* 17–18.

CROWHILL (6″) is so spelt 1696 *FF*. EASTACOTT is *Estcote* 1249 *Ass*. LILLY is *Lilleghe* 1291 Tax. NORTHLEIGH is *Northlegh* 1330 *SR* (p), *v.* leah.

Heanton Punchardon

HEANTON PUNCHARDON [heintən] 118 F 4

> *Hantona* 1086 DB
> *Hamtona* 1167 P (p), *Hampton* 1238 *Ass*
> *Hainton* 1213 FF
> *Hyaunton'* 1242 Fees 784, (*juxta Braunton*) 1302 *Ass, Heuan-tone* 1262 Exon, *Heanton* 1292 Ipm, 1303 FA, (*Punchardun*) 1297 Pat, (*juxta Barnestapla*) t. Ed 3 *Ass*
> *Yantone* 1291 Tax, *Yeanton* 1675 Ogilby

'At the high farm,' *v.* heah, tun. The place was held by Robert de *Ponte Cardonis* (i.e. thistle bridge) in DB, the ordinary French form *Punchardon* being found in 1215 (FF) and later records.

WRAFTON is *Wratheton* 1238 *Ass et freq* to 1340 *Ass, Wraghton* 1284 *Ass, Wrathton* 1412 IpmR, *Wroughton* 1738 *Recov. v.* tun. The first element may, as suggested by Blomé (20), be the OE *wraþu*, 'prop, support,' but the exact sense of the compound is uncertain. As the place lies low near the Taw estuary, the name might refer to a farm built near some erection used as a protection against floods.

WEST ASHFORD is *Westesford* 1242 Fees 784, *Westashford* 1303 FA. 'West' with reference to Ashford *supra* 24. CHIVENOR is *Chyvenor(e)* 1284 *Ass*, 1303 DA 11 (p), 1311 Exon (p), *Chivenore* 1285 Pat. '*Cifa*'s bank or shore,' *v.* ora. For this name cf. Chivington PN Wo 219. HARDING'S MILL (6″) is to be associated with the family of Robert *Heardyng* (1330 *SR*). HORRIDGE is *Harigge* 1288 FF, *Horugge* 1330 *SR* (p). 'Boundary ridge,' *v.* har. The farm lies on the parish boundary. MAINSTONE is *Meyneston* 1378 IpmR, *Maynston* 1400 DA 20. *v. s.n.* Mainstone *infra* 228.

Ilfracombe

ILFRACOMBE 118 B 4

Alfreincoma 1086 DB
Alferðingcoma 1167 P
Aufredyncomb 1208 PatR, *Alfrede(s)cumbe* 1234 Cl, 1249 FF
Alfrithecumb 1219 *Ass*, *Aufrithcumbe* 1244 *Ass*, *Aufridecumbe*
1233 Ch, 1261 Exon (p), 1269 Exon, *Alf-* 1249 *Ass*,
Aufricum(be) 1244 *Ass*, 1262–76 Exon, *Aufridycombe* 1291
Tax
Alfrincumbe 1242 Fees 784
Hilfardescumbe 1244 *Ass*
Ilfredecumb(e) 1262–76 Exon, 1274 Ipm, 1294 *Ass*, 1309 Ipm,
Ilfridec(o)umbe 1279 Ch, 1305 Ipm, *Ildefrithecumbe* 1290 Ch,
Ilfradiscombe 1328 FF
Hilfrincombe 1262–76 Exon
Ilvercombe 1302 Cl, *Ilfercomb* 1480 IpmR, *Ylfrycomb* 1346 FA
Elvertecombe 1322 Cl
Ilfordcomb 1667 Cai, *Ilfarcomb vulg. Ilfracomb* 1675 Ogilby

Probably '*Ælfred*'s combe,' *v.* ing, cumb. For the later
spellings with *i*, cf. Elmscott *infra* 73. The exact form of the
personal name involved is not certain. Some of the forms
suggest *Ælfriþ* or *Ælferhð*. The early spellings show curious
fluctuation between forms with *es* and *ing* as the connective
link between the two elements. The *ing*-forms are probably
responsible for the ultimate *s*-less compound.

CAMPSCOTT is *Kamescoth'* 1242 Fees 771, *Cambescote* 1326 Ipm,
Cammes- 1346 FA, *Cames-* 1371 IpmR. '*Camme*'s cot(e).' This
may, as suggested by Blomé (21), be the same *Camme* whose son
Bristric held the not far distant manor of Bugford in East Down
in 1086 (DB f. 126 b).

CHAMBERCOMBE is *Champernounyscomb* 1439 Exon, *Chambercomb*
1525 *AOMB* and is to be associated with the family of Henry de
Chambernon (1321 Exon), probably a descendant of the Oliver
de *Campo Ernulfi* whose heirs held the manor of Ilfracombe in
1242 (Fees 784).

HELE is *Hela* 1086 DB, *Hele* 1311 *Ass* (p), *Helemyll* 1525 *AOMB*.
This is the first example of a name which in the form *Hele* or

Heale is very common in Devon, and is occasionally found in Somerset. None of the Devon examples is found in a pre-Conquest form, but Heale in Curry Rivel (So) is found in a charter of Athelstan in the Muchelney Cartulary (38) in the form (*of*) *east heale*, and this makes it clear that the name goes back to OE *hēale*, the dative singular of healh. *Hele* would be the natural ME development of this in a stressed syllable, though in an unstressed syllable, with shortening of the vowel, OE *hēale* might become ME *hale*. Elsewhere in England in the fairly numerous places called simply *Hale* or *Hales* we have the distinctively Anglian form going back to OE *hāle*, without breaking of *æ* to *ea* before original *lh*. In non-Anglian England the *hale*-forms go back to an unlengthened OE *hĕale* or are due to the influence of the extremely numerous names with final unstressed -*hale*.

We have a few examples of *hale* in Devon. There is a Hale Farm in Honiton *infra* 640, which shows curious variation between the specifically Devon types and the more common one found elsewhere. So also we have traces of the *hale* forms in unstressed syllables in Cripple, Black Hall and Worthele *infra* 170, 304, 274.

LINCOMBE is *Lincoma* 1086 DB, -*cumba* 1198 BM, -*cumb(e)* 1200 FF, 1242 Fees 784, 1244 *Ass*, *Leyncombe* 1361 Cl. For this name *v.* Addenda *supra* lviii.

MULLACOTT is *Molacota*, *Malacota* 1086 DB, *Mullecoth*' 1242 Fees 787, *Mollecote* 1303 FA, 1330 *SR* (p), 1378 IpmR, *Mellecote* 1485 Ipm. Probably '*Molla*'s cot(e),' cf. PN La 119 *s.v.* Melling and John *Molle* (1373 Exon).

SCORE was the home of William *atte Score* (1330 *SR*). The place is on a steep hillside and we probably have the same unrecorded OE word discussed *s.n.* Shoreham (PN Sx 246). For initial *sc*, *v.* Introd. xxxv. See also Scur *supra* 34.

SHELFIN is *Sildesfen* 1167 P (p), *Schildisfene* 1329 DA 11 (p), *Shilfen* 1712 DA 20. '*Scyld*'s marsh land.' For the pers. name *Scyld* cf. Shelsley Beauchamp (PN Wo 76).

WARCOMBE is *Warcoma* 1086 DB, *Worcumb(e)* 1242 Fees 784, 1281 *Ass* (p), -*comb(e)* 1303 FA, 1356 AD iv, *Worthcumbe* 1314 Ipm, (*al. Worcumb*) 1316 Ipm, *Wercombe* 1327 Banco. This, as

Blomé suggests (22), may contain a river-name allied to the Celtic
Worica (*v.* Holder *s.n.*), but the river-name *Worf*, of varied
origin and going back either to *Worf* or *Worgh* (*v.* Ekwall RN
470), is more probable.

YARD FM (6″) is *Laierda* 1086 DB, *Yerd(e)* 1473 IpmR, 1499
Ipm, and was the home of William *atte Yurd* (1330 *SR*). There
are several places of this name in the county. All probably go
back to OE *gierd*, *gyrd*, 'area of land of varying extent, usually
30 acres,' i.e. a quarter-hide. *v. yard* sb. 2 in NED, sense 10,
where an example of its use for an area of land is quoted from
a Devon charter (BCS 721). The term *La Verge* found in the
early forms of some of these names is the corresponding French
word, *v.* Ducange *s.v. virga*. *La* in DB *Laierda* is the French
def. art.

BEERA, LANGLEIGH FM (6″), OAKRIDGE and SLADE were probably
the homes of Michael *atte Beare* (1408 *Ass*), William de *Lange-
legh* (1333 *SR*), John de *Okerigge* (ib.) and Gilbert *atte Slade*
(1330 *SR*), *v.* bearu, leah, slæd.

BICKENBRIDGE (6″) is *Bichingbrige* 1167 P (p), *Bickenbridge* 1641
SR. '*Bic(c)a*'s bridge,' *v.* ing and cf. Abbots Bickington *infra*
124. BICKLEIGHSCOMBE (6″) is *Bykelyscombe* 1443 *FF*. *Bekilles-
combe* 1561 *Deed*, and is to be associated with the family of
Robert *de Bikeleghe* (1321 Exon). BOWDEN (6″) is *Northbughedon*
1262 FF, *Lyttell Bowdon* 1503 Ipm. *v.* Bowden *supra* 37.
BURROW FM (6″) is *Borough* 1525 *AOMB*, *v.* beorg. DIBBON'S
LANE (6″) is to be associated with the family of John *Dobyn* (1330
SR). HORE DOWN is *Horedown* 1525 *AOMB*. As this is on the
parish boundary the meaning may be 'boundary hill,' *v.* har,
dun. HORNE FM (6″) is *Hurne* 1550 *AOMB* and was the home
of Walter *Inthehurne* (1333 *SR*), *v.* hyrne. KILLICLEAVE (6″) is
Kellicleave 1734 *Deed*, *v.* clif. LEE is *Legh* 1416 Exon, *v.* leah.
PLUDD. No forms have been noted, but the name is probably
identical with Pludda *infra* 467. There is marshy land here.
WARMSCOMBE is very likely identical with *Warmundesham* 1311
Ass, *Warmodesham* 1330 *SR* (p). '*Wǣrmund*'s ham(m).' WID-
MOUTH is *Wydmouth* 1529 *Recov*. 'Wide mouth,' referring to
the bay here. Cf. Widemouth (Co), *Widemutha* 1180 P,
Wydemuthe 1302 *Ass*.

Kentisbury

KENTISBURY 118 D 8

Chentesberia 1086 DB, *Kentesbir'* 1242 Fees 784, -*byri* 1275
    Exon, -*bury* 1316 FA
Kentelesberi 1260 Exon (p), -*bere* 1279 Ipm, 1303 FA, -*bur'*
    1281 *Ass*
Kantesbere 1274 Cl, *Kantelesberi* 1285 Ipm
Kynsbury 1523 *SR*

There was clearly a Cornish word *centel*, which must lie
behind such a p.n. as Tregantle (Co), DB *Argentel*, i.e. upon
centel. This may be connected with Welsh *cantel*, 'rim, circle,'
and *Centel* have been the old name for Kentisbury Down, a
circular hill on which tumuli are still found. The name would
then mean 'burh belonging to or by *Centel*.' The burh may be
the old 'camp' on Kentisbury Down.

BREADWICK

Breduica 1086 DB, *Bredewic*(*h*) 1198 FF, 1199 ChR, -*wike*
    1473 IpmR
Bradewic 1198 FF
Brudewyk 1234 Fees 396, *Bruddewyk* 1279 Ipm
Bridewyk 1242 Fees 772, -*wik* 1326 Ipm, *Northbridewyk* 1310
    Ass, *Bridwik* 1316 Ipm
Burdick 1809 M

The parallel of OE *bryda beorh* (KCD 1292) in Oxfordshire
suggests that we may have here a compound of OE *brȳd*, 'bride,
woman,' either in the genitive singular (*brȳde*) or plural (*brȳda*)
and wic. As with the 'maiden' names (cf. Maidenford *supra* 26),
it is impossible now to suggest the exact circumstances under
which such a name might be given.

PATCHOLE is *Patsola* 1086 DB, *Pacheshole* 1326 Ipm, 1333 *SR*
(p). Probably '*Pætti*'s hollow,' with the strong form of the pers.
name *P*(*e*)*at*(*t*)*a* found in *pattandene* (BCS 1307), Patney (W),
Peat(*t*)*anige* (BCS 1118) and Patton (Sa), *peattingtun* (BCS 587)
and early sound-substitution of *ch* for *ts*, cf. Patsford *infra* 52.
One might suggest '*Pæcci*'s hollow,' cf. Patchill *infra* 211, but we
have no parallel for 11th cent. substitution of *ts* for *ch*. *v*. holh.

KENTISBURY FORD, WAYTOWN and WEEK were probably the homes of William de *la Forde* (1244 *Ass*), Ralph de *la Weye* (1249 *Ass*) and Jordan de *Wike* (1238 *Ass*), v. weg, wic.

COWLEY is *Colleg(h)* 1244, 1249 *Ass* (p), v. Collacott *infra*. HOLLACOMBE is *Holecumbe* 1292 *Ass* (p). 'Hollow valley,' v. holh, cumb. LEY is *La Laye* 1249 *Ass*, *Legh* 1281, 1310 *Ass* (p), v. leah. PORT is *Port* 1809 M, v. Doggaport *infra* 95. PRESTON is *Prusteton* 1330, *Pruteston* 1333 *SR* (p). 'Priests' tun.' SEVEN ASH is *Sovenaisse* 1238 *Ass* (p), *-ayshe* 1330 *SR* (p), *Suvenass'* 1249 *Ass* (p), *Sevenash* 1326 Ipm, *Sonash* 1428 FA, *Sinash* 1765 D. 'Seven ashes,' cf. Seabeach (PN Sx 68). SILKENWORTHY is *Silkinford al. Silkingworth* 1737 FF.

Marwood

MARWOOD 118 E/F 6

> *Meroda, Merehoda, Mereuda* 1086 DB
> *Merew(o)de* 1219 FF, 1293 Ch, 1311 BM, 1343 Ipm
> *Churimerwod* 1242 Fees 787, *Cherchemerewode* 1256 FF,
>   *Chirchemerwode* 1345 *Ass*
> *Merwode* 1263 Exon, 1291 Tax

As there is no pool here the first element may, as suggested by Blomé (23), be OE (ge)mære, 'boundary,' the place being on the boundary between Braunton and Shirwell Hundreds. *Church* to distinguish it from Middle Marwood *infra* 52.

BLAKEWELL is *Blachewilla* 1086 DB, *Blakewill(e)* 1198 FF, 1242 Fees 784. 'Black stream or spring,' v. wielle.

SOUTH BURLAND (6") is *Bruneslond* 1244 *Ass* (p), *Brounland* 1289 *Ass*, *-lond* 1442 IpmR, *Brunelond* 1289 *Ass*. Probably 'brown land,' though the earliest forms suggest a pers. name *Brūn*.

COLLACOTT is *Colecote* 1333 *SR* (p). Names in *Col(l)-* are very common in Devon, as also in Somerset and north-east and east Cornwall. They may for convenience be divided into three groups: (*a*) those which show no medial *e* in the early spellings, (*b*) those which show a medial *e* but only one *l*, (*c*) those which show a medial *e* and a double *l* in at least the majority of early forms. The first group probably contains as first element the OE *col*, 'coal, charcoal,' perhaps referring to a locality where such

was burnt. The second and third groups are the most difficult. In the second group our choice lies between the pers.
name *Cola*, and the adj. *cōl*, 'cool.' The third group must contain as first element the OE pers. name *Col(l)a*, or in some few
cases—e.g. where compounded with broc—a river-name *Colle*
(*v.* Ekwall RN 85). In the majority of cases, at least in those
where a medial *e* appears in the early spellings, derivation from
the OE pers. name *Cola* is the most probable etymology.
Collaton in Malborough was held by one *Colo* or *Cole* TRE
(*v. infra* 307).

KENNACOTT is *Kiniuecota, Keniuecota* 1167 P (p), *Kynewecote*
1419 *Ass* (p). '*Cēngiefu's* or *Cynegiefu's* cot(e),' these being fem.
pers. names in OE.

KINGSHEANTON is *Hagintona* 1086 DB, *Hamtona* 1167 (p),
Kyngesheigham(p)ton 1387, 1394 Fine, *Kyngs Heaunton* 1400
DA 20. The DB form is probably an error and the history of the
name the same as that of Heanton *supra* 45. The Fine Roll
forms show duplication of the *high* element and folk-etymology
has also been at work. Cf. Highampton *infra* 145. It is not
known what *King* is referred to.

METCOMBE is *Metcoma* 1086 DB, *Medcome* 1244 *Ass* (p), *-cumbe*
1281 *Ass* (p), *Medecoumb* 1442 IpmR, *Meddecomb* 1501 Ipm.
'Meadow valley,' *v.* mæd, cumb.

MUDDIFORD is *Modeworthi* 1303 DA 11 (p), *Modworthy* 1400
DA 20, *Mud-* 1515–18 ECP 5, 191, *Mudford or Mudworthie* 1558
Deed. Probably '*Mōda's* worþig.' For interchange of *ford* and
worthy, *v. supra* 38.

PRIXFORD is *Pirkewurth* 1238 FF, *Pirkisworthe* 1319 Exon (p),
Pirkesworthi 1330, 1333 *SR* (p), *Pyrkesworthy* 1356 AD iv,
Prikesworthy or Pyrkesworthy 1499 Ipm. *v.* worþig. The first
element may be a British pers. name *Piroc*. This is not on record
but would be a derivative of *Pyr* (Chrest 158). Cf. also Manor-
bier (Pembr), *Maynaurpir, id est Mansio Pirri* c. 1185 Giraldus
Cambrensis, *Enispir* the old name for Caldy Island (Pembr),
Caldei quam Kambri Enispir id est Insula Pirri vocant c. 1185 (id.).

VARLEY is *Falleia* 1086 DB[1], *Fernlegh* 1330 *SR* (p), *Fer-* 1333 *SR* (p), *Ver-* 1486 Ipm. 'Bracken clearing,' *v.* fearn, leah.

WHIDDON is *Willedenna* 1086 DB, *Wyddene* 1242 Fees 775, *Wydedon* 1303 FA, *Wytedon* 1244 *Ass* (p), 1292 Ipm, *Witdedene* 1326 Ipm. The forms are too widely divergent for any etymology to be possible.

WHITEFIELD is *Witefella* 1086 DB, *Whytefeud, -feld* 1242 Fees 772, 787. 'White open country,' *v.* feld. The name *Whitefield* is fairly common in Devon, as elsewhere. In these names *white* may be used in the sense given by the EDD for that word, viz. 'dry open pasture ground in opposition to woodland and *black*-land growing heath.' Cf. the numerous names like Blackland, Blagdon, etc.

CROCKERS and SPENCER'S WOOD (6″) are probably to be associated with the families of William *Crokere* (1330 *SR*) and John *le Spenser* (1333 *SR*).

GUINEAFORD is *Giniver* c. 1800 Barum, *v.* Introd. xxxiv. HARTNOLL is *Hurtknoll* 1333 *SR* (p). 'Hart hill,' *v.* cnoll. HEWISH BARTON is *Hewish* 1765 D, *v.* hiwisc. HONEYWELL (6″) is *Huniwell* 1249 *Ass* (p), *Honiwell* 1681 Recov, and probably denoted a spring with sweet water, *v.* Honeychurch *infra* 165. LEE HO is *Legh* 1438 Exon, *v.* leah. MIDDLE MARWOOD is *Middelmorwude* (sic) 1234 Fees 396, *-merwode* 1242 Fees 784, *Myddel Marwode* 1491 Ipm. MILLTOWN is *Miltoune* 1609 Recov. PATSFORD is *Pattes-ford(e)* 1330 *SR* (p), 1394 *Ass*, 1441 IpmR. '*Pætti*'s ford,' cf. Patchole *supra* 49. SWINDON DOWN is *Swyndon* 1660 Recov, *Swindon al. Swinham* 1830 Recov. 'Swine hill,' *v.* dun. TOWN-RIDDEN (6″) is so spelt 1830 Recov. As this is just outside the village (*v.* tun), it probably means 'village clearing,' *v.* hryding. WESTCOTT is *Westecoth* 1242 Fees 774, *Westecotedoune* 1386 *Ass*.

Morthoe

MORTHOE 118 C 3

> *Morteho* 1086 DB *et passim* to 1450 IpmR with occasional forms *Morthe-* and *-hou, -how(e), -hoo, Mortaho* 1258 Exon
> *Marto* 1628 Barum 1, 62, *Moorthoe* 1739 FF

---

[1] The identification is not certain. It may refer to Voley in Parracombe *infra* 67, but no early forms of that name have been found.

This name must probably be taken along with the unidentified *mortan cumb* (BCS 479) in Wiltshire, Mortlake (Sr), DB *Mortelage*, Mortlock's Fm in Radwinter (Ess) 1201 FF *Mortlake*, Murtwell *infra* 301, *Moretor infra* 516, Mortham (PN NRY 30) and Mosterton (Do), DB *Mortesthorn*, and it must certainly be taken with the neighbouring North Morte. Morthoe and North Morte can have no relation to any stream. They are both on the tops of hills 400–500 ft. high, away from any stream. If we trace out the topography of *mortan cumb* in Grundy's analysis of BCS 479 (*Arch. Journ.* 76, 179) we find ourselves far away from any stream, and as Murtwell is high on a hillside, it is more likely that it takes its name from a spring than from a stream. Mosterton is on the Axe and so cannot contain a stream-name. Presumably there was some water which gave rise to the *lake* in Mortlake, but the only stream here is the Beverley Brook, which has an OE name (BCS 994). Mortlock's Fm is near a tiny tributary of the Pant. Mortham (NRY) is on the Greta; as this is a Scandinavian river-name the question of its earlier name must be left open. It is clear from this analysis that any assumption of a river-name *Morta* in England, as made by Blomé (24), is extremely doubtful and is certainly impossible for Mosterton, *mortan cumb*, Morthoe and North Morte. Professor Ekwall notes, so far as Morthoe itself is concerned, that by far the most prominent feature of the district is Morte Point and he suggests that *Morte* is the original name of the point and that this name is allied to the common Germanic stem found in Norwegian *murt*, 'small fish,' Eng. Dial. *murt*, 'small person,' Icel. *murtr*, 'short, stumpy,' MHG *murz*, 'stump' (cf. further Hellquist *s.v. mort*). If that is the case, we must assume that some at least of the other names given above contain a pers. name *Mort* or *Morta* derived from this stem and ultimately of nickname origin.

OUSSABOROUGH [ɔsəbʌrə] is *Asaberga* 1086 DB (Exon), *Aseberge* (Exch), *Osborough* 1827 G. The second element is beorg, 'hill.' The first element may, as suggested by Blomé (24), be the Scandinavian pers. name *Asa*, but the paucity of early spellings prevents any definite conclusion.

ROADWAY is *Radehida* 1086 DB, *-weye* 1242 Fees 792, 1270 *Ass*, 1303, 1316 FA, *-weie* 1333 SR (p). Probably 'red way,' the DB form being corrupt, cf. Raleigh *infra* 55. The soil is redder here than on the Morthoe side of the valley and a red stone is quarried near by (*ex inf.* Mr B. W. Oliver).

SHAFTSBOROUGH

> *Settesbergh* 1242 Fees 792
> *Schotteburgh* 1303 FA, *Shottes-* 1311, 1322 *Ass*, 1330 *SR* (all p), *Shotesberwe* 1325 *Ass*, *Shotisburgh* 1327 Banco
> *Shatesborough* 1809 M

'*Scot*'s hill,' *v.* beorg. *Scot* was here probably a pers. name rather than a national by-name, cf. Redin 23 and *Schottesdon* 1244 *Ass* (Devon). For the modern vowel, *v.* Introd. xxxiv.

SPREACOMBE is *Esprecoma* 1086 DB (Exon), *Sprecome* (Exch), *Sprecumb'* 1242 Fees 774, *Spreycomb* 1303 FA, *Spraycombe* 1380 Exon, *Sprycombe* 1385 Exon. 'Brushwood valley,' cf. Sprytown *infra* 208.

WOOLACOMBE

> *Wellecoma, Wolnecoma*[1] 1086 DB, *Wellecomb* 1301 Ipm
> *Wollecumb'* 1242 Fees 792 *et freq* to 1379 IpmR with variant spelling *-comb(e)*
> *Wullecumbe* 1244 *Ass*, *Wllecombe* 1275 RH (p)

Probably 'wolves' valley,' from OE *wulfa cumb, v.* cumb. The *n* in the DB form is probably an error for *u* (*v*).

BOROUGH is *Burgh* 1242 Fees 792, 1303 FA, 1327 Banco. Probably OE beorg, 'hill.' DAMAGE BARTON is *Damage* 1675 *FF*. EASEWELL is so spelt t. Jas 1 ECP. There is a spring here. MORTE BAY is *Mortbay* 1577 Saxton. MORTE STONE is *Mort Stone* (ib.). NORTH MORTE is *Murthe* 1244 *Ass* (p), *Morte* 1311 *Ass* (p), 1614 Barum, *Northmort* 1680 *FF*. For these names *v.* 53 *supra*. POOL was the home of Thomas *atte Pole* (1356 *Ass*). POTTER'S HILL is to be associated with the family of Thomas *Pottere* (1330 *SR*). TWITCHEN is *Twychyn* 1549 Pat. 'Crossways,' cf. Twitchen *infra* 57. Four tracks meet here.

Pilton, East and West

PILTON 118 G 6

> *Piltone wið Bearstaple* 10th (12th) Burghal Hidage, *Piltona*

---

[1] Corrected from *Welnecoma* in Exon DB.

1086 DB (Exon), *Wiltone* (Exch), *Pilton* 1121 France,
1167 P *et passim* with variant spelling *-tone*, *Pelleton* 1256
FF

'Farm by the creek,' *v.* pyll, tun, referring to the spot where
the little river Yeo enters the Taw and becomes tidal. For
Wiltone cf. Pickwell *supra* 44. *wið* here denotes 'opposite.'

PILLAND is *Pillanda* 1086 DB (Exon), *Welland* (Exch), *Pilland*
1157–60 France *et freq* with variant spellings *-land(e)*, *-lond(e)*,
Pylilond 1281 *Ass*, *Pileland* 1329 Ch. The 'pill' here must have
been the brooklet which rises near Pilland. Possibly in early
times it was a tidal creek or cove. For *W-*, cf. Pilton *supra*.

RALEIGH Ho [rɔˑli]

> *Radeleia* 1086 DB, *Radlega* 1174, 1176, 1180, 1181 P (p)
> *Raelega* 1107–28 (Ed 2) AD vi, 1161, 1171, 1172, 1175 P (p)
>   and 1174 P (ChancRoll), *Raalega* 1167 P
> *Ralega* 1160, 1163–6 P (p), *Ralegh* 1210 France (p) *et freq* to
>   16th century, *Ralegh juxta Barnstaple* 1370 *Ass*
> *Rawlegh* 1535 VE

Probably in this name as in Brayley and Roadway *supra* 34,
53, and Rowley *infra* 67, the *d* in the DB and the early Pipe Roll
forms is an error. The first element may be OE ræge, hence
'clearing of the wild she-goat.' The *d* may represent a French
clerk's attempt to deal with ME ȝ.

BEARA (6″) was the home of Robert *atte Beare* (1330 *SR*), *v.*
bearu. BRADIFORD Ho is *Bardeford* 1249 FF, *Bradeford juxta
Pilton* 1314 *Ass*, *Pillond juxta Bradeford* 1322 *Ass*. 'Wide ford.'
BURRIDGE. No forms have been found but it may be noted that
there is an ancient 'camp' here, *v.* burh. LITTABOURNE (6″) is
Lutteburne 1550 *Deeds Enrolled*, *v.* burna. POTTINGTON is
Potyngdon n.d. Oliver 203, *-ton* 1444 IpmR, *Petyngdon* 1435
Exon. Perhaps '*Potta's* farm,' *v.* ingtun. There is no hill here.
ROBOROUGH is *Rowborowe* 1679 *Deed*. 'Rough hill,' cf. Ro-
borough *infra* 118. TUTSHILL is *Tuttyshall in Pilton* 1533–8 ECP
7, 8, *Tyttishill or Titeshell* 1544 LP, *Tyttyshill* 1545 *Deeds
Enrolled*. The second element is probably 'hill,' the place
being on a hilltop. The first element looks like a pers. name but
the forms are too late for discussion. UPCOTT is *Uppecote* 1329

Exon. 'Higher cot(e).' YARNER WOOD (6″) is *wood of Yarvar* (sic) 1469 AD iii, *Yarnerwood* 1713 *Recov*, cf. Yarner *infra* 297.

Trentishoe

TRENTISHOE 118 B 9

Trendesholt 1086 DB

Trenlesho 1203 Cur, *Trendelesho* 1242 Fees 771, 1260 Exon, 1281 *Ass*, 1291 Tax, -*hou* 1326 Cl, -*hoo* 1326 Ipm, *Trenshoo* 1504–15 ECP 4, 276

Tryndesho 1441 Exon, *Trynshow* 1555 Wills

This is probably a compound of OE *trendel*, 'circle,' and hoh, as suggested by Blomé (26). Trentishoe Down is a circular hill and from it a high spur of land projects north-eastwards towards Trentishoe church. Hence, 'spur of (or by) the circular hill.'

SOUTH DEAN is *Deane* 1568 Deed, *Deane Downe* 1680 *Recov*, *v.* denu.

TATTISCOMBE is *Totescoma* 1086 DB, -*cumba* 1181 P (p), *Tottescumbe* 1310 Exon (p), -*comb* 1330 *SR* (p), 1346 FA, *Tatchcomb* 1630 Westcote. '*Tott*'s valley,' *v.* cumb. This pers. name is not recorded but would be the strong form of the well-evidenced *Totta*. For the 17th cent. spelling, cf. Titchberry *infra* 76.

II. SHIRWELL HUNDRED

Scireuuelle, -*uuille* 1084 Geld Roll, *Hundr de Schirewille* 1169 P

v. Shirwell *infra* 68.

Arlington

ARLINGTON 118 E 8

Alferdintona 1086 DB

Alureton c. 1200 BM, *Alfrintone* 1258–62 Exon

Auvrington 1242 Fees 782, *Aurington* 1258–62 Exon

Alrington(e) 1284 Exon, 1297 Pat, 1377 IpmR

Arlyngton 1550 *SR*

'*Ælfheard*'s farm,' *v.* ingtun.

HUCKHAM is *Hoccumb* 1238 *Ass*. The same name occurs *infra* 60 332, and we find the pers. name *atte Hocumbe* in Cheriton Fitz payne in 1333 (*SR*). This suggests a compound of OE *hoc* and *cumb* denoting a valley which had a definite twist in it, or into which projected a hook-shaped promontory of land.

TWITCHEN is *Tuchel* 1086 DB, *Twychene* 1281 *Ass* (p), 1330 *SR* (p), *Titchin* 1809 M. This is the OE *twicene*, 'crossways,' 'meeting of two ways.' Two tracks meet at the farm.

ARLINGTON BECCOTT is *Baccote juxta Alryngton* 1361 *Ass*, cf. Beccot *supra* 39. TIDICOMBE is *Tiddecumbe* 1244 *Ass* (p), '*Tid(d)a*'s valley.'

High Bray

HIGH BRAY 118 F/G 10

> (*æt*) *Bræg* c. 970 BCS 1253
> *Braia* 1086 DB, *brai* 1121 AC
> *Hautebray(e)* 1242 Fees 772, 1267 Exon, 1303 FA, 1326 Ipm, *Hautbrey* 1335 Exon
> *Heghebray* 1280 *Ass*, 1316 FA, 1334 *SR*, *-brey* 1346 *Ass*, *Heghbrey* 1347 FF, *Hyebray* 1448 Pat

Ekwall (RN 49) considers that Bray, though evidenced as a stream-name from the 13th cent. (*v. supra* 2), may originally have been a p.n. identified with Co, W *bre*, 'hill,' or OE *bræg*, 'brow.' High Bray stands on a well-marked hill and if of Celtic origin may possibly have been wrongly connected with the stream by the earliest English settlers. Bray in Morval and Brea in St Just (Co) are on hills and have similar early spellings and undoubtedly go back to the Celtic word.

GRATTON is *Gretedona* 1086 DB, *Gratedene* 1242 Fees 772, *Gretton* 1249 *Ass*, *Gratton* 1261 FF, *Gratton al. Gretton* 1326 Ipm. 'Big hill,' *v.* dun.

MUXWORTHY

> *Mixtewurthe* c. 1100 *AD* A 14252, *Mixeworth* 1279 *Ass* (p), *Myxe-* 1277 *Ass*
> *Mukeswurde* 1184 P (p)
> *Mexeworth* 1277 *Ass*
> *Muxaworthi* 1330 *SR* (p), *Moxworth* 1428 FA (p)

The *t* in the earliest form of this name is probably correct and in that case we must compare Mixnam (Sr), *Mixtenhamm* (BCS 34), both names alike going back to an OE **mixten*, a contamination of OE *meoxen*, 'dung,' and *mist*, or of **misten* and *meox*. Cf. Goth. *maihstus*, OHG *mist* and OHG *mistunnea*.

NATSLEY is *Nottesleye* 1330 *SR* (p), *Nottysley* 1442 IpmR. '*Hnott*'s clearing,' *v.* leah. The personal name *Hnott* from OE *hnot*, 'bald headed,' is first found on record in the 12th cent. in the form *Nhott*. Cf. Natsworthy *infra* 528.

OVIS [ɔfis] is *Houese* 1238 *Ass*, *Lunese* (sic) 1261 FF, *Ouese* 1408 IpmR, *Office* 1809 M, and was the home of Galfridus *atter Houese* (1333 *SR*). This is OE *ofes(e)*, 'edge,' a by-form of *efes*, 'eaves, border.' Cf. Woodovis *infra* 220 and *v.* PN Wo 391. It is preserved in the dialectal *ovvis*, recorded from Somerset. Ovis lies along the western border of the parish.

WHITEFIELD [witivəl] is *Witefelda*, *-fella* 1086 DB, *Whitefeld juxta Heghebray* 1306 *Ass*, *Whetefeld al. Whitfeld* 1326 Ipm. Cf. Whitefield *supra* 52.

BRAYFORD is so spelt in 1651 Exmoor. BRAYTOWN FM (6″) is possibly identical with *Bretton in Hautebrae* 1301 Ipm. This is a case of the Devon *town*, 'farm,' being added to the name of the village in which it is found, cf. *infra* 676. FULLAFORD is *Fuleford* 1281 *Ass* (p), *Follaver* 1678 Exmoor. 'Dirty ford,' *v.* ful and cf. Wallover *infra* 60. HOLE is *Overhole in Bray* 1423 IpmR, *Holebray* 1491 Ipm, *v.* Hole *supra* 43. KEDWORTHY is *Kydeworth* 1254 *Ass*, *Kedworthie* 1636 *FF*. Probably '*Cydda*'s farm,' *v.* worþig. LYDCOTT is *Litlecote* 1261 FF, *Litecote* 1330 *SR* (p), *Littecote* 1408 IpmR, *Lytlecote* 1442 IpmR. 'Little cot(e).' ROCKLEY (6″) is *Rokeleye* t. Edw 3 *Ass*. 'Rooks' clearing,' *v.* leah. WHITEFIELD DOWN is *Whettival Down* 1685 Exmoor, giving us the local pronunciation of Whitefield *supra*.

Brendon

BRENDON 118 B 12

> *Brandon(a)* 1086 DB, 1205 FF, *-dun*, *Bramdon* 12th Buckland
> *Bremdon(e)* 12th Buckland, 1291 Tax, 1328 Exon, *Brendon* 1275 RH
> *Bryndon* 1544 Wills

There can be little doubt that this name, found many times in Devon and three times in Cornwall, is a corruption of bremel and dun, 'bramble hill,' with early loss of *l* from the consonantal combination and assimilation of *md* to *nd*. The early forms with *a* for *e* are either AN spellings (cf. IPN 112) or have been influenced by the word *brame*, 'briar.'

BADGWORTHY COTTAGE (6″) and HILL [bædʒəri]

1. *Bicheordin* 1086 DB, *Bikeweithe* (sic) 1198 FF, *-wrthi* 1199 ChR *et freq* to 1301 Ipm with variant spelling *Byke-* and *-wurth*, *-worth(y)*, *Bygworthy* 1379 Cl, *Big-* 1379 IpmR
2. *Baggeworth*, *Baga Wordia* 12th Buckland, *Baggeworth(i)* 1244, 1289 Ass, *-worthy* 1425 MinAcct, *Bagewurth* 1249 Ass *Batchery* 1651 DA 39

The second element in this name is worþign, worþ or worþig. There seems from the earliest times to have been fluctuation between forms going back to a pers. name *Bic(c)a* (cf. Bickington *infra* 124) and a pers. name *Bacga* (cf. Bagga Tor *infra* 232). Both names are very common in Devon. How the confusion first arose we cannot say. Sometimes the *k* of *Bikke* was voiced to *g* and this may have helped the confusion. Later, [g] > [dʒ] in quite irregular fashion.

CHERITON is *Ciretona* 1086 DB, *Chirinton* 1198 FF, *Ceriton* 1205 FF, *Churiton* 1284 Ass. 'Farm by the church,' *v*. cyrice, tun. Here is the site of St Brendan's church. The 1198 form, unless it be a blunder, suggests an earlier *ciricean-tūn*, 'farm of the church.'

LANK COMBE is probably the DB *Lancoma*, stated to be a place added to the manor of Brendon, which paid geld for 1 ferding. The first element may, as suggested by Blomé (3), be OE *hlanc*, 'long, narrow'; OE lang is equally possible. Lank Combe is a long narrow valley running up from Badgworthy Water; it is now uninhabited, but in DB was the home of one villein.

LEEFORD is *Leoford* 1200 Cur, 1209 Oliver 347, *Lyweforda*, *Lewfordmede* 1425 MinAcct. The first element is probably OE *hlēow*, 'shelter,' the place lying in a valley with high hills on either side.

STRAYPARK CORNER (6″) is *le Strayerpark* 1425 MinAcct. This must contain OFr *estraieure*, 'goods left without an heir and hence passing to the lord' (Godefroi, *Dictionnaire de l'ancienne langue française s.v.*). Here as in Straypark *infra* 317, it has been reduced to the more common 'stray,' used of beasts found without an owner.

BIRCH WOOD (6") is *Birche Wood* 1563 DuCo. BRENDON COMMON is *la More de Bremdon* 1425 *MinAcct*. CLIFF WOOD (6") is *Highe Clif Wood* 1563 DuCo, v. clif. CRANSCOMBE is *Cranescomb* 1425 *MinAcct*. 'Crane's or heron's valley.' FARLEY is *Ferlee* 1198 FF, *Farlegh* 1281 Ass (p). 'Bracken clearing,' v. fearn, leah. HOCCOMBE is *Langhoccoumbe* 1339 Exmoor, cf. Huckham *supra* 56. MALMSMEAD is *Malsemede* 1425 *MinAcct*. SCOB HILL is *Scobbhyll* 1563 DuCo, v. Scoble *infra* 327. SHILSTONE is so spelt 1809 M, v. Shilstone *infra* 433. SLOCOMBESLADE (6") is *Slocumb* 1330 SR (p), *Slocomb* 1425 *MinAcct*. Probably 'sloe valley.' The 'slade' (v. slæd) is a late addition. TIPPACOTT is *Tibecote* 1249 Ass (p). '*Tibba*'s cot(e).' WATERLET LINHAY (6") is *Waterlett* 1525 AOMB. 'Water channel or leat,' cf. Leat *infra* 172, and *La Waterlate* 1238 Ass. For *Linhay*, v. 592 *infra*.

Challacombe

CHALLACOMBE [tʃɔləkum] 118 D 10

> *Celdecomba* 1086 DB, *Cheldecombe* 1438 IpmR
> *Caldecumba* 1167 P, *Chaudecumb'* 1242 Fees 772, *Chaldecumbe* 1244 *Ass*
> *Choldecomb(e)* 1326 Cl, 1346 FA, *Scoldecombe* 1330 Exon, *Cholcombe* 1428 FA, *Cholycombe* 1620 Wills
> 'Cold valley,' v. cald, cumb.

RADWORTHY [radəri] is *Radeuda* (sic) 1086 DB (Exon), *-ode* (Exch), *Radeweithi* (sic) 1198 FF, *-worth'* 1242 Fees 792, *-wrthi* 13th AD vi, *North Raddery* 1765 D. '*Rēada*'s farm' or '*Rǣda*'s farm,' v. worþig and cf. Ratton (PN Sx 424–5).

WALLOVER is *Waleurda* 1086 DB, *Walleworth'* 1242 Fees 772, *Waleworthy* 1244 *Ass*, *-worth* 1291 Tax, *Walworth(y)* 1346 FA, *Walliford al. Wallworthy al. Wooliford* 1673 Recov. 'Farm of the Britons or slaves,' v. wealh, worþig and Introd. xxxv. WALLOVER DOWN is *Wallyford Down head or Topp* 1678 Exmoor.

WHITEFIELD is *Witefella* 1086 DB, *Whitefelde* 1333 *SR* (p).
'White open space,' *v.* Whitefield *supra* 52.

BILL HILL STONE is *Billihillstone* 1678 Exmoor. BROADBARROW
STONE (6″) is *Broadburrough* 1678 Exmoor. BROCKENBURROW
LANE (6″) is so spelt in 1765 D. No barrows exist here now. BUS-
COMBE is *Berwordescomb* 1330 *SR* (p), *Buruardescomb* 1333 *SR*
(p), *Burscombe* 1765 D. '*Beornweard*'s combe.' GOAT COMBE
(6″) is *Gotecomb* 1330 *SR* (p), 'goats' combe.' LONGSTONE
BARROW is *Longstone ball* 1651 Exmoor. There is a tumulus here
and a 'Long Stone.' For 'ball,' *v. infra* 211. SADDLE STONE (6″)
is *Sadleystone ball, Sadleystone Combe* 1651 Exmoor. There is a
saddle-shaped stone here, an Exmoor Forest boundary mark.
SETTA BARROW is *Setteburrowh* 1651 Exmoor. There is a tumulus
here, *v.* beorg. SHOULSBARROW is *Solsbury Castle* 1630 Westcote, *Shrowlsbury Castle or Salusbury Castle* 1815 Exmoor. There
is an ancient 'castle' here, *v.* burh. SWINCOMBE is *Suncomb* 1330
SR (p), *Swinecomb* 1809 M, 'swine combe.' For the phonology
cf. Umborne *supra* 15. TWITCHEN is *North Twitchen in Challacombe* 1533–8 ECP 7, 338, *v.* Twitchen *supra* 57. WESTLAND is
Wistland in 1678 Exmoor. It is at the west end of the parish.
WITHECOMBE is *Whiddian Combe* 1678 Exmoor. WOOD BARROW
is *Woodberrowe* 1651 Exmoor. There is a tumulus here, *v.* beorg.

Charles

CHARLES 118 G 10

    Carmes 1086 DB

    Charnes 1242 Fees 784, 1244 *Ass*, 1279 Exon, 1284 *Ass*, 1309
      Exon, 1317 Exon, -*nis* 1275 RH, 1292 Cl, -*nys* 1285, 1303
      FA, 1292 Ipm, 1308 Exon

    Charles 1244 *Ass*, 1285 Pat, 1291 Tax, 1294 *Ass*, 1334 *SR*,
      -*leys* 1278 FF, -*lis* 1279 QW, -*lys* 1316 FA, *Charells* 1616
      Wills

This name is probably Celtic, containing the British words
corresponding to Co *carn*, 'rock,' and *lis, les*, 'court, palace',
(W *llys*). *v.* Introd. xxi.

MOCKHAM is *Mogescoma* 1086 DB, *Moccumb* 1285 Pat (p),
Mokcomb 1330 *SR* (p). Probably '*Mocca*'s valley,' *v.* cumb. Cf.
Muckwell *infra* 333.

BLAKEWELL, LANE, SLADE and STOCK were probably the homes of Gilbert de *Blakewill* (1333 *SR*), Robert *atte Lane* (1330 *SR*), Richard de *la Slade* (ib.) and Alma de *Stoke* (ib.). *v.* blæc, wielle, slæd, stocc.

HUDLEY MILL is *Huddeleyg'* 1306 *Ass* (p). '*Hud(d)a*'s clearing,' *v.* leah. LITTLE BRAY is *Little Braye* 1260 FF, in distinction from High Bray, *supra* 57. *Little* as opposed to High Bray *supra* 57. SHUTSCOMBE is *Shottescomb* 1330 *SR* (p). Probably '*Scot*'s combe,' cf. Shaftsborough *supra* 54. TOWNHILL (6″) is *Towne-hill* 1653 *FF*. WILCOMBE is *Wylecumbe* 1281 *Ass* (p), *Wylescomb* 1330 *SR* (p). Probably 'spring-combe,' cf. Welsford *infra* 77 and *v.* wiell(e). There are many springs in the valley here.

Countisbury

COUNTISBURY 118 B 12

Contesberia 1086 DB
Cuntesberia 1177 P, -*bir'* 1200 Cur, -*biry* 1209 Oliver 347, -*byr'* 1249 *Ass*, 1275 RH, *Countesbyre* 1291 Tax
Cuntebiria, Cintebiria 1222 Bracton
Cundeburye 1238 FF
Cunisbere 1577 Saxton, *Consberye* 1581 SR, *Cunsbery* 1629-57 Barum, 1, 59

Plummer was probably right (*Two Saxon Chronicles* ii, 93) in identifying this with the *arx Cynuit* of Asser (c. 54), a place near the Devon coast where Ubba, brother of Ivarr the Boneless, suffered defeat. This identification was criticised by Stevenson (Asser's *Life of Alfred*, p. 265, n. 3) on phonological and formal grounds. On the phonological side it should be pointed out that *Cynuit* is only one of the numerous Welsh spellings of Anglo-Saxon names found in Asser. *Cynuit* is for *Cunet* with the regular Welsh change of long *e* to *ui* or *oi*. The normal development of British *Cunet* is to *Kennet*, but Ekwall (RN 99) shows that in some names it developed to *Cunet*, *Cuned*, and ultimately to *Cound*. The final *d* for *t* is a late Welsh change, but the vocalic development is of earlier date and would explain the form of Countisbury. The name *Cunet* here must denote a hill and be related to Welsh *cwn*, 'height,' the place standing at an elevation of nearly 1000 feet, though less than half a mile from the sea.

It is to be noted that Asser says that the *arx cynuit* can only be approached from the eastern side. It is only on the eastern side that the approach to Countisbury Hill is in any way easy. On the formal side it is to be noted that genitival compounds of a Celtic first element and an English second element have their parallel in such names as *Andredes-weald, -ceaster*, etc., cf. also Kentisbury *supra* 49. burh is recorded in OE itself as a rendering of Latin *arx*.

COSGATE HILL (6") is *Corsneshet* 1219, *Corsnestake* 1279, *Cornesyete* 1298, *Cornesgate* 1301 Exmoor. The final element is clearly geat referring to an Exmoor Forest boundary gate. The first part of the name is obscure, but may contain the Celtic *cors*, 'bog, marsh,' cf. Coarsewell *infra* 285.

ASHTON is *Ashdene* 1330 DA 38 (p), *Aysshedene* 1333 *SR* (p), *Ashton* 1543 DA 38. 'Ash valley,' *v.* denu. CHUBHILL WOOD (6") is *Chubwyll wood* 1550 *AOMB*. COOMBE was the home of Roger *atte Combe* (1333 *SR*). DESOLATE FM is no doubt so called from its lonely position. DOGSWORTHY (6") is *Doggeworth* 1281 *Ass* (p). The first element seems to be OE *docga* or ME *dogge*, perhaps here used as a pers. name. WILSHAM is *Willmersham* 1426 IpmR. '*Wilmǣr*'s ham(m).' WINGATE is so spelt 1765 D. Cf. Wingate *infra* 145. It is in an exposed situation.

Loxhore

LOXHORE 118 E 8

> *Loches(s)ora* 1086 DB, *Lokesore* 1256 *Ass*, *Lokkesore* 1244 *Ass et freq* to 1324 Ipm with variant spellings *Lockes-, Lockis-*, and *-hore*
>
> *Logeshor'* 1238 *Ass* (p)
>
> Over-, *Nitherlockysore* 1303 FA, *Overalockissore juxta Shirewille* 1339 *Ass*
>
> '*Locc*'s bank or slope,' *v.* ora. Cf. Loxbeare *infra* 540.

COOMBE is *Cumb* 1254 *Ass* (p), *Combe* 1570 DA 38. HAMONDS (6") is to be associated with the family of Richard *Hamounde* (1544 *SR*). HILL was the home of Elias *atte Hille* 1333 *SR*. LOWER LOXHORE is *Nitherlockysore* 1303 FA, *Netherlokeshore* 1378 IpmR, *v. supra*. LOXHORE COTT is *Cote* 1751 *Recov*, *v.* cot(e). SMYTHAPARK is *Smethepath* 1270 *Ass* (p), *Smythe-path(e)* 1285 FA, 1359 *Ass*, *Smyththepath* 1310 *Ass*. 'Smooth path.' This must be the path which here follows the line of the hill.

Lynton

LYNTON 118 B 11

Linton(a) 1086 DB *et passim* with variant spelling *Lyn-*

'Farm by the river Lyn' (*supra* 9), *v.* tun.

CAFFINS HEANTON is *Hantona* 1086 DB, *Yanton* 1242 Fees 791, *Heanton* 1303 FA, *Hanton Coffyn* 1285 FA, *Coffyns Heannton* 1491 Ipm. 'At the high farm,' *v.* heah, tun. Hugo *Coffin* held the manor in 1242. Cf. Caffin's Cross in the same parish.

HOAROAK is *Horeoak Ball* 1651 DA 39, *Whoretarr, Whoretarr-combe, Whore Oake Ball* 1651 Exmoor. 'Boundary oak,' *v.* har. It is on the county boundary. For *Ball v. infra* 211. *tarr,* i.e. tor (*v.* torr), must refer to Hoaroak Hill (So)

ILKERTON

Incrintona 1086 DB (Exon), *Crintone* (Exch)
Hilcrinton 1242 Fees 792, 1285 FA, *Ilcrynton* 1346 FA
Westelcrilton 1289 *Ass*
Hykeryngton 1301 Ipm, *Hylkeryngton* 1379 IpmR

It looks as if this were a compound of a personal name and ingtun. Professor Ekwall suggests *Ielfgār* for *Ælfgār*, cf. Ilfracombe *supra* 46, Dr Ritter suggests *Hildegār*. No certainty is possible.

LYN, EAST and WEST, is *Lina* 1086 DB, *Lyn* 1242 Fees 792, 1275 RH, *Westlyn juxta Lynton* 1301 *Ass*, *Est-, Westlyn* 1303 FA. *v.* Lyn river *supra* 9.

LYNMOUTH[1] is *Lymmouth* 1330 *SR* (p), *-the* 1345 *Ass*. *Ley-mouth Harbour* 1679 DA 38. 'Mouth of the river Lyn,' *supra* 9.

SPARHANGER (6″) is *Sperhangre* 1238 *Ass* (p), 1244 *Ass*, 1333 *SR* (p), 1346 FA, *-anger* 1242 Fees 792 (p), *-angre* 1303 FA. The

---

[1] Lynmouth is partly in Countisbury parish.

first element may be OE *spere*, 'spear, lance,' the name possibly referring to a wood (*v.* hangra) which furnished material for such. Cf. Shebbear *infra* 107.

WOOLHANGER is *Wellangre* 1238 *Ass* (p), *Welanger* 1242 Fees 792, *Welhangre* 1301 Ipm, 1330 *SR* (p), 1346 FA, -*ger* 1434 IpmR, *Willhanger* 1756 *Deed*. 'Wooded slope by the spring(s),' *v.* wielle, hangra. There is still a wood here on the steep hillside at the source of two streams.

BARBROOK MILL is *Babbroke Mill* 1632 DA 38. BARHAM HILL is *Barram Common* 1691 Exmoor. BERRY'S (6") is to be associated with the family of Thomas *Bery* (1544 *SR*). BUTTER HILL is *Butterhill* 1593 *Recov*. Cf. Buttercombe *supra* 40. CHERRY BRIDGE is *Cheribridge* 1775 DA 38. CLEAVE (6") is *la Clive* 1244 *Ass*, *v.* clif. CREAL PLANTATION (6"), cf. *Creale comb* 1597 *Deed*. DEAN is *Dene* 1543 DA 38, *v.* denu. FURZEHILL is *Fershull* 1198 FF, *Furshille* 1242 Fees 792, *Forshull* 1301 Ipm. KIBSWORTHY (6") is *Kebsworthy* 1727 DA 38, *v.* worðig. LEE is *Legh* 1244 *Ass*, *v.* leah. LYN DOWN is *Lynedown* 1597 *Deed*, *v.* Lyn *supra* 64. METTICOMBE (6") is *Mettecombe* 1632 DA 38. RATSBURY (6") is *Radespree* 1242 Fees 792, *Radispreye* 1285 FA (p), *Radespreye* 1289 *Ass*, *Radispray* 1339 Cl. 'Red brushwood land,' cf. Sprytown *infra* 208. SHORTACOMBE COMMON (6") is *Shortecomb* 1330 *SR* (p). 'Short valley,' *v.* cumb. SIX ACRE FM is *Six Acre* 1543 DA 38. STOCK is *Stocke* 1276 *Ass*, *v.* stocc. THORNWORTHY is *Thornwrthy* 1275 RH (p), *Thorenworth* 1281 *Ass*, *Thorneworth* 1285 FA. 'Farm by the thorn tree' or 'thorn enclosure,' *v.* worðig.

Martinhoe

MARTINHOE 118 B 9

> *Matingeho* 1086 DB, 1196 P 17, 1219 *Ass*, *Mattynggeho* 1283 Exon
>
> *Mattynho* 1303 FA, *Mattinhoo* 1608 FF
>
> *Martenhoo al. Mattinghooe* 1702 *Recov*

'hoh of *Mætta*'s people,' *v.* ing. *Mætta* would be a pet form of an OE name in *Mæð*-. Cf. Matfen (PN NbDu 140), Mattingley (Ha), DB *Matingelege*, Mettaford, Matcott and

Matridge *infra* 78, 168, 442. There is a high spur of land here running out to the coast. The modern form may be partly due to the influence of the neighbouring Combe Martin *supra* 36.

CROSCOMBE

> *Craddokescumbe* 1249 *Ass*, *-comb* 1302 *Ass*, *Cradekescumbe* 1269 FF
> *Crad(d)escumb(e)* 1249 *Ass*, *Cradyscomb* 1333 *SR* (p)
> *Crokescomb* 1330 *SR* (p)

'*Cradoc*'s combe.' This is a British pers. name (W *Caradawg*, OBrit *Caratācos*).

KILLINGTON

> *Cheneoltona* 1086 DB
> *Kynewalton* 1238 *Ass*, 1262 FF, 1326 Ipm, *-wauthon* 1242 Fees 772, *Kynewelton* 1303 FA, 1333 *SR* (p)
> *Chilwenton* 1330 *SR* (p)
> *Kylweton* 1346 FA

Probably '*Cyneweald*'s farm,' *v.* tun. This may be shortened from earlier *Cynewealdingtun* or it may be an example of a compound without the usual genitival *s*. Cf. Kennerleigh *infra* 408.

KEMACOTT is *Chymecote* 1330 *SR* (p), *Kemecotte* 1537 *Recov* (p). '*Cyma*'s cot(e).' KITTITOE is *Ketecote* 1244 *Ass*, *Kytecote* 1333 *SR* (p). 'Kite' or '*Cȳta*'s cot(e),' cf. *cytanford* (KCD 714). MANNACOTT is *Manekot* 1219 *Ass*, *-cote* 1238 *Ass*, 1333 *SR* (p). '*Man(n)a*'s cot(e).' MILLTOWN was probably the home of Thomas *atte Mille* (1333 *SR*). For the 'town,' *v. infra* 676. RANSCOMBE COMBE (6") is *Rammescumbe* 1249 *Ass* (p), *Remmyscomb* 1399 *Ct*. Probably '*Hræfn*'s valley,' *v.* cumb. SLATTEN-SLADE is *Slatynslade* 1544 *SR*, *Slattenslade* 1659 *FF*, *v.* slæd.

Parracombe

PARRACOMBE 118 C 9

> *Pedracomba* 1086 DB
> *Parrecumb(e)* 1238 *Ass*, 1285 FA, *Parracombe* 1291 Tax
> *Perecumbe* 1281 *Ass*, *Pearecumbe* 1297 Pat, *-combe* 1307 Oliver 200, *Pearrecombe* 1308 Exon, *Piarecomb* 1303 FA
> *Parkcumbe* 1281 *Ass*

This is a difficult name. Probably Blomé's suggestion (7) is the best, viz. that it is from OE *pearroc-cumb*, 'valley marked (or distinguished) by an enclosure.' According to Mr Watkin there are the remains of a very early 'motte' or enclosure in the valley below. For the DB form we may compare Parrock (PN Sx 368), DB *Apedroc*. The later forms now brought to light are against Ekwall's tentative suggestion (RN 321), based on the DB form, of a river-name *Pedred* or Parret.

MIDDLETON, EAST and WEST, is *Mideltona* 1086 DB, *Middelton* 1242 Fees 772, *West-, Estmid(d)elton* 1480, 1482 IpmR. 'Middle farm,' *v.* tun. Why it is so called is not apparent.

ROWLEY

> *Rodeleia* 1086 DB, *Roeleia* 1195 FF
> *Rughelegh* 1242 Fees 772, *Roughlee* 1326 Ipm, *Rouw(e)legh* 1285, 1346 FA, *Roulegh* 1303 FA

'Rough clearing,' *v.* ruh, leah. For the DB spelling cf. Raleigh *supra* 55.

SKILLATON BRIDGE (6″) is *Skyliaton* 1281 Ass (p). This must take its name from some lost farm so called (*v.* tun). The first element is possibly to be connected with the stem **skell*, 'to resound,' found in OE *scyl*, 'shrill, sonorous' (*v.* Redin 23), from which a pers. name **Scyl(l)a* may have been formed. For initial *sk* and for *ia v.* Introd. xxxv, and cf. further Shilla Mill *infra* 220 and Skilgate (So), *Scheligate* DB, *Schillagate* 12th Buckland, *Scilegate* 1236 Fees, *Skilegate* 1242 Ass.

BODLEY is *Bodelegh* 1333 *SR* (p). '*Boda*'s clearing,' *v.* leah. HEALE is *Hele* 1481 IpmR and gave name to Henry de *Hele* (1333 *SR*), *v.* healh. HIGHLEY is *Heglegh* 1330 *SR* (p), *Heyley* 1702 ParReg. Probably 'hay clearing,' *v.* heg, leah. HOLWELL is *Halghewill* 1330 *SR* (p), *Westhollywell* 1545 *Deeds Enrolled*. 'Holy well.' There is one here. HOLWORTHY is *Holewurth* 1213 ClR, *Holleworthy* 1544 *SR*. 'Farm in the hollow,' *v.* holh, worðig. TUCKINGMILL (6″) is *Tokinmyll* 1543 *SR*, *Tucking Mill* 1816 ParReg. A 'tucking mill' is a fulling mill, *v.* NED *s.v.* The name is very common in Devon, but no other early example has been noted. VOLEY is *Foley* 1813, *Voley* 1818 ParReg, *v. s.n.* Varley *supra* 52. WALNER is so spelt 1797 *Recov.*

Shirwell

Shirwell 118 F 7

> *Sirewilla* 1086 DB (Exon), *-welle* (Exch), *Shirewelle* 1222
> Bracton *et passim* to 1346 FA with variant spelling *Shyre-*,
> *Schire-* and *-wille*
> *Sherewill* 1428 FA, *Scherrewylle* 1437 Exon

'Clear spring,' *v.* scir, wielle.

Brightlycott is *Brittecote* 1285 FA, *Brightlecote* 1310 *Ass*,
Barygthlecote 1346 FA, *Bryghtle-* 1351 *FF*, *Brightelecote* 1378
IpmR. '*Beorhtla*'s cot(e).' For this pers. name *v.* Brightling
PN Sx 470.

Plaistow is *Plei(e)stou* 1086 DB, *Pleistowe* 1166 RBE (p),
Plegestoue 1167 P (p), *Pleystowe* 1242 Fees 772, 1285 *FF*, FA,
1326 Ipm. *v.* plegstow.

Sepscott

> *Sebrescote* 1238 *Ass*, *Seberscote* 1333 *SR* (p), *Sebirscote* 1339
> *Ass* (p), *Sebryscote* 1451 IpmR
> *Sebrightescote* 1244 *Ass*, *Sebrittescote* 1244 *Ass* (p), *Sebrictescot*
> 1254 *Ass* (p), *Sebristescote* 1275 RH (p)
> *Schebescote* 1303 FA, *Sepescote* 1378 IpmR

'*Sæbeorht*'s cot(e),' cf. Sawbridgeworth (PN Herts 56),
pronounced [sæpsə].

Coxleigh is *Cokeslegh* 1238 FF, *Cocklegh* 1303 FA, *Cocosleg*
1317 Oliver 199, *Cockesleghe* 1319 *FF*. 'Cock's clearing' or
'*Cocc*'s clearing,' *v.* leah. South Hill is *Suthull* 1244 *Ass*.
Sloley is *Slaleg(e)* 1219 *Ass*, 1222 FF (p), *-legh* 1244 *Ass* (p),
Slolegh 1322 Misc. 'Sloe clearing,' *v.* leah. Upcott is *Uppecot*'
1333 *SR* (p). 'Higher cot(e).' Waytown is *Wayton* 1451 IpmR
and was the home of Henry *atte Weye* (1333 *SR*), *v.* weg. For
the 'town,' *v. infra* 676. Witchells is *Wichehole* 1423 IpmR.
'Wych-elm hollow' or 'witch-hole.' Woolley is *Wollegh* 1333
SR (p). Probably 'wolves' clearing,' *v.* leah and cf. Woolleigh
infra 87. Youlston is *Yoldeston* 1451 IpmR, *Yeolston* 1489
Ipm. 'Old stone.' *v.* Introd. lviii.

Stoke Rivers

STOKE RIVERS 118 F 8

Estocha 1086 DB (Exon), *Stoche* (Exch), *Stoke(s)* 1242 Fees
787, 1291 Tax

Stoke Ryvers 1285 FA, 1310 Ch, 1339 Ipm, *Stokerevers* 1403
Exon

v. stoc(c). In the 12th cent. the manor was held by the
Redvers or *Riveres* family, the first earls of Devon.

BARNACOTT is *Beardingecote* 1319 Exon (p), *Beardyngcote* 1330
SR (p), *Bernyngcote alias dicta Barncote* 1414 IpmR. *v. s.n.*
Barnstaple *supra* 25.

HAKEFORD is *Hakeford(e)* 1242 Fees 761, 1319 Exon (p), 1329
DA 11 (p), 1345 *Ass.* This is a difficult name. Blomé (9) may be
right in associating it with OE *haca*, 'bolt,' originally 'hook,'
used in some topographical sense, here of a thick tongue of land.
A personal name *Hac(c)a* is also possible. Cf. Haycroft *infra* 116.

KIMBLAND CROSS is *Chimelond* 13th AD vi (p), *Kymelonde* 1281
Ass, *-launde* 1291 Tax, 1319 Exon (p), *Kiemelonde* 1329 DA 11
(p), *Chymelond* 1330 SR (p). '*Cyma's* land.'

ORSWELL is *Ordeswell* 1244 *Ass*, *Orliswalle* 1319 Exon, *Horles-
walle* 1330 SR (all p). Probably '*Ordlāf's* spring,' as suggested
by Blomé (10). *v.* wielle and cf. *Orleswick* (PN Sx 325).

BEERA and BIRCH were the homes of John *atte Beare* and
William *atte Birche* (1333 SR), *v.* bearu.

BECCOTT is *Biccott* 1631 *Deed.* DAVIS (6″) is to be associated with
the family of William *Davy* (1544 SR). HORRIDGE is *Horigge*
1319 Exon (p), *Horugge* 1330 SR (p). The place not being on the
parish boundary the first element may be OE *horh*, 'dirt, mud.'
KNACKERSHOLE is *Nackers Hole* 1765 D, cf. the same name *infra*
227. YARDE is *Yard* 1809 M, *v. supra* 48.

I

III. HARTLAND HUNDRED

Hertilande 1084 Geld Roll, *-landa* 1131 P

v. Hartland *infra* 71.

Clovelly

CLOVELLY [klouv'eli]   127 A 5

Cloveleia 1086 DB (Exon), *-lie* (Exch)

Clovely 1242 Fees 780, 1275 RH, 1281, 1299 *Ass*, 1361 Ipm,
   -li 1276 Ipm, 1285 FA, 1314 Exon, *-ley(e)* 1281 *Ass*, 1298
   FF

Colf Ely 1290 Ch

Clofely 1296 Ipm, 13th *Deed*, *-li* 1306 *Ass*, *Cloyfely* 1371 Inq
   aqd

Clouvely 1361 Ipm

Clavellegh 1535 VE, *Clavelle* 1577 Saxton

This is a very difficult name. The persistent early spellings in
-li, *-ly*, show that the second element can hardly be OE leah (cf.
the spellings of Kelly *infra* 184), even if we assume that the
present accentuation on the second syllable is not old. If the
name is English it might be explained as a compound of OE
cloh, 'ravine,' and the word discussed under Velly (*infra* 76)
about four miles distant. If pre-English, the first element may,
as suggested in IPN 28, be a British word corresponding to
Welsh *clawdd*, 'ditch, pit, etc.,' the second element being either
the Old British pers. name *Beli* found in Trevilley (Co), or,
less likely, the Cornish *melyn*, 'mill,' which would leave the loss
of the final *n* unexplained. In each case the first element would
refer to the deep hollow or ravine in which the village of Clovelly
lies. For the change of *dd* (= *th*) to *f* Professor Max Förster
would compare Cardiff (Wales), olim *Caerdydd*.

HUGGLEPIT is *Hokilpit(h)* 1287 *Ass*, 1330 *SR*, *Hokylputt* 1333 *SR*,
Hoculpytt 1384 Exon (all p). This may be a compound of OE
hoc, hyll and pytt. The farm is situated on a high spur of land
above a deep valley. Blomé (27) quotes the parallel *hochylle* from
KCD 793 and 800.

STITWORTHY [stitəri] is *Stottewrth* 1238 *Ass* (p), *Scotteworth'*

1242 Fees 792, *Stotesworȝe* 1306 *Ass*, *Stot(t)eworthi* 1330, 1333 *SR* (p). 'Bullocks' farm.' *v.* stott, worþig.

WRINKLEBERRY is *Wynkenebiry* 1333 *SR* (p), *Winglebury* 1765 D. The forms are late and no certainty is possible, but we may have a compound of OE wincel and burh. Hence 'burh in the angle of land.' The hamlet stands at the head of a small deep-cut valley.

BURFORD is *Burforde* 1330, *Byreford* 1333 *SR* (p). The first element is probably burh. Blomé (27) suggests byre, 'byre,' but this element is never found in SCy names. BURNSTONE is *Borneston* 1319, 1320 *Ass* (p). '*Beorn*'s tun.' DOWNLAND is *Dounelonde* 1330 *SR* (p). 'Hill land,' *v.* dun. DYKE [dik] is *Westdich* 1333 *SR* (p), *v.* dic. There is a large earthwork here. EASTACOTT is *Estcote* 1281 *Ass* (p). It lies near the east border of the parish. GALLANTRY BOWER, *v. s.n.* Gallant Le Bower *infra* 302. HIGHWORTHY is *Hewurthi* 1330 *SR* (p). 'High worþig.' KENNERLAND is *Kynwarlonde* 1281 *Ass*, *Kenewarlond* 1333 *SR* (both p). Probably OE *Cynewarelond*, as suggested by Blomé (27), from an unrecorded OE feminine pers. name *Cynewaru*. SLADE is *La Slade* 1316 Ipm, *v.* slæd. SNACKSLAND is *Snackeslonde* 1301 DA 34 (p). The first element is probably the name of an early owner, bearing a nickname of ME origin derived from the noun *snack* in one of its various senses. THORNERY is *Thornwurthi* 1330 *SR* (p). *v.* Thornworthy *supra* 65. The modern spelling represents the common local pronunciation of final *-worthy*.

Hartland

HARTLAND 127 A 3

Heortigtunes 880–5 (c. 1000) BCS 553, *Hertitona* 1086 DB, (*H*)*ertinton* 1175, 1179 P, *Herctone* 1281 DA 34, *Harton* 1565, etc. *ParReg*, *Hurton towne* 1566 DA 34

Herti-, *Hirtilanda* 1167 P, 1169 France, *Hertland* 1196 P, *Hertiland* 1198 AC *et freq* to 1285 FA with var. spellings *-lond*, *-laund*, *Hurtelaund* 1287 Pat, *-londe* 1291 Tax, *Hurti-* 1354 Exon

The manor of *Heortigtun* probably took its name from the present Hartland village. The name *Hertiland* may well have arisen from the desire to find a more appropriate name for the very large manor and parish (17,000 acres) which centred around it. Blomé (27) and Karlström (PN in -*ing* 14) suggest that the first element is OE *heort-(i)eg*, 'stag island,' but it is impossible to see how the term 'island' even in the wider sense 'peninsula' can ever have been applied to any part of the town or hundred of Hartland. Alternatively Blomé suggests that we have OE *heortīe*, gen. sg. of *heort-ēa*, 'stag stream.' Harton might be named from the little stream on which it stands, but it is difficult to see how that little stream could have given name to the large area covered by the name Hartland. Alfred's *Heortigtun* may be a bad spelling for *Heortingtun* (cf. such spellings in Karlström (op. cit. 9–10) and the Pipe Roll forms), and all the *i*-forms be interpreted as from earlier *ing*-ones, though the uniform and early loss of the *ng* would be remarkable[1]. If that, however, is the correct explanation, we must take it that *Heort* was the one time lord alike of the village and of an appendent territory roughly identical with the later hundred. Cf. Hartington (Db). *Heort* is found as a pers. name in the Burton Cartulary in the early 12th cent. Cf. also OGer *Hiruz* (Förstemann PN 845) and Hurscott *infra* 351.

CHERISTOW is *Chircstoua* 1167 P (p), *capellam Sancte Wenne de Chirestowe* 1189 (1365) Oliver 207, *Cheristowe* 1301 Ipm, *Churstowe* 1400 Exon. The first element might be OE *cyric*, from Brit *cryc*, 'barrow, hill,' but as Mr Chope points out, there is neither barrow nor conspicuous hill here, whereas Cheristow has an ancient chapelry. The first element is therefore more likely to be cyrice, 'church,' and this would agree well with stow, cf. Churchstow *infra* 295. The dedication was to St Wenn, cf. the place of that name in Cornwall.

DOCTON is *Doketon(e)* 1319 Exon, 1330 *SR* (both p). 'Dock farm,' from OE *docce*, or '*Docca*'s farm,' with the name postulated by Ekwall (PN in -*ing* 77) for Docking (Nf) and probably found also in Dockworthy *infra* 363.

EDDISTONE [etsən] is *Eggeston(e)* 1299 Ipm, 1333 *SR* (p), *Egereston* 1301 Ipm, *Eagestone* (sic) 1301 DA 34, *Etson* 1565–1610

[1] Reaney (MLR 25, 494) noted the parallel of Donyland (Ess), *Dunninc land* BCS 1288, *Dunilanda* DB.

ParReg. Probably '*Ecghere*'s farm,' *v.* tun, with later sound-substitution of *ds* for ME *gg*. This is the reverse of the process discussed by Zachrisson (*Studien i Modern Språkvetenskap* 8, 123 ff). We may note similarly *ts* for *ch* in Pitsea (Ess), Titsey (Sr), Whitsbury (Ha), *v.* MLR 14, 342.

ELMSCOTT [emskət] is *Ilmundescote* 1281 *Ass*, *Ylmondescote*, *Ylmannescote* 1301 DA 34, *Hilmandyscote* 1333 SR (p), *Yelmescott*, *Emescott*, *Emenscott* 1566 DA 34. Probably '*Aelfmund*'s cottages,' *v.* cot(e), with the same type of OE dialectal variant **Ielfmund* as gave rise to the double forms of Ilfracombe *supra* 46. *Aelfmund* is not on record, but would be a regular formation.

EXMANSWORTHY [ekənzəri] is *Ikemaneswurda* 1167 P, *Hikmandesworth* 1330 SR, *Ekemandisworth* 1333 SR (all p), *Eokesmonsworthie* (sic), *Ookysmanysworthy* (sic), *Ekemysworthie*, *Ekesmanesworthy*, *Okornesory* 1566 DA 34, *Eccomsery* 1642 *ParReg*. Probably '*Ecgmund*'s worþig' with raising of *e* to *i* before following *k*.

FARFORD [værid] is *Fairford* 1332 DA 34 (p), *Furford*, *Ferford* 1566 (id.). Mr Chope suggests that the 14th cent. form may be an error and the real meaning be 'further ford' with reference to Ford *infra* 78, which is nearer the town.

FATACOTT is *Fattecot(e)* 1238, 1249 *Ass*, *Vattecote* 1370 Exon (all p), *Fatcat* 1682 *ParReg*. The first element is probably a late OE name of the nickname type from *fætta*, 'fat one,' hence '*Fat*'s cottages,' *v.* cot(e). Similarly Wallenberg in StudNP 2, 28.

FORCEWELL [fɔ·səl, fɔsəl] is *Fosfelle* 1299, *-felde* 1301 DA 34, *Forsewyll* 1566 DA 34, *Forcewell* 1695 *Recov*. This may be a compound of the Celtic word for 'ditch' (*v.* Voss *infra* 254) and OE feld. For *f* > *v* > *w* cf. Introd. xxxiv–v.

GALSHAM [gɔ·lsəm] is *Gallecusham* 1189 (1365) Oliver 207, *Galkysham* 1333 SR (p), 1577 Oliver 206, *Gallkisham* 1345 *Ass* (p). *v.* ham(m). The first element may be a British pers. name *Ga(l)oc*. This is not on record, but the simple *Gall* occurs in the Mabinogion, and Loth (Chrest 131) gives several instances of compounds such as *Gal-budic*, *-con*, *-du*, *-uuorveth*, etc.

GAWLISH is *Gavelersh* 1318 *Ass* (p), *-hersh* 1333 *SR* (p), *Gawlyche* 1566 DA 34. The name is a compound of OE *gafol*, 'tax, tribute,' and ersc, and must have originally denoted a piece of land leased or let for rent or services. Cf. Gavelacre (Ha), *Gavelacre* 1312 Ipm, *Gavelmede* (1228 Ch) in Hatfield Peverel (Ess), *Gavylmede* 1355 Cl (D), *Gavelefurlinges* 1199 FF (Nf) and Galford *infra* 187.

HESCOTT is *Hersecote* 1167 P (p), *Herscote* 1333 *SR* (p), *Herscoote, Harscott* 1566 DA 34. This name would seem to go with Harescombe and Haresfield, the names of adjacent Gloucestershire parishes of which the DB forms are *Harsecome* and *Hersefeld*. (For further forms *v.* PN Gl 78 and cf. Hersden in Sturry (K), *Hersyng'*, 1327 and 1333 *SR*.) The most natural explanation of these names is to assume that the places were owned by a man named *Hersa*, an unrecorded pers. name which would be the exact cognate of the much discussed OScand name *Hariso*. Cf. Zachrisson in *Festskrift til Finnur Jónsson*, 316 ff.

HINDHARTON (6″) is *Hyndehertone* 1299 Ipm, 1566 DA 34, *-herton* 1301 Ipm. This is clearly a compound of *Herton*, the alternative name for Hartland (*v. supra* 71–2) and an element *hind*. This is most probably the common adverb *hind*, the reference being to its position in relation to Hartland itself. Cf. the common Devon use of *yond* in Youngcott *infra* 216 and other names.

HOLE, NORTH and SOUTH, is *Hola* 1086 DB, *Hole* 1310 Seld 20, *Southhole juxta Stok* 1364 *Ass*, *Northehoole* 1566 DA 34. There are two farms called Hole, one in the extreme north and the other in the extreme south of the parish, the latter being the DB manor. Both lie in hollows.

KERNSTONE [kə·msən] is *Kyneman(e)ston(e)* 1249 *Ass*, 1256 FF, *Chynemaneston* 1254 *Ass*, *Kyrmeston* 1546 Oliver 216, *Ke(r)mson* 1566–1580 *ParReg*. Probably 'Cynemann's farm,' *v.* tun, but the second element is possibly stan, as there is a menhir or longstone not far off[1].

LONG FURLONG is *Langefurlang* 1238 FF, 1244 *Ass* (p), *Longfurland* 1565 *ParReg*. 'Long furlong,' i.e. furrow length, *v.* furlang.

---

[1] *Ex inf.* Mr R. P. Chope.

LUTSFORD is *Ludekeford* 1249 FF (p), *Lottekesford* 1301 DA 34
(p), *Luttekisforde* 1319 Exon (p), *Luttisford* 1570 *ParReg.*
'*Luttoc*'s ford.' This pers. name is not on independent record,
but would be a regular derivative of OE *Lutt* found in *luttes
crundel* BCS 327 and is found in ME field-names *Lutteke-
shel* (1291) and *Luttichesalre* (1361) in Devon. Cf. also Lutworthy and Liddington *infra* 401, 574 and *Ailric Lute filius* and
Lutting as pers. names in the Feudal Book of Abbot Baldwin
of Bury (c. 1150).

MARKADON is *Marcadene* 1189 (1365) Oliver 207, 1275 RH (p),
Markedene 1316 Exon (p), -*don* 1281 *Ass*. This place is, as
Mr Chope points out, on a hill forming the boundary between
the manors of Stoke and Harton so the meaning is probably
'boundary hill' (*v.* mearc), in spite of the predominance of
denu-forms.

MEDDON [meidən] is *Madona* 1086 DB, *Meddon*' 1234 Fees 400,
1279 Ipm, *Mededon* 1242 Fees 791, 1303 FA, *Westremeddon* 1316
Ass. 'Meadow hill,' *v.* mæd, dun.

MILFORD [milvəd] is *Meleforda* 1086 DB, *Milleford* 1238 *Ass*,
1310 Seld 20, *Mile-* 1249 FF, *Mule-* 1316 FA. OE *myln-ford*,
'mill-ford,' with early loss of *n*.

PUTSHOLE is *Puchelahole* 1301 Cl (p), *Puttishole, Pattyshole* 1546
Oliver. The first element is OE *pūcel*, 'goblin,' hence 'goblin's
hole.' For the substitution of *ts* for *ch*, *v. s.n.* Eddistone *supra*
72.

ROSEDOWN [ruˑzən] is *Rosdone* 1299 *Ass*, *Rousdon* 1301 DA 34.
This may be a hybrid name, the first element being the Co *ros*
(W *rhos*), 'moor, wasteland, etc.'

STOKE

   Nistenestoc 1086 DB, *Nectanestoke* 1189 (1365) Oliver 207
   Stoke Seneton 1276 QW, 1282 Oliver 208
   Stokes Seynt Nechan, Sancti Nythtan 1281 *Ass, Stoke Sancti
      Nectani* 1361 Exon

   v. stoc(c). The same dedication is found in St Nectan's in
St Winnow parish (Co), *capellæ Sancti Nictani* 1270 FF, *Seynt
Nightan* 1336 *Ass, Seynt Neighton* 1439 *FF*. This is the Irish

saint *Nechtan,* whose name appears in Welsh as *Neithon* (Mabinogion, Skene) and as *Neizan* or *Nizon* in Breton (NSB).

SUMMERWELL is *Somerwelle* 1274 BM, -*wille* 1330 *SR* (p). The name would have reference to a spring that is never dry, *v.* **wielle.** On the 6″ map an 'old reservoir.' is marked near the present farm, which may be on the site of the spring referred to.

TITCHBERRY is *Tetisbyr'* 1249 *Ass* (p), *Tettesbyry* 1308 Exon (p), -*bury* 1318 *Ass*, *Tyttesbury* 1396 Exon (p), *Titsbury* 1546 Oliver 206, *Tichbury* 1634 HMC 4, 572. '*Tetti*'s burh.' This pers. name is not on record but would be the strong form of *Tetta* (*v.* Tedburn *infra* 451) found in *Tettan monasterium* (BCS 59) and *Tettanbyrig* (BCS 1320), now Tetbury (Gl). Cf. also Tetsworth (O), *Tetteswrth(e)* 1209–12 Fees, 1278 RH. For *ch,* cf. *s.n.* Eddistone *supra* 72.

TOSBERRY is *Tosbi* 1167 P (p), -*biry* 1330 *SR* (p), *Tossebury* 1301 DA 34, -*bery* 1477 IpmR, *Tassebury* 1566 DA 34. Perhaps '*Tossa*'s burh.' This pers. name is not recorded but might be a pet form of *Torhtsige.* The parallel of Foston (PN NRY 39) quoted by Blomé (29) in support of *Tottesbyrig* is hardly applicable. That would not explain ME forms in *Tosse-*.

TRELLICK ['trelik] is *Trevelak* 1249 *Ass* (p), *Treverek* 1281 *Ass*, *Treveleck* 1333 *SR* (p), *Trelick* 1577 Oliver 206. This name is probably Celtic, the first element being the Co *tre, trev,* 'homestead,' etc. The second may be the pers. name *Eloc* found in the book of Llandaff. If, however, the *v* is here part of the second element this may be the Celtic pers. name *Maeloc.* If both elements are Celtic we must assume that English influence led to a change from [trev'elik] to ['trev(e)lik]. Cf. Trevellick in Michaelstow (Co), *Trevelek* 1327 *SR* (p), *Trevelek, Trevalek* 1338 *Rental.*

VELLY is *Felye* 1287 *Ass*, *Overefelye, atte Velye* 1301 DA 34, *la Felye* 1333 *SR* (p), *Velly* 1566 DA 34. This is a difficult name. An OE *fealge*, 'fallow land,' as suggested by Blomé (30) can hardly explain the later forms with *e.* This name offers some of the same difficulties as Felpham (PN Sx 140). There Professor Ekwall suggested that we probably had to start from a form *felg,* with a different vowel-grade *e,* related to OHG *felga,* 'a harrow.'

The exact meaning of OE *felg* is doubtful, but it might perhaps be used of 'fallow land,' cf. the similar relation of OE *fealga*, 'harrow,' to ME *falwe*, 'fallow land.' OE *felg* is actually on record in the sense 'felloe, felly.' This may ultimately be the same word. Hence perhaps 'fallow land.'

WARGERY is *Wardsworthe* 1570–4, *Wardsworthy* 1577, *Wargery* 1581, *Wardsery* 1618 ParReg. v. worþig. The first element may be the OE *weard*, 'watchman, guard, protector,' perhaps here used as a pers. name. Cf. the common surname *Ward*.

WELSFORD is *Welesford* 1262 FF, -*lys*- 1333 SR (p), *Wellesford* 1566 DA 34. Possibly 'ford of (or by) the spring.' There is a tradition of a well called Bradstones Well (*ex inf.* Mr R. P. Chope).

YAGLAND is *Yaggalond* 1320 Ass, *Yaggelande* 1381 Exon (p), *Yeageland* 1566 SR. This may be '*Eagga*'s land' as suggested by Blomé (30), with an unrecorded pers. name, a pet form of *Ēadgār*. (For *y*, *v*. Introd. xxxiii). The name *Geagga*, found in *Geaggan-treow* (KCD 650) is also possible, *v*. PN Wo 26, *s.n.* Hagtree for possible further examples.

ACKWORTHY is *Hec(k)worthy* 1570 ParReg, 1574 Ct, v. worþig. BAXWORTHY is *Badekeswurth* 1249 Ass, *Backasworthy* 1345 Ass (p), *Baxworthey* 1518–29 ECP 5, 315. '*B(e)adoc*'s worþig.' BECKLAND is *Bekeland* 1167 P (p), *Sowth Beckland* 1566 DA 34. '*Becca*'s land.' BERRY is *Bury* 1546 Oliver 206, v. burh. BITE-FORD is *Bytteford(e)* 1301 DA 34, 1333 SR (p). '*Bitta*'s ford,' cf. Bittadon *supra* 29. BLACKPOOL MILL is *Blackpole Mill* 1577 Oliver 206. BLAGDON is *Blakedon* 1238 Ass, 1301 DA 34, both (p). 'Dark hill,' v. blæc, dun. BLEGBERRY is *Blak(e)bur'* 1254, 1281 Ass, *Bleke-*, *Blyckebery* 1566 DA 34, v. blæc, burh. It adjoins the site of a castle. BRAWNS WOOD is *Brandeswoode* 1566 DA 34. *Braund* is a local surname still. BREMLIDGE (6″) is *Breme Rydge* 1566 DA 34, *Brimlidge* 1682 Rate-book. 'Bramble ridge.' BROWNSHAM is *Bronsham* 1564 ParReg, *Brownesham* 1566 DA 34, *Brownson* 1568 ParReg. '*Brūn*'s ham(m).' BURSDON [bə·zən] is *Burdesdon* 1301 DA 34. BUTTERBURY (6″) is *Boterbiri* 1301 Ipm, v. Buttercombe *supra* 40. DADWORTHY is *Doddeworthy* 1301 DA 34 (p), *Dodworthe* 1570 ParReg.

'*Dodda*'s worþig.' DEER PARK (6″) is *Deareparke* 1566 DA 34.
DEPTFORD [ditvəd] is *Dupeford* 1242 Fees 791, 1299 DA 34,
Depesforde al. Dupeford 1316 Ipm, *Ditford* 1682 *Rate-book*, *v.*
deop, ford. DOWN is *Downe* 1566 DA 34. FIREBEACON is *Fyrby-
kene* 1400 Exon, *Ester Fyerbycken, Sowth Fyerbyckon* 1566
DA 34. Self-explanatory. It is on a prominent hill. FORD is
la Forde 1301 DA 34. FOXHOLE (6″) is *Fochihole* 1301, *Fowche-
hole* 1566 DA 34. GOLDENPARK (6″) is *Middell Butterbury* or
Golden Parke 1566 DA 34. The later name possibly refers to a
field bright with yellow flowers, *v.* pearroc. GORVIN is *Garfen*
(sic) 1204 Cur, *Gorfenne* 1249 *Ass* (p), -*venne* 1281 *Ass* (p), *v.*
gor, fenn. GREENLAKE (6″) [grenlik] is *Grendicke* 1546 Oliver 217,
Grenlicke 1682 *Rate-book, Greenlake al. Grindlick* 1718 *Recov.*
Perhaps 'green dike,' *v.* dic, with later corruption. HARDIS-
WORTHY [ardzəri] is *Herdesworth(i)e* 1284 FA, 1301 Ipm,
1316 FA, -*worthe* 1325 Ipm, *Hardsery* 1580, *Hargary* 1682 *Par
Reg.* Probably '*Hererēd*'s worþig.' HARTLAND POINT is so spelt
1577 Saxton. HENDON MOOR (6″) [jenən] is *Yandon* 1333 *SR* (p),
Heawndon 1566 DA 34. 'At the high down,' *v.* heah, dun.
HENSTRIDGE WOOD (6″) is *Hengstrugge* 1281 *Ass* (p), *Hengestridge*
1566 DA 34. 'Stallion ridge,' cf. Henscott *infra* 132. HIGHFORD
is *Hayford* 1333 *SR* (p), *Hayvord* 1565 *ParReg.* Apparently
a compound of ford and heg or (ge)hæg, but as the site of the
ford is unknown no certainty is possible. HOLLOFORD is *Hol-
laford, Holyford* 1566 DA 34, *Holoford* 1581 *SR.* 'Ford in the
hollow.' LEIGH is *Leye* 1256 FF, *Leighe* 1546 Oliver 216, *v.* leah.
ST LEONARDS is *Saynte Leonards* 1546 Oliver 216. There was a
chapelry here. LOVELAND (6″) is *Loueland* 1581 *SR*, cf. the same
name *infra* 96. METTAFORD is *Meatteford* 1345 *Ass* (p), *Matte-
ford* 1566 DA 34, *Metford* 1593 *ParReg, v.* Martinhoe *supra* 65.
MOOR is *Moore* 1566 DA 34, *v.* mor. NATCOTT is *Notecote* 1238
Ass (p), *Nottecote* 1330 *SR* (p), *Nuttecote* 1492 Ipm, *Nottycott*
1566 DA 34. '*Hnotta*'s cot(e),' cf. Noddon *infra* 267. NETHER-
TON (6″) is *Nytheretoun* 1332 DA 34 (p). 'Lower farm,' *v.* tun.
NEWBERRY WOOD (6″) is *Newbery* 1546 Oliver 216, *v.* burh.
There is no earth-work here now. NEWTON is *Newton* 1546
Oliver 216. NORTON is *Northerton* 1281 *Ass* (p), *Norton* 1333
SR (p). '(More) north farm,' *v.* tun. It is north of Hartland.
PATTARD CROSS is *Patter, Pattermede* 1566 DA 34, *Patterd* 1566

SR. PHILHAM is *Fyleham* 1262 FF, *File-* 1321 Exon (p). Perhaps we may compare Fillham *infra* 285. PITT is *la Pytte* 1301 DA 34. PRUSTLEDGE WOOD (6") is *Prestlynch* 1546 Oliver 206. 'Priests' hlinc.' REEVE WOOD (6") is *Revewood* 1566 DA 34 and is perhaps to be associated with the family of Joel *Rene* (sic) (1332 DA 34). RETHERIDGE WOOD (6") is *Reddridge* 1566 DA 34. SECKINGTON is *Sygynton* 1333 *SR* (p), *Sekynton* 1505 Ipm. Possibly '*Sicga*'s farm,' *v.* ingtun. SOWDEN (6") is *Sower Downe* 1548 Pat, *Sowth Downe* 1566 DA 34. STADDON is *Stoddon* 1306 Ipm. 'Bullock hill,' *v.* stod, dun. STOWFORD (6") is *Stouford* 1330 *SR* (p), 1577 Oliver 206, *v.* Stowford *supra* 41. SUTTERLAND [sitəlænd] (6") is *Suttland* 1566 DA 34. Cf. Sittycleave *infra* 83. Sutterland lies just south of Hartland. THORNE (6") is *Thorn in Hertelond hundred* 1362 IpmR. TRUE is *Truwe* 1301 DA 34 (p), *atte Triwe* 1333 *SR* (p), *Trew* 1492 Ipm. '(At the) tree,' *v.* treow. WARMLEIGH is *Warmelegh* 1262 FF, *Werme-* 1332, 1566 DA 34, 'warm leah.' WEMBSWORTHY is *Wymandesworthy* 1301 DA 34, *Wymundesw(o)rthe* 1314 Exon, 1330 *SR* (all p), *Wemesworthy(e)* 1566 DA 34, *Wemsery* 1599 *ParReg.* '*Wīgmund*'s worþig.' YAPHAM is *Yeapeham, Yapham* 1301 DA 34 (p), *ʒapham* 1301 Ipm, *v.* ham(m). The first element is OE *gēap*, 'open, wide, extensive'; for the toponymic use of this word, *v.* Middendorff *s.v.* YOULDEN WOOD (6") is *Yholdedun* 1238 FF, 'old hill,' *v.* dun. 'Old' may have the sense of 'long under cultivation,' cf. Addenda *supra* lviii. YOULTREE CROSS (6") is *Yolletre* 1566 DA 34. 'Old tree.'

Welcombe

WELCOMBE 127 C 2

Walcoma 1086 DB

Welcuma 1189 (1365) Oliver, *Welcumb(e)* 1244 *Ass*, 1316 FA, -*come* 1338 Exon, *Welcombe juxta Bradeworthy* 1356 *Ass*

Welecumbe 1275 *FF*, *Wellecomb(e)* 1303 FA

Probably from OE *wiell(e)-cumb*, 'spring-valley.' There are several springs in the valley, including a 'St Nectan's Well' in the village and Well *infra* near by.

HOLLACOMBE (6"), KNAP WOOD (6"), MEAD, TREDOWN and WELL

(6″) were probably the homes of Walter de *Holecomb* (1330 *SR*),
Thomas *atte Knappe* (ib.), Reginald de *la Mede* (1333 *SR*),
William de *Doune* (1330 *SR*) (*v. s.n.* Tredown *infra* 146) and
Walter *atte Wille* (1333 *SR*), *v.* holh, cumb, cnæpp, mæd, dun,
wielle.

CHARTERSLAND (6″) is *Chartland* 1622 *Recov.* DARRACOTT is
Doddecote 1238 *Ass* (p). '*Dodda*'s cot(e),' cf. Darracott *supra* 43.
HENAFORD is *Henneford* 1238 *Ass*, 1301 DA 34, 1333 *SR* (all p),
'Ford frequented by water hens.' LEDDON (6″) is *Lydeton* 1301
DA 34 (p), *v.* tun. UNDERHILL (6″) is so spelt 1587 *Recov.*
UPCOTT is *Uppacote* 1301 DA 34 (p), *Uppecote in Welcom* 1485
Ipm. WITHEFORD (6″) is *Wythiford* 1330, *Whithiford* 1333 *SR*
(p), *v.* wiðig.

Woolfardisworthy

WOOLFARDISWORTHY [wulsəri] [ulsəri] 127 B 5

> *Olfereordi* 1086 DB (Exon), *Olvereword* (Exch)
> *Wulfrideswurd*'[1] 1230 P, *Wolfridesworthy* 1381 Exon
> *Wlfereswrthi* 1238 *Ass*, -*worth* 1261 Exon, *Wolfarysworth*' 1242
> Fees 780, -*fares*- 1242 Fees 758
> *Wolfardesworthi*[1] 1263 Exon, -*fradys*- c. 1310 Exon, *Wlfardes-
> worth*' 1350 Ipm
> *Wolfredesworthy* 1301 DA 34, -*ferdisworthe* 1319 Exon
> *Wollesworthye* 1550 Pat
> *Woolsry* 1629–57 Barum 1, 59, *Woolsery* 1686 Parkham
> ParReg
>
> '*Wulfheard*'s farm,' *v.* worþig.

ALMISTON [amsən]

> *Almerescota* 1086 DB
> *Alfmoreston* 1238 *Ass*
> *Almareston* 1238 *Ass*, -*meres*- 1242 Fees 775, 1285, 1303 FA,
> *Armareston* 1238 *Ass*
> *Ilmareston* 1244 *Ass* (p)
> *Ailmersdon* 1326 Ipm, *Ayl*- 1326 Cl
> *Umpson* 1765 D
> '*Aelfmǣr*'s farm,' *v.* tun. For the 1244 form, cf. Ilfracombe

---

[1] This may refer to Woolfardisworthy *infra* 399.

supra 46. For the change of second element, cf. Waddlestone *infra* 188.

ASHMANSWORTHY ['æʃənʒəri]

> *Essemundehorda* 1086 DB
> *Asmundeswrth'* 1242 Fees 786, *Hasmundesworthy* 1249 *Ass*,
>   *Ayshmundesworth(y)* 1316 FA
> *Esmundworthy* 1244 *Ass*
> *Ashmanesworth* 1292 Ipm
> *Asshmodesworth* 1306 *Ass*

'*Æscmund*'s worþig.'

BUCKS MILLS and CROSS is *Bochewys*, *Bochiywis* (sic) 1086 DB, *Bochiwis* 1167 P (p), *Buchiwises* 1238 *Ass* (p), *Bokish* 1311 FF, v. hiwisc. The first element is probably, as suggested by Mr Chope, the OE *bōc*, 'book,' used as in bocland to denote an estate or area held by charter. In the time of Edward the Confessor this manor was held by three thanes in parage. An alternative derivation would be to take the first element to be boc, 'beech,' but Mr Chope points out that the spot is not a favourable one for these trees.

HUDDISFORD [ʌtsvəˑd] is *Hodenysforde* 1330 *SR*, *Hodelysford* 1333 *SR* (p). The material is scanty, but the first element may be an *l*-derivative of the OE pers. name *Hodd(a)* or *Hud(a)*, cf. Huddlestone (PN Sx 237).

STROXWORTHY is *Strockeswrth* 1242 Fees 786 (p), *Northerestrokesworthy* 1289, 1351 *Ass*, *Strokesworth* 1378, 1423 IpmR. v. worþig. The name may well be of late origin and the first element be a ME surname *Stroke*, *Strocke*, of nickname origin, derived from ME *stroke*, *strocke*, 'stroke.'

FERNHAM (6″), FORDMILL, HOLE, KNAPP (6″), WEST MOOR, VENN and WALLAND were probably the homes of Hamund de *Fernham* (1333 SR), Robert de *Forda* (ib.), John *atte Hole* (ib.), Henry de *Cnappe* (1301 DA 34), Nicholas *atte More* (1330 SR), Philip *atte Fenne* (ib.), Walter de *la Walle* (1275 RH), and Richard *atte Walle* (1330 SR), v. ham(m), holh, cnæpp, mor, fenn.

ASHCROFT (6″) is *Ayscrofte* 1548 Pat, *Aisshe Croft* 1566 DA 34, *v.* croft. BITWORTHY is *Bitteworthe* 1256 *Ass*, *Bytteworthy* 1301 DA 34 (p). '*Bitta*'s farm,' *v.* worþig. Cf. Bittadon *supra* 29. CLAW CROSS is *Clawe* 1642 *FF*, *v.* Clawton *infra* 138. CLIFFORD is *Clifford* 1301 DA 34 (p), (*West*) 1318 Ch, (*Est*) 1492 Ipm, *v.* clif. There is a steep descent here. CRANFORD is *Cranford* 1275 RH (p), *Craneford* 1286 *Ass*, 1301 Ipm. 'Heron-frequented ford,' *v.* cran. DIPPLE (6″) is *Duphille* 1330 *SR* (p). This seems to be 'deep (? high) hill,' cf. Deepaller *infra* 544. DUERDON is *Durdon* 1333 *SR* (p), 1477 IpmR. 'Animal hill,' *v.* deor, dun. GORREL is *Gorwell* 1244 *Ass*. 'Dirty spring,' *v.* gor, wielle. LANE BARTON (6″) is *La Lane juxta Wolfedesworthi* (sic) 1286 *Ass*. LEWORTHY [ljuəri] is *Luueworth* 1238 *Ass* (p), *Loveworthi* 1330 *SR* (p). '*Lēofa*'s worþig,' cf. the same name *supra* 31. MARSHALL is *Meresfelle* 1281 *Ass* (p), *Mershfelde* 1330 *SR* (p). 'Marshy open space,' *v.* mersc, feld. RUNLAND is *Ronnelond* 1330 *SR* (p). The first element may, as suggested by Blomé (32), be OE *rynel*, 'stream,' with reference to Clifford Water near by. WEST TOWN is so spelt in 1765 (D) and is probably identical in site with *West Wullesworthy* (1566 DA 34). It is just west of Woolfardisworthy. For *town v. infra* 676.

Yarnscombe

YARNSCOMBE[1] 127 A 12

> *Herlescoma, Hernescoma* 1086 DB
> *Ernescumbe* 1238 *Ass et freq* to 1346 FA with variant spelling
>   *Ernnes-, Ernys-* and *-comb(e)*, (*Parva*) 1242 Fees 786
> *Jernescom* 1275 RH, *Yernesco(m)be* 1300 Ipm, 1303 FA
> *Yerscombe* 1413 *FF*, *Yarescombe* t. Eliz ChancP

'Eagle's combe,' *v.* earn, cumb.

DELLEY and DELWORTHY are *Dalilea* 1086 DB (Exon), *Dalilei* (Exch), *Dealleghe* 1330 *SR* (p), *Delworthy* 1756 Recov. '*Dealla*'s clearing' and 'farm,' *v.* leah, worþig. The same man probably gave name to both places, cf. Dalditch *infra* 582.

WARD gave name to Richard de *Warthe* (1330 *SR*). The place lies above a stream and the name must be OE *waroð*, 'bank, shore.' For such a use of ME *warth*, cf. 'Marsh lands called the *Warths* al. the new recovered grounds' (1652 *ParlSurv*, *Gl*).

---

[1] A detached part of Hartland Hundred.

CLEAVE, SHORTRIDGE and WESTCOTT (6″) were probably the homes of Adam *atte Clyve*, Henry de *Shortrugg'*, and William de *Westecote* (1330 *SR*), *v*. clif, cot(e).

HOOPERS and SAUNDERS (both 6″) are probably to be associated with the families of William *Hopere* and Richard *Saund'* (1333 *SR*).

BUDE (6″) is *Boghewode* 1330 *SR* (p). 'Curved wood,' *v. supra* 37 *s.n.* Bowden. CHAPPLE is *Cantaria Capelle Beati Johannis de Parva Ernyscumbe* 1310 Exon. COGWORTHY is *Koggeworth* 1270 *Ass* (p), *Coggworthy* 1663 *FF*. '*Cogga*'s worþig,' cf. *on coggan beame* BCS 1200 and Cople (PN BedsHu 90). CREALAKE (6″) is *Creulak(e)* 1330 *SR* (p), 1499 Ipm. 'Crow streamlet,' *v*. lacu, and Introd. xxxiii. CULVERHILL COPSE (6″) is *Culverwell* 1707 *Recov*, 'pigeon spring.' LANGLEY is *Westerelangeleye juxta Womberleghe* 1309 *FF*, *v*. lang, leah. LEY is *Leigh* 1809 M, *v*. leah. SHERWOOD GREEN is *Shirewode* 1238 *Ass* (p). 'Clear or bright wood.' SITTYCLEAVE (6″) is *Suttacliffe* 1638 *FF*, 1707 *Recov*, and was probably the home of Roger *de Southclyve* (1330 *SR*), cf. Sitcott *infra* 165, *v*. clif. STEEP HILL (6″) is *Stoophill* 1756 *Recov*. YEWKRIDGE (6″) is *Ykerigge* 1270 *Ass* (p), *Yawkeridge* 1683 *FF*.

IV. SHEBBEAR HUNDRED

Sheftbera 1167 P *et freq* to 1303 FA with variant spellings
    S(c)heft(e), *S(c)hef-*, *Scheftberga* 1170 P
Schafteberga 1171 P, *Schaftesberi* 1176 P

v. Shebbear *infra* 107. In the Geld Roll (1084) the hundred is called *Mertona* from Merton *infra* 99.

Abbotsham

ABBOTSHAM [æpsəm] 118 J 2

Hama 1086 DB
A(b)bedisham 1193 Oliver 95, 1269 Exon, *Abbudesham* 1238 *Ass*, *Abbodesham* 1282 Exon

v. ham(m). The manor was held by the abbot of Tavistock in 1086 (DB).

COMBE WALTER is *Comewater* 1561 *Deed* and was the home of *Walter de Combe* in 1333 (*SR*). For the form *water* cf. Ashwater *infra* 127.

CORNBOROUGH is so spelt in 1765 D. It seems to be identical with *Hornburgh* 1397, 1447, 1455, *Hurneburgh* 1474 AD vi, *Hornbrough* 1755 *Recov*. *v*. horn, beorg. horn may have referred to the prominent angle of land here. The change of initial consonant is apparently quite recent.

PUSEHILL is *Pueshille, Pyweshille* 1333 SR (p). This possibly contains the post-Conquest name *Pyw* found in Axminster in 1333 (*SR*). This is not the well-known Welsh *Pugh*, which is of much later date, but more probably the French surname *Puy*.

TEALTA (6″) is so spelt in 1662 *FF* and is to be associated with the family of Richard de *Talte* (1333 *SR*). This is clearly allied to OE *tealt*, 'unsteady.' Professor Ekwall notes that the verb *tilt*, a derivative of it, is used with the sense 'to slope' and suggests the possibility of an OE *tealt(e)*, 'slope.'

BOWOOD is *Westeraboue Wode* t. Ed 1 DA 33. As noted above (38 *n*. 2) this may be '(the more westerly place) above the wood.' For the comparative *wester* cf. Norton *supra* 78. BUCKLEIGH is *Bogheclyve* 1333 *SR* (p), *Boclyve* 1362 DA 33, 'Curved steep place,' *v*. clif and Bowden *supra* 37. CLAYCOTT (6″) is so spelt in 1741 (*FF*). CLIFTON (6″) is *Clyston al. Clyfton* 1576 *Deed*. KEENE is *tenement called Kene* 1569 *Deed*. LANGDON (6″) is *Est-, Westlangdon* 1569 *Deed*. 'Long hill,' *v*. dun. ORCHARD (6″) is so spelt 1569 DA 33. RIXLADE is so spelt 1691 *Recov*. SHAMLAND (6″) is *Sham(m)aland* 1670 *FF*, 1691 *Recov*. SPURLAND is *Spirelande* 1616 *FF*, cf. Spirewell *infra* 261.

Alwington

ALWINGTON 127 A 7

   Alwinetona 1086 DB

   Alwenton 1237 Cl, *Alwynton(e)* 1242 Fees 795 *et freq* to 1428
      FA, *Alwyngton* 1303, 1316 FA

   v. tun. The absence of medial *s* favours the OE feminine name *Ælfwynn* rather than the masculine *Ælfwine*. Cf. Blomé (33).

CARTLAND (6″) is *Karkelond(e)* 1330 *SR* (p), 1428 FA (p),

Karkaland t. Ed 3 DCo NQ 3, 164. The first element is possibly the Co *carrec*, 'rock.'

CHIDDLECOMBE is *Chittalacomtone* c. 1250 DCo NQ 3, 164, *Chitelhamcomb* 1330, *Chitelecomb* 1333 SR (p). It is very difficult to make any suggestion about this name. The first and earlier form here given makes Blomé's suggestion (33) OE *cietel-hæma-cumb* somewhat unlikely and the name had best remain unexplained. The relation of the forms to one another is difficult.

COCKINGTON is *Cokemeton* 1244, 1317 Ass, *Kokemeton* 1278 Ass, *Cokhampton* 1281 Ass, *Cokmanton* 1330 SR (all p). Here again the relation of the forms to one another is very difficult. It is uncertain if the form *Cokemanton* cited by Blomé (33) from a Fine of 1223 really refers to this place.

GILSCOTT [gilskət] is *Ghiliscote* c. 1250 DCo NQ 3, 164, *Gilscote* 1333 SR (p), *Gillescote* 1371 HMC iv (p). Blomé (33) suggests that we have here a pers. name of Celtic origin found also in the Durham *Liber Vitae* in the form *Gilla*. That name is clearly the Gaelic *gille*, 'servant,' which has no cognate in Welsh or Cornish. It is also unlikely that it would give rise to a name of strong form. There is evidence, however, for an OE name *Gylli* or *Gylla* in Gillingham (Do), *Gillingaham* ASC s.a. 1016 (c. 1150) (K), *Gillingeham* c. 975 (12th) BCS 1321. This is a more likely source for the present name. *Gylla* is probably an assimilated form from earlier *Gylda*. Cf. the use of *Gold-* in pers. names.

PORTLEDGE is *Porthlynche* 1318 HMC iv, *Port(e)lynche* 1345 Ass (p), 1384 IpmR, *Portelinche* 1420 IpmR, *Portlydge* 1577 Saxton. The hlinc or hill was probably named from the cove below, which bore the Celtic name *porth*, common in Cornwall, a loan-word from Latin.

FORD and WESTACOTT (6″) were the homes of Margaret *atte Forde* and John de *Westecote* (1330 SR).

BABBACOMBE is *Babbecumb* 1249 Ass (p), *Babecomb* 1330 SR (p). '*Babba*'s valley,' v. cumb. BAGGAPIT (6″) is *Bikepitte* 1345 Ass (p). DOTHERIDGE (6″) is *Dudderigge* c. 1250, *Dudarigge* t. Ed 2, *Dothderygge* 1434 DCo NQ 3, 164. Probably '*Dudda*'s ridge,' v. hrycg. DYDON (6″) is *Dyadone* 1333 SR, 1345 Ass (p). The OE

K

pers. name *Diga* is possible as the first element. DYMSDALE
WOOD (6″), cf. *Dymmyngesdale* (p.n.) and John D. in the same
context in HMC iv (1371). As the element *dale* is otherwise
unknown in Devon the name can hardly be of local origin.
GRATTON (6″) is *Grattone* 1330 *SR* (p). Perhaps 'great farm,'
v. tun. HOLE (6″) is *(la) Hole* 1249 *Ass* (p), c. 1250 DCo NQ
3, 164, *v.* holh. KNOTTY CORNER is so spelt 1765 D. PEPPER-
COMBE is *Pyppecombe* 1306 *Ass* (p). '*Pippa*'s valley,' *v.* cumb.
ROLLSTONE is *Raustone* c. 1250 DCo NQ 3, 164, *Roweston*
1294 *Ass*, cf. Rolstone *infra* 409. WARMSWORTHY COTTAGE (6″)
is *Warnisworthie* 1609 *Deed*, *v.* worþig. WINSCOTT is *Wynescot(e)*
1238, 1281 *Ass* (p). '*Wine*'s cot(e).' WOODTOWN is *Le Wode*
1294 *Ass*. For *town*, *v. infra* 676. SOUTH YEO is *atte Yo* 1375
(nom loc.), *Yoe* 1408 Exon, and was the home of Ralph *atte Ya*
(1330 *SR*). 'At the water,' *v. supra* 17–18.

Beaford

BEAFORD 127 D 12

Baverdona 1086 DB
Beauford 1238 *Ass et freq* to 1339 Ipm, *Beuford* 1242 Fees 788,
　Bew(e)ford 1249 *Ass*, 1435 Exon, *Beagheford* 1281 *Ass*
Bouford 1285 FA

The first element may be the OE *bēaw*, 'gadfly,' found in
Bowcombe *infra* 284, referring to a ford where these insects
worried the cattle. Blomé (33) suggests that the DB form may
represent an OE *bēaw-ford-dūn*, cf. Tiverton *infra* 541.

BLINSHAM

Blythemesham 1242 Fees 775, 1303 FA, *Blith-* 1314 *Ass*,
　Blythemisham juxta Chepyngtoriton 1361 *Ass*
Bilthemersham al. Blithemesham 1326 Ipm, *Bilchemersham*
　1326 Cl
Blymesham 1345 *Ass*, *-mys-* 1346 *Ass*

'*Bliðmǣr*'s ham(m)' as suggested by Blomé (33). If the second
element is hamm it may refer to the bend in the Torridge here.

STRAWBERRYHILL (6″). No forms have been noted, but a Mariota
de *Streuberihull* occurs in Fremington Hundred, not far distant,
in 1330 (*SR*).

WOOLLEIGH is *Oluelia* 1086 DB (Exon), *Ulvelie* (Exch), *Wlveleye* 1238 FF, *North-*, *Southwollegh* 1394 *Ass.* 'Wolves' clearing,' *v.* leah.

COMBE FM (6"), HOLE and UPCOTT[1] were probably the homes of Robert *atte Combe*, Gosse *atte Hole* and William de *Uppecote* (1330 *SR*), *v.* cumb, holh, cot(e).

BEAFORD MILL is *Beaufordmulne* 1359 *Ass.* CUPPER'S PIECE (6") is to be associated with the family of Hugo *Cupper* (1544 *SR*). HAREPATH is *Harepath* 1330 SR, *Herpathe* 1333 *SR* (p), *v.* herepæþ. There is a main road about half-a-mile to the east. PEARSON is *Periston* 1481 IpmR, *Peryeston* 1493 Ipm, *Persdon* 1563 *FF.* Probably a late compound, the first element being the name of a medieval owner. RAMSCLIFFE is *Ramscliffe* 1611 *FF.*

Bideford

BIDEFORD [bidifəd]   118 J 3

> *Bediford(a)* 1086 DB, 1201 Cur, 1202 FF, *Bedy-* 1356 *Ass*
> *Bedeford(e)* 1086 DB (Exch), 1210–12 RBE, 1261–8 Exon
> *Budiford* 1232 Pat, *Bude-* 1238 *Ass*, 1291 Tax
> *Bydiford* 1238 *Ass et freq* to 1314 Ipm with variant spelling
>   *Bidi-*, *Biddiford* 1632 Barum 1, 55
> *Bydeford* 1242 Fees 778 *et freq* with variant spelling *Bide-*
> *Byddeford* 1446 IpmR

This is a difficult name. Blomé (34) suggests a first element *byden* as found in Bidna *infra* 102, but this would not account for the persistent forms with medial *i*. It may well be for *Bȳdingford*, '*Bȳda*'s ford,' *Bȳda* being a recorded OE pers. name. For early loss of *ing*, cf. *s.n.* Hartland *supra* 71.

NOTE. ALLHALLAND ST is *Allhallow Street* 1673 DA 34. BUTT-GARDEN ST is *Buttgarden* 1673 DA 34, probably marking the site of ancient archery butts. GRENVILLE ST preserves the memory of the Grenville family, lords of the manor of Bideford from the time of the Conquest. HIGH ST is *magnus vicus* t. Edw 1 DA 33. MEDDON ST is *Maydenestrete* t. Edw 1 DA 33, *Mayden Street* 1673 DA 34, cf. Maidenford *supra* 26. MILL ST is so spelt 1673 DA 34. THE QUAY is *Old*, *New Key* 1673 DA 34.

ADJAVIN (6") is *Eggefen(n)* 1238 *Ass* (p), t. Edw 1 DA 33, *Ageven*

---

[1] *Northuppecott* 1547 Deeds Enrolled.

1492 Ipm. The OE pers. name *Ecga* is on record and the name may be 'Ecga's fenn,' with later lowering of *e* to *a*.

EAST-THE-WATER is probably an old settlement, for in 1489 there is mention of a grant to William Person 'of his tenement in Bydeford on the east side of the water called Torigge' (AD vi).

WINSFORD (6″) is *Wentesford* 1330 SR (p), *Wensford* 1441 DA 33. This may contain ME *went*, 'path, track,' hence 'ford of (or by) the track.'

BEARA (6″) and FORD HO were probably the homes of Richard *atte Beare* (1333 SR) and Richard Snelland de *la Forde* (1317 Ass), v. bearu.

BIDEFORD BRIDGE is *pontem de Bedeforde* 1342 Exon. BOWDIN (6″) is *Bowdon* 1487 Ipm, *Bowden Greene* 1624 *Deed*. 'Curved hill,' cf. Bowden *supra* 37. CADDSDOWN is probably to be associated with the family of Henry *Cadd* (1647 Wills). GAMMATON is *Galmyngton* 1330 SR (p), v. Galmpton *infra* 304. MORETON is *Mooretowne* 1624 *Deed*, v. mor. NORTHDOWN HOUSE (6″) is *Bynorthedone* t. Ed 1 DA 33. 'North of the down.' OLDISCLEAVE is *Hoddesclyve* 1330 SR (p). 'Hodd's clif.' UPCOTT is *Uppecote juxta Bidiford* 1298 Ass. WOODVILLE COTTAGES (6″) is *Woodwill in Bedyford* t. Jas 1 ECP. 'Spring by the wood,' v. Introd. xxxv.

Buckland Brewer

BUCKLAND BREWER 127 B 8

> *Bochelanda* 1086 DB, *Bockland* 1219 Ass, *Boclonde* 1269 Exon *Boclande Bruere* 1290 Ch, *Northboclaunde* 1312 Exon, *Bruweresboclond* 1360 Ass

v. bocland. William *Briwerre* held the manor in 1219 (*Ass* 180 m. 4). *North* to distinguish it from Buckland Filleigh *infra* 90.

ECKWORTHY is *Akewrthi* 1238 *Ass*, *Ekeworthi* 1321 Exon, 1330 SR, *Ekkeworthi* 1333 SR (all p). 'Ecca's farm,' v. worþig. Cf. Ecton (Nth), *Echentone* DB, *Ekinton* 1192 P, *Eketon* 1242 Fees.

GALSWORTHY [gælzəri]

> *Galeshora* 1086 DB, *Galles(h)oure* 1238 Ass (p), *Galeshore* 1244, 1249 *Ass* (p), 1330 SR (p), *Galsore* 1339 Ass (p), *Gallissore* 1422 IpmR

South Galesworthy 1616 *FF*, *Gallesworth al. Galsworthy* 1618
Depositions

Galsworthy is on the highest ground in the neighbourhood and
there is no stream here, so Blomé's river-name solution (35) will
not hold good. It is probably the Celtic name *Gall* of which we
have the diminutive *Galloc* in Galsham *supra* 73. The **ora** must
refer here to the slope of the hillside. The pronunciation locally
must have been *Galzery* with common preservation of syllabic
inflexion and then, since so many names like Woolfardisworthy
are pronounced with final -*zery* for original -*isworthy*, the name
seems to have been re-spelled and in its turn gave rise to a spelling pronunciation [gɔˑlzwəˑði].

GOUTISLAND is *Godekynnyslonde* 1330, -*es*- 1333 *SR* (p), *Gutsland*
1581 *SR*. The first element is probably, as suggested by Blomé
(36), a continental pers. name *Godekin*.

HELE is *Hela* 1086 DB and was the home of John *atte Hele* (1330
SR). *v*. Hele *supra* 46.

MUDDIPIT (6″) is *Modepitt(e)* 1287 *Ass* (p), 1373 IpmR, *Mody-
putte* 1330 *SR* (p), *Modipitte* 1333 *SR* (p). This may contain the
common adjective 'muddy' (first recorded in the 16th cent.),
deriving from the noun 'mud,' first occurring in the form *mode* in
the 14th cent.

ORLEIGH COURT is *Ordlegh* 1193 Oliver 95, *molend' de Ortheslegh*
1281 *Ass*, *Orleghmulle* 1330 *SR* (p), *Orlegh* 1416 Exon. *v*. leah.
The first element may be OE ord, 'point,' referring to the sharp
spur of land here.

SILKLAND (6″) is *Silkeland* 1238 *Ass*, *Sulkeland* 1249 *Ass*, -*londe*
1330, 1333 *SR* (p) and is perhaps to be associated with the family
of *Sulke*, of whom one William was living here in 1330 (*SR*).
Cf. Silkhay (Do), *Selkeheye* 1333 *SR* (p), with mention of
Andrew *Selk* in the same parish.

TYTHECOTT is *Tuddecote* 1238 *Ass* (p), *Todecote* 1394 *Ass*, 1491
Ipm, *Tothcote* 1496 AD vi, *Tothecoote* 1550 Pat. Probably
'*Tud(d)a*'s cot(e).' For interchange of *d* and *th*, *v*. Introd. xxxv.

VIELSTONE is *Vieleston* 1238 *Ass* (p), 1244 *Ass*, 1333 *SR* (p), *Vyel-*

1244 *Ass, Vileston Boklande* 1312 Ch, *Vealestone* 1330 *SR* (p).
This name, like Goutisland *supra* 89, probably contains as
first element a continental pers. name, but in this case the
name *Viel* (= Vitalis) is of French origin. A Ralph *Vitalis* held
manors in Shebbear Hundred in DB.

BURROW, CLEAVE (6″), PARK (6″) and THORNE were probably the
homes of John *atte Burghe* (1330 *SR*), Roger de *la Clyve* (1244
Ass), Robert *atte Parke* (1360 *Ass*) and Adam le *la Thorne* (1281
Ass). *v.* beorg, clif, pearroc.

BEARA is *Bere* 1219 FF (p), *atte Beare* 1333 *SR* (p), *v.* bearu.
BILSFORD is *Bylsford* 1330, *Bilsford* 1333 *SR* (p). Probably
'*Bill*'s ford.' BRADDON (6″) is so spelt 1496 AD vi. Probably
'broad hill,' *v.* dun. BRENDON (6″) is *Bremdon* 1281 *Ass* (p), *v.*
Brendon *supra* 58. COLLINGSDOWN is *Cullyngesdon(e)* 1383 *FF*,
1443 IpmR, *Colyngsdowen* 1563 *FF*. '*Culling*'s hill,' *v.* dun. The
name may be of OE or ME origin. CRANEHAM is *Cranham* 1330,
1333 *SR* (p). 'Heron ham(m).' GORWOOD is *Garwood* 1765 D.
HEMBURY CASTLE is *Henburye* 1550 Pat. 'High stronghold,' *v.*
heah, burh. There is an ancient camp here. HOLWELL is *Holi-
will(e)* 1330, 1333 *SR* (p), *Holewill* 1360 *Ass* (p). Probably 'well
in a hollow.' There is a spring here. LYNCH (6″) is *Lonche
Grove* 1546 *Deeds Enrolled*. MILFORD is *Mileford* 1330 *SR* (p).
NORTH WOOD (6″) is *Northewode* 1545 LP. SHORTRIDGE (6″) is
Shortrigh 1442 IpmR, *-rudge* 1563 *FF*. These three names
are self-explanatory. LOWER TWITCHEN (6″) is *Twichene* 1238
Ass (p), *Overe-, Nitheretochene* 1330 *SR* (p). 'Crossways,' *v.*
Twitchen *supra* 57. Several tracks meet here.

Buckland Filleigh

BUCKLAND FILLEIGH 127 E 9/10

> *Bochelan* 1086 DB, *Bokland* 1242 Fees 772
> *Suht Bokland* 1249 *Ass, Southboclande* 1268 Exon
> *Bokelondefilleghe* 1333 Exon
> *Bocland Hurtlegh* 1339 BM

v. bocland. Nicholas de *Fyleleye* held the manor in 1285 (FA);
he may have come from Filleigh *supra* 42. *South* to distinguish
from Buckland Brewer *supra* 88, *Hurtlegh* from the neighbouring manor of Hartleigh *infra* 91.

GRASCOTT

Greu(e)lcote 1268 DA 41
Greuliscote late Hy 3 BM, *Grewellescote* 1275 *Ass*, *Greu(e)lescote*
1275–1300 DA 41, 1281 *Ass* (p), 1309 BM, *Greuwelescote*
1281 *Ass*

The fuller forms given here show that the ME pers. name
which forms the first element here must be *Grewel* rather than
Greville, as suggested by Blomé (36). This might be a French
nickname, a derivative of *gru*, 'crane,' found in the form *gruel*
as the name of a young crane.

HARTLEIGH is *Hierlega* 1086 DB (Exon), *Herlege* (Exch),
Hertlegh' 1242 Fees 772, *Hurtlegh* 1281 DA 41 *et freq* to 1333
SR (p), *Hurte-* 1326 Ipm, 1384 BM. 'Hart-clearing,' *v.* leah.

WEST HEANTON is *Hanton(a)* 1086 DB, 1266 DA 41 (p), *Heanton*
1268 DA 41 (p), *Dainesheaunton* (sic) 1314 BM, *Davysheanton*
1420 Cl. 'At the high farm,' *v.* heah, tun. The identity of *Davy*
is not known.

AWSLAND is *Alsland al. Ashland* 1718 *Recov*. BARTON COTTAGES
(6″) is *the Barton* 1543 BM, *v.* beretun. BRADLEY is *Suth
Bradlegh* 1281–1300 BM, *v.* brad, leah. CHALHANGER (6″) is
Chealdhangre, Cholhangre early Ed 1, *Choldhangre* 1375 BM.
'Cold wooded-slope,' *v.* cald, hangra. DUCKPOOL (6″) is *Ducka-
pooll* 1718 *Recov*. GALMINGTON is *Galmeton* 1268 DA 41, 1268,
1274 BM, *Gelmeton* 1388 BM, *v.* Galmpton *infra* 304. HEMBURY
COTTAGES (6″) is *Henbury* c. 1285 DA 41, *Hembury* 1379 BM.
'(At) the high stronghold,' cf. same name *supra* 90. There is an
ancient camp here. HORRISLEW (6″) is *Horyslow* 1718 *Recov*.
Possibly 'dirty slough,' *v.* horh and cf. Slew *supra* 28. MODBURY
is *Madbury* 1718 *Recov*. This name may be identical with
Modbury *infra* 279. The petty sessions were held here in 1650
according to the 6″ map. WAY (6″) is *Way* 1549 BM. WOOD-
HEAD (6″) is so spelt 1718 *Recov*.

Bulkworthy

BULKWORTHY 127 D 7

Buchesurda, Bochesurde, -orda 1086 DB
Bulkewrth 1219 *Ass et freq* to 1462 IpmR with variant spellings

-*wrthy*, -*worth*, -*wurthi*, Bulkaworthy 1345 *Ass*, *Bulkeswort*
1229 Pat
Bolkeworth' 1242 Fees 797, 1279 Ipm, 1303 FA

The first element here is doubtless the pers. name found i
bulcan pytt (BCS 225) and Bulkeley (Ch). Hence '*Bulca*'s farm
v. worþig.

HANKFORD is *Hanecheforda* 1086 DB, *Hanekeford* 1313 *Ass*
Hankford 1458 IpmR. '*Haneca*'s ford' (over the Torridge). C
Hankham (PN Sx 447).

BOWER is *Boure* 1424, *Bowr* 1458 IpmR, *v.* bur. EASTACOTT i
Estecote 1330 *SR* (p), 1458 IpmR. HAYTOWN is *Heye* 143
IpmR, *Hey al. Heytowne* 1616 *Recov*, *v.* (ge)hæg. For *town*, *v*
infra 676. MERRIFIELD (6″) is *Muriefeld* 1238 *Ass*, *Mirifelde* 133
SR (p). Cf. Merrivale *infra* 247. STOWFORD is *Stafford* 1244 *As*
(p), *Stouford* 1333 *SR* (p), *v.* Stowford *supra* 41.

Frithelstock

FRITHELSTOCK [fristɔk] 127 B 9

Fredeletestoc 1086 DB (Exon), *Fredelestoch* (Exch)
Frithelaghestok 1223 Pat, *Frithelakestok(e)* 1224, 1228 FF
1238 *Ass*
Frithelarestok' 1235-6 Fees 561, *Fryth-* 1242 Fees 775
Frythelestoke 1269 Exon, *Frith-* 1287 Misc
Frydestoke 1445 Pat, *Frithelstocke al. Fristocke* t. Jas 1 EC
'*Friþulāc*'s stoc(c).'

ASH is *Aissa* 1086 DB, *Assh* 1303, *Ayssh* 1346 FA. The identifi
cation of the DB manor is not certain. It might also refer to As
in Petrockstow in the same Hundred.

CULLEIGH is *Colelia* 1086 DB, *College* 1228 FF, -*legh* 1330 *S*
(p), *Culelegh* 1238, 1244 *Ass* (p), *Kollelegh'* 1242 Fees 795
Colelegh 1275 RH (p), 1303 FA. 'Cool leah,' or '*Cola*'s leah,
v. Collacott *supra* 50. There is no stream here.

KNAWORTHY is *Knaworthi* 1330, 1333 *SR* (p), *Knavery* 157
Deed, *v.* worþig. The first element may be the OE *cnafa*, 'boy,
or possibly a pers. name *Cnafa*, as suggested by Blomé (38)
Cf. Knathorn *infra* 410. For *w* > *v* cf. Introd. xxxv.

PRIESTACOTT and PRESTON are *Priscotford* 1672 *Recov*, *Preston Hill* 1573 *Deed*, 'cot(e) and tun of the priests.' These two places, which are close together, are probably to be associated with the members of Frithelstock priory.

BEARA COTTAGE (6") and SOUTHCOTT were probably the homes of Henry *atte Beare* (1330 *SR*) and Robert de *Southcote* (1330 *SR*). The latter is *Southcott* (1573 *Deed*). *v.* bearu.

BIBBEAR is *Bubebury* 1281 *Ass* (p), *Bobburgh* 1333 *SR* (p), '*Bubba*'s burh.' HOLLAMOOR is *Holemore* 1244 *Ass* (p), 1462 IpmR, *v.* holh, mor. HORWOOD BARTON is *Horwode* 1330 *SR* (p). Probably 'dirty or muddy wood,' *v.* horh. MILFORD (6") is *Melleford* 1242 Fees 775, *Mileford* 1333 *SR* (p). SMITHACOTT is *Smythenecote* 1328 Exon (p), 1333 *SR* (p). 'Smiths' cot(e),' with a weak genitive plural in *-ene*. STRETCHACOTT is *Strecchecote* 1299 Ipm, *v.* Strashleigh *infra* 273.

Huish

HUISH 127 E 12

> *Ywis, Hywis* 1086 DB *et freq* with variant spellings *Hywis(c)h*, *Hywys(s)h*, (*juxta Merton*) 1410 *FF*

'Land for one household,' *v.* hiwisc.

HEANTON SATCHVILLE is *Hantona* 1086 DB, *Yauntone* 1242 Fees 785, *Heaunton Sechehevile* 1292 Ipm, (*Sechevil*) 1303 FA, (*Sachevylle*) 1377 Cl, *Heanton Sachevyld* 1428 FA. 'At the high farm,' *v.* heah, tun. John de *Sicca Villa* (i.e. *Secheville*) held the manor in 1242.

LOVISTONE is *Lovelleston'* 1242 Fees 779, *Loveleston* 1303 FA, and takes its name from the family of William *Lovel* who held the manor in 1303. Cf. IPN 132 and Loviston (Pemb), *Lovellestone* 1363 IpmR.

CLEMENT'S WOOD (6") is to be associated with the family of Stephen *Clement* (1544 *SR*). YEO (6") was probably the home of William *atte Ya* (1333 *SR*). 'At the water,' *v.* 17–18 *supra*.

Iddesleigh

IDDESLEIGH [idʒli] 127 F 13

> *Edeslega* 1086 DB, *Eddesleghe* 1291 Tax
> *Edwiesleghe* n.d. Buckland, *Edwislega* 1107 (1300) Ch, *-leg(he)*

1219 FF, 1242 Fees 779, 1260 Exon, *Edusleg(h)* 1277 Misc,
1281 *Ass*, 1285 FA

Edulvesly 1278 Pat, *Yedolvesleg* 1279 QW, *Edolveslegh* 1281
Ass

Ydusleghe 1296 Ipm, *Iduslegh* 1303 FA, *Yuddesleghe* 1308,
1320–4 Exon, *Yudeslegh* 1316 FA, 1340 *SR*

(Dughelond juxta) Eyddislegh 1339 *Ass*

Yiddesle 1330 *FF*, *Yeddeslegh* 1428 FA

Probably '*Ēadwig*'s clearing' (*v*. leah), though it is clear that
early confusion between *Ēadwig* and *Ēadwulf* took place. Cf.
Zachrisson, *Studier i Modern Språkvetenskap* 8, 130.

BRAMBLECOMBE is *Bremelcombe* 1086 DB, *-cumb* 1345 *Ass*. Self-
explanatory.

ASH HO is *Aisch* 1529–32 ECP 6, 20. BARWICK is *Berewyke* 1440
FF, *Barweeke al. Barricke* t. Eliz ChancP, *v*. berewic. BRIDGE
TOWN was the home of John *atte Brugge* 1333 *SR*. For *town*,
v. infra 676. BULLHEAD is *Boleheade* 1327 *Ass* (p), *-heved* 1330
SR (p), *-hed(ys)* 1402 Fine, 1440 *FF*, *-hede* 1475–85 ECP 2, 155.
'Bull's head,' cf. Farcet, PN BedsHu 185. HILL is *La Hille* 1242
Fees 779, *Hill in Yedeslegh* 1443 IpmR. NETHERCOTT BARTON
is *Nythercote* 1440 *FF*. 'Lower cot(e).' PIXTON is *Pikkestan*
1238 *Ass*. Professor Ekwall suggests that this may be a compound of *Picca*, the pers. name found in Pickworth (L), Pickwell (Lei) and stan. SMYTHSTONE (6″) is *Smythystone* 1440 *FF*,
Smithson t. Eliz ChancP. WALDONS is *Wallen* 1440 *FF*. WEEK
was the home of Roger de *Wic'* 13th Buckland, *v*. wic.

Landcross

LANDCROSS 127 A 9

Lanchers 1086 DB

Lancars(e) 1242 Fees 784, 1264 Exon, 1291 Tax, *-kars* 1285
FA, *-chars* 1348 Exon

Langkars 1292 Ipm, *-cars* 1316 FA, 1358 Ipm, 1446 Exon

Lancras 1318 Ch, *-crasse* 1624 Cai, *Landcross* 1822 Lysons

In view of the prominent rounded hill here it may well be
that Blomé (39) is right in suggesting a compound of OE *hlanc*,
'lank' and *ears*, 'arse.' For the use of such a word in hill and

other names cf. note by Mawer in Brownbill, *West Kirby and Hilbre* 312–13 *s.n.* Caldy.

PILLMOUTH is *Pilmouth* 1765 D. The Torridge is still tidal here, and the pyll is probably descriptive of the Yeo, which enters the main river at this point.

Langtree

LANGTREE 127 C 9

> *Langtrewa* 1086 DB, *Langetre* 1228 FF *et passim* with variant spelling *-trewe*, *-triwe*, *Langhetrewe* 1350 Ipm, *Langetreo* 1366 Exon

'Tall tree,' *v.* lang, treow. Cf. Langtree Hundred (O).

CHOLASH is *Chaldhasse, Chaldesasche* 1244 *Ass, Choldasshe* 1346 FA, *Coldeaisshe* 1350 Ipm, *Choldeaysche* 1540 *FF, Choldysshe* 1546 LP. 'Cold ash tree,' possibly with reference to some conspicuous tree in an exposed position. Cf. Cawthorn (PN NRY 78).

DOGGAPORT (6″) is *Thokirport* 1330, *-ker-* 1333 *SR* (p), 1346 *Ass* (p). The interpretation of *port* in Devon names (cf. *infra* 669) offers difficulties. Some of them, like Doggaport, can never have been 'towns,' the commonly recognised interpretation of OE port. Professor Ekwall and Dr Ritter agree in suggesting that the first element in this name may be OE *þocera*, genitive plural of an unrecorded *þoccere*, 'vagabond,' a derivative of OE *þocerian*, 'to run about.' The whole name, lit. 'tramps' town,' would then be one of derision, cf. Tad(d)iport, Beautiport and Lotherton *infra* 111, 122, 262, 581. Cf. also Introd. xxxv

HILLASHMOOR (6″) is *Illeryss* 1238 *Ass, Irissh al. Illerssh* 1390 Cl, *Yllers* 1408 *Ass* (p), *Illehershe* 1463 Pat, *Esthyllaryshe, Westhillarishe* 1555 *Deeds Enrolled*. This may be a compound of OE *igil, il*, 'hedgehog,' and ersc. Cf. Ilsham *infra* 519.

MUFFWORTHY (6″) is *Mokewrthe* 1244 *Ass* (p), *Moggewurthi* 1330 *SR* (p), *Moghworthi* 1333 *SR* (p), *Muckeworthe al. Muffworthie* t. Jas 1 ECP, *Muffery* or *Muggery* or *Mugworthy* or *Muckworthy* 1804 *Recov*. Probably 'Mocca's or Muc(c)a's worþig' with later development through g and gh [χ] to f as in Luffincott *infra* 152.

Mugberry in Stoke Climsland (Co), *Mokeworthi* 1338 *Rental*
Moggeworthy 1360 *Ass*, shows a different development.

THATTON (6") is *Thetton* 1288 *Ass*, 1333 *SR* (p), *v.* tun. The
first element is possibly OE *þæc*, 'covering, roof, thatch,' cf
Bratton *supra* 29.

BERRY CROSS, LANGTREE WEEK, SMALLRIDGE (6"), WATERTOWN
and WOODHOUSE[1] (6") were probably the homes of Philip de *Byry*
Richard de *Wyke* (1333 *SR*), William de *Smalerugge* (1330 *SR*)
Richard *atte Watere* (ib.) and Thomas *atte Wode* (1333 *SR*)
v. burh, hrycg, wic.

BEARE HO (6") is *Bernehouse al. Berehouse* 1390 Cl, *Bearhous*
1762 *Recov.* BROWNS is to be associated with the family of John
Broun (1330 *SR*). BUDA is *Bowode* 1287 *Ass, Boghe-* 1330 *SR*
Bou- 1333 *SR* (p). 'Curved wood,' cf. Bowden *supra* 37 and v
Introd. xxxvi. BURSTONE (WOOD) is *Burton, Burton Wood* t. Eliz
ChancP. LAMBERT is *Lampford* 1269 FF, *Lamford* 1296 Ipm
Lamford al. Lamberd 1563 *Deed.* 'Lamb ford,' cf. the same
name *infra* 155. LOVELAND (6") is *La Lovelonde* 1408 *Ass*
Cf. the same name *supra* 78. PUTSHOLE (6") is *Pyottsale* 1555
Deeds Enrolled. RIVATON is *Reveton(e)* 1314 Ch, 1330 *SR* (p)
Perhaps 'Reeve's farm,' cf. Riverton *infra* 351. STAPLETON is
Stapelton 1314 Ch, *Stapildon* 1330 *SR* (p), *Stapelton* 1420
IpmR, *v.* stapol, tun. STIBB CROSS is *Stibbe* 1330 *SR* (p), *Estybbe*
Weststybbe 1555 *Deeds Enrolled.* OE *stybbe*, 'stump, stub (of a
tree).' STOWFORD is *Stouford* 1330, 1333 *SR* (p), *Stauford* 1412
Exon, *v.* Stowford *supra* 41. SUDDON is *Soddon* 1333 *SR* (p)
Suddon 1581 *SR.* 'South of the hill,' *v.* dun. WITHECOTT is
Wydicote 1330, *Wydecote* 1333 *SR*, 1340 *Ass, Wida-* 1408 *As*
(all p). Probably 'withy cot(e).'

Littleham

LITTLEHAM 127 A 9

  Liteham 1086 DB, *Litelhama* 1107 (1300) Ch, *Lit(t)leham*
  1177 P, 1290 Ch, *Litelham juxta Bidford* 1361 *Ass*

v. ham(m).

APP'S LANE, FURLONG COTTAGE, HEALE HO and HOLE (all 6",

---

[1] *Wode* 1390 Cl.

were probably the homes of Robert *atte Apse* (1330 *SR*), John *atte Forlang* (1333 *SR*), Richard *atte Hele* (1330 *SR*), Baldwin *atte Hole* (1330 *SR*). *v.* æps, healh, holh.

HOLLAND (6″) is *Holond* 1394 *Ass*, *v.* holh, land. The farm is at the top of a valley. MIDDLE LANGDON (6″) is so spelt 1587 *Deed*. 'Long hill,' *v.* dun.

Peters Marland

PETERS MARLAND 127 D 10

> *Mirlanda* 1086 DB
>
> *Merlanda* 1184 P (p), *Petermerland* 1242 Fees 788, *Merlond(e) Sancti Petri* 1244 *Ass*, 1316 FA, 1431 IpmR, *Petrysmerlond* 1303 FA

This place and Merton *infra* 99 would seem to take their names from the river Mere which flows through the parishes. Since, however, no really early forms of this stream have been found (*supra* 10), it is more probable that mere originally denoted some large pool or stretch of marshy land extending over both parishes and that the stream is a late back-formation from the place-names. There is much marshland in the valley of the Mere. 'Peter' from the dedication of the church.

SWILLATON (6″) is *Sullyadon* 1238 *Ass*, *Suledon* 1244, 1249 *Ass* (p), *Sulle-* 1310 *Ass*, 1411 FF, *Swille-* 1313 *Ass* (p), *Swile-* 1330 *SR* (p). This name, like Swilly *infra* 241, may be connected with the OE *swylle* found in *swyllan healas*, a place on a stream (BCS 1036). Cf. OE *swilian*, 'to wash,' and see further *s.n.* Swale Bank (PN Sx 353). The ground here is marshy.

TWIGBEAR

> *Tucabera, Tuicaberia* 1086 DB (Exon), *Tu(i)chebere* (Exch)
>
> *Tukeber* 1238 *Ass* (p)
>
> *Twikeber* 1238 *Ass* (p) *et passim* to 1429 IpmR with variant spellings *Twyk(k)e-, Twycke-, Twicka-* and *-beare*
>
> *Twycbare* 1301 Ipm

The first element is probably identical with that of Twickenham (Mx), *Tuican hom* 704 BCS 111, *Tuicanhamm* 793 BCS 265, *Tuiccanham* 948 (c. 1200) BCS 860. No OE name *Twicca* is known, but we have a 9th cent. *Twicga*, the name of an

East Anglian moneyer, found again probably in Twigworth (Gl), *Twyggenuurthe* (1242) *v.* PN Gl *s.n. Twicca* may be an unvoiced pet-form of this. Such unvoicing offers the only reasonable explanation of such a name as the 11th cent. *Trump* from *Trumbeorht* and the common *Ecca* beside *Ecga. v.* bearu.

WEEK is *Wica* 1086 DB (Exon), *Wiche* (Exch), *Wyke* 1275 RH, 1330 *SR* (p), *v.* wic. Probably the dairy farm of the parish.

WINSCOTT is *Winescota* 1086 DB, *Wynscote* 1330 *SR* (p). 'Wine's cot(e).'

WINSWELL[1] is *Wivleswilla* 1086 DB (Exon), *Wifleswille* (Exch), *Wyveleswell* 1305 *Ass, Wyveliswille* 1321 *Ass, Wyllyswell* 1492 Ipm. '*Wifel*'s spring,' *v.* wielle.

WOOLLATON is *Wylleton* 1249 FF, 1346 FA, *Wyllaton* 1277 *Ass, Wiliton* 1428 FA, *Willeton al. Willington al. Welaton* 1616 *Deed.* Probably '*Willa*'s farm' rather than 'spring farm,' for there is no well or spring marked here on the 6″ map. *v.* tun.

EASTWOOD and YARD were probably the homes of John *Byeste-wode,* i.e. 'east of the wood' (1339 *Ass*) and William *atte Yurd* (1330 *SR*). For Yard *v. supra* 48.

ALSCOTT is *Alvardyscote* 1330, -*des*- 1333 *SR* (p), *Alescott al. Alvescott* 1563 *Deed.* '*Ælfheard*'s cot(e).' BUDA (6″) is *Estboue-wode, West Bouewode* 1289 *Ass, Estereboghewode* 1298 *Ass, Bowde* 1481 IpmR. 'Curved wood,' cf. same name *supra* 96. STONE is *Stone juxta Petrismerlond* 1377 IpmR and was the home of Roger *atte Stone* (1330 *SR*).

Meeth

MEETH 127 F 12

 Meda 1086 DB

 Meðe 1175 P, *Metha* 1180 P, (*la*) *Methe* 1209–62 Exon *et passim* to 1535 VE, *Mete* 1285 FA

 Lamee 1219 FF, *La Mehe* 1233 FF, *La Meye* 1242 Fees 785

---

[1] On the map are Winswell (hamlet) and Willeswell Moor. The first form is probably modern and due to association with the neighbouring Winscott. It is still Willeswell on the most recent 6″ map.

Mathe 1275 RH, *Meythe* 1585 BM

OE *mǣþe*, 'hayland,' as suggested by Blomé (42).

CROCKER'S, FRIAR'S and GIFFORD'S HELE are *Hela* 1086 DB, *Hele* 1242 Fees 788, 795, *Hele (le) Povere* 1288 *FF*, 1303 FA, *Hele Sechevill* 1303 FA, *Hele Pore* 1346 FA, *Hele Giffard* 1361 Cl, *Heele* 1377 Cl. *v.* Hele *supra* 46. The three farms trace their modern names to the families of Wm *Crocker* t. Ed 3 (Pole 379), Godfridus *Frye* (1428 FA) and Roger *Giffard* (1219 FF). Crocker's Hele was held by Richard de *Sechevil* in 1242 (Fees 795), Friar's Hele by William *le Poure* in 1278 (Ipm). These *Heles* and *Hele* in the neighbouring parish of Petrockstow are sufficiently far apart to make it clear that they must have been named independently and not from any one 'nook' of land.

STOCKLEIGH BARTON is *Estochelia* 1086 DB (Exon), *Stochelie* (Exch), *Stokkelegh* 1242 Fees 795, *Stockeleghe juxta Helestock-leghe* 1312 *FF*, *v.* stoc(c), leah and Addenda *supra* liii *s.n.* Yardley.

WOOLLADON is *Oladona* 1086 DB, *Wulledune* 1242 Fees 785, *Wolledon* 1378, 1423 IpmR, *Wolwedon* 1484 IpmR. Probably 'wolves' hill,' *v.* dun, though it is curious that the *v* should have been lost as early as DB.

BOURNA is *la burne* 1281 *Ass, atte Borne* 1330 *SR, atte Bourne* 1343 Cl (all p), *v.* burna. SHETSLADE (6″) is *Shittislade* 1621, *Shutslade* 1714 *Recov, v.* slæd. STOCKEY is *Stokheye* 1281 *Ass* (p), 1285 FA, *-hay(e)* 1333 *SR* (p), 1378 IpmR, *Stokkeheie* 1308 Exon (p), referring to an enclosure made with trunks or stumps. *v.* stoc(c), gehæg.

Merton

MERTON 127 D 11

Merton(a) 1086 DB *et passim, Mereton* 1175, 1196 P
Marton 1428 FA, 1675 Ogilby, *Martyn* 1535 VE, *Merton vulgo Martin* 1765 D

v. s.n. Peters Marland *supra* 97.

DUNSBEAR

Denesberga 1086 DB, *Denysbeare* 1388 IpmR
Dynesbere 1242 Fees 779, 1303 FA, *-beare* 1322 Exon, *-beri*

1350 Ipm, *Dinnesbere* 1244 *Ass*, *Dynnesbere* 1296 Ipm, *Dynsbere* 1329 Exon

Probably '*Dynni*'s wood,' *v.* bearu. Cf. Dinsley (Herts). *Deneslai* DB, *Dinesleg'* 1220 Fees, *Dinesle* 1234 *FF*, etc., with *i* and *y* and occasional *e* forms.

HASWELL COPSE (6″) is *Halswille* 1330 *SR* (p). Probably 'hazel spring,' *v.* hæsel, wielle. *Hals-* in Devon names may go back to OE *heals*, 'neck,' cf. Halsinger *supra* 33, or be a dialectal form of OE *hæsl*. Topographical considerations must largely determine one's choice of element in any particular name. *v.* Addenda lviii.

POTHERIDGE

Porriga 1086 DB, *Poderigg(e)* 1303 FA, 1329 Exon, 1378 IpmR, *-rug'* 1333 *SR* (p), *Podrige* 1375 Exon
Puderigge 1183 P, *-rug* 1237 Ch (p), *-righ'* 1242 Fees 785

'*Puda*'s ridge.' Cf. Putteridge (Herts), *Puderugge* 1240 *FF*, *Pudderigge* 1248 *Ass*, *Potherugge* 1303 FA, 1346 BM.

SPECCOTT BARTON is *Spececota* 1086 DB, *Speccote* 1185 P (p), *Spekcoth'* 1242 Fees 775, *Spekkecot* 1238 *Ass* (p), *Spekecote* 1256 FF, 1285 *Ass*, *Specke-* 1259 Exon

Blomé (43) suggests that the first element may be the OE **spæc*, 'brushwood,' assumed by Ekwall for Speke (La), PN La 110. Hence, 'cot(e) by the brushwood.' Wallenberg (StudNP 2, 89) suggests the pers. name *Spec(h)* found in DB (Beds). In that case we should, however, have expected some sign of genitival *s*.

COOMBE (6″), GREATWOOD, MOORHILL, NORTHDOWN (6″), YENDAMORE (6″) were probably the homes of Robert de *la Cumbe* (1285 *Ass*), Thomas *atte Wode* (1330 *SR*), Adam *atte More* (1333 *SR*), Adam *Bynorthedoune*, i.e. 'north of the down' (1330 *SR*), and William *Beyundemyre*, i.e. 'beyond the mire' (1333 *SR*), an interesting example of an early use in southern England of the NCy *mire*.

Monkleigh

MONKLEIGH 127 B 9

Lega 1086 DB, *Legh* t. Hy 1 Montacute
Munckenelegh 1244 *Ass*, *Monckeleghe* 1265 Exon, *Monekelegh* 1286 *Ass*

v. leah. The manor was granted to the monks of Montacute (So) t. Stephen.

ANNERY HO

Auri 1193 Oliver 95, *Aury* 1381 Exon, *Uppeaury* 1386 IpmR
Anerie 1238 *Ass*, *Anery* 1238 *Ass*, *Anry* 1278 Ipm, *Upanry*
1332 Ipm, *Annarye* 1577 Saxton

No explanation of this name can be offered. The *u*-forms are clearly due to errors of transcription.

DOWNES, KNOWLE (6″), LEY (6″), NORTHWAY (6″), SALTREN'S COTTAGES (6″) and UPCOTT were probably the homes of Nicholas *atte Doune*, John *atte Knolle*, Elizabeth *atte Leye*, John *Bynorthe-weye*, i.e. 'north of the way' (1330 *SR*), Henry de *Salterne* (1333 *SR*) and Walter de *Uppecote* (1330 *SR*), *v.* cnoll, leah, weg, ærn, cot(e).

LOOSEHAM (6″) is *Loseham* 1244 *Ass* (p), 1359 *Ass*. 'Pigsty ham(m),' *v.* hlose. PETTICOMBE is *Peatecumbe* 1363 HMC iv, 370, *Peadecombe* 1431 IpmR. ' *P(e)at(t)a*'s valley,' *v.* cumb and cf. Patchole *supra* 49.

Newton St Petrock

NEWTON ST PETROCK[1] 127 D 8

æt Nywantune 938 BCS 725, *Niweton* 1252 Ch, *Neweton juxta Sheftbere* 1292 *Ass*, (*prope Thorige*) 1299 Exon, *Nyweton Sancti Petroci* 1416 *FF*, *Nuton Petrocke* 1557 Wills
Nietona 1086 DB

'At the new farm,' *v.* niwe, tun. It was granted by King Athelstan in 938 to St Petrock's Monastery at Bodmin. It is by the Torridge.

DOWN is *Down* 1500 AD vi, *v.* dun. It may be the hill referred

---

[1] The boundaries of the Newton St Petrock charter (BCS 725) start from *wuduford*, i.e. Woodford Bridge, and go up-stream (i.e. up the Torridge) to the *lyttlan broc*, i.e. Cleave Lake, along the *broc* or Cleave Lake to the head of *hreodmor*, i.e. reedy swamp. There are *moors* or swamps on the northern side of the parish. Thence due south over the down (note the farm called *Down*) to the source of *loddan broc*. This must be the small stream which feeds Combe Lake, for the latter passes Ladford, earlier *Loddeford*, clearly containing the same first element. The boundary then goes down *loddan broc*, i.e. Combe Lake, to Torridge and back up Torridge to Woodford.

L

to in *on gerihte suð ofer dune* in the land boundaries of Newton, *v. supra* 101 n.

CLEAVE, LOWER COMBE, EAST and WEST HOLE (6″)[1], LANE (6″) and VENN[2] were probably the homes of Isabel *atte Clyve* (1330 *SR*), John *atte Combe* (1333 *SR*), Cristina *atte Hole* (1333 *SR*), William *atte Lane* (ib.) and William *atte Fenne* (1330 *SR*), *v.* clif, holh, fenn.

HOLWILL is *Holawille* 1319 *FF*, *v.* wielle. There is a slight hollow in the hillside here. SUDDON is *Soddone* 1330 *SR* (p), *Suddon* 1356 *Ass.* 'South hill,' *v.* dun.

Northam

NORTHAM 118 H 3

Northam 1086 DB *et freq, Norham* 1219, 1238 *Ass, Northeham* 1475–85 ECP 2, 439

'North ham(m)'; *north* probably in relation to Bideford, as opposed to Abbotsham to the west of that town.

APPLEDORE is *le Apildore in the manor of Northam* 1335 AD vi, *Apelder* 1347 Cl, *Apuldore* 1397 AD vi, *Appelthurre* 1401 Pat, *Appledoore* 1675 Ogilby. 'At the appletree,' *v.* apulder. The site of the town seems to be identical with the place called *Táwmuða* 1068 D (c. 1100) ASC, *in portu de Tauemuth* 1249 *Ass, Touemue* 1281 *Ass, villa de Tawe mouth* 1326 Barum, *Towemouth* 1356 *Ass, Toumouth* or *Pitt* 1770 Recov. *v.* Taw River *supra* 14.

BIDNA is so spelt in 1651 (*Recov*) and was the home of John *atte Bydene* (1330 *SR*). Blomé (44) suggests that in this name we have the OE *byden*, 'bushel, tub,' used in some topographical sense. This suggestion finds support in two OE examples noted by him. Beedon (Berks) is *Byden* (BCS 802, 1171), *Beden* (ib. 866) and is near the head of a long valley. Bidden (Ha) is *byden(e)* (KCD 783), and lies in a hollow. From the context it may be the name of a river, now the Whitewater, on which Bidden stands. Bidna itself lies in a hollow. Cf. further Bennah, Betham, *infra* 430, 398. The corresponding OGer word may possibly be found in the p.n. recorded under *Butino* in Förstemann (ON i, 654).

[1] *Estehole* 1501 Ipm, *Westhole* 1561 *FF*.   [2] *Fen* 1501 Ipm.

HYDE (6″) is *Westhede* 1520 AD vi and was the home of John *atte Hithe* (1333 *SR*) and Reynold *ate Hyth* (1335 AD vi). OE hyð, 'landing-place.'

TADWORTHY (6″) is *Tadyworthi* 1330 *SR* (p), *Tateworth* 1333 *SR* (p), *Tatworthy oth. Tadworthy* 1757 *Recov*. Probably ' *Tada*'s or *Tāta*'s worþig.'

WESTWARD HO! is a modern settlement which takes its name from the title of Charles Kingsley's novel, many of the scenes in which are laid in this neighbourhood.

BURROUGH, KNAPP (6″), ORCHARD HILL and WOODA (6″) were probably the homes of William *atte Burghe* (1330 *SR*), Richard *atte Knappe* (1333 *SR*), William de *Orchard* (ib.) and William *atte Wode* (ib.), *v.* beorg, cnæpp.

ASHRIDGE is *Aisserugia* 1156 France, *Ashrigg'* 1235, *Esserug'* 1236 Cl, *Aishrudge* 1632 *Recov*. Self-explanatory. BOTSHYDE (6″) is *Bothythe* 1397 AD vi. It adjoins Hyde *supra*. CHIRCOMBE (6″) is *Chercomb* 1765 D. DIDDYWELL is *Dodewille* 1330 *SR* (p), *-wylle* 1520 AD vi. '*Dudda*'s spring,' *v.* wielle. For the vowel *v.* Introd. xxxiv. DURRANT is to be associated with the family of Stephen *Duraunt* (1333 *SR*). HUBBASTONE (6″) is *Hubberstone* 1765 D, *v.* Asser (ed. Stevenson) 262 and Addenda lix. LENWOOD (6″) is *Lyndwode* 1330 *SR* (p). 'Limetree wood,' *v.* lind. MARSHFORD (6″), cf. *le Mersch* 1447 AD vi. NEWQUAY RIDGE (6″) is *the New Key* 1759 DKR 42. NORTHAM BURROWS is *Northam Borowes* 1632 *Recov*. 'Burrow' (from beorg) is here used probably of a sandy hillock, such as characterises this shore. PITT is *Toumouth oth. Pitt* 1770 *Recov, v. s.n.* Appledore *supra* 102. RALEIGH is *Rylegh* 1333 *SR* (p), *Ryley* 1695 *Recov*. Probably 'rye clearing,' *v.* leah, the modern form being corrupted through the influence of the well-known Devon surname. SILFORD is *Sulfford* 1333 *SR* (p). The first element may, as suggested by Blomé (44), be OE *syle*, 'miry spot.' Equally possible is OE *sulh-ford*, 'ford by the *sulh* or hollow,' cf. Silverton *infra* 569. UNDERBOROUGH (6″) is *Underburgh* 1330 *SR* (p), 1549 Pat. 'Under the hill' which rises to the south, *v.* beorg. WATERTOWN (6″) was probably the home of Ralph *ate Water* (1335 AD vi).

Parkham

PARKHAM 127 B 7

Percheham 1086 DB, *Perkham* 1381 BM
Parkeham 1242 Fees 785, 1269 FF, late Hy 3 BM, *Parkaham* 1281 *Ass*
Parcham 1254 FF, 1292 Ipm

This may represent an OE *pearroca ham(m)*, perhaps referring to a farm with small enclosures. *v.* pearroc, ham(m).

HALSBURY is *Halesbere, -bire* 1198 FF, *Halesbir'* 1237 Cl, 1275 RH (p), *-bury* 1238 *Ass*, *Hallesbur'* 1281 *Ass* (p). *v.* Halsdon *infra* 139. This place is on a neck of land and may be a compound of heals and burh, but the uniform spelling with medial *e* is surprising. See further Addenda *supra* lviii.

SEDBOROUGH

Sedeborga, Sedberga, Setleberga 1086 DB (Exon), *Seteberge* (Exch)
Sedbergh 1227 FineR, *Setysburg* 1433 IpmR
Seteburg(h) 1273 FF, 1333 *SR* (p), 1404 Exon

The second element is clearly OE beorg, 'hill.' The first is difficult. If the form *Setleberga* is correct we may have the OE setl, 'seat, sitting, assembly,' cf. Modbury *infra* 279. If the single spelling with *l* is assumed to be a mistake, as is most likely the case, we may compare Kingsett *infra* 201, which seems to contain as second element the OE *set*, 'seat, entrenchment, camp,' though there is no trace of any such here now.

WATERSHUTE was the home of Adam *atte Watershute* (1330 *SR*). The place stands at the source of a streamlet so that the meaning may, as suggested by Blomé (45), be 'place where the stream shoots forth, river-source.'

WORTHYGATE (6″) is *Wrdieta* 1086 DB, *Weredeget* 1193 Oliver 95, *in portu de Wordyate* 1281 *Ass*, *Wirtheyate* 1492 Ipm. This is probably a compound of OE worþ and geat, hence 'enclosure-gate,' denoting presumably a gate in the *hege* which surrounded it. The natural phonological development would have been to *Worthyate*, but in modern times StEng *gate* has taken the place of dialectal *yate*.

COURTICES (6″), HOOPS and HORNS CROSS are probably to be associated with the families of *Courtice* (1712 etc.), *Hooper* (1604 *et passim*) and *Horn(e)* (1537 *et passim*) ParReg.

SLOO and STONE were probably the homes of Henry de *la Sloo* (1330 *SR*), i.e. at the slough or marsh, and John *atte Stone* (1330 *SR*). The former is *Sloo* (1640 ParReg).

ASH, ASHMOOR BRIDGE (6″) are *Orshe* 1607, *Ash* 1648 ParReg, *Broadashmore* 1683 Recov. For intrusive *r*, *v*. Arscott *infra* 147. BABLEIGH is *Babelegh* 1504–15 ECP 4, 371. Probably '*Babba*'s leah.' BOCOMBE is so spelt 1680 *Recov*. BOWDEN (6″) is *Bogheton* 1330 *SR* (p), -*don* 1333 *SR* (p). 'Curved hill,' *v*. Bowden *supra* 37. BROADPARKHAM is *Brodperkham* 1411 IpmR. BULLAND (also BOLLAND WOOD (6″)) is *Bolleland* 1238 Ass, -*londe* 1281 *Ass* (p), *Northerebollelond* 1367 DA 33. 'Bulls' land.' CABBACOTT is *Cobbacote* 1306 *Ass* (p). '*Cobba*'s cot(e).' GOLDWORTHY is *Goldeworthy* 1325 *Ass*, 1389 FF, 1504 Ipm, *Gullorie* 1622 ParReg. '*Golda*'s farm,' *v*. worþig. HOLWELL is *Holywill* 1553 ParReg. MELBURY is *Melebyre* 1244 FF, cf. Melbury *infra* 130. For the interpretation *v*. *s.n.* Meldon *infra* 203. MOOR is *La More* 1312 AD vi, *v*. mor. NETHERCOTT is *Nethercote* 1492 Ipm.

Petrockstow

PETROCKSTOW 127 E 11

> *Petroc(h)estoua* 1086 DB, 1150 France
> *Patricstouwe* 1268 Exon, -*rikes*- 1334 *SR*, *Patrokestohe* 1270 Exon, *Patrichestowe* 1276 RH, *Paterikestowe* 1281 *Ass*, *Patrekestowe* 1281 *Ass*, *Patrikstawe* 1401 Exon
> *Pad(e)rokestowe* 1281 *Ass*, 1286 *SR*
> *Stowe Sancti Petroci* 1342 Exon
> *Padestowe* 1356 *Ass*, 1450 Pat, *Paddistowe* 1544 *SR*, *Padstowe al. Petrockstowe* 1618 FF, *Petherickstow vulgo Padstow* 1675 Ogilby

'Holy place of St Petrock,' to whom the church is dedicated, *v*. stow. Cf. Padstow (Co), *Sancte Petroces stow* ASC(C) *s.a.* 981, *Petrokestowe* 1297 Cl, *Patrikestowe* 1326 Pat, *Padrestowe* 1350 FF. *Petroc* is the W *Pedrawg*, Breton *Petroc*, *Petreuc*, *v*. NSB, *s.n.*

ALLISLAND [ɔ·slənd]

> *Aleslant* 1086 DB (Exon), *-land* (Exch), *-lond* 1290 Ipm (p)
> *Alleslond* 1219 *Ass*, 1350 Ipm, (*West-*) 1316 *Ass*, *Allislande*
> 1238 *Ass* (p), *-lond* 1388 IpmR
> *Haleyslond*' 1242 Fees 779, *Ayleslond* 1303 FA
> *Alselond* 1314 Cl, *Alslond* 1440 IpmR
> Probably '*Ælli*'s land.'

HEANTON BARTON is *Hantona* 1086 DB, *Heaunton* 1333 *SR* (p).
'At the high farm' (*v*. heah, tun), though it is really a little lower
than Netherton in the same parish.

HELE is *Hela* 1086 DB, *Hele* 1242 Fees 788, (*Godynd*) 1303,
(*Godyng*) 1346 FA. *v*. Hele *supra* 46. Johannes *Goding* held
the manor in 1242.

LITTLE MARLAND is *Merlanda* 1086 DB, *Merlond*, *Pye Merland*
1250 Cl, *Merlond Pye* 1303 FA. *v*. Peters Marland *supra* 97.
Pye looks like a manorial addition, but no such family has been
found in Devon.

VARLEYS (6") is *Ferleia* 1086 DB, *Fernlegh*, *Farnlegh* 1238 *Ass*,
Fernele 1273 FF, *Verlegh* 1330 *SR* (p), *Ferlegh juxta Paderstowe*
1356 *Ass*. 'Bracken clearing,' *v*. fearn, leah. The *s* is pseudo-
manorial. Cf. Varley Copse close at hand.

BURY, WESTACOTT and WOODA (6") were probably the homes of
William de *Biri* (1333 *SR*), German' de *Westecote* (1333 *SR*) and
Thomas *atte Wode* (1330 *SR*). *v*. burh, cot(e).

BRIGHTMANS HAYES [brɑ·nsi] is *Brightmanysheye* 1333 *SR* (p),
-mannes- 1411 *FF*, *Britensey* 1809 M, '*Beorhtman*'s enclosure,' *v*.
(ge)hæg. The name may, however, be of ME origin. CHELSDON
(6") is *Childedon*, *-ton* 1242 Fees 779, 782, *Chillesdon* 1303, 1346
FA, *v*. cild, dun. ZEAL (6") is *Sele* 1294 *Ass*, *v*. sele.

East Putford

EAST PUTFORD 127 C 6

> *Potiforda* 1086 DB, *Potteford* 1234 Fees 400, *Potteford Milite*
> 1346 FA
> *Putteford* 1242 Fees 797, *Est Putteford* 1316 FA

> *v*. West Putford *infra* 160. Robert *Mile* held the manor in
1234 and the heirs of Robert *Milo* in 1242.

MAMBURY is *Mambiri* 1330 *SR* (p), *Manbery* 1504–15 ECP 4, 371. *v.* burh. The first element may be the Celtic *maen*, 'stone,' as in Membury *infra* 644 or possibly the element noted under Mamhead *infra* 501.

LEY and VENN were probably the homes of John *atte Leye* and Roger *atte Fenne* (1330 *SR*), *v.* leah, fenn.

BOUNTIS THORNE is *Bountisthorne* 1431 IpmR and is to be associated with the family of Roger *Bountez* (1333 *SR*). NARRACOTT is *Northcote* 1292 *Ass* (p), *Norracott* 1752 *FF*. 'North cot(e).' It is at the north end of the parish. NUTTON (6″) is *Nottone* 1330 *SR* (p). 'Nut farm' or possibly '*Hnotta*'s farm,' *v.* tun. Cf. Natcott *supra* 78. SAXWORTHY (6″) is *Sexaworthi* 1330 *SR* (p). '*Seaxa*'s farm,' *v.* worþig. It is close to Sessacott *infra* 162. WINSLADE is *Wydeslade* 1360 *Ass*, (*al. Wyndslate*) 1550 Pat, *Wynslade al. Wydeslad* 1567 *Deeds Enrolled*. 'Wide slæd' or 'withy slæd,' *v.* wiðig.

Shebbear

SHEBBEAR 127 E 9

> (*of*) *Sceft beara* 1050–73 Earle, *Sepesberia* 1086 DB
> *Seftbia* 1167 P, *Scheaftberia* 1177 P, *Seftesberg* 1219 *Ass*,
>   *Schafbera* 1180 P, *-beria* 1194 P, *Shaftebeare* 1319 Ch
> *Syeftbere* 1262 Exon, *Sheftbeare* 1291 Tax, 1353 Ipm, *-biare*
>   1322 *Ass*, *Shieftbeare* 1358 Exon
> *Schebbeare* 1425 Exon

This is evidently a compound of OE *sceaft*, 'pole, shaft,' and bearu, but the exact sense of the compound is uncertain. Blomé (47) suggests that the name may have referred to a wood which furnished material for spears.

This name furnishes the only example in Devon of an OE form for one of the very numerous names in *-beer*, *-bear* or, independently, *Bere, Beere, Beare, Beara, Beera*. The early form of this name puts it beyond question that the source of that element is OE bearu. That word is a *wo*-stem in OE and it is curious that we find no trace of the inflected dative *bearwe*, which elsewhere in England has yielded *Barrow* (L, etc.). It would seem that in Devon the word bearu early went over to the declension of wudu, so closely allied to it in meaning, and that the dative was *beara*. This is further illustrated by the compound *ifigbearo* found in the Crediton charter (Crawford i). There we have *on ifigbearo...of ifigbeara*, a clear case of dative in *a* (cf. Stevenson's note, p. 50). The later phonological development illustrated by occasional *bare-*, more common *bere-*, and numerous *biare, byare, beare* spellings is curious. This element is often confused with beorg and even with the dative *byry* or *bery* from burh.

ALLACOTT is *Alvivecote* 1238 *Ass*, 1281 *Ass*, *Alvythecote* 1295 *Ass*, *Alveth(e)cote* 1333 *SR* (all p), 1426 Exon, *Alvecote* 1409 Exon. 'cot(e) of a woman named *Ælfgȳþ* or *Ælfgifu*.' Cf. Alvacott in Tamerton (Co), *Alvevacote* DB. For a similar confusion cf. Alvechurch PN Wo 332–3.

DURPLEY is *Durpleia* 1238 *Ass* (p), *-legh(e)* 1281 *Ass*, 1315 Exon (p), 1333 *SR* (p), *Durpelegh* 1244 *Ass* (p). This is OE *dēor-plega*, 'place where animals play,' as suggested by Blomé (47). Cf. Deerplay PN La 93, 263.

LADFORD is *Loddeford* 1244 *Ass* (p), 1406 Exon. In the boundaries of Newton St Petrock (BCS 725) the stream here is referred to as *loddan broc*, and both stream and ford probably contain the same first element *lodda*, perhaps the pers. name which lies behind Ludley (PN Sx 528) and is found in a strong form in Lodsworth (ib. 26) and Loddiswell *infra* 306.

LOVACOTT is *Lovecota* 1086 DB, *-cote* 1333 *SR* (p). The place takes its name from *Love* (Exch *Lofe*), the woman who held the manor TRE (DB 413 b). The OE form of her name would have been *Lufu*, gen. sing. *Lufe*.

PENNICKNOLD was the home of Adam de *Piliaknolle* (1333 *SR*). Probably '*Pil(l)a*'s cnoll or rounded hill,' cf. Pilistreet *infra* 173. For the *ia*, v. *supra* xxxvi.

VADDICOTT is *Faddecote* 1212 Fees 99, 1238 *Ass* (p), *Fade-* 1249 *Ass*, 1330 *SR* (p), 1386 IpmR, *Vade-* 1346 *Ass* (p). '*Fadda*'s cot(e),' cf. Fadmoor PN NRY 62.

WHITE was the home of Adam *atter Wayte* (1330) or de *la Wayte* (1333 *SR*) and William *atte Wayte* (1356 Exon). This is probably, as suggested by Blomé (47), the ME *wayte*, 'ambush, place where one lies in wait,' cf. *atte Waytehulle* (p) (1332 *SR*) in Dauntsey (W).

ASH (6″), BARN (6″), BERRY, FORDA (6″), FULFORD BRIDGE (6″),
SOUTH FURZE, HAY[1], MOORTOWN, WOODA (6″) and WOOTTON
were probably the homes of Robert de *Aysse* (1238 *Ass*), Walter
atte Berne (1330 *SR*), John *atter Biri* (1330 *SR*), Dobel de *la
Forda* (1238 *Ass*), William de *Foleford* (1333 *SR*), Ailmar de *la
Fursa* (1167 P) and Robert de *Southfors* (1330 *SR*), William de
la Heia (1238 *Ass*), Robert de *More* (1333 *SR*), John *atte Wode*
(1330 *SR*) and Isolda de *Wotton* (ib.). *v.* burh, ful, fyrs, (ge)hæg,
mor, wudu, tun.

BACKWAY is *Badekeweye* 1330 *SR* (p), *Backway* 1581 *SR*.
'*Beadeca*'s way or path.' BADWORTHY is *Badewurð* 1167 P (p),
Baddewrth 1238 *Ass* (p), *Badeworth(i)* 1254 *Ass*, 1330 *SR* (p).
'*Bada*'s farm,' *v.* worþig. BEARA (6″) is *Beare* 1609 *SR*, *v.* bearu.
BINWORTHY is *Bennewurð* 1167 P (p), *Bynnewurth* 1238 *Ass* (p),
-worth(i) 1244 *Ass*, 1330 *SR* (p). '*Bynna*'s farm,' *v.* worþig and
cf. Redin 60. CAUTE is *Cote* 1281 *Ass*, *Cot* 1765 D, *v.* cot(e).
DIPPERMILL (6″) is *Dupeford* 1306 *Ass*. 'Deep ford,' cf. Dipper-
town *infra* 200. HALWILL COTTAGES (6″) is *Halgwille juxta
Heworthy* 1322 *Ass*. 'Holy well.' HIGHWORTHY is *Heworthy*
1322 *Ass*. 'High farm,' *v.* worþig. HILL (6″) is *Hvlhey* 1504–15
ECP 4, 182, *v.* (ge)hæg. LIBBEAR BARTON is *Lipebear'* 1333 *SR*
(p), *v.* bearu. The first may be that found in Lipson *infra* 235.
PADDON is *Pattone* 1330 *SR* (p). Possibly '*Peatta*'s tun.' Cf.
Patchole *supra* 49. ROWDEN is *Ruedon* 1249 *Ass*, *Rouwedon* 1330
SR (p). 'Rough hill,' *v.* ruh, dun. WALTERSMOOR (6″) is to be
associated with the family of Richard *Walter* (1333 *SR*).
WORDEN was the home of Alwi de *la Wurða* 1167 P and Robert
atte Worthen 1333 *SR*, *v.* worþign.

Sheepwash

SHEEPWASH 127 F 10

Schepewast 1166 LN, *Sepewais* 1184 P, *Schepwayse* 1253 Ipm,
Shepwaysse 1276 Ipm, *Schipwaysche* 1346 FA, *Shiepwaysshe*
1358 Exon. The second element shows variant spellings
-wasse, -washe, -wesce, -wesse, -wesshe
Shipwaishe 1591 CtRequests, *Shipwash* 1675 Ogilby
Self-explanatory. The place is by the Torridge.

[1] *Hey* 1566 SR.

GORTLEIGH is *Golkele* 1249 *Ass*, *Gorgeleg'* 1276 RH, *Gorkelegh(e)* 1281 *Ass et freq* to 1341 Exon (p), (*West*) 1388 Fine. This may contain an OE pers. name *Gāroc(a)*, a diminutive of an OE *Gāra*, but no certainty is possible.

SWADDICOTT is *Surdecote* 1281 *Ass* (p), *Swerdecote* 1392 Exon (p), *Swardecot* 1765 D. This would seem to correspond to an OE *sweorda cot(e)*, 'cottage(s) of the swords,' but it is difficult to see how such a name could have arisen. Professor Ekwall and Dr Ritter agree in suggesting the possibility of an OE pers. name *Sweorda (cf. ON *Sverði*), while among other weapon-names Dr Ritter notes ON *Hiálmi*, *Skapti*, *Spióti*. Cf. also OE *Billa*. We have the strong form of this name in Swardeston (Nf), DB *Suerdestuna*.

DOWN FM (6″) is *Downe al. Tredowne* 1700 *Recov* and was the home of William *atte Doune* (1333 *SR*), cf. Tredown *infra* 146. GREGORY'S BRIDGE (6″), cf. *Gregorysland* 1383 IpmR. LAKE FM is *la Lake* 1266 DA 41. 'The stream,' v. lacu. SOUTH HILL is *Suthhulle* 1306 *Ass* (p). UPCOTT BARTON is *Upcote* 1243 FF, *Uppecote juxta Shipwasse* 1286 *Ass*. WOODA (6″) is *le Wode* 1501 Ipm and probably gave name to Adam *atte Wode* (1333 *SR*).

Little Torrington

LITTLE TORRINGTON 127 C 10

  Toritona 1086 DB, *Parva Toriton'* 1242 Fees 788, *parua Thorenton*, *Thorinton* 1249 *Ass*, *Little Torygton* 1411 Pat
  Liteltrorilanda 1086 DB

  'Farm by the Torridge' *supra* 14, v. tun. 'Little' as opposed to Great Torrington *infra* 123.

FRIZENHAM is *Friseham* 1086 DB, t. Hy 1 Montacute *et passim*, *Frisenham* 1333 *SR* (p). This is perhaps OE *Friesan-ham(m)*, 'Frisian's ham(m),' as suggested by Blomé (48). In OGer *Friso* is freely used as a pers. name, with a diminutive *Frisiko* (Förstemann PN 525) and there may have been a similar OE name.

HOLLAM is *Holnham* 1086 DB, 1330 *SR* (p), 1346 FA, *-am* 1242 Fees 788, 1345 *Ass*, *Holham* 1303 FA. 'Holly ham(m),' v. holegn.

SMYTHAM is *Esmitteham* 1086 DB, *Smitham* 1228 Bracton, *Smetham* 1229 FF, *Smetheham* 1238 *Ass*, *Smitheham* 1256 FF, 1289 *Ass*. Probably 'smiths' ham(m).' smeðe, 'smooth' is inapplicable.

TADDIPORT is *Tadyaport* late Hy 3 BM, *-ye-* 1311 Ipm, *-ia-* 1370 *Ass*, *Tadiaputt* 1333 SR (p), *Tadypitt* 1492 Ipm, *Tadyporte* 1364 *Ass*, 1443 *FF*. The same name occurs in Tawstock parish (*infra* 122) and in Veryan (Co). The first element is clearly OE *tadige*, 'toad,' and it looks as if the name may have had some contemptuous sense. Cf. Doggaport *supra* 95, and IPN 149.

CLEAVE and CROSS were probably the homes of Ralph *atte Clyve* (1333 *SR*) and Robert de *la Crosse* (1327 *Ass*), *v*. clif.

BAGBEAR is *Bagebere* 1244 FF, *Baggebeare* 1340 *Ass*, cf. Bagbeare *infra* 169. BOWDEN is *Boghedon* 1333 *SR* (p), cf. Bowden *supra* 37. WEST FORD is *Forde* 1229 FF, *La Forde juxta Parvam Toriton* 1311 *FF*. GRIBBLE INN is *Gribbell* 1622 *FF*, *v. s.n.* Gribbleford *infra* 143. NORTH HILL COTTAGES (6″) is *Northill* 1672 *Recov*. HOMER is *Holemere* 1281 *Ass* (p). 'Pool in the hollow,' *v*. holh, mere. WAYMOOR, cf. *Waye in the parish of Little Torinton* 1357 AD ii. WOODLAND is (*la*) *Wodelond* 1302 *Ass*, 1416 Exon.

Weare Gifford

WEARE GIFFORD [dʒifəd]   127 A/B 10

> *Wera* 1086 DB, *Were* 1219 *Ass et freq* to 1290 Ch, *Weregiffarde* 1328 Exon, *Ware* 1675 Ogilby

v. wer. The place lies by the river Torridge. The *Giffard* family is first mentioned in connexion with the place in 1219 (*Ass*).

GRENDESTOW (lost) is *Gorandestowe* 1279, *Gorontestowe* 1288, *Gorundestowe juxta Were* 1289, *Grendestowe* 1299 *Ass*. The name is possibly to be associated with the families of Walter *Gurand*, a juror of Torrington in 1238 (*Ass*), and Laurence *Goraund*, a juror of Fremington Hundred in 1249 (*Ass*). If so, it is an interesting case of stow being compounded with a post-Conquest pers. name.

HUXHILL

Hochesila 1086 DB, *Hokeshell* 1256 FF (p), *-hille* 1313 Exon
(p)
Hoxhull 1333 *SR* (p)

Probably '*Hōc*'s hill' as suggested by Blomé (49), but as there
is a well-marked spur of land here the first element may be OE
hoc, 'hook.'

LITTLE WEARE is *Litelwera* 1086 DB, *Littellawere* 1361 *Ass.*

CLEAVE (6″) is *Cleave* 1771 *Recov* and was the home of Nicholas
atte Clyve (1333 *SR*), *v.* clif. It is on a steep hillside. FOOTLANDS
(6″) is *Foolland* (sic) 1771 *Recov.* Cf. *Fotelands* t. Hy 8, Plym
Rec. LOWER NETHERDOWNS is *Netherdon* 1695 *Recov.* POOL-
STEPS (6″) is so spelt in 1771 *Recov.* SOUTHCOTT is *Southcot*
1492 Ipm. 'South' with reference to Park or Vinton. VINTON
is *Fenton* 1492 Ipm. 'Marsh farm,' *v.* fenn, tun.

V. FREMINGTON HUNDRED

Framintone 1084 Geld Roll, *Framiton* 1167 P, *Fremiton* 1238
Ass

v. Fremington *infra* 113.

Alverdiscott

ALVERDISCOTT [ɔ·lskət] 118 J 5

Alveredescota 1086 DB, *-kote* 1244 *Ass*, *Alvredescoth*' 1242
Fees 795
Alewardescot t. Ed 1 DA 33, *Alwardiscote* 1303 FA
Alvardiscote 1320 Exon, (*juxta Fremyngton*) 1346 *Ass*, *Alfar-
descote* 1329 Exon, *Alvarscot(t)e* 1449 Exon, *Alverscote* 1499
Ipm
Alvescote 1432–43 ECP 1, 56, *Alscote* c. 1550 Leland

'*Ælfrēd*'s cot(e).'

BULWORTHY is *Buleworthy* 1233 Cl, *Boleworth(y)*, *-i* 1242 Fees
779, 1303 FA, 1361 *Ass*, *Bulleworthy* 1499 Ipm. 'Bull farm,'
or *Bula*'s farm, *v.* worþig.

WEBBERY

Wibeberia 1086 DB (Exon), *Wiberie* (Exch)
Wibbebyria 1235 Bracton, *-bury* 1326 Ipm (p), *Wybbebeyre*
(sic) 1242 Fees 795, *-byre* 1244 *Ass*, *-bire* 1281 Exon (p)
Wybburi 1333 *SR* (p)
'*Wibba*'s burh.'

CLOGGSHILL CROSS and MATTHEW'S MILL are probably to be
associated with the families of John *Clogge* (1544 *SR*) and
William *Maththewe* (1525 *SR*).

BOROUGH, HAMPIT (6″) and NETHERCOTT were probably the homes
of John *atte Burghe* (1333 *SR*), Henry *atte Hamme* (1330 *SR*)
and Christina de *Nithercote* (1308 Cl). *v.* beorg, hamm, cot(e).

GARNACOTT is *Gornyngacote* 1320 *FF*, *v.* cot(e). The first element looks like a patronymic, but the single form is not enough
to go on, *v.* ing. HIGHER KINGDON (6″) is *Kyngdon* 1330 *SR* (p),
King- 1423 IpmR, cf. Kendon *infra* 470. KITSHAM (6″) is
Ketisham 1423 IpmR, *v.* ham(m). LASHINGCOTT MOOR was
perhaps the home of Robert de *Classyngcote* (1330 *SR*). LUP-
PINGCOTT is *Lopyngcote* 1385 Exon (p), *Lyppyncott, Luppyncott*
1525 *SR* (p). Possibly '*Loppa*'s cot(e),' *v.* ing and cf. *loppan
cumb* (BCS 828). OAKWORTHY (6″) is *West Okeworthy* 1663 *FF*,
Oakery 1809 M, *v.* worþig. SOUTHDOWN is *Suthdoune* 1311 Ch.
STONY CROSS is so spelt t. Eliz ChancP.

Fremington

FREMINGTON 118 G 5

Framintona 1086 DB, *Framigton* 1107–28 (t. Ed 2) AD vi,
    Framynton 1471 Barum ii, 236
Fremigtun 1107–28 (t. Ed 2) AD vi *et passim* with variant
    spellings *-ing-, -yng-, -in-*
Farmyngton 1577 Saxton

The forms point to the same OE pers. name *Fremma*
which lies behind Fremington (PN NRY 213) and Framfield
(PN Sx 392). The early forms with *a* are probably Anglo-Norman
spellings (IPN 112). It may be noted that in 1227 (Ch) there is
mention of a *Fremesmore* near by, probably named after the
same man.

GRABBISHAW is *Grobbes(c)haue* 1330 *SR* (p), 1399 *Ct*. This name may be of ME origin and contain ME *grobbe*, 'grub,' also, 'short, dwarfish fellow,' used as a surname. It should be noted, however, that already in OE we have a p.n. *grobbes dene* (BCS 552), which suggests that the *grobb* (whether as pers. name or significant word) goes back to Old English, though its meaning is obscure. Cf. also Grub (now Milton) Street in London, *Grobstrat* 1217–43 HMC ix, 8, *Grobbe-* 1277, *Grubbe-* 1281, *le Grubbestrete* 1332 Calendar of Wills in Hustings Court.

HOLLOWCOMBE is *Holcomma* 1086 DB (Exon), *Holecome* (Exch), *Hulecome* 1244 FF. 'Hollow valley,' *v.* cumb.

HOLMACOTT is *Hunemecote* 1270 *Ass* (p), *Honmanecote* 1330 *SR* (p), *-mene-* 1333 *SR* (p), *Holmenecote* 1399 *Ct*, *Hulmecote* 1420 IpmR. '*Hūneman*'s cot(e).' The later change of *n* to *l* may have been influenced by the family of Thomas *Holman* mentioned in a Fremington Court Roll of 1399. The absence of genitival *s* is noteworthy.

LITCHARDON is *Lychedone* 1333 *SR* (p), *Lycherton fild* 1499 Ipm, *v.* dun. The first element may, as suggested by Blomé (50), be OE lic, 'corpse,' hence 'corpses' down,' but the reason for the name is unknown. Possibly a gibbet once stood here.

LYDACOTT is *Levidyecot* 1281 *Ass* (p), *Levediecote* 1330 *SR* (p). Probably 'lady's cot(e),' from OE *hlǣfdige*, 'lady.'

KNOWLEHILL[1], MARSH (6″) and WOODLAND (6″) were probably the homes of Roisea *atte Knolle* (1333 *SR*), Walter *atte Mershe* (1330 *SR*) and William de *Wodelond* (1333 *SR*).

BARTRIDGE COMMON is *Bartridge* 1664 *Recov.* BICKINGTON is *Buckyngton* 1570, *Bukington* 1606 DA 38, cf. Abbots Bickington *infra* 124. BRYNSWORTHY is *Brendelwrd* 1195 FF. CLAYPIT COVERT (6″) is *Le Clay pittes* 1606 DA 38. COLLACOTT is *Colecota* 1195 FF, *-cote* 1330 *SR* (p), *v.* Collacott *supra* 50. COMBREW is *Comberewe* 1330 *SR* (p), cf. Cumery *infra* 268. FREMINGTON PILL (6″) is *Fremington Pille* 1566 *Deed*. 'Creek,' *v.* pyll. GULLINCOTT (6″) is probably identical with *Callyngcote* 1330 *SR* (p), 1399 *Ct*, *Gollingcott* 1620 *FF*. HORSACOTT is *Horsecote* 1399 *Ct*. 'Horse cot(e),' i.e. where horses were kept. KENNACOTT is

[1] *Knolles* 1419 Cl.

Kynecote, Kenecote 1345 *Ass, Cannacote* 1566 *Deed.* Perhaps
'*Cæna*'s cot(e),' cf. Kennacott in Poundstock (Co), *Kenecote*
1355 *Ass.* KNIGHTACOTT is *Knyghtacot* 1281 *Ass, v.* cniht,
cot(e). LOVEACOTT GREEN is *Luuetot* (sic) 1195 FF, *Lovecote*
1399 *Ct.* '*Lēofa*'s cot(e)' (masc.) or *Lufu*'s (fem.), cf. Lovacott
supra 108. PENHILL is *Penhull* 1281 *Ass* (p), *Penhill* 1752 *Recov.*
This is probably a hybrid name containing the British *pen*, 'head,
end,' and OE hyll. PYEWELL is *Piewille* 1301 Ipm. The name is
perhaps of ME origin denoting '(mag)pie spring' with *pie* from
OFr *pie* and wielle. ROOKABEAR is *Rokebe(a)re* 1195 FF, 1330
SR (p). 'Rook wood,' *v.* bearu. Cf. Rockbeare *infra* 594. ROOK'S
BRIDGE (6″) is probably to be associated with the family of John
Rok (1330 *SR*). LOWER YELLAND is *Yollelonde* 1330 *SR* (p).
Cf. Addenda lviii *supra.* YELLOWFORD (6″) is perhaps *Yolde-
port* 1326 Ipm, *Yaloporte* 1566 *Deed, Yolla port* 1752 *Recov.*
'The old port,' *v. s.n.* Doggaport *supra* 95.

Horwood

HORWOOD 118 J 4

Hareoda, Horew(o)da 1086 DB, *Harewde* 1219 FF
Horwude 1196 FF *et passim* with variant spelling *-wode, Hore-
wode* 1291 Tax, *Churchehorwode* 1356 *Ass*
Horwood al. Worewood 1692 *Recov*

The term *har* is commonly applied to a wood in OE and the
compound har-wudu would denote a grey wood. As this
compound would explain the early forms in *a*, with later regular
rounding to *o* before shortening took place, we are probably
right in assuming a first element har rather than hor, 'mud,'
which would leave the *a*-forms unexplained.

EAST BARTON and WEST BARTON are probably identical with
Westhorewod' 1242 Fees 773, *Esthorewode* 1242 Fees 791, 1361
Ass. PENHORWOOD (6″) is *Pinhorwod'* 1242 Fees 791, 1316 Ipm,
Pyn- 1303 FA. The sense of the first element is uncertain.

Huntshaw

HUNTSHAW 127 A 10/11

Huneseua 1086 DB
Honisseue 1230 Cl, *Hunishau(w)e* 1238 *Ass, Honeyshagh* 1322
   Misc, *Honyschawe* 1328 Exon, *-schaue* 1346 FA

Huns(c)haue 1242 Fees 785, 1339 Ipm, *Honchaue* 1291 Tax,
-*shagh* 1310 Ch, 1334 *SR*, -*shaue* 1316 FA, *Hundschaue* 1256
Ass

Huneshawa 1249 *Ass*, *Honesawe* 1277 Exon

'Honey-wood' or '*Hūn*'s wood.' *v.* sceaga and *s.n.* Honeychurch *infra* 165.

HAYCROFT is *Hakecrofte* 1275 RH (p), *Hag-* 1330 *SR* (p), *Hak-*
1364 *Ass*, *Hay-* 1483 IpmR. Names in *Hak-*, *Hack-* are fairly
common in Devon, *v. infra* 664. Blomé (9) suggests as first
element OE *haca*, 'hook, bolt,' used in some topographical
sense, cf. *le Hake* 1553 *Ct* (Clawton). In the present name the
word might refer to the hook of land just to the south of the
farm. Alternatively the first element may be the pers. name
Hac(c)a which occurs twice in the Devon DB (f. 388) as a holder
of land TRE.

KNOCKWORTHY is *Knokeworthy* 1327 Banco (p), -*thi* 1330 *SR*
(p). *v.* worþig. The first element is possibly the British word
corresponding to Welsh *cnwc*, 'hillock,' as suggested by Blomé
(39). Cf. Knook PN Wilts 109. The place stands high. Alternatively the first element may be a ME pers. name, cf. John *Knoke*
(1311 Exon).

BROWNSCOMBE is *Brownsham* 1765 D. GUSCOTT is *Godescote*
1386 IpmR. '*Gode*'s cot(e).' HADDACOTT CROSS is *Hadecote*
1386 IpmR. Perhaps '*Headda*'s cot(e).' HILL FM is *la Hylle
juxta Ernescumbe*, (i.e. Yarnscombe) 1292 *Ass*. It lies on the border of that parish. TWITCHEN is *le Twychene* 1244 *Ass* (p), *atte
Twichene* 1333 *SR* (p), cf. Twitchen *supra* 57. The place is at a
meeting of three ways. WAYHEAD (6″) was probably the home
of Richard *atte Weye* (1330 *SR*). WIGGADON is *Wigedon* 1249
Ass (p), *Wygge-* 1330 *SR* (p), *Wyghedon* 1377 FF. '*Wicga*'s hill,'
v. dun.

Instow

INSTOW 118 H 3

Johannesto 1086 DB (Exon), -*stou* (Exch)
Jonestowe 1242 Fees 779, *Yonestowe* 1291 Tax
Iouenestawe 1249 *Ass*
Yeonestowe 1260–80 Exon, ȝunstowe 1338 Exon

'Holy spot of St John,' *v.* stow. The church is dedicated to St John the Baptist.

BICKLETON is *Picaltona* 1086 DB, *Bykelton* 1281 *Ass*, 1297 Ipm, 1330 *SR* (p), *Bikel-* 1303 FA. Professor Ekwall and Dr Ritter agree in suggesting OE *Bicelantūn*, involving a pers. name **Bicela* which would be a diminutive of the exceedingly common Devon *Bic(c)a* (cf. Abbots Bickington *infra* 124). The DB form must be corrupt.

FULLINGCOTT is *Fughelyngcot* 1281 *Ass*, *Foullyngcote* 1421 IpmR, *Foughlyngcote* 1461 AD iii. '*Fugel*'s cot(e),' *v.* ing, or possibly, as the name may be of late origin, the first element is ME *fughelyng*, 'fowling,' hence 'cottage near which wild fowl are snared.'

RADDY is *(Le) Rodeheye* 1249 FF, 1281 *Ass* (p), *Rudehaye* 1281 *Ass* (p), *Roddehaye* 1330 *SR* (p), 1340 *Ass* (p). 'Reed enclosure,' i.e. 'enclosure by the reeds,' *v.* hreod, (ge)hæg.

WORLINGTON

> *Ulwritona* 1086 DB (Exon), *Uluretona* (Exch)
> *Wulwrinton* 1249 *Ass* (p)
> *Wolryngton* 1281 *Ass*, 1303 FA
> '*Wulfhere*'s farm,' *v.* ingtun.

VENN and SOUTH YEO (both 6″) were probably the homes of Henry *atte Fenne* (1330 *SR*) and William *atte Yo* (1333 *SR*). 'At the fen' and 'at the water,' *v. supra* 18.

HUISH is *Hiwis* 1205 FF, *Hywysh Beaupel* 1316 FA, *Hiwissh juxta Fremynton* 1316 *Ass*, *v.* hiwisc. Roger *Beupel* (i.e. 'fine skin') held the manor in 1242 (Fees). MULLINGAR is *Mulhangre* 1281 *Ass* (p), (*juxta Fremyngton*) 1314 *Ass*, *Moul(e)hangre* 1330 *SR* (p), 1421 IpmR. 'Mule slope,' *v.* hangra. ORCHARD is *Orchard* 1316 *Ass*, *Orchardmore* 1399 Ct. PAIGE's PILL (6″) is to be associated with the family of Thoma *Payge* (1544 *SR*). *v.* pyll.

M

Newton Tracy

NEWTON TRACY 118 J 5

Newentona 1086 DB, *Nywethon'* 1242 Fees 779, *Nyweton by Fremynton* 1327 Banco, *Newton Tracy* 1402 Inq aqd

'New farm,' *v.* niwe, tun. Henry de *Tracy* held the manor in 1242.

Roborough

ROBOROUGH 127 C 13

Raweberga 1086 DB, *Rauburga* 1193 Oliver 95

Ruaberga 1166 RBE (p), *Rugheberg'* 1242 Fees 773, 1244 *Ass*, *Roheberge, Rogheberhe* 1275 Exon

Rouberwe 1283 Exon, *Rouburgh juxta Beauford* 1349 *Ass*, (*juxta Chepyngtoryton*) 1356 *Ass*

Roweburghe 1291 Tax, 1384 Exon, *Rowaburgh juxta Beauforde* 1345 *Ass*, *Rouweburgh* 1346 FA

'Rough hill,' *v.* ruh, beorh. Cf. Roborough *infra* 225.

BARLINGTON

Beldrendilant, Baldrintona 1086 DB

Westbaldringthon' 1242 Fees 772, *Baldrin(g)ton* 1244 *Ass*, *Balryngton* 1303 FA

Barlinton 1326 Ipm

'*Bealdhere*'s farm' or possibly '*Bealdred*'s farm,' if we take the DB spelling to be an error for *Beldredinlant*, cf. Blomé (53).

EBBERLY HO is *Emberlegh* 1242 Fees 773, *Eberesleg* 1244 *Ass*, *Edberleg* 1249 FF, *Ebberlegh* 1310 FF, 1326 Ipm, 1330 *SR* (p), *Yabberley* 1641 *SR*. Probably '*Eadburg*'s leah,' the earliest form being corrupt. *Eadburg* is a woman's name in OE.

OWLACOMBE is *Ulacomba* 1086 DB (Exon), *Olecumbe* (Exch), *Ullecumb', Wollecumb'* 1242 Fees 775, *Oulecombe* 1326 Cl, (*juxta Beauford*) 1330 *Ass*. 'Owls' valley,' *v.* cumb.

SCOTTINGTON BARTON (6") is *Scotteneton* 1345 *Ass* (p). This may mean 'farm of the Scots,' referring perhaps to some stray Irish settlers.

VILLAVIN is *Fedaven* 1086 DB, *Feldefen* 1242 Fees 779, 1326 Ipm, *Midelfethelfenne, Middelfethesfenne* 1244 *Ass*, *Fellefenne*

303, 1316 FA, *Felesfenne* 1346 FA. Professor Ekwall and Dr Ritter agree in suggesting a pers. name as the first element. They take it to be an unrecorded OE *Fēþla* corresponding to OGer *Fandila* (Förstemann, PN 496), the diminutive of OHG *Fanto* (ib.), a name allied to OE *fēþa*, 'infantry,' *fēþe*, 'power of walking.'

WANSLEY BARTON is *Wanteslegh* 1238 *Ass*, 1242 Fees 773, *Wontes-* 1281 *Ass* (p), 1310 *FF*. '*Want*'s clearing,' v. leah. Cf. Wantley PN Sx 219.

COMBE BARTON and THORNDOWN (6″) were probably the homes of Richard de *la Cumbe* (1238 *Ass*) and John de *Thorndon* (1333 *SR*). v. dun.

CLISTON is *Clerkestone* 1333 *SR* (p), cf. Cliston *infra* 167, 316. RAPSON is *Robettesdon* 1330 *SR* (p), *Robyston* 1472 *FF*. Probably Robert's farm,' the name being of post-Conquest origin. Cf. Rabscott *infra* 344. SUGWORTHY is *Suggeworth* 1244 *Ass*, *-worthi* 1333 *SR* (p), *Suggaworthy* 1346 *Ass* (p), *Suggery* 1609 *FF*. '*Sucga*'s farm,' or possibly 'farm frequented by the *sugge*' (OE *sucga*), 'hedge-sparrow,' v. worþig. Cf. Sugworth (Berks). THELBRIDGE is *Thelbrigg* 1310 *FF* (p), 1318 *FF*, *Delbridge* 1740 *FF*. 'Plank bridge,' v. þelbrycg.

St Giles in the Wood

ST GILES IN THE WOOD 127 B 12

> *Stow St Giles* 1330 Inq aqd, *Ecclesia Sancti Egidii* 1379 Exon, *Seint Giles* 1501 Ipm, *Seynt Giles* 1529 Recov, *St Giles's* 1809 M

The parish takes its name from the dedication of the church to St Egidius, for which the popular English form, through Old French, was *Giles*. 'In the Wood' must be a quite recent addition to distinguish it from St Giles on the Heath *infra* 164. For the earliest form v. stow. Similarly for some parishes in Cornwall which now begin with 'Saint' we find stow in the earliest forms.

DODSCOTT

> *Dodecota* 1086 DB, *Dodescote* 1299 Ipm, 1354 *FF*, *-dis-* 1303 FA

Doddelescoth' 1242 Fees 774, *Dodeliscote* 1303 FA
Duddecoth' 1242 Fees 779

This place was held by one *Dodo* (Exch *Dode*) TRE (DB f. 388*b*), so that the later *l*-spellings are probably incorrect. '*Dodd*'s cot(e).'

HEALAND, NORTH and SOUTH, are *Healelonde* 1270 *Ass*, *la Hyales* 1280 DA 25, *Southeales* 1371 Cl. The second form suggests that the *land* is an addition to an earlier name *Heale*, dative singular of healh, 'nook of land.' If so we have an exceptional form *heale* in place of the usual *hele* found in Devon. Cf. Hele *supra* 46.

STEVENSTONE HO is *Steveneston(e)* 1242 Fees 779, 1376 Exon, *Stepheneston* t. Ed 3 *Ass*, -nis- 1346 FA, *Stephens-toun* now *Stenson* 1630 Westcote. This name probably goes back to some post-Conquest owner *Stephen*. Cf. the same name *infra* 456.

WHITSLEIGH is *Whiteslegh* 1238 *Ass* (p), *Whyteslegh(e)* 1242 Fees 779, 1310 *FF*, *Whitteneslegh* 1335 Ch, *Wyteslegh* 1346 FA. '*Hwīt*'s clearing,' *v.* leah.

PALMER'S HILL COPSE and WELSH'S COTTAGES (both 6″) are probably to be associated with the families of Alexander *Palmere* and Robert *Walsh* (1333 *SR*).

BEARA and LEY were probably the homes of Henry *atte Beare* (1330 *SR*) and Walter Faber de *Legh* (1244 *Ass*), *v.* bearu, leah.

BARNDOWN COTTAGES (6″) is *la Barnedoune* 1317 *Ass*. CRANFORD is *Cranford juxta Dodelescote* 1286 *Ass*, *Cranefordemore* 1317 *Ass*. 'Heron ford,' *v.* cran. GREAT HUISH [gəˑrtiʃ] is *Grythuissh* 1326 Ipm, *Grithiwissh* 1371 Cl, *v.* hiwisc. The first element is uncertain. HILL is *la Hulle* 1317 *Ass*. KINGSCOTT is *Kynscot* 1281 *Ass* (p), *Kynescote* 1330 SR (p), *Kynnescote* 1501 Ipm. '*Cyne*'s cot(e).' PEAGHAM BARTON [pegəm] is *Pagaham* 1333 *SR* (p), *Pageham* 1501 Ipm. '*Pæcga*'s ham(m),' cf. Pagham PN Sx 92. SWANNYCOMBE (6″) is *Swannacomb* 1765 D, cf. Swannaton *infra* 322. WARD is *Warde* 1529 *Recov*. This is on marshy ground by a small stream and may have the same etymology as Ward *supra* 82. WAY BARTON is *la Weye* 1309 Exon. The place is near a main road. WINSCOTT BARTON is *Winnescote* 1238 *Ass* (p). '*Wine*'s cot(e).' WORDEN'S COTTAGES (6″) was probably the home of Richard de *la Wrthen* (1281 *Ass*), *v.* worþign. The *s* may be pseudo-manorial.

Tawstock

TAWSTOCK 118 H 6

Tauestocha 1086 DB, *Taustoche* 1157–60 France, *Taustok'* 1212 Fees 97 *et freq*, (*al. dicta Toustoke*) c. 1400 Exon, *Tawestoke* 1279 Abbr
Toustok 1227 Ch, *Tostock* 1594 Cai

'stoc(c) by the river Taw,' *supra* 14.

HISCOTT is *Hengestecoth'* 1242 Fees 773, -*cote* 1326 Ipm, *Henxtecote* 1326 Ipm, *Heyscote* 1346 FA. 'Stallion farm,' *v.* hengest, cot(e).

LINSCOTT probably gave name to Thomas de *Clynggecote* (1330 SR), de *Clenchescote* (1333 SR), with subsequent loss of initial *c* by dissimilation, *v.* cot(e). For the first element we may perhaps compare *of clinca leage* BCS 943, and the pers. name *atte Clenche* 1327 SR (Berks). The significance of this element must remain obscure until we can identify the sites of various places with which it is associated. Middendorff (*s.v.*) takes it to be the same as Yorkshire *clink*, 'small crack, chink, crevice,' and LGer *klinke* used in much the same sense. Linscott is in a long deep-cut valley.

LOWER ROLLSTONE is *Roweston(e)* 1333 SR (p), 1390 Cl, and is perhaps to be associated with the family of Felice *Rowe* mentioned in the latter document in the same context.

ST JOHNS CHAPEL. Alexander *de Sancto Johanne* was living at Tawstock in 1330 and 1333 (*SR*). There was an ancient chapelry here of the Knights Templars, later of St John of Jerusalem, who have also left their trace in the parish in a farm called Templeton. Cf. Templeton *infra* 394.

SHORLEIGH (6") is found as the first part of the name *Shordelelane* 1390 Cl). Professor Ekwall notes that *shorde* is a ME form of OE *sceard*, 'notch, gap.'

SMEMINGTON is *Smimington* 1765 D and is probably identical with *Smythenaton* 1333 SR (p), -*ene-* t. Ed 3 *Ass* (p). If so, the first element is identical with that noted under Smithacott *supra* 93.

BRIDGETOWN, CLEAVE COPSE (6″), ROWDEN BARTON (6″), UPCOTT and WEEK were probably the homes of Alicia *atte Brugge* (1330 *SR*), Thomas *atte Clyve* (1333 *SR*), Philip de *Rowedon* (1330 *SR*), John de *Uppecote* (1333 *SR*) and Richard de *Wyke* (ib.). *v.* clif, ruh, dun, cot(e), wic.

BIRBROOK is *Bourbrok* 1330 *SR* (p), *v.* bur. The exact sense here is uncertain. CHARLACOTT is *Cherlecote* 1227 Ch, *Churlecote* 1330 *SR* (p), *v.* ceorl, cot(e). COLLABEAR is *Colebe(a)re* 1292 *Ass*, 1330 *SR* (p), *Collebiare* 1313 Exon (p). 'Colla's wood,' *v.* bearu. COMBE is *Combe* 1390 Cl. COMBER'S CROSS (6″) and WEEK are probably to be associated with the family of Robert and John *Comer* (1525 *SR*). CORFFE LODGE (6″) is *Corfe* 1755 *FF*. FISHLEY BARTON is *Fisshelegh* 1390 Cl. Cf. Fishleigh *infra* 143. The place is by the river Taw. HARRACOTT is *Harecote* 1330 *SR* (p), 1390 Cl. As the place is not near the parish boundary the first element must be either har in the sense of 'gray' or OE *hara*, 'hare.' HELE is *Hele* 1227 Ch, (*juxta Fremyngton*) 1339 *Ass*, *v.* healh. HERTON is *Hurdeton* 1330, 1333 *SR* (p), *Herton* 1392 AD vi, *v.* tun. The first element may be the gen. pl. of OE *heord*, 'flock, herd,' or hierde, 'shepherd.' HILDREW is *Hullerewe* 1330 *SR* (p), *Hilrewe* 1390 Cl. The name may have referred to a row of dwellings on the hill here. HOLLICK is *Holelake* 1399 *Ct.* 'Stream in the hollow,' *v.* holh, lacu. HOLY WELL is *Halghewillemede* 1390 Cl. LAKE is *Lake* 1390 Cl and was the home of Henry *atte Lake* (1330 *SR*), *v.* lacu. LANGHAM COTTAGES (6″) is *Langeham* 1227 Ch (p). 'Long ham(m).' MUZE (6″) was the home of Walter *atte Muse* (1333 *SR*). It is OE *mēos*, 'moss,' with the usual Devon u for *eo*. NOTTISTON is *Noteston* 1227 Ch, *Notteston* 1333 *SR* (p). 'Hnott's farm,' *v.* tun. Cf. Natsley *supra* 58. PILL is *the Pulle* 1390 Cl. 'Creek,' *v*, pyll. PRISTACOTT is *Prestecote* 1292 *Ass* (p), *Prustecote* 1333 *SR* (p). 'Priests' cot(e).' ROUNDSWELL is *Roundshill* 1675 Ogilby. RUSHCOTT is *Ridescote* 1227 Ch, *Radescote* 1292 *Ass* (p), *Rodescote* 1330 *SR* (p). SIDEHAM is *Sydenham* 1292 *Ass* (p), 'wide ham(m),' cf. Sydenham *infra* 209. TADIPORT (6″) is *Tadieport* 1330, 1333 *SR* (p). Cf. Taddiport *supra* 111. TENNA-

COTT is *Tunecote* 1227 Ch, *Tonne-* 1330 *SR* (p), *Tona-* 1333 *SR* (p). Probably '*Tun(n)a*'s cot(e).' VELLACOTT (6″) may be identical with *Wylyngcote* 1333 *SR* (p), hence '*Willa*'s cot(e),' *v.* ing. For interchange of *w* and *v*, *v.* Introd. xxxv.

Great Torrington

GREAT TORRINGTON[1] 127 B 10

> *Tori(n)tona* 1086 DB *et freq* to 1246 Ipm with variant spellings
> *Tory-*, *Thorin-*, *Tirinton* t. Hy 2 BM
> *Thorich* 1249 FF
> *Chippingtoriton* 1284 *Ass*, *Chepingtoryton juxta Were Giffard* 1316 *Ass*
> *Torytone Magna* 1366 Exon, *Turytone magna* 1370 Exon, *Mochel Torynton* 1443 FF

'Farm by the Torridge,' *supra* 14. 'Great' to distinguish from Little Torrington *supra* 110. 'Chipping,' i.e. with a market, *v.* cieping.

SHALLOWFORD COTTAGE (6″) is *Sholoford mill* 1371 Cl. This gives us an earlier form for the common word *shallow* than any hitherto recorded (*v.* NED *s.v.*).

BEAM MANSION is *la Beme* 1244 *Ass* (p), *Beme* 1424 IpmR. 'At the tree,' *v.* beam. BLAGDON (6″) is *Blakedon* 1244 *Ass* (p), 1531 Recov. 'Dark hill,' cf. Blagdon *supra* 77. CADDYWELL (6″) is *Cadewilpark juxta Chepingtoriton* 1310 *Ass*, *Cadewille park* 1371 Cl. '*Cada*'s spring,' *v.* wielle. CASTLE HILL, cf. *Castelwyke* 1371 Cl, *v.* wic. COOMBE is *la Cumbe* 1310 FF (p), *Combe* 1443 FF. HIGHER DARRACOTT is *Doddecote* 1322 FF, *Dodecote* 1330 SR (p). '*Dodda*'s cot(e),' cf. Darracott *supra* 43, 80. FURZE is *la Furze* 1244 *Ass* (p), *Forse* 1374 FF. HATCH MOOR is *Hatchmore* 1628 FF, *v.* hæcc. MOORTOWN is *More* 1475 IpmR, *v.* mor. NORWOOD (6″) is *Northwode* 1244 *Ass* (p), 1443 FF, *Bynorthewode* 1330 SR (p). 'North of the wood.' PRIESTACOTT MOOR is *Prestcot* 1281 *Ass* (p). 'Priests' cot(e).' SCHOOL LANE (6″), cf. *la Scolehouse* 1485 Ipm. WEEK, ALLEN'S, LITTLE (6″) and MIDDLE (6″) is *Wyk(e)* 1244 *Ass* (p), 1485 Ipm, *v.* wic. WOODHOUSE (6″), cf. *la Wode juxta Cheppinggetoryngton* 1306 *Ass*.

[1] CORNMARKET STREET is probably identical with *Cornstrete* 1345 DA 33. NEW STREET is *Nywestrete* 1434 IpmR. SOUTH STREET is *Southstreat* 1561 Deed. WELL STREET is *Wyllstreate* 1585 Deed.

Westleigh

WESTLEIGH 118 H 3

> Leia 1086 DB, *Weslega* 1086 DB, *Westlegh* 1238 FF, (*juxta Bideford*) 1303 *Ass*
>
> v. leah. 'West' to distinguish from Eastleigh *infra*.

EASTLEIGH is *Leia* 1086 DB, *Estlegh* 1242 Fees 792.

TAPELEY is *Tapeleia* 1086 DB, 1195 FF, *Tappeleg(he)* 1177 P (p) *et freq* to 1314 Exon. '*Tæppa*'s leah,' cf. Taplow PN Bk 231.

TREYHILL may be identical with *Ryhylle* 1281 *Ass* (p), the *t* being due to the common prefixing of the preposition *at*, v. Tapps *infra* 388. If so the meaning is simply 'rye hill.'

COMBE (6″), HILL HEAD (6″), SOUTHCOTT and WEACH BARTON were probably the homes of Matilda *atte Combe* (1330 *SR*), Richard *atte Hille* (1333 *SR*), Walter de *Southcote* (ib.) and Roger *atte Wyche*, i.e. 'at the wych elm' (1330 *SR*), v. cot(e), wice.

ASHRIDGE is *Aysshrygge* 1499 Ipm. BARNACOTT (6″) is *Bad(d)ing(e)-cot* 1229 Cl, 1229 FF (p), *Baddyngcote* 1286 *Ass*, 1330 *SR* (p). 'cot(e) of *Bad(d)a* or of *Bad(d)a*'s people,' v. ing. BRADAVIN is *Bradefenne* 1244 *Ass* (p), 1333 *SR* (p), -*vyne* 1330 *SR* (p). 'Wide marsh,' v. brad, fenn. MILLROW (6″) is *Milrew* 1658 FF, v. ræw. PILLHEAD is *Pilleheade* 1333 *SR* (p). It is at the top of a valley opening into the Torridge estuary, v. pyll. SYNCOCK'S CROSS (6″) is to be associated with the family of John *Symcock* (1544 *SR*).

VI. BLACK TORRINGTON HUNDRED

> *Toritone* 1084 Geld Roll, *Blachetoriton* 1167, 1168, 1175 P, *Blaketorrintun'* 1219 Fees 765
>
> v. Black Torrington *infra* 170.

Abbots Bickington

ABBOTS BICKINGTON 127 D 7

> *Bicatona* 1086 DB
> *Bechatona* 1189 (1465) Oliver 207
> *Bukyngton(e)* 1291 Tax, 1340 *SR*, *Bukynton* 1333 *SR*

Abbots Bekenton 1580 *Deed, Bekington al. Abbotsbekington*
1636 *Deed*

v. tun. The manor was held by Hartland Abbey already in 1189.
There are a large number of names in Devon which in their early
forms show a first element *Bike-, Byke-, Biche-* and the like, with
occasional *Bichen-, Byken-* and (more rarely) *Biching-, Byking-*,
the last being as a rule not found before the 13th cent. Some
of these names show *Buk-* forms (and the like) sporadically.
Others show such fairly persistently. The natural explanation of
these names is to take them as containing the gen. sg. of the
OE pers. names *Bic(c)a* or *Beocca* (*Biocca*), both of which are
well recorded from south-western England. *Beocca* is on record
from Dorset and is also clearly found in *beoccan brycg,* in the
Thorndon Hall charter (*infra* 296, n. 1). *Biche* was still used as
a Devon pers. name in DB. Presumably the names with persistent *Buk-* go back to OE *Beocca*, while those with occasional
Buk- go back rather to OE *Bic(c)a*, the *u* being due to labial
influence. *Bek-*forms (and the like) probably go back to OE
Beocca. It may be noted that the distribution of place-names
with initial *Bick-*, commonest in Devon and then next most frequent in Somerset, Hampshire and Wiltshire, corresponds to the
distribution of the pers. name as found in early documents. The
ing- forms may all be late developments but it may be noted that
already in the OE period we have in close proximity Bighton
(Ha), *Bicincgtun* BCS 1045, and *Bican hyrst* BCS 596. Blomé's
suggestion (58) for the *Buk-*names of a compound of *bīecn*, a
mutated form of *bēacen* (probably a back-formation from the
vb. *bīecnan*), fits neither the forms nor the general topography of
these places. There are as many in valleys as there are on hills.
He suggests for the *Bik-*names ME *bike*, 'bee-hive,' but here he
has misunderstood Zachrisson's comments on that word in
ZONF iv. 247. Zachrisson takes *bike* to be a ME back-formation
from the agent noun *bikere* and it cannot therefore be used in
explanation of names found already in Domesday, quite apart
from difficulties of form and sense involved in finding this word
in so many Devon p.n.'s.

CULSWORTHY (6″)

Colteshorda 1086 DB (Exch), *-worde* (Exch), *Colteswurða*

1175 P *et freq* to 1333 *SR* with variant spellings -*worth*,
-*worthi*
Culteswurth 1250 Fees 1426

'*Colt*'s farm,' *v.* worþig. *Colt* is not recorded as a pers. name,
but the name of the animal may well have been so used. Already
in OE we have a p.n. *coltan beorh* (BCS 734, an original charter),
which shows a weak pers. name formed from this word.

CHOLLATON is *Chalvedon* 1330 *SR* (p), 1504 Ipm. 'Calves' hill,'
v. dun. YOULDON (6") is *Yaldedon* 1249 *Ass.* 'Old hill,' i.e.
'long under cultivation,' cf. Youlden *supra* 79.

Ashbury

ASHBURY 127 J 11

   Esseberie 1086 DB, -*biry* 1223 Pat
   Asebiria 1136 France, *Assebure* 1238 *Ass*, *Ashbiry* 1291 Tax
   Aissebyri 1274 Exon, *Aysshebyry* 1276 Cl

'burh by the ashtree,' *v.* æsc, burh. There are no remains of
any earthworks here now.

SCOBCHESTER is *Scobbechestre* 1242 Fees 788, 1303 FA, 1330 *SR*
(p), *Scobe-* 1378 IpmR, *Scobchester* 1500 Ipm. Blomé (135)
quotes the probable parallels *scobbanora* (BCS 932) and *scobban
byrgels* (KCD 673) in illustration of the first element, which must
be an unrecorded pers. name *Sc(e)obba*; the second is ceaster,
but nothing is known of any early fortification here. For initial
sc, v. Introd. xxxv.

WADLAND BARTON is *Wadeland* 1244 *Ass*, -*lond(e)* 1270, 1288
Ass. Cf. Wadland in Liskeard (Co), *Wadelond* 1333 *FF*, and
Wadfast in Whitstone (Co), *Wadefeste* DB, *Wadefast* 1303,
Wadvast 1346 FA. As all these three places are by streams the
first element may be OE wæd, 'ford.' In the case of the first
two, OE wad, 'woad,' is also possible though the persistent
medial *e* suggests that in the Devon name at any rate we may
have the pers. name *Wada*.

BLAGDON is *Blakedon* 1458 *FF*. 'Dark hill,' *v.* blæc, dun.
PINNACLE is *Pynkhulle* 1359 *Ass*, *Pynacle* 1612 *Recov.* Probably
'*Pinca*'s hill,' the later form being corrupt. Cf. Pinkworthy
infra 388.

Ashwater

ASHWATER 137 A 6

Aissa 1086 DB
Esse Valteri 1270 Exon, *Esshe fil Walteri* 1281 *Ass, Essefitz-walteri* 1302 BM, *Asshefitz Wauter* 1327 Banco
Aswalter 1285 FA, *Essewautier* 1311 Exon (p), *Essewalter* 1326 Ipm, *Aysshewater* 1385 BM
Exe t. Ed 1-2 BM

v. æsc. *Walter* may have been *Walter* de Doneheved who held the manor in 1270 (Exon). The manor seems to have been first named after one Walter and then after his son, who presumably bore the same name. Cf. Bridgwater (So), *Brugie* DB, *Brug' Walteri* 1155-8 (1334) Ch, *Brigewauter* 1248 Ass.

ARSCOTT is *Ayshcote* 1330, *Arscote* 1333 *SR* (p). One might possibly compare Arscott *infra* 147 were it not that in the latter name *Ars-* is clearly a late corruption of *Ash-*. In this name it is difficult to see how *Ars-* arose already in the first half of the 14th cent. Possibly the first form is corrupt and the first element may be ersc, hence, 'cottage by the earsh-land.' We may, at least in the second Arscott, have the common Devon dialectal development of [æʃ] to [ɑ·ʃ] found in *splash, wash* and *ash* itself. Cf. Arson *infra* 356 and Ash in Parkham *supra* 105.

GRINDSWORTHY is *Gryndeworthi* 1330 *SR* (p), *Gryndesworthy* 1516 *Recov.* Blomé's first suggestion (135) that we have here the OE pers. name *Grind* is perhaps the most likely, though the authority for that name is not very strong and its origin disputed (Björkman ZEN 39). Blomé's alternative derivation from OE **grinde*, 'gravel, shingle,' does not suit the locality (*ex inf.* the Rev. G. D. Melhuish).

HENFORD is *Hindefort* 1086 DB, *-ford* 1238, 1244 *Ass, Hynde-* 1242 Fees 794, *Hynte-* 1238 *Ass.* 'Hinds' ford.'

QUODITCH is *Quidhiwis* 1249 *Ass* (p), *-hiwische* 1318 Exon (p), *Quydiche* 1609 FF, *Cowditch* 1765 D. This is probably a compound of OE *cwēad*, 'dung, filth,' and hiwisc, 'land to support a family,' hence perhaps 'dirty land' or 'well-manured land.' Cf. Quidhampton (PN W 138), Quidhampton (Ha), *Quedamtone* 1337 Ch, and Quither *infra* 216.

VIZA was the home of John de *la Vise* (1330 *SR*), de *la Vyse* (1333 *SR*). Elsewhere in the county we have Vizacombe *infra* 151 and Vyse Wood in Morthoe for which no early forms have been noted. Outside Devon occur Devizes (PN W 69), which stood close to the meeting of the boundaries separating two of the bishop's manors from one of the king's, the precincts of the castle lying in two separate hundreds (Gentleman's Magazine 1863, pp. 475 ff.). We may note further Pipewell Abbey (Nth), referred to in 1143 (Dugd v, 434) as *Sancta Marie de Divisis*, which is on the boundaries of Rothwell and Corby Hundreds. We have pers. names *atte Vise* (1327 *SR*) (W), *atte Vyse* (1327 *SR*) (W), *atte Vyse* (1332 *SR*) (K) and *de la Vise* 1287 *Ass* (Herts). Of the three Devon places, Vyse Wood is on the borders of the parishes of Morthoe and West Down. The other two places are not near the parish boundary, but may have been on the dividing line between the manors of Ashwater and Henford, and Inwardleigh and Curworthy respectively. It is clear that in all the names we have a short form of OFr *devise*, 'division, boundary,' as suggested by Ekblom (PN W loc. cit.).

BRADDON, BURROW[1], HEATH (6″), LANGAFORD, NORTHEND (6″) and VENN were probably the homes of William de *Braddon* (1330 *SR*), Richard *atte Burghe* (id.), John de *la Hethe* (1333 *SR*), Gilbert de *Langeford* (1238 *Ass*), John de *Northende* (1333 *SR*), and Philip de *la Fenne* (id.). *v.* brad, dun, beorg, lang, fenn. There is a tumulus by Burrow.

BLAGATON is *Estblakedon* 1330 *SR* (p). 'Dark hill,' cf. Blagdon *supra* 77. CLAWFORD is *Clouford(a)* 1330 *SR* (p), 1362 *Ass*, *v.* Clawton *infra* 138. CLAW MOOR is *Clawmoore* 1663 *Recov*, *v.* Clawton *infra* 138. EASTDOWN is *Estdowne* 1592 *SR*. HEGGADON is *Heghedon(e)* 1330, 1333 *SR* (p). Possibly 'high hill,' *v.* heah, dun. For the modern *g*, cf. Wagaford *infra* 171. HUNSCOTT is *Hunescote* 1249 *Ass* (p), *Hunscote* 1451 IpmR. '*Hūn*'s cot(e).' LARKWORTHY is *Leverekewurth* 1244 *Ass*, *Leverkeworthi* 1330 *SR* (both p). 'Lark farm,' *v.* worþig. LUCKCROFT is *Lokcroft* 1322 *Ass*, -*krofte* 1329 *Ass*, *Lukcrofte* 1330 *SR* (all p). The first element is possibly OE loc(a), 'enclosure.' MOORHAY is *Morehay* 1464 *FF* and MORCOMBE WOOD is *Morcomb(e)* 1333

---

[1] *Boroughes* 1624 *Recov.*

SR (p), 1491 Ipm. *v.* mor, (ge)hæg, cumb. MUCKWORTHY is *Mokeworth(y)* 1423, 1451 IpmR, *Muck-* 1611 *Recov.* '*Mocca*'s or *Muca*'s worþig.' HIGHER PRESTACOTT is *Prustecote* 1337 Pat, *Pristacott* 1621 *Recov.* 'Priests' cot(e).' RENSON is *Raynston* 1621 *Recov.* STATFOLD is *Stottefold* 1500 Ipm, *Weststatfold* 1621 *Recov.* 'Bullock enclosure,' *v.* stott, fal(o)d. SWINGDON is *Swyndon* 1296 *Ass* (p). 'Swine hill,' *v.* dun. WESTDOWN is *le Wesdone al. la Done* 1302 BM.

Beaworthy

BEAWORTHY [bɑueri] 127 H 9

Begeurda 1086 DB, *Begehworth(i)* 1285 FA
Beghworthy 1242 Fees 788, *Begheworthy* 1359 Exon
Beworthy 1281 *Ass*, 1316 FA, 1339, 1345 *Ass*, *-the* 1291 Tax, *-thi* 1323 Exon
Beuworthi 1340 *Ass*, *-y* 1346 FA, *Beworthy vulgo Bowery* 1765 D

'Farm of *Bǣga* or *Bēaga*,' *v.* worþig. Cf. Richard *Beagha*, a juror in Kenton (D) in 1275 (RH).

BEAMSWORTHY is *Baldemundeswurthe* 1249 *Ass*, *Bealmundesworthi* 1318 *Ass*, *Balmandesworth* 1333 *SR* (p), *Bealmesworthy* 1418 *Ass*. '*Bealdmund*'s farm,' *v.* worþig.

BURDEN is *Buredon* 1262 FF, *Byrydon* 1330 *SR* (p), *Byri-* 1314, 1343 BM. The place is on the hill crowned by Broadbury Castle and it is probable that the dun took its name from this earthwork. *v.* burh.

HIGH HAYNE (6″) was the home of Martin de *la Heghen* (1333 *SR*). Names in *hayes, hayne* are found throughout Devon and are especially common in the south-east of the county. They probably all derive from ME *hay*, OE (ge)hæg, 'enclosure.' Since in the east of the county the element is as a rule compounded with the name of a medieval owner, or is added at a late stage to some already existing monosyllabic p.n. such as Stone, Coombe, Wood, Ford, etc., it is likely that in nearly all cases we have to do with names of ME origin in which the word had come to have little more than the sense of 'farm' or 'holding' (cf. the manorial use of *bury* in Ess, Herts and Mx and EPN *s.v.* burh). Thus Alexanderhayes *infra* 616 is better rendered 'Alexander's farm' or 'holding,' than 'enclosures.' The variation between forms *heghes* and *heghen* in ME has usually been explained as due to alternation between nom. pl. and dat. pl. (OE *gehægum*). Such frequent use of a dative plural in place-names has no parallel outside Anglian and Anglo-Scandinavian England (cf. Mawer, *Problems of Place Name Study* 14) and considering the late origin of most of these names would be remarkable anywhere. Rather, the form *heghen* is to be taken as the weak plural of *hegh*, existing side by side with the more common and regular *heghes*. Such might well be found in Devon where ME weak forms are specially common (cf. also Willing, Pitten, Fursdon *infra* 263, 278, 311). *v.* Introd. xxxvi.

MADWORTHY is *Mad(d)eworth* 1270, 1285 *Ass*, *-wrthy* 1286 *Ass*, *Madeford* 1303 FA. The pers. name *Mada* is not on independent record but is found in Madeley (St), earlier *Madanlieg* (BCS 1312), Madingley (PN C 67) and Madington (PN W 119). Cf. OGer *Mado* (Förstemann PN 1108). It would be a regular pet-form for a *Mæð*-name. Hence 'Mada's farm,' *v.* worþig.

MANSDITCH is *Manship(p)esdich(e)* 1333 *SR* (p), 1339, 1340 *Ass*, *Manyspesdyche* 1458 FF. This is a compound of OE *(ge)mænscipe*, 'community,' and dic, hence 'ditch or dyke marking off the land of such'; it is by the parish and hundred boundary. Cf. the use of *gemænness* in Sussex (PN Sx 536, 560). The dic may be the main Holsworthy-Okehampton road, which here forms the parish boundary. The farm lies by this road.

MELBURY (6") is *Meleberia* 1086 DB, *-bir* 1238 *Ass*, *-bery* 1303 FA, *Mellebir* 1238 *Ass*, *Milbury* 1428 FA. *v. s.n.* Meldon *infra* 203.

ALDERFORD, PRESTACOTT and VENN were probably the homes of Roger de *Allerford* (1330 *SR*), John de *Prustecote* (1330 *SR*) and Henry de *la Fenne* (1339 *Ass*), *v.* preost, cot(e), fenn.

BROADBURY DOWN is *Brodebury* 1440 *FF*, *Broadbury Down* 1791 *Recov*, *v.* burh. There is an ancient camp here. BROADMOOR COTTAGES (6") is *Brademore* 1310 Seld 22. COXWALL is *Cokkys-wall* 1330 SR, *Cokes-* 1333 SR (p), *Cokys-* 1458 FF. 'Cocc's wall.' As this is close by Broadbury Castle, the 'wall' may be some part of its outworks. PATCHACOTT is *Pec(c)hecote* 1250 Misc(p), 1256 *Ass, Pacchecote al. Pashecote* 1389 IpmR, *Paysshecote* 1424 IpmR. '*Pæcca*'s cot(e),' cf. Patcham (PN Sx 293). TUTCHENOR (6″) is *Twychene juxta Beworth* 1288 *Ass*. 'Crossways,' *v.* Twitchen *supra* 57. Final *or* is a vulgarisation of final syllabic *e*. Cf. Introd. xxxvi. WEEKS-IN-THE-MOOR is probably identical with *Weekemore* 1631 *FF, v.* wic, mor. It has a damp and bleak situation near Venn Down. WIGDON (6″) is *Wyggedon* 1458 *FF*. Cf. Wiggadon *supra* 116.

Belstone

BELSTONE 137 A 13

> *Bellestam* (sic) 1086 DB
>
> *Belstana* 1166 LN, *Belestan* 1167 P, 1231 Pat (p), 1254 FF, *Belestone* 1259 Exon, *Belston* 1292 Ipm
>
> *Ballestan* 1238 *Ass*

A compound of OE *belle*, 'bell,' and stan. According to LGS 96, "the bellstone was a remarkably fine logan rock that rolled like a ship in a gale....It has been thrown down and broken up by quarrymen."

LAKE, EAST and WEST, is *La Lake juxta Belston* 1285 *Ass* and was the home of *Simon atter Lake* 1333 SR, *v.* lacu. PRIESTACOTT is *Prestacoats* 1725 Recov, *v.* preost, cot(e).

Bradford

BRADFORD 127 F 8

> *Bradefort* 1086 DB, *-ford(e)* 1242 Fees 784, 796, *Bradafford* 1346 FA
>
> *Brodford* 1524 SR

'Wide ford,' over the Torridge.

BASON is *Baddestan* 1244 *Ass, -stone* 1249 *Ass* (p), *Badeston* 1333 SR (p), *Bedeston* 1330 SR (p). '*Bad(d)a*'s stone.'

DUNSLAND Ho and CROSS

> *Doneslanda* 1086 DB, *-laund* 1286 *Ass* (p)
>
> *Dunneslond* 1229 Pat, *-lande* 1412 FF, *Dunesland* 1238, 1244 *Ass* (p), *Dunsland Crosse* 1532 Dartmoor

'*Dun(n)*'s land,' cf. the same name *infra* 152.

HENSCOTT is *Hainghestecota, Engestecota* 1086 DB, *Hengestecoth'*
1242 Fees 772, *Heyng(e)stecote* 1244 *Ass* (p), 1330 *SR* (p),
Ynestecote 1303 FA, *Heynstecote* 1333 *SR* (p), *Endscot* 1809 M.
'Stallion cottages,' i.e. cottages near which such were kept.

LASHBROOK is *Lachebroc* 1086 DB (Exon), *Loche-* (Exch),
Lachebrok 1346 FA, *(Mulys)* 1444 IpmR, *Lec(c)hebrok* 1238 *Ass*,
1303, 1316, 1428 FA, 1378 IpmR. 'Sluggish stream,' *v.* lache,
broc. This was probably the nameless stream just south of the
farm. Cf. Lashbrook (PN O 143). John de *Molis* held the manor
in 1242, John de *Mules* in 1284.

RIGHTADOWN is *Rythtedon, Est-, Westritedon* 1244 *Ass, Westrhitte-
don* 1262 FF, *Ryghtadon* 1333 *SR* (p), *Estryghtedon* 1418 *Ass,
West Ryghtedon* 1429 *FF*. This must be a compound of OE *riht*,
'straight,' and dun, the name being descriptive of the long hill
here.

BOVACOTT is *Bovycott* 1542 *Deed, Bovacott* 1680 *FF*. FLARES is
Flayers 1462 IpmR and is probably to be associated with the
family of John *Floyer* (1330 *SR*). HIGHSTEAD is *Hestede* 1620
FF. 'High place,' *v.* stede. HOLEMOOR is *Holemore* 1623 *Ct*.
'Hollow marshy spot,' *v.* holh, mor. KENNELAND is *Kenelonde*
1330, *Kynalonde* 1333 *SR* (p). KITHILL is *Kytehele* 1284 *Ass*,
1333 *SR* (p). 'Kite nook,' *v.* healh. MIDDLECOTT was the home
of Henry de *Midelcote* (1333 *SR*), *v.* cot(e). PRIESTCOTT is
Prestecote 1352 Pat. 'Priests' cottage(s).' STADSON is *Stodesdon*
1249 *Ass* (p), *Stottesdon* 1284 *Ass* (p), *Stottys-* 1431 IpmR,
Stoddisdon 1485 Ipm. 'Hill of either the stod or the stott.'

Bradworthy

BRADWORTHY 127 D 5

    Bravordina 1086 DB (Exon), *Brawardine* (Exch), *Brawrthi*
    1196 FF, *-worthy* 1233 Cl

    Bradew(o)rth 1231 Pat, 1279 Ipm, *-worthi* 13th *Torre, Brad-
    worthy* 1461 IpmR

    Broworthon 1285 FA, *Brodworthie* 1524 *SR, Broadworthie*
    1605 Wills

    'Wide estate,' *v.* brad, worþign.

ALFARDISWORTHY [ɔ·lzəri]

> *Alfardesworth'* 1242 Fees 792, *Alfardisworth(y)* 1346 FA
> *Alfrydesworth(y)* 1270 *Ass*, *-fredes-* 1328 *FF*, *-frythes-* 1423 *FF*
> *Alferysworthy* 1316 FA, *Alfresworthe* 1379 IpmR, *Alsworthy*
>   1525 *Recov*

'*Aelfheard*'s worþig.'

ASH, EAST and WEST, is *Aissa* 1086 DB, *Eisse* 1196 FF, *Estere Esse, Westeresse* 1279 Ipm.

ATWORTHY is *Attewurth* 1228 FF, *-worth* 1242 Fees 791, *-wrthy* 1279 Ipm (p). '*Aetta*'s farm,' *v.* worþig.

BREXWORTHY

> *Bristeleshorda* 1086 DB (Exon), *Bristelsworde* (Exch),
>   *Brichteleswurða* 1167 P (p), *Brictenestworth* 1303 FA
> *Brighteneswych'* 1242 Fees 791, *-w(o)rthy* 1279 Ipm, 1316 FA,
>   *Britennysworthi* 1330 *SR* (p)

'*Beorhtel*'s worþ.' For this pers. name, *v.* Bricklehurst PN Sx 451. Some of the forms show common confusion of *l* and *n*.

HORTON is *Hortona* 1086 DB, *Hort(h)on* 1242 Fees 772, 1279 Ipm. 'Dirty farm,' *v.* horh, tun.

INSTAPLE

> *Esastapla* 1086 DB
> *Hethestapele* 1242 Fees 792
> *Henstaple* 1244 *Ass* (p), *Euestapel* (sic) 1303 FA, *Enstaple* 1314
>   Exon (p), *Yenstaple* 1314 Exon (p), 1431, 1458 IpmR

Professor Ekwall suggests OE *hǣðena-stapol* as the OE form of this name. One might interpret this as referring to some pillar or landmark which the Saxon invaders associated with earlier heathen worship. It may have stood on the site of the present Instaple Cross. *v.* stapol.

KIMWORTHY

> *Chemeworda* 1086 DB
> *Kimewrthi* 1219 *Ass*, *-wurth* 1228 FF, *Kymeworth* 1303 FA,
>   1330 *SR* (p)
> *Kemmeworth'* 1242 Fees 756, 773, *Kemworthy* 1390 Cl

'The worþig of one *Cyma*, or possibly *Cymma*,' a pet-form of *Cynemǣr* or some similar name.

LIMSCOTT

> *Lefwinescote* 1196 FF, *-wynes-* 1234 Fees 400, *Lywynescote* 1238 *Ass* (p), *Lewenescoth'* 1242 Fees 791, *Lyvenescot* 1275 RH (p)
> *Luwyniscot* 1279 Ipm, *Luwenescote* 1303 FA, *Luvenescote* 1333 *SR* (p), *Lunescote* 1428 FA (p)

'*Lēofwine*'s cot(e).' Cf. Lympstone *infra* 591.

REDMONSFORD (6″) is *Redefenneford* 1464 IpmR, *Redfenford* 1493 Ipm, (*or Redmansford*) 1634 *Deed*. 'Ford by the reed marsh,' *v*. fenn.

TRENTWORTHY (6″) is *Trentaworth* 1333 *SR*, *Trenteworthy* 1353 *Ass*, *Trende-* 1356 *Ass* (all p), *Trent Tree* 1765 D. The forms are too late for any satisfactory solution to be offered. There is no stream here, even if one could have a compound of worþig and a stream-name. It is just possible that the first element is OE *trendel*, 'circle,' hence 'circular enclosure.' The last form is evidently an attempt to represent the local pronunciation [trentəri], cf. Great Tree *infra* 433.

WRANGWORTHY (6″)

> *Wrangaworth* 1313 *Ass* (p), *Wrange(s)worth* 1320 *Ass*, 1333 *SR* (p), *-thi* 1360 *Ass* (p), *Wranggeworthy* 1492 Ipm

Presumably this is from OE *wrang*, 'crooked,' and worþ(ig), hence 'crooked enclosure.' Cf. Wrangaton *infra* 286.

EAST YOULSTONE is *Yulkesdon juxta Bradeworthy* 1353 *Ass*. Across the county boundary in Cornwall is West Youlstone, *Yulkesdon* 1302 *Ass*, *ʒolkesdone* 1310 Exon (p), *Yolkesdon* 1476 FF. The first element here is probably a late OE or early ME pers. name *Geoloc*, 'little yellow one.' Hence, '*Geoloc*'s dun.'

HEATH and WHITELY were probably the homes of John de *la Hethe* (1333 *SR*) and Ralph de *Whiteley* (1330 *SR*), *v*. leah.

BERRIDON is *Bearedon* 1333 *SR*, *Bera-* 1364 *Ass* (p), *v*. bearu, dun. BLATCHBOROUGH is *Blachesburgh* 1353 *Ass*, 1356 *FF*, *Blachborowe* 1581 *SR*. '*Blæcci*'s hill,' cf. Blachford *infra* 269. CLEVERDON is *Cleverdon* 1279 Ipm, 1330 *SR* (p). 'Clover hill,' *v*. clæfre, dun. DINWORTHY is *Dunneworth'* 1242 Fees 791,

Donnewrth' 1279 Ipm, *Donnaworthi* 1333 *SR* (p), *Dunworthy* 1499 Ipm. '*Dunna's* worþig.' WEST DOWN Ho is *Dune* 1242 Fees 791, *La Doune* 1279 Ipm. DURAL (6″) is *Durhille* 1330 *SR* (p), cf. Duerdon *supra* 82. FORD COTTAGES (6″) is *La Forde* 1279 Ipm. GREADON is *Graddon* 1330 *SR* (p). 'Great hill,' *v.* dun. HOLYROOD is *Hollowood* 1809 M, 1827 G. LEYLAND COTTAGES (6″) are probably on land called *La Leye* 1279 Ipm, *v.* leah. NEWLAND is *Niweland'* 1242 Fees 773, *Southnywelond juxta Holdesworthy* 1332 *Ass.* RYALL is *Ryhulle* 1279 Ipm. 'Rye hill,' cf. Royal Fm in Elsted (Sr), *Riehull* 1128 Dugd, *Ryhall* 1341 Pat. STOWFORD is *Stauford* 1238 *Ass*, *Stovorde* 1279 Ipm, *Stoneford* 1303 FA, *v.* Stowford *supra* 41. WATERLAND (6″) is *Waterlond* 1518–29 ECP 5, 546, *a justment called Waterlond* 1539 CtAugm, cf. Justment *infra* 449. WORDEN is *Worthy* 1242 Fees 791, *Northerewrthy, Suthewrth* 1279 Ipm, *la Worthyn* 1333 *SR* (p), 1410 *FF*, *Worthen* 1346 FA, *v.* worþign.

Bridgerule

BRIDGERULE[1] 127 G 4

> *Brige* 1086 DB, *Brugia* 1121 AC
>
> *Briggeroald* 1238 *Ass*, *Brigge Rowalde* 1291 Tax, *Bryggeruwel* 1393 Exon
>
> *Bruge Ruardi* 1242 Fees 787, *Brugeroward* 1281 *Ass*

The place takes its name from the *Ruald* who held the manor in 1086 (DB f. 411). The bridge is over the Tamar. Cf. Bridgwater (So) *s.n.* Ashwater *supra* 127.

LODGEWORTHY is *Lowdeswothe, Lowdeshowe, Ludeswothe, Loudesho, Lodishowe* 13th Launceston, *Lowdisworthie al. Ludsworthy* 1698 Recov. The second element in this name is probably worþ in spite of the confusion of the early forms. The first is the pers. name *Hlūd* found in OE *Hludesbeorh* (BCS 741), now Luddesdown (K). The name may, however, be of ME origin, from the corresponding ME surname *Lowde*.

TACKBEAR

> *Tacabeara* 1086 DB (Exon), *-bere* (Exch) *et passim* to 1400 Pat with variant spellings *Tacke-, Takke-* and *-bere*
>
> *Tekebeare* 1447 IpmR, *Tegebere* 1491 Ipm

[1] The part of Bridgerule parish lying to the west of the Tamar was formerly in Cornwall.

This p.n., Takeley (Ess), DB *Tacheleia*, and Tackley (O), DB *Tachelie*, *Takkelea* 1175 P, *Tackele* 1196 FF, suggest an OE pers. name *Tæcca*, probably a reduced form of the recorded *Tætica*, hence 'Tæcca's wood,' v. bearu.

FURZE (6″) and NORTON [nɔ·dən] were probably the homes of Thomas de *Forse* and Thomas de *Nordon* (1330 *SR*), and John de *Northdon* 1370 *Launceston*, v. norþ, dun.

BOROUGH is *Burewe* 1303 FA, *in Burgo* 1306 FA, *Burgh* 1428 FA, v. beorg. DUX is *Dok(h)ersh* 1330 SR (p), *Dux al. Duckis* 1676 FF. 'Duck ersc.' HOLLADON is *Holedon* 1333 *SR* (p). The farm is situated above a hollow area below a hill, v. holh, dun. KNOWLE is *Knolle* 1306, 1346 FA, v. cnoll. LITTLEBRIDGE is *Parvo Ponte* 1303, 1306 FA, *Lytelbrigge* 1417 IpmR. MERRIFIELD is *Murifeld* 1302 *Ass* (p), *Miryfeld* t. Ed 1 *Launceston* (p), *Meryfeld* 1427 *Ass*, v. Merrivale *infra* 247. NEWACOTT is *Niwecot* 1202 P, *Newecote* 1302 *Ass*. 'New cot(e).' SIMONSHAM (6″) [senzəm] is *Simondesham* 1303, 1346 FA, *Symundisham* 1306 FA, *Sensham* 1667 FF. '*Sige-mund*'s ham(m).' TATSON is *Tottesduna* t. Hy 2 (14th) *Launceston*, *Totesdon* 1249 *Ass* (p), *Tottesdon(e)* 1270 *Ass*, 1330 *SR* (p), '*Tott*'s hill,' v. dun.

Broadwood Kelly

BROADWOOD KELLY 127 F 14

> *Bradehoda* 1086 DB, -*wode* 1175 P
> *Brawode Kelly* 1261 Exon, *Brodwode Kelly* 1291 Tax, *Brode-wodkelle* 1346 FA

'Wide wood,' v. brad. The manor was held by William de *Kelly* in 1242 (Fees 784). He probably took his name from Kelly *infra* 184.

BRIXTON BARTON

> *Bristanestona* 1086 DB, *Bryxstaneston* 1270 *Ass*, *Brightenyston* 1333 *SR* (p), *Brixton* 1316 FA, *Brixiston* 1346 Pat (p)
> *Brigteneston'* 1242 Fees 784, *Bricsteneston* 1249 *Ass*, *Brex-teneston* 1285 FA, *Bryxsteneston* 1303 FA

'*Beorhtstān*'s tun.'

CORSTONE is *Corbineston* 1242 Fees 784, *Corbeston* 1373 IpmR,

Corpyston 1445 IpmR. It takes its name from Peter *Corbin* who held the manor in 1242. *v.* tun and IPN 118, 132.

INGLEIGH GREEN[1]

> *Genelie* 1086 DB, *-leye* 1263 Ipm
> *Jonelegh* 1242 Fees 788
> *Inneleghe* 1295 Ipm, *Yn(n)elegh* 1303, 1346 FA
> *Yennelegh* 1326 FF
> *Indeley* t. Eliz ChancP

Blomé (140) is possibly right in taking the first element here to be a pers. name *Gēana*, but the phonology of the later forms is difficult. *v.* leah.

LEWERSLAND is *Luwardeslond, Luuerdesland* 14th *Launceston, Luwardesland* 1660 *Recov,* '*Lēofweard*'s land.'

MIDDLECOTT is *Mildelcota* 1086 DB and was the home of Gilbert de *Middelcote* (1330 *SR*).

SPLATT. This is clearly the dialect word *splot(t), splat,* defined by the NED as 'plot of land' and by the EDD as 'a plot or little piece of ground,' used in this sense in Co, D, and So. It may be noted that the word occurs in Devon as early as the year 963 when we find *on clænan splott* in the land boundaries of Clyst St George, *v. infra* 585 n.

BARNTOWN and UPCOTT were probably the homes of William de *la Berne* (1318 *Ass*) and Alice de *Uppecote* (1330 *SR*), *v.* cot(e). For 'town,' *v. infra* 676.

CHUBHOUSE (6″) is *Chubbehowse* 1609 *FF*. CLARKE'S TOWN (6″) is *Clarkestone* 1563 *FF*, cf. Cliston *infra* 167, 316. HAWKSLAND is *Haukeslond* 1333 *SR* (p). HOGSLAND is *Hoggeslond* 1330 *SR* (p). MOISTOWN (6″) is probably to be associated with the family of John *Moys* (14th *Launceston*). EAST NETHERCOTT (6″) is *Nithercote juxta Brodewodekelly* 1318 *Ass*. PATTILAND (6″) is *Patlande* 1563 *FF*. REDHAYS is *Rodhey* 1563 *FF*. Perhaps 'enclosure by the reeds,' *v.* hreod, (ge)hæg. The place lies by a stream. TAYLOR'S DOWN is *Taylersdon* 1637 *FF*. WALSON is *Walston* 1563 *FF*. WOODCROFT is *Wodecrofte* 1494 *FF*, *v.* croft.

---

[1] Further trace of the old forms of this name seems to be found in YENNE PARK (6″) just to the east of Ingleigh.

Clawton

CLAWTON   127 J 6

Clauetona 1086 DB, *Clavatona* 1088 Totnes
Clauton' 1242 Fees 775 *et passim*

This place-name must clearly be considered together with
Clawford and Claw Moor *supra* 128, higher up the river Claw
supra 3, on which Clawton stands. This would suggest at first
sight that *Claw* must be a genuine river-name, otherwise one
has to assume a large measure of coincidence, but along with
these names must go Claw Cross *supra* 82, where we have uncompounded *Claw* and no possibility of a river, and Claw *infra*
381[1]. Cf. also the field and minor names *le Clawes* 1525 *AOMB*
(Woodbury, D), *ate Clauwe* (p) in a *SR* for 1332 (Sr), *la Clawe*
1336 Ipm (Martock, So), *le Clawe* 1326, 1510 *Ct* (Thorpe,
Sr). All these are against any river-name solution but point
equally clearly to some toponymic term. It can only be suggested
that the common OE *clawu* by some local custom was used in
Devon and elsewhere of land whose topography suggested a claw
or something cloven. It is impossible to discover the exact
application of the names now. Ekwall (RN 80) suggests that at
least in the case of Clawton the reference may be to a tongue of
land between two streams. If this is correct the stream-name is
a back-formation.

CROSWORTHY (lost)[2] is *Crosworthy* 1641 *Recov* and is probably to
be associated with the family of Robert de *Craftesworthy* (1322
Ass) and Baldwin de *Kraftesworthi* (1333 *SR*). This name is
probably of ME origin, with the ME surname *Craft* as a first
element (cf. Weekley, *Surnames* 219).

TINACRE is *Tinacre* 1239 FF, *Tyn-* 1242 Fees 775, *Tyne-* 1428
FA, *Tenaker* 1535 VE. 'Ten acres.' For *Tin-*, cf. Tinhead (W),
Tenhyde 1316 FA, and the old form of Teignhead *infra* 459-
60.

NORTH and SOUTH BEER, EASTACOMBE and FORDA COTTAGE (6")
were probably the homes of Hugo de *Bere* (1330 *SR*), Walter de

---

[1] There are also a Claw Copse in Huntshaw and in Tawstock, a Claw Moor
in Fremington and The Claws in Gidleigh.
[2] According to the Rev. G. D. Melhuish the name is preserved as *Crossery*,
a group of fields on Coffcott farm.

Estecombe (1330 *SR*) and Richard de *la Forde* (1238 *Ass*), *v.* bearu, cumb.

AFFALAND is *Affelanda* 1175 P (p), *Affelond* 1457 IpmR. '*Æffa*'s land.' BLAGDON is *Blakedon(e)* 1238 *Ass* (p), 1242 Fees 775. 'Dark hill.' CHOLCH is possibly identical with *Chollyswyk* 1330 *SR* (p). Cf. Cholwich *infra* 269. COFFCOTT GREEN [kɔˈkət] is *Coffyncott* 1544 *SR*, *Corfingcott* 1595 *Churchwardens Accounts*[1], *Coscott* (sic) 1641 *Recov.* EASTDOWN is *Byestedone* 1242 Fees 775. 'East of the down.' FERNHILL is *Fernhille* 1242 Fees 775. GUNNACOTT is *Godenecote* 1330 *SR* (p), *Gunnacott* 1690, *Gonna-* 1693 *FF.* Possibly '*Godwine*'s cot(e),' but the material is insufficient for certainty. HERDICOTT is *Hurdecote* 1281 *Ass* (p), *Herdacott* 1641 *Recov.* 'Shepherds' cot(e),' cf. Herdwick *infra* 149. HORSLETT is *Horseland* 1765 D, 1809 M. KEMPTHORNE is *Kymethorn(e)* 1238 *Ass* (p), 1242 Fees 775, 1303 FA, *Kymel-* 1346 FA. '*Cyma*'s thorntree,' cf. Kimworthy *supra* 133. KENNICOTT is *Kennycott* 1586 *Recov*, cf. Kennacott *supra* 51, 114. LANGDON is *Langedon* 1333 SR (p), 1418 IpmR. 'Long hill,' *v.* dun. LAYHAY is *Lehay* 1765 D. LEWORTHY is *Loveworth'* 1242 Fees 775, 1341 Ipm, *-thy* 1345 *Ass*, *Leuwurth* 1249 *Ass*. '*Lēofa*'s farm,' *v.* worþig. NORTHDOWN is *Northdowne* 1641 *Recov.* SELLICK is *Sallack* 1610 *FF*, *Zellake* 1628 *Deed*, *v.* lacu. WESTDOWN is *Westerdoune* 1641 *Recov.*

Cookbury

COOKBURY   127 F 8

> *Cukebyr'* 1242 Fees 788
>
> *Kokebyry* 1270 *Ass*, *Cokebiry* 1291 Tax, *-bery* 1303 FA, *-bury* 1420 IpmR

'*Cuc(c)a*'s burh.' This pers. name is not on record but is apparently found in *cucanhealas* (BCS 936) in a Gloucestershire charter. Cf. also *cuceleshylle* (KCD 741) in a Dorsetshire charter, involving apparently a diminutive of this name.

COOKBURY WICK is *Wicha* 1086 DB, *Wika* 1198 FF, *Cokebury-wike* 1420 IpmR, *v.* wic. Probably the dairy farm of Cookbury.

HALSDON BARTON is *Halesdon(e)* 1242 Fees 788, (*juxta Haldes-*

[1] *Ex inf.* Rev. G. D. Melhuish.

wrth') 1295 *Ass*, Halsdon 1303 FA, 1333 *SR* (p). This is probably
a compound of OE *heals*, 'neck,' and *dun*. Halsdon is on a hill
lying between two valleys. Cf. Halsbury *supra* 104 and Addenda
lviii.

VAGLEFIELD

> *Faklefeld* 1238 *Ass* (p)
> *Fagelefenne* 1242 Fees 788
> *Faggelefeld* 1244 *Ass*, *Fagle*- 1303 FA, *Fagheles*- 1244 *Ass*, *Fa-*
>   *gele*- 1311 Exon (p), *Fagil*- 1340 *Ass* (p), *Faggales*- 1346 FA
> *Falighfeld* 1428 FA

Blomé (141) suggests that the first element is a metathesised
form of OE *fealh*, ME *falegh*, 'fallow,' but such metathesis, even
if it were possible, could not yield *Fakle*- or *Fagele*-. More probably it is the diminutive *Fæccela* of the pers. name *Facca* found
in Faccombe (Ha), *Faccancumb* Thorpe 534, and *Faccanlea* (Wa),
BCS 1232. Cf. *Fache* in the Selby Cartulary i, 205, 224 (13th)
and OGer *Facho*, *Fachil*(*o*) (Förstemann PN 493). Intervocalic
k is often voiced to *g*.

STAPLEDON is *Stapeldun* 1228 FF, -*don* 1242 Fees 788. 'Hill
marked by a post or boundary-mark of some kind,' *v.* stapol,
dun. UPCOTT is *Uppecoth*' 1242 Fees 788. 'High cot(e),' *v.* uppe.

Exbourne

EXBOURNE 127 H 14

> *Hechesburne*, *Etcheborna* 1086 DB (Exon), *Echeburne* (Exch)
> *Yekesburn*(*e*) 1242 Fees 784, 1292 Ipm, -*bourne* 1292 Cl,
>   *Yekkes*- 1242 Fees 789, *Yeks*- 1297 Pat
> *Hecesburn*(*e*) 1266 Exon, *Ekes*- 1285, 1303 FA, -*borne* 1291
>   Tax
> *Ikysbourne* 1375 Exon
> *Axbourne* 1740 FF

Blomé (141) is probably right in interpreting this as 'cuckoo's
stream' from OE *gēac* and burna. We might have expected some
ME forms in *Yak*(*k*)*es*-, cf. Yaxley (PN BedsHu 202), but
Professor Ekwall notes that late WS *ēa* tended to become *ē*
not only before *c* but also after *g*.

BUSKIN is *Busken* 1353 *Ass* and was the home of Nicholas *atte*

Busken (1329 *Ass*), *atte Bosken* (1330 *SR*). This is the weak plural *busken* of *busk*, from a lost OE *busc*, 'wood.' See further PN BedsHu 227 *s.n.* Warboys and p. xli of the same volume.

COXWELL is *Cokkyswall* 1330 *SR* (p), *-kes-* 1377 Cl, *Cokyswill* 1461 IpmR. This may be '*Cocc*'s spring' or 'spring of the (wood)cock,' though as Wallenberg notes (StudNP 2, 98), the *wall*-forms suggest OE *weall*[1]. In that case the sense is obscure. It has a parallel, possibly more easily explicable, in Coxwall *supra* 130.

HOLE FM, NARRACOTT, and WOODHALL were probably the homes of Richard *atte Hole*, Stephen de *Northcote* and Stephen *atte Wodehall* (1330 *SR*), *v.* holh, cot(e), heall.

CHATTAFIN is *Chatevenne* 1330 *SR* (p). '*Ceatta*'s fenn.' SHILSTONE is *Shilston by Okhampton* 1464 Pat, *v.* Shilstone *infra* 433. SWANSTONE is so spelt in 1685 *FF*. WATERHOUSE is so spelt in 1738 *Recov.*

Halwill

HALWILL   127 H 8

> *Halgewilla* 1086 DB, *-wille* 1291 Tax, *Halga-* 1285 FA
> *Haliwill* 1228 FF, *Halywell* 1296 Ipm
> *Hal(e)ghewill(e)* 1242 Fees 778, 1283 Exon, (*juxta Blake-toriton*) 1318 *Ass*, *Halleghwille* 1355 Exon

The place takes its name from a 'holy well' which still exists, with the ruins of a chapel by it (LGS).

BRENDON is *Bremdon* 1330 *SR* (p). Perhaps 'bramble down,' *v.* Brendon *supra* 58. CROFT is *Crofte juxta Haleghewill* 1288 *Ass*, *v.* croft. FOXHOLE is *Fox(h)ole* 1238 *Ass*, 1333 *SR* (p). HALWILL MOOR is *Halgewilmore* 1269 FF. HENDERBARROW is *Hyndeburgh* 1330 *SR*, *-bury* 1333 *SR* (p). 'Hinds' hill,' *v.* beorg. STOWFORD is *Stonford* 1309 Cl (p), *Stouford juxta Begheworth* 1322 *Ass*, *Stouford* 1330 *SR* (p), *v.* Stowford *supra* 41. UPCOTT is *Uppecote in Halghewill* 1396 IpmR.

---

[1] It is worth noting perhaps that in the Homme charter (BCS 451) dealt with *infra* 264, we have a twice-repeated *wælle* for *wielle*, which suggests that this form may occasionally have been used in Devon and account for ME *wall*.

Hatherleigh

HATHERLEIGH 127 G 12

Hadreleia 1086 DB (Exon), *Adrelie* (Exch)
Hatherlegam 1193 Oliver 95 *et passim* with variant spellings
-legh(e)
Hatherley al. Hetherley 1675 Ogilby

This name raises the problem of a large number of names containing *Hather-, Hether-, Hader-, Heder-,* as their first element in their ME forms. In addition to this name we may note in Devon Hatherton, Hathercombe, Hatherland, *Hetherland,* Hatherleigh and Heathercombe *infra* (*v.* Index). Elsewhere we have Heatherton in Bradford (So), *Hederdon* 1277 FF, *Hetherden* 1456 AD i; Hatherleigh in Holton (Do), *Hatherlegh* 1277 *Ass,* 1309 Ipm; Hatherley (Gl), *Athelai* DB, *Haiderleie* c. 1150 BM, *Heitherleia* 1210 Gl Corpn. Records, *Hatherlege, Hetherlege,* 1221 *Ass*; Hatherden in Andover (Ha), *Hadredena* c. 1110 (15th) Dugd, *Hetherdene* 1235, 1256 *Ass, Hatherdene* 1256 *Ass*; Hatherton (Ch), *Haretone* 1086 DB, *Hatherton* c. 1307 St Werburgh Cartulary. For none of these have we any OE forms, but we have one for Hatherton (St). In the Wolverhampton charter of 996 this is *Hage(n)þorndun* (Dugd vi, 1443). It is DB *Hargedone,* 13th cent. *Hather-, Hetherden.* This makes it clear that it is just possible that all these contain as their first element OE *haguþorn, hægþorn,* 'hawthorn,' with loss of *n* from the consonant groups *rnd, rnl,* as early as DB, and variant *Hather-, Hether-, Haider-, Heither-* forms which reflect the ME variants *hawethorne, heythorne.* It is a little surprising, however, if this is the history of these names, that the *aw* and the *n* have disappeared so completely in all the various examples, and the question may be raised whether we may not have, in some of these names at least, the ancestor of the common word *heather.* That has hitherto only been noted from the North of England and from Scotland in ME documents, where it takes the forms *hather, hadder, hedder.* The origin of this word is obscure (*v.* NED *s.v.*). That it might be used in place-names is shown by Heather (Lei), *Hadre* DB, *Hether* 1221 Cur, *Hethere,* 1428 FA but there is no evidence that the word *heather* was in common use in Southern England until modern times and there is no evidence for the presence of the plant itself at many of the places in question. It is of course possible that the term, if it was in use, had not the same significance as it had in the north of England. It might denote heathland generally, not necessarily a place where the plant we know as heather grows. There may have been an OE *hǣðra or *hǣðor with a stem-extension of the same type as that found in ME polre (OE *pōlra) from pōl, 'pool,' telgor from telga. It would presumably denote a heath-grown place, v. Addenda supra lix.

ESSWORTHY is Esseworth' 1283 Ass, Esseworthi 1330 SR (p), v. worþig. The first element may be a personal name Essa. This is not on record, but might be a pet-form of such an OE pers. name as Ēadsige.

FISHLEIGH[1] is Fislega 1228 FF, -legh 1242 Fees 781, Fisseleg 1244 Ass, Middelfishlegh(e) 1302 Ass, 1318 FF, Westfuslegh 1362 AD ii, Fishleghe 1408 IpmR. This name seems to be a compound of OE fisc, 'fish,' and leah, but the reason for such a name is obscure. Cf. Fishley (Nf), Fischele 1278, Fisshele, Fyshele 1295 Ipm.

GRIBBLEFORD BRIDGE is Gribbelthward 1532 Dartmoor. The first element here is clearly the Devon, Dorset and Cornwall gribble, 'crabtree' or 'blackthorn.' The earliest reference in the NED is dated 1518, but already in the 1330 SR we have Walter atte Gribbele in Crediton and Grybbelparke in 1386 (Ct) in Dartmoor. -thward in 1532 is probably a bad form for -ford.

LYDBRIDGE is Ludebrugg' 1330 SR (p), Lydebrigge 1483 IpmR. This is a difficult name. The river here is the Lew, but Blomé (143) suggests that this part of it was also called Lyde (cf. Ekwall RN 272 ff.).

PULWORTHY

West Pulewrth' 1242 Fees 784, Pulleworthy 1492 Ipm
Est, West Poleworth(y) 1303 FA, Yestpoleworthi 1339 Exon, Polleworthy 1346 Ass

Both East and West Pulworthy are far from streams and one

---

[1] West Fishleigh (6″) is still marked on the map, as also Stone Fishleigh, Bishop's F., Spear's F., Arnold's F. and Grove's F. Which of these was 'Middle' is not clear.

must therefore take the first element to be the pers. name *Pulla,
probably found in Polehanger (PN BedsHu 172) and Pul-
borough (PN Sx 152) and certainly found in a diminutive form
in Pulloxhill (PN BedsHu 160). For the latter cf. also Pulsford
infra 525.

SELDON is *Seledon* 1244 *Ass* (p), *Seldene* 1269 Misc (p), *Seldon*
1333 *SR* (p), v. dun. The first element is probably OE *sele*,
'building,' as suggested by Blomé (144). Cf. Zeal *infra* 292.

CLEAVE[1], CROSSPARK (6″) and LONGHAM BRIDGE (6″) were
probably the homes of Roger de *la Clyve* (1330 *SR*), Robert
atte Crosse (1333 *SR*) and Adam de *Langham* (1330 *SR*). v. clif,
lang, ham(m).

BIDDICOMBE (6″) is *Bytcombe* 1550 *Deeds Enrolled*. BREMRIDGE
is *Bromeridge al. Bremeridge* 1551 Pat. DECKPORT is *Dykerport*
1330 *SR*, cf. Doggaport *supra* 95. GRUDGEWORTHY (6″) is
Griggeworthi 1330 *SR* (p). HANNABOROUGH is *Haneburge* 1228
FF, *-bergh* 1242 Fees 781, *-burgh* 1303 FA, v. beorg. The first
element is OE *hana*, 'cock,' cf. Handborough (PN O 120). HOLE-
PARK is *Hole, Holeparkes* 1550 *Deeds Enrolled*, v. holh. HURL-
BRIDGE is *Hurdlebrygge* 1424 Exon, *-bridge* c. 1630 Pole. The
meaning may have been 'bridge (i.e. causeway) formed by
hurdles.' The stream here is a small one. KERSWELL is *Carswill*
1303 FA, 1330 *SR* (p). 'Cress spring,' v. wielle. LAKE is *Over-
lake* 1779 Recov. 'Streamlet,' v. lacu. LANGABEAR is *Lange-
be(a)re* 1238 *Ass*, 1242 Fees 781, v. lang, bearu. LEWER is
Liwere 1249 *Ass* (p), *Lywere* 1279, 1285 *Ass*, 1333 *SR* (p) and is
probably a compound of the river-name Lew and OE wer, 'weir,
fishing-pool.' LITTLEWOOD is so spelt 1551 Pat. LOCKS PARK is
to be associated with the family of John *Locke* (t. Eliz *SR*).
MARSHFORD is *Marmenesford* 1303 FA, *Marmesford* 1333 *SR*
(p). MARYMEAD (6″) is *St Mary Meade* 1550 *Deeds Enrolled*.
MEDLAND is *Medelond* 1333 *SR* (p). 'Meadow land,' v. mæd.
PASSAFORD is *Paseford* 1238 *Ass*, 1333 *SR* (p). '*Passa's* ford.'
PRESSLAND is *Pruteslond* (sic) 1370 *Ass*. Perhaps 'priest's land.'
RUNNON MOOR is *Renden* 1551 Pat, *Rundon Moor* 1809 M.
STAPLEFORD is *Stapelford* 1270 *Ass*. 'Ford marked by a staple
or post.' STRAWBRIDGE is probably identical with *Stowbrigge*

---

[1] *Clife* 1581 *SR*.

1532 Dartmoor. UPCOTT is *Uppecote juxta Hatherlegh 1454 FF*. GREAT VELLIFORD is *Filleford 1292 Ass, Ville-* 1303 FA, *Valleyford* 1809 M, cf. Filleigh *supra* 42. WATERHOUSE is *Waterhowsen* 1518–29 ECP 5, 335 and was probably the home of William de *la Watere* (1330 *SR*). WINGATE (6″) is *Wyndeyate* 1550 *Deeds Enrolled*. 'Windy gate.' The place is on a hill in an exposed position. WOODHOUSE (6″) is so spelt 1663 *Recov*. YOULABERRY (6″) is *Yoldeberie* 1606 Wills. 'The old burh.'

Highampton

HIGHAMPTON 127 G 10

> *Hantona* 1086 DB (Exon), *Hanitone* (Exch), *Hanton* 1285 FA
> *Heantone* 1282 Exon, *Heghanton* 1303 FA, *Hehampton* 1318
>   Ch, *Hegheheauntone* 1330 Exon, *Hegheamton* 1336 *Ass*,
> *Hegheyampton* 1372 *AD* C 8194, *Highanton* 1492 Ipm

'The high farm,' *v.* heah, tun. Later, when the meaning of the first element had been forgotten, the ME *hegh(e)*, 'high,' was added.

LYDACOTT is *Ludecote* 1292 Ipm, 1303, 1346 FA, 1412 *FF*, 1492 Ipm. No certainty is possible. One might suggest that the first element was a river-name *Lyde* (cf. Lydford *infra* 191) used here of Pulworthy Water, though there is no parallel for a compound of cot(e) with a river-name. The absence of such a compound may, however, be merely a chance. Alternatively we may have the OE pers. name *Luda* with common development of *u* to *i* before a dental. Hence '*Luda*'s cottage(s).'

STEWDON is *Styvadon* 1333 *SR*, *Styvedon* 1345 *Ass* (p), *Stefedon* t. Hy 8 *Rental*. This p.n., like Steventon (Berks), *Stifingehæme gemæra* BCS 1142, and (Ha), DB *Stivetone*, Stewley (So), 1225 *Ass Stiuelegh*, Steeton (Y), *Styfington* and *Styfetun* c. 1025 (EHR 28, 16), must contain a pers. name *Stifa*, a derivative of the adj. *stif*, 'rigid.' The entire absence of *u*-forms in all these names is somewhat against OE *Styfa*, as suggested by Blomé (144). *Stifa* or *Styfa* would alike suit Steventon (PN BedsHu 46).

STOCKLEIGH is *Estocheleia* 1086 DB (Exon), *Stochelie* (Exch), *v.* stocc, leah and Addenda *supra* liii *s.n.* Yardley.

BURDON is *Buredon* 1262 FF, *Bordon* 1303 FA, *Burdon* 1333 *SR* (p), *v.* burh, dun. There is no burh here now. COOMBE is *Combe* 1491 Ipm. ODHAM is *Wodeham* 1281 *Ass* (p), *Wodham* 1340 *Ass* (p). 'Wood ham(m).' For loss of initial *w*, cf. Oatnell, Odle *infra* 207, 642. TOTLEIGH BARTON is *Totele(g)* 1244, 1285 *Ass* (p), *-leye* 1289 Ipm, *Totteleg* 1249 *Ass*, *-ley* 1493 Ipm. '*Tot(t)a*'s clearing,' *v.* leah. TOWN BARTON (6″) was probably the home of Adam de *la Tune* (1244 *Ass*). It is hard by the village. UPCOTT is *Uppecote* 1333 SR (p). 'Higher cot(e).' VENTON is *Fenton(e)* 1314 Ch, 1330 SR (p). 'Marsh farm,' *v.* fenn, tun.

Hollacombe

HOLLACOMBE 127 G 7

> *Holecoma* 1086 DB, *-cumbe* 1238 *Ass*, *Holecombe juxta Holdes-worthy* 1299 Exon

'Hollow valley,' *v.* holh, cumb.

EASTCOMBE and WESTCOMBE are *Estecomb* 1279 Ipm, *Westecom(b)e* 1339 *Ass* (p), 1431 IpmR. Probably 'east and west of the combe,' the farms being so situated. *v.* Introd. *supra* xxxvii.

NORTH and SOUTH (6″) HEADON. *Suhtynedon, Suhynedon* 1249 *Ass*, *Hynedon* 1330, *Hyna-* 1333 SR (p). *v.* higna, dun. The reference must be to land belonging to some household or community, not necessarily religious. Cf. *hina land* (BCS 542) and *hine hylle* (BCS 890), in a ME text. The 'household' may possibly be that of the neighbouring royal manor of Holsworthy.

TREDOWN [trə'daun] was the home of Richard *atter Doune* (1330 SR), i.e. 'at the down.' *Tre* here represents ME *atter* = OE *æt ðære*, 'at the' (fem.), *atter doune* being later wrongly divided as *at tredown*. Cf. Trelana, Treleigh *infra* 163, 210. This development is very common also in East Cornwall, but there it may have been influenced by the numerous Celtic names beginning with *Tre-*.

HAYNE and WHITECROFT were probably the homes of Richard *atte Heghen* (1330 SR), *v.* Hayne *supra* 129 and Ong' de *White-croft* (1333 SR), *v.* croft.

Holsworthy

HOLSWORTHY [hɔlzəri] 127 G 6

> *Haldeurdi* 1086 DB (Exon), *Haldeword* (Exch)

Halleswrthia late 12th BM *et freq* to 1291 Tax with variant
spellings -*worth(e)*, -*wordi*

Haldewurth 1228 FF, *Aldeswrh'* 1257 Ipm, *Haldeswrthy* 1277
Ass et passim to 1389 AD iv, with variant spellings -*wrthi*,
-*worth*

Holdesworthe 1308 Exon, *Hollesworthi* 1327 *Ass*, *Holdisworth
et non Haldisworth* 1330 *Ass*, *Houlsworthy* 1675 Ogilby,
Holsworthy vulgo Holsery 1765 D

Healdesworthe c. 1320 Exon, *Hyallesworthi* 1326 Exon

This place must be considered along with *healdesuuyrth* in a
Sussex charter (BCS 197), cited by Blomé (145), Holdstrong
infra 188 and Halsworthy *infra* 520, all alike containing a first
element *Healdes*-. The triple occurrence of this otherwise unrecorded element in genitival form is in favour of interpreting it
as a pers. name *Heald*, rather than a common noun (*ge*)*heald*,
'stronghold,' postulated by Blomé or an unmutated OE *heald*,
'slope,' allied to OE *hielde*. If it is a pers. name it must be
derived from OE *heald*, 'bent.' Cf. also Holdworth (Y), DB
Haldeuurde, Holdsworth (Y) 1276 RH *Haldewrthe*, and the pers.
name *Halda* recorded in OE, apparently the weak form of this
name.

ARSCOTT is *Essecote* 1238 *Ass*, *Esshecote* 1277 *Ass* (p), *Asshecote
juxta Haldesworth* 1292 *Ass*, *Ayshcote* 1333 *SR* (p), *Arscott*
1563 *FF*. 'Ash cot(e),' i.e. 'by the ash trees.' For the later forms
cf. Arscott *supra* 127.

CHASTY is *Chagkesti* 1238 *Ass* (p), *Chaghesty* 1391 *FF*, *Chagestye*
1412 IpmR. 'Path overgrown with gorse or broom,' *v.* stig, and
cf. Chagford *infra* 424.

CHILSWORTHY

Chelesorda 1086 DB (Exon), -*worde* (Exch)

Chelewrth' 1210 RBE, -*worth* 1233 Pat, -*wurth* 1276 Cl

Chilleswrth' 1238 *Ass*

Chelliswrth' 1242 Fees 613, *Cheles*- 1249, 1278 *Ass*, *Chelles-
worth* 1275 RH

Chulaworth 1272 Ipm, *Chulesw(o)rth* 1278, 1281 *Ass*, *Chulles-
worthi* 1310 Exon (p), *Chulysworthy* 1316 FA

'*Cēol's* farm,' *v.* worþ. Chilsworthy in Calstock (Co) has the
same history.

RATHERTON is *Rit(t)hedon* 1238 *Ass*, 1330 *SR* (p), *Ritherdon* 1281 *Ass* (p), 1333 *SR* (p), 1391 *FF*, *Ryderdon* 1428 FA (p). In spite of the absence of *u*-forms we are probably right in interpreting this as 'cattle-hill,' from OE hryðer and dun.

RHUDE is *Northrude juxta Wyke Sancti Pancracii* 1311 *Ass*, (*juxta Haldesworthy*) 1314 *Ass*, *Roude* 1326 Ipm, *Northrude* 1615 *Recov*. It was the home of Mabilla Blonche *atte Rude* (1333 *SR*). This may be OE *hrēod*, 'reed,' referring to the marshy land just below the farm. The meaning in that case would probably be 'land where reeds grow,' as suggested by Blomé (145). Cf. Rhudemead (6″) in Pancrasweek, similarly situated.

SIMPSON is *Synnyaneston, Sinnaneston* 1281 *Ass* (p), *Syneston* 1333 *SR* (p), *Symmeston* 1390 *FF*, *Symeston* 1413 Exon, *Simpston* 1472 IpmR, *v.* tun. The first element is difficult. It may be a ME pers. name, ultimately of Celtic origin, cf. *Siniaun Mab Idnevyd* 1205 (1295) Ch, a witness to a charter of Valle Crucis Abbey (Wales).

THORNE is *Torna* 1086 DB, *Thorne* 1242 Fees 773, 1377 Exon. Self-explanatory.

TREWYN is *Trewene* 1311, *la Treawen* 1312, *Cantaria atte Trewen juxta Hallisworthy* 1337, *Capelle atte Trewe* 1348 Exon, *atte Trewyn* (nom. loc.) 1411 *FF*, *Trwen* 1438 Exon. This is not a Celtic name, but English, the meaning being simply 'at the trees,' with the weak plural form *trewen*, cf. Train *infra* 261.

VOGNACOTT is *Fuggincote* 1279 *Ass*, *Fuggyng-* 1305 *Ass*, *Foggyng-* 1330 *SR* (all p). The first element in the light of fuller forms is probably *Fucga*, a weak form of the first element in the p.n. *fucges flodan* (BCS 674), rather than the *Focga* of the Devon *focgan igeðas* (*v. s.n.* Voghay *infra* 457), as suggested by Blomé (146). The *ing* is probably connective.

YELLOWLAND and YOULDON are *Yeoldelonde* 1390 *FF*, *Yoldon* 1330 *SR* (p), *Yeol-* 1333 *SR* (p), *Yoldedon* 1390 AD iv. 'Old land' and 'hill,' *v.* dun. 'Old' probably meaning 'long under cultivation'. Cf. Addenda *supra* lviii.

BARROW (6″), HOLE and SOUTHCOMBE were probably the homes of Roger *atte Burghe* (1333 *SR*), *v.* beorg, Gregory de *la Hole*

(1314 Exon), *v.* holh, and Nicholas de *Bysouthecombe* (1333 *SR*), i.e. 'south of the combe.'

COLE's MILL (6″) and GEARNES are probably to be associated with the families of John *Colle* (1524 *SR*) and Alice *Gearne* (1627 Wills).

BABINGTON is *Babbedon* 1295 *Ass* (p), 1399 *Ct* (p), *Babedon juxta Haldesworthi* 1305 *Ass.* '*Babba*'s hill,' *v.* dun. BRENDON FM is *Brendon*, *Breyndon* 1314 *Ass*, *Bremdon* 1295, 1351 *Ass* (all p). Possibly 'bramble hill,' *v.* Brendon *supra* 58. BURSCOTT (6″) is *Burstenyscote* 1330 *SR* (p), *Buscote* 1472 IpmR. '*Beorhtwine*'s cot(e).' CRANBURY is *Cranebir*' 1238 *Ass* (p), *Cran(e)byr*' 1244 *Ass* (p), *Crambury* 1615 *FF*. 'Crane (heron) frequented burh.' FEATHERLANDS (6″) is *Fetherlande* 1563 *FF*. GREYLAND is *Greylond* 1541 *Recov*, *Grayland* 1639 *FF*. HERDWICK is *Hardwick al. Hurdweke* 1669 *Recov*, *v.* heordewic. HONEYCROFT is *Honecroft* 1314 Exon, 1333 *SR* (p). 'Honey croft' or '*Hūna*'s croft,' *v.* Honeychurch *infra* 165. KEEPHILL is *Kephilparks* 1562 *FF*. LAKES is *Est Lake*, *West Lake* 1390 *FF* and was the home of Editha *atter Lake* (1330 *SR*), *v.* lacu. LAMERTON is *Lomedon* 1305 *Ass* (p), *Lamerton* 1663 *Recov*, *Lomedon al. Lamerton* 1699 *Deed*, *v.* dun. The first element is obscure. It may be OE *lamba*, 'lambs'.' MANWORTHY COTTAGES (6″) is *Manewurthe* 1181 P (p), *Manewrth* 1219 *Ass*, *Mannewrthy* 1239 *FF*, *Manneworthy-mylle* 1410 *FF*. '*Man(n)a*'s farm,' *v.* worþig. MERRYFIELD is *Muriafeld* 1281 *Ass* (p), *Miriafeld juxta Holdesworth* 1345 *Ass*, *Merryville* 1809 M, *v.* Merrivale *infra* 247. NEWCOURT is *New-cotte* t. Hy 8 *Rental.* 'New cot(e).' SOLDON is *Soldon* 1313 *Ass*. Probably a compound of sol and dun, 'hill marked by a miry pool.' SOUTHCOTT is *Suthcote* 1238 *Ass* (p), 1276 Ipm. STADDON is *Stoddon* 1238 *Ass*, 1333 *SR* (p). 'Bullock hill,' *v.* stott, dun, or 'stud hill,' *v.* stod. STANBURY CROSS is *Stanbury* 1669 *Recov*, *v.* stan, burh. There are no remains here now. UGWORTHY is *Uggeworthi* 1308 Exon, 1330 *SR*, *Ugga-* 1340 *Ass* (all p). '*Ucga*'s farm,' *v.* worþig, cf. Ugborough *infra* 284. WHIMBLE is *Wimble* 1686 *FF*.

Inwardleigh

INWARDLEIGH [inəli, iŋəli] 127 H 12

Lega 1086 DB

o

Inwardlgh' (sic) 1242 Fees 784, *Inwardesle* 1267 *Ass*, *In(d)war-
legh* 1285, 1303 FA, *Inewardleghe* 1291 Tax, *Inwardisleghe*
1311 Exon (p), *Inworde-* 1329 Exon
Enwarle 1426 EEW, *Inworley* 1538–44 ECP 8, 170
Inwardleigh vulgo Ingerleigh 1765 D, (*oth. Inwarley*) 1769
Recov

v. leah. This place derives its name from *Inwar* (DB Exch
Inewar) who held the manor TRE (DB f. 291 b). *Inwar* is an
Anglo-Scandinavian name, the equivalent of ON *Ívarr*.

CURWORTHY

Corneurde 1086 DB
Curewrthi 1219 *Ass*, -*wrthy* 1238 *Ass*, -*worth(i)* 1242 Fees 789,
1378 IpmR, *Cureworthy* 1492 Ipm
Coreworthy 1316 FA, (*juxta Inworthlegh*) 1356 *Ass*

Blomé (146) is certainly right in pointing out here that whatever may be the history of *Corn-* in other names, the persistent *u*
in the forms of this name compels us to treat it apart. He suggests
that the first element is OE *cweorn(e)*, 'hand-mill.' Hence 'mill-
farm.' For loss of *n*, cf. Corhampton (Ha), *Cornhamton* 1225
BM.

OAK is *Acha* 1086 DB, *Oke* 1477 *FF*.

WIDEFIELD is *Witefelda* 1086 DB, *Whitefeld* 1242 Fees 789,
Widefeld 1284, *Wydefolde* 1316 FA, *v.* Whitefield *supra* 52.

BUTTERFORD (6″) is *Boterford* 1330 *SR* (p), *v.* Buttercombe
supra 40. DOWNHOUSE (6″) is *Downehowses* 1663 Recov. EAST-
WOOD (6″) is *Byestewode* 1351 *Ass*. 'East of the wood.' ELLMEAD
is *Elmede* 1333 *SR* (p). FOLLY GATE is so spelt in 1809 M.
HEATH HILL (6″) was the home of Henry de *Hethe* 1333 *SR*.
HORRALAKE is *Horelake* 1562 *FF*. Probably 'dirty streamlet,'
v. lacu and cf. Holyford *infra* 622. LURCHARDON is *Lurchydon*
1533–8 ECP 6, 267. MEAD is *le Mede* 1499 Ipm, *v.* mæd.
MERRIFIELD (6″) is *Murifelde* 1353 *Ass* (p), *Merefylde* 1562 *FF*,
cf. Merrivale *infra* 247. MISDON is *Myston* 1345 *Ass* (p),
Miston 1609 *FF*. Probably 'mist hill,' *v.* dun and cf. Mis Tor
infra 195. NARRACOTT is *Northecote* 1333 *SR* (p), 1370 *Ass*,
Northcote juxta Hatherlegh 1449 *FF*. 'North cot(e).' NORTH-
WOOD is so spelt in 1783 Recov and was probably the home of

Nicholas de *la Wode* (1333 *SR*). PADSON is *Pattesdone* 1330 *SR*
(p), *Paddiston* 1562 *FF*, cf. Patchole *supra* 49. ROSENCOMBE
(6″) is *Rosedoncomb* 1562 *FF*, cf. Rosedown *supra* 75. SMALL-
WORTHY is *Smaleworthi* 1330 *SR* (p). 'Narrow estate,' *v.* smæl,
worþig. STOCKEN is *la Stocken* 1333 *SR* (p), *v.* stoc(c). For the
en, *v.s.n.* Hayne *supra* 129. TONGUELAND (6″) is *Tongesland* 1633
FF. It is a piece of land situated in a fork between two roads.
VIZACOMBE (6″) is *Visacomb* 1562 *FF*, *v.* Viza *supra* 128. WAY-
TOWN is *Waye* 1387 Fine, *Wey al. Wey Town* 1782 *Recov*, *v.* weg.
WESTACOMBE is *Westcumbe* 1219 *FF*, *Bywestecomb* 1330 *SR*,
Biwestecoumbe 1356 *Ass* (p). 'West of the valley,' *v.* cumb.
WESTACOTT is *Westecot* 1242 Fees 784, *Wescote* 1378 IpmR.

Jacobstowe

JACOBSTOWE 127 H 13

> *Jacopstoue* 1331 Exon, *Jacobstouwe* 1334 *SR*, *Jacobestauwe*
> 1349 *Ass*
> *Stowe Sancti Jacobi* 1353 *Ass*, 1395 *FF*, (*Stawe*) 1408 *Ass*,
> 1535 VE
> *Stawe Seint Jake* 1387 Fine

'Holy spot of St Jacob (James),' *v.* stow and cf. Jacobstow
(Co). The church is dedicated to St James. The reference
Jacobestow (1297 Pat) may be to either the Devon or the
Cornish place of this name.

BROOMFORD MANOR is *Branford'* 1242 Fees 781, *Bronford* 1333
SR (p), *Brom(p)ford(e)* 1408 *Ass* (p), 1409 IpmR, *Brampford*
1428 FA. The first element may be either brame or brom. *mf* in
some forms becomes *nf* by dissimilation, cf. Brendon *supra* 58.

NORTH PIEND is *La Pynd* 1303 FA and was the home of Walter
de *la Pynda* (1333 *SR*). This is the OE *pynd*, 'enclosure,' discussed under Pen Hill (PN Sx 200).

COMBE and CROFT were probably the homes of Roger de *la
Cumbe* (1244 *Ass*) and William *atte Croft* (1408 *Ass*), *v.* cumb,
croft.

CADHAM is *Cadeham* 1219 *Ass*, *Kadeham* 1249 *Ass* (p). 'Cada's
ham(m).' DORNAFORD is *Dorneford* 1219 *FF*, *Derne-* 1303 FA,

Durne- 1333 *SR* (p), 1356 *Ass.* 'Secret or hidden ford' (over the Okement), *v.* dierne. DUNSLAND COURT is *Dunessland'* 1228 Bracton, *Doneslonde* 1228 FF (p), 1286 *Ass*, *Dunesland* 1244 *Ass*, *Douneslond* 1491 Ipm. Probably '*Dunn*'s land,' *v. supra* 131. *Doun* may be for *Donn.* RISDON is *Risdon* 1219 FF, 1317 *Ass* (p), *Rysdon* 1333 *SR* (p). 'Brushwood hill,' *v.* hris. STOCKBEARE is *Stokbere* 1270 *Ass*, *Stokebeare* 1409 IpmR, *v.* stoc(c), bearu.

Luffincott

LUFFINCOTT[1] 137 A 5

    Leghyngecoth' (sic) 1242 Fees 787

    Lughyngecot' 1242 Fees 787, *Lughyngcote* 1330 *SR*

    Luffingecote 1275 Exon, *Luffyncote* 1428 FA, *Luffencote* 1577 Saxton

    Loghingecote 1285 FA, -ynge- 1303 FA, 1324 *Ass*, -yng- 1339 *Ass*, *Logghyng-* 1350 Exon, *Loyʒhincote* 1291 Tax

    Loghynton que vocatur Loghyngecote 1346 FA

    Lyghingcote 1364 Fine

'cot(e) of *Luhha*'s people,' *v.* ing. For interchange of cote and tun cf. Waddlestone *infra* 188 and Almiston *supra* 80.

EAST and WEST PEEK are *Pech* 1086 DB, t. Ed 1 *Launceston*, *Westpyk* t. Ed 1 *Launceston*, *Estpyke* 1330 *SR* (p), 1418 IpmR, *Pyk* 1333 *SR* (p), *Pike* 1481 *Cl.* The early forms of this name offer difficulties. One would, apart from the forms in *pyke, pike*, explain it in the same way as Peek *infra* 285, from OE *pēac.* That word should not give a series of forms *pyke, pike*, but as they are comparatively late and not without parallel in the Peek which certainly comes from *pēac*, we should not perhaps lay too much stress on the irregularity. Cf. further Cowley Peak (Gl) *somet de Pik de Covele* 1316 St Peter Gl.

HENDON is *Heaundone* 1330 *SR* (p). 'At the high hill,' *v.* heah, dun. WORDEN is *la Worthen* 1330 *SR* (p), *v.* worþign.

Milton Damarel

MILTON DAMAREL 127 E 7

    Mideltona 1086 DB

    Middelton 1238 FF, 1285 FA, (*Albemarl*) 1314 Ch

---

[1] In DB this place seems to have been included under the manor of *Tamerlanda, v.* Tamar River *supra* 13.

Milton Daumarle 1339 *Ass*, (*Daubmarle*) 1345 *Ass*

'Middle farm,' *v.* tun. Why so called it is impossible to say. The manor was held by Robert de *Albamarla* in 1086. See further *s.n.* Sydenham Damarel *infra* 209.

DERWORTHY is *Dirreworth* 1219 *Ass*, *Dyraworthy* 1270 *Ass*, *Direworth*(*i*) 1313 *Ass*, 1330 *SR* (p). Cf. also Derrill and Derriton *infra* 163, 164, *Byrhsige Dyrincg* (BCS 1064) and (*to*) *dyran treowe* (BCS 721). All these contain as first element a pers. name *Dȳra* or *Dīera* (*v.* Redin 47). This survived in Devon into ME times, a John *Dyra* and a Peter *Dira* appearing in the Bishop's Registers 1308–1310.

GIDCOTT is *Gildescota* 1086 DB, *Giddecoth'* 1242 Fees 788, *Gydekote* 1244 *Ass*, *Gidicote* 1244 FF, *Gydi-* 1303 FA, *Gyde-* 1346, 1428 FA, *Gide-* 1420 IpmR. Probably '*Gydda*'s cot(e),' the *l* in the DB form being a mistake.

WOODFORD BRIDGE is (*on*) *wuduford*, (*to*) *wuduforda* 938 BCS 725, *Wodeford Brygge* 1398 Exon. Self-explanatory.

DOWN (6″) and VENNGREEN[1] were probably the homes of John *atter Doune* and John *atte Fenne* (1333 *SR*), *v.* dun, fenn.

BUTTERMOOR is *Buttermoor* 1809 M, *v.* Buttercombe *supra* 40. GRAWLEY is *Grovelegh* 1488 Ipm, *Grawley* 1681 FF, *v.* grafa, leah. KITTABOROUGH (6″) is *Keytberyhill* 1612 Recov, *Kitteberry* 1681 Recov. NORTHTOWN (6″) is *Milton Myll al. Northtowne* 1612 Recov. WALDON is *Waldon*(*e*) 1330 *SR* (p), 1492 Ipm. Cf. next name. WALLAND is *Waleland* 1249 *Ass* (p). Possibly OE *Wēala land*, 'land occupied by Britons or serfs,' *v.* wealh. WHITEBEAR is *Whitebeare* 1317 Exon (p), 1421 IpmR, *v.* bearu. WITHYPOOL BRIDGE (6″) is *Wydepol* 1281 *Ass*.

Monk Okehampton

MONK OKEHAMPTON 127 G 13

Monacochamentona 1086 DB (Exon), *Monuchementone* (Exch) *Munekeokementon* 1242 Fees 784, *Monkochmentone* 1265 Exon *Monk Oakinton* 1675 Ogilby, *Monke Ockhampton oth. Monk Ockington* 1759 *Recov*

[1] *Vendowne, Vengreene* 1681 *Recov.*

'Farm on the river Okement' (*supra* 11). In DB the manor belonged to Baldwin the sheriff, having been in the possession of one *Olnot* (i.e. *Wulfnōþ*) TRE. If the place was ever monastic property it must have been at some date before the 11th cent. We have further trace of these holders in Monkleigh *infra* and Monk's Mill Fm (6″), just over the border in Hatherleigh parish.

BEER and BURROW (6″) were probably the homes of Stephen de *Bere* (1330 *SR*) and Nicholas de *la Burghe* (1333 *SR*), *v*. bearu, beorg.

MONKLEIGH (6″) is *Monkeclyve* 1333 *SR* (p). 'The monks' clif.' WOOD BARTON is *Wode* t. Hy 8 *Rental*.

Northcott

NORTHCOTT 137 B 5

> *Northcote* 1263 FF (Co), (*juxta Boyton*) 1345 *Ass*, *Northecote juxta Loghincote* 1378 IpmR

This was formerly a part of Boyton parish in Cornwall. Why 'north' is not clear. It is south of Luffincott, east of Boyton.

Northlew

NORTHLEW 127 H 11

> *Leuia* 1086 DB, *Lewe* 1274 Ipm
>
> *Liw* 1228 FF, *Lyu* 1242 Fees 778, *Lyu Toritune, -tone* 1258 Exon
>
> *North Lyu* 1316 FA, *Northleu* t. Ed 3 BM, *Northlieu* 1353 *FF*

The place takes its name from the river on which it is situated (*supra* 8). *North* to distinguish from Lewtrenchard *infra* 187. Why *Toritune* (i.e. Torrington) is not clear.

GORHUISH, HIGHER and LOWER [gɔriʃ], is *Gohewis* (sic) 1086 DB, *Gorehiwiss'* 1242 Fees 784, *-hiwishe* 1378 IpmR, *Gorhywys* 1285 FA. 'Dirty estate,' *v*. gor, hiwisc.

EAST and WEST KIMBER

> *Chiempabera* 1086 DB (Exon), *Chempebere* (Exch), *Kyempe-biare* 1311 Exon (p)

Kemppebere 1242 Fees 788, *Kempeberg* 1244 *Ass* (p), *-bere* 1276 Ipm, *West Kempebeare* 1310 Seld 22
Kymbeare 1336 Ipm (p)

The first element is apparently OE *cempa*, 'warrior, soldier,' but whether used as a significant word or as a late OE pers. name it is impossible to say. Cf. the common use of *Kemp(e)* as a surname. *v.* bearu.

GREAT RUTLEIGH is *Radecliva* 1086 DB, *Estradeclive* 1286 *Ass*, *Radeclyve* 1333 *SR* (p), *Rutleigh* 1809 M. 'Red clif.' Cf. Rackley (So), *Radeclive* c. 1200 Wells, 1248 FF.

EASTCOTT, LAKE[1], LAND'S END[2] and WATERHOUSE (6″) were probably the homes of Jordan de *Estkote* (1244 *Ass*), Nicholas *atte Lake* (1333 *SR*), Nicholas de *Londeshende* (ib.) and Alice *atte Watere* (1330 *SR*), *v.* cot(e), lacu. Land's End is at one end of the parish, cf. the same name *infra* 404.

BLACKWORTHY is *Blakeworthy* 1285 *Ass*, *Blakesworthi* 1330 *SR*, *Blakeworth* 1333 *SR* (all p). '*Blaca*'s farm,' *v.* worþig. BOLLAND is *Boueland* 1581 *SR*. 'Curved piece of land,' *v. s.n.* Bowden *supra* 37. CROWDEN is *Crowedon* 1330 *SR* (p), *Crowdon* 1607 *Recov*. 'Crow-hill,' *v.* dun. DURDON CROSS is *Durdon Cross* 1532 Dartmoor, *Duredon* 1562 FF. Cf. Duerdon *supra* 82. EAST-COMBE (6″) is *Estecumbe juxta Wadelond* 1305 *Ass*, *Byestecombe* 1330 *SR* (p). 'East of the valley,' *v.* cumb. FORDA TOWN (6″) is *Fordetowne* 1616 *Recov*. For the *town*, *v. infra* 676. GREEN-DOWN is *Grendon* 1346 FA. HARRATHORN is *Harethorn* 1249 *Ass* (p), *Hore-* 1396 Cl. Probably 'boundary thorntree,' *v.* har, þorn. The place is about 300 yards from the parish bound-ary. HEATH is *Heathe* 1616 *Recov*. HOLLOWAY WOOD (6″) is *Holewaye* 1333 *SR* (p), *-weye* 1370 Exon. LAMBERT is *Lamford* 1333 *SR* (p). 'Lamb ford,' cf. the same name *supra* 96. MILLTOWN, cf. *Milleham*, *Lewe mille* t. Hy 8 *Rental*. MOOR TOWN is *More* 1458 FF, *v.* mor. NORLEY is *Norleighford* 1663 *Recov*, *v.* norþ, leah. SOUTHCOMBE (6″) is *Southecomb* t. Hy 8 *Rental*. WHIDDON is *Whetedon* 1249 *Ass* (p), *Wheddon* t. Eliz *SR* (p). 'Wheat hill,' *v.* dun. WORTH is *Este-*, *Westewerthe* t. Hy 8 *Rental*, *v.* worþ. SOUTH YEO is *Southeyeo* t. Hy 8 *Rental*. 'South of the water,' *v.* Yeo *supra* 18. It lies south of the river Lew.

---

[1] *Lake* 1616 *Recov*.   [2] *Londesende* 1440 FF.

Pancrasweek

PANCRASWEEK 127 F 4

> *Pancradeswike* 1197 FF, *Pancrastwik* 1234 Fees 399, *Pan-*
> *kardeswik'* 1242 Fees 791
> *Wykepranhard* 1285 FA, *Prankardiswyk* 1303 FA, *Prangar-*
> *deswik al. Prankardiswyk* 1316 Ipm, *Prankerdeswyk* 1374
> *FF*
> *Wyke Sci Pancratii* 13th *Torre,* 1291, 1340 *FF, Capella de*
> *Wike* 1291 Tax, *Wyk Sancti Pancracii* 1346 FA
> *Weeke St. Prancars* 1570 *Deed*

v. wic. The church is dedicated to St Pancras (Pancratius).
Cf. Germansweek *infra* 183 and Week St Mary (Co). The early
forms offer difficulties. They can be explained in two ways.
Either there was a popular form *Pancart* for *Pancratius,* which
under the influence of English names in *-hard* was changed to
Pank(h)ard and with further insertion of a second *r* to *Prank-*
(h)ard, or the association of the parish name with the dedication
of the parish church is a piece of folk-etymology, and the real
name of the village was derived from some late settler bearing
the name *Pancoard* (Förstemann PN 243), of Continental
Germanic origin.

DEXBEER

> *Diakanesbere* 1197 FF, *-ken-* 1199 FF, *Dyakenes-* 1234 Fees
> 396,*Yakenesbear* 1279 Ipm
> *Decnesbere* 1242 Fees 791, *Dekenisbere* 1316 Ipm
> *Dyakesbere* 1303 FA, *Dekysbeare* 1491 Ipm

v. bearu. The first element answers to OE *dīacon,* 'deacon,'
but the reason for the name is not known.

DUNSDON is *Dunewinusdona* (sic), *Denewynesdone* 1086 DB
(Exon), *-winesdone* (Exch), *Dunwinesdon* 1197 FF, *Donnysdone*
1330 *SR* (p). '*Dunnewine's* hill,' *v.* dun. *Dunnewine* is on record
as the name of a Devon witness.

HAMSWORTHY

> *Hermondesworda* 1086 DB (Exon), *Hermodesword* (Exch)
> *Hermodeswortha* 1166 RBE, *-wurth* 1234 Fees 396

Her(e)man(n)eswrth(i) 1197, 1199 FF, 1242 Fees 791, 1279 Ipm
Hermandeswo(r)th 1316 Ipm, 1333 *SR* (p)
Westharmesworthie 1550 Pat

This is probably '*Heremōd*'s **worþig**,' but there was early confusion with other OE pers. names such as *Heremund* and *Hereman*. Cf. Harmondsworth (PN Mx 40).

KINGFORD is *Kinkeford* 1244 *Ass*, *Kyngford(e)* 1311 Exon, 1330 *SR* (p). Possibly OE *cyne-ford*, 'royal ford,' with common later assimilation to a more usual type. It is not far north of the Stratton-Holsworthy road, which links up royal manors.

LUFFLAND is *Loffeland* 1303, *Luffe Londe* 1314 *Ass*. This probably contains the same pers. name found in Luffenhall (Herts), *Luffenhale* (BCS 737). See further under Lovaton *infra* 449.

VIRWORTHY is *Fereordin, -urdi* 1086 DB, *Firaworthi* 1313 Exon (p), *Vireworth(y)* 1316 FA, *Veraworthy* 1350 Ipm. Probably 'farther farm,' as suggested by Blomé (151). *v.* worþig, worþign. The place is at the extreme north end of the parish and the adjective may have reference to its position in relation to Hamsworthy which is nearer Pancrasweek village.

VENN and WOOD FM were probably the homes of Osbert de *la Fenne* (1333 *SR*), *v.* fenn, and John de *la Wode* (1316 Ipm).

ALDERCOTT is *Aluethecote* 1281 *Ass*. 'cot(e) of a woman named *Ælfgȳþ*.' BRENDON is *Brendon* 1333 *SR* (p), *v. supra* 58. BROOMHILL is *Bramble* 1765 D. HEADON (6″) is *Heddon* 1333 *SR* (p). Probably 'heath hill,' *v.* dun, cf. Headon (Wt), *Hetdene* 1324 Misc. HUDSON is *Huddesdun* 1238 *Ass* (p), *-don* 1279 Ipm, 1303 FA, *Huttesdon* 1242 Fees 791, *Hudesdone al. Huddisdon* 1316 Ipm. '*Hudd*'s hill,' *v.* dun. LUTSON is *Luttysdon* 1397, *-tes-* 1458 IpmR. Perhaps '*Lutt*'s hill,' *v.* dun, and cf. Lutsford *supra* 75. PITWORTHY is *Pedeworthy* 1281 *Ass*, *Pitaworth* 1333 *SR* (p), *v.* worþig. PUCKLAND is *Pokelonde* 1330 *SR* (p). 'Goblin land,' *v.* puca. SHILLAND is *Shillond* 1333 *SR* (p), *v.* scylf, land. There is a fairly steep slope here. SLADE (6″) is *Slade* 1458 IpmR, *v.* slæd. TAMARSTONE is *Tamer Stone* 1765 D. Stones are marked here by the river Tamar. YOULDEN is *Yoldon* 1333 *SR* (p), cf. Youldon *supra* 148.

North Petherwin

NORTH PETHERWIN 137 B/C 3

> *Pidrewin* 1138–55 (13th) Exon, *Nordpydrewyn* 1269 Exon
> *North Piderwine* 1259 Exon, *Northpiderwyne* 1283 Exon, 1286 Ass, *Northpiderwyn* 1341, 1361, -*pyder-* 1426, 1427 Exon
> *Northpederwyn* 1346 Pat, *North Pederwyn* 1432 Pat, 1551 Deeds Enrolled
> *Northpytherwyn* 1581 *FF*

This place and South Petherwin in Cornwall[1] are some miles apart and, as they have no natural feature in common, such as a river or hill, it is probable that the name was originally that of a district or large area. This is rendered probable by the fact that there is a Cornish hundred named Pyder (*Piderscire* 1185, *Piðersire* 1186, *Pidelescira* 1187 P, *Pidelsir, Pidersir* 1201 *Ass*, *Pidre* 1274 RH, *Pydrisire* 1303, *Pydreshire* 1306 FA, *Pythreshir* 1338 *Rental*). Petherwin probably contains the same word, the additional element being the British *vindo (W *gwyn*), 'white.'

BODGATE [bɔdʒət] is *Bodget* 1286 *Ass* (p), *Bodgyete* 1364 *Ass* (p), *Bageyeat al. Bodgate* 1661 *Recov*, *Bagyeat al. Badgeyeat al. Bodgate* 1718 *Recov*. This is a difficult name. We are just on the Cornish border and it may be that the first element is British *bod*, 'house,' common in Cornwall. If so, we should have to take the second element as British *cet*, 'wood,' with an otherwise unparalleled ME development to *get, gyet*. The only alternative possibility is to take the name as derived from OE *Bodangeat*, '*Boda*'s gate,' *v.* geat.

BRAZACOTT is *Brosiacote* 1330, *Brosyngacote* 1333 *SR* (p), *Brassacott* 1618 *FF*, *v.* cot(e). There is no English pers. name corresponding to the first element of this name, but there was a Richard *Brosia* taxed under Plymouth in the 1330 *SR*, cf. also Johannes *Brosya* in Lesnewth Hundred (Co) 1428 FA. This may contain the Co *bras*, 'big,' W *bras*, 'thick, fat, coarse,' used as a pers. name, though that name has not been found as an element in Cornish p.n.'s. For the *ia* spelling, *v. supra* xxxvi.

[1] *Suthpydrewyn* 1269, *Pitherwyne* 1274 Exon, *Pydrywyn* 1292 *Ass*, etc.

CLUBWORTHY is *Clobiry* 1322 *Ass*, 1330 *SR*, *-bury* 1333 *SR* (all p), *Clowbery* 1639 *FF*, *Clobbery* 1807 *Recov*. This name is clearly a compound of burh. The first element may have reference to the site of the burh on a rounded hill. There is no OE word *clobb* with this sense on record, but we may compare Cornish *clob*, 'clod or lump of earth' and Danish *klub*, 'knoll,' earlier 'lump of earth.' It is clear that the *worthy* is a quite recent inverted spelling due to the fact that this terminal element is commonly pronounced [əri] in Devon names.

HELLESCOTT is *Hilscote* 1330, *Hulscote* 1333 *SR* (p), *Hulscott* 1537 *Deed*, *Hilscott* 1658 *FF*. Blomé (151) may be right in adducing the parallel of *hylsan seohtra* from a Sx charter (BCS 50) and we may also compare *Hilsefenne* (1408 *Ass*), a field-name in Saltash (Co). OHG *hulsa* (earlier *hulisa*), 'shell, covering,' may have had an OE cognate *hylse*. A compound *hylse-cot* would be an exact parallel to Hulcott (PN Bk 152), containing OE *huluc*, 'husk,' later 'hovel.'

KERSWORTHY is *Casteswurth* 1228 FF, *Catteswurthi* 1249 *Ass* (p), *Castesworthy* 1270 *Ass*, *Keastesworthi* 1330 *SR* (p), *Carsworthy* 1551 *Deeds Enrolled*, 1612 *Recov*, *Kersworthy al. Kearsworthy al. Catisworthy* 1762 *Recov*. v. worþig. For the first element we may compare Keason (Co), *Kestingtun* c. 1150 (1348) Pat, *Keyston* 1571 *FF*, and Lankeast (Co), *Lankest* 1364 *Ass*, 1380 FF. Loth (Chrest. 19) notes *Cast* as the name of a Breton saint, possibly derived from the Lat *castus*. There seems to be no evidence that this was used as an ordinary pers. name in British, but it may possibly be connected with the Cornish surname *Keast*.

PENROSE [pen'ru·z] is *Penros(e)* 1249 *Ass* (p), 1544 *SR*, *Penrowse* 1673 *FF*. This is a Celtic name, the elements corresponding to Co *pen*, 'head, end, top,' and *ros*, 'moor, heath.' The p.n. is common in Cornwall and also in Wales (Penrhos).

BOLESBRIDGE and DAWS are probably to be associated with the families of John *Bole* (t. Eliz *SR*), and William *Dawe* (1550 *SR*).

BILLACOTT is *Byllyngcote* 1330 *SR* (p), *Byllacott* 1606 *FF*. Probably '*Billa*'s cot(e).' COLLACOTT is *Collaco* ... 1544 *SR*. '*Col(l)a*'s cot(e).' COPTHORNE is *Cobthorne* 1612 *FF*. FORDA was the home of Roger *atte Forde* 1330 *SR*. GODCOTT is *Godecot(e)*

1286 *Ass*, 1330 *SR* (p), *Goddacott* 1612 *Recov.* '*Goda*'s cot(e).'
KENNACOTT is *Kinnacott* 1612 *Recov.* KILFORD is *Kyllaford*
1611, *Kilford* 1638 *FF.* MAXWORTHY is so spelt t. Jas 1 ECP
174, 1626 *FF*, v. worþig. NESCOTT is so spelt 1717 *Recov.* PAT-
TACOTT is *Pattecote* 1306 *Ass*, 1308 Exon (both p). '*P(e)at(t)a*'s
cot(e).' SLIDDON is *Sliddon* 1680 *FF*, *Sluddon* 1707 *Recov.*
STENHILL is *Stanenehall* 1333 *SR* (p), *Stenhill, Stainehill* 1701
Recov. The first element is OE *stænen*, 'stony.' The second is
uncertain. TASCOTT is *Tascot(t)* 1544 *SR*, 1619 *FF.* TRILLACOTT
is so spelt 1694 *Recov.* TROSWELL is *Treswell* 1249 *Ass* (p),
Tros(s)well 1661 *FF*, 1717 *Recov.* WEBWORTHY is *Wibworthie*
1669 *FF*, v. worþig. Cf. Webbery *supra* 113. WESTON is *Weston*
1249 *Ass* (p), 1579 BM. 'West farm,' v. tun. This must be in
relation to Werrington. MIDDLE WHITELEY is *Whytele(ye)* 1249
Ass (p), 1330 *SR* (p), *Midelwhytelegh* 1366 Pat. 'White leah.'
WIGGATON is *Wigadon* 1612 *Recov.* WINNACOTT is *Wynnecott*
1544 *SR*, *Whenacott* 1592 *SR*, *Whinnacott* 1699 *FF.* WINSDON
is *Wynnysdone* 1330 *SR* (p), *Wynnesdon* 1333 *SR* (p). This is
perhaps '*Wine*'s hill,' v. dun. It is doubtful if Winnacott contains the same first element. YOUNGCOTT is so spelt 1694 *Recov*,
cf. Youngcott *infra* 216.

West Putford

WEST PUTFORD   127 C 6

  Poteforda, Podiforda 1086 DB
  Puteford 1238 *Ass*, *Putteford(e)* 1238 *Ass et freq* to 1311 Exon,
      Westerputford 1270 *Ass*, (*West*) 1394 *Ass*
  Westpotteford 1314 *Ass*

'*Putta*'s ford.' *West* to distinguish from East Putford *supra*
106.

COLSCOTT is *Colscote* 1330 *SR* (p) and is very likely identical
with *Colsouenescota* 1086 DB. If so, the meaning is '*Colswegen*'s
cot(e),' *Colswegen* being an Anglo-Scandinavian pers. name
found already in Devon c. 1100 (Earle 263) in the form *Colswein*.
Cf. also *Colsweineston* 1195 FF (Devon).

CORY is *Curri* 1219 *Ass*, *Cory* 1330, 1333 *SR*, 1339 *Ass* (all p),
Cory Mills 1723 *Recov.* For parallels for this name cf. Ekwall
RN 97 *s.n.* Cory. All the places with which Ekwall deals can be

clearly referred to rivers, but Cory is definitely not on a river but in a little hollow opening out from the valley of the Torridge. Ekwall explains Cory as a river-name containing perhaps a W root *ceu*, 'hollow,' so that the term *Cory* might be used in the first instance of a valley and then of the stream flowing through it. For the river-name *v.* Corrie Brook *supra* 3. This explanation seems more likely than Blomé's attempt (152) to connect it with Celtic *kuros*, 'circle.' The semicircle of which he speaks here and in connexion with Coryton is very vague and shadowy.

KISMELDON (BRIDGE)

> *Kestelmeledon* 1219 *Ass*
> *Kystemeldon'* 1242 Fees 787, 1330 *SR* (p), *Kiste-* 1244 *Ass* (p)
> *Kystumelbregg, Kistelmelebrigge* 1279 Ipm, *Custummelbrigge* 1283 Pat
> *Kytelmelbrig' al. Kustemelebrugg'* 1283 Ipm, *Kystemele Brugg* 1366 Ch
> *Kystermeldon* 1303 FA, *Kistermelebrigge* 1318 Ch
> *Kestmelbrug* 1343, 1346 Ipm

The etymology of this name is suggested in EPN *s.v.* cristelmæl. This word, which has a metathesised form *cyrstelmæl*, denotes a cross or crucifix. It is found five times in lists of boundaries in OE charters, the most interesting reference being to one standing on a watch-hill (*wearddune þær þæt cristelmæl stod* BCS 1176). It is compounded with ac (BCS 204) and beam (BCS 919), denoting apparently an oak or other tree on which there was a crucifix, and with leah in the unidentified *cristemeleighe* (BCS 768) in Dorset. It would seem to be a variant by dissimilation of a more regular *cristenmæl*, i.e. Christian sign, found in a different text of BCS 919. The down and bridge seem independently to have been named from the same cross.

JULIANS PUTFORD is *Choleputteford* 1464 IpmR, *Putford Jelyan al. Cholly Putford* 1556 *Deed*, where a Thomas Wade and *Jelyan* his wife are mentioned in connexion with the place. The name is probably identical with the earlier manor of *Churiputteford* 1242 Fees 787, *Churc Potford* 1303, *Churche Poteford* 1346 FA with later common confusion of *r* and *l*. If so, the first element may be *cyric*, 'barrow,' as the farm is not near the parish church.

THRIVERTON is *Thevedryngh* 1281 *Ass, Thevethryng* 1330 *SR* (p). The early forms suggest a place-name of the derisive nickname type, derived from OE *þēofa þring,* 'crowd of thieves.' For further parallels *v.* Thuborough *infra* 168. The curious corruption in modern times is difficult of explanation.

FIELD IRISH is *Yeriche* 1507 HMC v, 571, *Feildirish* 1672 *FF, Irish* or *Yerish* 1737 *Recov.* Probably OE ersc, 'stubble field,' cf. Irish in St Breward (Co), *Arishes* c. 1550 *Rental, Erish* 1701 *FF.* IDDLECOTT (6″) is *Idelcote* 1428 FA (p), 1493 Ipm. 'Empty cot(e).' EAST LOVELAKE (6″) is *Lovelake* 1330 *SR* (p), *Lillake* 1729 *Recov.* '*Lēofa*'s stream,' *v.* lacu. SESSACOTT is *Saxecot'* 1219 *Ass, Sessecot(h)e* 1238 *Ass* (p), 1242 Fees 792, 1303 FA, *Sassacote* 1315 Exon (p). Probably '*Seaxa*'s cot(e),' cf. Sessingham PN Sx 410 and Saxworthy *supra* 107. SILWORTHY is *Selewrth'* 1238 *Ass,* 1279 Ipm, *-wurth* 1249 *Ass, -worthy* 1320 *Ass, Selaworthi* t. Ed 3 *Ass.* Possibly a compound of OE sele and worþig. VOLEHOUSE is *la Foghelhuse* 1292 *Ass, Foghelhous,* 1423 *FF.* The NED first records the word *fowl-house* from 1839. WEDFIELD is *Wydefeld* 1330 *SR* (p), *Wydefyld* 1430 BM. 'Wide open land,' *v.* feld. NORTH WORTHEN (6″) is *Northworthen* 1729 *Recov, v.* worþign.

Pyworthy

PYWORTHY 127 G 5

   Paorda 1086 DB

   Peworthy 1239 Ch, *-wrthe* 1261–8 Exon, *-wrthi* 1287 Cl

   Peywrth 1249 *Ass*

   Pyworthe 1291 Tax, *-thy* 1310 Ipm, *-thi* 1341 Ipm, *Piworthi* 1330 *SR,* Exon

   Pyheworthi 1309 Exon, *Pieworthy* 1434 Exon

   Puworthi 1401 Pat

   Pyworthy al. Pury 1547 LP, *Pyworthy oth. Puworthy oth. Pury* 1786 *Recov*

Blomé (153) takes the first element to be OE *pīe,* 'insect.' Professor Ekwall would take it to be the same word used as a nickname. He notes the neighbouring Hopworthy as containing OE *hoppa,* 'grasshopper,' which might similarly be used as a nickname. Cf. OGer *Huppo* (Förstemann PN 936).

BRADFORD is *Bradefort* 1086 DB. 'Wide ford,' *v.* brad.

CRINACOTT is *Frenecoth'* 1242 Fees 775, -*cot(e)* 1303 FA, 1306 Ipm, *Frenakote* 1244 *Ass*, *Frenycott* 1586 *Recov*, *Crinecot* 1809 M. The first element here is probably the Anglo-Scandinavian pers. name *Fræna* found as a signatory to a Devon charter of 930 (BCS 1343). No explanation of the later corruption can be offered.

DERRILL [dəˑl]

> *Dir(e)hill(e)* 1201 Cur (p), 1238 *Ass* (p), *Dyrehill* 1244 *Ass* (p), *Direhille juxta Haldesworthy* 1304 *Ass*, *Derehulle* 1278 *Ass* (p), *Derhille* 1300 Misc (p)

v. Derworthy *supra* 153. Possibly the same person gave name to this place and to Derriton *infra* 164, 210.

HOPWORTHY is *Hoppeworthe* 1318 Exon (p), -*thi* 1333 *SR* (p), *Hopworthy* 1464 IpmR. This may be either 'grasshopper farm' or '*Hoppa*'s farm,' *v. supra* 162; cf. Hopcott (So), *Hoppecot* 1387 FF.

KILLATREE is *Kiletre* 1242 Fees 775, *Killetruwe* 1249 *Ass*, -*trewe* 1303 FA, *Kyletru* 1330 *SR* (p), *Keletre* or *Kylketre* 1492 Ipm, *Kelytre* t. Hy 8 *FF*. '*Cylla*'s tree.'

PARNACOTT

> *Parnyngcot* 1306 *Ass*
> *Pyarnygacote* 1311 Exon, *Parny'acote* 1330 *SR* (p)
> *Permaniacote* 1315 Exon (p)
> *Pernycote* 1330 Exon (p), *Pernyngcote*, *Pernyacote* 1345 *Ass* (p)

This name must remain an unsolved problem. It looks like an ing(a) derivative of a root *pearn-, but no such word o pers. name is known.

TINNEY is *Tuneo* 1529-32 ECP 6, 169, *Tyneowe* 1550 Pat. 'Between the waters.' It is situated on a spur of land between the Derrill Water and the Tamar. See further *s.n.* Tinhay and Twinyeo *infra* 190, 479.

KNOWLE, MARSH, MOOR COTTAGES (6") and TRELANA were probably the homes of Richard de *Knolle* (1333 *SR*), John *atte Mershe* (1333 *SR*), Hamund *atte More* (1330 *SR*), and John *atte Lane* (1330 *SR*). *v.* cnoll, mor and Tredown *supra* 146.

Bounds Cross is probably to be associated with the family of William *Bound* (t. Eliz *SR*). Derriton is *Direton* 1238 *Ass*, *Dyreton* 1278 *Ass* (p), *v.* Derworthy *supra* 153. Holemoor (6″) is *Holemor juxta Pyworthy* 1289 *Ass*, *v.* holh, mor. There is marshy ground here and a slight hollow. Northmoor (6″) is *Northmore* 1529–32 ECP 6, 169. Pinkworthy is *Hier Pinkeworthie* 1623 *Ct.* It may be identical with Pinkworthy in Oakford *infra* 388. Hence, 'Pinca's worþig.' Thorndon is *Thorndone juxta Pyworthy* 1307 *FF.* 'Thorn hill,' *v.* dun. Villavin is *Fellefen* 1709 *FF.* Possibly we should compare Villavin *supra* 118. Winscott is *Winescoth'* 1242 Fees 775, *Wynscote* 1303 FA. '*Wine*'s cot(e).' Worthen is *la Worthen* 1330 *SR* (p), *la Worthyn* 1333 *SR* (p), *v.* worþign. Yeomadon is *Yamedon* 1330, *Yeame-* 1333 *SR* (p). 'Éama's hill,' *v.* dun.

St Giles on the Heath

St Giles on the Heath 137 B 5

> capella Sancti Egidii 1202 (14th) *Launceston*, 1291 Tax, (*parochia*) 1532 *Recov*
>
> St Gylses en le Hethe 1585 Deeds Enrolled, St Gyles in le Hethe 1585 Recov

The place takes its name from the dedication of its church to St Giles (Egidius).

Carey Barton is *Cary* 1242 Fees 794 *et freq* to 1350 Ipm with variant spellings *Kary, Kari, Kyari* t. Hy 3 Harl (p), *Keary* 1333 *SR* (p), *Uppekary* 1296 *FF.* The place takes its name from the river Carey, *supra* 3.

Panson is *Panestan* 1086 DB, *Panneston* 1238 *Ass* (p), 1242 Fees ,81, 1303 FA, *Paneston* 1356 *Ass*, *Overpanston* 1438 BM. The name must have referred to a stone of some particular shape as in Mis Tor Pan *infra* 196.

Pinslow is *Pinteslo* 1244 *Ass*, *Penteslo* 1330 *SR* (p). This is a difficult name. The second element is probably sloh, 'marsh, slough.' Professor Ekwall suggests that the first element may be ME *pint* or *pintel*, a short name for the common plant cuckoo-pint or -pintle, which grows in marshy places.

Chapmans Well (hamlet) is probably to be associated with the family of Walter *Chepman* (1330 *SR*). Haukadon is *Hauekedon*

1242 Fees 781, 1303 FA. 'Hawks' hill,' *v.* dun. HELE is *Hele* 1765 D, *v.* Hele *supra* 46. PETER'S FINGER is so spelt in 1765 D. SITCOTT is *S(o)uthcote* 1302 *Ass*, 1330 *SR* (p), *Sutcote* 1532 *Recov*. 'South cot(e)' with reference to Carey Barton to the north. Cf. Sittycleave *supra* 83.

Sampford Courtenay

SAMPFORD COURTENAY 127 H 15

> *Sanfort* 1086 DB, *-ford* 1242 Cl, 1248 Ipm, *Sandfort* 1093
> France
> *Saunforde Curtenay* 1262 Exon, *Sampford* 1274 Ipm

'Sandy ford' (over the Taw). The association of the *C(o)urtenay* family with the place goes back to 1242 (Cl).

CORSCOMBE

> *Cockescumb'* 1242 Fees 784, *Cokescomb* 1333 *SR* (p), *Cockys-*
> *combe* 1345 *Ass* (p), *Cokkes-* 1378 IpmR
> *Coklescumbe* 1244 *Ass*, *-combe* 1330 *SR* (p)
> *Coscombe* t. Ed 6 *Rental*

v. cumb. Probably 'cock's combe' or '*Cocc*'s combe,' but if the spellings with *l* are to be taken into account we may compare Curscombe *infra* 563.

HALFORD seems to be identical with *Herpeford* 1242 Fees 784, *Herpford* 1303 FA, *Herford* 1428 FA. If so, the name is identical with Harpford *infra* 590, i.e. 'ford by the herepæð.' There is a road here but not a main one.

HONEYCHURCH[1]

> *Honechercha* 1086 DB (Exon), *-cherde* (sic) (Exch)
> *Hunichirche* 1238 *Ass*, *-church'* 1242 Fees 784, *Honycherche*
> 1261 *Ass*, 1303 FA, 1378 IpmR, *-churche* 1316, 1428 FA,
> 1425 IpmR, 1535 VE
> *Hunecherche* 1244 *Ass*

Honey is found in Devon in many modern p.n.'s in combination with cyrice, clif, cot(e) (3), croft, land, tun (2), wielle (2). In most cases there is not enough evidence to decide between

---

[1] Formerly a separate parish.

P

OE *hunig*, 'honey,' and the OE pers. name *Hūna*, the sole exception being Honiton *infra* 639. Where compounded with *wielle* the epithet may refer to the sweetness of the water or to a stream where bees swarmed in pollarded willows and the like (cf. Honeybrook PN Wo 12, and Addenda to PN NRY xliv). In combination with other elements[1] the name may refer to a place where bees were kept. The present name is more difficult, but the Rev. G. D. Melhuish notes that it might have referred to bees swarming under the eaves of the church, and Mr R. P. Chope notes that such honey-making still takes place in the church at Hartland. The preponderance of early spellings with medial *i* or *y*, moreover, seems to be against a pers. name *Hūna* in this name.

LYDCOTT is *Lewidecot'* 1242 Fees 784, *Ludecote* 1303 FA, 1378 IpmR. '*Lēofgȳþ*'s cot(e),' this being a feminine pers. name in OE.

REDDAWAY is *Radeweye* 1238 *Ass et freq* to 1310 *Ass* with variant spelling -*weie*. 'Red way or track.' The soil here is red sandstone.

STICKLEPATH is *Stikelepethe* 1280 Exon, -*pathe* 1292 Ipm, *Stikilpath juxta Saunford Curtenay* 1309 Orig, *Stigylpath* 1329 Exon, *Stikilepath* 1396 Exon. 'Steep path,' *v.* sticol. There is a sharp ascent here over a spur of the moor.

TRECOTT is *Trycote* 1296 *Ass* (p), *Tricote* 1330 SR (p), *Tricott, Tryckott* t. Ed 6 *Rental*. Professor Ekwall suggests a compound of OE treo, 'tree,' and cot(e), 'cottages by the tree,' with the same shortening and raising of the vowel as in ME *sik* from OE *sēoc*. Cf. also Tricombe *infra* 628.

WILLEY is *Wythelgh'* (sic) 1242 Fees 784, *Wygelege* 1244 FF, *Wyghelegh* 1292 Ipm, 1378 IpmR, *Wytelegh* 1303 FA, *Waghelegh* 1346 FA, *Wyggelegh* 1377 Cl. Probably '*Wīga*'s leah,' some of the forms being corrupt.

APPLEDORE is *Apildorneford* 1330 SR (p). Probably 'appletree

---

[1] Cf. Honeybourne (PN Wo 264), Honicombe (Co), *Honyacomb* 1338 *Rental*, Honiton (Co), *Huniton* 1208–13 Fees (p), *Honyton* 1397 *Rental*, Hunnyhill (Wt), *Hunyhille* 1275 FF, Honeyborough (Pembrokeshire), *Honiborth* 1325 Ipm, *Honyburgh* 1334 Cymmrodorion Rec. Soc. 4, 63, *Honyfeld* 1504–15 ECP 4, 197 (Devon).

ford.' BEAUMEAD is *Boghemede* 1306 *Ass*, 1330 *SR* (p). 'Curved meadow,' cf. Bowden *supra* 37. BEER was the home of John *atte Beare* (1330 *SR*). BEERHILL is *Bearehill* t. Ed 6 *Rental*, *v*. bearu. BERRY DOWN is *Berye downe* 1550 *AOMB*, *v*. burh. There are no remains here now. BROOK FM is *Broke* t. Ed 6 *Rental*. CLISTON is *Clerkeston* 1333 *SR* (p), *Cliston* t. Ed 6 *Rental*, *Clesson* 1592 *SR*, cf. Cliston *infra* 316. COLDACOTT (6″) is *Caldecote* 1238 *Ass* (p). 'Cold cottages,' *v*. cald, cot(e). COMBE FM (6″) is *Combe* t. Ed 6 *Rental*. DORNAFORD (6″) is *Durneford* 1242 Fees 784, 1244 *Ass*, *Dorne-* 1330 *SR* (p). 'Secret or hidden ford,' cf. same name *supra* 151. FRANKLAND is *Franklond* t. Ed 6 *Rental*. Perhaps '*Franca*'s land,' cf. Frankaborough *infra* 179. FULLAFORD is *Foleford* 1378 IpmR. 'Dirty ford,' *v*. ful. HATHERTON is *Hatherdon* 1418 *Ass* (p), *-downe* t. Ed 6 *Rental*, *v*. Hatherleigh *supra* 142. HAYRISH (6″) is *Hayrish juxta Tawe* 1637 *Recov*. HONEYCOTT (6″) is *Honycott* t. Ed 6 *Rental*. Probably selfexplanatory. HUCKLAND CROSS (6″) is *Hokelandes* 1412 *FF*, *v*. hoc, land. The meaning is doubtful; it may refer to the triangular area here enclosed between two roads. INCOTT is *Yundecote* 1330 *SR* (p). 'Further cot(e)' or 'beyond the cot(e).' LANGABEER is *Langbeare* t. Ed 6 *Rental*. LANGMEAD is *Langemede* 1238 *Ass* (p), *v*. lang, bearu, mæd. OXENPARK BARN (6″) is *Oxenpark* 1618 *Recov*. PITT (6″) is *Pithayes* 1616 *Recov*. For *hayes*, *v. supra* 129. RAT COMBE is *Radcombe* t. Ed 6 *Rental*. Probably 'red valley,' *v*. cumb. The soil here is red sandstone. ROWDEN is *Rughedon* 1244 *Ass* (p), *Rowedon* 1330 *SR* (p). 'Rough hill,' *v*. ruh, dun. ROWTRY (6″) is *Routrewe* 1283 *Ass* (p), *Rowtre* 1500 Ipm. 'Rough tree,' probably referring to some gnarled and ancient one serving as a landmark. SLADE (6″) is *Slade* 1592 *Recov*, *v*. slæd. SOLLAND is *Sandlond* 1330 *SR* (p), *Sanlond in manerio de Sandford Curtenay* t. Ed 6 *Rental*. 'Sandy land.' UNDERDOWN is *Underdowne* t. Ed 3 *Ass*. VENTOWN is *Fennetowne* t. Ed 6 *Rental*, *v*. fenn. For *town*, *v. infra* 676. WESTACOTT is *Westecot(e)*' 1242 Fees 784, 1303 FA. WHITELY MOORS is *Whitleymore* 1504 Ipm. Probably 'white clearing,' *v*. leah. WITHEYBROOK (6″) is *Wythibrok juxta Saunford Curtenay* 1291 *Ass*, *Wethybroke* 1523 *Recov*. WOOD is *at Wood* t. Ed 6 *Rental*. YONDHILL (6″) is *Yundehill* t. Ed 6 *Rental*. 'Beyond the hill,' *v*. Indicombe *supra* 35.

Sutcombe

SUTCOMBE 127 E 6

> *Sutecoma* 1086 DB
> *Suttecumb'* 1242 Fees 772 *et freq* to 1428 FA with variant
>   spelling -*combe*, *Suttacombe* 1339 *Ass*, 1421 Exon
> *Suthtecumbe* 1268 Exon, *Suthcombe* 1291 Tax, *Southecomb*
>   1303 FA
> *Sottecome* 1281 *Ass*, -*cumbe* 1299 Cl, -*combe* 1299 Ipm

Persistent *utt* in the early forms of this name must lead us to
associate it with Sotwell (Berks), *Suttan wille* BCS 810, and
Suttanurde (BCS 864). All alike point to an obscure *Sutta* as
a pers. name. Later some of the spellings show association with
South-names like Sutton.

THUBOROUGH

> *Teweberia* 1086 DB
> *Thefebergh'* 1242 Fees 787, *Thefbergh* 1326 Cl (p)
> *Thuuaburg*(*h*) 1346 FA, *Thuue*- 1411 *FF*, *Thuburgh* 1492 Ipm

Probably 'thieves' hill,' as suggested by Blomé (156). Cf.
Dupath in Callington (Co), *Theuepath* 1324 *Ass*, *Thuvepath* 1345
Ass, *Thewpath al. Dewpath* 1706 *Recov*, *þeofa cumb* BCS 1319
and Thriverton *supra* 162.

LANE[1] and UPCOTT[1] were probably the homes of John *atte Lane*
and Thomas de *Uppecote* (1330 *SR*), *v.* cot(e).

BILLHOLE is *Billehole* 1333 *SR*, 1345 *Ass* (p). '*Billa*'s hollow,'
v. holh. BRENDON is *Bremdon* 1330 *SR* (p). Probably 'bramble-
hill,' *v.* dun, and cf. Brendon *supra* 58. HEDDON is *Hetdoun*
1339, 1340 *Ass* (p). 'Heath hill,' *v.* hæþ, dun. MATCOTT is
Mattecote 1244 *Ass*, 1321 Exon, 1330 *SR* (all p). '*Mætta*'s
cot(e),' cf. Martinhoe *supra* 65. NORTHCOTT is *Northcote* 1276
Ass, 1533 *Recov*. STONE (lost) is *Stane* 1242 Fees 791, (*La*) 1279
Ipm. 'At the stone.'

Tetcott

TETCOTT 127 J 5

> *Tetecot*(*a*) 1086 DB, 1217 PatR, *Tettecot*(*e*)' 1238 *Ass et freq*
>   to 1346 FA

---

[1] *Lana* 1581 *SR, Upcott* 1609 *SR.*

Teticote 1210–12 RBE, *Tetticot'* 1242 Fees 794
Tedecot' 1225 ClR

'*Tetta*'s cot(e).' Cf. Tedburn *infra* 451.

BELLAND is *Boghelond* 1330 *SR* (p). 'Curved land,' *v.* Bowden *supra* 37. The place is situated on a spur of land. Cf. Bolland *supra* 155.

LANA, MOORTOWN, NETHERCOTT and VEARNDON were probably the homes of Lucas *atter Lane*, John *atte More* (1330 *SR*), Robert de *Nithercote* (1333 *SR*), and John de *Ferndone*, i.e. 'bracken hill' (1330 *SR*), *v.* mor, cot(e), dun.

Thornbury

THORNBURY 127 F 7

Torneberia 1086 DB, *-bury* 1193 Oliver 95
Thornebiria 1224 Bracton, *Thornbir'* 1242 Fees 781

v. þorn, burh.

LITTLE LASHBROOK is *Lechebroch* 1219 *Ass*, *Little Lechebroc* 1228 FF, *Lettellelechebrok* 1256 *Ass*, *Lychebrok* 1286 *Ass*. 'Sluggish stream,' cf. Lashbrook *supra* 132.

WONFORD

Wenforda 1086 DB
Wantford 1230 P (p), *Wanford* 1244 FF, 1303 FA, (*West-*)
   1330 *SR* (p)
Waunford 1333 *SR* (p)

The first element in this difficult name may, as suggested by Professor Ekwall, be OE *wægn*, 'wagon,' the whole name being descriptive of a ford which would carry a wagon. Cf. Fatherford *infra* 202.

BERRY and WOODACOTT were probably the homes of William de *la Beara* (1316 *Ass*) and Aungere de *Wodecote* (1330 *SR*), *v.* bearu, cot(e).

BAGBEARE is *Baggebere* 1333 *SR* (p). '*Bacga*'s wood,' *v.* bearu. LASHBROOK WEEK was the home of Thomas de *Wike* (1333 *SR*), *v.* wic. LEY (6″) is *Legh* 1400 Exon, *v.* leah. LOPTHORNE (6″) is *Loppedethorn* 1287 *Ass*, *Loppidethorne* 1333 *SR* (p), *Loppethorn*

1366 *FF* (p). 'Lopped or pollarded thorntree,' cf. Lapthorne *infra* 281, 323. THORNE is *Thorn* 1492 Ipm.

Black Torrington

BLACK TORRINGTON 127 G 9

> *Torintona* 1086 DB, *Blaketorrintun* 1219 Fees 264, *-thorenton* 1227 Ch, *-torintone* 1277 Exon, *-toryngtone* 1359 Exon
> *Blachetoriton(a)* 1167 P *et freq* to 1316 FA, with variant spelling *Blake-*

'Farm on the Torridge,' *supra* 14. According to Mr E. T. Abell the river here has a blackish colour, which it loses three miles further down.

BRAUNDSWORTHY is *Brendeswurth* 1238 *Ass*, *-worth* 1269 Misc, 1276 Ipm (p), *Brandeswrthy* 1299 Ipm. '*Brand*'s worþig.' The phonology is difficult but alternative forms *Brand-Brend* may have arisen through the common alternation of ME *brante-brente* and *brande-brende*.

CRIPPLE (6″) is *Cripple* 1744 *Recov* and may be identical with *Cromhale* 1333 *SR*, 1340 *Ass* (p). The connexion of the earliest and latest forms is probable and the development must have been from *crumhale* to *crump(h)ale* and then, with a common development of *u* to *i* before nasals, to *crimple* and so by folk-etymology to *cripple*. The place lies in a crook in the river and the name is probably a compound of *crumb*, 'crooked,' and *healh*.

KNEELA (6″) is *la Knylle* 1304 *Ass* (p), *atte Knylle* 1330 *SR* (p). This is from OE *cnyll*, 'knoll,' *v.* Knell(e) in PN Sx (169, 528). A further example of this word occurs in the pers. name *atte Knulle* in a Hants *SR* of 1327. Cf. also Oatnell *infra* 207.

BEARA COURT, FORDA FM, HAYNE, HOLE, LEY and TREW were probably the homes of Nicholas *atte Beare* (1330 *SR*), Adam *atte Forde* (1333 *SR*), Henry *atte Heghen* (ib.), *v.* Hayne *supra* 129, William *atte Hole* (1330 *SR*), John *atter Leye* (1333 *SR*) and Richard de *la Triwe* (1244 *Ass*). *v.* bearu, holh, leah, treow.

BUCKPITT (6″) is *Bukapitte* 1313, *Bockapitte* 1321 Exon (p), *Bokeputte* 1333 *SR* (p). Probably 'bucks' hollow.' BUTTERBEARE is *Boterbeare* 1304 *Ass*, *Boterebere* 1340 *Ass* (p), *v.* Butter-

combe *supra* 40. CHILLA is *Chille* 1330 *SR* (p). COHAM [ku·m]
is *Cuham* 1230 P (p), *Coham* 1304 *Ass* (p), 1464 *Cl*, *Couham* 1333
SR (p). 'Cow ham(m).' CRAYTHORNE is *Crowethorne* 1311
Exon (p). 'Crow thorntree,' *v.* Introd. xxxiii. GRADDON is
Gratedon 1244 *Ass* (p), *Graddon* 1492 Ipm. 'Great hill,' *v.* dun.
HIGHWEEK is *Highwick* 1765 D, *v.* wic. KINGSMOOR is *Kinges-
more* 1249 *Ass*. Black Torrington was a royal manor in 1086
(DB). UPCOTT is *Uppecote* 1270 *Ass*. WAGAFORD WATER is
Wagheford 1244 *Ass* (p). The first element may be identical with
that found in Warne *infra* 201, and refer to a ford which has not
a very firm bottom. HIGHER WHITELEIGH is *Wyteleghe* 1307
Ipm, *Whi(t)teleye* 1312 Cl, 1313 Ipm. 'White leah.'

Werrington

WERRINGTON 137 C 4

Uluredintona, Olwritona 1086 DB, *Vlredintona* 1086 DB (Co)
Wlurintona t. Wm 2 Oliver 89

Wulryngton 1193 Oliver 95, *Wolringtone* t. Hy 3 BM, *Wol-
    rington juxta Lifton* 1296 *Ass*, *Wolryngton Abbatis* 1316 FA
Wulfrinton 1249 *Ass*, *Wlfrintone* 1265 Exon, *Wolverinton* 1285
    FA
Worryngton Abbatis 1324 *Ass*, *Werington* 1593 *FF*, *Worriton*
    1675 Ogilby

'*Wulfræd*'s farm,' *v.* ingtun. The manor originally belonged
to Tavistock Abbey which regained it in 1096.

STOWSDON is *Stovisdon(e)* t. Hy 3 *Harl*, 1612 *Recov*. This may,
as suggested by Blomé (158), be from OE *Stūfesdūn*, '*Stūf*'s hill,'
v. dun.

YEOLMBRIDGE [joumbridʒ] is *Yambrigge* t. Hy 3 *Harl*, *Yombrigge*
1308 Exon (p), *Ialmebryge* 1518–29 ECP 5, 276. Professor Ekwall
suggests that this is from OE *ēa-hamm-brycg*, 'bridge by the
river meadow.' The *l* in the 16th cent. and modern forms offers
difficulties, but it may be noted that it seems never to have been
pronounced and may be inorganic.

BRIDGETOWN[1], GROVETOWN, HAM MILL and SUTTON TOWN
were probably the homes of Peter de *Brugge*, John *atte Grove*,
Everard *atte Hamme* and Ralph de *Sutton* (1330 *SR*), *v.* ham(m).

---

[1] *Bridgtowne* 1629 *Deed*.

As Sutton Town is north of Werrington and not distinctively south of any particular settlement, Ralph de *Sutton* may have come from a Sutton elsewhere.

COLMANS, MARSHALL[1] and PEPPERSHILL are probably to be associated with the family of Walter *Colman* (1524 *SR*), Nicholas *Marshal* (1330 *SR*) and William *Pipard* (1333 *SR*).

BULLAPIT is *Bolapitte* t. Hy 3 *Harl*, *Boleputte* 1322, 1324 *Ass* (p). 'Bulls' hollow.' CULLACOTT is *Coulecote* 1330 *SR* (p). Probably '*Cula*'s cot(e).' The modern and ME spellings show it to be of different origin from Collacott *supra* 50. DAISYLAND (6″) is *Daiseyland* 1733 *Recov*. DOWNHAYS is *Dounheghes next Tamur* 1391 *FF*. 'Hill enclosure(s),' *v*. dun, (ge)hæg. DRUXTON is *Durkestonbrugge* 1370 *Launceston*, *Druxton* 1678 *FF*, *v*. tun. The first element may be a ME pers. name from OE *deorc*, 'dark,' cf. Ditsworthy *infra* 239. EGGBEAR is *Eggebear*, *Egkebear* 1238 *Ass*, *Eggebe(a)re* 1296 *Ass*, 1330 *SR* (all p), *Eggbeare* 1378 IpmR. '*Ecga*'s bearu.' HESSACOTT is *Hirscote* 1330 *SR* (p). The first element is possibly identical with that of Hescott *supra* 74. HORREL gave name to Henry *atte Horehole* (1345 *Ass*). 'Dirty hollow,' *v*. horh, holh. LANGDON is *Langedone* 1365 *FF*. 'Long hill,' *v*. dun. LEAT gave name to John *atte Lete* (1330 *SR*). This is OE *gelæt*, 'watercourse, leat, channel.' There is a mill-leat close at hand. POLAPIT TAMAR is *Poolapit Tamer al. Colehouse super Tamer* 1625 *Deed*, *v*. pol, pytt. For the alternative name *v*. Collacott *supra* 50. RADFORD is *Radeford* 1202 (14th) *Launceston* (p). Cf. Radford *infra* 257. TAMERTOWN is *Tamer Town* 1765 *D*. TETTARIDGE is *Titteridge* 1760, 1772 *Recov*. WORMSLAND was the home of Stephen de *Wormyslond* 1202 (14th) *Launceston*. The first element is probably a ME surname *Worm* or less likely the OE *wyrm*, 'snake.'

VII. LIFTON HUNDRED

Listona 1084 Geld Roll
Liftune 1167 P, *Liftona* 1168 P
v. Lifton *infra* 188.

[1] *Marshall* 1551 *Deeds Enrolled*.

Bradstone

BRADSTONE [brasən] 137 E 6

> (*of*) *brada stane*, (*æt*) *bradan stane* c. 970 BCS 1246, *Bradestana*
> 1086 DB, *-tona* 1174–83 BM, *-tane* 1242 Fees 789. Further
> forms are without interest except: *Bradenestan* 1244 *Ass*,
> *Braston* 1539 LP, *Bradstone al. Braston* 1699 *Recov*

'At the broad stone,' *v.* brad, stan. This is possibly the one
marked on the 6″ map near the present church.

GREYSTONE BRIDGE is *Greyston Brygge next Tamer* 1438 Exon,
taking its name from Greystone in Cornwall, *Greyston* 1333 FF,
1426 IpmR.

PILISTREET is *Pillestrete* 1281 *Ass*, *Pilestret* 1330 *SR*, *Pelestret*
1333 *SR* (all p). The first element is a pers. name *Pila*, which is
apparently found in Pillaton (Co), DB *Piletone*, 1291 Tax *Pyla-
tone*. Cf. also Pilmoor PN NRY 23. The exact meaning of the
second element is not clear, but two ancient trackways met in
this parish[1].

BAUCOMBE is *Baucomb* 1301 Ipm, 1330 *SR* (p), *v.* Bowcombe
infra 284. FELLDOWNHEAD is *Velldownhead* 1729 *Deed*. HOLLAND
is *Holond(e)* 1281 *Ass*, 1318 *Deed* (both p), *v.* holh and land. The
farm lies in a valley. TORR (6″) was the home of John *atte Torre*
1330 *SR*, *v.* torr.

Bratton Clovelly

BRATTON CLOVELLY 137 B 9

> *Bratona* 1086 DB, *Bratton(e)* 1242 Fees 785 *et freq* to 1427
> *Ass*, (*Clavyle*) 1279 Ipm, (*Clovyle*) 1547 *Deed*, (*Clovelleigh*)
> 1625 Wills
> *Bracton Clavile* 1331 Ipm
> *Bretton* 1367 Pat

For the interpretation of this name *v.* Bratton Fleming *supra*
29. Roger de *Clavill'* held land in Bratton in 1254 (Cl), and,
according to Pole, in 1248 Sir Roger *Claville* married Joan,
daughter of Hamelin de Deaudon, lord of the manor of Bratton.

---

[1] *Ex inf.* Miss Kelly.

This family-name was later corrupted owing to the influence of the place-name Clovelly *supra* 70.

BOASLEY [bouzli]

> (*æt*) *borslea* c. 970 BCS 1247, *Borslegh* 1316 FA, *Borsleie alias Borslegh* 1316 Ipm
> *Bosleia* 1086 DB
> *Boreslegh* 1286 Ipm, 1411 Exon, *Borseley* 1733 *Recov*

This name seems to contain the same first element as Boscombe (W), 1199 *Borscumbe* (PN W 30). No OE word *bors* is known, but it is possible that such existed. The common word *burr* is generally taken to be a Scandinavian loan word (cf. Norw, Dan, Sw *borre*, with the same sense), going back to an IE root **bhers* which, with a different ablaut vowel and suffixed *t*, is familiar to us in *bristle* from OE *byrstel*. *bors* may be an old plant-name denoting something of a spiky or bristling nature. Such a word might well be found compounded with leah or cumb. Risdon and Fursdon *infra* 176, 177, close at hand, are names of a similar nature.

BREAZLE [breizəl]

> *Breulishill* 1238 *Ass*, -*les*- 1244 *Ass* (p)
> *Brewlleshull* 1238 *Ass*
> *Breweleshull* 1287, 1288 *Ass*, -*lyshill* 1288 *Deed*
> *North Breysell* 1609 FF, *Bresell* 1728 *Recov*

An OE word has here been added to an earlier Celtic placename as in Dunterton *infra* 182. Cf. *Breulis*, a place-name occurring in the Redon Cartulary (334). The second element of this is probably the British word meaning 'court' or 'palace,' perhaps used of a chieftain's residence (W *llys*, Co, Br *lis*, *les*). The first is difficult. It may be identical with Celtic *briva*, 'bridge, ford' (there is a stream here), *v*. Holder 610 and cf. Kellybray (Co), *Kellibregh*, *Killibreu* t. Ed 1, *Kellybreu*, *Kellibrey* 1338 *Rental*. The name *Breulis* would then mean 'court by the bridge or ford.'

CHIMSWORTHY

> *Chemesworthi* 1286 *Ass*, -*ysworth*(*y*) 1378 DA 27, 1533–8 ECP 6, 267

Tymeworth 1286, 1314 *Ass* (p), *Tymmeworth* 1287 *Ass* (p), 1296 DA 27
Themeswrth' 1287 *Ass* (p)

v. worðig. The first element is perhaps a pers. name **Cemmi*, a pet-form of *Cēolmǣr*, but it might equally well be a reduction of *Cēolmǣr* itself, considering the lateness of the earliest form. The *T*-forms are almost certainly erroneous.

CULMPIT (6″) is *Culme Pitt* 1724 *Recov*. Cf. also *Culmehill* 1520 *Ct* (Luppitt) and the entry "3 lime kilns, 2 *Culme* pits..." (1797 *Recov*). The first element is probably identical with *culm*, 'soot, smut, coal dust, slack' (NED *s.v.*), 'slack of bituminous coal used for burning lime and for drying malt' (EDD *s.v.*). The term is on record from Devon and Somerset.

ELLACOTT is *Allecote* 1281 *Ass* (p), *Ayl(l)ecote* 1286 *SR* (p), 1311 Exon (p), 1322 *Ass* (p), *Aille-* 1317 Exon (p), 1353 FF. 'Ægela's cot(e).' This name is not recorded, but would be a weak form of *Ægel* (*v.* PN Bk 145).

GUSCOTT (6″) is *Godescota* 1086 DB, *-cot(e)* 1238 *Ass* (p), *Godiscote* 1303 FA. 'Gode's cot(e),' cf. Godsworthy *infra* 232.

HEADSON is *Hiddelesdon* 1244 *Ass* (p), *Hiddeston* 1330 *SR* (p), *Hiddestone brygge* 1408 DA 27, *Hyddysdon* 1505 Ipm. The first element is a pers. name *Hiddel*, an *l*-derivative of *Hiddi*. The forms are insufficient to decide whether the second element was dun or tun.

MAINDEA [mendə] is *la Mened* 1228 FF (p), *atte Menegh* 1279 *Ass* (p), *atte Menede* 1330 *SR* (p), *Meyndey* 1566 DA 27. This is probably a Celtic name corresponding to Cornish *meneth*, 'hill' (W *mynydd*). There is a well-marked hill just to the north of the farm. The final vowel may be due to the influence of such Devonshire names as Forda, Beera, Wooda, etc., *v.* Introd. xxxvi.

METHERALL is *Middelhull(e)* 1302 *Ass* (p), 1333 *SR* (p), 1351 Deed, *Metherell* 1722 *Recov*. 'Middle hill.' For the development cf. Metherall *infra* 427 and Metherall (Co), *Middylhille* 1327 *SR*, *Middelhill* 1338 Rental, *Midderhull* 1399 *Ct*.

REDSTONE is *Roddekeston* 1330 *SR* (p), *Raddockeston, Ruddok-kyston* 1501 ECP 4, 54, 59, *Rudston* 1533–8 ECP 6, 267.

'*Ruddoc*'s farm,' *v.* tun. This pers. name is not recorded but would be a regular diminutive of *Rudda* (Redin 108).

REED is *Estrude* 1504–15 ECP 4, 243, *Reed* 1686 *FF*, *Rood* 1765 D. This is probably OE hreod, 'reed,' the first form showing the usual Devon *u* for OE *ēo*. There is much marshy land near this spot.

SWADDLEDOWN is *Swatheledoune* 1366 *Ass*, (*aliter dicta Landone*) 1528 DA 27, and is to be associated with the family of John *Swathela* (1330 *SR*).

VOADEN is *Fochedone* 1377, *Vowedone* 1378, *Fowedone* 1408 DA 27 (all p), *Vawden* 1707 *Recov.* *v.* dun. The first element is OE fag, 'variegated,' and must refer to some particular colouring of the soil here. Cf. Fawdon (PN NbDu 82).

VOULSDON CROSS is *Fokelesdune* 1228 FF (p), *Voghelesdon* 14th, *Foelesdone* 1377, *Vol(l)ysdon* 1566 DA 27. *v.* dun. The first element is almost certainly the OE pers. name *Fugul*, cf. Fugglestone (PN W 87).

SOUTH BARTON (6″) and BURROW were probably the homes of Walter de *Berton* (1333 *SR*), William *atte Burgh* (1330 *SR*). *v.* beretun, beorg.

BANNADON is *Bannadon* 1656 *FF*, *v.* dun. BLACKBROOM is *Blackbroome al.* *Blackabroome* 1719 *Deed*. BLAGROW is *Blagrove al.* *Blackgrove* 1770 *Recov.* Self-explanatory. BROADCROFT is *Broadacraft* 1707 *Recov*, *v.* brad, croft. BROCKSCOMBE is *Brokkescombe* 1365 *FF*, *Brokes-* 1458 *FF*. Possibly 'badger's combe' (*v.* brocc), though the presence of Brock's Common just by suggests that we may have to do with a ME surname *Brocke*. CALEHOUSE (6″) is *Calwehous*, *Calewhouse* 1432 DA 27. The first element is probably OE calu, 'bare.' FURSDON is *Fursdon* 1228 FF (p), *Suthforsdon* 1279 *Ass*, *North-* 1330 *SR* (p). 'Furze hill,' *v.* fyrs, dun. LANGWORTHY is *Langewrthi* 1244 *Ass* (p), *Langworthy* 1505 Ipm. 'Long worðig.' MORSON is *Morystone* 1416 DA 27 (p), *v.* tun. The form is too late for any interpretation of the first element to be suggested beyond saying that it is probably a pers. name[1]. NORTHCOMBE is *Northcumb* 1279 Ipm, *v.* cumb. In the

---

[1] There is a place called *Moreleston* mentioned in 1327 (*FF*), but there is nothing to prove that it refers to this place. Its first element seems to be the OFr pers. name *Morel* (*Moreau*).

same document there is mention of a *Southcumb*. RISDON is *Reysdone, Rysdone, Ryssdone* 1408–37 DA 27. The first element may be hris. Hence 'hill overgrown with brushwood,' *v.* dun. WRIXHILL is *Wykyshille* 1378, *Wrixell Bridge* 1684 DA 27. Perhaps identical in origin with Wrixhill *infra* 182, but the forms are too few for certainty.

Bridestowe

BRIDESTOWE [bridistou] 137 B/C 10

> *Bridestou* 1086 DB, *-owe* 1221–30 Fees 1443, 1249 *Ass, Brydestou* 1259–79 Exon
> *Biritestowa* 12th Oliver, *Byrightestowe* 1242 Fees 786, *Brightesstowe* 1242 Fees 756, *Brithtestawe* 1249 *Ass, Briʒtestowe* 1259–79 Exon, 1281 *Ass*
> *Brigidestowe* 1259–79 Exon, *Stowe Scē Brigide* 1299 *Ass*
> *Brittestowe* 1303 FA, 1334 Exon, (*juxta Lydeford*) 1340 *Ass, Brithstowe* 1350 Pat
> *Briddestowe* 1391 Exon, *Breddestawe* 1539 LP
> *Bristow* 1428 FA

'Holy place of St Brigid (Bridget),' the Irish saint to whom the church is dedicated. *v.* stow. Cf. Bridstow (PN He 27).

BATTISHILL is *Batesilla* 1086 DB, *-hill* 1238 *Ass* (p), *Batteshull* 1330 *SR* (p), 1351 *Deed, Battishullwode* 1351 *Deed, Batsell* 1544 *SR.* '*Bætti*'s hill,' *v.* hyll. This pers. name is not on record but would be the strong form of OE *Bata. v.* PN Wo 162.

BIDLAKE is *Bydelak(e)* 1238, 1270 *Ass* (p), 1296 *Ass*, 1306 *FF, Westera-* 1330 *Ass, Biddelake* 1333 *SR* (p), *Bydde-* 1428 FA (p). '*Bid(d)a*'s streamlet,' *v.* lacu. Alternatively *Byde* may be a stream-name, cf. Bidwell *infra* 410.

CHURNDON is *Cherendon* 1279 *Ass, Churn-* 1325 *Ass* (p), 1330 *SR* (p), *Chern-* 1372 *FF, Charnedon* 1586 *FF.* This is a difficult name. We have in a court roll of 1420 reference to a place called *Churne* in Pinhoe parish. Both there and in Churndon we may have the Cornish equivalent of Welsh *cern*, 'side of the head,' 'side of a steep hill,' Breton *kern*, 'crown of the head' (cf. RN 80 *s.n.* Churnet). Such a term might be compounded with dun. A river-name *Churn* is out of the question here as Churndon is on the Lew, which is probably an ancient river-name.

COBHAM WEEK (6″) is *Cobbehammyswyk* 1377 *FF*, *Weke Cobham* 1500 Ipm, *v.* wic. It was held by John *Cobbeham* in 1377.

COMBEBOW is *Comba, Cumba* 1086 DB, *Combe Bowe* 1699 *Recov. v.* cumb. 'Bow' refers to the bridge here over the river Lew. Cf. Bow *infra* 315.

EBSWORTHY TOWN

> *Etboldus Wrda, Boldesworda* 1086 DB, *Eboldesworthi* 1333 *SR* (p)
> *Egbollesworth* 1270 *Ass*, *-bolis-* 1334 *SR* (p), *Ekbolisworthi* 1330 *SR* (p)
> *Ebbolisworthy* 1313 *Ass* (p), *Ebbelesworth* 1355 Pat (p)
> *Embollesworthi* 1330 *Ass* (p)
> *Ebsworth* 1442 Dartmoor

'*Ecgbeald*'s worðig.' The second DB form is perhaps due to a misunderstanding of *Et-*, *Et* being taken for the preposition æt.

FERNWORTHY is *Fernewrda, -urda* 1086 DB, *Ferneworthy* 1306 *Ass* (p). 'Bracken worðig.'

KERSFORD is *Carsforda, Casforda* 1086 DB, *Carsford* 1330 *SR* (p). 'Cress ford,' *v.* cærse.

MILLATON HO is *Millenton* 1238 *Ass*, *Mille-* 1317 *Ass*, *Milla-* 1330 *SR* (all p). '*Milla*'s farm,' *Milla* being a pet-form for an OE pers. name in *Mild-*. The early spellings are against our taking the first element to be OE *myln*, 'mill.'

SPRIGHILL (6″) is *Sprighill* 1378 *Ct* (p), 1612 *FF*. This place is probably to be associated with the family of Richard *Spryg*, who was living near here in 1414 (Exon).

WAY is *Weia* 1086 DB, and was the home of Geoffrey *atte Weye* (1330 *SR*). *v.* weg.

BEARA DOWN, STONE and WOODHEAD were the homes of Jordan *atte Beare* (1330 *SR*), Richard *atte Stone* (ib.), and Nicholas de *le Wode* (1270 *Ass*). *v.* bearu.

BLACKABROOM is *Blakebrom(e)* 1319 Exon (p), 1412 *Ct*, 1500 Ipm, *Blackbrome wall* 1576 *DuCo*. BRAMBLEHAM (6″) is *Bremilham*

1330 *SR* (p), *Bremleham* 1593 *Recov*, *v.* bremel. The second element may be hamm, the place lying in a bend in the river Lyd. CRANDFORD (6″) is *Craneford* 1238 *Ass* (p), *Estera-* 1335 *Ass* (p), *Cranford* 1500 Ipm. 'Heron-ford,' *v.* cran. LEAWOOD Ho is *Lywode* 1500 Ipm, *Leywood* 1518–29 ECP 5, 528. SHORTACOMBE is *Sortecumb* 1270 *Ass*. WOODFORDHAM is *Woodford* 1504–15 ECP 4, 337.

Broadwoodwidger

BROADWOODWIDGER [bradud]   137 C 7

> *Brade(w)oda* 1086 DB, *Bradwode* 1282 Exon
> *Brawod'* 1242 Fees 776, (*Vypund*) 1273 Exon
> *Brodewode* 1279 Cl, *Brodwod* 1303 FA, *Brod(e)wode Wyger*
>   1306 Ipm, 1332 Pat

'Broad wood,' *v.* brad, wudu. The manor was held in 1242 by Richard de *Veteri Ponte* (i.e. *Vypund*), but had passed to the *Wyger* family by 1273.

BANBURY is *Barnebur* 1238 *Ass*, *Westbernebir'* 1249 *Ass*, *Bornebury* 1372 FF, *-byry* 1394 *Ass*, *West-*, *Estbornebury* 1386 *Ass*, *West Bonbury* 1758 *Deed*. '*Beorna*'s burh.'

BECKETT is *Bykecote, -i-* 1242 Fees 794, 1284 FA, 1333 *SR* (p), (*juxta More*) 1311 *Ass*, *Bykkecoth'* 1242 Fees 755. '*Bic(c)a*'s cot(e),' *v.* Abbots Bickington *supra* 124.

BRIDGEPARK (6″) is *Bryse Park, otherwise Bruyshe Park* 1598 DA 33, *Brush Park* 1765 D. Cf. also *Brusche Close* 1507 DA 33. The first element is clearly *brush*, 'brushwood,' *v.* NED *s.v. Park* probably denotes a small enclosure.

DOWNACAREY is *Kari* 1086 DB, *Doune Cary* 1371 IpmR, *Brodewodecary* 1394 *Ass*, *Douncary* 1418 IpmR. The place takes its name from its position on a hill above the Carey river *supra* 3. For the medial syllable *v.* Introd. xxxvi.

FRANKABOROUGH is *Frankebergh* 1238 *Ass* (p), *-borowe* 1504–15 ECP 4, 337. '*Franca*'s hill,' *v.* beorh. Cf. Frankley (PN Wo 346).

KELLACOTT is *Chaluecot* 1228 FF, *Calewecot'* 1244 *Ass*, *Calwecote* 1244, 1335 *Ass*, 1438 BM, *Caluwecot* 1244 *Ass*. 'Bare cot(e),' cf. Calehouse *supra* 176.

LUGWORTHY is *Loggeworthi, -y* 1333 *SR* (p), 1436 *Deed, Lugga-, Loggaworthi* 1345 *Ass, Luggery* 1728 *Recov. v.* **worþig**. The first element must be a late pers. name ***Lugga**. This is not recorded but may be related to *Lucc(a)*, which is well evidenced. Cf. such pairs as *Pubba, Puppa, Wocca, Wogga* (v. Ogwell *infra* 461), etc.

MOOR is *Mora* 1086 DB, *La More* 1205 FF, *More Veteris Pontis* 1306 Ipm. *v.* mor. For the manorial addition *v.* Broadwood *supra* 179.

NORTON is *Nortona* 1086 DB, *Nort(h)on* 1242 Fees 776, (*Beauceyn*) 1305 Ipm. 'North farm,' *v.* tun. Richard *Baucan* held the manor in 1242.

REXON is *Ryggeston* 1249 *Ass* (p), *Reggeston* 1386 *Ass, Rexton* 1505 Ipm. No likely suggestion can be offered for this name. A compound *hrycg-stan*, 'ridge-stone,' is possible but does not seem particularly apt for the topography and no stone survives here. The later *e* also offers difficulties.

WESTMANTON is *Westmanatune* 13th *Deed*. 'tun of the west men.' The place lies at the extreme west of the parish.

COMBE[1], COMBESHEAD, CROSS, FERNHILL, HOLE, NETHERCOTT (6″), UPCOTT[2], and VENN were probably the homes of Roger de *Combe* (1330 *SR*), John de *Comeshevd* (1281 *Ass*), Johanna *atte Crosse* (1330 *SR*), Milo de *Fernhull* (ib.), John de *Hole* (1333 *SR*), John de *Nithercote* (1249 *Ass*), John de *Uppecote* (1333 *SR*), and Adam *Attefenne* (1288 *Ass*). *v.* cumb, holh, cot(e), fenn.

BRINSON is *Brinestune* 13th *Deed* (p), *Brineston* 1244 FF, *Breneston* 1275 RH (p). '*Brȳni*'s tun.' COBDEN is *Cobedon* 1351 *Ass* (p), *Cobdon* 1438 BM. '*Cobba*'s dun.' DOWNTOWN is *Dountone* 1422 DA 27. EASTLAKE is *Byestelake* 1244 *Ass*. 'East of the stream,' *v.* lacu. GOODACRE is *Gotaker* 1249 *Ass, -acre* 1320 *Ass*, 1330 *SR* (p). 'Goat field,' *v.* gat, æcer. GRINACOMBE is *Grenacumbe* 1313 Exon (p), *Grenecombe* 1330 *SR* (p), 1544 *Recov.* 'Green valley.' GROVE is *Northgrove* 1606 Wills. HUNTSDOWN is *Hounddown* 1809 M. IVYHOUSE COTTAGES (6″) is *Ivyhouse* 1686 *FF*. NAITHWOOD is *Bynethewode juxta Brodewodewyger*

---

[1] *Combehay* 1345 *Ass, v.* Hayne *supra* 129.
[2] *Uppecote* 1438 BM.

1361 *Ass*. 'Beneath the wood,' cf. Neadon *infra* 424. SHALLA-
FORD is *Shaldeford* 1238 *Ass* (p), *Scholdeford* 1280 *Ass*, *Sholaforde*
1577 *SR*. 'Shallow ford,' *v.* sceald. SLEW is *la Slo* 1347 Exon.
OE *sloh*, 'mire, slough.' STADDON is *Stoddon* 1330 *SR* (p).
This is probably the same name as Staddon *supra* 149. THORN-
DON HO is *Thorndon* 1438 BM. THORNE is *Thorne* 1324 Ipm,
Thornwyger 1422 IpmR, *v.* Broadwood *supra* 179. TREDOWN
[trədɑun] is *atte Doune* 1345 *Ass* (p), *Tredowne* 1628 *Recov*,
Terdowne 1671 *FF*, *v.* dun. 'At the down,' *v.* Tredown *supra*
146. WESTWEEK is *Westwyke* 1411 Exon, *v.* wic. WITHERDON
is *Wetherdon* 1330 *SR* (p), *v.* dun. The first element is OE
weðer, 'sheep,' cf. Weatherhill (Sr), 1332 SR *Wetherhulle*.

Coryton

CORYTON [kɔritən] 137 D 8

    (*æt*) *curitune*, (*æt*) *curritune*, (*æt*) *curri tune* c. 970 BCS 1246,
      1249, *Curiton(e)* 1238 Cl, 1242 Fees 757, 1261, 1279 Exon,
      (*juxta Lydeford*) 1339 *Ass*, *Cureton* 1377 *SR*
    Coriton(a) 1086 DB, 1236 Cl, 1284 FA, *Corryton* 1293 Pat,
      Coreton c. 1420 Exon
    Coryngton 1547 *SR*

Ekwall (RN 97) suggests that the first element may be an old
name of the river Lyd, there being mention also of a *Curiford*
(1242 Fees 773), *Coryfforde* (1346 FA), and a place in the parish
CORYHILL, for which no early forms have been found. This is
very likely, since Lyd is an English name and the river must
have had an earlier British name. For this river-name *v.* Cory
supra 160.

EASTCOTT is *Estkote* 1249 *Ass*, *v.* cot(e). KIDKNOWLE (6″) is *Kite-
cnolle* 1244 *Ass* (p), 1316 *Ass*, *Kyte*- 1330 *SR* (p). 'Kite hill,' *v.*
cnoll. KNOWLE is *Cnolle* 1249 *Ass*. LONGHAM is so spelt in 1642
(*FF*). Probably 'long hamm.' The farm lies by the river Lyd.
PARK COTTAGE (6″) was perhaps the home of Robert *in the Park*
(1304 *Ass*).

Q

Dunterton

DUNTERTON 137 F 6

Dondritona 1086 DB
Dunterdune 1242 Fees 786, -*tone* 1242 Fees 756, 1244 *Ass*,
  1265 Misc, 1284 FA, *Donterton* 1291 Tax
Duntretone 1301 *Ass*, *Doun*- 1319 *Ass*, 1394 Exon
Dunderton, *Dunderdon* 1434 Exon

The OE *tun* has here been added to an earlier Celtic name as
in Breazle *supra* 174. The first syllable is the OBrit **duno*- (W, Co
din), 'fort, castle.' This is masculine, so in the consequent
absence of lenition the second element must be a word beginning
with *t*. Possibly this is Co *trev* (W *tref*), 'homestead, village,'
the final consonant being lost early, as in Cornish names generally.
Duntref would be an ancient compound with the defining element first, corresponding to the late Cornish place-name Treen,
Tredyn 1304 *Ass*, *Trethyn* 1314, 1321 *Ass*, with the elements in
the reverse order. The *din* is the ancient castle here, which was
probably once an important stronghold guarding the passage of
the Tamar. OBrit *duno*-, should give Welsh and Cornish *din*, but
the *u* forms seem to be preserved in some place-names, e.g.
Dunchideock *infra* 495, Dunmeer and Dunveth (Co).

DUNTERUE WOOD on a spur of land projecting into the Tamar
also contains this old Celtic name. It is *Donterhowe* 1566 DA 43,
Dunterhow 1677 *Recov*. *v*. hoh.

WRIXHILL

Wrikeshull 1219 *Ass*, *Wrikkeshill* 1566 DA 43
Wyrkeshalle 1265 Misc, -*hulle* 1301 *Ass* (p), *Wirkeshill* 1353
  FF
Werkeshulle 1281 *Ass* (p)

The first element is either a Celtic pers. name *Guirec*, recorded by Loth (*Noms des Saints Bretons*), of which the British
form would be **Wiroc* or it may, as suggested by Professor
Ekwall, be a strong variant of the weak English pers. name
which seems to lie behind Wrickton (Sa), *Wyrketon* 1255 RH,
Wirketon 1263 Ipm.

EASTACOTT is *Estcote* 1301 *Ass* (p), 1516 *Recov*. HARDSTONE is

Hardston 1379 IpmR, *Harestone* 1566 DA 43, *Herston* 1610 *SR*. 'Hard stone' or '*Hearda*'s stone.'

Lucy Cleave Wood (6") is *Lowsye Cliff* 1566 DA 43, *v.* clif. Possibly the first element is the OE hlose, 'pig-sty.' Sherrill is *Shirewill* 1330 *SR* (p), *Sherewyll* 1566 DA 43. 'Clear spring,' *v.* scir, wielle. Woodtown is *la Wode* 1249 *Ass*, *Woodtown* 1729 *Deed*. For *town*, *v. infra* 676.

Germansweek

Germansweek 137 A 8

> *Wica* 1086 DB, *Wyk Langeford* 1285 FA, *Wyke Germyn* 1458 *FF*, *Wykejarmen* 1474 FF, *Germaneswyk* 1468 Pat, *Germans Weeke* 1699 Recov, *Jermans Week al. Weeke Langford* 1728 Recov

v. wic. The dedication of the church is to St *Germanus* of Auxerre, who is also commemorated at St Germans (Co). *Wyk Langeford* has reference to a manor in Germansweek held by Richard de *Langeford* in 1242 (Fees 785).

Bovey is *Bovy* 1242 Fees 755, 1333 *SR* (both p), *Bovye* 1569 *Deed*. This looks as if it was the same name as Bovey *infra* 466. That is a river-name, but this Bovey lies on a ridge between two streams, so it seems difficult to think it can be a stream-name. It might be manorial, it might be for OE *bufan ie*, 'above the water.' No certainty is possible.

Seccombe is *Seccomb(e)* 1310 *Deed*, 1330 *SR* (p), 1404 *Ass*. Probably '*Secca*'s combe.' The pers. name *Secca* (cf. OGer *Secco*) is recorded in *Widsith* and found in Seckington (Wa), ASC *s.a.* 755 *Seccan dun*, and in *Seccan ham* KCD 898.

Southweek is *Wyca, Wiche* 1086 DB, *Sudwik'* 1242 Fees 756, *Southwyke* 1279 Ipm, *v.* wic. It lies south of Germansweek. There is a Westweek in Broadwoodwidger to the west.

Toft is *La Toffe* 1310 Exon, *Toff* 1333 *SR* (p), *Tuffe* 1674 *FF*. This is probably the ME word *tuff(e), tuft(e)*, 'tuft, clump, small group of trees or bushes, grassy hillock, etc.,' *v.* NED *s.v. tuft*. Cf. Tuffland *infra* 268.

Eworthy is *Yworthy* 1468 Pat, *Yewry* 1765 D. Probably 'yew

worðig,' *v.* iw. WORTHA is *Westwurtha juxta Bratton* 1320 *Ass,*
v. worþ. For the final vowel, *v.* Introd. xxxvi. East and West
Wortha Fms are marked on the 6″ map.

Kelly

KELLY 137 E 7

> *Chenleia* 1086 DB (Exon), *Chenleie* (Exch)
> *Chelli* 1166 RBE (p), *Kelli* 1219 *Ass et freq* to 1391 Exon with
>   variant form *Kelly, Kelle juxta Bradiston* 1346 *Ass, Kellegh*
>   1428 FA
> *Killi* 1219 *Ass*

The DB form is exceptional and may probably be disregarded.
If so, the name is clearly of Celtic origin corresponding to Co
celli, 'wood, grove,' common in Cornish place-names (Pengelly,
Killigrew, etc.). There is still a fair amount of woodland in the
parish.

BILLACOMBE is *Billercombe* 1319 *Ass* (p), 1482 IpmR, *Biler-* 1333
SR (p), *Bilricomb* 1330 *SR* (p). *v.* cumb. The first element is
very probably OE *billere,* dial. *bilders, billers,* used in Devon of
the cow-parsnip and in Cornwall of the water-dropwort (*v.*
NED *s.v. bilders*). Cf. Bilbrook (St), *Bilrebroch* DB, *Bilrebroch,*
Billebroc 13th (PN St) and Bilbrook in Old Cleeve (So), *Bilrebroc*
n.d. AD iv, *Byllerebroke* 1527 AD iii.

SHUTE (6″) is *Shuteland* 1482 IpmR and was the home of
Augustin *atte Schute* (1333 *SR*). This name, for which a more
complete run of forms will be found under Shute *infra* 417, goes
back to OE *scīete,* a side form of sceat, for a fuller discussion of
which see PN Wo 180 *s.n.* Cockshoot Fm. It may be added that
this place like many of the Devon Shutes lies in or near an angle
of the parish boundaries.

HALL and KELLYBEARE are *Hole, Beare* 1562 *FF* and were the
homes of Nicholas *atte Hole* and Martin *atte Beare* (1330 *SR*).
v. holh, bearu.

BOROUGH is *Burgh* 1407, 1482 IpmR, *v.* beorg. There is a hill
here, the highest land in the parish. CLEAVE (6″) is *Clyff* 1562 *FF,*
v. clif. HORNBROOK is *Hornebrok(e)* 1325 *Ass,* 1482 IpmR, *v.*
horn, broc. There is a spur of land above the little stream here.

MEADWELL is *Medwell* 1219 *Ass* (p), *-will(e)* 1242 Fees 786, 1275 RH (p), 1330 *SR* (p), *Medewelle* 1378 IpmR, 'meadow spring,' v. mæd, wielle. SMITHSON (6") is *Smetheston* 1238 *Ass* (p), *Smyston* 1562 *FF*. Probably 'smooth stone.' WINBROOK is *Wunbrok* 1317 *Ass* (p), *Wonbrok(e)* 1330 *SR* (p), 1482 IpmR. The vowel of the first element is too uncertain to allow of any etymology. YEOMANS is *Yomans* 1562 *FF*, deriving probably from a former owner.

Lamerton

LAMERTON [læmətən] 137 F 8

> (*of*) *lamburnan* (dat.) c. 970 BCS 1247
> *Lambretona* 1086 DB, *Lamberton(e)* 1232 Ch, 1238 *Ass*, 1265 Exon, 1284 FA
> *Lamerton'* 1242 Fees 756 *et passim*, *Lammerton* 1749 *FF*

'tun by the Lumburn stream,' v. *supra* 9. The earliest reference is to a place, not to the river. Probably the river-name, like Meavy *infra* 229, applied then to the whole manor.

CHADDLEHANGER [tʃæliŋgər]

> *Cheldesangre* 1238 *Ass* (p), *Chedelhanger* 1521 *Recov*
> *Chadelhangre* 1304 *Ass*, 1330 *SR* (p), *-dil-* 1330 *Ass*
> *Challinger* 1708 *Recov*

'*Ceadela*'s hangra,' or possibly 'cold spring *hangra*.' v. ceald, wielle, the place being near the source of a stream. Cf. Channey Grove (Berks) *Chaderhangra* 1175, *Chedelhangre* 1185 P, *Chadelhengre* 1231 Hurley Charters.

COLLACOMBE BARTON is *Colacoma* 1086 DB, *Collecumb'* 1242 Fees 789, *Cullecumb* 1242 Fees 756, 1284 FA, *Culecumb* 1244 *Ass*, *Colecumbe* 1244 *Ass*, *-comb* 1303 FA, 1330 *SR* (p). '*Cula's* cumb,' Cf. Culham (O), *Culanham* BCS 352.

HARTWELL is *Herdewill'* 1242 Fees 781, *Hertewill juxta Dount'ton* 1319 *Ass*, *Hurtwille juxta Dunterton* 1320 *Ass*. 'Hart spring,' i.e. where they watered, v. wielle. The second and third forms above would seem to refer to this place though Dunterton is in fact some miles distant.

HURLDITCH COURT is *Whurueldych* 1351 *Ass*, *Wyrueldyche* 1365 *Ass*, *Whyr-* 1413 *Ass*, *Hurueldych* 1475–85 ECP 2, 220. 'Circular

ditch,' v. hwyrfel, dic. The place is situated in a pan or circular
hollow (J.J.A.), but the exact sense of dic is uncertain. Cf. *on ða
hwyrfeldic* (BCS 670) and *to hwerfeldice* (KCD 705).

LAMERHOOE is *Lamerhowe* 1562 *FF*. The name may be a compound of OE *lambra*, genitive plural of lamb, and hoh, referring
to the spur of land running into the Tamar here. Mr Alexander
suggests, however, that the name Lamburn may at an early date
have been applied to the whole parish and that hoh, like tun,
refers to an area included in the manor. Cf. Dunterton and
Dunterue *supra* 182.

OTTERY

   Odetreu 1086 DB, *Odatrew* 1193 Oliver 95, *Odetrewe* 1504
      Ipm, *Oddetrewe* 1242 Fees 757, 1303, 1316 FA
   Ottrewe, Odytre 1413 *Ass*, *Ottrewe al. Ottrey* 1540 Oliver

'*Od(d)a*'s tree,' v. treow. This may have been a boundary
mark, since the place is situated on the border of Lamerton and
Tavistock parishes.

PITTESCOMBE is *Puttokescumbe* 1238 *Ass* (p). This may mean
'kite's combe' from ME *puttock*, 'kite.' Alternatively the first
element may be a derivative of the OE pers. name *Putta*. The
modern form shows the not uncommon Devon change of *u* to *i*.
v. Introd. *supra* xxxiv.

VENN HO and TREVENN (6") are *Fenn* 1488 (*Rental*), *Treven* 1586,
1670 (*Deed*). v. fenn. These places are near together by the
Lumburn stream and the names are probably identical, *tre*
representing ME *atter* as in Tredown *supra* 146.

WILLESTREW is *Wilavestreu* 1086 DB, *Willestre* 1242 Fees 789,
-truwe 1284 FA, *Weleuestre* 1244 *Ass*, *Wylestrewe, Wylestredoune*
1413 *Ass*. '*Wīglāf*'s tree.'

ATWATER COTTAGES (6") is *Atwater* in 1751 *Recov*. CAPELTOR
(6") is *Gabletor wood* t. Jas 1 ECP 328. CHOLWELL may have
been the home of Hamelin *Coldewylle* (1428 FA). 'Cold spring,'
v. cald, wielle. A small brook rises here. COMBE is *Thercomb*
1562 *FF*. *Ther* is ME (*at*) *ther*, 'at the.' GRENOVEN WOOD is
Grengfenne juxta Lamerton 1288 *Ass*. 'Green marshy place.' For

the medial vowel, *v.* Introd. xxxvi. HAYCOMBE (6″) is *Haycomb* 1365 *Ass*, *v.* cumb. It is near Haye. HAYE, GREAT, is *Le Heie* 1238 *Ass*, *v.* (ge)hæg. HILL is *Hyltowne* 1558–79 ECP. For the *town*, *v. infra* 676. PITLAND is *Pitlonde* 1457 *FF*. 'Land in the hollow.' RUSHFORD is so spelt in 1765 D. SLEW WOOD (6″) is *Slowe wood* t. Jas 1 ECP 328, cf. Slew *supra* 28. THEALE (6″) is *Ouerethele juxta Lamerton* 1361 *Ass*, *v.* þel. There is a small stream here crossed by a footbridge. 'Over' presumably in contrast to some other footbridge. WIDSLADE (6″) is *Wideslad'* 1203 Cur, *Wydeslade* 1413 *Ass*. 'The wide slæd.' WOODLEY is *Wodelygh juxta Lamerton* 1345 *Ass*, *v.* wudu, leah.

Lewtrenchard

LEWTRENCHARD [trænʃəd] 137 D 8

> *Leuya, Lewe* 1086 DB, *Lewe juxta Raddon* 1298 *Ass*
> *Lyu* 1238 FF, 1242 Fees 786, 1284 FA, (*Trencharde*) 1261 Exon
> *Lyw(e)* 1242 Fees 757, 1303 FA, *Liw* 1244 *Ass*, 1274 Exon, *Lewtrancharde* 1431 Exon
> *Trenchardeslieu* 1316 *Ass*

The place takes its name from the river on which it is situated (*v. supra* 8). The family of *Trenchard* is first mentioned in connexion with the place in 1238 (FF), but a Ricard *Trencard* occurs in the county as early as c. 1100 (Earle 258). Cf. Coombe Trenchard *infra* 188.

BEECHCOMBE

> *Biddelescumb(e)* 1244 *Ass*
> *Bittelescumbe* 1244 *Ass* (p), *-combe* 1356 *Ass*, *Bitelescumb* 1270 *Ass*, *-iscombe* 1330 *SR* (p)
> *Bikelliscumbe* 1244 *Ass* (p)
> *Bitchcombe al. Biddescombe* 1739 *Recov*

'*Bittel*'s cumb.' *Bittel* is not on record but would be an *l*-derivative of the pers. name *Bitta* apparently found in *bittan cnoll* (BCS 1080). Cf. Bittleford *infra* 526. The modern *Beech-* is probably a euphemism. Cf. Beechburn (PN NbDu 16).

GALFORD [gælvərd] is *Galford(e)* 1544 *SR*, 1625 *FF* and is probably identical with the place called *Gafulford, Gafolford*[1] in the ASC (*s.a.* 823), the site of a battle between the Britons and the men of Devon. The first element is probably OE *gafol*, 'tax, duty,' perhaps referring to a ford where payment was exacted for passage. The OE *gafol*, 'fork,' is unlikely on topographical grounds. There is a ford here but no fork for some 1½ miles.

HOLDSTRONG (6")

> *Hawlestorn* 1238 *Ass*
> *Holdesthorn* 1244 *Ass*, -*torne* 1314 *Ass*, -*disthorn* 1249 *Ass*,
>   *Holesthorn* 1305 *Ass*, *Holstorne* 1333 *SR* (p)
> *Hyalde(s)thorn* 1249 *Ass*

The second element is OE *þorn*. The first is probably the pers. name discussed under Holsworthy *supra* 146.

WADDLESTONE is *Wadelescota* 1086 DB, *Wadeleston'* 1242 Fees 786, 1303 FA, *Wath-* 1249 *Ass*, *Warstrong* 1809 M. It takes its name from *Wadell'*, the holder of the manor TRE (DB). For the change of second element cf. Almiston and Luffincott *supra* 80, 152.

COOMBE TRENCHARD (6"), FOXCOMBE, and WOODA were probably the homes of Reginald de *Cumb* (1244 *Ass*), John de *Foxcombe* (1330 *SR*), and Robert *atte Wode* (ib.).

BURLEY DOWN is *Burlegh* 1244 *Ass* (p), v. burh, leah. There are ancient 'camps' here. GALFORD DOWN is *Galfer Downe* t. Hy 8 FF, v. *supra* 187. LEWDOWN is *Leywedon* 1270 *Ass*.

Lifton

LIFTON 137 D 6

> (*æt*) *Liwtune* 880–5 (c. 1000) BCS 553[2], (*fram*) *liwtune* c. 970 BCS 1247
> *Listona* 1086 DB
> *Leftun* 1155 RBE, -*ton* 1209 Pap, 1227 Pat
> *Liftuna* 1158 P *et passim* to 1331 Ipm, with variant spellings *Lyf-* and -*ton(e)*

---

[1] The identification was first suggested by the late Rev. S. Baring Gould.

[2] This identification of the manor of *Liwtun* in Alfred's will receives strong support from the fact that *Liston* in DB was held TRE by Queen Edith. It is extremely likely also that we have a further reference to this place in the *Leowtun* (BCS 677) where Æthelstan held his court in November 931.

'Farm by the river Lew,' *v.* tun. A change of *w* to *v* is evidenced in some Devon names, though usually at a later date. Cf. Meavy *infra* 229, and Introd. xxxv. In this case the *v* may well have been early unvoiced to *f* before *t*. For the reverse development cf. Woolscroft in Poundstock (Co), *Foghelescroft*, *Foglescroft* 1302 *Ass*, *Foulescroft* 1508 *FF*. Mr Alexander suggests that in early times the lower Lyd was called the Lew, the upper Lyd the Cory (*v.* Coryton *supra* 181), in other words that the Lew was regarded as the main stream, the Cory as its tributary.

ASHLEIGH is *Assileia* 1086 DB (Exon), *Aisselie* (Exch), *Asseleg* 1228 FF, *Esselegh* 1242 Fees 756, *Asshelegh juxta Kelly* 1323 *Ass*. *v.* æsc, leah.

CARLEY is *Carleg'* 1230 P, *-legh(e)* 1238, 1281 *Ass*, *-leye* 1287 *FF*, *Kearlegh* 1330 *Ass* (all p), *v.* leah. It is difficult to find any OE word to account for the first element of this name. It is likely therefore that we have here the Co *car* (*caer*), 'fort, camp,' common in Cornish place-names. It is true that no remains of any camp are visible at this spot, but the same is the case with many Cornish place-names containing this word. The place is so near the Cornish border that it is quite possible that the whole name is British, the second element being a word equivalent to W *llech*, 'flat-stone,' which is apparently found in many Cornish names in *leigh*, *e.g.* Treleigh, Fenterleigh (olim *Trelegh, Funtenlegh*).

COOKWORTHY, HIGHER and LOWER

    Kokewrthy 1238 *Ass* (p), *Cokewurthi* 1244 *Ass* (p), *-worthe* 1308 Exon (p), *-worthi* 1330 *SR* (p)

    Cockewrthi 1238 *Ass* (p), *Cookeworthy al. Cockworthy* 1690 Deed

    Nitheracokaworthi 1299 DA 33

'The worðig of *Coc(ca)*.' Cf. Cockbury (Gl), BCS 246 *Coccanburh*.

GATHERLEY is *Ghiderlega, Gyderlega* t. Hy 2 (14th), *Gyderleg*, *Giderleg* 14th *Launceston*, *Gatherley* 1606 *FF*. Professor Ekwall suggests the possibility of OE *gýþrife*, 'cockle,' as the first element in this name. *v.* leah. Hence, 'clearing where cockle grows.'

HUNTFORD (lost) is *Hunteneford* 1299 DA 33, 1333 *SR* (both p), *Hunt(a)ford* 1677, 1750 *Recov.* 'The huntsmen's ford.' Cf. Huntingford (Gl), *huntena forda* BCS 764.

MARKSTONE (6″) is *Markeston* 1319 *Ass* (p), 1415 *Ass*, *Markstone* 1529 ECP 6, 69. Probably 'boundary stone,' *v.* mearc. The farm is at the boundary mark of three parishes.

MOONHOUSE is *Monyshous* 1422 DA 33, *Monehouse* t. Hy 6 IpmR and is probably to be associated with the family of Martin *Mona* (1299 DA 33).

POLSON, POLSON BRIDGE (6″) is *Pouleston Brigge* 1338 *Rental*, *Polstun bridge* c. 1550 Leland. The ME form suggests that the original vowel was long. The name may therefore be a compound of 'pool' and 'stone,' possibly referring to some stone here by the river, marking the boundary between Devon and Cornwall. Alternatively the first element may be the personal name *Paul*, when the name would be of late formation and denote 'Paul's farm.' *v.* tun.

TINHAY is *Bituinia* 1194 P, *Tuneo* 1316 Pat (p), *Tenyowe* 1486–1515 ECP 3, 168, *Twyneow* c. 1500 PlymRec. The meaning is 'between the waters,' the place being on a tongue of land between the Thrushel and Lyd rivers. Cf. Tinney *supra* 163 and Twinyeo *infra* 479.

TURCHINGTON [titʃiŋtən] is *T(h)ycheneton* 14th *Launceston* and was the home of Peter de *Tuchenaton* (1333 *SR*). 'Farm at the crossways,' *v.* tun and cf. Twitchen *supra* 57. Three or four tracks meet here.

BEARA, COMBE (6″), HEALE, SMALLACOMBE, STONE[1], WELLTOWN (6″), and YEAT, were probably the homes of Andrew de *Bere* (1277 *Ass*), John Brok' de *Combe* (1322 *Ass*), William *atte Hele* (1333 *SR*), John de *Smalecombe* (ib.), Henry *atte Stone* (ib.), John *atte Wille* (ib.), and Martin *atte Yate* (ib.). *v.* bearu, cumb, healh, smæl, wielle, geat.

CAWDRON (6″) is *Coddethorn* 1330 *SR* (p), *Cadron* 1765 D. '*Codda*'s thorntree.' CROSSTOWN (6″) is *Crossetowne* 1677 *Recov.*

---

[1] *Lyftenstone* 1426 Pat.

For *town*, *v. infra* 676. KINGSWELL (6″) is *Kingswill* 1677
Recov. Lifton was a 'royal' manor as early as the time of King
Alfred. LAKE is *Lake* 1504–15 ECP 4, 292. 'Streamlet,' *v.* lacu.
LIFTONDOWN (hamlet) is *Lifton Downe* 1737 *FF*. NETHERCOTT
(6″) is *Nythercote* 1547 *SR*. LIFTON PARK is *Parke* 1299 DA 33.
v. pearroc. WHITELY is *Wytteleye* 1311 *Ass* (p), *Witley* 1765 D.
Probably 'white clearing,' *v.* leah. WOOLADON is *Nythere-
wolvedon* 1322 *Ass*. 'Wolves' hill,' *v.* dun, neoðere. WORTHAM
is *Michilworthene* 1475–85 ECP 2, 220. *v.* mycel, worþign.

Lydford

LYDFORD (with Dartmoor Forest)[1] 137 D 10[2]

(*to*) *Hlidan* c. 910 (12th) BCS 1335, *Hlydanforda* c. 1000
   (997 C, D) ASC
Lydanford 979–1016 Coins
Hlidaford 1018 (11th) Crawf 4, c. 1120 (997 E) ASC
Lideforda, Lidefort 1086 DB, *Lydeford* 1232–9 Ch *et passim*,
   with variant spelling *Lide-, Lydaford* 1346 *Ass, Lydyforde*
   1390 Exon
Lidesford' 1181 P
Liddeford' 1230 P, 1238 *Ass*
Ludeford(e) 1232–9 Ch *et freq* to 1392 Exon, *Ludford* 1379
   MinAcct

'Ford over the river Lyd.' For the stream-name *v. supra* 9.

AMICOMBE HILL is *Aunnacomb* (sic) 1346 Dartmoor, *Ame-* 1355
DuCo, Amma- MinAcct, 1364 *DuCo, Amme-* 1352 *MinAcct*. The
'combe' must have been one of the valleys below, perhaps that
to the east. The first element is uncertain.

BABENY is *Babbeneye* 1260 Exon, *Babenny* 1303 Dartmoor,
Babenay 1317 Pat (p), *Babeney* 1481, 1497 *Ct, Beubeney, Bew-
beney* 1588 *DuCo*. '*Babba*'s well-watered land.' *v.* eg. The farm
lies by the Walla Brook.

---

[1] The parish of Lydford is the largest in England, extending over nearly
60,000 acres. It includes the whole of the ancient area known as Dartmoor
Forest, the boundaries of which were first fixed in a perambulation of 1240,
and have remained practically unaltered to the present day.
[2] Part of the parish is to be found in 138 D, E, F, G, H and J.

BELLEVER

> Welford 1355 DuCo, Weleford 1477 DuCo, 1481 Ct, Wellafo*
> Mills, Willaford Mylls 1579 DuCo
> Bellab(o)ur 1608, 1609 DuCo
> Bellaford 1663 DuCo, 1702 Dartmoor
> Bellefor 1736 DuCo

Probably a compound of wielle and ford. Confusion of w a*
v is common in SW dialects and interchange of v (f) and b
evidenced in Broxwater (Co), Froxewade 1289 Ass.

BELLEVER TOR is probably named after the farm. For the mode*
form of the name v. Introd. xxxiv.

BRIMPTS

> Bremstout(e) 1307 Dartmoor, 1317 Pat (p), 1347 DuCo, 14*
> Ct, Bremp- t. Hy 6 Ct, Bremestowte 1481 Ct
> Brynstowte 1443 Ct
> Bremst 1611 DuCo, Bremst otherwise Brymst 1613 DuC*
> Bromist 1736 DuCo

The second element in this name is found also in Stou*
Stouthaies, Winstout, Southill (v. Index) and probably in Sto*
(So) for which no early forms have been noted. These places a*
all on or by well-marked hills and the forms point to an OE *st*
used to denote such. In ON we have stútr, which stands *
ablaut relation to OE stott, used of a bull, and also of the bu*
end of a horn, a stumpy thing. The root idea behind stútr*
probably something stumpy. Such a term might well be used *
a rounded hill of a certain shape and would furnish a clo*
parallel to the history of the word peak, similarly used of a hi*
(cf. Mawer, Problems of PN Study, 71). The first element *
probably OE bremel, hence 'bramble-grown hill.'

CATER'S BEAM is so spelt in 1809 (M). Beam is found in ma*
old Dartmoor minor names, e.g. Lapwyll beme, Yealbroke ben*
1538, Bollamerebeym 1539, Peppercornebeme 1611. R. H. Wor*
(DA 58, 360) suggests that the word was a mining ter*
perhaps referring to the 'rocking beam' of a pump used f*
mining purposes.

COCKS HILL is Cockshull 1573 Ct. It must be identical with th* hill called *Mewyburgh(e)* in the 1240 Perambulation (Dartmoor)[1]. The Buckland Cartulary copy of this has *Meweburghe*.

CONIES DOWN is probably identical with the spot called *Condyshull* 1346 Dartmoor, *Condeshull* 1352 *MinAcct*. The forms are late but it may be that in the first element we have an old hill-name identical with that found in Countisbury *supra* 62. It is clear that the modern form has been influenced by association with ME *coney*, 'rabbit.'

CRANMERE POOL is *Cremere in Thertmore* c. 1470 WmWo, *Crau Meer or Cran Meer Pool* 695 Camden, *Crau Mere Pool vulgo Cran-mere* 1765 D. The name was originally 'crow mere' rather than 'crane (or heron) mere.' Cranmere Pool is an insignificant pool in the heart of Dartmoor, but it is famous as being the source of the Teign, the Dart, the Tavy and the Okement rivers. For the form *Cremere, v.* Introd. xxxiii.

CROCKERN TOR is *Crokkerntor, Crockerntor* 1481 *Ct.* The Tor takes its name from Crockern Fm (6″). This is a compound of OE *crocc*, 'pot, vessel, crock,' and *ærn*, referring possibly to a house where pots were made or found. Cf. Crockernwell *infra* 428 and Potterne (W).

CUT HILL takes its name from *Cut Lane* near by. This is defined as 'a track or way formed by removing the soft surface soil and leaving exposed the harder and often stony subsoil; a way artificially cut through a mire' (DA 58, 362).

DUNNABRIDGE (6″)

> *Donebrugge* 1305 Dartmoor, *Donabrigge* 1358 Dartmoor
> *Dunbrigge* 1347 Dartmoor, *-brugge* 1356 DuCo, *Dunbruggeford* 1379 DuCo
> *Dounbriggesforth* 1365 DuCo
> *Dounebrigge* 1377 DuCo, *Donaghbrigg Hill* 1403 Dartmoor, *Donabrighull* 1417 DuCo
> *Dounabridge al. Denybridge* 1579 Dartmoor

'Bridge by the down,' *v.* dun, referring to a bridge over the Dart here. There is a hill near by. For the medial syllable, *v.* Introd. xxxvi.

---

[1] In the perambulation it is the one point between Mis Tor and Lynch Tor and therefore cannot be named from the river Meavy as suggested by Ekwall (RN 262), unless indeed Meavy was also the old name for the Walkham.

DUNNA GOAT is *the gate called Dunyng gate* 1588 *DuCo, Dunyng Yeate* (ib.). The 'gate' must have been one of the forest boundary marks.

EYLESBARROW is *Elysburgh(e), Elesburghe* 1240 Dartmoor, *Elesburghe* 1240 Buckfast, *Gyllesburghe* (sic) 1291 (1408) Dartmoor, *Elysburghe* 1444 Dartmoor, *Ellysburgh* 1481 *Ct.* '*Elli*'s barrow,' *v.* beorg. This was an ancient forest boundary mark and the tumuli still existing here probably mark the site of some ancient burial-place.

HESSARY TORS

> *Hysfothere, aliam Hysfothere* 1240 Buckfast
> *Hysfothre, Ysfo(r)ther(e), Esforthere, Heghysfoder* 1240 *Peramb*
> *Hysfochres* (sic) 1408 Dartmoor
> *Hoggysfoder(e)* 1481 Ct
> great, little *Hisworthie* 1608 Dartmoor
> *Easter and Souther Hissary* 1702 Dartmoor

No certain explanation of this name can be offered. It is possible that it may be a compound of OE *hīehst*, 'highest,' and the word *foðer* found in Fatherford *infra* 202, but the sense of the compound is obscure. For the phonology, *v.* Introd. xxxiv–v.

HEXWORTHY [hæksəri]

> *Hextenesworth'* 1317 Pat (p), *Hextenworth* 1344 Dartmoor (p)
> *Hextworthy, Bysouthhexworthi* 1379 Dartmoor, *Hextesworthy*
>   1417 *Ct, Hexteworthy* 1481 *Ct*
> *Haxary* 1809 M.

In 1417 there is mention of William *Hexta* of *Hextesworthy* and in 1481 of Robert *Hexte* of *Hexteworthy*. It is fairly certain therefore that the place took its name from an ancestor of these men, and since the element worðig was in living use at a comparatively late date the name may not go back much earlier than the first record of the place. The earliest form of the pers. name appears to be *Hexten*, the ME representative of OE *Hēahstān*.

HUCCABY is *la Woghebye* 1296 Rowe (p), *Woghby* 1317 Pat (p), *Woghebi* 1340 SR (p), *Hogheby(e)* 1417 Ct, *Hoockaby* 1573 Ct, *Hookeby* 1608 DuCo. This is probably a compound of OE woh, 'crooked,' and byge, 'bend, curve,' referring to the big loop of the

West Dart here. For loss of initial *w*, cf. Oatnell and Odle *infra* 207, 642.

HUNTINGDON WARREN is *Huntyndon* 1481 *Ct*, *Huntingdon* 1598 *DuCo*. The forms are too late to enable us to settle the first element with certainty, but it may well be OE *huntena*, hence 'huntsmen's hill.' Cf. *Huntford supra* 190.

LAUGHTER HOLE, LAUGHTER TOR [la·tər]

> *Laddretorre* 1362 Dartmoor, 1417 *DuCo*, *Ladretorcomb* 1379 *MinAcct*, *Laddertorcomb* 1416 Dartmoor
> *Leddertor* 1476 Dartmoor, *Leddercombe* 1475 *DuCo*, *Lethertorrehall* 1557 *DuCo*
> *Liddercomb* 1476 Dartmoor
> *Lodercombe* 1555 *DuCo*, *Loterholl* 1616 *DuCo*
> *Lartercombfoote* 1609 *DuCo*, *Laster Hole*, *Laughter Combe* 1702 Dartmoor

The first element may be a Celtic word corresponding to Welsh *llethr*, Co *ledr*, 'slope, cliff, declivity,' with early attempts at folk-etymology. A possible further example of this name is found in Leather Tor *infra* 245.

LYNCH TOR is identical with the spot called *Lullingesfote*, *Lullyngyssete*, *-ingessete* in the 1240 Perambulation, but it is not quite clear if the modern name is a corruption of this or whether it is a new name (*v*. hlinc). The early forms suggest that *Lulling* was the name of the hill rather than of some man, *fote* ('foot') and *sete* referring to its foot and summit, *v*. Kingsett *infra* 201. In 1608 (Dartmoor) the spot is called *Luntesborowe*, i.e. 'tumulus of some man named *Lunt*,' a name which is apparently preserved in LIMSBARROW (6"), a tumulus on the tor.

MERRIPIT is *Meriput* 1344 Dartmoor (p), *Mirapyt* 1347 *DuCo* (p), *Myrapytte*, *atte Myrypytte* 1417 *Ct*, *Merepyt* 1481 *Ct*, *Merepitt* 1585 Dartmoor. 'Pleasant hollow,' *v*. myrig.

GREAT MIS TOR is *Mystorre*, *per medium Mytorystor* (sic) 1240 *Peramb* (other versions have *per medium mistum*, *per mediam Mistmore*), *Mystorre* 1240 Buckfast, *Mistorr* 1291 (1408) Dartmoor, *Mistorr moore* 1608 Dartmoor. The meaning may be simply 'mist tor,' perhaps because the tor was more fre-

quently enshrouded in mist or fog than others in the neighbourhood. We may possibly compare Misdon *supra* 150.

MIS TOR PAN is *Mistorpanna* 1291 (1408) Dartmoor. It is a
circular rock basin or 'pan' on the tor.

NUN'S CROSS or SIWARD'S CROSS (6″) is (*ad*) *crucem Sywardi* 1240
Peramb, (*usque*) *Crucem Sywarde* 1240 Buckfast, *crucem Silwardi*
(sic) 1291 (1408), *Seawards Crosse* 1608, *Nannecross* 1699 Dartmoor. This is an ancient forest boundary mark and must take
its name from some unknown man named *Sigeweard*. The reason
for the present name is unknown.

PIZWELL

>*Pushylle* 1260 Exon, *-hull* 1355 *DuCo*, *-hill* 1452 *MinAcct*,
>Pusshill* 1260 Dartmoor
>*Pishull* 1305 Dartmoor, 1347 *MinAcct*, *Pys-* 1417 *Ct*, *Pysehyll*
>1443 *Ct* (p)
>*Pesehill* t. Hy 6 *Ct*, 1578 *DuCo*, *Peselford*, *Peselsmyth* 1521
>Dartmoor

'Pease hill,' i.e. where they were grown. For the form *Pus-*,
cf. Posbrook, PN Sx 187.

POSTBRIDGE is *a stone bridge of 3 arches called Post bridg* 1675
Ogilby, *Poststone Bridge* 1720 Crossing. There is an ancient
'clapper' bridge here which was in existence centuries before
the present road-bridge. Presumably the name 'post' was
added when the bridge began to carry an important post-road.

PRINCE HALL

>*Prinshill* 1521 Dartmoor, *Prynshull* 1555 *DuCo*
>*Prynshall* 1533 Dartmoor, 1535, 1555 *DuCo*, *Prins-* 1541
>*DuCo*
>*Princehall* 1561 *DuCo*

The forms are not sufficiently early for certainty. The place
may derive from a medieval owner *Prynn*, the name having been
altered later owing to the fact that it was a Duchy of Cornwall
possession and as such belonged to the *Prince* of Wales. The
farm is in a hollow and the *hill* must be that behind it.

PRINCETOWN is a modern settlement which has grown up round

the well-known prison here, originally built in 1808 for French and American prisoners of war. It took its name from the Prince Regent, afterwards George IV.

RUNNAGE

> *Renewych* 1317 Pat (p)
> *Renewith* 1365 *DuCo*, 1379 Dartmoor, *-wich* 1386 *MinAcct*,
>   *Renwige* 1608 *DuCo*, *Rennidge* 1702 Dartmoor
> *Reynweche* 1452 *MinAcct*
> *Rynneweche* 1474 *Ct*, 1477 *DuCo*
> *Ranage* 1666 Dartmoor

The forms are too late for any certainty, but Professor Ekwall and Dr Ritter agree in suggesting a pers. name *Rægna as the first element, a shortened form of one of the OE names in *Rægen-, Regen-*. Hence 'Rægna's farm,' v. wic. If that is the case, we have an example of a rare formation, viz. wic with a pers. name.

RYDER'S HILL. In the 1240 Perambulation in the Buckfast Cartulary it is called *Gnatteshulle* and *Gnatesburghe*. Later forms are *Gnatteshill, Gnattleshill, Knattleburroughe* 1608 Dartmoor, *Knattleburroughe called in old records Gnatteshill* 1608 *DuCo, Knatteshill* 1786 *DuCo, Ryders Hill* 1827 G. The *Gn-* forms seem to be the correct ones. The name may mean 'gnat's hill' or perhaps '*Gnat's* hill,' *Gnat* (OE *gnæt*) being here a pers. name of ME origin. Cf. Great Gnats' Head, 2 miles to the west.

SHERBERTON is *Sherborne* 1358 Dartmoor, *Shirburnecroft* 1379 *MinAcct, Sherborne Croft* 1476 Dartmoor, *Sherborton* 1736, *Sherburn* or *Sherberton* 1813 *DuCo*. The name must originally have designated a piece of land or 'croft' by the Swincombe (earlier *Sherborne*) River *supra* 13. For the late addition of 'ton,' cf. Yelverton *infra* 225.

TWO BRIDGES is *Tobrygge* t. Hy 6 *Ct, terr' vocat' too bridge* 1573 *Ct, Two Bridges* 1659 *FF*. The meaning is probably simply 'at the bridge,' with the common Devon use of *to* (later corrupted to *two*) for *at*. Cf. Staverton Bridge *infra* 521.

WATERN TOR is *Walterysdoune* 1481 *Ct, Waterdown(e)* 1520 Dartmoor, 1555 *DuCo, Waterdontorr* 1609 Rowe, *Walter Tor*

R

1702 Dartmoor. If the earliest form refers to this place the meaning is 'Walter's hill,' cf. Bridgewater (So), earlier *Bruge Walteri*. In any case *Watern* is clearly a corruption of *Waterdon*.

WISTMAN'S WOOD is so spelt by Risdon (c. 1630). This is a wood of stunted oaks by the Dart. *Wistman* is locally thought to refer to the Devil, the first syllable being the Devon dialect *wisht*, 'eerie, uncanny.' The wood is in a lonely situation and its general appearance strange and gloomy.

ASSYCOMBE is *Assecomb* 1488 *DuCo*, 1514 *Ct*. Probably 'asses' combe,' i.e. where they grazed. BEARDOWN is *Berdon* 1498 *Ct*, *Bear Down* 1808 *DuCo*. v. dun. BRAT TOR is *Bradetorre* 1386 *MinAcct*. 'Broad torr.' BROWNBERRY (6") is *Brembery* 1563, 1608 *DuCo*, *Bremberry al. Brounberry* 1585, *Bromebury* 1586 Dartmoor. Probably 'bramble burh,' v. bremel. CHERRYBROOK FM is *Churybrokset* 1347 Dartmoor. v. Cherrybrook *supra* 3. For *set*, cf. Kingsett *infra* 201. CHITTAFORD DOWN (6") is *Chiteford* 1379 *MinAcct*. CROW TOR is *Crewtor* 1346, *Crewetorre* 1347 Dartmoor. 'Crow-torr,' v. Introd. xxxiii. DARTMEET is *Dartameet* 1616 *DuCo*, -met 1689 Dartmoor. The spot where the E. and W. Dart rivers join. DOWNTOWN is *la Doune* 1344 Dartmoor, *Dounton* n.d. Dartmoor. v. dun. For the *town*, v. *infra* 676. DURY is *terram de Dury* 1390 *Ct* and is probably to be associated with the family of Richard *Dury* (1344 Dartmoor). ERME HEAD is *Ermehede* 1474 *Ct*. The source of the Erme river *supra* 5. FERNWORTHY is *Vernaworthy* 1355 *DuCo*, *Ferne-* 1377 *Ct*, *Vernworthie* 1524 *SR*, *Fernworthy Yeat* 1579 Dartmoor. 'Bracken worðig.' FICES WELL is *Fices Well, Fitzwell* 1702 Dartmoor. The well was built by John *Fitz* of Tavistock in 1568 (LGS 254). FOX TOR is *Foxtorre Combe* 1444 Dartmoor, *Foxtorcomb* t. Hy 6 *Ct*. FUR TOR is *Vurtorre* 1346 Dartmoor, *Forterfote* 1528 *DuCo*. The first element might be OE *fierra*, ME *furre*, 'further.' It is in a remote situation. GRIMS GROVE (6") is *Grymesgrove* in 1240 *Peramb*. 'Grim's grove,' v. Grimspound *infra* 482. HARTLAND TOR is *Herterland(e)* 1521, 1540 Dartmoor. *Herter* is probably for earlier *Hertetor*, 'hart torr.' HOUND TOR is *Parva Hunde Torre, Parva Houndetor* 1240 *Peramb*. 'Hounds' torr' or '*Hunda*'s torr.' KITTY TOR is *Kit Tor* 1808 *DuCo*. Possibly 'kite torr.' KNEESET TORS are *Great, Little*

Kneeset 1827 G. For *set*, cf. Kingsett *infra* 201. LAKEHEAD
HILL is *Lakehevede* 1347 Dartmoor. 'Stream head,' *v.* lacu.
LINTS·TOR is *Linx Tor* 1765 D. MILL TOR is *Milltor* (1532
Dartmoor) and was possibly earlier 'middle tor' from its position
midway between Oke Tor and Yes Tor. OKE TOR is *Hoctor* 1808
DuCo. PLYM HEAD is *Plimheadd* 1608 Dartmoor. The source of
the river Plym. RENDLESTONE is *a great stone called Roundle* 1675
Ogilby, *Rundlestone* 1702 Dartmoor. 'Circular stone,' *v. rundle,
roundel* (NED). RIDDON is *Riddon* 1488 *DuCo,* 1585 Dartmoor,
Reddon 1586, *Ryddon* 1589 Dartmoor. Perhaps 'hill cleared of
undergrowth, etc.,' *v.* ridde, dun. ROUGH TOR [rɑutər] is
Rowetor 1532 Dartmoor. 'Rough tor,' cf. Rough Tor (Co),
Roghe-, Rowetorr 1284 FF. SKIR HILL is *Est Skurhill* 1619 *FF.*
For initial *sk, v.* Introd. xxxv. There is also a SKIRFORD close at
hand. It may be that the adjective was first applied to the ford,
of which it could more naturally be used, *v.* scir. SMITH HILL
is *Smithill* 1808 *DuCo.* STANNON TOR is *Stannon* 1702 Dartmoor. Stannon (Co) is *Staundon, Stondon* 1401 *Ct.* 'Stone hill.'
STEEPERTON TOR is *Steapedon* 1346 Dartmoor, t. Hy 6 *MinAcct,
Stapedon* 1355 *DuCo.* 'Steep hill,' *v.* dun. SWINCOMBE is
Swynecomb 1514 *Ct, Swenecombford* 1609 *DuCo, Swancombe*
1702 Dartmoor. 'Swine combe.' For the later vowel, cf. Swana-
ford *infra* 424. THIRLSTONE is *Therle-, Thurlestone* 1240 *Peramb.*
A forest boundary mark. The name means 'holed stone,' re-
ferring to an ancient stone on the hill here. Cf. Thurlestone *infra*
312. TOR ROYAL is a modern house erected c. 1800 (J. J. A.).
VARRACOMBE is *Fayrecombe* t. Hy 6 *Ct.* The first element is clearly
OE *fæger*, 'fair, beautiful.' WHITE BARROW is *Whytaburghe,
Westere Whyteburghe* 1240 Buckfast, *Ester Whyteburghe* 1240
Dartmoor, *Wyteburgh* 1377 *Ct.* 'White hill,' *v.* beorg. WILD
TOR is *Willtorrwill* 1702 Dartmoor. There is a well marked near
by (6").

Marystow

MARYSTOW 137 E 8

> (*Ecclesia*) *Sancte Marie Stou, Stowe* 1266–78 Exon, *Stowe
> Beate Marie* 1282 Exon, *Stowe Sanctae Mariae* 1341 *FF
> Marystowe* 1334, *Seyntmariestowe* 1394 Exon, *Stowemary*
> t. Hy 8 *Star Chamber, Marystow* or *Marstow* 1790 *Recov*

'Holy spot of St Mary,' *v.* stow.

CHOLWELL is *Cholewill* 1244 *Ass*, *Chaldewell* 1270 *Ass*, *-wille* 1341 *FF*, *Chollewill* 1330 *SR* (p). 'Cold spring,' *v.* cald, wielle.

DIPPERTOWN is *Dupeford* 1244 *Ass*, 1341 *FF*. 'Deep ford,' cf. Dipper (Co), *Dupeford* 1322 FF, 1349 Ipm, *Dupford* 1464 *Rental*, *Dypper* 1695 Camden. For *town*, *v. infra* 676.

RADDON is *Ratdona* 1086 DB, *Raddun(e)* 1197 FF, 1242 Fees 795, *-don(e)* 1242 Fees 757, 1272 Ipm, *West Raddon juxta Lyfton* 1299 *Ass*, *Reddoñ* 1216 ClR. Probably 'red hill,' *v.* read, dun.

SYDENHAM is *Sidreham* 1086 DB, *Parva Sideham* 1242 Fees 776, *Sydeham*, *Shydeham* 1284 FA, *Parva Sydenham* 1303 FA, *Little Sythenham* 1382 *FF*. 'At the wide hamm,' *v.* sid. There is comparatively flat ground here by the Lyd. For the DB form, *v.* IPN 107.

WARRACOTT is probably identical with *Woruegate* 1333 *SR* (p), 1335 *Ass*. *v.* geat. The first element may be OE *weorf*, 'cattle, beast of burden,' hence, 'gate of the cattle.' For interchange of *cott* and *gate* cf. Portgate *infra* 208.

LEE, THORNE, and TREHILL were the homes of John *atter Lighe* (1327 *Ass*), Walter *atte Thorne* (1330 *SR*), and William *attar Hulle* (1339 *Ass*). *v.* leah and cf. Tredown *supra* 146.

ALLERFORD is *Aureford* 1242 Fees 757, *Alreford* 1330 *SR* (p), *Alresford* 1346 FA. 'Alder ford.' BULLHILL (6″) is *Bolehull(e)* 1330 *SR* (p), 1382 *FF*. LEE DOWNS is *Leghdon* 1341 *FF*. ROUTER is *Rowetorr* 1461 *FF*, *Roughtor* 1765 D. Cf. Rough Tor *supra* 199. SOUTHDOWN (6″) is so spelt in 1729 *Deed*. TIBRIDGE is *Tibberigge* 1394 *Ass*. '*Tibba*'s ridge,' cf. Tippacott *supra* 60.

Marytavy

MARYTAVY 137 F 10

> *Tavi* 1086 DB, *Tavy* 1242 Fees 776, (*St Mary*) 1290 Ipm, (*ecclesia*) *Sancte Marie de Tavi* 1270 Exon
> *Tavymarie* 1412 Exon, *Marytauey* 1577 Saxton

Both this settlement and Petertavy *infra* 231 were at first called simply Tavy after the river by which they are situated, *supra* 14. Later the two places were distinguished by the dedication of their churches to St Mary and St Peter.

BURNTOWN (6″) is *Berna* 1086 DB, *Burne* 1330 *SR* (p), *Borne Towne* 1563 *FF*. 'At the stream,' v. **burna**. For *town, v. infra* 676.

KINGSETT is *Kyngsete* 1417 *Ct* (p), *Kyngesset* 1478 *Ct* (p), *Kingsett* 1648 *Recov*. This name is found again in Widdecombe and Walkhampton *infra* 529, 245. All three places are situated on or below prominent hills and it is likely that they were originally hill-names, 'king's seat' signifying perhaps a lofty spot. Cf. Arthur's Seat in Edinburgh, Kingsettle Hill in Brewham (So), *Kingesettle* 1251 Ch, Kingsettle Fm in Gillingham (Do), *Kyngessettle* 1327 *SR* (p).

WARNE, NORTH and SOUTH

Wagesfella 1086 DB
Wag(h)efen(n)e 1242 Fees 776, 1303 FA, 1305 Ipm, 1330 *SR* (p), 1423 IpmR, (*juxta Tauistok*) 1310 *Ass*, *Waghfen* 1394 *Ass*
Wawefenne 1284 FA, *Waufen* 1428 FA, *Waven* 1488 *Rental*

The first element is probably connected with the stem *wag-* found in OE *wagian*, 'to shake,' of which Ekwall (RN 439) suggests we have a noun-derivative in Wawne (Y). The same compound is found in the form *wagufen* in the Thorndon Hall Charter (*v. infra* 296 *n*. 1). The whole name would mean 'quaking marsh,' v. **fenn**.

WRINGWORTHY is *Weringuerda, Weringheorda* 1086 DB, *Wringeworthy* 1238 FF, *Wringe-, Wryngeworthe* 1488 *Rental*. v. **worþig**. *Wring* occurs in So as a stream-name (RN 474) and here it may be the earlier name of the small tributary of the Tavy now called 'the Burne.' But since Devon names in *-worthy* are seldom compounded with a descriptive element, it is perhaps more likely that **Wringa* was a pers. name, probably related to the verb *wringan*, 'to wring, twist, squeeze' (cf. RN *loc cit.*). Curiously enough, there are four Wringworthys in Cornwall. This on the whole favours a significant first element, but it is difficult to suggest its source or to determine its sense.

BLACKDOWN is *Blakedon* 1345 *Deed, Blackdowne* 1563 *FF*. CREASON is *Creston* 1697 *Recov*. HARFORD BRIDGE is *Hartforde Yeate* 1589 Dartmoor, *Hartfordbridge* 1639 *Recov*. 'Hart ford.

HORNDON is *Horndon* 1284 Misc, 1333 *SR* (p). *v.* horn, dun.
There is a spur of land here running down into the Tavy. LEY
(6") is *Leye* 1443 *FF*. *v.* leah. WHITESTONE (6") is so spelt in
1651 *Recov.*

Okehampton and Okehampton Hamlets

OKEHAMPTON [ɔkiŋtən, ɔkəntən] 137 A 12

(*æt*) *ocmund tune,* (*æt*) *ocmond tune* c. 970 BCS 1245
Ochenemitona 1086 DB
Okementon(a) 1167 P, 1275 RH, *Ock-* 1238 FF, *Okemanton*
1238 *Ass*
Okematon' 1219 *Ass,* -*eton'* 1242 Fees 756, *Okemptone* 1261
Exon, *Ockamaton* early Hy 3 BM
Ocumptona 1222 Bracton, *Okumpton* 1274 Ipm, *Ocumtune*
1275 RH
Ochanton 1284 FA, *Okhamptone* 1316 FA, *Castalokampton*
1349 *Ass,* *Castel Okhampton* 1351 *Ass*
Okington 1543 LP, *Okenton* t. Hy 8 Dartmoor

'tun by the river Okement' (*supra* 11). The name was later
associated with the common terminal -*hampton*, but the local
pronunciation [ɔkiŋtən, ɔkəntən] still survives among old people
in the district.

ALFORDON is *Alfardesdune* 1242 Fees 756, 785, *Alfarsdone* 1330
SR (p), *Alferdisdon* 1333 *SR* (p). '*Ælfheard*'s hill,' *v.* dun.

BOWERLAND is *La Bourlonde* 1292 Ipm, *Bowrelond* 1532 Dartmoor, and gave name to Margery *atte Bourlond* 1330 *SR*. This
is OE *būrland,* 'land occupied by peasants,' from *būr,* 'peasant.'

CHICHACOTT [tʃisəkət] is *Cicecota* 1086 DB, *Chichecot'* 1276 *Ass*
(p), *Chechecotte* 1549 Pat, *Churchcott* t. Eliz ChancP. '*Cicca*'s
cote.' Cf. Chicheley (PN Bk 33).

FATHERFORD is *Foddreford* 1296 Rowe 294, *Foderford* 1340 *SR,*
Foddyrford 1361 *Ass* (all p). The first element is probably OE
foðer, 'load, cartload,' the meaning being a ford over which a
cartload could pass. Cf. Barford (PN BedsHu 50).

FOWLEY is *Foleleghe* 1267 Exon (p), *Folingelegh* 1280 *FF,* *Folle*
1462 Pat. '*Fola*'s clearing,' *v.* ing, leah. The late appearance of

inge in this name is difficult to account for unless we assume that the earlier form is really elliptical for a fuller *Foling(e)leghe*. This pers. name is not recorded, but would be the OE *fola*, 'foal,' used as a pers. name. Cf. William *Folia* 1330 *SR* (D).

GLENDON is *Glindon* 1238 *Ass*, *Glyndon* 1330 *SR* (both p). *v.* dun. This is a difficult name. Association with the East Sussex Glynde (PN Sx 352), which seems never to be found outside that area, is out of the question. Possibly we have a hybrid compound of Cornish *glen*, *glin*, 'valley,' cf. Glynn (Co), and dun, hence 'hill by or above the valley.' A well marked valley runs into the hill on which Glendon stands.

HALSTOCK is *Halgestoke* 1240 Dartmoor, *Holstocke Ball* 1622 *DuCo*. 'Holy place,' *v.* stoc. There was an ancient chapel here, dedicated to St Michael, which is mentioned in the 1240 Perambulation of Dartmoor. For *Ball*, *v. infra* 211.

HIGH WILLHAYS [wiliz] is *Hight Wyll* 1532 Dartmoor, *High Willows* 1827 G. This is the highest point of Dartmoor (2039 ft.), and the name may be simply a compound of 'high' and 'well' (spring). It is really a part of Yes Tor and in early times the latter name was probably applied to the whole hill. The later additional syllable is hard to explain. It looks like the common *hay(s)*, 'enclosure,' with phonetic reduction in the unstressed syllable.

KIGBEARE

> *Cacheberga* 1086 DB, *Cakeber(e)* 1242 Fees 784, 1303 FA, 1333 Ch, *Cacke-* 1343 Cl
> *Kadekeber'* 1256 *Ass*, *Cadeke-* 1303 FA, 1310 Ipm, 1378 IpmR, *Cadekbear* 1391 IpmR, *Catokebeare* 1441 IpmR

v. bearu. The first element may be the Celtic pers. name *Cadoc*, **Catawc*, a derivative of *cad*, 'battle,' *v.* Förster KW 180. Alternatively it might be a diminutive of OE *Cada*, which is however itself a Celtic loan-name. Cf. Cadson in St Ive (Co), *Cadokestun* 12th (1348) Pat, *Cadeston* 1365 FF. The absence of inflexional *s* suggests a weak derivative of this pers. name.

MELDON is *Meledon(e)* 1175 P *et freq* to 1292 Ipm with var. spelling *-dune*, *Melledon* 1244 *Ass* (p). The first element in this

name would seem to be identical with that found in Melbury
supra 105, 130, Milbury and Melhuish *infra* 496, 452. We must
probably take with them Melbury Abbas (Do), *Meleburg*,
Mealeburg in BCS 970 (late copy), Melbury Bubb (Do), 1297
Pat *Melebury*, Melcombe Regis (Do), DB *Melcome*, 1280 Ch
Melecumbe and Melcombe Horsley (Do), 1285 FA *Melecumbe*
and Melplash (Do), 1303 FA *Meleplays*. The place-name which
may give the clue to this group of names is Millbarrow Down
(Ha), which appears as *meolæn beorge* (BCS 620), copy of original
charter[1], *mælan beorh* (ib. 622), *mælan beorge* (BCS 1077), the
last three being from the Codex Wintoniensis. It is difficult to
know what authority to give to the form in BCS 620, especially as
it is inconsistent with the later development and the charter
cannot be contemporary. Toller (B.T. Supplt. *s.v. mæle*) suggests
that we have here an OE adjective *mæle*, 'spotted, variegated,'
hitherto only noted in the compound *unmæle*, 'not spotted.' For
such an epithet applied to ground cf. the common use of OE
fah, 'stained, variegated' (*v.* Voaden *supra* 176). Zachrisson
(*Romans, Kelts and Saxons* 52–3), offers different explanations
of this element, viz. (1) that it is the Old Celtic *mailo-*, 'bare,
bald,' (2) that it is that word substantivised to denote 'bare hill.'
The first explanation can hardly hold good, for it involves the use
of a British adjective and that in an inflected form before an
English noun. Such a formation is without parallel. It should
be added perhaps that as the Melburys and Milbury contain
burh rather than beorg as their second element, one would have
to interpret these names as 'bare burh,' a name which does not
seem very likely, and not as 'bare hill.' With regard to (2) there
seems to be no evidence for the use of the adjective *mailo-* as a
noun denoting a hill in early times, for Meole (Sa) is a difficult
name which is capable of a different explanation (cf. Ekwall RN
287), and no example of such a place-name has been found in
Cornwall. It would also leave the persistent inflexional syllable
unexplained and could not be used in explanation of the Mel-
combes and Melplash[2].

---

[1] The form *meolanbeorge* in BCS 621 is copied from BCS 620.

[2] Since this note was written, Ekwall (NoB 17, 168) has advanced the same
explanation for Meldon as that put forward here and suggests that in some
of the *Mel*-names, as in Melhuish *infra* 452, we may have a pers. name
Mægla, Mæla.

PUDSON is *Poddesdon* 1244 *Ass* (p), *Puddesdon* 1270 *Ass* (p), *v.* dun. The first element may be the strong form of the OE pers. name *Podda* (Redin 107), cf. also *to poddan beorge* (BCS 1072). It may be noted that there was a William de *Podehongre* in the parish in 1330 (*SR*), suggesting that there was also in the parish a hangra or hillside named after the same man. The single form shows the weak inflection but it may be that in the late OE period at any rate the weak or strong form of a pers. name could be used indifferently for the same individual.

VELLAKE CORNER is *atte Villelake* 1378 *Ct* (nom. loc.), *Villake* or *Velelake* 1653 DA 31. *v.* lacu. The first element is doubtful, but may be the obsolete plant-name *fille* (NED *s.v.*), used for various plants.

YES TOR is *Ernestorre, Yernestorr* in the various copies of the 1240 Perambulation. It is spelt *Yerneristorre* in the Buckfast Cartulary, but this must be an error. Donne's map (1765) has *Yestor*. The meaning is 'eagle's *tor*,' *v.* earn. Cf. Easdon *infra* 482 and the later forms of Yarnscombe *supra* 82.

BEARE BRIDGE (6″), HIGHER BOWDEN, NORTHWOOD[1] FM (6″), HIGHER UPCOTT and YELLAND were probably the homes of Richard *atte Beare* (1333 *SR*), John de *Boghedon* (ib.), cf. Bowden *supra* 37, William *Bynorthewode*, i.e. 'north of the wood' (1330 *SR*), John de *Uppecot* (1275 RH), and John de *Holdelond* (1333 *SR*). *v.* bearu, uppe, cot(e), and cf. Addenda *supra* lviii.

ABBEYFORD (6″) is *Abbyford* 1657 *Recov.* BLACK DOWN is *Blakedown* 1392 *FF.* BLACK TOR is *Blacktorr hedge* 1569 *DuCo.* BRIGHTLEY is *Bristleghe* 1344 Exon, *Brightlegh juxta Okhampton* 1378 IpmR. *v.* beorht, leah. CROFT is *Craffte* 1242 Fees 784, *Crofte juxta Ayshbury* 1340 *Ass,* (*juxta Northlyeu*) 1356 *Ass,* *v.* croft. DREW'S COTTAGE (6″) is to be associated with the family of Henry *Drew* (1591 *SR*). ESTRAYER PARK probably has the same history as Straypark *supra* 59. HILLTOWN is *Hille* 1657 *Recov.* For *town, v. infra* 676. HOOK is *La Hoke* 1242 Fees 756. *v.* hoc. HUGHSLADE is *Houslade* 1827 G. *v.* slæd. KENNEL WOOD (6″) is probably to be associated with the family of John

---

[1] *Northwoods* 1657 *Recov.*

Kynewyll (1361 *Ass*), *Kynewelle* (1370 *Ass*). Perhaps 'Cyna's spring,' *v.* wielle. KNOWLE is so spelt 1657 *Recov. v.* cnoll. MADDAFORD is *Maddeford* 1285 Ipm, *Made-* 1356 *Ass, v.* Madworthy *supra* 130. MOORGATE (6″) is *Moretowne Yeat* 1585 Dartmoor and was the home of Richard de *la More* 1267 Exon. It was one of the openings into Dartmoor Forest. *v.* geat. SANDY FORD is *Langaford al. Sandyford* 1608 *DuCo.* SOUTHCOTT is *Southcote* 1458 *FF. v.* cot(e). 'South,' apparently in relation to Nethercott in Okehampton. STENG-A-TOR [stiŋkətɔ·r] is *Steinegtor* 1608 Dartmoor, *Steinigtorr, Stynkatorr* 1608 *DuCo.* STERRAGE WOOD (6″) is *Storedge wood* 1550 *AOMB.* STOCKLEY is *Stockelgh'* (sic) 1242 Fees 786, *Stockelegh* 1333 *SR* (p). *v.* stoc(c), leah and Addenda *supra* liii, *s.n.* Yardley. YOULDITCH is *Yoldedych* 1339 *Ass* (p), *Yoldeche* 1461 IpmR. 'Old ditch.'

Sourton

SOURTON [suˑrtən] 137 B 11

(*of*) *swuran tune* c. 970 BCS 1247, *Surintona* 1086 DB
Suret(h)on' c. 1200 (15th) *Torre*, 1242 Fees 756, 773, *Surton* 1249 *Ass*, 1284 FA
Sourton(e) 1286 Ipm, 1303 FA, 1331 Ipm, (*juxta Bridestowe*) 1339 *Ass*
Sworton 1577 Saxton, *Sowerton* 1577 *SR*, 1701 *Recov, Soreton oth. Sourton* 1782 *Recov*

'Farm of or by the neck or col,' *v.* sweora, tun. The hill on the east side of Sourton separates two deep-cut valleys. For loss of *w*, cf. Sorley *infra* 296.

DIGGAPORT (6″) is *Digeport* 1219, 1238 *Ass*, 1301 Ipm, *Dyge-* 1238 *Ass*, 1458 IpmR, *Dike-* 1238 *Ass* (p), *Dygge-* 1286 *SR*, 1330 *SR* (p). '*Dycga*'s port,' but the meaning of the second element is not clear. Cf. Doggaport *supra* 95. For the p.n. *Dycga, v.* Redin 63.

EAST LINNACOMBE is *Lonecomb(e)* 1333 *SR* (p), 1345 *Ass* (p). It is doubtful if it is identical with *Ledencomb* 1595 *Ct, Leden combe* 1595 Dartmoor, *Ludon Comb* 1584 (ib.), *Ludden Comb* 1585 (ib.). The last two forms may refer to LUDDON about three miles distant but also in the parish. *Leden* may be a stream-name (*Co ledan*, W *llydan*, 'broad'). Cf. RN 242.

OATNELL is *Wodeknylle* 1330, 1333 *SR* (p), *Uttknyll* 1544 *SR*, *Wotnell* 1827 G. A compound of OE wudu, 'wood,' and *cnyll*, 'knoll.' *v.* Kneela *supra* 170. For loss of initial *w*, cf. Odle *infra* 642.

PITTSWORTHY (6″) is *Pittelesworthy* 1310 *Ass*, *Pittesworthi* 1330 *SR* (p). '*Pyttel*'s worðig.' The p.n. *Pyttel* occurs also in Pitshanger (Mx), *Putteleshangre* 1274 *Ass* and *pyttelles ford* BCS 1074 (So).

PREWLEY is *Prinelegh* (sic) 1380 Pat (p), *Prynelegh* (sic) 1439 IpmR, *Preuelegh* 1481 *Ct*, *Preely more* 1579, *Preveley moore* 1584 Dartmoor. Professor Ekwall suggests that the first element here may be the plant-name *privet*. The history of that word is obscure, but there is some evidence for earlier forms *pryvet*, *prevet*, which would explain the forms of the Devon name. *v.* NED *s.v. privet* and leah.

NORTH RUSSELL is *Nordthrossille* 1262 FF, *Northrissel(l)* 1275 RH, 1286 Ipm, *-ryssel* 1281 *Ass*, *Northrisschel* 1303 FA, *North Phrisshel* 1326 Ipm, *Northtrusshele* 1356 *Ass*. North Russell stands on an arm of the Thrushel (*v. supra* 14), near its source, this arm probably being distinguished as 'North Thrushel.'

CLEAVE[1], COOMBE[1], FORDA[2], LAKE, EAST TORR[3], and WEEK[4] were probably the homes of Walter *atte Clyve* (1330 *SR*), Richard *atte Westerecomb* (1333 *SR*), Nicholas *atte Forde* (ib.), Cristina *atte Lake* (1330 *SR*), Ralph *atte Torre* (ib.), and Thomas *atte Wyke* (ib.). *v.* clif, cumb, lacu, torr, wic.

BLATCHFORD is *Blaccheford* c. 1200 (15th) *Torre*, *Blacheford* 1330 *SR* (p), *Blecheford* 1445 *Deed*. The first element is probably the pers. name *Blæcca* found also in Blachford *infra* 269. COLLAVEN is *Colefenne* 1333 *SR* (p). *v.* Collacott *supra* 50. HEWTON is *Hueton* 1262 FF, *Houghton* t. Eliz ChancP. The early forms are scanty, but the name may be identical in origin with Houghton *infra* 267. HURSDON is *Hurlesdon* 1330, *Herlesdon* 1333 *SR* (p). Possibly '*Heor(uw)ulf*'s hill,' *v.* dun. Cf. Harlesden (Mx), *Herulvestune* 1086 DB, but *Herleston* in 1197 (HMC App. ix, 12). KNOWLE is *Knoll* 1827 G. *v.* cnoll. LILLICRAPP (6″) is probably

---

[1] *Clyve, Comb*, 1381 BM. [2] *Forde* 1544 *SR*.
[3] There was also a *West Tor* (1504 Ipm). [4] *Wike* 1544 *SR*.

to be associated with the family of Peter *Liliecrop*, i.e. 'Whitehead' (1330 *SR*). POOL is *Pole* 1458 IpmR. SOUTHERLY is *Southeleye* 1412 *Ass*, *Sowtherley* 1579 Dartmoor. *v.* leah. For the medial syllable, *v.* Introd. xxxvi. THORNDON is *Thorndon* 1244 *Ass*. 'Thorn hill,' *v.* dun.

Stowford

STOWFORD [stoufəd] 137 C 8

Estatforda 1086 DB (Exon), *Staford* DB (Exch)
Stafford(e) 1242 Fees 757, 1264 Exon, 1265 Misc, 1291 Tax
Stoford juxta Meleford 1287 *Ass*
Stauford 1330 *SR*
Stouford 1349 Exon, (*juxta Lyfton*) 1306 *Ass*

For a discussion of this name, *v.* Stowford *supra* 41.

ARRACOTT is *Tadiecote* 1327 *Ass* (p), *Tadecote* 1330 *SR* (p), *Taddacote* 1333 *SR* (p), *Adecote* 1394 *Ass*, *Addecote* 1546 *Recov*, *Arracott oth. Addacott* 1774 *Recov*. *v.* cot(e). The first element is OE *tadige*, 'toad,' perhaps because these creatures were especially numerous on this particular settlement, which lies low near the river Lew. The modern development shows loss of initial *t* as explained *s.v.* æt in EPN, and the same change of *d* to *r* as in Darracott *supra* 43, 80.

BARBARYBALL is *Bobrifal* (sic) 1330 *SR* (p), *Babryhille* 1546 *Recov*, *Babriballe* 1570 *Ct*. The forms are insufficient for any interpretation to be offered, beyond the suggestion that the name may contain the British *bri*, 'hill.' In later times there has been much confusion in the final element.

MILFORD is *Melefort* 1086 DB, *-ford* 1242 Fees 756, *Mileford* 1303 FA, 1333 *SR* (p), *Muleford* 1316 FA, *Milford* 1326 Ipm, *Melleford juxta Liston* 1365 *FF*. Probably self-explanatory.

PORTGATE is *Porteyetepark* t. Hy 6 *Ct*, *Portcot oth. Portgate* 1774 *Recov*. This hamlet is situated beside the main road from Exeter to Launceston, which would have been described as a *port weg* in OE times. *Portgate* (*v.* geat) may have been the name for a gate on such a road. Cf. Portgate (PN NbDu 159).

SPRYTOWN is *Sprei* 1086 DB, *Spray* 1179 P (p), *Spree* 1242 Fees 789, *Sprey(e)* 1276 Ipm, 1284 FA, (*juxta Lifton*) 1311 *Ass*, *Sprey-*

town 1610 *SR*, *Sprytown* 1729 *Recov.* The same element is found in Spurway, Spreyton, Sprydoncote *infra* 388, 446, 577, and in Sprecott, Spreacombe and Ratsbury *supra* 31, 54, 65. Outside the county we may note Sparcombe in Exford (So), *Spracombe-sheved* 1298 Exmoor, *le Spray juxta Oterburn* (Ha) 1306 *Ass*, *le Spraye*, *le Spray grene* 1350 AD i (Berks) and the pers. name (de) *Spray* 1327 *SR* (W). All these names contain the word *spray* for which NED gives the meanings, 'collection of slender or small twigs,' 'fine brushwood,' 'hazel, birch or other twigs used for thatching,' etc. The sense in place-names must have been that of land overgrown with brushwood. It may be noted that the word is here carried back some 200 years earlier than its first mention in the NED (1297).

BROADMOORHEAD is *Brode Moore* 1614 *Deed*. COOMBE (6″) was the home of John Beare de *Comb* (1333 *SR*). HAYNE is *la Heyghen* 1287, 1288 *Ass* (p), *v. supra* 129. ROWDEN is *Rowedon* 1330 *SR* (p). Probably 'rough hill,' *v.* ruh, dun. TOWNLEIGH is *Townley* 1546 *Recov*, *v.* tun, leah. Cf. Townley, PN La 84 and Tunley *infra* 307. The sense of the compound is uncertain.

Sydenham Damarel

SYDENHAM DAMAREL 137 G 7

> *Sidelham* 1086 DB, *Sideham* 1201 FF, (*Aumarle*) 1306 Ipm
> *Sidenham* 1283 *Ass*, (*Albemarlie*) 1297 Pat, (*Daumarll*) 1303 FA, (*juxta Lamerton*) 1339 *Ass*, (*Daumarle*) 1340 Ipm, *Ciddenham* 1428 FA

'(At the) wide ham(m).' The village does not lie low, so that the second element must be ham, or else hamm in the sense of enclosure. Johannes de *Alba Mara* or de *Albemarle* is first mentioned in connexion with the manor in 1242 (Fees) and the modern *Damarel* is for earlier *D'Albemarle*. *Albemarle* commonly develops to *Aumerle* and this in combination with initial *d* has given the present *Damarel*.

BIRDSHAM (6″) is *Berdesham*, *Birdesham* 1318 *Deed*, *Briddesham* 1333 *SR* (p), *Berdisham al. Berdysham* 1344 BM. '*Brid(d)*'s ham(m).' For *Bridd*, *v.* Redin 18. It is apparently the OE *bridd*, 'young bird,' used as a pers. name.

HORSEBRIDGE is *Havtesbrygge* 1437 Exon, *Hautesbrygge, Hawtys-*

brygge 1478 WmWo, *Hantesbrigg* (sic), *Hawtesbrigge* c. 1550
Leland. Probably the name is of late origin involving a pers.
name of ME origin, viz. a surname *le haut* of nickname-type
from OFr *halt, haut.*

PORTONTOWN is *Portingatone* late 13th *Deed, -yngton* 1330 *SR*
(p), *-yngatoñ* 1365 *Ass* (p). 'tun of *Port* or of *Port*'s people,' *v.*
ing. For the pers. name *Port, v.* Portslade (PN Sx 289). There
is no large town or any harbour near which would allow us to
associate the name with OE *port* as a significant word.

DERRITON (6″) is *Direton* 1330 *SR* (p), *Dyreton, Diraton* 1339
BM. See further under Derworthy *supra* 153. HARDMEAD (6″)
is *Hardmede* late 13th *Deed, Harde-* 1318 *Deed.* 'Hard meadow,'
v. mæd. REDFORD (6″) is *Radeford* 1292 *Ass* (p). 'Red ford.'
TOWNLAKE was the home of Richard *atte Tounlake* 1330 *SR*,
v. tun, lacu. The name is not easy to explain as there is no stream
near by. TRELEIGH (6″) was the home of John *atter Leghe* (1330
SR). It is *Treleghe* 1562 *FF.* 'At the leah.' See further *s.n.*
Tredown *supra* 146. WONWOOD is *Wonnewode* 1283 *Ass*, 1330
SR (p), *Woonwood* 1610 Wills. *v.* Wonwell *infra* 279.

Thrushelton

THRUSHELTON 137 C 8

> *Tresetone* 1086 DB, *-a* 1088 Totnes
> *Thrisselton'* 1242 Fees 757, 1303 FA, *Thrysselton juxta*
> *Bratton* 1336 *Ass*
> *Thrysshelton* 1242 Fees 776 *et freq* to 1334 *SR* with variant
> spellings in *i* and *sch*
> *Trisselton* 1284 FA, *Trisshelton juxta Stouford* 1313 *Ass*
> *Thrushelton* 1306 Ipm, *Trusshilton* 1364 *Ass, Trussell(ton)*
> 1428 FA
> *Treshalton* 1502 ECP 4, 94

> *v.* tun. Ekwall (RN 406) takes the first element of this name
to be OE *þryscele,* 'thrush,' which survives in Devon dialect as
thrishel (*v.* EDD *s.v.*). Cf. also Thurlescombe *infra* 551, and *la*
Throsalbeare 1470 *Ct.* The river Thrushel (*supra* 14) is probably
an early back-formation from the p.n.

AXWORTHY is *Arkeswrthi* 1238 *Ass, -worthe* 1244 *Ass, -worthi*

1330, 1333 *SR* (all p), *Axworthy* 1737 *Deed. v.* worðig. The first element is probably a pers. name *Earric, a pet form of *Eardric* as suggested for Alkesford (PN Sx 370).

DRINGWELL is *Tringewelle* 1281 *Ass* (p), *Tryngwyll* 1515–18 ECP 5, 52, *Tringwill al. Dringwill* 1609 *Deed.* The first element may be connected with OE ðring, 'crowd, pressure, commotion,' ðringan, 'to press, crowd, throng,' in which case the reference must have been to a much used or much frequented spring.

PATCHILL is *Pacheshill juxta Trisselton* 1283 *Ass*, *-hulle* 1330 *SR* (p), *Paccheshulle* 1399 Exon (p). '*Pæcci*'s hill.'

THRUSHELBALL (6″) is *Throshilball* 1529–32 ECP 6, 153. 'Hill by the Thrushel river.' The word *ball*, used to denote a rounded hill, is confined to Somerset and Devon. The earliest dated example is that found in the pers. name John *att' Balle* (1327 *SR*), (So). The earliest occurrence of the word in a Devon place-name is in 1429, *v. infra* 688.

TREBICK is *Trybuke* 1408, *Trebek* 1482 DA 27 (both p), *Trybuk* 1544 *FF.* The forms are too late and too few for any certain etymology to be suggested. If the name is Celtic it may contain the British words corresponding to W *tref*, 'homestead,' and *bychan*, 'little.' Cf. Trebeigh (Co), *Trebichen* DB, *Trebygha* 1360 *Ass.*

ALDER is *Aller* t. Hy 8 *FF, v.* alor. BROADLEY is *Bradelegh* 1330 *SR* (p), *Bradlegh Mede* 1505 Ipm, *v.* brad, leah. BURSCOTT is *Buttescott* 1518–29 ECP 5, 528, *v.* cot(e). CANNONBARN is *Canbarn* 1535 VE. It was a grange belonging to the canons of Plympton Priory. Cf. Canonbury (Mx). HUDDISPIT is *Whit(e)-spit(t)* 1809 M, 1827 G. KILSON (6″) is *Kyleston* 1330 *SR* (p), *Killesdon* 1356 *Ass.* '*Cylli*'s tun or dun.' LEIGH was the home of John *atter Leghe* 1330 *SR, v.* leah. LOBHILL CROSS is *Lubewell* 1249 *Ass* (p), *Lobbawylle* 1313 *Ass*, *Lobbewille* 1330 *SR* (p). For the interpretation *v. s.n.* Lobb *supra* 33. ORCHARD is *Orcherd* 1242 Fees 786, *Orchard juxta Bratton* 1301 *Ass, v.* orceard. WHITEABOROUGH (6″) is *Whyttaborough* 1727 *Deed.* WHITELEY is *Whithelegh* 1306 Ipm, *Whitteleye* 1316 Cl. 'White clearing,' *v.* leah. WHITEROW is *Whitrowe* 1720 *Recov.* WIDDACOMBE (6″)

is *Wydecomb* 1282 *Ass*, 1330 *SR* (both p). 'Wide valley,' *v.*
cumb. WOLLACOTT is *Wlnethecote* 1238 *Ass* (p), *Wolnethecote*
1330 *SR* (p), *Wolthecote* 1356, 1364 *Ass*, *Wolcote* 1428 FA.
'*Wulfnōþ*'s cot(e),' with absence of genitival *s*. WONNACOTT is
Wonnecote 1238 *Ass*, *-kote* 1279 *Ass* (p). *v.* Wonwell *infra* 279.
WORTHAM was the home of William *atte Wurthen* 1330 *SR*. It is
Taworthan 1415 *Ass*, *v.* worþign. *Ta* is probably from ME *atte*,
v. s.n. Tredown *supra* 146. WREYS BARTON is *Wreies* 1505 Ipm
and is to be associated with the family of Stephen *le Wrey* mentioned in connexion with Thrushelton in 1313 (*Ass*). *v.* beretun.

Virginstow

VIRGINSTOW 137 B 6

> *Virginestowe* 1174–83 BM, *Virgenestowe* 1278–80 Exon, 1394
> *Ass*, *-ystouwe* 1334 *SR*
> *Virstawe* 1463 Pat

'Holy place of the virgin,' *v.* stow. The reference is not to the
Virgin Mary but to St Bridget the Virgin to whom the church is
dedicated.

BRADAFORD is *Bradeford(a)* 1086 DB, 1303 FA, *Brodeforde* 1602
FF. 'Wide ford' (over the Carey river). *v.* brad. For the medial
vowel, *v.* Introd. xxxvi.

SCOTLAND is so spelt in 1827 (G). This name occurs also in
Bridgerule and Morchard Bishop parishes, though no early forms
have been found, and a further example has already been noted
in Sussex. The only early form noted is that for Scotland in
Godshill (Wt), which appears as *Skotland* in 1354 and 1371 (*Ct*).
Land so called was probably subject to some payment or
customary tax. For such use of *scot*, *v.* NED *s.v. scot* sb. 2.

TILLESLOW

> *Tornelowa* (sic) 1086 DB
> *Tullesho, Tuleslo* 1238 *Ass* (p), *Tullesle* 1242 Fees 794, *-sclo*
> 1249 *Ass*, *-slo* 1284 FA
> *Tolleslo* 1303 FA, *Tolyslo* 1334 *SR*, *Toleslo* 1346 FA
> *Turislo* 1324 Ipm, *Tuslow* 1728 Recov

Probably '*Tulla*'s slough or miry place,' *v.* sloh. For this pers.
name cf. *Snelling Tullinges sunu* (Earle 262) in a Devon document

of c. 1090, and Tulwick (Berks) *Tullewyk* 1284 *Ass.* The absence of *gh* spellings for the second element is curious.

CROWSNEST is *Creweneste* 1281 *Ass* (p), *Crowness* 1675 Ogilby. 'Crow's nest.' For names of this kind, *v.* Crowneast (PN Wo 91). DOWNEYCROFT is *Downa Croft* 1674 *FF*, 'hill croft.' For the medial syllable, *v.* Introd. xxxvi. MIDDLECOTT is *Middelcoth'* 1242 Fees 788, 'middle cot(e).' It lies between Ashwater and Virginstow.

VIII. TAVISTOCK HUNDRED

Tauistoke 1187 P, *Tauistok* 1238 *Ass*

v. Tavistock *infra* 217. At the time of the DB survey this hundred was included under Lifton *supra* 172. It was first created a separate hundred by a charter of Henry I, dated 1116 (DA 47, 376).

Brentor

BRENTOR 137 E 9

(*apud*) *Brentam* t. Hy 2 Oliver 135, *Brenta* 1238, 1244 *Ass*, *Brente* 1228 FF (p)
Brienta 1228 FF (p), *Northbrienta* 1322 *Ass*
Brentetor(re) 1232 Cl, Ch, 1302 *Ass*, 1309 Exon (p), *Brente Torre* 1281 *Ass*
Brintetorre 1265 Exon, *Bryntetor* 1488 *Rental*
Brendetorre 1287 Pat, *Bremptetorre* 1299 *Ass*
Brentor 1423 *Deed, Brenter* 1648 *Depositions*

This place and Brent (So), *Brente* 725 (14th) BCS, *Brenteknol* 1288 FF, are both isolated steep hills and Brent *infra* 290 is near a prominent hill though not an isolated one. In PN Sx 256, Ekwall suggests that these names may contain a lost noun-derivative of OE *brant*, 'steep.'

BRINSABATCH (6″) is *Bremysbatch, Brymmysbatch(e)* 1488 *Rental, Brensabeche* 1670 *FF.* Possibly '*Brēme*'s stream,' *v.* bæc. The stream is that now called 'the Burn.'

s

LIDDATON GREEN

Lideltona 1086 DB

Liddintone 1166 RBE (p), *Estlidinton* 1256 *Ass*, *Lyditune* 1272 Ipm

Liddeton(e) 1166 LN (p), 1193 Oliver 95, *Lideton* 1228 FF, *Lydeton* 1238 *Ass* (p), 1330 *SR* (p), *West Lidethon* 1242 Fees 78, *Estlideton* 1256 *Ass*

Westledeton 1408 *Ass*

v. tun. The place presumably takes its name from the river Lyd, *v. supra* 9, though no spellings with a *u* have been found. The OE form was either *Hlydantūn* or perhaps *Hlydingtūn.* Cf. *Tæfingstoc* for Tavistock *infra* 217.

WAS TOR is *Wassetorre* 1445 *Deed*, *Was Tor* 1488 *Rental.* 'Wassa's torr.' This is probably a Celtic pers. name which occurs in the Bodmin manumissions (KCD 971) in the form *Was(s)o*, and in the p.n. Trewassa (Co), *Trewassa* 1284 *Ass*, 1302 Pat, *Trewasse* 1386 IpmR.

WATERVALE [-vɑːl] is *Waterfale* 1167 P (p), *Watrifalla* t. Hy 2 Oliver 135, *Waterfalle* 1282 (1328) Ch, 1291 Tax, *Waterifalla* 1330 *SR* (p), the name referring to a waterfall on the river Lyd. The OE form is *wætergefeal* and the *ge* has left its trace in the *i* of the second and last forms. Higher Watervale Fm is nearly a mile from the fall, but Lower Watervale is not far from it.

ASHELTOR WOOD (6″) is *Aisheltor* 1640 FF. BOWDENHILL (6″) is *Boghedon* 1285 FF, *Bowedon* 1516 *Recov.* 'Curved hill,' *v. supra* 37. BROADRIDGE WOOD is *Broderidge Wood* 1740 *Recov.* BURN-VILLE, BURN LANE (6″) is *Burnlane* 1765 D, *Burn, Burnville* 1827 G. *v.* burna. There is a small stream here. *ville* is a modern addition (J. J. A.). HEATHFIELD is *Brenthethfeld* 1423 *Deed*, *Hethfelde* 1488 *Rental.* 'Waste land by Brent (Tor).' HOLYEAT is *Hole, Hoole* 1488 *Rental*, *Holeyate* 1732 *Recov*, *v.* holh. The farm lies in a valley. *yate* is the dialect form of *gate*, *v.* geat. LANGSTONE is *Langestanam* t. Hy 2 Oliver 135, *Langastane* 1282 (1328) Ch. 'The long stone.' There is no trace of this here now. MONK-STONE is *Monkiston* 1770 *Recov.* The manor of Brentor belonged to the monks of Tavistock Abbey. PRESCOMBE (6″) is *Prustecombe* 1445 *Deed.* 'Priests' valley,' *v.* cumb. ROWDEN is *Rughadona*

t. Hy 2 Oliver 135, *Roggadonne* 1351 *Deed*. 'Rough hill,' cf.
Rough Tor *supra* 199. WOODMANSWELL is *Wudemanneswella*
t. Hy 2 Oliver 135. 'Woodman's spring,' *v.* wielle. Alternatively
the first element may be a pers. name *Wudumann*.

Milton Abbot

MILTON ABBOT 137 F 7

> *Mideltona* 1086 DB, *Middelton Abbots* 1297 Pat, *Myddeltone
> al. Myltone* 1391 Exon

'Middle farm,' *v.* tun. As early as DB the manor belonged to
Tavistock Abbey. 'Middle' perhaps with reference to Dunterton and Lamerton.

CARDWELL (6″) is *Kerdewell* 1238 *Ass* (p), *Kerdauuylle* 1275 RH
(p), *Kerdewyll* late 13th *Deed*. '*Cærda*'s spring,' *v.* wielle. Cf.
Cardington (PN BedsHu 88). It is curious that a William *Kerda*
was living at Tavistock in 1333 (*SR*).

EDGCUMBE is *Egghacombe* 1275 RH (p), *Eggecumbe* 1281 *Ass* (p),
-comb(e) 1330 *SR* (p), 1435 Exon (p), 1493 Ipm, *Egecombe* 1381
Exon (p), *Eghcombe* 1412 *Deed*, 1488 *Rental*, *Eggelcumbe* 1281
Ass (p). Probably '*Ecga*'s valley,' *v.* cumb.

FOGHANGER [fɔgnər]

> *Foghauer* (sic) 1242 Fees 781
> *Foggehanger* 1244 *Ass*, *Foghangre* 1346 FA, *-ger* 1504 Ipm
> *Froggaanger* 1285 FA
> *Foghehangre* 1330 *SR* (p), *-gher* 1365 *Ass*, *-ger* 1375 *Ct*

Probably '*Focga*'s slope,' *v.* hangra. For the pers. name
Focga, *v.* Voghay *infra* 457. Alternatively one may have
a compound of hangra and the dialectal *fog*.

LANDSKERRY (6″) is *Lanskery* 1544 *SR*, *Landsgerry* 1729 *Deed*.
As the place is near the parish boundary the name clearly
derives from OE *landscearu*, 'boundary, landmark.' For the *s(k)*
v. Introd. xxxv and Stevenson's note in the *Crawford Charters*,
p. 48. He there points out that the term is distinctively south-
western, only being found once elsewhere, viz. in an 11th cent.
Northamptonshire Charter (KCD 736). In East Devon *land-
score* is common as the name of a boundary lane. We also have

landshare, 'headland in a field,' and *landsherd*, 'ridge or strip of untilled land between two crops or marking a boundary.'

LEIGH BARTON is *Lega* 1086 DB, 1174–83 BM, *Leghe* 1291 Tax *Legh Champeaus* 1303 FA. *v.* leah. Alicia de *Campell*' held the manor in 1242 (Fees 781).

POFLET (6″) is *Poghelippe* 1242 Fees 781, -*lyp(e)* 1296 *Deed Poghlippe* 1303 FA, *Poggelyp* 1346 FA, *Poghlep, Poghlup* 1412 *Deed*. '*Poh(h)a*'s hlype.' There is a dip down to a little stream here and up again (J. J. A.). The persistent *gh* makes OE *puca*, 'goblin,' improbable.

QUITHER is *Queder* 1281 *Ass* (p), -*dre* 1284 FA, *Quederne* 1330, 1333 *SR* (p), 1412 *Deed*, *Quydor, Quyderin* 1488 *Rental*. The name is probably a compound of OE *cwēad*, 'dung, dirt,' and ærn, 'house.' Cf. Quoditch *supra* 127 and *v.* Mixerne (Gl), *s.v.* ærn.

TUELLDOWN [tuˑəl] is *Tuywelle* 1349 BM, *Twywille* 1412 *Deed*, *Twywell, Twyvell* 1414 *Deed*. A compound of OE *twī*, 'double' (as in the p.n. Twyford) and wielle, 'spring.' Cf. Twywell (Nth), *Tuiwella* D̄B, *Tuywell* 1235 Cl. There are numerous springs in the neighbourhood and about half a mile east of Tuell there is a double spring.

YOUNGCOTT (6″) is *Iundcot* late 13th *Deed*, *Yuncote* 1276 *FF*, *Hundcot* 1284 FA, *Hyndcote, Yundcote al. Hundcote* 1336 BM, *Youngcott* 1658 BM. *v.* cot(e). For the first element, *v.* Indicombe *supra* 35. Youngcott is a stage further away from Milton than Hardicott and the name means 'beyond the cottages (at Hardicott).'

LONGBROOK and UPPATON were the homes of Robert de *Langebrok* and Robert de *Uppeton* (1330 *SR*). *v.* broc, tun.

BECKADON (6″) is *Byketon* 1330 *SR* (p), 1391 BM, and BECKWELL (6″) is *Bikewill* 1238 *Ass* (p). These names contain as first element a pers. name *Bic(c)a*, *v.* Abbots Bickington *supra* 124. BEERA is *la Bere* 1244 *Ass* (p), *Atbeare* 1412 *Deed*, *v.* bearu. BROADTOWN (6″) is *Bradtowne* 1615 *Rental*, *v.* tun. BURNSHALL is *Burnardeshalle* 1330 *SR* (p), *Bernardshall* 1488 *Rental*. The first element may be the OE pers. name *Beornheard*, but more likely the place is of post-Conquest origin and contains the corresponding OGer name. CHILLATON is *Childeton'* 1242 Fees 781, *Chillatun* 1284 FA, *Chilleton* 1303 FA. *v.* cild, tun. ENDSLEIGH COTTAGE is *Inneslegh* 1378 Oliver 91. *v.* leah. FORD is *Ford* 1336 BM. HARDICOTT is *Hardecote* 1370 Exon (p), 1488 *Rental, -cott* 1521 BM. '*Hearda's* cot(e).' NARRACOTT is *Northecote* 1244 *Ass* (p), 1323 *Ass* (p), 1413 *Ass.* 'North cot(e),' cf. Narracott *passim.* RAMSDOWN PLANTATION is *Ramsdowne* 1601 *Recov.* SHORTBURN is *Shurtburn* 1518–29 ECP 5, 494. SOUTHCOMBE is *Southcombe* 1372 BM, *v.* cumb. WEEK is *la Wike* 1238 *Ass* (p), *Wyk'* 1242 Fees 781. *v.* wic. WESTCOTT is *Westecote* 1353 Pat. 'West' in relation to Brentor and not to Milton Abbott. WILLESLEY [wilzli] is *Wilselegh* 1282 *Ass, Wylshlegh* 1488 *Rental.* Perhaps '*Wilsige's* leah,' but the forms are too few for certainty.

Tavistock and Tavistock Hamlets

TAVISTOCK 137 G 9

> (*at*) *Tauistoce* 981 (13th) KCD 629, *Attavistoce* 981 (1348) BM
> (*æt*) *Tefing stoce* c. 1000 (997 E), *Tæfingstoc* c. 1120 (997 E) ASC, 1046 (12th) KCD 1334
> *Tæuistoc, Tæfistoc* c. 1000 Saints, *Tauistoc(h)* c. 1115 BM, 1131, 1160 P, *Tauystok juxta Lamerton* 1321 *Ass*
> *Tavestocha* 1086 DB, *-stok* 1270 Pat
> *Tastocke* 1602 Cai
> 'stoc by the river Tavy' *supra* 14. For the *-ing-, v.* PN NRY 77 *s.n.* Sinnington.

AZORES [æzəriz][1]

> *Hauesworth'* 1242 Fees 781, *-worthy* 1392 FF
> *Hasworth(y)* 1284 FA
> *Haverisworthy* 1353 Pat
> *Hawesworthie, Husworthie* 1488 *Rental, Haysworthy al. Hassory* 1598 *Deed*
> If the 1353 form is to be trusted the name may be interpreted '*Hæfer's* worþig,' cf. Haversham (PN Bk 8).

[1] Surviving as the name of a group of fields in Kilworthy Fm. (*Ex inf.* Mr J. J. Alexander.)

BANNAWELL[1] (6″) is *Banewelle* 1320, *-will* 1438 *Deed, Banawylle* 1337 AD iii. Probably '*Bana*'s spring,' *v.* wielle, though *banan-wylle*, 'slayer's spring,' or even *bānawylle*, 'spring of the bones,' is just possible. Cf. Banwell (So), *æt Bananwylle* BCS 612.

BOWRISH COTTAGES (6″) is *Borhiwis* 1238 FF, *Burhywis* 1277 Misc, *Bowrehuish, Bourehuishe* 1488 *Rental*. Apparently a compound of bur, 'peasant,' and hiwisc, i.e. a hiwisc of land on which a peasant or peasants were settled. Cf. Bowerland *supra* 202.

CREBOR (6″)

> *Crevebere* 1166 RBE (p)
> *Crievebere* 1193 Oliver 95 (p)
> *Crauber* 1228 FF, *Crauweber* 1244 *Ass* (p)
> *Crewebeȓ* 1238 *Ass, -byar'* 1275 RH (p), *atte Crewebeare* 1324 *Ass* (p), *-beare* 1330 *SR* (p), *Crewebeara juxta Tauystoke* 1339 *Ass, Crewbere* 1414 *Deed*
> *Creubere* 1242 Fees 781
> *Creber* 1530 *Deed*

'Crow wood,' *v.* bearu. For the form *crewe, v.* Introd. xxxiii.

CROWNDALE is *Crundel* 1244 *Ass* (p), *Croundel* 1330 *SR* (p), 1348 Ipm, *-dale* 1342 *Deed, -dil* 1355 BM, *-dell* 1488 *Rental. v.* crundel. There is an old quarry in the immediate neighbourhood.

GULWORTHY is *Goleworthe, Coleworthie* 1414 *Deed, Goleworthi* 1431 Pat, *Gule-, Gulleworthie* 1488 *Rental, Golyworthy* 1542 *Deeds Enrolled, Gulworthy al. Gullaford* 1598 *Deed. v.* worþig. A Roger *Golle* was taxed under Tavistock in 1333 (*SR*) and the place must have taken its name from him or from his family. For a similar example of a probable late compound of worþig, *v.* Hexworthy *supra* 194.

HURDWICK is *Hurdewik(e)* 1275 Oliver 96 *et passim* to 1498 Ipm, *Herdewyk* 1281 *Ass, Hordeswike* 1291 Tax, *Howrdeweke* 1514 AD i. *v.* heordewic.

INDESCOMBE (6″) is *Entescombe* 1340 Inq aqd, *Entyscomb(e)* 1375, *Endes-* 1483, *Endis-* 1488, *Indes-* 1500 *Deed*. The first element

---

[1] Now the name of a street in Tavistock.

might be OE *ent*, 'giant.' Hence, 'giant's valley,' cf. Thursden (PN La 85) from OE *þyrs*, 'giant.' In the 1488 Rental the Walla-brook stream which flows down this valley is called *Endlesbrooke*. Its relation to Indescombe is obscure.

MILEMEAD (6″) is *Milimet* 1238 FF, 1275 RH (p), *Melemet* 1310 *Ass* (p), *Milemete* 1330 *SR* (p), *Mylemete* 1402 *Deed*. This name involves the same word as is found in *to mil gemete* BCS 955, *on ðæt milgemæt* KCD 673, apparently a compound of *mil*, 'mile,' and *(ge)met*, 'measure, space, boundary, limit.' The place probably takes its name from an old milestone, as it is about a mile distant from Tavistock on the road to the north-west.

NUTLEY (6″) is *Nutlegh* 1238 *Ass* (p), *Notteleye* 1250 Fees 1251 (p), *-legh* 1303 FA, *Noteleghe* 1339 *Ass*, *Nutteleghe*, *Noteleghe* 1416 *Deed*. 'Nut-tree wood,' *v.* leah.

PARSWELL is *Pashull* 1244 *Ass* (p), *Pashill juxta Tauystok* 1345 *Ass*, *Passehille juxta Tauistoke* 1345, 1346 *Ass*, *Passehull* 1423 FF, *Pashill al. Passell* 1551, 1585 AD v. '*Passa*'s hill.' For the p.n. *Passa*, *v.* Redin 106. For the dialectal pronunciation, cf. Arscott *supra* 127 and Introd. *supra* xxxiii.

PETTYPACE (lost)[1] is *Petypaswyke juxta Tavystoke* 1345 *Ass*, *Wykepatipas* 1382 *Deed*, *Petipaswyke* 1411 FF, *Petipaslond* 1488 *Rental*. *v.* wic. The name is to be associated with the family of William *Petitpas* (1249 *Ass*), probably a pers. name of the nick-name type, referring to a man who took little steps when walking.

PIXON LANE (6″) is *Piggeston, Pigeston, Pyxton* 1488 *Rental*. The first element may be ME *pigge*, used perhaps as a pers. name.

RUBBYTOWN is *Rubes in Wodeovis* 1488 *Rental*. Thomas *Rubye* sold land in 'Woodovyse' to John Brent sometime before 1488. The land he sold is called *Smythland* and probably was later called *Rubbytown* or *Ruby*'s (*ex inf.* Mr J. J. Alexander). This Thomas *Rubye* may well have been of the same family as Roger *Rubi*, a witness to a charter granting land in the neighbouring district of Foghanger in 1185 (Buckland). For further names of this type, cf. Sparkaton, Prowtytown *infra* 231, 248.

---

[1] According to Mr Alexander, the name survives as that of a field adjoining Pickpocket Lane (6″).

RUMONSLEIGH COTTAGES (6″) is *Rumonslegh* 1349 *FF, Remmenlegh juxta Tavystoke* 1371 IpmR, *Romanesleghe* 1416 *Deed.* 'Rumon's leah,' referring to St Rumon, the patron saint of Tavistock Abbey. The name is found also in Ruan Major and Minor (Co) and goes back ultimately to the Latin *Romanus.*

SHILLA MILL is *Shildemyll* 1488 *Rental, Shellamyll* 1606 DCo NQ 10, 103. The same name in Cornwall is *Shillamille* 1670 *Recov.* Possibly the *d* is an error and in both names we have the word *shill,* 'sonorous, resonant,' applied to the sound of the mill. Cf. Skillaton *supra* 67.

STILESWEEK (6″) is *Stoileswike* 1340 Inq aqd, *Staylesweke* 1488 *Rental,* and is probably to be associated with the family of Stephen *Stoyl,* who held the manor of Foghanger (*supra* 215) in 1284 (FA). *v.* wic.

WHITHAM (6″) is *Wyteham* 1291 Tax, *Whytteham* 1303 FA, *Whiteham* 1346 FA, *Dudruyswyteham juxta Tavystoke* 1362 *Ass, Barkeswhiteham, Berkhamstead Whiteham* 1488 *Rental. v.* hwit, ham(m). Nicholas *Berchamstede* held land in Tavistock in 1405 (*Deed*). No trace of the name *Dudruys,* presumably a feudal addition, has been discovered. The name of this manor at one time survived only in a group of fields near Whitchurch Down, but has recently been revived in *Whitham* Park, a new district laid out in 1927 (J. J. A.).

WILMINSTONE [wilmistən] is *Wynemerestona* 13th Oliver 89, *Wynemaneston* 1228 FF (p), *Ovrewynmereston juxta Tauystok* 1305 *Ass, Wilmerston* 1394 *Ass, Wilmeston* 1488 *Rental, Wimpson* 1605 Wills. '*Winemǣr*'s tun.' The second form quoted above shows confusion with the OE pers. name *Wineman.*

WOODOVIS is *Wodeheuese* 1244 *Ass* (p), 1330 *SR* (p), *Wodeuesse juxta Tauistoke* 1346 *Ass, Wodeuese* t. Ed 3 *Ass, Wodewys, Odewys, Wodeovese, Wodeovys* 1488 *Rental.* 'At the wood-edge,' *v.* efese. Cf. Woodsaws (Co), *Wodesouse, Wodeseuese* 1296 *Ass, Wodesouese, Wodesauese* 1302 *Ass.* The modern form has probably been influenced by the dialectal *ovvis,* recorded from Somerset, and used commonly in Devon, a closely allied word.

LANGFORD and WELL (6″) were probably the homes of Nicholas

de *Langeford* (1330 *SR*), and William *Atauuylle*, i.e. 'at the spring' (1275 RH). *v.* wielle.

ABBOTSFIELD is a house built and named c. 1853 (*ex inf.* Mr J. J. Alexander). ARTISCOMBE is *Arthcombe* 1415 *Deed*, *Artescombe* 1488 *Rental*. BLANCHDOWN WOOD is *Blanchdon* 1488 *Rental*, *Blanchelond wood* 1514 *Deed*. BRISCOTTS COTTAGE (6″) is to be associated with Peter de *Brettenescote* (1244 *Ass*). '*Beorhtwine*'s cote.' The *s* is probably pseudo-manorial. BROADWELL is *Brodewyll* 1488 *Rental*. 'Wide spring,' *v.* brad, wielle. BUCTOR is *Buketor* 1414 *Deed*, *Bucketor* 1488 *Rental*, *Bukterwode* 1518–29 ECP. The first element is probably OE *bucca*, 'buck, he-goat, male deer,' or a pers. name *Bucca* derived from the animal. BURNFORD is *Burneford* 1311 Cl (p), *Burneford al. Burne* 1488 *Rental*. 'Ford over the Burn,' i.e. the stream here so called. *v.* burna. CHIPSHOP is so spelt in 1765 (D). Mr Alexander suggests that the name may have come into existence during the mining period, i.e. c. 1660. CRELAKE (6″) is *Crewelake* 1381 *Deed*, 1488 *Rental*, *Crelake* t. Eliz ChancP. 'Crow streamlet,' *v.* lacu and Introd. *supra* xxxiii. DOWNHOUSE is *Uppedoune al. Dounehouse* 1488 *Rental*. FITZFORD COTTAGES (6″) is *Fytzford* 1583 *DuCo* and derives its name from the family of John *Fitz*, M.P. for Tavistock in 1427, who owned land here. Cf. Fices Well *supra* 198. GRAMMERBY WOOD [græməbai] is *Greymerby* 1488 *Rental*. Probably 'grey pool bend,' the second element being OE *byge*, 'curve, bend,' referring to the wide curve made by the Walla Brook here. Cf. Huccaby *supra* 194. GRENDON is *Grenedene* 1311 Cl, *-don* 1330 SR (p), 1488 *Rental*. 'Green valley,' *v.* denu. HARTSHOLE is *Hurtishole* 1299 *Ass*, *-tes-* 1330 *SR* (p), 'hart's hollow,' *v.* holh. HATCHWOOD is *Hatchwode* 1488 *Rental* and was probably the home of Thomas *atte Hacche* (1330 *SR*). *v.* hæcc. HELE is *Hele* 1274 Ipm, *la Hele* late 13th *Deed*, 1281 *Ass* (p). Cf. Hele *supra* 46. HOCKLAKE (6″) is *Hawklake, Hawkslake* 1488 *Rental*. 'Hawk streamlet,' *v.* lacu. IMPHAM (6″) is *Impeham*, *Ympham wood* 1488 *Rental*. KIL-WORTHY is *Kyleworthi* 1323 *Ass*, 1330 SR (p), *Kilaworth* 1334 *SR* (p), *Kellworthi* 1447 *Deed*. '*Cylla*'s worþig.' KINGFORD is *Kyngesford* 1281 *Ass* (p), *Kyngford juxta Tavistoke* 1349 *Ass*. LUSCOMBE DOWN (6″) is *Liscomb or Luscomb Down* 1488 *Rental*.

Probably 'pigsty valley,' *v.* hlose, cumb. MADDACLEAVE WOOD is *Maderclif* 1378 Oliver 89. 'Steep hillside where madder grew,' *v.* clif and cf. Maddacombe *infra* 505. MANA BUTTS. Cf. *Butt Park* 1587 AD *v.* The name must have reference to archery butts. The first element is possibly that found in Manadon *infra* 246. MORWELL is *Morwalla* 1194 P, *Morwille* 1291 Tax, *Morewell* 1394 *Ass. v.* mor, wielle. MORWELL DOWN is *Morewyldowne* 1488 *Rental.* MORWELLHAM is *Morwelham* 1244 *Ass* (p), *Morwilham* 1349 BM, *Morlam* 1675 Ogilby. *v.* ham(m). There is flat land here by the Tamar. NEWTON is *Nywyton juxta Tauystoke* 1351 *Ass.* 'New tun.' OGBEAR is *Ogbere* 1238 *Ass* (p), *Ok-* 1242 Fees 781, *Ockbyar* 1296 *Deed* (p), *Okebeare juxta Tavistok* 1311 Orig. 'Oak wood,' *v.* bearu. PARKWOOD is *Parkewode* 1417 *Ct*, and was probably the home of Walter *in the parke* (1330 *SR*). *v.* pearroc. PARTICLIFFE WOOD (6″) is *Pearteclive* 1488 *Rental.* Possibly '*Pearta*'s steep hillside,' *v.* clif. For this pers. name *v.* PN BedsHu 16 *s.n.* Pertenhall. RADGE (6″) is *Radersh* 1238 *Ass* (p), *Raddershe juxta Tauystok* 1345 *Ass*, *Radyssh* 1482 IpmR. 'Red earsh,' *v.* ersc. RAMSHAM WOOD (6″) is *Ramesham* 1488 *Rental. v.* ham(m). The first element is OE *ramm*, 'ram,' here perhaps used as a pers. name. SANDYPARK (6″) is *Sondep'ke* 1447 *Deed.* SHEEPRIDGE (6″) is *Shiprigge*, *Shiprig* 1488 *Rental.* Self-explanatory. TAVITON is *Tavyton* 1284 FA, 1321 *Ass*, 1355 BM. 'Farm by the Tavy,' *v.* tun. The present farm is at a little distance from the river, but the original site of the settlement was at the spot now called Mount Tavy.

IX. ROBOROUGH HUNDRED

Roggebere 1181 P, *Ruggeberge* 1184 P
Ruweberga 1187 P, *Rugheberegh* 1238 *Ass*, *-berewe* 1280 Oliver 382, *Rughbergh* 1318 Misc
Rokeberg 1261 Pat
Roweberwe 1284 FA, *Rogheberg* 1303 FA

The meaning is 'rough hill,' *v.* ruh, beorg. The name is taken from Roborough in Buckland *infra* 225. In the Geld Roll (1084) the hundred is called *Walchentone* from Walkhampton *infra* 243.

Bere Ferrers

BERE FERRERS 144 B 9

Birlanda 1086 DB, *Birlond* 1318 Fine, 1319 Orig
Ber 1242 Fees 796, 1258–79 Exon, (*juxta Tauistok*) 1311 *Ass*,
   Bere 1301 Ipm, 1331 Cl, *Bere Ferers* 1389 Cl, *Bereferres*
   1428 FA
Byr 1281 *Ass et passim* to 1377 *SR, Byr Fer(r)ers* 1306, 1318
   Ass, 1327, 1338 Pat, *Byrferers* 1340 *FF, Byre Ferers* 1316
   FA, *Bireferers* 1328 Pat
Bire 1369 Pat
Beyrferes 1419 *FF*, *-ferres* 1426 *MinAcct*

It is impossible to offer any satisfactory explanation of this
name. It is clearly not the common Devon *beere, beare,* from
OE bearu (cf. Shebbear *supra* 107), neither is it NCy byre,
'byre.' William *de Ferers* held the manor in 1242 and Sir
Reginald *de Ferariis* was patron of the church in 1258 (Exon).

BERE ALSTON

Alphameston que est hamella de Byrfferers 1339 *Ass*
Berealmiston 1433–72 ECP 2, 28
Berealbeston 1542 *Deeds Enrolled, -bis-* 1615 *Rental*
Berealston 1549 HMC ix, 279, *Alson* 1675 Ogilby, *Allmeston
   al. Alson al. Alveston* 1686 *Recov*

'*Ælfhelm*'s tun.' Cf. Yealmpstone *infra* 254. The centre of
population has now shifted from Bere Ferrers to this place.

BRAUNDER (6″) was the home of John Stacy *at Brande* (1524 *SR*),
of Bronder (1525 *SR*). This must contain OE *brand*, 'burning,
used in the sense 'place where burning has taken place.' For
final *er, v.* Introd. xxxvi.

GAWTON is *Goueton* 1311 *Ass, Estgouaton juxta Tauystok* 1346
Ass, Gawton 1496 Ipm. *v.* Goveton *infra* 318.

RUMLEIGH is *Romeley* 1298 *Ass, Rumlegh(e)* 1311, 1339 *Ass* (p),
Romlegh 1321 *Ass* (p), 1333 *SR* (p), *Rommelegh* 1345 *Ass.*
Probably a compound of rum and leah, 'wide clearing.' Cf.
Romiley (Ch).

WARD is *Ward* 1571 *SR* and was the home of Robert *atte Warde*

(1309 Exon) and Walter fil. William *atte Netherwarthe* (1345 *Ass*). This is the same name as Ward *supra* 82, the place lying by the river Tamar.

BIRCH (6″) and HOLE were the homes of John Benet *at Byrch* (1524 *SR*), and Simon *atte Hole* (1333 *SR*), v. holh.

ASHEN is *Aishdon al. Aishton* 1665 *Deed*. The second element is probably dun. Hence, 'ash hill.' EZONRIDGE (6″) is *Esenridge* 1604 *FF*. KINGSWELL (6″) is *Kingishill* 1615 *Rental*. There is a spring here, so the second element may be *well*. LEIGH is *Legh* 1284 FA, *Treley in Beer Ferris* 1533–8 ECP 7, 136. v. leah and Tredown *supra* 146. LOCKRIDGE FM (6″) is *Lokryge Hille al. Higesbale* 1453 Pat. 'Ridge with a loc or enclosure.' The alternative name contains the word *ball*, 'hill,' v. *supra* 211. SLIME-FORD (6″) is *Slymford* 1335 *Ass*. The first element is probably OE *slim*, 'slime, mud,' cf. Slimeford (Co), *Slymford* 1399 *Ct*. TUCKERMARSH is *Tuckmarsh al. Tuckamarsh* 1665 *Deed*. Possibly the first element is the OE pers. name *Tucca* (Redin 111). WATTONS (6″) is to be associated with the family of Roger de *Wadeton* (1333 *SR*). The p.n. may be derived from the name of this family or more likely the *s* is pseudo-manorial and the name may mean '*Wada*'s farm,' v. tun. WELL (6″) is *Wille* 1625 *Recov*, 'at the spring,' v. wielle. WHITSAM is *Wittesham Doune* 1452 Pat.

Bickleigh

BICKLEIGH 144 B 11

  Bicheleia 1086 DB, *Bickeleye* 1261 Pat
  Bikeleg(he), *-y-* 1225 Pat (p) *et freq* to 1291 Tax, (*juxta Boclond*) 1292 *Ass*
  Bikleg 1263 Ipm
  '*Bica*'s leah.' v. Abbots Bickington *supra* 124.

DARKLAKE (6″) is *Durkelake* 1498 *Ct*. 'Dark streamlet,' v. lacu. HAM is *Hamelonde* 1336 BM, *Ham* 1515–18 ECP 5, 136. v. hamm. There is flat land here by the Plym. HELE is *Heale ferme* 1547 Dartmoor, v. Hele *supra* 46. UPPERTON is *Uppeton* 1281 *Ass* (p), v. uppe, tun. WOOLWELL is *Wolewell* 1281 *Ass* (p), *-wille* 1291 (1408) Dartmoor, *Wollewell* 1286 *Ass*. Probably 'wolves' spring,' v. wielle. Cf. Woolacombe *supra* 54.

Buckland Monachorum

BUCKLAND MONACHORUM [mən'ækərəm] 137 J 10
   (*of*) *bóc lande* c. 970 BCS 1247, *bocsætena higweg* 1031 KCD
   744
Bochelanda 1086 DB, *Boclaund* 1234 Fees 401
Further forms are without interest except:
Bockelonde 1271–6 Exon, *Boclonde Monachorum* 1291 Tax,
   (*Abbatis*) 1316 FA, *Monkyn Bockelond* 1525 *SR*

v. bocland. *Monachorum* refers to the monks of the abbey
founded here in 1278. *bocsætena higweg* must refer to a 'hay
(waggon) road' used by the inhabitants of Buckland. For *sæte*,
cf. *s.n.* Broadwas (PN Wo 103).

ALSTON is (*Oppeton juxta*) *Halpiston* 1323 *Ass.* It is identical
with Alston *infra* 330 and with Albaston in Calstock (Co),
Alpeston, Alpiston 1338 *Rental, Alpeston* 1357, *Albeston* 1399 *Ct.*
These forms are probably reductions of an earlier *Ælfbeorhtestun*,
i.e. *Ælfbeorht*'s *tun, v.* tun. For the unvoicing of *b*, cf. Alpraham
(Ch), *Alburgham* DB, *Alpraham* 1310 St Werburgh Cart.,
Ashprington *infra* 314 and Alperton (Mx), *Alprinton* 1199 FF,
which seems to contain the same pers. name as Alston itself.

DIDHAM is *Dudenham* 1281 *Ass* (p), *Dydeham* 1281 *Ass* (p),
Dideham 1312 Cl (p), *Dedeham* 1542 Oliver. '*Dydda*'s ham(m).'
This pers. name is not recorded but is found in *to dyddan þorne*
BCS 596 and enters into Didcot(e) (Berks, Gl).

HARROWBEER (6″) is *Baraberga* 1096 France, *Harebere* 1546 LP,
Herrabere 1591 *SR, Harrabeare* 1624 *FF.* If the *b* in the earliest
form is a clerical error for *h*, the first element may be OE *hara*,
'hare.' With the great gap in forms between 1096 and 1546 it is
difficult to be sure if the second element is berg or bearu. We
clearly have the second of these words in Harrowbarrow (Co),
Harebeare 1313 Fine, *Estharabyar'* 1324 *Ass.*

ROBOROUGH DOWN is *Rueberge* 1114–16 BM, *Roweberwe* 1284
FA, *Rouburgh juxta Tavistoke* 1387 *FF, Litilholt on Rowberdon*
1540 *Deed, Rowborough Downe* 1624 *Recov.* 'Rough hill,' *v.*
ruh, beorh, dun, holt.

YELVERTON is *Elleford, Ellefordlak* 1291 (1408) Dartmoor,
Elverton 1765 D. '*Ella*'s ford,' or possibly 'elder tree ford,' *v.*

ellen. For the modern addition of *ton*, cf. Dippertown *supra* 200. For *lak*, *v.* lacu. The *y* in the modern form is a 19th cent. addition. The farm is still called Elfordtown (6"). Yelverton is the dialectal form adopted by the G.W.R. when the station was built in 1859 (J. J. A.).

AXTOWN is *Axtowne* 1625 *Recov* and is probably to be associated with the family of Gilbert *Axsa* (1333 *SR*). For names of this type, cf. Rubbytown *supra* 219. BALSTONE is *Balson* 1684 *Recov*. BERRA TOR is *Berrytor* t. Jas 1 ECP. As there is a camp here the first element is possibly burh. BICKHAM is *Bykecombe* 1291 Tax, *Bycacumbayoneda* 1291 (1408) Dartmoor. *v.* Abbots Bickington *supra* 124. *Yoneda* may be for *yond*, 'further,' curiously suffixed to the name. The final *a* is the common Devon syllabic ending, *v.* Introd. xxxvi. BROOM (6") was the home of William de *la Bromen* (1306 *Ass*). The 14th cent. form represents the ME weak plural form, *v.* Pitten *infra* 263. BUCKTOR is *Buckatordowne* 1613 *Recov*. 'Bucks' tor' or '*Bucca*'s tor.' COOMBE is *Combe* 1710 *Recov*. COPPICETOWN is *Cuppers al. Copper Towne* 1710 *Recov*. As the pers. name *le Coppere* occurs in the 1333 *SR*, the name is clearly a corruption of 'Copper's town.' CRAPSTONE is *Crap Stone* 1678 *Deed*. CUMEREW [kʌmeri] is *Comerewe* 1624 *Recov*. *v.* Cumery *infra* 268. CUXTON (6") is *Coxton* 1546 LP. FAIRTOWN (6") is *Fairplace* 1684 *Recov*. FREESABERE (6") is *Heresabere* t. Eliz ChancP, *Fresaber* 1684 *Recov*. *v.* bearu. Probably the *He* is an error for *F*. HARWOOD is *Harewode* 1403 Oliver. 'Hare wood.' HELLINGTOWN is *Hillyngton* 1525 *SR*, *Hellingtowne* 1591 *SR*. LOPWELL is *la Lobbapilla* 1291 (1408) Dartmoor. *v.* Lobb *supra* 33. The pyll must be the stream which joins the Tavy here. LUDBROOK (6") is *Ludbrooke* 1684 *Recov*. Probably 'loud stream,' cf. Ludbrook *infra* 285. MABOR (6") is *Mayburgh* 1546 LP. MILTONCOMBE is *Milton* 1546 LP. NETHERTON (6") is so spelt 1546 LP. 'Lower farm,' *v.* tun. POUND is so spelt in 1765 D. 'Cattle enclosure.' SOUTH WOOD is *Sowthewoode* 1546 LP. SOWTON is *Suthetone* 1313 *Ass* (p), *Southton* 16th Oliver 381. 'South farm,' *v.* tun and cf. Sowton *infra* 233. UPHILL is *Uppehull* 1340 *SR* (p), *Uphill* 16th Oliver 381. UPPATON is *Upton* 1249 *Ass* (p), *Oppeton juxta Halpiston* 1323 *Ass*. 'Higher farm,' *v.* tun. WINSBEER (6") is *Winsbeare* 1710 *Recov*. *v.* bearu. YEOLAND is *Yeoland* 16th Oliver 381, *Yolland* 1624 *Recov*.

Compton

COMPTON 144 D 10

Contona 1086 DB

Cumpton 1234 Fees 401, 1279 Ipm, *Comp-* 1242 Fees 789,
1333 Ipm, *Comton* 1284 FA, *Cumbeton* 1285 Ipm

'Valley farm,' *v.* cumb, tun. The place is still usually known
as *Compton Giffard* from the family which held the manor in the
13th and 14th centuries (*v.* Fees 401, 789, FA 1284, etc.).

Egg Buckland

EGG BUCKLAND 144 C 10

Bochelanda 1086 DB, *Eckebokelond* 1221 Cl

Further forms for the second element are unnecessary. For
the first element may be noted *Ecke-* 1242 Fees 789, 1261 Exon,
Hecke- 1275 RH, Exon, *Eke-* 1279 Ipm, 1291 Tax, *Heke-* 1284
FA, *Eccke-* 1308–14 Exon, *Egge-* 1340 *SR*.

v. bocland. There is no reason to doubt that the distinctive
first element is derived from *Hece* (Exch DB *Heche*), who held
the manor TRE (Exon DB f. 327 *b*). The OE form of his name
was probably *Ecca*, with inorganic *h* in DB.

COLERIDGE (6″) is *Colrige* 1086 DB, *-rig* 1284 FA, *-rugge* 1303
FA, *-rigge* 1318 FF, (*juxta Ekkebouklond*) 1323 *Ass*, *Courig* 1242
Fees 776. The first element is probably col, 'charcoal,' from its
being burnt on this ridge. Cf. Coleridge *infra* 332.

CROWN HILL is a modern name invented c. 1880. The place was
earlier called *Nackershole* 1765 D, *Nackers Hole, Knackers Hole*
in a map of 1823 (*ex inf.* Mrs Rose-Troup). The meaning of this
name (cf. Knackers Knowle *infra* 324) is uncertain, but it was
clearly a term of contempt. Cf. Knackers Hole (PN Wo 49).

EFFORD is *Eppeford* 1186 P, 1242 Fees 789, *Efford* 1284 FA,
Ebford 1306 *Ass*. The parallels of Efford *infra* 251, 266, 278,
Efford in Stratton (Co), *Ebbeford* 1183 P, 1202, 1256 FF, on
the estuary of the Bude river, Efford in Milton (Ha), 1242 Fees
Ebbeford, on Avon Water, a tidal creek, make it probable that this
name is to be interpreted as 'ford passable at ebb-tide,' referring
to a passage over the Plym estuary.

LEIGHAM is *Legham* 1242 Fees 776, 1303 FA, (*juxta Plympton*) 1316 *Ass*, *Ley-* 1318 Ch, *Lyg-* 1365 *FF*. The first element is probably OE læge, 'fallow.' Cf. Leigham in Streatham (Sr), *Leygham* 1164 P, *Legham* 1302 Abbr.

MAINSTONE (6″) is *Mainston* 1201 FF, *la Maynstane* 1256 *Ass* (p), *la Maynston* 1298 *Ass* (p), *Meynston* 1392 IpmR, *Maynston-crossa*, *Maynstonkvilla* 1291 (1408) Dartmoor. This may be a hybrid name, the first part being a British word corresponding to W, Co *maen*, 'stone,' cf. *to þæm mægen stane* BCS 723, a Devon charter, *to mægen stanes dene* BCS 1072 (Wiltshire), *oð þone mægen stan* BCS 491 (Berkshire), also Mainstone *supra* 45. In that case we must take the OE spelling *mægen* to be a pseudo-etymological spelling due to association with *mægen*, 'strength.' Professor Ekwall would take it to have been *mægen-stan*, 'mighty rock,' from the first. In the metres of the OE Boethius *mægenstan* renders the *micel stan*, *i.e.* great-stone, of the prose version. The *kvilla* of the 1408 form may be a transcription error for *Knilla*, *v. s.n.* Kneela *supra* 170.

WIDEY [waidi] is *Wida* 1086 DB, *Widhi* t. Hy 2 Oliver 135, *Wythy* 1242 Fees 789, 1284 FA, *-i* 1333 SR (p), *-ey* 1428 FA, *Widie* 1282 (1328) Ch. This is probably the OE wiðig, 'withy.' For the *d* forms, cf. Widdecombe *infra* 526.

AUSTIN is perhaps to be associated with the family of John *Austyn* (1333 *SR*). For omission of the genitival *s*, cf. Durrant *supra* 103. BIRCHAM (6″) is *Byrcheham* 1270 *Ass* (p). 'Birch ham(m).' BOWDEN is *Boghedon juxta Ekebokelond* 1321 *Ass*. 'Curved hill,' *v.* Bowden *supra* 37. COLWILL is *Colewell*, *-will* 1281 *Ass* (p), *-vill* 1336 Ipm. *v.* Collacott *supra* 50. CRABTREE is *the Crabe Tree* 1598 PlymRec. DERRIFORD is so spelt 1827 G and is possibly to be associated with the family of John *Derye* (1571 *SR*). FROGMORE is *Frogmere* 1572 AddCh. 'Frog pool,' *v.* mere. PLYM BRIDGE is *Plymbrydge* 1525 *AOMB* 385. POOL (6″) is *Poole* 1572 AddCh. SHALLAFORD (6″) is *Shallowford*, *Shellaver* 1627 Deed. For the second form, *v.* Introd. xxxiv. SMALLACK (6″) is so spelt 1827 G. Probably 'narrow streamlet,' *v.* lacu.

Meavy

MEAVY [meivi] 137 J 11

Mæwi 1031 KCD 744[1]
Mewi (4), *Metwi* (1) 1086 DB, *Mewy* 1263–6 Exon, (*juxta Bokelond*) 1346 *Ass*
Meuwy 1284 FA, 1377 *SR*, *Mewey* t. Mary *MinAcct*
Mevie 1571 *SR*, *Meavie* 1589 *Deed*

The village takes its name from the river on which it stands (*v. supra* 9). In 1342 (Pat) there is a curious reference to the 'church of Seintmevy,' no doubt a mistake.

BRISWORTHY [brisəri]

Brutereswurdam t. Hy 2 Oliver 135
Brytenesworh 1270 *Ass*, *Brittenesworth(y)* 1303 FA
Brythtesworthy 1346 FA, *Bryghtesworthy* 1386 *Ass*, t. Hy 6 Ct, *Brightesworth* 1505 Dartmoor
Brisworthy 1584 Dartmoor, *Brissery* 1827 G

v. worðig. The first element is the OE pers. name *Beorhtwine* with common confusion of *n* and *r* in the first form.

CADOVER BRIDGE and CADWORTHY FM (6″) are *Cadewurdam* t. Hy 2 Oliver 135, -*worth(i)* 1284 FA, *Cadaworth* 1291 (1408) Dartmoor, *Cadworthy* 1493 Ipm, *West Cadworthy al. Caddaver* 1773 Deed, (*de*) *ponte de Cadaworth* 1291 (1408) Dartmoor. '*Cada*'s farm,' *v.* worþig. For the modern form, *v.* Introd. xxxv. The bridge preserves the local pronunciation of the farm name.

CALLISHAM DOWN [kælisəm] is *Calyngisham* 1486–1515 ECP 3, 293, *Calysham* 1553 Deed, *Callisham* 1698 *FF. v.* ham(m). The first element would seem to be a pers. name, perhaps of ME origin. Alternatively it might perhaps contain ME *calenge*, 'challenge,' 'claim' (cf. Callanswood PN Wo 218 and Callingwood PN St 30), hence 'ham(m) of (or in) dispute,' but the forms are too late for any certainty.

GOODAMEAVY is *Godemewy* 1242 Fees 776, 1333 *SR* (p), *Gode Meuwy* 1284 FA, *Gode Mewy* 1292 *Ass*, *Good a mewye* 1557

---

[1] KCD 744 is a grant of half a hide of land at Meavy. It is impossible to identify the defining boundaries except for the reference to the 'hay road' of the people of Buckland (Monachorum), *v. supra* 225.

Deed. The first element is probably the ME representative of the OE pers. name *Goda* and the name would mean '*Goda*'s settlement by the Meavy.' Cf. Babcary (So), *Babakari* DB, *Babbekari* 1242 Ass, from the OE pers. name *Babba* and the river-name *Carey*, and Uffculme *infra* 537.

GRATTON is *Gropeton* 1242 Fees 776, 1303 FA, 1306 Ipm, *-toune* 1291 Tax, *Cropeton* 1291 (1408) Dartmoor, *Grapton al. Gratton* 1688 *Recov*. There is an OE *grōp*, denoting a ditch or drain (cf. Förstemann ON i, 1117). We may possibly have this word or an allied weak form in this name. Gratton lies in a hollow, but the whole matter is very difficult. Equally difficult is Grappenhall (Ch), DB *Gropenhale*. This is in a slight depression on a small stream, possibly another *grop*. In the Devon name the stream is the Meavy so that Gratton can hardly take its name from the stream itself. A pers. name *Gropa* is also possible.

HOO MEAVY is *Hughemewy* 1242 Fees 795, *Hewemewy* 1244 *Ass*, *Huge Meuwy* 1284 FA, *Hughmewey* 1303 FA, *Howe Mewy* 1564 *Deed*. It is difficult to be sure about this name but as Goodameavy seems to contain the name of its sometime owner or holder, so also Hoo Meavy may contain ME *Hewe, Hue, Hughe*, 'Hugh.' Cf. Adam *Hugha* found in Hartland Hundred in 1333 (*SR*). It may be noted that there were four manors of *Mewi* in DB but none of them was held by either a *Goda* or a *Hugh*, so that both names, if not of pre-Conquest origin, must derive from some unrecorded 12th cent. holders.

LOVATON is *Lovyeton* 1242 Fees 789, 1378 IpmR, *Loveton* 1273 Cl, *(Bastard)* 1303 FA, *Loviaton* 1284 FA, *Louyngton* 1505 Dartmoor. *v.* tun. The first element must be a pers. name *Lufa* or *Lēofa* with the intrusive vowel noticed *supra* xxxvi. Cf. also William *Lovya* and Robert *Lovye* 1309, 1318 Exon. Baldwin *le Bastard* held the manor in 1284 (FA).

SHILLIBEER (lost) is *Shullebere* 1333 SR (p), *-beare* 1517 *Recov*, *Shullabeare al. Shullabeare Towne in the parish of Mewie* 1587 *Deed*. The name is probably a compound of scylf and bearu.

YENNADON is *Yhanedouna* 13th *Deed*, *Yanedonecrosse* 1291 (1408) Dartmoor. '*Ēana*'s hill,' *v.* dun. Cf. to eanan leage BCS 624.

CATSTOR DOWN is *Cattestorre* 1340 SR (p), *Cattysterre* 1486-

1515 ECP 3, 293. 'Torr frequented by the (wild) cat.' DURANCE (6″) is *Tixtent otherwise called Duraunce* 1486–1515 ECP 3, 293 and is probably to be associated with the family of Reginald *Durante* (1430 *Ct*). GREENWELL (6″) is *Grenewell* 1181 P (p), *-will* 1517 *Recov*. LAKE is *Lak* 1291 (1408) Dartmoor, *v.* lacu. There is a small stream here. LYNCH COMMON is *Lunche* 1595 PlymRec, *Linch* 1740 *Recov*, *v.* hlinc. MARCHANT'S CROSS is referred to as *Smalacumbacrosse* in a perambulation of 1291 (1408) (Dartmoor). *v.* smæl, cumb. The later name might be connected with the family of *Marchaund*, found in Tavistock in 1281 (*Ass*). SPARKATON (6″) is *Lake al. Higher Lake al. Sparkatowne* in 1589 *Deed* and is to be associated with the family of Robert *Sparke* (1238 *Ass*). Cf. Rubbytown *supra* 219. URGLES (6″) is *Urggelegh* 1423 IpmR. WIGFORD DOWN is so spelt in 1827 G and is possibly to be associated with Andrew de *Wigheworthi* who held Fernhill in Shaugh in 1306 (Ipm). He may have come from Wigford *infra* 306. WILLAKE (6″) is so spelt in 1745 *Recov*. *v.* lacu.

Petertavy

PETERTAVY [piˑtəteivi, pit-] 137 F 10

    Tawi 1086 DB, *Taui* 1165 P

    (*ecclesia*) *Petri Tavy* 1270 Exon, *Tavy Beati Petri* 1291 Tax,
        Tavy Sancti Petri 1318 Exon

    Peterestavi 1276 Exon, 1295 Ipm, *Petrestauy juxta Tauistok*
        1313 *Ass*, *Petterstavy* 1583 *FF*

    Patrystavy 1434 Pat, *Patryxtavy* 1535 LP

'(Church of) St Peter by the Tavy.' *v.* Marytavy *supra* 200. The two latest forms seem to have been influenced by the name *Patrick*. The two elements should be pronounced as one word with unifying stress on the first syllable.

BROUSENTOR (6″) is *Brounstountor* 1403 Dartmoor, *Brounsdontor* 1603 *DuCo*, *Brounson Tor* 1765 D. In 1340 (*SR*) there is mention of a John de *Brouneston*, which suggests that *Brouneston* is a lost place from which the *tor* took its name. The farm is probably to be associated with John *Broun* mentioned in the same subsidy-roll, the meaning being thus 'Brown's farm,' *v.* tun.

CUDLIPPTOWN is *Cudelipe* 1114–19 BM, *-lip(p)* 1238 *Ass,* *Codelip(p)* 1238 *Ass,* 1428 FA, *-lepe* 1303 FA, *Cuddelypp* 1474 *Ct,* *Cudliptowne* 1641 *FF.* '*Cud(d)a*'s hlype.' As usual in such names it is difficult to say just what the 'leap' was. Possibly it has reference to the stream here. For the *town, v. infra* 676.

GODSWORTHY is *Godesworthi* 1238 *Ass,* 1340 *SR* (p), *Godewurthi* 1244 *Ass* (p), *Goddesworthy* 1514 *Ct.* '*Gōde*'s worðig,' cf. Guscott *supra* 175.

LANGSFORD (6″) is *Lanxford oth. Lanxkarford oth. Langsford* 1785 *Recov.* The first element is OE *landscearu,* 'boundary, landmark.' It is near the parish boundary. Cf. Landskerry *supra* 215.

LAUNCESTON MOOR is *Langeston More* 1488 *Rental.* 'Long stone moor,' referring to the menhir near by. The modern form is corrupt.

SMEARDON DOWN [smə·n] is *Smerdon* 1340 *SR* (p), 1346 *Ass* (p), 1497 *Deed, Smardon Downe* 1561 *FF. v.* smeoru, dun. The name was probably applied to the hill because it gave rich pasturage. Cf. St Martin's Down (Wt), *Smeredon(e)* 1313 Ch, 1324 Misc.

WAPSWORTHY is *Werbricheswurdh'* 1230 P (p), *Werbrightewrthy* 1238 FF, *-briteswurth* 1244 *Ass, Warbritteswurth* 1244 *Ass, Werbrightesworthy* 1394 *FF, Warpisworthy* t. Hy 6 *Ct, Werpys-* 1514 *Ct.* '*Wǣrbeorht*'s worðig. Cf. Warbrightsleigh *infra* 394.

WILLSWORTHY is *Wifleurde* 1086 DB, *Wiueleswrth* 1219, 1249 *Ass, Wyvelesworth'* 1242 Fees 789, *Wevelesworth* 1342 *Deed, Wenelesworthi* (sic) 1378 IpmR. '*Wifel*'s worðig.' This pers. name, though not on independent record, is very common in p.n.'s.

BAGGA TOR is *Baketorre* 1238 *Ass* (p), *Bagge-* 1333 *SR* (p), *Bagetor* 1488 *Rental.* '*Bacga*'s torr' or '*Bacca*'s.' BEARDON is *Buredone, Burydon'* 1242 Fees 756. *v.* burh, dun. BROADMOOR (6″) is *Brademore* 1345 *Deed, Brodmore* 1598 *Recov.* BUTTERBERRY (local) is *Boterworthi* 1330 *SR* (p), 1408 *Ass* (p), t. Hy 6 *Ct, -ie* 1488 *Rental, Butreworthy* 1342 Pat (p). 'Butter worðig,' cf. Buttercombe *supra* 40. CHURCHTOWN (6″) is *Churchetowne* 1621

Recov. For *town*, *v. infra* 676. CLAY TOR is *Claytorre* 1665
Dartmoor. COX TOR is *Bowren al. Cockestorre* 1618 *FF*. The
later name may derive from some man named *Cock.* GER TOR is
Gordetorre 1306 *Ass* (p). The first element is perhaps a man's
name; a William *Gurde* occurs in Tavistock (late 13th *AddCh*).
HARRAGROVE is *Haregrave* 1238 *Ass* (p), 1274 Ipm, *Hargrave*
1274 Ipm, *Haregrove* 1394 *Ass.* 'Hare grove' or 'grey-grove,'
v. hara, har. HILLTOWN is *Hill Towne* 1720 *Recov.* For *town*,
v. infra 676. LONGBETTOR (6″) is probably referred to in *Beator-
yeate* (1514 *Ct*), the *long* being a later addition. Cf. Beetor
infra 470. *Yeate* = 'gate,' *v.* geat. NATTOR is *Gnattorr'* 1340
SR (p), 1352 *MinAcct*, *Gnatetorre* 1355 *DuCo*, *Gnatorre* 1347
Dartmoor. 'Gnat torr,' cf. Gnatham *infra* 245. REDFORD (6″) is
Redeford 1342 *Deed.* 'Red ford' or 'reed-ford.' ROOS TOR is
Rulestorre 1665 Dartmoor. SOWTONTOWN (6″) is *Sutheton* 1249
Ass, (*juxta Petres Tawy*) 1288 *Ass*, *Sowton Towne* 1598 *Recov.*
'South farm.' It lies due south of Petertavy village. For the
additional *town*, *v. infra* 676. STANDON is *Standune, Stondon'*
1242 Fees 756. 'Stone hill,' *v.* dun. TORTOWN is *Torre al.
Torre Towne* 1711 *Recov.* For the *town*, *v. infra* 676. TWIST
(6″) is *Twyste* 1502 *DuCo*. This may be the ordinary word
'twist.' There is a sharp bend in the lane here[1]. WEDLAKE is
Wydelake 1518–29 ECP 5, 285. 'Wide stream,' *v.* lacu. WHITE
TOR is *Whittor* 1779 *Recov.* Probably 'white torr,' the modern
form being a 'restored spelling.' WILL (6″) was the home of
Walter *atte Wille* 1342 (Pat). 'At the spring,' *v.* wielle.

Plymouth

PLYMOUTH 144 D 9/10

Plymmue 1230 Lib, 1254 Worth, -*muth* 1318 Misc, *Plimmue*
1231, *Plimmuth, Plinemuth* 1234 Cl, *Plympmouthe* 1353
Ass

Plummuth 1281 *Ass*, 1318 Misc, (*ad portum de*) 1331 Orig,
-*mouthe* 1377, 1384 Exon, *Plumpmuth* 1307 Cl

Pleymuth 1292 Pat, *Plemmuth* 1297 Pat, 1350 Cl, -*mewe* 1322
Pat

Sutton Prior vulgariter Plymmouth nuncupatur c. 1450 Oliver
144

---

[1] *Ex inf.* Mr J. J. Alexander.

v. Plym river *supra* 12. The earliest forms refer to the harbour and estuary, the older name for the parish being Sutton *infra* 236.

NOTE. PLYMOUTH STREET NAMES. The original town of Plymouth was of small extent, being limited chiefly to the area round Sutton Pool (*infra* 236). Of old names the following may be noted, the spellings unless otherwise stated being taken from PlymRec.

BATTER ST is so spelt in 1626. BILBURY ST is *Billabiri Strete* 1342, 1476. There was also a *bilbury brigge* 1506. This is possibly *Billa*'s burh. BRETON SIDE is *Britayn side* c. 1493, cf. Bartholomew Street in Exeter *supra* 21. BUCKWELL ST is *Buckwell strete, Buckwyllane* c. 1493. CATHERINE ST is *St Catherines lane* 1641, from the chapel of this dedication on the Hoe (*infra* 235). CATTEDOWN ST is *Cat strete* c. 1493, *Katt strete* late 15th. Cf. Cattewater *infra.* FINEWELL ST is *Fynewyl stret* c. 1493. FRIARS LANE is *The Fryers lane* 1517, cf. also *Fryerie Greene, White Fryers Gate, Friary Garden* 1587. The order of the Friars Minor had a house here (cf. Pat 1386). GREEN ST is *green street* 1706. HIGH ST is *Hygh strete* c. 1493. KINTERBURY ST is *Kynterbury Street* 1537. *v.* Kinterbury (*infra* 241). LAMBHAY ST is *the Lambe hay* 1627. 'Lamb enclosure,' *v.* (ge)hæg. LOO ST is *Loostreete* 1588, possibly containing the word *loose,* 'pigsty,' *v.* hlose. MARKET ST is *the Market Street* 1520 HMC ix, *Marget Street* 1537. MILL ST, cf. *Old Mill Lane* 1616. NEW ST is *Sperkes newe streate* 1584, *a new street paved leading towards the new key* 1584. NUTTE ST is *Nutte streete* 1459, *Notestrete* c. 1493. ST ANDREWS ST is *Seynte Andrewes streate* 1577, from the old church of St Andrew. SOUTHSIDE ST is so spelt 1591. It leads to *Southeside Kaye* (1584) referring to an old quay or wharf here. STILLMAN ST is *Stylmanstrete* 1412, possibly from a man named *Stil(e)-man.* TOTHILL ROAD must be near the spot called *Totehill* in 1641, i.e. 'look-out hill' (*v.* PN Sx 31). TREVILLE ST takes its name from one Richard *Trevill,* a wealthy merchant in Elizabeth's reign. VAUXHALL ST is a corruption of *Foxhole* (1491, 1598, 1661)[1]. WEEK ST is *Wike street* 1585. There may have once been some dairy farm here. *v.* wic. WHIMPLE ST is *Wympelstrete* 1493, *Wympilstrete* 1518 HMC 9, *Whimplestreate* 1577, possibly from the sale of 'wimples' or veils here. The word is recorded from c. 1242 (NED *s.v.*). WOLSDON ST is *Woolster Street* 1637 *Deed,* 1706. If the earlier forms are correct, the name may derive from the 'woolsters' or wool staplers who lived here.

CATTEDOWN, CATTEWATER are *la Catte* 1249 *Ass* (p), 1281 *Ass,* *atte Katte* 1333 *SR* (p), *le Catte* t. Hy 7 PlymRec, *Cattedowne* 1621 *Recov, Cat Water* 1577 Saxton. The 1249 and 1333 references refer respectively to a certain Richard de *la Catte* and Richard *atte Katte.* More important is the 1281 reference, first noted by Ekwall (RN 329), in which certain people were drowned

---

[1] *Ex inf.* Mr C. W. Bracken, to whom we owe access to the volume of records which give most of the early forms of these names.

in a small boat *apud la Catte*. The preposition *apud* suggests that *Catte* was not the name of the estuary at that time but some feature on its shores. There can be little doubt that *Katte* is the common animal name and that some feature in the topography of the district suggested the use of the term. The growth of modern Plymouth makes it impossible to identify that feature. In the course of time the name came to be compounded with Down and also with Water, the name of the estuary below, and with street, as in *Catstrete* the old form of Cattedown St *supra* 234.

COXSIDE (6″) (district) is *Cocke syde* 1591, *Cockshedd lane* 1605 PlymRec, *Cockside* 1661 Worth, and is possibly to be associated with the family of Richard *Cokke* of Plymouth (1468 Pat). *Side* may in that case have the sense 'end,' quarter of the town.

THE HOE. One John *atter Howe* was living here in 1330 (*SR*), while in 1370 (Exon) we have reference to 'capella Sancte Katerine *atte Howe*.' Leland calls it 'the How.' This is a point of comparatively high land projecting into Plymouth Harbour. *v.* hoh. There was an ancient chapelry here.

LIPSON (6″)
> *Lisistona* 1086 DB
> *Lipston* 1238 *Ass*, *Lyp-* 1270 *Ass*, 1346 FA, (*juxta Compton*) 1364 *Ass*
> *Lippeston'* 1242 Fees 796, 1291 Misc, *-stan* 1249 *Ass*
> *Loppeston* 1284 FA
> *Lepston* 1303 FA

The DB form (if it belongs here) is obviously corrupt. If the original second element was *stan*, the name may be an OE compound of this word and *lippa*, 'lip,' perhaps referring to some stone of a peculiar shape or appearance. Professor Ekwall suggests OE *hliep-stan*, 'leap-stone,' i.e. a mounting stone.

MILLBAY is *the Mylle Bay* c. 1550 Leland. The spot was earlier known as *Surepola(m)* 13th, *mill de pourepolemulle* (sic) 1387 HMC, ix, 274, *Sourepol* 1368 Oliver, *Sourepolemylle* 1373 Worth. This would mean literally 'sour pool,' perhaps because its water was brackish.

MUTLEY is *Modleia* 1086 DB, *Motlegh(e)* 1311 Exon (p), 1333

SR (p), *Motelegh* 1492 Ipm. Perhaps a compound of OE (ge)mot, 'meeting' and leah. Cf. *in gemotleage* BCS 476, *to gemot leage* BCS 1213.

SUTTON (6″) is *Sutona* 1086 DB, *Sutton(e)* 1201 FF, *Sud-* 1201 Cur, *Suth-* 1264 Exon, 1281 *Ass, pola de Sutton* 1275 RH, *Sottone* 1291 Tax, *Sytton* 1319 Ipm. 'South farm,' perhaps with reference to Stoke (*infra* 240). This was the original name of the area now called Plymouth, that name being at first applied only to the harbour (*v. supra* 233–4). The name *Sutton* survives in *Sutton* Pool. In medieval times there were two manors of Sutton, namely Sutton *Prior*, held by Plympton Priory, and Sutton *Vautort*, held by the family of *Vautort* or de *Valle Torta* (*v.* FA 340, 354, 380).

DRAKE'S ISLAND was formerly *isle of St Nicholas* 1396 Cl, *Insula Sancti Nicholai* 1478 WmWo, *Sent Nicholas Ilond* 1573 Plym Rec, from a chapel of St Nicholas on it. The later name is due to association with Sir Francis Drake. HOUNDISCOMBE (6″) is *Hundescumb* 1244 *Ass, -combe* 1477 IpmR, *Hondescumbe* 1318 *FF*. '*Hund*'s cumb' or 'hound's cumb.' MANNAMEAD (6″) is *Manna-meads* 1841 DA 28, 761. Cf. Manadon *infra* 246. MOUNT BATTEN derives its name from Admiral *Batten*, governor of the fort here during the Civil War (1642–9). It was earlier known as *Hostert* (1296 *Ass*), *Hoe Stert* (1598 PlymRec), *v.* Hoe *supra* 235 and steort. Hence, 'end of the hoe.' MOUNT GOLD derives from Colonel William *Gould*, governor of Plymouth garrison during the Civil War. PEVERELL is a new district, the name having been suggested by the adjacent Weston Peverell *infra* 246. THORN PARK (6″) is *thorne hylle þke* t. Hy 7 PlymRec. LOWER VENN (6″) is *Fenne al. Venne* t. Eliz ChancP 3, and was the home of William *atte Fenne* (1333 *SR*). *v.* fenn.

St Budeaux

ST BUDEAUX [bʌdəks]   144 C 8

> *Seynt Bodokkys* 1520 *Recov*, (*Budoks*) 1553 *FF, St Budox* 1624 *Recov, Saint Budeaux* or *Saint Buddox* 1796 *Recov* (*cum*) *capellis S'cor' Budoc' et* ... 1535 VE
> *St Botake* 1539 LP, *S. Budok chirch* c. 1550 Leland

This parish (the earlier name for which was Budshead *infra*) takes its name from the Celtic saint *Budoc* to whom the church was dedicated. Cf. Budock (Co), *ecclesie sancti Budoci* 1208 ClR. The name *Budoc(k)* goes back to OBritish *Boudicco(s)*, of which the fem. *Boudicca* is well known in the corrupt form *Boadicea*.

BUDSHEAD

> *Bucheside* 1086 DB
>
> *Buddekeshyde, -hide* 1242 Fees 789, *Budekeside* 1263 Ipm, *Budokyshyde* 1440 Exon
>
> *Bodekesid(e)* 1263 Ipm, *Bodekeshid* 1284 FA, *Bottekeshide* 1313 Exon (p), -*ok*- 1333, 1334 SR (p)
>
> *Butshead al. Boxhead al. Budocoshide al. St Budeox* 1671 Deed

'The hide of land of St Budoc,' *v. supra.*

LITTLE ERNESETTLE is *Yernessetle* 1281 Ass (p), *Ernessetle* 1282 (1328) Ch, *Nythere Ernessettle* 1320 Ass, *Ernissetle* 1321 Exon (p), *Yernesetele* 1383 FF (p). The name may be a compound of OE *earn*, 'eagle,' and *setl*, 'seat, sitting,' etc., referring to the slight elevation here above the Tamar. Alternatively *Earn* may have been used as a pers. name. Cf. *to hafocys setle* KCD 832 (Devon).

HONICKNOWLE [hʌniknoul]

> *Hanenchelola* 1086 DB, *Haneknolle* 1219 Ass, -*cnolle* 1228 FF, 1242 Fees 796, *Hanknolle* 1246 Ipm, *Hony Knoll* 1737 FF

'*Hana*'s' or '*Haneca*'s knoll,' *v.* cnoll. The DB form is corrupt.

KING'S TAMERTON is *Tanbretona* 1086 DB, *Kyngestamerton* 1281 Ass, *Kyngestomerton juxta Sutton Prioris* 1339 Ass. 'tun on the Tamar.' The manor was held by the king as early as DB and was thus distinguished from Tamerton Foliot *infra* 242.

WHITLEIGH HALL is *Witelie, -leia* 1086 DB, -*le* 1218 FF, *Whytelegh* 1242 Fees 777, 789, *Wittelegh* 1284 FA, *West Whyteleghe* 1405 FF. 'White leah.'

AGATON is *Haketon* 1333 SR (p), *Agaton* 1626 Recov. The forms are too few to interpret with safety. If the initial *h* is incorrect, the first element may be the pers. name *Aca*. WOODLAND is *Woodland* 1641 Recov.

Sampford Spiney

SAMPFORD SPINEY 137 H 11

Sanford(a) 1086 DB, 1242 Fees 789, Saunford 1234 Fees 398,
1237 Cl, (Spinee) 1281 Ass, Sam- 1262 Ipm, Samp- 1291
Tax

Saundford Spyneye 1304 Ass, Saunford Spenee 1346 Ass

'Sand(y) ford' (over the Walkham river). The manor was held
by Gerard de Spineto in 1234 (Fees 398).

HUCKWORTHY [hʌkəri] is Hokebere 1238 Ass, Hoghe- 1281 Ass,
Hocbeare 1304 Ass, Hocke- 1305 Ass (all p), Huckery Mill 1677
Recov. v. hoc, bearu. There is a spur of land here above the
Walkham. The second element has been wrongly written -worthy
in modern times, owing to the fact that most names with this
terminal are locally pronounced with final [əri].

MONKSWELL (6″) is Mankeswill(e) 1340 SR, -kys- 1365 Ct, -kis-
1377 Ct (p), Manteswille 1365 Ct. 'Manec's spring,' v. wielle.
The weak form Maneca occurs in Redin (157), a diminutive of
the OE pers. name Mann or Mana. Cf. Manxey (PN Sx 445).

STOURTOWN (6″) is Sturrtown 1740 Recov and is probably to be
associated with the family of Nicholas atte Sturte (1377 Ct) and
Willelmus Sturte (1428 FA). v. steort. The farm lies on a well-
marked tongue of land. See, however, Walkham river supra 16.

BROOK is Brooke 1712 Rental. DUNRIDGE is Donerigga, Donerigge-
forde 13th Deed. v. dun. EASTONTOWN (6″) is Byestedon 1340
SR (p), Estedon 1377 Ct (p), 1417 Ct, Easton Towne 1677 Recov.
'East of the down.' FOXHAMS is Foxesham 1669, 1742 FF. HOLE-
TOWN (6″) is Hole Towne 1677 Recov. LEETOWN (6″) is Lygh 1291
(1408) Dartmoor, Legh in Sanford Spynee 1314 Pat. WOODTOWN
is atte Wode 1378 Ct (nom. loc.). v. holh, leah, wudu. For the
addition of town, v. infra 676.

Sheepstor

SHEEPSTOR 137 J 12

Sitelestorra 1168 P (p), Sytelestorre 1242 Fees

Schetelestorre 1181 P (p), 1356 Exon

Schitelestor(re) 1219 Ass, -tar 1303 FA, Schytlestorre 1375
Exon

Scitelstor 1244 *Ass, Skytelestor* 1262 Ipm
Schidistorre 1378 IpmR, *Scitestorr(e)* 1408 Dartmoor, *Shittys-*
    1422 *Ass, Shettes-* 1453 Pat, *Shittes-* 1474 *Ct*
Shistor 1547 Dartmoor
Shepystorr 1574 *Deed, Shipstor* 1607 *Recov, Shetelstor now*
    Shepstor c. 1620 Risdon
Shippistor al. Shittistor 1691 *Recov, Sheepstor al. Shittestor*
    1695 *Recov*

The first element might be the OE pers. name *Scyttel* (cf.
Shillington PN BedsHu 173), but it is perhaps more likely that
we have here the OE *scyttel(s)*, 'bar, bolt.' The *tor* is suggestive
of such when viewed from certain points. The substitution of *p*
for *t* was probably an attempt to prevent the unpleasant suggestions of the old form of the name.

DITSWORTHY WARREN [ditsəri] is *Durkesworth(y)* 1474 *Ct*,
Durkysworthi 1481 *Ct*. The identification is not certain, but is
highly probable. If correct, the first element is perhaps the OE
deorc, ME *durke*, 'dark,' etc., used as a ME pers. name. Cf.
John *Durke* 1333 *SR* (Devon), Druxton *supra* 172, and Dassells
Green (Herts), *Derkeshale* n.d. AD iv, 1287 *Ass*, 1307 *SR* (p).

PLYM STEPS is *Plymystappys* 1498 *Ct*, and is called *Plymcrundla*
in 1291 (1408) Dartmoor. Plym Steps is an ancient ford of
stepping stones on the southern branch of the Abbot's Way, an
old track leading from Buckfast to Buckland Abbey. There are
ancient 'hut circles' here situated in an oval depression. *Crundel*
is probably used in its original sense of 'curved valley.' Cf. also
Stepps in Advent (Co) *Heghstappe* 1334 *Ct*, 1338 *Rental, Hye*
Stepps 1638 *FF*, at a crossing of the river Camel.

RINGMOOR DOWN is *Rydemore* 1291 (1408) Dartmoor, *Rynmore*
1535 VE, 1547 Dartmoor, *Ridemore Down al. Ringmore Downe*
t. Eliz ChancP 1, 401. The first element may be ME *ridde*, referring to a moor cleared of undergrowth, etc. *v*. Ringmore
infra 283.

CHUBSTON COTTAGE (6″) is *Chubbeston* 1375 *Ct* and is probably
to be associated with the family of Walter *Chubba* (14th *Deed*).
COLLYTON (6″) is *Collatowne* 1691 *Recov*. EVIL COMBE (6″) is
probably the place called *Great Evell* 1611 *Deed*. GUTTER TOR

is *Gotetorre* 1281 *Ass* (p), 1317 Pat (p), *Gotterknap* 1539 *Deed*.
'Goats' *tor*,' *v*. gat, cnæpp. HARTER TOR is *Hartor Tor* 1827 G.
Probably 'hart *tor*,' the second *tor* being redundant. LONGSTONE
(6") is so spelt in 1694 *Recov*. No *menhir* exists here now.
NARRATOR (6") is *Narrow Tor* 1827 G. The farm lies on the north
side of 'Sheeps Tor and probably goes back to a ME *Bynorthe-
torre*, 'north of the *tor*,' *v. supra* xxxvii. PORTLAND LANE (6") is
Portlandhead t. Hy 6 *Ct*. The meaning of *port* here is as usual
doubtful, *v*. Doggaport *supra* 95. SHEEPS TOR (the tor) is *la
Torr apud Shitestorr* 1291 (1408) Dartmoor, *Shepystor Downe*
1576 *Deed*. SMALLCOMBE (6") is *Smalacumba* 1291 (1408) Dartmoor. 'Narrow combe,' *v*. smæl. YELLOWMEAD is *Yalmede* 1249
Ass (p), *Yoldmede* 1281 *Ass* (p), *Yollameade al. Oldmeade* 1607
Recov, *Yollmead Down* 1718 *Deed*. 'Old meadowland.' For *old*,
v. Addenda *supra* lviii. YEO FM (6"). Cf. *Yeofford* 1691 *Recov*
and *v*. Yeo *supra* 17–18.

Stoke Damarel

STOKE DAMAREL[1] (Devonport) 144 D 9

> *Stoches* 1086 DB, *Stoke* 1086 DB, 1238 FF, *Stoca* 1174–83
> BM, *Stokes* 1242 Fees 789
>
> *Stok Aubemarl* 1281 *Ass*, *Stokeda(u)marle* 1311, 1382 Exon,
> *Stoke Daumarle* 1316 FA, (*Daun-*) 1341 Ipm

v. stoc(c). The manor was held by Robert de *Albamarla* in
1086 (DB) and by Ralph de *Aubemarle* in 1238 FF (called
Radulfus de *Alba Mare* 1242 Fees 789). For the later form of
the pers. name, cf. Sydenham Damarel *supra* 209.

CAMEL'S HEAD (district) (6") is *Kemel* 1286 *SR* (p), 1318 *Ass* (p),
1386 *Ass*, *-ell* 1386 *Ass*, 1400 Exon, 1405 *FF*. The name seems
to be identical with Kemble (Gl) *Kemele* 682 (15th) BCS 63,
Kemeleshage 956 (15th) BCS 922. This is probably a British
name. Professor Ekwall suggests connexion with *Camulos*, the
name of a Celtic deity.

DEVONPORT. This district was earlier known as *Plymouth Dock*,
the name being changed to *Devonport* in 1824 (Worth). *Devon
Port* appears in 1827 G.

---

[1] Now included within the modern borough of Devonport.

FORD (district) was probably the home of Nicholas de *la Forde* (1238 *Ass*) and John *atte Forde* (1333 *SR*). The ford was over a creek of the Hamoaze.

KEYHAM is *Kaine Place Creke* c. 1550 Leland, *Keame* t. Eliz Worth, 1629 *FF*, 1643 Worth, *Came* 1765 D. The forms are too late for any etymology to be suggested, but it is clear that the *-ham* is quite modern. Leland's spelling is probably a mistake for *Kame*.

KINTERBURY HO (6″) is *Kenteburi* 1291 Tax, *-bery* 1346 FA, *Kynteberi* 1330 *SR* (p). *v.* burh. No suggestion can be made for the interpretation of the first element unless it is to be associated with Walter *Kynta*, taxed in the 1333 *SR*. It is on the river Tamar so cannot contain a river-name *Kent* or the like.

BARNE BARTON (6″) is *East, West, Barne* 1639 *Recov*. MOOR FM was the home of Thomas *atte More* 1345 *Ass*. MORICE TOWN (district) (6″) takes its name from the family of Sir William *Morice*, who purchased the manor of Stoke in 1667 from Sir Charles Wise (J. J. A.). MOUNT WISE (district) takes its name from the family just mentioned. Still earlier Sir Thomas and Arthur *Wyes* are mentioned in connexion with Stoke (t. Jas 1 ECP 193). PENNYCOMEQUICK (6″) is *Penicomequick* 1643 Worth, *penny comequicke* 1650 PlymRec. Probably a nickname for a prosperous farm. Cf. Make-em-rich (Nb). PENNYCROSS is *Penycrosse* t. Eliz ChancP 1, *Penny Crosse beakeo͞* (sic) t. Eliz Worth. HIGHER SWILLY (6″) is *Swilley* 1577 *SR*, 1682 *FF*. It is probably the ModEng *swilly*, 'hollow place, gutter washed out by the soil, etc.,' *v.* NED. The place lies low.

Stonehouse

STONEHOUSE 144 E 9

Stanehus 1086 DB, *Stanhus(e)* 1238 *Ass* (p), 1242 Fees (p)
Stonehouse 1314 Ipm, *Eststonhouse juxta Sutton Prioris* 1356
    Ass, Esterestonhouse 1370 *FF, Westestonhouse* 1480 IpmR

Self-explanatory.

Tamerton Foliot

TAMERTON FOLIOT 144 B 9
> *Tambretone* 1086 DB, *Tamerton* 1242 Fees 789, *Tamereton Foliot* 1262 Ipm
> *Taverton* 1675 Ogilby

'tun by the Tamar' (*supra* 13). The *Foliot* family held the manor from 1242 (Fees 789).

BELLIVER (6") is *Bellewurthi* 1244 *Ass* (p), -*worthy* 1317 *Ass* (p), 1377 *Deed.* '*Bella*'s worðig.' For the modern development, cf. Cadover *supra* 229.

BLAXTON is *Blachestane* 1086 DB, *Blakestana* t. Hy 2 Oliver 135, -*ne* 1242 Fees 789, *ferry of Blakeston* 1263 Ipm, *Blakeston Martynes* 1377 Cl. 'At the black stone.' No trace of such now exists. It is possible, however, that Blaxton and Whitson *infra* 243 refer respectively to Blaxton and Whitson Crosses. For *Martynes*, *v.* Maristow *infra*.

HAXTER (6") is *Haggestor(e)* 1383 *FF*, 1458 *Cl*, 1459 *FF*. '*Hæcgi*'s tor.' See further *s.n.* Haxton *supra* 31.

HORSHAM is *Horsham* 1270 *Ass* (p), 1306 *Ass*, 1326 *FF*, *Elyshorsham* 1543 BM. 'Horse ham(m).' No explanation of *Elys*- can be offered.

MARISTOW is *capellam S. Martini de Blakestana* t. Hy 2 Oliver 135, *Martynescombe* 1291 Tax, *Martinstowe* 1346 Inq aqd, *Martyn(e)stowe* 1378 IpmR, 1535 VE, *Martynstowe al. Maristowe* 1550 Pat, *Markistowe al. Maristowe* t. Eliz ChancP. *v.* stow. There was a chapel here dedicated to St Martin, attached to the manor of Blaxton. The reason for the later corruption is not certain but it may be due to the fact that the manor was held by Plympton Priory, the dedication of which was to St Mary.

PORSHAM [pɔ·rsəm] is *Portesham* 1244 *Ass*, 1383, 1459 *FF*, -*tis*- t. Ed 3 *Ass*. '*Port*'s ham(m).' For the pers. name, *v.* Redin 22. It occurs also in Portisham (Do), *Porteshamme* 1024 KCD 741.

WARLEIGH HO is *Wardlegh* 1242 Fees 789, *Warlegh(e)* 1270, 1345 *Ass*, 1378 IpmR, 1493 Ipm. *v.* weard, leah. There may have been some watch place or defence post here at the period when the country across the Tamar was still hostile. Another possibility is that we have OE *waroð*, 'shore,' which elsewhere in the county has yielded *warth* and *ward*, cf. Ward *supra* 82.

HAYSEND (6″), POUND CROSS and SOUTHWAY (6″) were the homes of John de *Hayeshende*, Walter *atte Poune* (sic), and Robert *Bysoutheweye*, i.e. 'south of the way' (1333 *SR*). *v.* (ge)hæg, pund.

COPPERS and WEBBERS (both 6″) are to be associated with the families of Richard *le Coppere* and Nicholas *le Webbere* (1333 *SR*). The first is *Copereslond* in 1383 *FF*.

ASHLEIGH BARTON is *Asseleg'* 1244 *Ass* (p), *Ayshlegh* 1333 *SR* (p), *Southaysshelegh* 1383 *FF*. *v.* leah. BROADLEY (6″) is *Bradelegh* 1383 *FF*, *Broadley* 1630 *Recov*. *v.* brad, leah. CANN HOUSE (6″) is *Canne park* 1543 *CtAugm*, *Cannhouse* 1697 *Recov*. See Canna *infra* 481. HENWELL (6″) is *Hynwell* 1263 FF, *Hyndwille Sowth Hyndefyld* 1538–44 ECP 8, 100. 'Hind spring,' i.e. where they watered, or 'monks' spring,' *v.* higna, wielle. LOOSELEIGH (6″) is *Losele(y)gh(e)* 1498 *Ct*, 1543 *CtAugm*. 'Pigsty clearing,' *v.* hlose, leah. WHITSON FM (6″) is *Wyston* 1383 *FF*. Probably 'white stone.' WIDEWELL (6″) is *Widwell* 1615 *Rental*.

Walkhampton

WALKHAMPTON [wækiŋtən], [wækətən] 137 J 11

> *Walchentone* 1084 Geld Roll, *Walchinton* 1187 P
> *Wachetona* 1086 DB
> *Walcom(e)ton*, *-cam(e)ton* 13th *Deed*
> *Walkamton(e)* 1258–76 Exon, 1262 Ipm, 1328 Exon, *-campton* 1261 Pat, 1262 Ipm, *-tamton* 1284 FA
> *Walkham(p)ton(e)* 1270 *Ass*, 1274 *FF*, 1306 *Ass*, *Walke-* 1306 Orig
> *Walcumlond* 1281 *Ass*
> *Wakampton* 1291 Exon, *Wakington* 1675 Ogilby
> *Walkyn(g)ton* 1548 Pat, t. Hy 8 Dartmoor, *-ington* 1733 *DuCo*

The relation of the forms of this name to one another and to those of the river Walkham on which it stands is a difficult one. Ekwall (RN 431) is probably right in taking the river-name to be a back-formation from an original *Wealchǣmatun*. The relation of such a form to the three earliest ones is difficult. If we may judge by other *hǣmatūn*-names, that compound would not readily be reduced to *-entone*, *-intun* in the 11th and 12th cents. Those forms look more like a *tūn* development of a yet earlier river-name *Wealca* (the rolling one), suggested by Ekwall (loc. cit.). If so, we must assume an alternative form of that name formed by adding *hǣma* to the first part of the name. Cf. Strettington (PN Sx 68), which seems originally to have been simply *Strǣt-tūn* and later *Strǣthǣma-tūn*.

BURHAM (6″) is *la Burghen* 13th *Deed*, *atte Burghen* 1377 *Ct*. This may represent a weak plural of either OE burh or beorg. Burham lies on the side of a valley but there are no earthworks or barrows now present which might have given rise to the name.

CRIPTOR (6″) is *Crepetorre* 1317 Pat, *Crupetorre* 1330 *SR* (both p). The first element is probably the OE *crype*, 'narrow passage, drain,' discussed under Crypt (PN Sx 16). The farm lies in a hollow.

DITTISHAM [ditsəm] is *Dodelesham* 1281 *Ass* (p), *Dodesham* 1356 Exon, *Dyttesham* 16th Oliver 381. '*Dod(d)el*'s ham(m).' This pers. name is not recorded, but would be a regular *l*-derivative of OE *Dod(d)a*. For the modern *i*, *v*. Introd. xxxiv.

DOUSLAND [dɑuzlənd] is *Dovesland* late 13th *Deed* (p), *Douseland* 1653 *FF*. Probably the first element is a pers. name of ME origin.

EGGWORTHY Ho [ekəri] is *Hekewrthi* 1238 *Ass*, *Ekeworthi* 1281 *Ass*, 1333 *SR*, *Eckeworthy* 1345 *Ass* (all p). '*Ecca*'s worðig.' Cf. Eckworthy *supra* 88.

HUCKEN TOR is *Hulkynctore* 16th Oliver 381, and near by must have lived Agnes *atte Holk* (1317 Pat), and Richard *atte Hulken* (1340 *SR*). The first element seems to be identical with that found in Sandick *infra* 352, Gunoak Wood (Co), *Gomholke* 1338 *Rental*, *Adelhulke* Hy 8 *Rental* (Loddiswell, D), *on sand holcan* 1044 OS Facs ii, Exeter xii (Dawlish, D), and *on dod holcan* KCD 739. All these names seem to contain the OE *holc(a)*, 'hole,' 'cavity,' a derivative of *hol*, 'hollow,' etc. In the present name the reference is doubtless to the rock-basins on the tor here.

NORSWORTHY [nɔzwəˈði, nɔzəri] (6″) is *Northisworthi* 1384 *Ct*, *Northesworthy* c. 1410 *Ct*, *-ysworthy* 1417 *Ct* (all p). *v.* worðig. *North* is probably here a pers. name of ME origin.

ROWTRUNDLE (6″) is *Rowetrendell* 1417 *Ct*. 'The rough circle,' *v.* ruh, trynde. The reference is clearly to the ancient hut-circle near the farm.

COMBSHEAD TOR, HOLEWELL, KNOWLE (6″)[1], WAYTOWN (6″), and WELLTOWN (6″), were probably the homes of Warin de *Cumbesheved* (1281 *Ass*), Roger de *Halghewille*, i.e. 'holy well' (1333 *SR*), Richard de *la Knolle* (1244 *Ass*), William *atte Weye* (1314 *Ass*), and Geoffrey *atte Welle* (1412 *AddCh*), *v.* cumb, cnoll, weg, wielle.

BLACK TOR is *Blacktorr* 1611 *Deed*. CLASIWELL POOL is *Clasiewell* 1638 DCo NQ 12, 239. CRAMBER TOR is *Cramberplana* 1611 *Deed*. DAVYTOWN is *Croftum David* 14th *Deed*, *Davyton* 1516, *-towne* 1576 *Deed*. Cf. Rubbytown *supra* 219. DEANCOMBE (6″) is *Denecomb(e)* 1317 Pat, 1340 *SR* (both p), *Den Combe* 1444 Dartmoor. FOGGINTOR is *Vokketorre* 1408 *Ass*. FURZETOR is *Forsetor* 16th Oliver 381. GNATHAM BARTON is *Gnatham* 1311 Exon, *Gnatt-* 1611 *Deed*. *v.* ham(m). The first element would seem to be OE *gnæt*, 'gnat,' cf. Gnatham in Stoke Climsland (Co), *Gnattham* 1301 *MinAcct*, and Midgham (PN Berks 57). HOLLOW TOR is *Hollowetorre* 1385 *Ct*. HORSYEAT (6″) is *Horsyet* 1378 *Ct* (p). 'Horse-gate,' *v.* geat. KINGSE(A)T (6″) is *Kyngessete* 1333 *SR* (p), *Kynggissete* 1377 *Ct* (p). *v.* Kingsett *supra* 201. LEATHER TOR is *Lodertorre* 1317 Pat (p) and is probably of the same origin as Laughter Tor *supra* 195, the vowel of the early form being a scribal error. LOWERY is *Loueworþe* 1256 *Ass* (p), *-worth* 1340 *SR* (p), *-worthy* 1417 *Ct* (p). 'Lēofa's' or '*Lufa*'s worþig.' MIDDLEWORTH is *Midlesworth* 1281 *Ass* (p), *Middelworthi* 1303 DA 8, 314 (p), *-y* 1375 *Ct*. 'Middle worþig,' from its position between Deancombe and Norsworthy. NEWLEYCOMBE LAKE (6″) is *Newelcombe* 1444 Dartmoor, t. Hy 6 *Ct*. PARKTOWN (6″) is *Le Parke* 16th Oliver 381, *v.* pearroc. For *town*, *v. infra* 676. PEEK HILL is *Pykehyll* 1525 *SR*, *Pyke* 16th Oliver. *v.* Peek *supra* 152. RIDDY PIT (6″) is *Reedapitt*

---

[1] *Knoll* 1584 FF.

1611 *Deed.* 'Reed hollow.' SHARPITOR is *Sharpetorre* 1342 Pat (p), *Sharpatorr, Sharpatorrbeme* 1611 *Deed.* Self-explanatory. For *beme, v.* Cater's Beam *supra* 192. STANLAKE is (*la*) *Stenylak* 1281 *Ass* (p), 1340 *SR* (p), *Stenelake* 16th Oliver 381. 'Stony streamlet,' *v.* lacu. The first element is OE *stǽnig*, 'stony.' YELLOWMEADE (6″) is *la Hollemede* 1256 *Ass* (p). If the *h* is inorganic we may compare Yellowmead *supra* 240.

Weston Peverel

WESTON PEVEREL 144 C 9

Weston(*a*) 1086 DB, 1228 FF, 1242 Fees 776, 1259 Ipm

'West farm,' with reference perhaps to Egg Buckland to the east and Sutton to the south. The Peverel family, which is first mentioned in connexion with the place in 1228 (FF), was probably a branch of the family of Hugo *Pyperellus* who held the East Devon manor of Sampford Peverel *infra* 551.

BURRINGTON, BURRINGTON FM (6″) and BURRATON FM (6″), all close together, represent *Buretona* 1086 DB, *Boreton* 1333 *SR* (p), *Ass* (p), *Boryton* 1555 *Recov.* Cf. Burraton *infra* 272 and Burraton in Stoke Climsland (Co), *Boraton* 1338 *Rental, Boreton* 1439 *FF.* The most likely suggestion for these names is that they all alike go back to OE (*ge*)*būra tūn*, 'peasants' farm,' from OE *būr*, 'boor, peasant.' Cf. similar compounds of swan.

HAM is *terram de Hamma* t. Hy 2 Oliver 135, *Westoneshamme* 1201 FF, (*juxta Sutton Prioris*) 1286 *Ass, Westounesham* 1291 Tax. *v.* hamm and Hamoaze *supra* 20.

MANADON is *Manedona* 1086 DB, *Manedon*(*e*) 1242 Fees 776, 1303 FA, (*juxta Plympmouth*) 1356 *Ass.* The first element here is not uncommon in Devon names, *v. infra* 667. In field-names we find also *Manne mede* 1509, *Mannemede* 1452 *Ct, Meneweye* 1368 IpmR and *Little Menepark* 1691 *Deed*, all in Devon. Outside the county may be noted *on gemanan hylle* BCS 670 (So), *to mænan leage* BCS 622, 731 (Ha), *to mæne lege* BCS 1119 (So), *Menemede* t. Hy 7 *Rental* (Wt), *la Menewode* c. 1265 (Ha), *on þone gemænen þorn* KCD 783 (Ha) and Menmarsh (O) 1278 RH *Menemers.* All these names contain the OE (*ge*)*mǽne*, 'common,' 'general,' and may refer either to some natural feature belonging to the whole village or community, or possibly in some cases to some particular object marking the boundary between two or more estates. See further Manhood (PN Sx 79).

TORR is *Overtorre* 1524 *Deed* and was the home of Claricia *atte Torre* (1339 *Ass*). *v.* torr.

Whitchurch

WHITCHURCH 137 H 10

> *Wicerce* 1086 DB, *Wicherche* 1166, *Witcherche* 1167 P
> *Whitechirche* 1238 *Ass*, *Whit-* 1290 Ch, *Whytecherch'* 1242
> Fees 769, *Whitechurche juxta Tavystoke* 1370 *FF*

There are many places of this name in England. The meaning 'stone church,' suggested as a possibility in PN Bk 86, may be the correct one here. Mr Alexander points out that most Devon churches would probably have been built of wood in Saxon times except where granite from Dartmoor was available, as here. In the adjacent parish of Tavistock wood was plentiful.

GRIMSTONE is *Ingrameston* 1427 *FF*, *Engrymston in Whitchurch* 1518–29 ECP 5, 439, and evidently contains as first element the continental pers. name *Ingram*. The modern form is doubtless due to mistaken division of the name into *in Grimston*.

HORRABRIDGE is *Horebrigge* 1345 *Ass*, 1377 *Ct*, *Le Horebrugg* 1348 BM, *la Horabrigḡ* t. Ed 3 *Ass*, *Hollowbridge* 1675 Ogilby. 'Boundary bridge,' *v.* har. The bridge here over the Walkham is at the boundary of three parishes, and there is an old boundary stone on the bridge (J. J. A.). Cf. Harrowbridge (Co), *la Horabrigge* 1302 *Ass*, *Horebrigge* 1470 *FF*, on the boundary between St Cleer, St Neot and Altarnon parishes.

MERRIVALE is *Miryfeld* 1307 *Ass*, *Meri-* 1377 *Ct*, *Mere-* 1474 *Ct* (all p), *Merivill* 1612 *FF*, *Merrifield* 1751 *Recov*, *Merriville Bridge* 1765 D. 'Pleasant open space,' *v.* myrig, feld. Cf. Marvell (Wt), *Merifelde*, 13th *Carisbrook Deed*.

PENNATON [peniŋtən] is *Penyton* 1314 *Ass*, (*juxta Tauystok*) 1322, 1325 *Ass*. The name seems to be identical with Pennington (La), the first element of which Ekwall takes to be the OE *pening*, 'penny.' The meaning of such a name is not clear.

PROWTYTOWN (6″) is *Prowta towne al. Wobadge* 1651 *Recov* and is to be associated with the family of Thomas *Prouta* (1340 *SR*). Cf. Rubbytown *supra* 219. The alternative name looks like a compound of woh and bæc, i.e. 'crooked stream,' but there is none near.

WALREDDON [wɔ·ldərn]

> *Walradene* 1329 *Ass* (p), 1346 *Ass*, -*radan* 1401 Exon, -*reden* 1421 Exon
> *Weldraden* 1349 *FF*
> *Waldron* 1719 *FF*

This is a difficult name but Professor Ekwall may well be right in suggesting that we have to do with an OE *Wēala-rǣden*, 'community of Britons.' The place is very near the Cornish border.

WHITCHURCH DOWN is *Werydon* 1488 *Rental*, 1613 *Recov*, *Werydown* 1518–29 ECP 5, 558, *Whitchurch downe* 1653 *Recov*, *Whitchurch Down* oth. *Werry Down* 1803 *Recov*. The forms are too late for certainty, but *wer(r)y* may go back to OE *wearg*, 'outlaw, criminal,' and the name refer to a hill on which a gibbet was erected. Cf. Wreighill (PN NbDu 220).

ASH (6″), MOORTOWN[1], TOR, VENN[2] (6″) and WOODTOWN were probably the homes of John de *Aysshe* (1333 *SR*), William *atte More* (1340 *SR*), William *atte Torre* (ib.), William *atte Fenne* (1313 *Ass*), and Ralph *atte Wode* (1333 *SR*). *v.* mor, torr, fenn.

ANDERTON is *Underdon* 1270 *Ass*, 1355 BM. 'Below the down.' Anderton (Co) has the same history. BOYTON (6″) is *Bawton* 1518–29 ECP 5, 558, *Easter Bowton* 1613 *Recov*. CASEYTOWN is *Casytown* 1518–29 ECP 5, 558, *Casetowne* 1616 *FF*, the first element being probably a former owner's name. Cf. Rubbytown *supra* 219. CHOLLACOTT is *Cholcote* 1482 IpmR, *Chaldecote* 1500 Ipm. 'Cold cot(e),' *v.* cald. COLLATON is *Coleton* 1408 *Ass* (p), 1445 *Deed*, *Collyton* t. Eliz ChancP 1. *v.* Collacott *supra* 50. DENNITHORNE is *Donethorn* 1327 Banco, *Donnethorne* 1380 *FF*, *Dunethorn* 1417 *Ct*. 'Dunna's thornbush.' DOWN-HOUSE is *Donhous* t. Hy 6 *Ct*, *Downhowsen* 1518–29 ECP 5, 558.

---

[1] Cf. *Moreyate*, i.e. 'moor gate' 1518–29 ECP.
[2] *Fennetown* 1518–29 ECP.

Self-explanatory. The second form preserves the old weak pl.
FULLAMOOR (6″) is *Folamor* 1346 *Ass* (p) and probably contains
as first element OE fola, 'foal.' GRENOFEN is *Grenefenne* 1238
Ass (p), 1294 *Ass*, *Grenefen in parochia de Whitechurche* t. Hy 6
Ct. 'At the green marsh.' HECKLAKE (6″) and HECKWOOD are
Heckelake 1435 *Deed* (p), *Hikewode* 1408 *Ass* (p). HIGHLAND (6″)
is *Hillond* 1615 *Rental.* HOLWELL is *Holiewille* 1353 Pat, *Halghewille in parochia de Whytechurch* 1417 *Ct*, *Hallowyll* 1514 *Ct.*
'Holy well.' LONGFORD is *Langeford* 1238 *Ass.* OAKLEY is
Oklegh 1518–29 ECP 5, 558. 'Oak clearing or wood,' *v.* leah.
PEW TOR is *Pewterdowne* 1697 *Recov.* PLASTER DOWN is *Play-
sterdown* 1518–29 ECP 5, 558. The form is late but the first
element may be a corruption of plegstow. Cf. Plestor in Sel-
borne (Ha), the name for the space in the centre of the village,
presumably an ancient place for games. RIXHILL is *Ryck hill*
1573 *Ct.* SHORTS DOWN (6″) is *Shortysdown* 1518–29 ECP 5,
558. *Short* was probably the name of a medieval holder. SORT-
RIDGE is *Shorterugg'* 1333 *SR* (p), *Short(e)rigge* 1346 *Ass*, 1349
FF. Self-explanatory. STENTAFORD LAND is *Stentaford* 1364
Ass, *Stenteford* 1408 *Ass* (p), *(land)* 1632 *Recov.* The first element is OE *stæniht*, 'stony.' WILSETTON (6″) is *Wylsheton* 1486–
1515 ECP 3, 322.

X. PLYMPTON HUNDRED

Plintona 1084 Geld Roll, *Plimton* 1187 P, 1238 *Ass*

v. Plympton *infra* 251.

Brixton

BRIXTON [briksən]   144 E 12

Brisestona   1086 DB

Brikeston'   1200 Cur, 1201 FF, 1306 *Ass*, 1376 Pat, *Brixton*
1284 FA, t. Ed 1 Ipm, *Bryokeston* 1346 *Ass*

Brigston   1242 Fees 776

v. tun. The first element is perhaps the old Celtic pers. name
Brioc(Chest 111), cf. Brixham, Marshall, Branscombe (*infra* 507,
498, 620). The DB form is probably an error, but the later
forms do not favour the OE pers. name *Beorhtsige*.

BUTLASS is *Plethameston* c. 1250 *Deed, Plethemeston juxta Plumptone* 1296 FF, *Pled(a)meston(e)* c. 1300 *Deed, Buttelers* 1504 Ipm, *Butlers al. Plethmeston* 1605 *Deed.* Probably 'Pleghelm's farm,' though the change of *g* to *th* is difficult to account for. The later name is to be associated with the farm of Richard *Butler* who was living in the parish in 1525 (*SR*).

CHITTLEBURN (6″) is *Chichelesberia* 1086 DB, *-burgh* 1238 *Ass*, 1284, 1303 FA, 1305 Ipm, *Chicheburgh* 1242 Fees 794, *Chicheleburgh* 1302 *Ass.* 'Ciccel's burh.' The pers. name is not on record, but would be a regular *l*-derivative of *Cicca* (*v.* Chichacott *supra* 202). On the common confusion of burh and burna in later forms, *v.* PN NbDu 270.

COFFLETE is *Cokflute* 1244 *Ass*, 1284 FA, 1310 Ipm, *Cokeflet* 1244 *Ass, Cokflete* 1284 AD i, *Coc-* 1291 *Ass. v.* fleot. The first element may well be the river-name noted under Cofford *infra* 500.

GOODAMOOR is *Godemore* 1343 *FF* (p). 'Goda's mor.' It may be noted that one *Godo* held the adjacent manor of Hemerdon in 1086 (DB f. 115 *a*).

GORLOFEN is *Gorlowesfenne* 1281 *Ass, Gorlowefenne* 1284 FA, *Gorlefenne* 1330 *SR* (p), *Gorleven* 1433–72 ECP 2, 4. The name seems to be a triple compound of gor, hlaw and fenn, meaning 'the marshy land by the muddy hill or mound.'

HALWELL is *Hagawila* (sic) 1086 DB, *Hal(e)gh(e)well'* 1242 Fees 776, 1284, 1303 FA, *Haliwill* 1249 *Ass* (p). 'Holy well.'

HARESTON is *Harestana* 1086 DB, *-ne* 1242 Fees 796, *-ston* 1301 Ipm. As the farm is close by the parish boundary this may be from OE *hārstān*, 'grey stone,' 'boundary stone,' but one would have expected ME *horestone*, unless the vowel was early shortened. Alternatively the first element may be *hara*, 'hare,' but the sense of such a compound is obscure.

EAST and WEST SHERFORD is *Sirefort* 1086 DB (Exon), *-d* (Exch), *Scyreford, Westscireford* t. Hy 2 Oliver 135, *Shire-* 1242 Fees 794. 'Clear ford,' *v.* scir.

SPRIDDLESTONE is *Espredelestona* 1086 DB, *Spridleston* 1238 *Ass* (p), *Sprideleston* 1284 FA, 1328 *FF*, cf. Spridlington (L), DB *Spredelintone, Sperlinctone*, Lindsey Survey *Spridlinctuna, Spritlingtuna*. In post-Conquest times *Sprydel* is found in Devon as a surname (cf. Spriddlescombe *infra* 280), so that it is clear we have a pers. name here, but its origin is obscure.

VEALEHOLME (6″) is *Velehalle* 1336, 1344 Ipm, 1373 Cl, *Vealehall, Vealholme* 1550 *FF*, and is probably to be associated with the family of Peter de *Veel* (1373 Cl).

WINSTON is *Winestona* 1086 DB, *Wyneston* 1284, 1303 FA, *Wynneston* 1284 AD i, *Wynston Rauf* 1337 Ipm. '*Wine*'s farm,' *v.* tun. The identity of *Rauf* is unknown.

WIVERTON is *Wyuerton* 1292 *Ass* (p), *Wayfreton* 1550 *FF*, *Wifferton Cross* 1638 *Deed*, *Weyferton* 1704 *Recov*. Possibly '*Wīgferð*'s farm,' but the forms are too late for certainty. For absence of the genitival *s*, cf. Killington *supra* 66.

WOLLATON is *Olvievetona* 1086 DB (Exon), *Ulvevetone* (Exch), *Woluiueton* 1244 *Ass* (p), *Wolvyngton* 1346 FA, *Wollington oth*. *Wolvington oth*. *Wollaton* 1821 *Recov*. '*Wulfgiefu*'s tun,' this being a feminine pers. name in OE.

COMBE, FORDBROOK[1] (6″), SLEW (6″), TORR[2] FM (6″) and VENN FM (6″) were probably the homes of Richard de *Cumbe* (1281 *Ass*), Thomas *atte Forde* (1330 *SR*), Richard *atte Slo* (1327 Banco), cf. Slew *supra* 28, Robert *atte Torre* (1330 *SR*) and Richard de la *Fenne* (1281 *Ass*). *v.* cumb, torr, fen.

CATSON GREEN (6″) is possibly to be associated with the family of John *Caston* of Plympton (1571 *SR*). EFFORD is *Ebford* t. Hy 2 Oliver 135, cf. Efford *supra* 227. WAPPLEWELL (6″) is *Whapleswell* 1683 *Recov*.

Plympton St Mary

PLYMPTON 144 D 11

Plymentun 904 (13th) BCS 610
Plimtun 1131 Earle, *Plimton(a)* t. Stephen BM, 1219 FF,
    Plimpton 1225 Pat, *Plym(p)*- 1244–62 Ipm

---

[1] So spelt 1765 D.   [2] *Torr* 1683 *Recov*.

Plintona 1086 DB, *Plinton* 1179 P, 1217 Pat, 1238 *Ass*, 1263 Ipm

Plumton(e) 1166 RBE, 1245 Ipm, 1263–73 BM, *Plumpton* 1238 *Ass*, 1263 Ipm, 1275 RH

Ekwall (RN 328) takes this name to be a compound of OE *plȳme*, 'plum-tree' and tun, the river-name Plym being a back-formation (*v. supra* 12). This is very probable, especially as there is no Celtic root from which the river-name could be derived.

BACCAMOOR (6″) is *Bachemora* 1086 DB, *Bacche-* 1168 P, *Backe-more* 1242 Fees 794, 1285 FA, *Bakkemor* 1324 Ipm. '*Bacca*'s mor,' cf. *baccan mor* (BCS 982).

BATTISFORD (6″) is *Botesforda* 1086 DB, *Bottesford* 1245 Ipm, 1311 *Ass*, 1392 IpmR, *Botelesforde* 1295 FF. '*Bott(e)*'s ford,' *Bott(e)* being the strong form of the OE pers. name *Botta*. The 1295 form seems to point to an *l*-derivative of the same name.

BICKFORD TOWN (6″) is *Bicheforda* 1086 DB, *Bykeford* 1242 Fees 788 (p), 1340 Ipm, *Byckfordetoune* 1571 *SR*. '*Bi(c)ca*'s ford.' *v.* Abbots Bickington *supra* 124. For the addition of 'town,' *v. infra* 676, and cf. Cudlipptown *supra* 232.

BORINGDON [bɔritən]

Borington 1279 *Ass*, -*in(g)don* 1279, 1286 *Ass*, -*yngdone* 1291 Tax

Burningdon 1286 *Ass*

Boraton 1320 *Ass* (p), -*e*- 1330 *SR* (p)

Burrowtown 1675 Ogilby

There is an old camp or burh here, so it seems likely that the name is a compound of that word, though its exact form is uncertain. Possibly it is a compound of burh and dun, with connective ing.

CHALLONSLEIGH is *Lega* 1086 DB, *Legh'* 1242 Fees 789, *Legh Chaluns* 1284 FA, 1286 *Ass*, *Chalonsleye* 1330 Pat, *Chanounsleghe* 1376 Exon. *v.* leah. The family of *Chalun(s)* held the manor from the 13th cent. (Fees 789, 1284 FA).

DRAKELAND CORNER is so spelt in 1622 *FF*, and is probably to be associated with the family of Ralph *Drake* (1374 *SR*).

ELFORDLEIGH [elvəli] is *Lega* 1086 DB, *Elford leigh* 1689 *FF*, *Elfordleigh oth. Elverley* 1739 *Recov. v.* leah. The distinctive first element may be derived from the family of Thomas *Elfforde*, who was living in the parish in 1571 (*SR*).

FLANKWELL (lost) is *Wlaunkewill* 1244 *Ass* (p), *Wlonkewill(e)* 1420 IpmR, 1425 *FF*, *Flankwell* 15th ECP 2, 548. '*Wlanca*'s spring,' *v.* wielle. Cf. Longslow (PN Sa 145) and Lancing (PN Sx 199). For initial *f, v.* Introd. xxxv.

HEMERDON [heməden]

> *Hainemardun* 1086 DB
> *Henemerdona* t. Hy 2 Oliver 135, 1282 (1328) Ch, *-mordon* 1262 Ipm, *Henmerdone* 1263 Exon (p), *Hennemer(e)don(e)* 1285 FA, 1338, 1372 Exon, *Henemeredon juxta Plympton* 1297 *FF*, *Henemeresdon* 1303 FA
> *Hemmerdone* 1597 DCo NQ 3, 110

This is probably a triple compound of henn, mere and dun, meaning 'the hill by the hen-pool.'

HOLLAND (6″) is *Honeland(a)* 1086 DB, 1284 FA, *-londe* 1330 *SR* (p), *Hunelaunde* 1242 Fees 794, *Honylond* 1467 IpmR. '*Hūna*'s land.'

LANGAGE is *Langehewis* 1086 DB, *-hiwis* t. Hy 2 Oliver 135, *-hywys* 1291 Tax, *Langishe* 1629 *FF*. 'The long hiwisc.'

LOUGHTOR MILLS (6″) is *Lochetora* 1086 DB, *Lughetor(re)* 1238 FF, 1242 Fees 794, 1284 FA, 1356 *Ass*, *Loghhatorre* 1304 *Ass*, *Loghetorre* 1356 *Ass*, *Lukketore* 1249 *Ass* (p). '*Luh(h)a*'s torr.' For this pers. name, cf. Loughton (PN Bk 20).

SPURHAM (6″) is *Spurham* 1244 *Ass*, *Sporeham* 1330 *SR* (p). It seems to be a compound of OE *spora*, 'spur' and ham(m). The farm lies low by the river Erme near a slight projecting hill.

TORRIDGE (6″) is *Tori, Torix* 1086 DB, *Little Torryz* 1238 FF, *Toryz juxta Plumtone* 1291 *FF*, *Toryz* 1303 FA, *Torigge* 1285 FA, 1310 Ipm, (*juxta Plympton*) 1346 *Ass*, *Torrig(g)e* 1341 Ipm, *Tourigg* 1346 FA. *v.* Tory Brook *supra* 15.

TUXTON FM is *Tuxton* 1515–18 ECP 5, 40. An earlier spelling is provided by the surname (de) *Tukkeston* (1340 *SR sub*

Barnstaple). The first element is a strong form of the OE pers. name *Tucca* (Redin III). Cf. Tuxwell (So), *Tocheswelle* DB, *Tukeswell(e)* 1226, 1228 FF, and Tuxlith (PN Sx 45).

Voss is *Fosse* 1504 Ipm, and was the home of Robert *atte Fosse* 1330 *SR*. This may be the English word *foss*, 'ditch, dike, etc.,' though the NED records no earlier instance than c. 1400. Alternatively we may have the Co *fos*, used in the same sense, a borrowing from the Latin *fossa*. The 6″ map reveals nothing which might give a clue as to the exact sense of the name.

WALFORD (lost) is *Waleforda* 1086 DB (Exon), *Waliforde* (Exch), *Waleford* 1242 Fees 794, 1303 FA, *Wyleford* 1285 FA, *Walles-ford* 1346 FA, *Walford* 1428 FA. 'Ford of the Britons,' *v.* wealh.

WOODFORD is *Odeforda* 1086 DB, *Wodeford* 1242 Fees 794.

YEALMPSTONE [jempsən] is *Alfelmestone* 1086 DB, *Alfemeston(a)* t. Hy 2 Oliver 135, 1285 FA, *Alfameston* 1303 FA, *Alphameston juxta Wenbury* 1318 *Ass*, *Yemston* 1704 *Recov*. '*Ælfhelm*'s tun.' Cf. Bere Alston *supra* 223.

BRIDGE (6″), FORD (6″), HAY FM, SOUTHWOOD (6″) and YOLLANDS (6″) were probably the homes of Alicia atte *Brugge* (1333 *SR*), Richard atte *Forde* (ib.), John de la *Heye* (1281 *Ass*), William *Bysouthewode*, i.e. 'south of the wood' (1330 *SR*), and Gilbert de *Oldelond* (1333 *SR*), *v.* (ge)hæg and Addenda lviii *supra*.

APPLETHORN SLADE (6″) is *Happeldoreslade* 1291 Tax, *Apple-thorneslade* t. Eliz *LRMB* 191. 'Apple-tree slæd,' *v.* apulder. The modern form is due to folk etymology. BICKHAM (6″) is *Bykenham* 1333 *SR* (p). '*Bic(c)a*'s ham(m).' BIRCHLAND (6″) is *Bircheland* c. 1480 ECP 2, 194. BLACKLANDS is *Blakelond* c. 1480 ECP 2, 194, *Blacklande* t. Eliz ChancP. Cf. Whitefield *supra* 52. BUDE (6″) is *Bouwode juxta Plympton* 1322 *Ass*, *Bouewod* 1325 *Ass*. Possibly 'above wood,' *v. s.n.* Bowden *supra* 38 n 2. CANN COTTAGES (6″) and WOOD are to be identified with *Canhaye* 1638 *Deed*. For the first element, cf. Canna *infra* 481. CHADDLE-WOOD is *Chadelwode* 1387 Cl, 1445 IpmR, *Chaddlewood* or *Chadlood* 1767 *Recov*. As the forms are late and there are many springs in the neighbourhood this may be from *ceald wielle wudu*, 'wood by the cold spring.' COLEBROOK is *Colbroc* t. Hy 2 Oliver 135, 1282 (1328) Ch, (*juxta Plympton*) 1340 *Ass*, *Colebrok* 1281 *Ass*. COLLAFORD (6″) is *Coleford* 1285 Ch, 1330 *SR* (both p), *Collyfforde* 1504 Ipm. *v.* Collacott *supra* 50. COMBE FM is *Combe Pryor al. Lower Combe* 1638 *Recov*. The place belonged to Plympton Priory. CROWNHILL is *Crownewyll Wood* 1547 *DuCo*. HARDWICK is *Erdewik, Herdewik* 1245, 1263 Ipm. *v.* heordewic. HEATHFOWL COTTAGE (6″) is *Hethfeld juxta Plympton* 1279 *Ass*. 'Waste land,' cf. Heathfield 265 *infra*. HEMERDON BALL (hill) is *Hemmerdone Ball* 1597 DCo NQ 3, 110. *v.* Hemerdon *supra* 253. For *ball*, *v. supra* 211. HITCHCOMBE is *Hitchcomb* 1809 M. HOUNDALL (6″) is *Houndehulle* 1330 *SR* (p). 'Hounds' hill.' LEE MILL BRIDGE is *Leghbrygge* 1414 Exon, *Legh Mille* 1437 Pat. LEY (6″) is *La Lye* 1281 *Ass* (p), *Legh* 1337 Ipm. *v.* leah. LOBB FM (6″) is *aquam de Lobbe* 1356 *Ass*. *v.* Lobb *supra* 33. The 'water' must be Smallhanger Brook *supra* 13. MERAFIELD is *Merefeild* 1615 *Recov*. MOOR FM (6″) is *La More* 1291 Tax. *v.* mor. NEWNHAM is *Niweham* 1292 Ipm, *Niwenham* 1325 Ipm (p), *Nyuwenham* 1330 *SR* (p). *v.* niwe, ham(m). RIDGEWAY is *Ryggeweystrete* 1281 *Ass*, *Ryggeweye juxta Plympton* 1302 *Ass*. The ridgeway is the main Exeter-Plymouth road. SALTRAM is *Salterham* 1249 *Ass* (p), *Saltram* 1263, 1504 Ipm. It is probably a compound of OE *sealtera*, 'salters' (gen. pl.) and ham(m). SHERWELL (6″) is *Shirewell(e)* 1238 *Ass* (p). 'Clear spring,' *v.* scir, wielle. SMALLHANGER is *Smalhangr'* 1330 *SR* (p), *Smallhanger* 1505 BM. 'Narrow slope,' *v.* smæl, hangra. SMITHALEIGH is *Smitha leighe* 1617 *FF* and was probably the home of Guydo *atter Smytthe* 1333 *SR*. 'At the smithy,' cf. Hammersmith (Mx), *Hameresmythe* 1312 Seld 33. SPARKWELL is *Sparchewelle* 1167 P (p), *Sperkwill* 1330 *SR* (p). *v.* Sparkwell *infra* 520. UNDERWOOD (district) is *Underwood* 1649 *Recov*. 'Below the wood.' VENTON is *Fenton'* 1242 Fees 796, *Venton* 1301 Ipm. fenn, tun. WIXENFORD is so spelt in 1782 *Recov*.

Plympton Erle or St Maurice (6″)

PLYMPTON ERLE 144 D 11

   Plympton Comitis 1299 *Ass*, (*Erle*) 15th ECP 1, 260, (*Earls*) 1485 Ipm

This was the town which grew up around the castle which formed the head of the Honour of Plympton, held by the Redvers earls of Devon. The parish is now commonly named after the dedication of the parish church to St Maurice, in contrast to Plympton St Mary *supra* 251.

Plymstock

PLYMSTOCK 144 E 10

> *Plemestocha* 1086 DB
> *Plumstok* 1228 FF
> *Plimstok* 1244, 1281 *Ass*, *Plimp-* 1284 FA

The meaning is either 'plum-tree stocc' or 'stocc near the Plym river.' *v.* Plympton, Plym *supra* 251–2, 12.

ELBURTON is *Aliberton* 1254, *Ailberton* 1423, *Aylberton* 1480, *Elberton* 1485 Pat, (*in Plympstock*) t. Jas 1 ECP 310. Probably '*Æþelbeorht's* farm,' *v.* tun. Cf. Aylburton (PN Gl 13). For the absence of a genitival *s*, cf. Wiverton *supra* 251; or it may be, as the earliest form is dated 1254, that the original form was *Aeþelberhtingtun*, *v.* ingtun.

GOOSEWELL is *Gosewella* 1086 DB, *-will'* 1242 Fees 789, 'goose-spring,' *v.* wielle.

HOOE (FMS) are *Ho* 1086 DB, 1201 FF, *Hoo* 1200 Cur, 1246 Ipm, *Westho* 1279 Ipm, *Estho* 1303 FA. *v.* hoh. There is a well-marked spur of land here.

ORESTON is *Worston Passage* 1466 Pat, *Horstone* t. Eliz Worth, *Oriston* 1739 Camden. It is just possible that the first element may be har. The stone was clearly one used to mark a passage. If so, the *w* spelling must be parallel to the 15th cent. *whole* for *hole*. Cf. Warstock PN Wo 357.

POMPHLETT is *Ponnaflute* 1330 *SR* (p), *Ponneflut* 1333 *SR* (p). The first element may be the OE pers. name *Pun(n)a*, which is found in Poynings (PN Sx 286), but the forms are too late for any certainty. The second element is fleot, referring to the tidal creek here which opens into the Cattewater.

STADDISCOMBE is *Stotescoma* 1086 DB, *-cumbe* 1281 *Ass*, *-coumbe* 1305 Ipm, *-comb* 1334 *SR*, *Stottescumb* 1284 FA, *-combe* 1364

Ass, -tys- 1427 *FF, Stottecumb'* 1242 Fees 776, *Stodescumbe* 1288 *Ass* (p)

STADDON is *Estotdona* 1086 DB, *Stoddune* 1242 Fees 794. 'Bullock valley and hill,' *v.* stott, cumb, dun.

TURNCHAPEL is *Tan Chapel* 1765 D, *Turn Chapel* 1827 G. There was formerly a chapel dedicated to *St Anne* here. For the later corruption, cf. *Tooley* Street (Southwark, Sr) from *St Olave*.

BLACKHALL (6″) is *la Blakehall* 1249 *Ass* (p). *v.* heall. COMBE is *Combe* 1591 *Recov. v.* cumb. HIGHCOMBE (6″) is *Haycomb* 1364 *Ass. v.* heg or (ge)hæg, cumb. LEYFORD (6″) is so spelt 1558–79 ECP. RADFORD is *Reddeford* 1249 *Ass* (p), *Radeford* 1275 RH (p), 1284 FA, (*juxta Plympstoke*) 1306 *Ass, Radford* 1485 Ipm. 'Red ford.'

Revelstoke

REVELSTOKE[1] (locally STOKE) 144 G 12

> *Rawelestok* 1219 *Ass, Ravelsto(c)ke* 1546, 1571 *SR*
> *Rewelstoke* 1418 AD vi, *Reuelstok* 1500 *FF, Revelstok(e)* 1525 *SR*, 1535 VE
> *Roulestok* 1441 Exon, *Rolstoke* 1538 LP

v. stoc(c). The place must take its name from the *Revel* family which became important in the south-west in the 12th cent. Richard *Revel* was sheriff of Devon in the reign of Richard I.

NOSS MAYO is *Nesse Matheu* 1286 BM, *La Nasse* 1309 Cl, *Nasse* 1316 FA, 1400 Exon, *Nasse Mayow* 1418 AD vi, *Nasmayowe* 1472 Pat. *v.* næss. The place is on a point of land between two creeks. *Mayo* (*Mayow, Maheu*) represents the OFr form of *Matthew*, referring to *Matheu* filius Johannis, who held the manors of Noss, Yealmpton, etc. (1284, 1303, 1316 FA, 1309 Cl).

WORSWELL is *Wyresfeld* 1239 Ch, *Wursfeld* 1244 *Ass, Worsfeld-hamme* 1310 Ipm, *Worsfelde* 1333 *SR* (p), *Worswell* 1670 *Recov*. This is a difficult name. Professor Ekwall and Dr Ritter suggest the possibility of derivation from OE *Wigheres-feld*, with rounding of *i* to *u* after *w*. Alternatively Professor Ekwall suggests the possibility of a compound of OE *wiersta*, 'worst.'

---

[1] Not marked by name on the newest 1″ map.

COMBE FM and MIDDLECOMBE (both 6″) are *Combe* 1670 *Recov*, *Midelcombe* 1530 *Ct*. *v*. cumb. NETTON is *Neatteton* 1333 *SR* (p). 'Cattle farm,' *v*. neat, tun. Cf. Netton (PN W 130). ROWDEN is *Rowdon* 1765 D. Probably 'rough hill,' *v*. ruh, dun and cf. Rowden *supra* 209, 214.

Shaugh

SHAUGH [ʃei] 144 B 11

>*Escaga* 1086 DB (Exon), *Scage* (Exch), *Scaghes* t. Hy 2 Oliver 135
>*Saghe* 1218 FF, 1242 Fees 776
>*Shaue* 1281 *Ass*, (*La*) *S(c)hagh* 1303 FA *et passim*
>*Schyaghe* 1310 Exon (p), *Sheagh* 1535 VE, *Shea* 1584 Wills
>*Shaff* 1584 *Recov*, *Shaghe al. Shave* 1587 *Recov*, *Shaye* t. Hy 8 Dartmoor

v. sceaga. There is still much woodland in the parish. The parish is sometimes known as Shaugh Prior (*Pryoursheagh* 1559 *Deed*), from the fact that the manor from the earliest times belonged to Plympton Priory. The pronunciation of the place-name among old people is [ʃei], probably for earlier [ʃeiv] or [ʃeif]. *v*. Introd. xxxv.

BEATLAND CORNER is *la Beate, Beathlonde* 14th *Deed*. It is probably the word *beat*, 'turf pared off the ground for burning,' *v*. beat, beatland, in NED and EDD.

BRIXTON BARTON

>*Bristrichestona* 1086 DB (Exon), *Brictricestone* (Exch)
>*Brigtricheston'* 1242 Fees 794, *Brightricheston* 1316 FA
>*Britricheston* 1244 *Ass* (p), 1303 FA, *Brixton* 1428 FA

'*Beorhtric*'s tun.'

COLDSTONE is *Coltrestan* 1086 DB, *Codelston* 1346 *Ass* (p), *Culterstone al. Colestone* 1668 *Recov*. Apparently a compound of OE *culter*, 'coulter,' and stan, 'stone,' though the reason for the name is unknown.

COLLARD is *Colritte juxta Plympton* 1289 *Ass*, *Colritte* 1333 *SR* (p), *Kaldrade* or *Callard* 1486–1515 ECP 3, 162. The name may be a compound of OE *col*, 'coal, charcoal,' and *ryt*, 'brushwood,

rubbish for burning.' Cf. Rutt *infra* 286. The 6″ map marks
THE RUTS near by, a piece of waste land.

FAUNSTONE is *Faunteston* 1339 *Ass*, *Faundeston* 1346 *Ass* (both
p). The name is probably to be associated with the family of
Samson *le Enfaunt*, a juror of Plympton Hundred in 1249 (*Ass*).
Cf. Fonston (Co), *Fonteston*, *Faunteston* 1284 *Ass*, *Fanteston*
1311 *Ass*. For OFr *faunt* as a surname, cf. Weekley, *Surnames*
245, 247. Hence, '*Faunt*'s farm,' *v.* tun.

FERNHILL is *Fernehella* 1086 DB, *Fernhille* 1242 Fees 775, *-hulle*
1306 Ipm, *Farnhill* 1291 (1408) Dartmoor. 'Bracken hill,' *v.*
fearn, hyll.

PETHILL (6″)

   Pidehel(e) 1086 DB, 1330 *SR* (p)
   Puddehell 1238 *Ass* (p), *Pudehel* 1291 (1408) Dartmoor
   Pythehele 1394 *Ass*, *Pithehele* 1490 Ipm

   Probably '*Pyd(d)a*'s healh,' with later confusion of unstressed
second elements.

PORTWORTHY is *Porteworthy* 1322, 1329 *Ass* (p), 1333 *SR* (p),
Pourtewurthe 1474 *Ct* (p), *Portaver* 1587 *Recov*. '*Porta*'s worþig.'
For the pers. name, *v.* Portontown *supra* 210. For the last form,
cf. Cadover *supra* 229.

PURPS (6″) is *Purpris* 1291 (1408) Dartmoor, and was the home
of John *atte Purpris* 1330, *atte Purp'se* 1333 *SR*. This is the OFr
pourprise, 'a close or enclosure,' properly the past participle of
OFr *pourprendre*, 'to take away entirely,' *v.* NED *s.n.* It was
a legal term used in the case of encroachments upon the property
of a community or of the crown. Cf. Purprise, PN SWY 234.

TROWLESWORTHY WARREN [trɔlzeri] is *Travaylesworth* 1244,
1281 *Ass*, *Travailesworth* 1291 (1408) Dartmoor, *Trailesworthi*
1334 *Ass* (all p). The first element here is almost certainly a pers.
name of ME origin. Cf. *Travell* in Weekley, *Surnames* 222.

BLACKALDER COTTAGES (6″) is *Blakalre* 1333 *SR* (p), *Blakaller*
1443 *Ct*. *v.* alor. HARSCOMBE is *Hescumbe* 1291 (1408) Dartmoor. HAWKS TOR is *Haneketorr* 1291 (1408) Dartmoor. The
13th cent. form should no doubt read *Hau-*. HEN TOR is *Hynde-*

torr 1375 *Ct* (p), *Hynde-, Hende-, Hentorre* 1474 *Ct.* 'Hinds' torr.' HENWOOD is *Indewood* 1650 *Recov* and was the home of Thomas *Byundewode* 1333 *SR.* 'Beyond the wood,' *v.* Indicombe *supra* 35. HOLLOWGREEP (6″) is *Holygripe* 1352 *SR*, cf. *grip* sb. 2 (NED), 'furrow, trench.' The farm lies in a hollow. HUXTON (6″) is *Hokestone* 1330 *SR* (p), *Huckestone* 1571 *SR.* This may be '*Huc(c)*'s farm,' *v.* tun. LANGCOMBE HEAD is *Lancomhille* 1365 *Ass. v.* lang, cumb. LEE MOOR is *Leemore* 649 *FF*, *Leigh Moore* 1695 *Recov.* The moor must be named after some lost place *Lee*, *v.* leah. NETHERSHAUGH (6″) is *Nythereshagh* 1330 *SR* (p), i.e. lower Shaugh. *v.* neoðera. NORTH WOOD is *Northwood* 1515–18 ECP 5, 40. SADDLESBOROUGH (hill) (6″) is *Sedilburghhill* 1474 *Ct* and is so called from its shape. *v.* beorh. SHADEN MOOR is probably for *Shaugh down moor* (Crossing). It lies above Shaugh village. TORYCOMBE (6″) is *Torrycomb* 1479 Dartmoor, *Torycomb Wode* 1514 *Ct. v.* Tory Brook *supra* 15. TRINAMAN'S WOOD (6″) is to be associated with the family of Jeffrey *Trenaman* of Walkhampton (1635 Wills). WHITTABOROUGH (6″) is *Whitaburrowe* 1611 *Deed.* Probably 'white hill,' *v.* beorg. WOTTER is *Wodetorre* 1263 Ipm, *Wottorre* 1345 *Ass*, *Wottor* 1445 IpmR. 'Wood tor.'

Wembury

WEMBURY 144 F 10

Weybiria   t. Hy 1 (1329) Oliver 134
Wenbiria   t. Hy 2 Oliver 135, *Wenbir* 1238 *Ass*, *-bury* 1318 *Ass*
Wembir   1238 *Ass*, *-bury* 1359 *Ass*
Wymbury   1283 *Ass*, 1386 Exon
Waynbury   1365 *MinAcct*

This place has been identified by some with the *Wicganbeorh* of the ASC (*s.a.* 851), but in view of the early spellings given above, this is impossible. The second element is burh. The first is difficult. It may be *Wægan*, gen. sg. of a pers. name *Wæga*, a pet-form of one of the rare OE names in *Wæg-*.

DOWN THOMAS is *Dona* 1086 DB, *Donne, Dunne* 1285 FA, *La Doune* 1303 Ipm, *Doune Thomas* 1316 FA. *v.* dun. The place is on a prominent hill. *Thomas* was probably *Thomas* le Squier mentioned in FA (1346).

LANGDON COURT is *Langadona* 1086 DB, *Oueralangadone* 1322 BM. 'Long hill,' *v.* dun.

SPIREWELL (6″) is *Spirewell* 1238 *Ass*, -*wylle* 1381 Exon (p), *Spurewille* 1333 *SR* (p). The first element is probably the word *spire* (OE *spīr*), for which the NED gives a meaning 'reeds, sedges,' found in SW dialects.

FORD (6″) and TRAIN (6″) were the homes of Richard atte *Forde* (1330 *SR*), Thomas *atte Trewen* (1311 *Ass*) and Thomas *atte Nitheretreawen* (1330 *SR*). 'At the trees,' cf. Trewyn *supra* 148.

PAIGE'S FM, PRINCE FM and TAYLOR'S FM (all 6″) are probably to be associated with the families of William *Page* (1346 FA), John *Pryn* (1591 *SR*) and Richard *le Taillour* (1333 *SR*).

BOVISAND is *Bouy Sand* 1690 Map[1], *Bovey Sand* 1765 D. HOLLACOMBE WOOD (6″) is *Holecumbe juxta Sprydeleston* 1298 *Ass*. 'Hollow valley,' *v.* cumb. KNIGHTON is *Knytheteton* (sic) 1281 *Ass* (p), *Knyghton in Wenbury* 1548 Pat. *v.* cniht, tun. MEW STONE (rock in sea) is *Meweston* 1383 Fine. The first element is OE *mǣw*, 'seagull, mew.' RANELEIGH [rænəli] is *Ranelegh* 1515–18 ECP 5, 40, -*leygh* 1562 *FF*. This may contain OE *rāna*, gen. pl. of *rā*, 'roe,' the vowel being early shortened in the trisyllable. *v.* leah. WEST WEMBURY (6″) is *Westwenbury* 1577 *SR*.

Yealmpton

YEALMPTON [jæmptən] 144 E 12

Elintona 1086 DB

Alentone 1205 FF, *Almenton* 1249 *Ass*

Yalminton 1244 *Ass*, *Ealmintone* 1270 Exon, *Yalmetun* 1275 RH, *Yalmton* 1297 Pat, *Ealmeton* 1418 AD vi

Ylampton 1287 Pat, *Yalumptone* 1291 Tax, *Yalampton* 1303 FA, *Yhal-* 1309 Ch, 1310 Ipm, *Yalempton juxta Plympton* 1313 *Ass*, *Yealampton* 1375 *Ct*, *Yelhampton* 1429 Pat

Yampton al. Yealmpton 1670 Recov

'Farm by the Yealm river,' *supra* 17, *v.* tun.

DUNSTONE is *Donestantona* 1086 DB (Exon), -*stanestone* (Exch), *Dunestaneston* 1201 FF, *Dunstanestun* 1204 Cur, -*ton juxta*

¹ *Ex. inf.* Mr C. W. Bracken.

Ermyngton 1325 *Ass*, *Dunston in the parish of Yalmeton* 1489
Ipm. 'Dunstan's tun.'

HURDLECOMBE (6″) is *Hudelacumbe* 1275 RH (p), *Hodelacomb*
1330 *SR* (p), *Hothelecombe juxta Yalampton* 1364 *Ass*. '*Hudela*'s
valley,' *v.* cumb. This pers. name is not recorded, but would be
a regular *l*-derivative of *Huda*. Cf. Huddlestone (PN Sx 237)
and Walter *Hodyl* 1372 Exon (D).

LOTHERTON BRIDGE

> *Lodreton* 1219 FF, *Lodder-* 1303 FA, (*juxta Plympton*) 1329,
> 1334 *Ass*, *Loder-* 1337 Ipm, *Loddereton juxta Ermyngton*
> 1323 *Ass*
> *Louderetune* 1238 *Ass*

The first element points to OE *loddere*, 'beggar,' which may
have given rise to a contemptuous farm-name. Cf. *to loddera
beorge* BCS 981, Lattiford (So), *Lodreford* DB, *Loderford* 1242
Ass, 1303 FA, *Lotherford* 1226 FF (p) and Doggaport *supra* 95.

LYNEHAM is *Lineham* 1238 *Ass* (p), *Lin-* 1254 *Ass* (p), 1285 Ch
(p), *Lyn-* 1374 Exon. *v.* ham(m). The first element must be OE
lin, 'flax.'

TREBY [tri·bi] is *Driby* 1275 RH, *Dryby* 1281 *Ass* (both p). This
name may be a compound of the OE *drȳge*, 'dry,' and *byge*,
'curve, bend,' found also in Huccaby, Grammerby (*supra* 194,
221). There is a slight bend here formed by the junction of a
small stream with the Yealm river.

WILBURTON is *Wilberdon* 1311 *Ass* (p), 1428 FA (p), *Wyl-* 1333
SR (p). Probably '*Wilburh*'s down,' *Wilburh* being a fem. pers.
name in OE. Cf. Wilburton (C), *on Wilburhtune* BCS 1268.

WINSOR is *Winlesore* 1202 FF, *Wyndesore* 1309 Ch, 1310, 1341
Ipm, *Wyndesore, Wynsore* 1500 Ipm. This name clearly contains
the same elements as Windsor (Berks) 1050–65 BM *Windlesora*,
DB *Windesore*, Windsor (Do) DB *Windresoria*, 1278–84 Ipm
Wyndelsore and Winsor (Ha) *Windlesor* (1236 *Ass*). The second
element is ora, 'bank.' The first is a pers. name found also in
Windlesham (Sr), *Windlesham* (1227 Ch) and an unidentified
wyndelescumb (BCS 721) in the bounds of Topsham (D). All
these point to a pers. name *Windel*, a diminutive of the *Wind(a)

which lies behind Wyndham (PN Sx 213). There is some evidence for OGer pers. names *Windo, Windulo* (cf. Förstemann PN 1618). Further examples of the name Windsor are noted in Hemyock and Luppitt *infra* 618, 644, unfortunately only with late forms. There is a Windsor in Lanreath and a Winsor in Lansallos in Cornwall, for which the earliest forms are *Wyndesore* (1327 *SR*), and there is a Windsor in Lamphey (Pembroke), *Wyndlehor* 13th *AD, Wyndesore* 1275 *AD*. At first sight this suggests a curious preference for the association of the pers. name *Windel* and ora, but it should be noted that some of these may contain *Winel* rather than *Windel*, and that one or more of the places, and this is specially true of the Pembrokeshire one, may have been named in direct imitation of the famous Berkshire Windsor.

WORSTON is *Wluretheston* 1219 *Ass* (p), *Wolryggeston* 1281 *Ass* (p), *Wolrichton* 1310 Ipm, *Wolricheston* 1333 *SR* (p). '*Wulfric's* tun.'

HERNE[1], WOOD COTTAGE[2], and YEO[3] (all 6″) were the homes of John in the *Hurne* (1333 *SR*), *v.* hyrne, John atte *Wode* (ib.), Alvī de *la Ya* (1238 *Ass*) and Roger *atte Yo* (1333 *SR*), i.e. 'at the water,' *v. supra* 17–18.

BUTLAND (6″) is *Botelond* 1496 Ipm. KITLEY is *Kitelhey* 1310 Ipm, *Kytelegh* 1333 *SR* (p). Probably 'kite-clearing,' *v.* leah, the *h* in the first form being a clerical error. LONGBROOK is *Langebroke* 1531 *Ct.* OAKHILL BARN (6″) is *Okewyll* 1531 *Ct.* 'Oak spring,' *v.* wielle. ORCHARD FM is *Orchard* 1809 M. PITTEN is *Pyttyn* 1472 Pat, *Westpytten* 1499 Ipm and was the home of Thomas *atte Pitte* (1333 *SR*). 'The hollows,' the name being the weak plural of pytt. YEALMBRIDGE [jæmbridȝ] is *Yalmebrugge* 1531 *Ct, Yaulm bridge* c. 1550 Leland. It may be the bridge referred to as *inter pontem Martini et Almenton* in 1249 *Ass*.

---

[1] *Herne* 1670 *Recov.*   [2] *Wode* 1496 Ipm.
[3] *Yeo Cross* 1712 *Deed.*

XI. ERMINGTON HUNDRED

Erminton(a) 1131, 1181, 1187 P, 1238 *Ass*

v. Ermington *infra* 272. In the Geld Roll (1084) the hundred is called *Alleriga*, a name not found again. The meaning may have been '*Ælla's* ridge.'

The South Hams

This is the name given to the fertile district lying between Plymouth and the Dart estuary and bounded on the north by Dartmoor. It is called *Southhammes* 1396 Exon, *the Southhammes* c. 1550 Leland. Cf. also Charleton *infra* 319. The application of the term hamm here is not clear. It is tempting to associate with this district the grant of 20 hides of land *on Homme* (BCS 451) made by Aethelwulf in 846. The boundaries of that grant are very difficult to determine. It clearly has to do with land in the neighbourhood of that granted in the Thorndon Hall Charter (*v. infra* 296 n. 1), for among the boundary-points we have (in this order) *græwanstan, afene, sueordleage wælle, wulfwælles heafod, wealdenesford*, which must be the same points as *afne, græwan stane, wealdingford, wulfwyllesheafod, swurdleg wyll* in the Thorndon Hall Charter, mentioned in that order. *Afene* is the Avon *supra* 1, *sueordleage* would seem to be Sorley *infra* 296. The boundaries also include a *ðyrelan stan* close by the sea and this would seem to be Thurlestone *infra* 312. The next point in the boundaries is *smalan cumb*, and this tends to confirm the Thurlestone identification, as Mollycombe in Thurlestone is earlier *Smalacombe, v. infra* 312. Beyond that it is difficult to go. There is clearly some crossing of the boundaries of the two areas and we cannot determine the area of *Homme* beyond saying that it included at least the territory between Kingsbridge estuary and the sea five miles to the west. We may have traces of another *hamm* in the place-name Stokenham, earlier *Stoke in Hamme* (*v. infra* 331). This *hamm* was possibly the eastern half of the peninsula between the Kingsbridge estuary and the sea on the east. The two *hamms* may have been known as 'The south *hamms*' from their extreme southerly position[1], but *hamm* must

[1] There is a *Northamme* in Loddiswell, cf. Ham *infra* 306.

in that case have been used of an area far larger than has hitherto ever been suggested for that term. Such a suggestion receives some confirmation perhaps from the curious use of *homme* in BCS 410 where *Beornwyn* retired to Devon and took up her share of the inheritance in the place called *Derentunehomme*. *Derentune* is clearly Dartington *infra* 297. It looks as if *homme* was used of the whole district around *Derentune*. *v.* Addenda lix.

Aveton Giffard

AVETON GIFFARD [ɔ·tən dʒifəd] 145 F 2

> *Aveton(e)* 1086 DB, 1242 Fees 789, 1259 Exon, (*Giffard*) 1276 Ipm, (*Jefford*) 1441 Moulton
> *Aventon* 1239 Ch, 1281 *Ass*, 1510 *Deed*
> *Awton Gifford* 1546 SR, *Aveton Gifford al. Awton Gifford* 1562 *Deed*

'Farm by the river Avon' (*supra* 1). Walter *Giffard* held the manor in 1242 (Fees 769).

HARRATON is *Harewodeton* 1244 *Ass* (p), *Harwodetone, -wedetone* 1274, 1286 Exon (p), *Harweton* 1316 AD vi (p). 'Grey wood farm' or perhaps 'boundary wood farm,' *v.* har, the place lying near the parish boundary.

HEATHFIELD is *Hetfelt* 1086 DB, *-feld* 1244 *Ass*, 1296 AD vi, *Hethfeld'tone* 1242 Fees 771, *Hethfeld(e)* 1291 Tax, (*juxta Magna Modbury*) 1324 *Ass*, *Hethefeld juxta Aveton Gyffard* 1345 *Ass*. 'Waste land,' cf. Heathfield *supra* 214.

IDSTON

> *Hyddeston* 1238 *Ass* (p)
> *Eddestone* 1287 *Ass*
> *Iccheston* 1330 SR (p), 1339 *Ass* (p)
> *Yedeston* 1346, 1428 FA, *Yeddistone* 1430 FF, *Yeddes-* 1466–83 ECP 1, 356

Probably '*Geddi*'s farm,' *v.* tun. This pers. name is found also in Yeading (Mx), *Geddingas* 793 (12th) BCS 182, *æt Geddincggum* 825 BCS 384.

LIXTON is *Lyvegherston* 1296 AD vi, *Liv(e)ger(e)ston* 1417 AD vi, *Lygiston* 1421 AD vi, *Lyxton* 1507 AD iii. The place took its name from the family of William *Lyvegher* (1296 AD vi) and

John *Liveger* (1386 *Ass* 1495 m. 26). *v.* tun. It may be noted that the name *Liueger* (i.e. *Lēofgār*) is on record in Devon c. 1100 (Earle 259).

STADBURY is *Stotberia* 1086 DB, *Stodbire* 1242 Fees 771, *-byri* 1270 Ipm, *-byry* 1298 *MinAcct*, *-bury* 1303 FA, *-bery* 1340 Ipm. *v.* stod, burh.

WIZALLER is *Wierdesalre* 1296 AD vi (p), *Wyardesallre* 1305 *Ass* (p), *Werdesallere* 1310 Exon (p), *Wyddesallar* 1538–44 ECP 8, 263, *Wisaller* 1744 *FF*. '*Wīgheard*'s alder,' *v.* alor.

YABBACOMBE (6″) is *Yabbecombe* 1339 *Ass* (p), 1376 Exon (p). '*Eabba*'s valley,' *v.* cumb. Cf. Yapton (PN Sx 144) and *on eabbincg wylle* BCS 480.

HEATH (6″) and TORR (6″) were the homes of Richard *atte Hethe* and Richard *atte Torre* (1333 *SR*). *v.* hæð, torr.

ASHFORD is *Ayshford* 1339 *Ass* (p), *Aysheford* 1568 *Recov*. BABLAND is *Bablandcrosse* 1712 *Deed*. '*Babba*'s land,' cf. Babbacombe *supra* 85. BENNICK (6″) is *Bynek* 1489 Ipm. BURN COTTAGES (6″) is *Burne* 1515–18 ECP 4, 540. CHANTRY is *Chantrey* 1744 *FF*. CHILLATON is so spelt 1740 *FF*. Cf. Chillaton *supra* 217. COMBE (6″) is *Come* 1201 FF, *Cumba* 1296 AD vi (p). *v.* cumb. COPYTHORN CROSS (6″) is *Cappathorn* 1753 *FF*. Probably 'copped thorn.' DAMEREL'S COMBE (6″) is to be associated with the family of John *Daumarle* (1330 *SR*). EFFORD (6″) is *Suth Ebbeford juxta Stodbur* 1302 *Ass*. 'Ford passable at ebb tide,' *v. supra* 227. FISHLEIGH is *Fishley* 1598 *Deed*. Cf. Fishleigh *supra* 143. SPICERSCOMBE (6″) is so spelt 1619 *FF*. STOCKADON is *Stoketon* 1249 *Ass* (p), *-don* 1412 *FF*. Probably 'hill of the stumps,' *v.* stocc, dun. TITWELL (6″) is *Tetewill(e)* 1291 Tax, *Totte-* 1303 FA, *Tette-* 1357 Ipm. '*Tetta*'s spring,' *v.* wielle. Cf. Tedburn *infra* 451. WAKEHAM is *Overe Wakaham* 1313 *Ass*, *Wakham* 1322 *Ass* (p). '*Waca*'s ham(m),' cf. Wakeham (PN Sx 43). WATERHEAD is so spelt in 1627 *Recov*.

Bigbury

BIGBURY 145 G 2

> *Bicheberia* 1086 DB, 1166 P
> *Bickeberi* 1201 Cur *et passim* to 1332 Pat, with variant spellings *Bik(k)e-*, *Byke-*, *-biry*, *-bury*, *Bikesbury* 1357 Pat

Bukebur̄ 1238 *Ass, Bukkebury* 1379 IpmR
Bekebyry 1420 Exon
Byggebury 1485 Pat
'*Bi(c)ca*'s burh.' See further *s.n.* Abbots Bickington *supra* 124.

BOROUGH ISLAND is *the Boro' Island* 1667 DKR 40, 145, *Borough*
or *Bur Isle* 1765 D. There was an ancient chapel here called
'chapel of St Michael de *la Burgh*,' 1411 Exon, the beorg or hill
being that on which the chapel stands.

HINGSTON is *Hyndestan* 1238 *Ass*, 1244 *Ass* (p), *-ne* 1284 *Ass*,
Hyndeston, Hendeston 1427 *Ass, Hengeston* 1489 Ipm. 'Hinds'
stone,' perhaps some ancient boundary mark.

HOUGHTON

Hugheton' 1242 Fees 770, 1303 FA, 1330 *SR* (p)
Hueton 1249 *Ass*
Huginton 1249 *Ass* (p)
Hugaton 1301 Ipm
Hogeton, Hoggeton 1346 FA
Hoghton 1428 FA

This is a difficult name. We may perhaps suggest an unrecorded OE pers. name *Huhha* or *Huga*, hence '*Huhha's* or
Huga's farm.' The other possibility is that we have ME *Hughe*,
Huwe (cf. Hoo Meavy *supra* 230), a pers. name which appears in
1333 (*SR*) as *Hugha*. This would suit Hewton *supra* 207 and
Howton in Moretonhampstead *infra* 485 better, where we have
no forms with *-inton* or with *gg*. Houghton in High Week does
show forms with double *g*.

NODDON (6″) is *Nottedon(e)* 1242 Fees 770, 1330 *SR* (p), 1346
FA, *-dowene* 1286 Exon, *-ton* 1303 FA, *Noddon* 1489 Ipm.
Probably '*Hnotta's* hill,' *v.* dun. Cf. Natsley *supra* 58, *Hnottan ford* (BCS 1217) and *on hnottan mære* (BCS 491), also
Wymond *Notte* (1319 Exon). Notter Tor in Linkinhorne (Co),
Nottetorre t. Hy 1 (1378) Pat, suggests, however, that we may
have in some cases a descriptive element such as OE *hnott*,
'bare,' etc., used in some topographical sense. Cf. also Natton-
hole *infra* 433.

TUFFLAND is *Tuffelonde* 1286 Exon, *Toffalonde* 1330 *SR* (p). This name contains the ME *tuffe*, *tufte*, discussed under Toft *supra* 183.

BOARSHILL (6″) is *Boryshulle* 1330 *SR* (p). The first element must be OE bar, 'boar,' cf. Boarzell (PN Sx 451). CHALLON'S COMBE is probably to be associated with the family of John *Chalons* of Ermington (1571 *SR*) and Nicholas *Challons* of Modbury (1603 Wills). *v.* cumb. COMBE FM (6″) is *Combe in the parish of Byggebury* 1485 Pat. CUMERY is *Comereuwe* c. 1280 Exon, *Comberewe* 1414 *FF*. 'Row of houses along the valley,' *v.* cumb, ræw. Cf. Cumerew *supra* 226. EASTON (6″) is *Southestone* c. 1280 Exon, *Esteton* 1330 *SR* (p). 'East farm,' *v.* tun. It lies NE of Bigbury. The first form is for 'South Easton.' FROGLAND (6″) is *Frogeland al. Vrogland* 1613 Recov. HEXDOWN (6″) is *Bigbury-down al. Hexte-down* t. Eliz ChancP. *Hexte* may be for OE *hiehsta*, ME *hexte*, 'highest.' HOLWELL (6″) is *Halewill'* 1242 Fees 770, *Holewell* 1303 FA, *Holwell* 1489 Ipm. Probably 'holy well.' There is a 'holy' well marked here. KNOWLE (6″) is *Knoll* 1478 BM. *v.* cnoll. ST MILBURGA'S ORATORY (6″) is *Capella Sancte Milburge* 1381, 1425 Exon. The dedication is presumably to *St Mildburh*, abbess of Wenlock.

Cornwood

CORNWOOD 144 C 13

> *Cornehuda* 1086 DB (Exon), -*hode* (Exch)
> *Curnwod'* 1242 Fees 796, *Cournewode* 1404 *Ass*
> *Cornewud* 1249 *Ass*, *Cornewode* 1283 Exon, 1337 *FF*, *Cornne-* 1337 Ipm
> *Cornwode* 1263 Exon, 1276 Ipm, 1283 *Ass*, 1291 Tax, 1297 Pat
> *Cornwood vulg. Curlewood* 1675 Ogilby

Names in *Corn-* are always difficult. In Devon we have the present name, a lost *Cornewode* (1238 *Ass*) in Bampton Hundred, Cornworthy (*infra* 320), Corringdon and Corndon (*infra* 290, 426), and a *Curnbroke* 1291 and *Corndich* 1297 (*AddCh*). Cf. also Corneal in St Dominick (Co), *Cornhele* 1305, 1404 *Ass*, 1427 IpmR. All these names may, of course, contain the OE *corn*, 'crane,' discussed under Cornwood (PN Wo 54), but in view of the numerous early spellings with *ou* or *u*, other alternatives are possible, e.g. British words corresponding to W *corn*, 'horn,' or *cwrn*, 'spire, pile, knob.' Cf. the use of OE *horn* in place-names.

BLACHFORD

> *Blacheorda, -urde* 1086 DB
> *Blechewrth* 1219 FF
> *Uvereblachesuurthe, Nythereblachesworth'* 1242 Fees 771, 795, *Overe-, Nithereblaccheworth(y)* 1303 FA, *Blayccheworthy* 1520 BM
> *Blachesworthi* 1324 Ipm, 1334 *Ass*
> *Blachford oth. Blachworthy* 1740 *Recov*

'*Blæcci*'s or *Blæcca*'s worþig.' Cf. Bletchingley (Sr), *Blaching-lei* DB, *Blechingelegam* 1210 RBE. For the interchange of *ford* and *worthy*, v. Introd. xxxv.

BROOMAGE (6″) is *Bromwic* 1249 *Ass*, *Bromwych, Nytherbrom-wyche, Nether Bromeweche* 1282 BM. 'Broom farm,' v. wic.

CHOLWICH TOWN [tʃɔlidʒ]

> *Cholles-, Caldes-, Calleswyht, Choldeswych, Cholsweche* 13th BM
> *Chaldeswych* 1249 FF
> *Chaldewyth* 1274 *FF*
> *Chollewyche* 1304 *Ass*, *Cholleswyche* 1314 Exon
> *Chailleswych* 1313 *Ass*
> *Cheldeswych* t. Ed 3 *Ass* (p)

This is a difficult name. The second element is wic, 'farm,' with the same palatalised development as in Fuge and Fuidge *infra* 316, 446, and Runnage and Broomage *supra* 197, 269. Professor Ekwall suggests that the first element may be OE *cealdost*, Southern ME *choldest*, 'coldest.' It stands on the edge of the Moor, some seven hundred feet up.

DINNATON

> *Dinin-, Dunitona* 1086 DB
> *Dynenton* 1242 Fees 796, *Dynyngton* 1303 FA, 1330 *SR* (p), *Dynn-* 1428 FA

This is probably from OE *Dynning-tūn*, i.e. '*Dynna*'s farm,' v. ingtun. It may be that *Dynna* is to be identified with the

Donna (Exch *Donno*) who held the manor TRE, with a rare though not unparalleled rendering of OE *y* by *o* before *n* in DB.

FARDEL

> *Ferdendel*(*la*) 1086 DB
> *Ferthedel*(*e*) 1219 FF, 1242 Fees 796, 13th Buckfast (p)
> *Furthedel* 1303 FA, *Furdedell* 1370, a. 1416 BM
> *Fyrdell* 1370 BM

This must be the OE *feorða*(*n*) *dǣl*(*e*), 'fourth part.' *v. fardel* in NED. The place may originally have formed part of some larger estate[1]. See further Addenda *supra* lix.

LUTTON is *Luttat*(*h*)*on* 1242 Fees 770, t. Hy 3 BM, *Lude-* 1242 Fees 796, *Lutte-* t. Hy 3 BM, *Locton* 1337 Ipm, *Lotteton* 1356 *Ass*. '*Lutta*'s farm,' *v.* tun. For this pers. name, *v.* PN Bk 186 and Lutworthy *infra* 401.

PENN MOOR is *Penmore Common* t. Hy 8 CtRequests, *Penmore* 1547 *FF*, *moore of Penn* 1605 *Deed*. This is probably the British *pen*, 'head, top,' perhaps referring originally to Penn Beacon, the highest point of the moor.

ROOK is *Roke* 1325 *Ass* (p), *Westroke* 1334 *Ass*, *Roka*, *Est Roke* 1337 BM, *West Rake* 1348 Ipm. 'At the oak,' cf. Rock (PN Wo 69).

STALL MOOR, STALLDOWN BARROW (6″) are *Staledon* 1474 *Ct*, 1479 Rowe, *Stealdon* 1479, *Stayldon* 1586 Dartmoor, *Stallmoor* 1792 *Recov*. *v.* dun. The first element is clearly OE *steall*, 'stall, stable,' possibly with some such sense as that found for *stodfald* (IPN 150). There are several enclosures marked on the Moor on the 6″ map.

YADSWORTHY is *Yodesworth* 1330 *SR* (p), *Yeodesworthi* 1333 *SR* (p), *Yeaddsworthy* 1481 *Ct* (p), *Yeaddisworthy*, *Yeaddisford* 1563 *FF*. *v.* worðig. The first element is clearly a pers. name found also in Yeatson *infra* 315. It looks like a strong form of the pers. name *Eada*, with the common Devon development of *ea* to *eo*.

BRIDGE FM (6″), COMBE (6″), FORD BARN (6″), HANGER[2], HELE[3],

---

[1] After this was written Professor Zachrisson suggested independently the same solution of the name (*Jespersen Miscellany* 40–1).

[2] *Hanger* 1403 BM, *Hangerdown* 1533 *Deed*.

[3] *Southehele* c. 1420 *Ct*.

MILL WOOD and COTTAGES (6″), MOOR CROSS, PARKLAND[1] (6″), SLADE, STERT[2], STONE (6″), TOR and YEO COTTAGES (6″) were probably the homes of Alfred *atte Brugge* (1330 *SR*), Walter de *Combe* (ib.), Benedict *atte Forde* (ib.), William *atte Hangher* (ib.), William *atte Hele* (1438 Exon), John *atte Mulle* (1333 *SR*), Walter *atte More* (1330 *SR*), John *atte Parke* (1333 *SR*), John *atte Slade* (1330 *SR*), Gilbert *atte Sturte* (ib.), John *atte Stone* (ib.), Reginald *atte Torre* (ib.), and Thomas Kyng de *la Yo* (1334 *Ass*). i.e. 'at the water,' *v. supra* 17–18. *v.* cumb, hangra, healh, mor, pearroc, slæd, steort (there is a tongue of land here), torr.

BROOK BARN (6″) is *Broke* 1291 Tax. CORNTOWN (6″) is *Corne Towne* t. Jas 1, *Cornetowne* 1670 *Recov*, and is perhaps identical with *Cornwodaton* 1330 *SR* (p), *v. supra* 268. DELAMORE HO is *Dallamore* 1723 *Recov*. DENDLES WOOD (6″) is *Dendals* 1815 *Recov*. GOODABROOK WOOD (6″) is *Goodebrooke* 1605 *Deed*. Cf. Goodamoor *supra* 250. HARROWTHORNE PLANTATION (6″) is *Harethorn* 1249 *Ass* (p), *Harrathorne* 1740 *Recov*. The first element is most likely OE har in the sense 'grey,' since the wood is not on the parish boundary. HAWNS was the home of Richard *atte Haghene* (1330 *SR*). This is the weak plural of OE *haga*, 'hedge,' 'enclosure.' HEDDON DOWN is *Headon* 1627 BM. Probably 'heath down.' HOUNDLE (6″) is *Hundehole* 1314 *Ass*, *Hounde-* 1403 BM. 'Hounds' hollow' or '*Hunda*'s hollow,' *v.* holh. LANGHAM BRIDGE (6″) is *Langham* 1301, 1490 Ipm. *v.* ham(m). PITHILL is *Pudehele* 1306 *Ass* (p), *Pide-* 1330 *SR* (p), *Pyda-* 1333 *SR* (p). '*Pydda*'s healh,' cf. Pethill *supra* 259. SHELL TOP (hill) is so called from its resemblance to a limpet shell (Moore 23). SHERWILL (6″) is *Shirewille juxta Erminton* 1283 *Ass*, *Sherewell* 1438 Exon (p). 'Clear spring,' *v.* scir, wielle. STORRIDGE WOOD (6″) is *Storidge* 1604 *Deed*. Cf. Storridge *infra* 310. TOLCHMOOR GATE is *Torchȝete, Torcheate, Torychyete* 1332 BM. The first element is a stream-name found in Torycombe to the south. For *yete, v.* geat. UPPATON (6″) is *Uppaton* 1314 *Ass*. WATERCOMBE (6″) is *Watercomb* t. Hy 6 *Ct*. WILKEY'S MOOR (6″) is *Welkersmore* 1330 *SR* (p), *Whelkersmore* t. Eliz ChancP. WISDOME is *Wisdome* 1618 BM and is possibly to be associated with the family of John de *Wymesdone* (1316 Exon).

---

[1] *La Parke* 1404 BM.   [2] *Sterte* 1497 Ipm.

YEALM HEAD is *Yalme hede* 1477 *DuCo*, the source of the Yealm river *supra* 17.

Ermington

ERMINGTON 145 E 1

> *Ermentona, Hermentona* 1086 DB, *Ermintona* t. Hy 2 Oliver
> 135 *et passim* with variant spellings -*ing*-, -*yng*-
> *Armyngton* 1614 *FF*

'Farm on the River Erme,' *v.* Erme *supra* 5.

BURRATON is *Bureton* t. Hy 2 Oliver 135, 1330 *Ch*, *Bouratone* 1276 RH (p), *Buratona* 1282 (1328) *Ch*, *Boraton* 1366 *Ch*, -*e*- 1425 *FF*, *Burraton* t. Ed 4 BM, 1501 Ipm. This is probably from OE (*ge*)*būra-tūn*, 'farm of the peasants,' *v.* bur, tun, and cf. Bourton *infra* 505.

CLICKLAND is *Clegland* 1238 *Ass* (p), *Clekelond(e)* 1278 *Ass*, 1330 *SR* (p), *Clakelonde* 1333 *SR* (p). The first element may be identical with the word *cleaca* found in the land-boundaries of a charter relating to Meavy (D), in 1031 (KCD 744). This word, for which Bosworth-Toller gives the meaning of 'stepping-stone,' is possibly of Celtic origin and related to the W *cleg*, 'hard mass, lump,' *clegyr*, 'cliff, rock.' There is a small stream here by Clickland farm which might once have been fordable by means of stepping-stones.

COYTON is *Coditon* 1244 *Ass*, *Codyaton* 1299 *Ass*, -*ia*- 1330, 1333 *SR* (all p). Perhaps '*Coda*'s farm,' *v.* ingtun. See further under Wonwell *infra* 279.

KEATON is *Cauton* 1330 *SR* (p), *Keaton juxta Worthy* 1424 *FF*, *Keaton* c. 1430 *Ct*, *Kayton* 1481 IpmR, (or *Keyton*) 1504 Ipm. The forms are difficult to reconcile with one another. Professor Förster suggests that the first element may be the Cornish *ke*, Welsh *cae* (from *cai), 'enclosure, field.' There are on the modern map Keaton and Caton on either side of the Erme river, presumably the same name.

PENQUIT [pænkit]

> *Pencoyt* 1238 *Ass* (p), (*juxta Magna Modbury*) 1289 *Ass*,
> (*juxta Ermyngton*) 1329 *Ass*, -*koyt* 1290 Oliver 299, -*quoit*
> 1291 Tax, -*quit* c. 1400 Exon, -*quite* c. 1480 ECP 2, 215
> *Pinquitt* 1609 *Deed*, *Panquett* 1748 *Deed*

This name is Celtic, the elements corresponding to modern W *pen*, 'head, end, top,' and *coed*, 'wood.' It is interesting as being an example of an isolated British place-name in an essentially English area. Cf. Penketh (PN La 106), where reference is made to the parallel name Penquite (Co).

PRESTON

> *Prutestan* 1204 Cur (p), *Pruteston* 1303 Ch (p), (*juxta Loddiswell*) c. 1400 Exon, *Prustston* 1501 Ipm, *Prutteston al. Pruston* 1737 FF
>
> *Prouteston(e)* 1310 Exon (p), 1330 SR (p), *Proutt-* 1339 Ass *Prutastone(s)lond* 1425 AD iii

The second element is stan. The first is probably a post-Conquest pers. name *Prut*, 'proud one.' Cf. Roger *Prowt* (1333 SR) in Holbeton, an adjacent parish.

SEXTON (6″)

> *Secoteston* 1281 *Ass* (p), *Shecoteston* 1329 *Ass*
> *Sheccodeston* 1333 *SR* (p)
> *Shettokeston* 1334 *Ass* (p)
> *Shakeston* 1433–72 ECP 2, 25
> *Shexton al. Shekerston* 1560 *Deeds Enrolled*
> *Sexton al. Shecodeston* 1621–5 ECP 94

The place derives its name from the family of Richard *Sheccoc* mentioned in 1199 (FF), *v.* tun. There was a Richard *Scheccote* still living here in 1333 (*SR*). It is impossible to determine the correct early form of this name, since *c* and *t* are commonly confused in ME script.

STRASHLEIGH is *Strecchelegh* 1285 *Ass*, 1330 SR (p), *Strecheleghe* 1319 Exon (p), *Strachlegh* 1442 AD iv. A pers. name **Strecca* is not on record in OE but is found (t. Hy 1) in Wiltshire in the form *Strecce* (Harl 61 f. 40 *b*) and in the Devon pers. name *Stretche* (1275 RH), cf. also Stretchacott *supra* 93, Stretchford *infra* 521, and Stretcholt (So), *Stretheholt* 1242 Ass, *Streccholt* 1344 Ipm, and *Strecchhull* 1306 *Ass* (Devon). In all of these a pers. name is a possibility, but it is clear from Stretch Down *infra* 396, that *strecche* could also be used as a topographical term. Doubtless it is the word *stretch*, 'expanse of territory,' hitherto only recorded from a much later date. *v.* leah.

SWAINSTONE (6″) is *Swinstanam* t. Hy 2 Oliver 135, *Swynestona* 1282 (1328) Ch, *Swynyston* 1330 *SR* (p), *Sweyneston* 1353 *Ass*. This seems to be a compound of 'swine' and 'stone,' though the sense is obscure. The modern form is quite irregular, cf. however Swanaford *infra* 424.

WORTHELE

> *Ordihella* 1086 DB
> *Wurdihel* t. Hy 2 Oliver 135, *-thi-* 1226 FF, *-le* 1230 Pat
> *Worthihal(e)* 1239 Ch, 1296 *Ass*, *-the-* 1345 Ipm, *-thy-* 1377 Cl
> *Worthyel* 1242 Fees 776, *-yhele* 1242 Fees 770, *-ehele* c. 1250
>   *Ch*, 1303 FA, Misc
> *Worthele* 1341 Ipm

Apparently a compound of worþig and healh, denoting '*healh* marked by an enclosure,' though it is unusual for the former word to occur as the first element in place-names. Cf. Wortheal (So, olim Do), *Worthiale* 1427 FF[1].

STRODE[2], THORNHAM, VENN COTTAGES (6″) and WESTLAKE were probably the homes of Gervas de *Strode* (1238 *Ass*), Simon *atte Thorne* (1330 *SR*), Ranulph de *la Fenne* (1306 *Ass*), and Richard *Bywestelake*, i.e. 'west of the streamlet' (1333 *SR*). *v.* strod, fenn, lacu.

BEACH FM (6″) is *Beach* 1775 *Recov*. BROOK is *Broke* 1515–18 ECP 5, 91. CADLEIGH PARK is *Cadelegh(e)* 1351 *Ass*, 1438 *FF*. '*Cada*'s clearing,' *v.* leah. CLEEVE is *La Cleve* 1291 Tax, *La Clyve* 1303 FA. *v.* clif. COBHILL (6″), cf. *Cobbelond* 1489 Ipm and Cobley *infra* 370. HOLLOWCOMBE is *Holecombeslad* n.d. AD ii, *Holcombe* 1469 IpmR. *v.* holh, cumb. HUNSDON is *Honesdon* 1333, 1340 *SR* (p), *Honnesdon* 1438 *FF*, *Hounstonysforde* 1502 AD ii. '*Hūn*'s hill,' *v.* dun. MEADWELL COPSE (6″) is *Medwill* 1238 *Ass* (p), *Medewyll* 1501 Ipm. 'Meadow spring,' *v.* mæd, wielle. WEST PARK (6″), cf. *La Southpark* 1325 Ipm. STIBB (6″) was the home of Alice *atte Stibbe* (1333 *SR*). 'Stump,' *v.* Stibb *supra* 96. UPTON (6″) is *Uppaton juxta Ermynton* 1310 *Ass*. WHIPPLE'S COTTAGE (6″) is *Whiphills* 1683 *Recov*. WOODLAND is *La Wdeland* 1219 *Ass*, *Wodelond* 1414 Exon.

---

[1] *Ex. inf.* Mr A. Fägersten.
[2] *West Strode* 1550 Pat, *Stroude*, c. 1620 Risdon.

Harford

HARFORD 145 C 1

Hereford(a) 1086 DB, 1175 P (p), 1242 Fees 796, 1301 Ipm, *Esthereford juxta Ermyngton* 1286 *Ass*, *(juxta Uggeburgh)* 1304 *Ass*, *West Hereford* 1289 *Ass*
Herforde 1291 Tax, 1299 Ipm

The name is identical with Hereford (He), the first element being the OE *here*, 'army.'

STOWFORD HO is *Stoford* 1280 AD vi, 1400 Exon, *Stouford juxta Ermynton* 1313 *Ass*. *v*. Stowford *supra* 41.

COMBESHEAD[1] (6″), MEADS (6″) and TORLANDS BARN[2] (6″) were the homes of John de *Comeshevede* (1330 *SR*), Edward *Bytharmede*, i.e. 'by the mead' (1333 *SR*), and Richard *atte Torre* (ib.). *v*. cumb, torr.

BLACKLAND CORNER (6″) is *Blacklands* 1685 *Deed*. BROOMHILL is *Brimhill* 1765 D. BULLAVEN (6″) is *Bulefen* 1175 P, *Bolefenne* 1330 *SR* (p), 1340 *Ass* (p). 'Bulls' marsh,' *v*. fenn. BURFORD DOWN is *Burfort, Burford Downes* 1681 *Deed, Recov*. *v*. burh. Perhaps this referred to some place defending the ford over the Erme here. HARFORD MOOR is *Hartford More* 1685 *Recov*. LUKESLAND is *Lukesland* 1675 *FF* and is to be associated with the family of John *Lucas* (1330 *SR*). HIGHER and LOWER PILES is *Pyles Wood* 1542 *DuCo*. Cf. Pilemoor *infra* 420.

Holbeton

HOLBETON [hɔbətən], [houbətən] 144 F 13

Holbouton 1229 FF
Houbauton, Houbouton 1238 *Ass*
Holbogatone 1245–57 Exon, *-boggeton* 1256 FF, *-boheton* 1275 RH, *-bogh(e)-* 1289 Misc, 1291 Tax, 1303, 1346 FA, *-boughe-* 1328 Exon
Holebouton 1249 *Ass*, 1342 *FF, Holboweton* 1278 *Ass*, 1279 Ipm, *-bouethon* 1289 Misc, *Holbeton* 1444 *FF*

The name is a triple compound of OE holh, boga (*v*. Bowden *supra* 37) and tun, the whole meaning 'farm in the hollow bend.'

---

[1] *Comeshed* 1576 SR   [2] *Torland* 1529–32 ECP 6, 191.

ALSTON HALL is *Alnatheston* 1228 FF (p), 1238 *Ass* (p), 1244 *Ass*, *Alnethestan* 1230 P (p), -*ton'* 1242 Fees 795, 1244 *Ass* (p), FF (p), -*nedeston'* 1242 Fees 770, *Ailnateston* 1238 *Ass* (p), *Aylnetheston* 1244 *Ass* (p), FF (p), *Aleneston* 1303 FA, *Alnestone juxta Battekesburgh* 1304 *Ass*. '*Æþelnōþ*'s tun.'

BATTISBOROUGH HO

  Bac(h)etesberia 1086 DB
  Battekesbergh' 1242 Fees 771, -*burh*, -*burne* 1275 RH, *Battokesburgh(e)* 1291 Tax, 1303 FA

'**Bat(t)oc*'s hill,' *v.* beorg. This pers. name is not on record, but would be a regular derivative of *Bat(t)a*. *v.* Batton *infra* 333. The DB form shows transposition of *c* and *t*.

CAULSTON is *Calsinton(e)* 1238 *Ass*, 1242 Fees 795, -*yng*- 1303 FA, 1438 *FF*, *Kalsyngthon* 1242 Fees 770. We seem to have a pers. name *Calmund* in Calmsden (Gl), *Kalemundesdene*, *Calmundesden* BCS 466, and *Calnōþ* in Candlesby (L) DB *Calnodesbi*. These three place-names suggest the possibility of a series of OE pers. names with a first element *calu*-, 'bald.' In that case Caulston must be '*Calusige*'s farm,' *v.* ingtun.

FLETE

  Flutes 1086 DB, *Flutte* 1340 Ipm, *Flute Damarle* 1396 AD iv
  Flete 1198 Abbr, 1224 Bracton, 1238 *Ass* (p), *Flethe* 1242 Fees 770
  Flitte 1303 Misc, *Flitte Daumarle* 1334 *SR*

v. fleot. The name probably denoted the spot where the Erme became navigable, or the point to which the tide reached. Guy de *Alba Marl* held the manor in 1198 (Abbr). Cf. Sydenham and Stoke Damarel *supra* 209, 240.

LAMBSIDE

  Lammeseta 1086 DB
  Lamside 1242 Fees 770, 1278 *Ass*, 1346 FA, (*Crispyn*) 1291 Tax, *Lame*- 1244 *Ass*, -*syde* 1278 *Ass*
  Lamsede 1242 Fees 795, 786
  Lampside 1303 FA, -*syde* 1377 Cl
  Lammyshyde 1316 FA

This would seem, as suggested by Professor Ekwall, to be a

compound of OE **lamb** and **side**, hence, 'lamb hill.' The word
side is not on record in a topographical sense in OE but it is
found as early as DB in Side (Gl).

LUSON

> *Loveston, Leueston* 1238 *Ass* (p)
> *Lyveston* 1244 *Ass*
> *Luueston(e)* c. 1300 *Ch*, 1330, 1333 *SR* (p), *Luvystone* 1313
> Exon (p)
> *Luueneston* 1340 *SR* (p)
> *Luyston* 1489 Ipm
> *Leveston al. Lueston* 1566 *Deed, Lewiston* 1576 *SR*

'*Lēof*'s tun.' If stress is to be laid on the 1340 form, the earlier
forms may well be a reduction of the full *Lēofwinestun*, '*Lēofwine*'s farm.'

MEMBLAND HALL

> *Mimidlanda* 1086 DB
> *Mimminlande, Mimming-* 1238 *Ass* (p), *Mymmyngelonde* 1297
> Exon (p), *Mim(m)-* 1310 Exon (p), 1330 *SR* (p), *Mymmyngs-
> lond* 1501 Ipm
> *Mimilaunde* 1242 Fees 795
> *Memmyslonde* 1261 Exon (p)

Ekwall (RN 294) suggests tentatively that the first element
may be an old stream-name identical in origin with Mint (We),
earlier *Mymid*. If that is correct, we must assume that *Mimidland*
was early reduced to *Mimiland* and that the name was then
re-fashioned to *Mimingland* under the influence of other names
in which, by the reverse process, *-ingland* had been reduced to
-iland. Cf. Hartland *supra* 71.

MOTHECOMBE [mʌdikum] is *Muthecumb(e)* 13th AD i (p), 1244
Ass (p), 1275 Misc, *Mode-* 1238 *Ass* (p), *Mouthecombe* 1330 *SR*,
1342 Exon (p), *Mowdecombe* 1375 Exon (p). The valley was
probably so called because it opens into the estuary of the Erme
river just at its mouth. *v.* muþa, cumb.

RAMSLAND is *Remmyslonde* 1313, 1321 Exon (p), *Rammeslond(e)*
1325 *Ass* (p), 1330 *SR* (p). Probably '*Hræfn*'s land.'

Y

SCOBBISCOMBE is *Scobiscombe* 1819 *Recov* and is probably identical with *Scotescombe in Holbogheton* 1440 IpmR. Doubtless the earlier form is a mistake and the first element identical with that of Scoble *infra* 327.

BOROUGH[1] (6″), FORD[2], FURSDON (6″), HAYE[3] (6″), HOLE[4] were probably the homes of John *atte Overeburgh* (1330 *SR*) or Thomas *atte Nytherburgh* (1333 *SR*), Agnes *atte Forde* (1330 *SR*), William *atte Forsen* (1330, 1333 *SR*), Thomas *atte Hay(e)* (ib.), and Thomas Lange *atte Hole* (1327 Banco). *v.* beorg, fyrs, (ge)hæg, holh. For *atte Forsen, v. supra* 129–30.

ADDISTONE (6″) is *Addeston* 1238 *Ass*, 1303 Ch, *-stane* 1242 Fees 769 (all p). '*Ædda's* stone.' BROWNSWELL (6″) is *Brounyswill(e)* 1330 *SR* (p), 1381 *FF*. '*Brūn's* spring,' *v.* wielle. CARSWELL (6″) is *Carsewell* 1281 *Ass*, *Carswill* 1333 *SR* (p), 1501 Ipm. 'Cress spring.' COMBE (6″) is *Nethre Cumbe juxta Holbouton* 1298 *Ass*, *Overcombe* 1503 Ipm. EFFORD HO is *Ebford* 1281 *Ass* (p), *Efford in parochia de Holbeton* 1444 *FF*. *v.* Efford *supra* 227. PAMFLETE is *Pamflette* 1620 *FF*. The form is too late for anything to be said beyond the fact that the second element is fleot. POOL is *Poole* 1501 Ipm. WHITEMOOR is *Whytemore* 1483 IpmR. YARNIN-KNOWLE WOOD (6″) is *Yernecnolle* 1324 Ipm. 'Eagles' hill,' *v.* earn, cnoll.

Ivybridge

IVYBRIDGE[5] 144 D 14

Ponte Ederoso (abl.) 1280 AD vi

Ivebrugge 1292 *Ass*, *Yvebrygg* 1395–1419 Exon, *Ivebrigge* 1500 Ipm

Ivybrygg' 1313 *Ass* (p), *-brigg'* 1314, 1316 *Ass*, *Ivy Bridge* c. 1550 Leland

Brigg, Brygg c. 1400 Exon

The name was probably descriptive of the ancient bridge here over the Erme, on the main Exeter-Plymouth road.

GODWELL is *Godewill* t. Hy 8 *CtWards*. HENLAKE DOWN is *Henlake* 1629 *Recov. v.* lacu.

---

[1] *Burgh* 1478 BM.
[2] *Ford* 1448 IpmR.
[3] *Haie* 1610 SR.
[4] *Hole* 1448 IpmR.
[5] A modern parish formed in 1894 from Ermington and Ugborough.

Kingston

KINGSTON 145 F 1

Kingeston(e) 1242 Fees 771 *et passim* to 1394 *Ass* with variant
spelling *Kyng-*, (*juxta Ermington*) 1284 *Ass*, (*juxta Byke-
bury*) 1386, 1394 *Ass*

'King's farm,' but the exact royal owner is unknown. *v.* tun.

LANGSTONE is *Langeston* 1324, 1489 Ipm, 1330 *SR* (p). Self-
explanatory, but no stone exists here now. In 1288 and 1295
(*Ass*) there are references to *Clerkeslangestone* and *Fuggeslangaston*
which must preserve the names of early tenants, not traced.

WONWELL COURT

Womgwylle 1245–57 Exon, *Wonigwill* 1275 RH (p)
Womewelle 1259 Exon, *Wonyawell* 1329 *Ass* (p)
Wonywell(e) 1281, 1288 *Ass*
Wonyng(es)well 1281 *Ass* (p)

We have in OE pers. names *Wunbeald*, *Wuncild*, *Wunstan*
which seem to contain an element *Wun-* (cf. Sweet OET 559).
A pet-form *Wun(n)a* for one of these names seems here to be
linked with wielle by the connective use of ing. The same name
seems to be found in Wonwood, Wonnacott and Wonham *supra*
210, 212, *infra* 532.

Modbury

MODBURY[1] 145 E 1

Motberia, -bilia 1086 DB
Modberi(a) 1174–83 BM, 1181 P, *-bury* 1238 *Ass*, *-beregh* 1276
    Cl, *-byry* 1278 Misc, 1291 Tax, *Mychel Modbury* 1480–3
    ECP 2, 309, *Modeberyburgh* 1368 *FF*
Motberia 1185 P, *-bur'* 1281 *Ass*, *-bury* 1333 Ipm

This is probably a compound of OE *gemōt*, 'meeting-place'
(*v.* Mutley *supra* 235), and burh. Cf. *on ðæne gemot beorh* BCS
392. Possibly it was at an early date the hundred meeting-place.

BROWNSTON is *Brunardeston* 1219 FF, 1242 Fees 771, *Bron-* 1295

---

[1] BACK ST is *Backelane* 1568 *Deed*. BROWNSTON ST is *Brounstonstrete* 1568
Deed, leading to Brownston *infra*. GALPIN ST is *Golepynstrete* 1530 BM,
Galluppingstrete al. Galstrete al. Leightrete 1568 *Deed*, of obscure origin.
POUNDWELL ST is *Pounstrete, Pounwell* 1568 *Deed*.

Ch, Brinewardiston 1227 FF, *Brunewardestuna* 1231 Bracton, *Brouniston* 1290 *Ch*, *-nes-* 1331 *Ch*, *Brunarston* c. 1300 *Ch*. '*Brūnweard*'s tun.'

EDMESTON is *Yedmareston* 1242 Fees 796, *Edmereston* 1275 RH (p), 1289 *FF*, *Edmyston* 1490 Ipm, *Edmeston al. Empston* 1638 *Recov.* '*Ēadmǣr*'s tun.'

GOUTSFORD BRIDGE is *Goudenesford* 1281 *Ass* (p), 1327 *Ass, -nys-* 1330 *SR*(p), *Godenesford* 1304 *Ass* (p). Possibly '*Goldwine*'s ford.'

JEWELSCOMBE (lost) is *Joelescumbe juxta Modburi* 1298 *Ass*, *Julyscomb* 1417 *Ct*. The first element is the OFr pers. name *Iohel*. A Thomas fil. *Joel* was juror in Plympton Hundred in 1238 (*Ass*).

LEIGH is *Lega* 1086 DB, *Legh'* 1242 Fees 776, (*Britevile*) 1276 Ipm, *Leyebretavyle* 1282 *FF*, *Brytevyleslegh* 1332 Ipm, *Lye Derrant* 1530 BM. *v.* leah. The manor was held by Wido de *Brettevil'* in 1242 (Fees 776). The *Derrant* is unknown.

OLDAPORT is *La Yoldeporte* 1310 *FF*, *La Porte in parochia de Modbury* 1332 Exon. 'The old *port*,' referring to the curious fortified remains here by a creek of the Erme estuary. "There are remains of walls and round towers, by some esteemed Roman work. They are a puzzle to the antiquary, and only the spade will determine to what period they belong." (LGS.)

ORCHETON is *Orcartona* 1086 DB, *Orcherdton'* 1242 Fees 770, *Orcherton* 1290 *FF*, *Orchardton* 1303 FA. *v.* orceard, tun.

SHILSTON BARTON

   Silfestana 1086 DB, *Silvestane* 1242 Fees 771, *Schilveston*
      1244 *Ass, Sh-* 1493 Ipm
   Scillestane 1265 Misc (p)
   Schelston 1284 AD i

   'At the shelving stone,' i.e. cromlech. *v.* Shilstone *infra* 433. At this particular place no trace of such survives.

SPRIDDLESCOMBE (6") is *Comba* 1086 DB, *Cumb Spridel* 1242 Fees 770, *Spridelcumb* 1242 Fees 796, *Spridlescombe* 1301 Ipm. *v.* cumb. William *Sprydel* held the manor in 1346 (FA). In 1242 (Fees) it was held by the *Peverel* family, but the *Spridel* family may have been sub-tenants.

STOCKENBRIDGE is *Stokkenebrugg'* 1330 *SR* (p), *Stokenebrigge* 1361, 1366 *Ass*, *Stoken-* 1493 Ipm, *Stokyng-* 1495 Ipm. 'Bridge made of stocks or logs,' *v.* stoccen. Cf. Stockbridge (PN Sx 14).

STOLIFORD is *Stolyford* 1330 *SR* (p), 1423 IpmR, *Stoliford*, *Sterliford* 1489 Ipm. The forms are rather late, but the name may be a compound of stan, leah and ford.

WHYMPSTON HO is *Wymundeston* 1242 Fees 796, 1298 *Ass*, 1324 Ipm, *-mond-* 1249 *Ass*, 1423 IpmR, *Wymston* 1421 Cl. '*Wigmund*'s farm,' *v.* tun.

AYLESTON (6″) is *Ayleston* 1388 *FF*. Possibly '*Ægel*'s tun.' BUTLAND is *Buttelond* 1238 *Ass* (p), *Bottelonde* 1311 Exon (p), *-a-* 1330 *SR* (p), *Butlond* 1502 AD ii. '*Butta*'s land.' COMBE is *Combe* 1333 *SR* (p), *Gurrantiscomb al. Combdowne in Modbury* 1515–18 ECP 4, 408. CROPPIN'S COMBE (6″) is *Croppingiscombe* 1550 *Deed* and is to be associated with the family of Richard *Croppyng* (1333 *SR*). NORTH GREENOVENS (6″) is *Grenefen(ne)* 1298 *Ass*, 1460 AD vi. 'Green fenn,' cf. same name *supra* 186, 249. KNIGHTONCOMBE (6″) is *Knyghtescombe* 1418 *FF*. Perhaps 'combe of the cniht,' but if the place is of ME origin it may contain as first element the name of a former owner. LAPTHORNE (6″) is *Loppedethorn* 1330 *SR* (p), *-nne* 1347 Ipm. 'At the pollarded (lopped) thorntree.' LITTLE MODBURY is *Parva Modbyr'* 1242 Fees 795, *Lytelemodbury* 1356 *Ass*. SHEARLANGSTONE is *Shearlangston* 1776 *Recov*. SHEEPHAM is *Schypham* n.d. AD iv, *Schip-* 1244 *Ass* (p), *Sypeham* 1269, *Chipham* 1271 FF, *S(c)hepham* 1301 Ipm, 1420 IpmR. 'Sheep ham(m).' STUBSTON is so spelt in 1679 *Recov*. SWANBRIDGE MILL (6″) is *Swyne Bridge* 1568 *Deed*. TRAINE (6″) is *Treawen* 1388 *FF*, *Trewen* 1469 IpmR, and was the home of John Tirry *atte Trewen* 1370 *Ass*. 'At the trees,' cf. Train *supra* 261. WEEKE is *Weeke* 1684 *Recov*, *v.* wic. WHEATPARK WOOD (6″), cf. *Wheatland* t. Eliz ChancP. WIDLAND (6″) is *Wydialond* 1330 *SR* (p). The ME form favours *withy* rather than *wide* as the first element. YARNICOMBE is *Yornecumbe* 1238 *Ass*, *-comb* 1333 *SR* (p), *Yernecomb* 1306 *Ass* (p), *Yeornecombe juxta Modbury* 1345 *Ass*. 'Eagles' valley,' *v.* earn, cumb. For the *Y-*, *v.* Introd. xxxiii.

Newton Ferrers

NEWTON FERRERS 144 F 11

Niwetona 1086 DB, *Nyweton* 1242 Fees 796, *Niweton al. Niweton Fereirs* 1306 Ipm

Newenton 1249 *Ass*, *Newintone* 1279 Exon, *Newenton Ferers* 1328 Cl

Newaton Ferys 1412 Exon

'New farm,' *v.* niwe, tun. The manor was held by the family of *Ferrers* (Fees 796, *Ass* 176 m. 32, Ipm 1306).

BLOWDEN (6″) is *Blowedoune* 1270 DA 48, *-don* 1330 *SR* (p). 'Cold, exposed hill,' *v.* bla(w), dun. Cf. Blofield (Nf), *Blafelda*, *Blawfelle*, *Blauuefelda* 1086 DB[1], Blurridge *supra* 28, and *Blowelond* 1378 IpmR (Devon).

CREACOMBE

Crawecome 1086 DB, *Craucombe* 1231 FF (p), *Crauwecumba* 1231 Bracton

Creuecumbe 1238 *Ass* (p), *Crewecumb* c. 1300, *-comb* 1356 *Ch*, *Crencomb* (sic) 1421 IpmR

'Crow cumb,' *v.* Introd. xxxiii.

PUSLINCH [pʌzlidʒ]

Pusling 1238 *Ass*, *Posling* 1254 *Ass*

Puselynch 1242 Fees 796

Poselinch 1242 Fees 770, 1328 *FF*, 1337 Ipm, *Posylynch* 1346 FA, *Posselynch* 1428 FA, *Poslinchbrigg* 1289 Misc

Pyselynch 1303 FA

This may be a compound of OE pise (*peose*), 'pease,' and hlinc. Cf. Posbrooks (PN Sx 187). Hence, 'hill where pease grow.'

WRESCOMBE is *Wrescomb* 1281 *Ass* (p). This may contain as first element OE *wræst*, 'thicket,' cf. PN BedsHu 62.

ASHCOMBE (6″) is *Assecumb* 1254 *Ass*, *Aysshecomb* 1330 *SR* (p), *v.* cumb. BRIDGEND is *Briggeyend* 1417–39 *Ct*. BROWNSTONE is *Bromeston* 1281 *Ass*, *-mys-* 1330 *SR* (p), 1337 Ipm. The modern

---

[1] *Ex inf.* Dr O. K. Schram.

form is clearly corrupt but it is difficult to see whence *Bromeston* can be derived. CLANICOMBE is *Clenacombe* 1619 *Recov.* *v.* Clanacombe *infra* 312. COLLATON is *Coleton* 1330 *SR* (p). *v.* Collacott *supra* 50. CRAWL WOOD (6″) is *Crawlwood* 1775 *Recov.* CREBAR (6″) is *Crewebere* 1330 *SR* (p). Cf. Crebor *supra* 218. GNATON HALL is *Westgnatton* 1587 *Recov.* Perhaps 'gnat infested tun,' cf. Gnatham *supra* 245. HORSEWELLS (6″) is *Halswill* 1330 *SR* (p), *Haslewell* 1709 *Recov.* 'Hazel spring.' PRESTON is *Preston* 1278 *Ass*, *Pruston* 1427 *FF*. 'Priests' tun.' SHORTAFLETE CREEK (6″) is *Shortaflett* 1587 *Recov.* 'Short creek,' *v.* fleot. TORR was the home of Robert *atte Torre* (1330 *SR*).

Ringmore

RINGMORE 145 G 1

Reimora 1086 DB

Ridmor(e) 1242 Fees 770, t. Ed 1 Ipm, 1284 Exon, 1291 Tax, *Ryd-* 1244 FF, 1333, 1336 BM

Redmore 1242 Fees 795, *Redemore* 1329 FF

Ridemor(e) 1249 *Ass*, 1303 FA, *Ryde-* 1281 *Ass*, 1381 Exon, *Rydy-* 1281 *Ass*

Ryn(n)mor(e) 1434 Exon, 1438 BM, *Rynne-* 1434 Exon

Reynmore, Reymmore 1435 Pat, *Rymmore* 1436 BM

Ryngemore 1600 BM

This is probably a compound of *ridde* and *mor* signifying a tract of land cleared of wood or undergrowth. OE hreod, 'reed,' is also just possible. The same name occurs *supra* 239, and *infra* 460. In all cases the modern form must have been influenced by the word *ring*.

MARWELL (6″) is *Merlewill* 1260 Ipm, *-well* 1281 *Ass* (p), 1303 FA, *Marlewille* 1324 Ipm, *Merwyll* 1421 IpmR. *v.* wielle. The first element is no doubt identical with that of Marlborough (W), *Merleberge* DB, *æt Mærle beorge* 1110 ASC and Malborough *infra* 307. This is a pers. name *Mǣrla*, an *l*-derivative of *Mǣra*. Cf. OGer *Merila, Merlus* (Förstemann PN 1102).

OKENBURY

Ocheneberia 1086 DB, *Ockenbury* 1726 FF

Wockenebery 1303 FA, *-bury* 1324 Ipm, *Wokkenebiri* 1324 Ipm, *Wokynbury* 1410 Exon

Professor Ekwall suggests that the first element may be OE
Woccena, genitive plural of *Woccan*, a tribal name related to the
pers. name *Wocc* found in Woking, etc. Such a name would
only be possible in Devon if it was due to the migration to this
region at an early date of a folk previously settled further east,
which retained its original name in its new settlement. Cf.
Whitsun Brook (PN Wo 16).

Ugborough

UGBOROUGH 145 D 2

Ulgeberge 1086 DB
Uggeberge 1200 ChR, *Ugge-*, *Uggabergh* 1242 Fees 771, 789,
1244 *Ass*
Oggeberg 1262 Ipm, *-burghe* 1291 Tax
Uggebyri, Huggeburne 1266–74 Exon, *Uggaburga* 1282 (1328)
Ch, *-ghe* 1306 *Ch*, *Uga-* c. 1300 *Ch*
Ugborough al. Ubbourowe 1570 *Deed*

'*Ucga*'s hill,' *v.* beorh. This pers. name may be inferred from
ucganford (BCS 1030), now Ugford (W).

BOWCOMBE

Baucumb 1238 FF (p) *et freq* to 1297 Pat with variant spellings
-comb, -cume
Beaucumbe 1308 Exon (p), *-combe* 1312 Exon (p), 1490 Ipm
Bawecumbe 1310 Exon (p)

v. cumb. The first element is possibly OE *bēaw*, 'gad-fly,'
referring to a valley infested by this insect. Cf. Beaford *supra* 86.

BROADAFORD (6″) is *Bradeforda* 1086 DB, *-ford'* 1242 Fees 770.
'Wide ford.'

CANTRELL (6″) gave name to Robert de *Canterhulle* (1330 *SR*),
de *Canterhill* (1333 *SR*). Possibly *canter* is for *cantel* by dissimilation. If so, we may perhaps compare Tregantle (Co),
Argantel 1086 DB[1], *Tregantel* 1303, 1306 FA, in which the
second element is probably a Cornish word corresponding to the
Welsh *cantel(l)*, 'circle, rim.' Cantrell is on the slopes of a
circular hill.

---

[1] The first syllable is Cornish *ar*, 'upon.'

CHESTON is *Cherteston* 1198 FF, *Cheston* 1679 *Recov.* This may contain the element *cert* found in Churt (Sr), BCS 65 *Cert.* If so, the name means 'farm of or by the rough land.'

COARSEWELL is *Coresfeld(e)* 1198 FF, *Cors-* 1330, 1333 *SR* (p), *Coryswyll* 1499 Ipm. *v.* feld. The first element is probably the Celtic word *cors*, 'bog, marsh.' Cf. Corsley (PN Sx 371).

FILLHAM is *Filidhamme* 1244 *Ass*, *Filetham* 1322 *Ass* (p), *-it-* 1330 *SR* (p), *Vilet-* 1336 *Ass*, *Filham* 1605 BM. 'Hay enclosure' *v.* filipe, hamm. Cf. Feltham (So), *Fylet hamme*, *Fælet hamme* 882 BCS 550, *Filed hamme* 956 BCS 923, *Filetham* 1255 FF.

LANGFORD BARTON is *Langeforda* 1086 DB, *-de* 1198 FF, *Langa-ford le Estre* 1279 Ipm, *Langeford lestr'* or *Langefordestrete* 1331 Ipm, *Langeford Lestre juxta Blakehalle* 1361 *Ass*. 'Long ford.' Galfridus de *Lestre* held the manor in 1198 (FF) and Robert del *Estre* in 1257 (FF).

LUDBROOK

    Lodrebroc, Ludebroca, Lodebroc 1086 DB
    Ludebrok 1238 FF, 1242 Fees 796, *North-, Sout-* 1303 FA,   *Suth Ludbrok* 1490 Ipm
    Loddebroc 1238 *Ass* (p), *-ok* 1316 FA
    Luddebrok 1244 *Ass* (p)
    Loudebrok c. 1280 *Ch*, 1333 *SR* (p), *-ck* c. 1300 *Ch*, *Nort-*   1306 (1586) *Ch*
    Lodbrok, South Lodbrok 1301 Ipm

The name must have originally referred to the stream here still called *Lud* Brook. The meaning is 'loud brook.'

MARRIDGE is *Marigge* 1276 *Ass* (p), t. Hy 6 IpmR, *-rugge* 1330 *SR* (p), *Maurigge* 1290 Oliver 299, *Marrigge* 1333 *SR* (p). The 1290 form is difficult to reconcile with the others and the interpretation of the name must remain uncertain. *v.* Addenda *supra* lx.

PEEK (6″)

    Pech 1086 DB, *Pek'* 1242 Fees 796 *et freq* to 1336 *Ass* with   variant spellings *Peke, Pek, Westpek* 1306 *Ass*, *Peck* 1303   FA
    Pyek 1333 *SR* (p), *Est Pyk* 1382 *FF*
    Pykedon 1498 *Ct*, *Pigedone* c. 1580 DA 61

East Peek and West Peek are two farms adjacent to the hills now called Eastern and Western Beacon. In both cases we have probably an old hill-name from OE *pēac*, for which *v.* PN BedsHu *s.n.* Pegsdon, and Mawer, *Problems of PN Study* 71. According to Crossing (77) the old people still talk of *Picken* Hill. This may be a corruption of earlier Peak Down Hill and have itself given rise to the present-day *Beacon*.

QUICKBEAM HILL is *Quykbeme* 1474 *Ct*, 1479 Dartmoor. The OE compound *cwicbeam* existed, but it is uncertain to what tree it refers (*v.* NED *s.v.*). In south-western dialects, however, the 'quickbeam' is always used of the mountain ash. A single tree of this kind, though small, would have been a conspicuous landmark on the bleak open moorland here.

RUTT (6″) was the home of Guydo *atte Rytte* (1333 *SR*), Thomas *atte Rette* (1340, 1347 *SR*), and Richard *atte Ryte* (1412 *Ct*). This is OE *ryt*, 'rubbish for burning,' cf. Collard *supra* 258 and Rat (PN Sx 499).

THREE BARROWS HILL is *Thribiriburghe* 1240 Buckfast, "a certain great heap of stones by the name of *Tryberie Boroughs al. Tre Boroughs*, being the middle heap of three heaps of stones here" (1557 Dartmoor), *Threberis* c. 1580 DA 61. It is clear that in this name beorg must have the sense of 'heap' or 'mound.'

TURTLEY is *Thurreclyve* 1320 *Ass* (p), *Turaclyve* 1330 *SR* (p), *Tirraclyve* 1333 *SR* (p), *Turtlay oth. Turcliff* 1768 Recov. 'Dry slope,' *v.* clif. The first element must be the OE *ðyrre*, 'dry, withered,' referring to the bare hillside here. Cf. Therfield (Herts) *þyrefeld* 796 (12th) BCS 281, *Derevelde* 1086 DB, *Thirefeld* t. Hy 2 Dugd ii, 228, t. Ric 1 (1301) Ch.

VENN is *Fen* 1086 DB, and was the home of Jordan *atte Fenne* (1330 *SR*). *v.* fenn.

WITCHCOMBE is *Wydescomb(e)* 1330, 1333 *SR* (p), 1364 *Ass* (p), -*dis*- c. 1430 *Ct*. The first element is probably a pers. name of ME origin.

WRANGATON is *Wrangeton* 1244 *Ass* (p) *et freq* to 1346 FA. *v.* tun. The first element may be a pers. name *Wranga*, cf. Osbert *Wrange* 1182 P. Here, however, and in Wrangworthy (*supra*

134), it is equally possible that we have the OE adjective *wrang*, 'crooked, twisted,' from which this pers. name is derived. Cf. *on wrangan hylle* BCS 832, and *Wrangeheygh* (1511 *Newnham*).

ZEASTON was the home of William *atte Soueston* (1330 *SR*) and Stephen *atte Seuenston* (1374 *Ass*). The meaning is clearly 'at the seven stones,' but there are no remains of such here now. Cf. Soussons *infra* 482.

BARONS HILL[1], BOLTERSCOMBE[2], DAVEYS CROSS, FOWELSCOMBE[3], and SPURRELLS CROSS are probably to be associated with the families of Hugo *Baron* (1330 *SR*), Alexander *Boltere* (1330 *SR*), John *David* (1330 *SR*), Thomas *Fogelle* (1375 Exon) and Johannes *Fowell* (1428 FA), and Thomas *Spurwell* of Harford (1634 Wills).

COMBE CROSS (6″), FORDER (6″), HAY (6″), WARE (6″), WELL CROSS, YEO, and YOLLANDBROOK (6″) were probably the homes of Isabella de *Combe* (1330 *SR*), Henry *atte Forde* (1333 *SR*), Richard *Inthehaye* (1330 *SR*), Walter *atte Were* (ib.), Richard *atte Wille* (ib.), Hugo de *la Yeo* (1333 *SR*), i.e. 'at the water,' *v. supra* 17–18, William *Attenoldelonde* (1244 *Ass*) and Hugo *atte Oldelond* (1333 *SR*), cf. Addenda *supra* lviii. *v.* cumb, (ge)hæg, wer, wielle.

BITTAFORD BRIDGE is *Bittiford* 1677, *Bitta-* 1699 *Recov*. BLACKADON FM (6″) is *Bla(c)kedon* 1311 *Ass* (p), 1330 *SR* (p). 'Black hill,' *v.* dun. BUTTERDON HILL is *Butterdone* c. 1580 DA 61. *v.* Buttercombe *supra* 40. CANNAMORE (6″) is *Kanemor* 1219 *Ass*. See Canna *infra* 481. CUTWELLWALLS is *Cotewill* 1219 *Ass*, *Cuttewell* 1500 Ipm. '*Cotta*'s spring,' *v.* wielle. DENNIS HILL is *Deynyshyll* 1542 *Depositions*, *Denyshill* 1550 Pat, deriving from some medieval owner. DUNWELL is *Dunewell(e)* 1238 FF (p), *Done-* 1278 *Ass* (p), *Dunnewill* 1306 Ch, *-na-* 1333 *SR* (p). '*Dunna*'s spring.' EARLSCOMBE MILL (6″) is *Erlescombe* 1312 Exon (p), *Yorlescombe* 1330 *SR* (p), *Yerles-* 1352 FF. 'Earl's combe.' The count of Mortain held four manors in the parish in DB. ENNATON CROSS (6″) is *Innaton juxta Modbiry* 1311 *Ass*, *Eneton* 1439 *Deed*, *Enyton Downe* 1550 Pat. '*In(n)a*'s tun.

---

[1] *Baronshill* 1619 *FF*.
[2] *Bolterescumbe* 1276 *Ass* (p), *Bolterscombe* 1330 *SR* (p), t. Hy 6 IpmR.
[3] *Foulescombe* t. Hy 6 IpmR.

GLASSCOMBE CORNER (6″) is *Glascumb* 1316 Pat, *-combe* 1685 *Recov.* The first element is a stream-name, *v.* Glaze Brook *supra* 6. HAREDON (6″) is *Har(e)don* 1301 *Ass*, 1330 *SR* (p), *Haradon* 1356 *Ass, Est Haredon* 1576 *Recov.* 'Hare hill,' *v.* har, dun. HILLHEAD is *Hille* 1440 *FF.* HOOKMOOR CROSS (6″) is *Hokemore* 1316 Pat, *Huckemore* 1550 Pat, *Hockemore* 1610 *Recov. v.* hoc, mor. The name is descriptive of the ridge of waste land here. HUNGERS-COMBE (6″) is *Hungariscombe* 1421 Cl, *Hungeres-* 1454 *FF.* '*Hūngār's* combe.' LEIGH (6″) is *Legh* 1242 Fees 770, *Leghe* 1330 *SR* (p). *v.* leah. MONKSMOOR (6″) is *Mounkysmore* 1541 *Deed.* NEWLANDS is *Newelonde* 1306 *FF.* OWLEY is *Hululeg', Huleleg'* 1249 *Ass, Ulleghe* 1256 FF, *Oulalegh* 1333 *SR* (p). 'Owl wood or clearing,' *v.* leah. SHELLWOOD (6″) is *Shelwood* 1550 Pat, *Shil-* 1717 *Recov.* Probably 'wood on the shelf or terrace of land,' *v.* scylf. SHUTE is *le Shuta* 1394 *Ass* and was the home of Robert *atte Schute* 1333 *SR. v.* Shute *supra* 184. STONE (6″) is *Stane* 1198 FF and was the home of Alvred *atte Stone* (1333 *SR*). UGBOROUGH MOOR is *Uggbroghe Moor* 1557 Dartmoor. WATER-MAN (6″) is perhaps to be associated with the family of Thomas *Waterman* of *Upharadon* (1421 Pat), i.e. Haredon *supra.* WHITEHOUSE (6″) is *Whytehous* 1440 *FF.* WHITELEY (6″) is *Whitelegh* 1324 Ipm. *v.* leah. WOOD is *Wode* 1504 Ipm. WOODLAND (6″) is *Wodelonde* 1284 *Ass.*

XII. STANBOROUGH HUNDRED

Stanberg(h)(a) 1159, 1182 P, 1219 Fees 262, 1238 *Ass*
Stanburg(h)e 1187 P, 1275 RH, 1295 Ipm
Stanbrug 1251 Fees 1264

The Hundred presumably takes its name from Stanborough in Halwell *infra* 324, though that place is now just outside the Hundred boundary. In the Geld Roll (1084) the Hundred is called *Dippeforda* from Diptford *infra* 299.

West Alvington

WEST ALVINGTON [ɔ·lviŋtən] 145 H 3

Alvintona 1086 DB, *Alvint', Aufint'* 1212 Fees 99, *Aufinton* 1237 Cl, 1244 Fees 1386, *Auffyngton* 1315 Ipm

Alfinton(e) 1232 Cl, 1270 Exon, *-tune* 1269 Ipm, *-fyn-* 1237
  Ch, *-fing-* 1242 Fees 766, *-fyng-* 1275 RH
Offinton 1232 Cl, *Affinton* 1285 FA
Alvyngetone 1328 Totnes, *Alvyngton al. West Alvyngton* 1551
  Deed

'*Ælf(a)*'s farm,' *v.* ingtun. Cf. Alphington *infra* 422. Possibly
it is *West* in relation to that place.

BAGTON is *Bachedona* 1086 DB, *Baketon(e)* 1238 *Ass*, 1285 FA,
1327 *Ass* (p), *Backe-* 1310 *FF*, *Bagkethon*' 1242 Fees 766,
Baggeton(e) 1242 Fees 795, 1428 FA. '*Bacca*'s farm,' *v.* tun.
Cf. Baccamoor *supra* 252. The *d* appears only in DB and is
probably incorrect, since the farm is not on a hill.

BOWRINGSLEIGH is *Bowryngislegh* 1505 Ipm and is to be associated with the family of Stephen *Bouryng* (1333 *SR*). *v.* leah.

HEDDISWELL is *Hyddeswille* 1306 *Ass* (p), *Hydeswill* 1330 *SR*
(p), *Hidys-* 1333 *SR* (p), *Hid(d)is-* 1348 *FF*, 1505 Ipm. '*Hiddi*'s
spring,' *v.* wielle. For the pers. name, *v.* Redin 127.

WOOLSTON is *Ulsistona* 1086 DB, *Wols(t)ingthon*' 1242 Fees 777,
Wolseton 1285 FA, *Wolsatone* 1312 BM. '*Wulfsige*'s tun.'

AUTON is *Auueton* 1249 *Ass*, *Aueton* 1330, 1333 *SR* (p). Probably
'*Afa*'s tun.' It is not near the river Avon. COLLAPIT BRIDGE is
Coleputte 1249 *Ass*, 1310 *FF*, *-pitte* 1328 Exon, 1330 *SR* (all p),
-putte 1384 *FF*. *v.* Collacott *supra* 50. EASTON is *Esteton* 1333
SR (p). 'East tun.' GERSTON is *Garston* 1493 Ipm. *v.* gærstun.
LONGBROOK (6″) is *Langebrok* 1330 *SR* (p). NORDEN is *Northdon*
1384 *FF*, *Norden* 1567 BM. 'North hill,' *v.* dun. OLDAWAY is
Yolleweye 1330 *SR* (p), *Oldeweye* 1436 IpmR. *v.* Introd. xxxiii.
SOCKWELL (6″) is *Sackwill* 1617 *Deed*. TICKETWOOD (6″) is
Tacket Wood 1584 *Deed*, *Tackett Woode* 1605 Recov. WESTON
(6″) is *Weston* 1368 IpmR. WOODHOUSE (6″) is *Wodehous* 1384
FF. YARNACOMBE CROSS (6″) is *Westyernecumbe juxta Kyngesbrigg* 1316 *Ass*, *Yarnecomb* 1330 *SR* (p). 'Eagles' valley,' *v.*
earn, cumb. YOUNGCOMBE is *Youncomb* 1430 IpmR, *Yoncombe*
1613 *FF*. Perhaps from OE *ēowena-cumb*, 'ewes' valley,' *v.*
cumb.

South Brent

Sᴏᴜᴛʜ Bʀᴇɴᴛ 145 C 2/3

> *Brenta* 1086 DB, 1238 *Ass*, *Brenth'* 1242 Fees 767, *Brente*
> 1244 *Ass et freq* to 1337 Exon, *-tte* 1268 Exon, (*juxta Ugge-*
> *burgh*) 1322, 1325 *Ass*, *Southbrynt* 1497 Ct, *Brent al. South-*
> *brent* 1714 *Recov*

The name has the same history as Brentor (*supra* 213) and
refers to the prominent Brent Hill, just above the village. *South*
to distinguish it from a former *Ouera Brenta* (1304 *Ass*), which
was apparently the name of a settlement further up the Avon.

Bᴀʀʟᴇʏᴄᴏᴍʙᴇ (6″) is *Barlecumbe* 1297 *Add*, *Burlacomb* 1330 *SR*
(p), *Barlecomb* 1333 *SR* (p), 1472–85 ECP 2, 258. This may be
from OE *Bǣrelan cumb*, with the same diminutive pers. name that
is found in Birling (PN Sx 417) and in several other place-names.
The 1330 form must be an error.

Bᴜʟʟʜᴏʀɴsᴛᴏɴᴇ is *Bolehorn(e)ston* 1287 *Add* (p), *Bulhornston al.*
Bulston 1574 *Add*. This would seem to mean 'bull horn stone,'
with reference to a stone of some particular shape, but no such
stone is known here now.

Cʜᴀʀғᴏʀᴅ

> (*of*) *cyric forda* c. 970 BCS 1247[1]
> *Chereforda* 1086 DB
> *Churcheford* 1412 *Ass* (p), *Churforde* 1426 DA 45, *Chirche-*
> *ford* 1543 *Recov*

Probably 'church-ford,' i.e. perhaps 'ford on the way to the
church' (cf. Ekwall, *Studies* 40).

Cᴏʀʀɪɴɢᴅᴏɴ (6″) and Cᴏʀʀɪɴɢᴅᴏɴ Bᴀʟʟ

> *Correndon* 1284 *Add*, *Correndon Ball* 1575 *Deed*, 1805 *Recov*
> *Corndon* 1288 Orig (p), 1292 *Add*, 1306 *Ass* (p), *Corndon al.*
>   *Coringdon* 1561 *Add*
> *Curndon* 1291 *Add*

In the last reference given there is mention also of a *Curnbroke*
(1291) and *Corndich* (1297), both in this locality. For the interpretation, *v. s.n.* Cornwood *supra* 268. For *ball, v. supra* 211.

---

[1] The identification is not certain as most of the places mentioned in this
manumission are in the neighbourhood of Tavistock.

CUTTLEFORD (6″) is *Cotelaforde* 1297 DA 45, *Coteleford* 1333 *SR* (p), 1339 *Ass* (p). '*Cottela*'s ford.' This pers. name is not recorded, but would be a regular *l*-derivative of OE *Cotta*. Cf. Cotleigh *infra* 625. Alternatively the name may be a triple compound of cot(e), leah, and ford.

DIDWORTHY [didəvər] is *Duddewrth(e)* 13th Buckfast (p), 1238 *Ass* (p), *Dodeworthi* 1333 *SR* (p). '*Dudda*'s worþig.' For the modern vowel, *v*. Introd. xxxiv.

DOWNSTOW is *Duntestorr*' 1238 *Ass* (p), *Dountestorr*' 1330 *SR* (p), *Dunstorre* 1464 DA 45, *Downster* 1724 *Recov*. '*Dunt*'s torr.' This pers. name is not actually found, but seems to be the first element of Dunsfold (Sr), *Duntesfolde* 1291 Tax, *Dontesfold* 1303 Ch and Duntisbourne (Gl), 1102 *Dontesborne* PN Gl 56. For the modern form cf. Winstow *infra* 480.

ELWELL is *Enewell* 1201 FF, *Ellewill* 1306 *Ass*, 1333 *SR* (p), *Enwell* 1427 IpmR. 'Elder-tree spring,' *v*. ellen, wielle.

GINGAFORD (6″) [giŋgəfəd] is *Geyngford* 1330 *SR* (p). The first element is possibly the word discussed under Gingerland *infra* 556.

HARBOURNEFORD is *Herberneford(a)* 1086 DB (Exon), 1176 P, *Hurburneford* 1238 *Ass*, 1279 DA 45 (p), *-berne-* 1242 Fees 782, 1326 Ipm, *Northhurberneford* 1345 *Ass*. 'Ford over the Harbourne river,' *v*. *supra* 7.

PALSTONE is *Pallyngeston* 1270 *Ass*, *Pallingston* 1298 *Add*. '*Palling*'s farm,' *v*. tun. This pers. name appears as the first element of Paddenswick[1] (Mx), *Palyngewyk* 1270 FF, *Pallyngeswyk* 1380 BM, Pat, *Palyngeswyke* 1487 Ipm and is recorded as *Palinc* in a Lincs Assize Roll of 1219.

PENNATON (6″) is *Pynnaton* 1292 *Add*, 1340 *Ass* (p), *Pynaton* 1330 *SR* (p), *Pin(n)aton* 1422 DA 45. '*Pinna*'s farm,' *v*. tun. The pers. name *Pinna* may be inferred from *pinnan rode* KCD 967. Cf. also Pinner PN Mx 69.

STIDSTON is *Stidewardesdoune* 1309 Exon (p), *-ton* 1410 BM, *Stitewardeston(e)* 1310 Exon (p), 1333 *SR* (p), *Styddeston* 1489 BM. '*Stiþweard*'s tun.'

---

[1] Now Ravenscourt Park.

STIPPADON is *Stibeton* 1333 *SR* (p), *Stybedon* 1443 *Ct* (p). This is probably from OE *stybbatūn* or *stybbadūn*, 'farm' or 'hill of the stumps.' Cf. Stibb *supra* 96.

BEARA[1], CHAPEL (6″), FORDER (6″), HORSEBROOK and LEIGH GRANGE were the homes of Isabella *atte Beare* (1330 *SR*), Richard *atte Chapele* (1333 *SR*), William de *la Forde* (1279 *Add*), Cristina de *Horsbrok* (1330 *SR*) and Hugo de *la Ley* (1297 *Add*). *v.* bearu, broc, leah.

AISH is *Esse* 1280, *Ayshe* 1599 *Add.* BADWORTHY [bædəvə] is *Bad(e)worth(y)* 1291 *Add*, 1417 *Ct*, -*thi* 1347 *SR* (p), *Westbadworthie al. Baddaford* 1569 *Add.* 'Bada's worþig.' BINNAMORE is *Bynnemore* 14th *Add.* 'Bynna's mor.' BLACK TOR is *la Blaketor*' 1291 *Add.* BRENT HILL is *Brentedone* 1374 Exon. BRENT MOOR is *Brentamore, Mora de Brenta* 1240 Buckfast. BROAD MOOR (6″) is *Bradamore* 1650 *Recov.* DOCKWELL is *Docwille* 1294 *Ass* (p), *Dockwell* 1347 *SR* (p). 'Spring where dock grows.' GISPERDOWN [gispədɑun] (6″) is *Gispdowne* 1664 *Recov.* KERSWILL is *Karswill* 1285 FA, *Carswell* 1306 *Ass* (p). 'Cress spring.' LINCOMBE is *Lyncombe* 1306 *Ass* (p), 1478 BM, *Lincoumbe* 1315 *FF*, *Lynecomb* 1330 *SR* (p). *v.* Addenda *supra* lviii. LISBURNE is *Lesborne* 1333 *SR* (p). *v.* burna. The first element may be OE læs, 'pasture.' LUTTON is *Lodeton* 1289 DA 45, *Ludeton* 1296 *Add.* Perhaps 'Luda's farm,' *v.* tun. MOORE is *La More* 1297 *Add*, *Estmore* 1559 DA 45. SHIPLEY BRIDGE is *Schepelegh* 1291 *Add*, *Shiplegh juxta Overa Brenta* 1304 *Ass.* 'Sheep clearing,' *v.* leah. THYNACOMBE BARN (6″) is *Thenacombe* 1284 *Add*, *Thynna-* 1560 DA 45. Possibly 'thin valley,' cf. Thinwood (Co), *Thynnewode* 1289 *Ass.* TREELAND (6″) is *Treuwelond* 1306 *Ass* (p), *Trewland* 1312 DA 45, *Treawelond* 1330 *SR* (p). 'Tree-covered land.' WEBLAND (6″) is *Wibbalonde* 1297 *Add*, *Wybbelonde* 1330 *SR* (p). 'Wibba's land.' WONTON is *Wondeton* 1333 *SR* (p). YALLAND is *la Yoldelande* 1291 *Add*, *Yollelonde* 1330 *SR* (p). Cf. Addenda *supra* lviii. ZEAL is *Sele* 1279 *Add. v.* sele.

[1] *la Beare* 1291 *Add.*

Buckfastleigh

BUCKFASTLEIGH [bʌkfəst'li·] 145 A 4

Legh 1286 *SR*, *Leghe Bu(c)festre* 13th Buckfast, 1310 Exon
Bucfasteneslegh 1306 *Ass*, *Boc-*, *Bok-* 1314 *Ass*, *Bucfastenlegh*
1353 Ch
Bokfastlegh(e) 1334 *SR*, *Buc-* 1349 Exon, *Bukfastley* 1374
Exon
Bookefasteligh 1538 DA 28

The leah in or near Buckfast *infra*. For another name of this
type, cf. Grimpstonleigh *infra* 313.

BUCKFAST

on Bucfæsten 1046 KCD 1334, *Bucfesten*, *-fasten* 13th Buckfast
Bulfestra 1086 DB (Exon), *Bucfestre* (Exch)
Bucfastria 1136 France, *Buch-* 1150 France, *Bucfest'* 1186–90
HMC iv, 55, *Buckfestr'* 1228 id. 66, *Bucfestre* c. 1270 Gerv,
1286 *Ass*, *Buffestr(e)* 1251 Cl, 1263 Exon
Buckefast' 1286 *Ass*, *Bucfast(e)* 1286 *Ass*, 1353 Ch, 1357 Ipm,
-fest 1368, *Bukfast* 1302 Cl
Bugwastene 1292 BM

The name is apparently a compound of OE *buc*, 'buck,' and
fæsten, 'stronghold,' possibly used of a thicket where a *buck*
once took shelter. The *r* is an AN spelling, cf. IPN 106,
strengthened perhaps by the existence of an OE form *fæstern*
side by side with *fæsten*. Cf. The Vasterne on the outskirts of
Reading.

BUTTON (6″) is *Bodetone*, *Boda-*, *Budetune*, *Buddetun* 13th Buckfast, *Bodeton* 1276 RH, 1318 BM, *Boddeton* 1276 Ipm and perhaps
takes its name from the family of Theobald *Budde* mentioned in
the Buckfast Cartulary (f. 236).

CHALK FORD (6″) is *Chelkeford* 1474 Ct, *Chalkford gate* 1571
DuCo. There is no chalk here, but the forms are late and may
possibly go back to an OE *cealfloc(a) ford*, 'ford by the calf
enclosure.' Cf. Challock (K) *æt cealflocan* 833 BCS 412.

COLSTON is *Couleton* 1345 DA 28, *-la-* 1400 BM, *Cowla-* 1558–79
ECP, *Coleton in parochia de Bukfastlegh* 1463 FF and perhaps
takes its name from the family of Thomas *Cole* mentioned in
1345 (DA 28). *v.* tun.

HAWSON COURT is *Hosefenne* 13th Buckfast, 1314 *Ass*, 1343 BM. *v*. fenn. The first element may be the genitive plural of OE *hōs*, 'short tendril,' cf. the pers. name *atte Hose* (1314 *Ass*) and *aqua vocata Hosebrok* (1345 *Ass*). This latter stream-name is a parallel to Hurstbourne (Ha), *Hysseburna* (BCS 553) and *hyssa pol* (BCS 595) from the allied OE *hyse*, 'tendril.' Hence, 'marsh of the tendrils,' referring possibly to some marsh-plant.

KILBURY HO (6″) is *Killebiria* t. Hy 2 Oliver 135, -*byry* 13th Buckfast, -*byre* 1242 Fees 771, *Kyllebery*, *Kilebyre* 13th Buckfast, *Kellebir'* 1275 RH, *Kilebury juxta Bokfasteneslegh* 1314 *Ass*. '*Cylla*'s burh.'

LAMBS DOWN. In the Buckfast Cartulary (13th) the valley below is referred to as *Lambescumbe*, *Lombescumbe*, *Lomescome*. The singular form shows that we have to do with a 13th cent. owner rather than with the animal. For the spellings with *o*, cf. Lamerton *supra* 149, Lambscombe *infra* 345.

PUPERS HILL[1] is *Popaburghe* 1240, *Pubbaburga* 13th Buckfast, *Poweburghys forest* 1481 Ct, *Puppers* 1809 M. '*Pubba*'s burh.' Cf. Publow (So), *Pubbelowe* 1258, 1308 FF.

SCORRITON is *Scoriaton(e)* 13th Buckfast, 1292 BM, 1346 FA, *Scoryaton juxta Bukfast* 1294 *Ass*. The first element is difficult, it may be a pers. name as in Scarhill *infra* 449. Alternatively, as the place is on a steep hillside, we may have the element noted under Score *supra* 47. For the medial *ia*, *v*. Introd. xxxv.

SNOWDON (hill) is *Snoudon* 1238, 1244 *Ass*, *Snowdon* 1384 *DuCo*. The name may have arisen from some occasion when the hill was specially deep in snow or because the snow lies specially late here. Cf. the same name 311 *infra*.

WALLAFORD is *Walleworthe* 13th Buckfast, -*th(i)* 1285 FA, *Waldeworth(y)* 1346 FA, *Walwrthy* 1326 Ipm, *Walworthie al. Walford* t. Eliz *LRMB* 191. The forms of the first element vary too widely for any solution to be possible.

COMBE and FORDER (6″) were the homes of Richard de *Cumbe* (13th Buckfast) and John de *la Forde* (1244 *Ass*).

AUSTIN'S BRIDGE is to be associated with the family of William

---

[1] *Puppers Hill* (old 1″).

Austyn (1330 *SR*). BIGADON HO is *Byketon* 1333 *SR* (p),
Bigadon 1636 *FF*. Cf. Bickaton *infra* 509. BOSSELLPARK (6″) is
Borshill t. Eliz *LRMB*, cf. Boasley *supra* 174. BOWDEN (6″) is
Steneneboghedon juxta Bocfasteneslegh 1314 *Ass*, *Bowedon* 1463
FF. 'Stony curved hill,' cf. Bowden and Stenhill *supra* 37, 160.
BOWERDON is *Bowrton* 1550 *AOMB*, *Bowerton* 1680 *Recov.*
BRAMBLEBY (6″) is *Bremelby* t. Hy 8 Dartmoor. The second
element is the OE word *byge* discussed under Huccaby *supra*
194. BROOK HO is *Broke* 1463 *FF*. BUCKFASTLEIGH MOOR is
Bukfastmore 1240 Buckfast. BURCHETTS WOOD (6″), cf. *Byrcherd
Parke, Byrgerd Ball* t. Hy 8 Dartmoor. CULLAFORD (6″) is *Colle-
forde* 1344 BM. *v.* Collacott *supra* 50. FULLAFORD (6″) is
Fouleforde 13th Buckfast, *Fuleford* 1244 *Ass*. 'Dirty ford,' *v.* ful.
GREENDOWN (6″) is *Grendon* 1596 DKR 38, 360. *v.* dun. HAP-
STEAD is *Hapstrete* 1600 *SR*. For interchange of stede and stræt,
cf. True Street *infra* 506. HAYFORD is *Hayforde* 1463 *FF*. HEM-
BURY CASTLE is *vetus castellum quod dicitur Hembire* 13th Buckfast. Probably OE (*æt þære*) *hēan byrig*, 'at the high burh.' There
is an ancient camp here. HIGHER TOWN and LOWER TOWN (6″)
are *le hyer towne, Lower towne* t. Eliz *LRMB*. HOCKMOOR (6″)
is *Howkemer wood* t. Hy 8 Dartmoor. LAKEMOOR (6″) is *Lake
more* 1613 *FF*. *v.* lacu. MERRIFIELD (6″) is *Meryfyld* 1563 DA
31, *Merifeild* 1661 *Recov*. *v.* Merrivale *supra* 247. NEWPARK (6″)
is *Neweparke* t. Hy 8 Dartmoor. NORTHWOOD is *Northwoode* t.
Hy 8 Dartmoor. RILL is *Rill* t. Jas 1 ECP. Probably ME *at ther
hille*, 'at the hill,' cf. Rill *infra* 606. WARMMACOMBE (6″) is *Werme-
cumbe* 13th Buckfast, *Warmecombe* 1474 *Ct*, 1618 BM. 'The
warm combe,' cf. *wearman dene* BCS 1282.

Churchstow

CHURCHSTOW [tʃəˑstou] 145 G 3

> *Churechestowe* 1242 Fees 767, *Churicstowe* 1291 Tax
> *Chyristowe* 1244 *Ass*, *Chyre-* 1281 *Ass*, *Chirstowe Sancte
> Marie juxta Kyngesbrigge* 1379 Exon
> *Churestowe* 1276 RH, 1308 Exon, *Churstowe juxta Aveton
> Giffard* 1318 *Ass*
> *Chirchstowe* 1297 Pat
> *Churche Stoke* 1459 BM, *Chestow* 1577 Saxton

The name is a compound of OE cirice and stow.

COMBE ROYAL is *Cumbe* 1086 DB, *Cumb Ruel* 1303 FA, *Ruwel-cumbe* 1282 Pat. Further forms for the manorial addition are *Regis* 1346 FA, *Riall* 1368 IpmR, *Real* 1369 Cl, *Roiel* 1387 Cl, *Rouell* 1423 IpmR, *Ryall* 1428 FA. In 1346 (FA) Hugo de Cheverestone held the manor and it is stated that one 'Willelmus *Royel* quondam tenuit.'

ELSTON is *Aylleston(e)* 1312 *FF*, 1357 Ipm, *Ayleston juxta Kyngesbrigge* 1360 *FF*, *Ayleston* 1423 IpmR. '*Ægel*'s farm,' *v.* tun.

LEIGH is *Lega* 1086 DB, *Leghe* 1200 Cur, *Legh Tuzseyns* 1267 *Ass*, *Lecch All Saints* 1297 Ipm, *Alhalghenelegh* 1377 HMC xv, App. 7, *Alhalwenlegh* 1393 *FF*. *v.* leah. There was formerly a small monastic cell here attached to Buckland abbey. Hence, 'All Saints' or 'All Hallows.'

RAKE is *Rak(e)* 1228 FF (p), 1242 Fees 776, 1373 Exon. It is probably the OE *hraca*, 'throat,' used topographically as in *andlang cumbes hracan* (BCS 970). *v.* also EDD. The farm lies at the point where the Avon valley narrows.

SORLEY[1] is *Sueordleage (wælle)* 947 BCS 451, *(æt) swurdleage, swurdleg (wyll)* 962, Thorndon Hall Charter, *Surleia* 1086 DB, *-legh* 1242 Fees 776, 1249 *Ass*, 1284 *Ass*, *Sourlegh* 1284 *Ass*, *Sor-* 1285 FA. The name must be a compound of OE *sweord*, 'sword' and leah, but the meaning of such a place-name is obscure. Cf. Swaddicott *supra* 110, and for the early loss of *w*, cf. Sourton *supra* 206.

WARCOMBE is *Worcumbe* 1228 FF, *Wercumb* 1238 FF, *Ass*, 1249 *Ass* (p), 1316 FA, *Warcumbe* 1238 *Ass*, *Werecumbe* 1244 *Ass*, *Werecumbe juxta Alvyngton* 1345 *Ass*. 'Weir valley,' *v.* wer, cumb. The place lies near the Avon.

CULVERWELL (6") is *Culverwell, Culvereswyll* 1244 *Ass* (p), *Colverewill* 1333 *SR* (p). 'Dove-spring,' *v.* culfre, wielle.

---

[1] In DA 61, 250 Mrs Rose-Troup prints a hitherto unknown Anglo-Saxon charter of Edgar, preserved at Thorndon Hall, Essex. It is a grant of land in a place called *æt swurdleage*. The boundaries are difficult to follow but they include *cingesbricge* (Kingsbridge), a river called *afne* (dat.) (the Avon *supra* 1) and *beoccan bricge* which may well have been near Bickham *infra* 304, as they contain the same personal name. See also 264 *supra*.

HOLDITCH (6″) is *Holedich* 1244 *Ass* (p), *Holdich* 1289 DA 45 (p). 'Hollow ditch,' *v.* holh, dic. MERRIFIELD is *Meriafeld* 1283 DA 45, *Mirifelde* 1330 *SR* (p), *Myrefelde* 1414 *FF*. 'Pleasant open space,' *v.* Merrivale *supra* 247. NUCKWELL is *Nokewille* 1414 *FF*, *Nochwell* 1520 DA 45. Perhaps ME (*att*)*en oke wille*, 'at the oak spring.' OSBORNE NEWTON is *Niweton* 1244 *Ass* (p), *Nywe-* 1414 *FF*, *Osborne Newton* or *Newton* 1823 *Recov*, and takes its distinctive prefix from the family of George *Osburne* (1672 *SR*). VENN is *Fenne* t. Ed i BM, *le Fenne* 1394 *Ass*. *v.* fenn.

Dartington

DARTINGTON 145 B 5

> *Derentunehomm* 833 (c. 1400) BCS 410
> *Dertrintona* 1086 DB, *Dertinton(ia)* 1162–5 Totnes *et freq* to 1282 Ipm with variant spelling *-ing-*
> *Derdington*' 1176 P

'Farm on the river Dart' (*supra* 4). For the *homm* in the earliest form, *v. s.n.* South Hams *supra* 264. There is a great bend (*v.* hamm) in the Dart here but the context in which the form *Derentunehomm* occurs hardly allows of our taking the name to refer to this.

COPLAND is *Coperenesland* 1333 *SR* (p), *Coppislond* 1505 Ipm, *Coperislond* 1548 Pat. The first form is probably an error for *Copeneresland* with the same family name *Copenere* noted under Cadbury Barton *infra* 377.

HOOD is *Hode* 1183 P (p) *et freq* to 1326 Ipm, *Hoode* 1372 *FF*. It is OE *hōd*, 'hood,' and must have referred to the curious shape of the hill near the farm, now called Hood Ball (*v.* 211 *supra*).

TIGLEY is *Tiggele*, *Tiggelegh* 1399 *Ct*. '*Tigga*'s leah.'' This pers. name is not recorded, but might be a pet form of an OE name such as *Tīdgār*.

YARNER is *Yornere* 1333 *SR* (p), *Yerner* 1399 *Ct*, *Yearner* t. Ed 6 *Rental*. Possibly 'Eagle slope or bank,' *v.* ora. Cf. Yarner *supra* 56.

ALLERTON is *Alreton* 1330 *SR* (p), *Allerton* t. Ed 6 *Rental*. 'Alder farm,' *v.* alor, tun. BELLEIGH is *Bealdelegh* 1330 *SR* (p), *Bealle-* 1333 *SR* (p). '*Bealda*'s leah,' cf. Bellamarsh *infra* 479. BILLANY

(6″) is *Byllynghaghe* 1333 *SR* (p), *Bellynghey* 1550 Pat. '*Billa*'s enclosure,' *v.* ing, (ge)hæg. BROOK is *Browking* 1550 Pat, *Brokyn* 1563 *FF*. COBBERTON (6″) is *Cobeton(e)* 1313 HMC iii, 343, 1333 *SR*, *Cobbeton* 1327 *Ass*, 1330 *SR* (all p). '*Cobba*'s farm,' *v.* tun. COXSLAKE (6″) is *Cokkyslak* 1330 *SR* (p), *Cokkeslake* 1333 *SR* (p), *Cokyslake* t. Ed 6 *Rental*. 'Cock's streamlet' or '*Cocc*'s streamlet,' *v.* lacu. DRORIDGE (6″) is *Dryerugge* 1330 *SR* (p), *Drierig*' 1399 *Ct*. 'Dry ridge.' HUXHAM'S CROSS is to be associated with the family of *Huxham* found in Harberton in 1563 and in Totnes in 1709 (Wills). They must have come from Huxham *infra* 443. NORTH WOOD (6″) is *Northe wood* 1550 *AOMB* 431. PETOE (6″) is *Paytow* 1399 *Ct* and is to be associated with Thomas de *Peyto* (1319 Exon), who presumably came from Poitou (France). PUDDAVEN is *Podefenne* 1330 *SR* (p), 1365 *Ass*, -*fen* 1399 *Ct*. '*Pud(d)a*'s or *Pod(d)a*'s marshy spot,' *v.* fenn. REDLAKE CROSS (6″) is *Redelake* t. Ed 6 *Rental*. *v.* lacu. SHINNERS BRIDGE is to be associated with the family of John *Shynner* (1581 *SR*). STAPLE is *Stapell, Staple* t. Ed 6 *Rental*. *v.* stapol. VENTON is *Fenton* 1242 Fees 781, 1303 FA. 'Marshy farm,' *v.* fenn, tun. WEEK is *Wike* 1399 *Ct, Weke* t. Ed 6 *Rental* and was the home of Sarra *atte Wyke* (1330 *SR*). *v.* wic. WESTCOMBE is *Wascombe* 1330 *SR* (p), 1551 *Deeds Enrolled*, t. Ed 6 *Rental, Waysshcombe* 1551 *Deeds Enrolled, Washecombe* t. Ed 6 *Rental*. 'Sheepwash valley,' *v.* (ge)wæsc, cumb.

Dean Prior

DEAN PRIOR 145 B 3

> *Dena* 1086 DB, *La Dene* 1244 FF, *Dene Prioris* 1316 FA, *Dene Pryour* 1415 Exon, *Niderdenam* t. Hy 2 Oliver 135, *Nitheredene* 1242 Fees 781, *Netherden* 1326 Ipm
> *Over(e)dene* 1242 Fees 781, 1244 FF

v. denu. The manor was held from the 11th cent. by the priors of Plympton Priory. *Over* Dean must refer to the part of Dean around the church, *Nether* Dean to the place now called simply Dean, in the valley below. *v.* neoðera.

SKERRATON

> *Siredona* 1086 DB
> *Scyredun, Schiredon* 1212 Fees 98, *Sciredune* 1244 Fees 1386, *Sciredon* t. Hy 3 Dartmoor, *Shyradon* 1425 Pat

Skiredon 1228 Cl, *Skyredon* 1248 Ipm, 1320 Ipm, *-dun'* 1250
Fees 1250, *Skyrredon* 1320 Ipm, *Skyredon yeate* t. Hy 6 *Ct*,
Skeredon 1466 Pat, *Skyrdonyeate* 1481 *Ct*

This is probably a compound of OE scir (adj.) and dun.
Hence, 'bright hill.' For the initial *sk*, *v.* Introd. xxxv. Cf.
Burngullow (Co), *Brongolou* 1296 *Ass*, *Bronwolou* 1311 AD iv
and *Bren-golou* Chrest 191 with the same meaning (cf. W *goleu*,
'bright, light').

ADDISLADE is *Tadyeslade* 1306 *Ass* (p), *Tadiaslad* 1310 *FF*,
Addeslade 1587 *Recov*. 'Toad valley,' *v.* slæd. For loss of initial
t, cf. Arracott *supra* 208. BARRALL'S COTTAGE (6″) may be
identical with *Berehill* 1460 *FF*. 'Barley hill,' *v.* bere. DEAN-
COMBE is *Dencomb* t. Hy 6 *Ct*, *Denecome* 1481 *Ct*, *v.* denu, cumb.
MOORS HEAD (6″) is *Morisheaved* 1340 *SR* (p), *Moryshede* 1460
FF. The *moor* (*v.* mor) is that referred to in *Morlaund juxta
Overedene* 1291 *Ass*. NURSTON is *Nuston* 1593 DA 26. SMALL-
COMBE (6″) was the home of Henry de *Smalecomb* (1330 *SR*).
'Narrow valley,' *v.* smæl, cumb. TORDEAN is *Tordeane* 1566
Recov and is to be associated with John de *la Torre* (1286 *Ass*).
v. torr. VENN BRIDGE CROSS, cf. *Venvorda* 1312 Exon. *v.* fenn,
ford. ZEMPSON is *Siweneston* 1340 *SR* (p), *Sempeston* 1593 DA
26. '*Sigewine*'s tun,' cf. Simpson *infra* 301.

Diptford

DIPTFORD [dipfəd] 145 D 3/4
Depeforda 1086 DB *et freq* to 1428 FA, *Diepeford'* 1230 P
Dupeford 1267 Ipm, *Duppe-* 1303 FA, 1385 Pat, *Dup-* 1306
FA
Ditford 1671 *Recov*
'Deep ford,' over the Avon. Cf. Deptford (K).

BEENLEIGH
Benleia 1086 DB, *-legh* 1242 Fees 766, 790
Beneleg' 1219 *Ass*
Bunelee 1238 *Ass* (p)
Binnelegh 1244 *Ass* (p), *Bine-* 1276 Ipm, *Bynne-* 1311 *Ass* (p),
1330 *SR* (p), 1495 Ipm, *Byne-* 1377 Cl
This name must clearly be taken with Beneknowle *infra* 301,

one mile to the east. It is difficult to be certain about the names. The forms perhaps favour OE *bēona*, 'of the bees,' rather than *Bynna(n)* from the pers. name *Bynna*, but on the other hand adjacent places are more likely to have been named from one man than from bees. *v.* leah.

CRABADON is *Crabbeton* 1306 *Ass*, 1330 *SR* (both p). 'Crab apple farm,' *v.* tun, and cf. Crabbet (PN Sx 281).

CURTISKNOWLE

>   *Cortescanola* 1086 DB, -*knoll* 1285 FA, 1325 Cl
>   *Curtescnolle* 1242 Fees 795, -*knolle* 1297 FF
>   *Courtescnolle* 1242 Fees 766, -*knoll* 1303 FA, -*cnoll* 1322 Misc
>   *Goosnoll al. Courtesknoll* 1767 Recov

'*Curt*'s hill,' *v.* cnoll. This pers. name is not recorded but would correspond to the weak *Curta* or *Corta* found in Corburn (PN NRY 14), and Courteenhall (Nth) *Cortenhale* DB, 1195 P, *Curtehala* 1316 Ch. Cf. also Coursehill Fm (O) *Curteshull* (1328 Ch) and a lost *Curteshale* in Rowington (Wa), *Curteshale* c. 1250 *Harl* 1708.

FARLEIGH is *Ferleia* 1086 DB, *Fernlegh* 1279 Ipm. 'Bracken clearing,' *v.* fearn, leah.

GARA BRIDGE is *Garebridge* c. 1550 Leland. Close at hand is GARA LAND (6″) in N. Huish parish. Both alike must be connected with Dionis' de *Gare* (1333 *SR*), *v.* gara. This may have referred to the angle of land in the Avon valley here. The phonology is difficult. One would have expected ME *gore* in 1333 in Devon. The *a* in the compounds Gara Bridge and Land might be due to early shortening of the vowel before it developed to *o*.

HOLSOME is *Haulesham* 1244 *Ass* (p), *Holsome* 1593 *SR*, and may involve an OE pers. name *Hagol*. *v.* ham(m).

LAPLAND BARN (6″) is *Lappelond(e)* 1303 FA, 1330 *SR* (p). The first element may be the OE *læppa*, 'piece, portion, section, etc.,' but the exact sense of the compound is not clear. One has also to bear in mind the possibility of the unexplained first element found in Lapworth (Wa), *Hlappawurþin* BCS 356.

TENNATON (6″) is *Tuneton* 1244 *Ass* (p), 1244 Fees 1386, 1276 RH. '*Tun(n)a*'s tun.'

WAGLAND (6″) is *Wagelond* 1303 FA, *Wagghe-* 1303 FA, *Wagge-* 1346 FA, 1431 *FF*, *Waghe-* 1356 *Ass*. The first element is probably allied to that discussed under Warne *supra* 201. Cf. the relation of ME *waggen* to ME *wawen* from OE *wagian*. There is a stream here and some marshy land.

CHAPPLELANDS (6″), CLEAVE and STERT were the homes of Walter atte *Chapele* (1330 *SR*), John *atte Clyve* (1394 *Ass*) and Richard de *la Sturte* (1244 *Ass*). *v.* clif, steort.

ASHWELL is *Assewyll* 1244 *Ass*, 1244 Fees 1386, *Asswelle* 1275 RH. 'Spring by the ash,' *v.* wielle. BENEKNOWLE is *Bineknoll* 1330, *Buneknolle* 1333 *SR* (p). *v.* Beenleigh *supra* 299. BLACKWELL (6″) is *Blackewill* 1581 *SR*. 'Dark spring,' *v.* wielle. BRADRIDGE HO is possibly identical with *Brodech juxta Dupeford* 1303 *Ass*, *Brodeache* 1306 *Ass* (p), *Brodeche* 1320 *Ass* (p). 'Wide oak,' cf. Whitnage, Bradninch *infra* 553, 555. COOMBE (6″) and COMBESHEAD CROSS are *Combe*, *Comshed* 1576 *SR*, *Combshed* 1648 *Recov*. CREBER (6″) is *Crowbere*, *Croubere*, *Crowberewe* 1281 *Ass*. 'Crow wood,' *v.* Crebor *supra* 218. FROGWELL is *Frogwyll* 1518 *Recov*. HORNER is *Horner* 1244 Fees 1386, 1244 *Ass*, *Hornore*, *Horn'e* 1275 RH. *v.* horn, ora. The place is on a hill slope near a slight spur of land. LARCOMBE is *Levercombe* 1228 FF, *Leverecome* 1296 *Ass* (p). 'Wild iris valley,' *v.* læfer, cumb. MURTWELL is *Mortewill* 1330 *SR* (p). *v.* Morthoe *supra* 52. NEWHOUSE (6″) is so spelt 1671 *Recov*. NEW WELL (6″) is *Newell* 1671 *Recov*. SIMPSON is *Siwineston* 1244 *Ass* (p), *Symyston* 1394 *Ass*. '*Sigewine*'s tun,' cf. Zempson *supra* 299. TRIMSWELL (6″) is probably to be associated with the family of Lucia de *Tunemanneswell* mentioned in connexion with Diptford in 1244 *Ass*. WATERGATE is *Wateryett* 1671 *Recov*.

Holne

HOLNE [houl] 138 J 3

> *Holla* 1086 DB
> *Holne, -a* 1166 RBE *et passim* to 1413 IpmR, *Olna* 1175, 1176
>   P, (*Abbatis*) 1276 Ipm, (*Buzun*) 1285 FA, *Sutholne* 13th
>   Buckfast, *Northholne* 1408 IpmR
> *Holme* 1211 RBE, 1384 Pat

Hunne 1219 Fees 265, *Hounne* 1242 Fees 778, 1243 FF,
(*Ergiuleys*) 1242 Fees 778
Holle 1423 Exon, 1481 *Ct*, *Holl* 1535 VE, *Hole al. Holne* 1714
Recov

'Place abounding in holly,' *v.* holegn. William *Buzun* held
one of the manors in 1242 (Fees). Other parts of the manor were
held by Buckfast Abbey and the family of *Urgeleys* or *Ergiuleys*
(Buckfast 126, 1303 FA, Ch).

COMBESTONE [kʌmstən] is *Comereston* 1333 *SR* (p), *Comerston*
1347 *SR* (p), 1474 *Ct*, *Comberstone* 1702 Dartmoor, *Cumston*
1809 M. The first element may be a ME surname *Comere*, of
nickname origin. The second may be either stan or tun. Hence,
'*Comer's* farm' or 'stone.' Cf. John *le Comere* (1316 Pat) in Stoke
Gabriel parish *infra* and Comber's Cross *supra* 122.

GALLANT LE BOWER is *Gallant Bower* 1809 M. Cf. *Gallants
Bower* 1758 *Recov*, apparently in Exminster parish. Gallant
Bower and Gallantry Bower are names occurring elsewhere in
England, possibly referring to secluded spots suitable for lovers'
meeting-places. 'Gallant Le' may be a corruption of 'Gallantry.'
Miss Lega-Weekes, however, has shown (DA 61, 237) that
Gallants Bower in Dartmouth, though spelt *Gallante's Bower* in
1646, was earlier *Galions Boure* (1463 *Pat*). This suggests that
in some cases, at least where the name occurs on the coast, we
may have reference to some secluded spot which gave shelter to
galleons or other ships.

STOKE is *Estocha* 1086 DB (Exon), *Stoche* (Exch). *v.* stoc(c).

BENJIE TOR is *Benchey* t. Eliz DA 28. HOLNE MOOR is *Sow-
tholnemore* 13th Buckfast. LANGAFORD (6″) is *Langeforde* 13th
Buckfast. LITTLECOMBE is *Lytlecombe* 1544 *Deeds Enrolled*.
MICHELCOMBE [mʌtʃikəm] is *Michelcombe* 1408 IpmR, 1481 *Ct*.
'Big valley,' *v.* micel, cumb. RIDGE CROSS (6″) is *Byridge* 1629
DA 31. 'By the ridge.' SHUTTAFORD is *Suteforde* 13th Buckfast,
Shuttaford 1711 *FF*. *v.* Shute *supra* 184. It is in the extreme
south-east corner of the parish. STADDICOMBE (6″) is *Stotte-
cumbe* 1292 Ipm, *Stuttecombe* 1420 IpmR. 'Bullocks' valley,' *v.*
stott, cumb. STEART (6″) was the home of John *atte Sturte* (1333
SR). *v.* steort. STOODLEY is *Stodlega* 13th Buckfast. *v.* stod,
leah. WOTTON (6″) is *Wotton* 1330 *SR* (p). 'Wood farm,' *v.* tun.

North Huish

NORTH HUISH 145 D 3

> *Hewis* 1086 DB, *Hiwiss'* 1242 Fees 795, *Hywysh* 1291 Tax,
> *Hewysshe* 1364 Exon, *Northywys* 1285 FA

v. hiwisc. *North* to distinguish from South Huish *infra* 304.

AVON WICK is on the Avon but the name is modern and was coined c. 1878. The spot was earlier called *Newhouse* (*ex inf.* Mr J. J. Alexander). .

BROADLEY is *Bradeleia* 1086 DB, *-legh* 1242 Fees 766. 'Wide clearing,' *v.* brad, leah.

BUTTERFORD is *Botreforda* 1086 DB, *Buterford* 1242 Fees 776, *Boter-* 1303 FA. *v.* Buttercombe *supra* 40.

COLMER is *Colemor(e)* 1242 Fees 780, 1328 *Ass* (p). '*Cola's* mor.' Possibly this was the same man who held the manor of Lupridge TRE (DB f. 397).

LUPRIDGE

> *Olperiga, Luperiga, Kluperiga, Loperige* 1086 DB
> *Luperige* 1242 Fees 769
> *Loperige* 1242 Fees 780, *-rigg* 1341 Ipm, *Lopruge* 1309 Ch
> *Lopperigge* 1290 Oliver 299, 1301 Ipm
> *Lupperugge* 1303 FA, *-rygge* 1303 Misc

Professor Ekwall and Dr Ritter agree in suggesting a pers. name *Hluppa* as the first element in the name. Hence, '*Hluppa's* ridge,' *v.* hrycg.

PENSON is *Payneston* 1334, 1340, 1377 *SR*, 1379 IpmR, *Payns-* c. 1430 *Ct*, *Painson* t. Jas 1 ECP. The first element looks like the French pers. name *Payn(e)*, though this family has not been noted in connexion with the place.

RUTHERFORD (lost) is *Ruthereford* 1334 DA 28, *Rotheraford*, *Rotherneforde* 1343 BM *Rotherneford al. Rotherford in North Huish* 1536 Deed, *Rutherforde combe* 1812 Recov. 'Cattle ford,' *v.* hryðer.

WHEELDON (6")

> Whiueldon 1249 Ass (p), Wheveldon 1437 IpmR
> Werheldon 1322 Ass (p), 1330 SR (p)
> Wiheldon 1499 Ipm, Whyledon 1520 BM, Wheldon al. Whevel-
> don 1614 Deed

'Circular hill,' v. hwyrfel, dun. Cf. Hurlditch supra 185.

COMBE (6") and LEY were the homes of Nicholas de Combe and Roger atte Leye (1333 SR), v. cumb, leah.

BICKHAM BRIDGE is Bykecomb 1330 SR (p), Bykcome in North Hewys 1392 IpmR. 'Beoc(c)a's cumb,' v. supra 296 n. BLACK HALL is la Blakehale 1238 Ass (p), -halle 1330, 1333 SR (p), 1362 Ass. The earliest form suggests that the original second element was healh. FORD (6") is Forde 1453 FF. HART'S WOOD (6") is to be associated with the family of Henry Hert (1571 SR). HASWELL is Halswall 1299 Ass (p), Halsewyll 1515–18 ECP 5, 162. Probably 'hazel spring,' v. hæsel, wielle. HAWKERIDGE COPSE (6") is Haukerig 1350 Ipm, Hawkridge 1602 AD v. NORRIS is Norreis c. 1630 Pole, Norris 1670 FF and is to be associated with the family of John Noreys (1333 SR). WHETCOMBE is Wetecomb 1330 SR (p), Whetcombe 1594 Recov. 'Wheat valley,' v. cumb.

South Huish

SOUTH HUISH 145 H 2

> Heuis 1086 DB, Hywis 1242 Fees 766, Suthhywish juxta
> Kyngesbrigg' 1302 Ass

> v. supra 303.

GALMPTON [gæmptən]

> Walenimtona 1086 DB (Exon), Walementone (Exch)
> Gamelton' 1231 Cl
> Yalmeton 1238 Ass
> Gaumeton 1242 Fees 795, Galmaton 1244 FF, -me- 1285 FA,
> 1303 FA, 1325 Ipm, Northgalmatone 1304 Ass, Gealmeton
> 1428 FA
> Gaylmington 1281 Ass

This name must be taken together with Galmpton infra 511 and Gammaton and Galmington supra 88, 91, and also with

Galmington and Galhampton (So). For Galmington we have *Galmetone* (1199 FF), *Galameton* (1225 Ass) and for Galhampton *Galampton* (1248 FF). Professor Ekwall suggests that all these names alike go back to an OE *gafolmanna-tūn*, 'farm inhabited by rent-paying peasants.' Cf. OE *gafolswān*, 'rent-paying peasant,' and ME *gavelmanni* recorded in Kent in the 13th cent. (Neilson's *Customary Rents* 8, 42, 44).

BURLEIGH is *Burlegh* 1238 *Ass*, *Borlegh* 1333 *SR* (p), *Bourlegh* 1356 *Ass* (p). *v.* burh, leah. There is an old camp near by.
WITHYMORE (6") is *Widemore* 1238 *Ass* (p), 1242 Fees 764 (p), *Wydi-* 1244 *Ass* (p), *Widi-* 1244 FF, *Wyte-*, *Wythe-* 1249 *Ass*, *Wydya-* 1324 Ipm, *Whithi-* 1330 *SR* (p). *v.* wiðig, mor.

Kingsbridge and Dodbrooke

KINGSBRIDGE (with DODBROOKE) 145 G 4

(*to*) *cinges bricge* 962 Thorndon Hall Charter
Kingesbrig' 1230 P, (*burg' de*) 1244 *Ass*

It is clear that the name goes back to Saxon times, but the exact royal owner is unknown. The bridge was from early times an important one crossing the end of the long creek known as Kingsbridge estuary.

DODBROOKE

Dodebroca 1086 DB (Exon), *-och* (Exch), *Dodebrok(e)* 1276 RH, 1291 Tax, 1412 AD i, *Doddebrok'* 1242 Fees 786, 1249 *Ass*, 1284 FA, *Doddebroke Borwe* 1313 Seld 36, *Dodebrok-burgh* 1395 *FF*
Dud(d)ebroc 1219 FF (p), *Duddebroc* 1219 *Ass*
Dodbroke 1257 Ch

'*Dodda's* brook,' *v.* broc.

ADDLEHOLE (6") is so spelt in 1765 D. Cf. *Addelhole* t. Ed 6 *Rental* (Kenton). The first element may be the OE *adela*, 'dirt, filth.'

CENTRY is *Lydstone al. Centry al. Sentry* 1768 Recov. *Sentry* is a local corruption of 'sanctuary' in the sense of consecrated ground, etc. Cf. St Cherries *infra* 447.

Loddiswell

LODDISWELL [lɔdzwəl] 145 F 3

> *Lodeswilla* 1086 DB *et passim* to 1345 *Ass* with variant
> spellings *-well(e)*, *-will(e)*, *Lodiswell* 1205 FF, *-will'* 1242
> Fees 98
> *Lodgewyll* 1552 *Deed*, *Lodswell* 1684 *Recov*
> *Ladeswill* t. Jas 1 ECP
> '*Lodd*'s spring,' *v*. wielle. Cf. Lodsworth PN Sx 26.

HATCH is *Hach'* 1242 Fees 777, *Hache Arundel* 1260 FF, *Hacche*
1269 Ipm. *v*. hæcc. John de *Arundel* held the manor in 1242
(Fees).

TOPSHAM BRIDGE. This name is probably manorial in origin.
Richard de *Toppesham* held one *ferling* in Loddiswell parish in
1262 (Ch), deriving his name presumably from Topsham *infra*
454. *v*. Addenda *supra* lix, *s.n.* Fardel.

WIGFORD is *Wigewrth* 1249 *Ass*, *Wykewurthy* 1262 Ch, *Wyge-
worth'* 1310 *Ass*, *Wygheworthi* 1330 *SR*, *Wygge-* 1333 *SR* (all p),
Wigford al. Wigworthy 1714 *Recov*. '*Wicga*'s worþig.'

YANSTON is *Youineston, Yeovineston* 13th *Torre, Yeuengeston*
1330 *SR* (p), *Yungeston* 1410 Exon, *Yengestone* 1421 Exon,
Yongeston n.d. Oliver 183 (p), 1475 IpmR, 1493 Ipm, *Yeanston*
1626 *Recov*. Perhaps '*Gefwine*'s farm,' *v*. tun.

COMBE and WEEKE were the homes of John de *Combe* and John
atte Wyke (1330 *SR*). *v*. cumb, wic.

BLACKDOWN CAMP is *Blakedoune* 1546 LP. *v*. dun. COURT HO
(6″) is *Courte* 1600 *SR*. CRANNACOMBE (6″) is *Cranacombe in
Ladeswill* t. Jas 1 ECP, *Crannacombe* 1624 *FF*. 'Herons' valley,'
v. cumb. HAM is *Northamme* 1242 Fees 766, *Ham in Lodeswell*
1484 IpmR. *v*. hamm. HAZELWOOD is *Halsewood* 1614 *Recov*
and is possibly identical with *Haselholt* 1262 Ch. 'Hazel wood.'
HEATHFIELD BARTON is *Hethfelde* 1310 *Ass*, 1330 *SR* (both p).
v. *supra* 265. READS (6″) is to be associated with the family of
Henry *le Red* (1330 *SR*). REVETON (6″) is *Reveton* 1485 Ipm.
Probably 'reeve's farm,' *v*. tun. Cf. Riverton *infra* 351 and
Reaveley PN NbDu 163. STANTON is *Staunton* 1262 Ch, *Stanton*

1330 *SR* (p). 'Stone enclosure,' *v.* tun. TUNLEY (6") is *Tonleigh* 1600 *SR*. Possibly so called because near the tun or village. Cf. Townleigh *supra* 209.

Malborough

MALBOROUGH [mɔ·lbərə] 145 J 3

> *Malleberg(e)* 1249 *Ass*, 1270 FF, *-bergh* 1281 *Ass*, *-beregh* 1289 *Ass*, *-burgh(e)* 1310 *Ass*, 1356 Ipm, *Malbergh* 1362 Pat
> *Marleberg(e)* 1270 Exon, 1281, 1289 *Ass*, *Marlburrough* 1561 Moulton
> *Merleberg'* 1275 RH, *-burgh* 1431 Pat
> *Maulborrough* 1751 *Recov*

'*Mǣrla*'s hill,' *v.* beorg and cf. Marwell *supra* 283.

ALSTON is *Alwinestona* 1086 DB, *Alwiston* 1228 *FF*, *-wys-* 1478 AD vi, *Alwyneston* 1285 FA. The place takes its name from one *Alwin* who held the manor TRE (DB f. 322 *b*). *Alwin* is for earlier OE *Ælfwine*.

BOLBERRY

> *Boltesberia, Boteberia, Botestesberia* 1086 DB
> *Boltebyry* 1224 FF *et freq* to 1333 Ipm with variant spellings *-bure, -bir(y), -byr(e), -bury, Parva Boltebure* 1238 *Ass*, *Mochele Boltebury* 1346 FA
> *Bultebyr'* 1249 *Ass*, *Magna Bultebur'* 1288 *Ass*
> *Little Baltesbiry* 1310 Ipm

It is probable that *Bolt* was the name of the stretch of land terminating at one end in Bolt Head (*Bult poynt* 1577 Saxton) and at the other in Bolt Tail (*Bolt Tail* 1765 D). *Boltbay* (1451 Pat) may have reference to Salcombe estuary. *Bolt* is probably the ordinary word *bolt* used in a topographical sense to describe the straight stretch of high coast land here as viewed from the sea. There are no remains of a burh here now.

CHURCHILL (6") is *Curcheswille* 1201 FF (p), *-well* 1286 *Ass*, *Corcheswille juxta Malleburgh* 1296 *Ass*. 'Spring of or by the hill or barrow,' *v.* wielle. For *cyric*, *v.* Churchill PN Wo 106.

COLLATON is *Coletona* 1086 DB, *Colethon'* 1242 Fees 777, taking its name from one *Colo* or *Cole* who held the manor TRE (DB f. 322). The earlier OE form would have been *Cola*.

HOPE is *la Hope* 1281 *Ass, atte Hope* 1330 *SR* (p), 1394 *Ass* (p), *Hope-Key* c. 1620 Risdon. This is probably the OE *hop*, though it is tempting to derive the name from ON *hóp*, 'bay, inlet,' were there other evidence of Scandinavian p.n.'s in the neighbourhood. Hope is a little fishing hamlet and small harbour sheltered by Bolt Head.

ILTON

> *Edetona* 1086 DB (Exon), *Eddetone* (Exch)
>
> *Edelton* 1201 FF, 1238 *Ass, Edilton* 1285 FA, *Etheldon* 1371 IpmR, *Edilton al. Ethelton* 1499 BM
>
> *Ydelthon'* 1242 Fees 777, -*ton* 1244 *Ass* (p)
>
> *Yedelthone* 1242 Fees 766, -*ton* 1310 Seld 20, 1368 IpmR, *Yeldetone* 1309 Exon, *Yediltone* 1328 Exon, *Yeltone* 1374 Exon

Possibly from OE *Ēadhildetūn*, '*Ēadhild*'s farm,' as suggested by Dr Schram. *Eadhild* is a woman's name in OE.

SEWER is *Sura* 1086 DB, *Sure* 1242 Fees 777, 1285 FA, *Shoure* 1243 FF, *Soure* 1275 RH *et freq* to 1499 BM. This may be the OE plant-name *sūre*, 'sorrel.'

YARDE is *la Verge* 1228 FF (p), (*Alwyneston cum*) *Virga* 1303 FA, *atte Yurd* 1330 *SR* (p), *Yarde* 1566 *Recov. v.* Yard *supra* 48.

COMBE and SOUTHDOWN were the homes of Matthew *Inthecombe* and Walter *Bysouthedon*, i.e. 'south of the down' (1333 *SR*). The first is *Combe* (1698 *Deed*).

FURZEDOWN (6″) is *Fursen* t. Hy 8 *MinAcct*, representing the weak plural of OE *fyrs*, 'furze,' cf. Fursdon *supra* 278. HORSCOMBE CROSS (6″) is *Horscumbe* 1310 *Ass, Horsecombe* 1482 IpmR. 'Horse valley,' *v.* cumb. LINCOMBE is *Lyncombe* 1478 AD vi (p). *v.* Addenda *supra* lviii. MARYKNOWLE (6″) is *Mare Knol* 1243 FF, *Marecnoll* 1244 *Ass*, 1249 FF. As this is on the parish boundary, it is probably OE (*ge*)*mǣre-cnoll*, 'boundary-hill,' cf. Mary Brook (PN Wo 13). *v.* cnoll. REW is *Rewe* 1303 FA, and was the home of Andrew *atte Rewe* 1330 *SR. v.* ræw. STAREHOLE BAY is *Sterewyll* t. Hy 8 *MinAcct. v.* wielle. The first element may be either *stær*, 'starling,' or *stēor*, 'bullock.' WEST PORTLEMOUTH is *Westportelemuth* 1292 *Ass*, 1311 *Ass, West-*

portlesmuthe 1306 *FF*, *Portelmuth juxta Malleburgh* 1313 *Ass.*
v. Portlemouth *infra* 328.

South Milton

SOUTH MILTON 145 H 3

> *Mideltona* 1086 DB, *Middelton juxta Kingesbrigg'* 1285 *Ass*,
> *Milton* 1428 FA

'Middle farm,' *v.* tun. Perhaps so called because midway
between South Huish and Churchstow.

COLLACOTT (6″) is to be associated with John Hengeston de
Colacote 1571 *SR*. If this is a proper place-name, the meaning
is '*Cola*'s cot(e),' but since the second element cot(e) is found
nowhere else in the South Hams, it is highly probable that the
name is of manorial origin, deriving from a man who came from
one of the numerous Collacotts in North Devon.

HIGHER KERSE (6″) was the home of Ralph *atte Karsen* (1330 *SR*),
atte Carse (1333 *SR*), i.e. 'at the cress place,' the earlier form
representing the weak plural, cf. *supra* 130.

WHITLOCKSWORTHY (6″) is *Wylakesworth* 1244 *Ass* (p), *Wyght-
locks Worthy* 1391 *FF*, *White Loxworthy* t. Eliz *LRMB* 191.
'*Wihtlāc*'s worþig,' the name having been later influenced by the
ME surname *Whitelock(s)*.

DIDWELL (6″) is *Dudewell* 1244 *Ass* (p), *Dodewille* 1330 *SR* (p),
1339 *Ass* (p), 1414 *FF*, *Dedewille* 1452 *FF*. '*Dudda*'s spring,'
v. wielle. HOLWELL is *la Kersehalewell* 1309 *FF*, *Holywille* 1448
FF. 'Holy well.' The first element must be OE cærs, 'cress.'
HORSWELL HO is *Horswell(e)* 1238 *Ass* (p), 1282 FF, *Horsewell*
1244 *Ass*. SUTTON is *Sutton juxta Middelton* 1296 *Ass*. 'South
farm,' *v.* tun. TRENDWELL (6″) is *Trendelwell* 1309 *FF*. 'Circular
stream or spring,' *v.* trynde, and cf. Trundlebeer *infra* 450.
UPTON is *Uppetone* 1242 Fees 795, *Uppeton juxta Kyngesbrugg'*
1321 *Ass*. 'Higher farm,' *v.* tun. It lies above South Milton.

Moreleigh

MORELEIGH 145 E 4

> *Morlei* 1086 DB *et freq* with variant spelling *-legh(e)*,
> *Moorley* 1610 *SR*

v. mor, leah.

AA

CHILLEY is *Childelegh* 1330 *SR* (p), *Chyllegh* 1449 *FF. v.* cild, leah. STONE FM was the home of William *atte Stone* (1333 *SR*). STORRIDGE is *Star(r)ig* 1242 Fees 765, 790, *Storigge* 1311 Exon, 1348 Ipm. Probably 'stone ridge.' *v.* stan, hrycg.

Rattery

RATTERY 145 B 4

    Ratreu 1086 DB, *Ratreueford* 1219 *Ass*
    Radetre c. 1240 Lives, *Radetru* 1314 *Ass* (p), *-trewe* 1316 FA, *trowe* 1327, 1346 Pat
    Rattre 1242 Fees 766, *Rattrew, Raktrue* 1270 Exon, *Rattriwe* 1276 RH, *-tru* 1284 Exon, *Ratterie* 1675 Ogilby
    Ratworthie al. Rattre 1620 *Inst* (PRO)

'At the red tree,' *v.* treow. *Ratworthie* is an inverted spelling. So many names in *worthy* are reduced in speech to a final *-ery* that a final *-ery* is sometimes re-spelled as *worthy*.

BULKAMORE is *Bolkemore* 1260 HMC iii 343, 1330 *SR* (p). 'Bullocks' moor,' or possibly '*Bulca*'s moor,' *v.* mor and cf. Bulkworthy *supra* 91.

LUSCOMBE is *Loscumma* 1086 DB, *Luscumba* 13th Buckfast (p), *-be* 1228, 1238 FF, *Loscumb Baruge* 1285 FA, *Loscome* 1303 FA, *Luscombe, Loscombe Bernage* 1326 Ipm. Probably 'pigsty valley,' *v.* hlose, cumb. Jurdan *Barnage* held the manor in 1242 (Fees 765).

MARLEY HO is *Merlegh(e)* 1242 Fees 781, 1285 FA, 1326 Ipm, *Marlegh* 1428 FA. 'Boundary clearing,' *v.* (ge)mære, leah. The place lies near the parish boundary.

VELWELL

    Falewill 1249 *Ass* (p), *-well* 1254 *Ass* (p), 1424 Exon, *Phalewille* 1281 Exon (p), *Valewyll* 1417 Exon (p), *Fallewille* 1426 FF, *Faliwelle* 1469 IpmR
    Vealewille 1330 *SR* (p)

    v. wielle. The first element is probably the OE adjective *fealu*, 'yellow, dusky, dark.'

WHITEOXEN is *Whittekesdon* 1242 Fees 782, *Wittekesdon* 1285 FA, *Whyttokesdon* 1303 FA, *Whittockesden* 1326 Ipm. '*Hwītuc*'s hill,' *v.* dun. The same pers. name is found in White Ox Mead (So), *Witochesmede* DB, *Whittukesmed* 1225 Ass, and in *hwittuces hlæwe* BCS 908.

BEARA (6″) and KNOWLE (6″) were the homes of Stephen de *la Bare* (1281 Exon) and Ralph *atte Beare* (1333 *SR*) and John *atte Knolle* (ib.). *v.* bearu, cnoll. The latter is *Knoll* 1593 *SR*.

BROWNSTON is *Brounston* 1330 *SR* (p). '*Brūn*'s tun.' CHOLWELL is *Chollewill* 1333 *SR* (p). 'Cold spring,' *v.* cald, wielle. CULVERLANE (6″) is so spelt 1765 D. ME *culver*, 'dove, pigeon.' HATCHLAND (6″) is *Hachelonde* 1563 *FF. v.* hæcc. HOLWELL BARN (6″) is *Hollewille* 1281 Exon (p), *Hole-* 1333 *SR* (p). 'Spring in the hollow,' *v.* holh, wielle. KERATON (6″) is *Coryaton* 1330 *SR* (p). SNOWDON (6″) is *Snauedon* 1298 *Ass*, *Snouwedon* 1330 *SR* (p). Cf. Snowdon *supra* 294. VENTONHILLS (6″) is *Fenton* 1249 *Ass* (p), 1326 Ipm. 'Farm in the marshy spot,' *v.* fenn, tun. WILLING is *Wyllen* 1515–18 ECP 5, 165 and was the home of Margery *atte Wille* 1330 *SR*. 'At the spring(s),' *v.* wielle. The later and modern forms seem to go back to the OE weak plural. YELLAND is *la Yaldelonde* 1275 RH (p), *la Yollalonde* 1365 HMC iii, 342 (p). *v.* Addenda *supra* lviii.

Salcombe

SALCOMBE 145 J 4

> *Saltecumbe* 1244 *Ass et freq* to 1464 IpmR with variant spelling *Salt-* and *-combe*, *Saltcombe by Ethelton* 1369 Pat
> *Salcume juxta Kinggesbrigg* 1286 *Ass*

'Salt combe,' perhaps with reference to the making of salt in salt-pans in this creek. *Ethelton* is Ilton *supra* 308.

BATSON is *Badestana* 1086 DB, *-ne* 1201 FF (p), 1244 *Ass*, *-ston* 1289 *Ass*, *Baddestane* 1242 Fees 765, 796, *-ston* 1301 Ipm, 1478 AD vi. '*Bada*'s stone.' Cf. Bason *supra* 131.

SHADYCOMBE (6″) is *Shabecombe* 1429 AD i, *Schabbecombe in the tithing of Baddeston* 1478 AD vi, *Shabbacombe in Salcombe* 1668 Deed. With the same history as Scabbacombe *infra* 509, except for initial *sh*.

Thurlestone

THURLESTONE 145 H 2

(*fram*) *ðyrelan stan* 845 BCS 451
Torlestan 1086 DB, *Thorlestone* 1279 Exon
Thurlestan(*e*) 1238 *Ass*, 1242 Fees 777, *Thurelston* 1362 Pat
Therlestan(*e*) 1238 *Ass*, 1242 Fees 766, -*ston* 1243 FF
Threlleston 1421 Exon, *Thrulston* 1546 *SR*

The place takes its name from a rock on the coast here, pierced by a natural hole. *v.* þyrel, stan.

AUNEMOUTH is *Avenemue* 1286 Ipm, -*mouth* 1401 *FF*, *Hauene-mouth* 1316 Pat, *Almouth al. Awmuth* 1600 *Recov.* 'At the mouth of the Avon' (*supra* 1).

BUCKLAND is *Bochelanda* 1086 DB, *Bocland*' 1242 Fees 776. *v.* bocland.

CLANACOMBE is *Clenecumbe* 1316 Pat, *Clenecombe juxta Thorleston* 1330 *Ass*, *Clanacombe* t. Eliz ChancP. 'Clean valley,' i.e. clear of undergrowth or bushes, *v.* clæne, cumb.

MOLLYCOMBE (6″) is very likely identical with *Smalacombe* 1619 *Recov.* 'Narrow valley,' *v.* smæl, cumb. If this is correct (*v. supra* 264) it is the (*oð*) *smalan cumb* of BCS 451.

NORTH UPTON, WHITLEY and WORTHY were probably the homes of John de *Uppeton* (1330 *SR*), Alan de *Whiteleie* (ib.) and Thomas *atte Worthy* (1316 Pat). *v.* hwit, tun, leah, worþig. The last is *Worthy* 1401 *FF*.

Woodleigh

WOODLEIGH 145 F 4

(*æt*) *Wudeleage* 1008–12 Crawford 10[1]
Odelea 1086 DB, *Wodelegh*' 1242 Fees 765, *Wodelegh juxta Lodeswell*(*e*) 1338 FF, 1339 *Ass*
v. leah.

CAPTON is *Cop*(*p*)*eton* 1330, 1333 *SR* (p). Either 'hill farm' from ME *coppe*, 'hill summit,' or '*Coppa*'s farm,' cf. *Coppan ford* KCD 699.

[1] The identification is not certain.

GRIMPSTONLEIGH (6″) is *Lege* 1086 DB, *Grymeston cu' Legh* 1340 *SR*, *Grymstonlegh* t. Ed 3 *Ass*, *Grymestoneslegh* 1394 *Ass. v.* leah. The place was later held by Robert de *Grimeston* who held also the manor of Grimston in Blackawton *infra* 316.

HALSTOW (lost) is *Haletrou* (sic) 1086 DB, *Halestowe* 1244 *Ass* (p), 1249 *Ass* (p), *Halstowe* 1449 *FF*, 1493 Ipm, *Halstowde* (sic) 1504–15 ECP 4, 226. Probably 'holy spot,' *v.* halig, stow. The DB form, if it belongs here, must be a scribal error.

HENDHAM is *Hyndham* 1330 *SR* (p), *Hendhame* 1653 *FF*. 'Hinds' ham(m).' MORECOMBE (6″) is *Morcomb(e)* 1330 *SR* (p), 1449 *FF*. *v.* mor, cumb. PRESTON is *Prusteton* 1303 *Ass* (p), *Pruston* 1330 *SR* (p), *Prusteston juxta Loddiswell* 1419 Exon. 'Priest's or priests' farm,' *v.* tun. WOOD BARTON (6″) is *Le Wode* 1420 Exon and was the home of Walter *atte Wode* (1333 *SR*). WOOLCOMBE BARN (6″) is *Wollecombe* 1449 *FF*. Probably 'wolves' valley,' *v.* cumb, and cf. Woolley, Wolborough *infra* 468, 524. WOTTON (6″) is *Odeton juxta Lodeswill* 1305 *Ass*, *Wotton* 1330 *SR* (p). 'Wood farm,' *v.* tun. YEO (6″) is *Yeo* 1505 Ipm and was the home of Geoffrey de *la Ya* (1242 Fees) and Nicholas *atte Yo* (1330 *SR*). 'At the water,' *v. supra* 17–18.

XIII. COLERIDGE HUNDRED

Curigge 1238 *Ass*, *Courigḡ* 1244 *Ass*
Colrig 1276 RH, *Colerigh* 1284 FA, *Colrigg* 1309 Ch

v. Coleridge *infra* 332. In the Geld Roll (1084) the hundred is called *Cadelintona*, presumably from Chillington in Stokenham *infra* 332.

East Allington

EAST ALLINGTON 145 F 5

Alintone, -na 1086 DB, *-yn-* 1268–75 Exon, 1312 BM, *Alenton* 1239 Ch, *-in-* 1285 FA, *Alynton Cryspyn* 1346 FA
Alingeton 1219 FF
Allyngthon' 1242 Fees 766, *Alyngtone* 1291 Tax, 1337 Cl, *Alyngton Crespyn* 1303 FA, *Eastallyngton* 1581 *SR*
Aylington' 1242 Fees 777

'Ælla's farm,' *v.* ingtun. Gilbert *Crespin* held the manor in 1242 (Fees 777). *East* as opposed to *South* Allington *infra* 320.

FALLAPIT HO is *Vialepitte* 1316 Exon (p), *Falepitte* 1321 *Ass* (p), *Valeputte, -pitte* 1339 *Ass. v.* pytt. For the first element, *v.* Velwell *supra* 310. The soil here is loamy.

FLEAR is *La Flere* 1268 FF, *La Fler* 1291 Tax, *Fleere* 1417 FF. This may be derived from OE *flǣre*, 'ear-lap, ear-lobe,' the term having been applied to the steep tongue of land between the two streams here.

RIMPSTONE is *Remmyston, Rempeston* 1330 *SR* (p), *Rymmyston, Rymston* 1500 Ipm, *Rimson* 1672 *SR*. Probably '*Hræfn*'s farm,' *v.* tun.

COLE'S CROSS and PINHEY'S CROSS are to be associated with the families of Martin *Cole* (1571 *SR*) and John *Penhay* (t. Hy 8 *Ct*).

LOWER NORTON, PITT FM and VENN (6″) were probably the homes of John de *Norton* (1333 *SR*), Richard atte *Putte* (1330 *SR*) and Ralph de *Fenne* (1321 *Ass*). *v.* norþ, tun, pytt, fenn.

COLEHANGER is *Colehanger* t. Eliz ChancP 1, 1616 *FF. v.* hangra and Collacott *supra* 50. COMBE is *Combe* 1312 BM. *v.* cumb. CROSS (6″) is *Crosse* 1455 IpmR, (*in the parish of Alyngton*) 1503 Ipm. CUTTERY FM is *Cuttrye* 1591 *Depositions, Cutterey* 1619 *Recov.* HARLESTON is *Harliston* 1252 FF, -*les-* 1333 *SR* (p), 1363, 1423 IpmR. '*Herel*'s or *Herewulf*'s farm,' *v.* tun. Cf. Harlington, PN BedsHu 123. HORSEWELL COTTAGE (6″) is *Halswill* 1333 *SR* (p). Probably 'hazel spring,' cf. Horsewells *supra* 283. KELLATON is *Keleton* 1254 *Ass* (p). KNIGHTON is *Knyghteton* 1383 FF, *Knytheton* 1422 IpmR. *v.* cniht, tun. LIPTON is so spelt 1661 *Recov.* NUTCOMBE is *Notcomb* 1330 *SR* (p), *Notte-comb(e)* 1333 *SR* (p), 1430 FF, *Nuttecomb* 1505 Ipm. Probably 'nut valley,' *v.* hnutu, cumb. LOWER WALLATON CROSS is possibly to be associated with Odo de *Welredon* 1333 *SR*. Cf. Walreddon *supra* 248.

Ashprington

ASHPRINGTON 145 C/D 6

Aisbertona 1086 DB

Asprinton(a) 1088 Totnes, 1187 P, 1260 Exon, 1340 Pat, *Ass*-1260 Exon

Aysprington(e) 1143 Totnes, 1308 Exon, *As-* 1238 *Ass*, 1260
Exon, *Aisspryngton* 1450 *FF*
Asperyngton 1316 FA
Ayshprynton 1327 Banco, *Aysshprington* 1365 *Ass*, *Asshpring-
tone* 1352 Exon, *-yng-* 1370 Orig, *Aschprengton* 1443–50
ECP 1, 120
Ashbrenton t. Jas 1 ECP 313

Probably 'farm of *Æscbeorht* (*Æscbriht*) or *Æscbeorn*,' *v.* ingtun. For the *p*, cf. Alston *supra* 225.

BOW BRIDGE (6″), with Bow, is *Steuenebogh* 1315 Totnes, *Stene-
bowe* 1453 *FF*, *Bowbridge* c. 1550 Leland, and refers to the bridge
here over the Harbourne river. Cf. Bow (Mx). *steuen* is a mis-
reading for *stenen* (OE *stænen*, 'stony, of stone'). Cf. Stonebow
PN Wo 167.

SHARPHAM HO is *Sharpeham* 1249 *Ass* (p), *Sherpham* 1340 *Ass*,
1377 HMC v, 604. 'The sharp hamm,' referring to the prominent bend in the Dart here.

YEATSON is *Yodeston* 1281 *Ass* (p), *Yeodesten* (sic) 1386 HMC xv,
App. 7. This seems to contain the same pers. name found in
Yadsworthy *supra* 270.

HAM REACH is *la Hamme* 1334 Exon. *v.* hamm. The reference
is to the big bend in the river here. PAINSFORD is *Pynesford* 1411
Exon, 1438 *FF*, 1480 Pat. TORCOMBE (6″) is *East Torcombe* 1639
FF. It is very doubtful if it can be the place called *Tybbecombe
juxta Aisspryngton* 1450 *FF*, *Tikcombe* 1501 Seld 16. This seems
to contain as first element the OE pers. name *Tibba*. TUCKENHAY
is *Tokenhey* 1550 *AOMB*. Possibly 'at the oak enclosure,' *v.* æt,
(ge)hæg, and Tapps *infra* 388. WORLD'S END (6″) is *Worlds End*
1765 D. The place is in a lonely situation by the Dart at the
extreme north-east corner of the parish.

Blackawton

BLACKAWTON 145 E 6

Auetona 1086 DB *et freq* to 1266 Exon with variant spellings
 Ave-, *-ton(e)*
Blakeaueton(e) 1281 *Ass*, 1308 Exon, *Blakaueton* 1284 FA,

1338 AD iv, *Blakauueton* 1291 *Ass, Blake Aueton* 1303 FA,
Ave- 1330 Exon
Blackawton al. Blackaveton 1671 *Deed*

This may be '*Afa*'s farm,' *v.* tun, but it is possible that
the first element is a stream-name 'Avon,' as in Aveton Giffard
supra 265. If so it must have been an earlier name of the Gara
river *supra* 6. The significance of the element *Black* is obscure.

CLISTON is *Clerkeston* 1311 *Ass*, 1333 *SR, -kys-* 1330 *SR, Clyston*
1516 BM. This name is identical with Cliston *supra* 167. The
meaning must be 'farm of the cleric or priest or of a man named
Clerke.' For the modern form, cf. Ditsworthy *supra* 239.

FUGE is *Fuwyche* 1269, 1425 *FF, Fewche* 13th (15th) *Torre,
Fuwiche* 1330 *FF, Fuyche* 1333 *SR* (p), *Feweche* 1481 *Cl, Fuyge*
1534 *Recov.* This may be a compound of OE *feoh*, 'cattle,' and
wic. Cf. Cowick *infra* 438.

GRIMSTON is *Grismetone* (sic) 1086 DB, *Grimeston'* 1242 Fees
790 *et freq* to 1359 Ipm with variant spelling *Grymes-, Grimston*
1284 FA. '*Grim*'s farm,' *v.* tun. This pers. name is not necessarily of Scandinavian origin (cf. PN Wo 126). It is found as the
name of the holder of the manor of Thrushelton in DB (TRE)
and also in Grimscott (Co), *Grymescote* 1311 *Ass*.

OLDSTONE is *Olvyston* 1330, *Olvestone* 1333 *SR* (p), *Ouldstone*
1551 DA 32. '*Ulf*'s farm,' *v.* tun. *Úlfr* is an ON pers. name.
This place and the neighbouring *Grimston* may both alike take
their names from late Anglo-Scandinavian settlers.

SHEARSTON is *Schinreston* 13th (15th) *Torre, Shynnerston* 1330
SR (p), *Scynneriston* 1333 *SR* (p). The first element is probably
the ME surname *Shinner*. Cf. Shinners Bridge *supra* 298. This
ME surname is, as suggested by Professor Ekwall, derived
from OE *scinnere*, 'magician.'

HIGHER and LOWER WADSTRAY are *Wadestrew* 1330, *Wadest'we*
1333 *SR* (p). '*Wade*'s tree.' This pers. name is recorded by
Redin (130), but is somewhat doubtful. Cf. Wadswick (W)
Wadeswica 12th BM. There is no stream here, so the first element
cannot be wæd.

COMBE FM, FORDER, and STONE FM were the homes of Isabella
de *Combe* (1330 *SR*), Peter *atte Forde* (ib.), and William *atte
Stone* (ib.). *v.* **cumb, stan.** For final *er* in Forder, *v.* Introd. xxxvi.

BLACKWELL (6″) is so spelt in 1583 DA 32. BOWDEN is *Boghedon*
1330 *SR* (p). *v.* Bowden *supra* 37. BURLESTONE is *Burlaueston*'
1249 *Ass* (p), *Borlaveston* 1269 FF. '*Beornlāf*'s tun.' COTTER-
BURY BARTON is *Cottebyri* 1318 Totnes (p), -*bury* 1415 Exon (p),
Cottaberye 1593 DA 26. '*Cotta*'s burh.' DALLACOMBE is *Dala-
combe* 1569 *Recov* and is probably to be associated with the
family of William *Dalla* (1333 *SR*). DREYTON is *Dreyton* 1285
Ass, 1694 FF. *v.* **dræg, tun.** EASTDOWN is *Estdoune* 1569 *Recov*.
GREENSWOOD is so spelt in 1611 FF. HARTLEY is *Westhurtlegh*
13th Oliver, *Hurtlegh* 1322 *Ass* (p), *Hurtelegh* 1422 *Ass*.
'Hart clearing,' *v.* **heorot, leah.** HILLAWAY (6″) is *Hillawayes*
1712 *Recov*. HUTCHERLEIGH is *Hucheslegh* 1428 Pat, *Huchley*
1563 FF, *Hitchesley* 1732 FF. Cf. Hutcherton *infra* 352.
LARCOMBE (6″) is *Levercumbe* 1244 *Ass* (p), *Leverkecomb* 1320
Ass (p), *Lercomb* 1333 *SR* (p). 'Lark cumb.' MILLCOMBE was
the home of Richard *atte Milcombe* 1409 *Ass* (p). PADDLELAKE
(6″) is so spelt in 1730 *Recov*. *v.* **lacu.** PASTURE FM is *Pasture*
1678 *Recov*. PRUSTON BARTON is *Pristeton* 1249 *Ass*, *Preston* 1320
Ass (p). 'Priests' farm,' *v.* **tun.** SECCOMBE is *Secumb* 1238 FF.
'*Secca*'s valley,' *v.* **cumb,** and cf. Seccombe *supra* 183. SHEP-
LEGH COURT is *Shippele* 1313 *Ass* (p), *Schippelegh* 1319 *Ass* (p).
'Sheep clearing,' *v.* **leah.** SOUTHWOOD is so spelt in 1575 DA 32.
STRAYPARK (6″) is *Strayer Park* 1761 *Recov*. *v.* Straypark *supra*
59. STRETE is *Strete* 1244 *Ass* (p) *et freq* to 1359 *Ass*. *v.* **stræt.**
The place is on a main road, which was probably an ancient
trackway. SWEETSTONE is *Sweteston* 1330 *SR* (p). The first
element appears to be the ordinary adjective, here possibly
used as a ME pers. name. ULCOMBE PLANTATION (6″) is *Oule-
comb* 1330 *SR* (p). 'Owl combe.' WASHWALK is *Whaste Whalke*
1656 *Deed*, *Washweek al. Washwalk* 1746 FF.

Buckland-Tout-Saints

BUCKLAND-TOUT-SAINTS 145 G 4

Bochelanda 1086 DB, *Bocland* 1238 FF, 1242 Fees 780
Bokelonde Touseyne 1479 FF, *Bukland Towesende* 1501 Pat,

Buckelande Towson 1562 *FF*, *West Bokelond juxta Kinges brigge* 1391 *FF*

v. boclond. The family de *Tuz Seinz* is first mentioned in connexion with the place in 1238 (FF). Cf. Towsington *infra* 497.

BEARSCOMBE is earlier *Wodemaneston'* 1242 Fees 780, 1303 FA, *Wodemaneston juxta Kyngesbrigge* 1306 *Ass*, *Bearescombe al. Woodmaston* 1688 *Recov.* This place corresponds to the manor of *Bochelanda*, which was held by one *Odeman* (i.e. *Wodeman*) TRE (DB f. 396 *b*). The modern name is to be associated with the family of *Beare.* Cf. John *Beare* of Bearscombe, M.P. for Tavistock in 1685 (DA 42, 277).

GOVETON is *Gouedon* 1244 *Ass* (p), *Goueton(e)* 1330 *SR* (p), 1372 Exon (p), 1500 Ipm, *Goton al. Goveton* 1686 *Recov.* A William *Gova* was living at Sigdon *infra* in 1372 (Exon) and an ancestor of his probably gave name to this place. This pers. name may be identical with the Cornish *gof*, 'smith.' Cf. Gawton *supra* 223.

LIDSTONE is *Lydestone* 1291 Tax, *Lyuedeston* early 14th, *-dis-* 1392 BM, *Lyvedston* 1333 *SR* (p), *Lyvediston al. Lydiston* 1433 AD i (p). Dr Ritter suggests OE *Lēofgȳðestān*, 'stone of a woman named *Lēofgȳð.*' *v.* stan. Professor Ekwall suggests a pers. name *Lēofede*, which is actually on record as *Leouede* in Devon (Earle 262). In that case the second element would be tun.

SIGDON is *Siggedone* 1238 *Ass*, *Sygedon(e)* 1291 Tax, 1314 Ipm, *Syggedon* 1333 *SR* (p). '*Sicga*'s hill,' *v.* dun.

BLACKRIDGE CROSS (6″) is *Blackridge* 1688 *Recov.* BOROUGH is *Burgh'*, *Bergh'* 1242 Fees 777, *Burgh juxta Kyngesbrygge* 1314 *Ass*, *Bergh juxta Kyngesbrugge* 1321 *Ass.* 'Hill,' *v.* beorg. COURT-LANDS is *Cotelond* 1333 *SR* (p), *Cottelond* 1437 Exon. *v.* cot(e). CRIMPS CROSS (6″) is *Crympes* 1688 *Recov* and is to be associated with the family of Richard *Crempa* (1333 *SR*). CROFT is *Croft* 1504 *FF. v.* croft. SLADE is *Slade More* 1417 AD vi. *v.* slæd. TORR (6″) was the home of John *atte Torre* 1333 *SR. v.* torr.

Charleton

CHARLETON 145 H 4

Cheletona 1086 DB

Cherleton(e) 1242 Fees 768, 1291 Tax, (*juxta Kyngesbrigg*) 1311 *Ass*

Churleton(e) 1267 Ipm, 1316 FA, 1328 Exon, *Cheorletone* 1329 Exon

Charleton in Southammes 1396–1408 Exon, *Chorleton* 1408 Exon

v. ceorl, tun.

CLEAVEHOUSE (6″) was probably the home of John de *Clyve* (1333 SR), *v.* clif. CROFT (6″) is *Croft* 1525 *SR. v.* croft. EAST CHARLETON is called *Eastown* in 1765 D. FROGMORE is *Froggemere* 1522 *Recov.* 'Frog pool,' *v.* mere.

Chivelstone

CHIVELSTONE 145 J 5

Cheveletona 1086 DB

Chevelestuna 1133–8 Totnes, *-ton(e)* 1225 Pat, 1238 FF, 1242 Fees 795, 1284 FA, 1291 Tax, *-lys-* 1346 FA

Cheveryston 1316 FA

Chyvelston 1428 FA, *Chilston oth. Chivilston* 1734 *Recov*

Cheleston 1546 *SR*

'*Ceofel*'s farm,' *v.* tun. *Ceofel* being a diminutive of OE *Ceofa.* Cf. also Chelson *infra* 595 and Chilswell (Berks) *Cheveles-, Chiveleswell* 1244 FF, *Chiefleswelle* c. 1200 Abingdon.

FORD is *Forda* 1086 DB, *Ford juxta Alington* 1422 IpmR.

EAST PRAWLE

Prenla 1086 DB

Pratt 1169 P (p), *Pral* 1254 *Ass* (p), 1285, 1316 FA, 1334, 1340 *SR*

Praule 1203 Cur (p) *et freq* to 1308 Exon (p), *Praulle* 1242 Fees 786

Prahulle, Prahelle 1204 Cur (p)

Prahall 1214 HMC xv App. 7 (p)

Prawle Point is a prominent headland, and Professor Ekwall

writes as follows: "The name means 'look-out hill.' The first element is connected with OE *beprīwan*, 'to wink the eye,' *prēowthwīl*, 'twinkling of an eye.' From this was formed a noun *prāw* or *prǣw* (or both), the common base being an *a*-stem **praiwaz, -iz*, meaning 'the act of peering.' The OE name may be *Prāwhyll* or *Prǣwhyll* or else *Prāhyll*, *Prǣhyll*. A base **praiwa* (**praiwi*) would give us *prā* and *prāw*, *prǣ* and *prǣw*, side by side. Perhaps *Prǣhyll* is most likely." See more fully Ekwall, *Studies* 79–80.

SOUTH ALLINGTON is *Alinton* 1284 FA, *Southalyngton juxta Chevelistone* 1320 *FF. v.* East Allington *supra* 313. BOROUGH is *Bourrough* t. Hy 8 *Ct. v.* beorg. WOODCOMBE is *Wodecomb* 1330 *SR* (p). *v.* cumb.

Cornworthy

CORNWORTHY 145 D 6/7

   Corneorda 1086 DB

   Corneworthi 1205 FF *et freq* to 1291 Tax with variant spellings -wrth(e), -wordi, -wrthy, *Westcorneworthy* 1322 *Ass*, *Up-corneworthy* 1292 *FF*

   Cornnewrth' 1242 Fees 795, -worthe 1310 Exon

   Cornworth(i) 1250 Cl, 1297 Pat

   v. worþig. The first element has been discussed under Corn-wood *supra* 268. *West* and *Up* to distinguish from East Corn-worthy *infra*.

ALLALEIGH is *Alelege* 1238 FF, -legh 1303 FA, *Halilegh* 1238 *Ass*, *Allelegh* 1330 *SR* (p). 'Æl(l)a's leah.'

GITCOMBE is *Gydyacomb(e)* 1327 Banco, 1333 *SR* (p), *Gydicombe* 1330 *SR* (p). The first element may be a ME pers. name, cf. Henry *Gidya* and Roger *Gydie* 1330, 1333 *SR* and Introd. xxxv.

TIDEFORD [taidifəd] is *Tidewrthi* 1238 *Ass* (p), *Tiddewurdi* 1244 *Ass* (p), *Tideworth* 1272 Ipm, *Tyde-* 1327 Banco, *Tydeworthy juxta Westcorneworthy* 1322 *Ass*, *Tiddesworth* 1376 Pat. 'Tid(d)a's worþig.' Cf. *on tiddan cumb* BCS 1002.

BROADRIDGE is *Broderidge* 1617 Recov. EAST CORNWORTHY is *Estcorn(e)w(o)rthy* 1291 Pat, 1324 *Ass*. HIGHER DINNICOMBE is *Dinnicomb* 1714 Recov. WOOLCOMBE is *Wolcomb* 1333 *SR* (p). Perhaps 'wolves' valley,' *v.* cumb.

Dartmouth

DARTMOUTH 145 E 8

(*to*) *Dærentamuðan* 11th (1049) ASC
(*to*) *Dertamuðan* 11th (1050) ASC, *Dertemuthe* 1231 Cl *et freq*
to 1377 Cl with variant spelling -*mue*, *Deretemuwe* 1233
Bracton, *Dertesmuth'* 1234 Cl, *Dartemuth* 1265 Abbr
Clifton Dertemuth juxta Kyngeswere 1307 *Ass*, (*juxta Stoke-
flemyng*) 1313 *Ass*, *Clifton Dertemuth and Hardenesse* 1327
Orig, *Clifftoundertemouthe Hardenasse* 1416 AD vi, *Darte-
mouth Hardenysse* 1516, 1522 BM
Southtoundertemouth 1416 AD vi

'At the mouth of the Dart' (*supra* 4). The borough of
Dartmouth consisted originally of three distinct places, Clifton
infra, Dartmouth, and Hardness. The last name (*v.* næss) refers
to the ridge of land running from Townstal *infra* to the ferry
(*ex inf.* Mr H. Watkin).

NOTE. HIGHER STREET is *The Heigh Streat* 1561 *Deed*. SMITH
STREET is *Smiþenestrete* 13th, *Smythenestrete* 1390 HMC v. 'Smiths'
street.' In 1388 there is mention also of a *Monkenestrete* (HMC v).
'Monks' street.'

CROWTHER'S HILL (6″) is *Croterhill* 1478 HMC v, and is probably
to be associated with *Crowetorre* 1420 HMC v. 'Crow torr.'

TOWNSTAL is *Dunestal* 1086 DB, *Tunistal* c. 1200, *Tunestalle*
1224-44 HMC v, 599, *Tounstall(e)* 1247 Oliver, 1346 FA, (*juxta
Dertemouth*) 1373 *FF*, *Tunstealle* t. Ed 1 HMC v, 599, *Toster*
1675 Ogilby. *v.* tunsteall.

WARFLEET is *Welflut* t. Ed 1, *Walflete* 1410, *Walfletcrosse*
1478 HMC v. The first element is probably the OE weall in
some sense, perhaps that of earthwork or rampart. The second
is fleot, referring to the little creek here.

BAYARD'S COVE CASTLE (6″) is *Bayardscove* 1351 HMC v, 601.
BLACKSTONE POINT is *Blakeston* 1306 Pat. CLIFTON (6″) is
Clifton(e) t. Ed 1 HMC v, 601, (*upon Dertemuth*) 1302 Ch,
(*Manstell*)[1] 1368 IpmR. *v. supra.* COMBE POINT is *Cumb(e)*

---

[1] Possibly a corruption of the name of the family of (de) *Mortellis, Morcellis
Morceaux*, who held the manors of Stoke Fleming and Townstal in DB.

t. Ed 1 HMC v, 600 (p), 1470 IpmR. *v.* cumb. NORTON is *Northton* 1284 FA, *Dertemouthe juxta Norton* 1314 *Ass, Norton* 1336 Ch, (*juxta Stoke Flemmyng*) 1364 *Ass.* 'North farm,' *v.* tun. OLD MILL CREEK is *Old Mylle Creke* c. 1550 Leland. SOUTHTOWN (lost) is *Southtondertemouthe* 1356 *Ass, Southton* 1472 IpmR. SWANNATON is *Swaneton(e)* 1322 *Ass*, 1330 *SR* (both p). 'Peasants' farm,' *v.* swan, tun.

Dittisham

DITTISHAM [ditsəm, ditʃəm] 145 D 8

   Didasam 1086 DB

   Didisham 1230 P (p), 1285 FA, *-es-* 1276 Ipm, 1285 *Ass*,
     1303, 1316 FA, *Dydes-* 1281 *Ass*, 1291 Tax, 1297 Pat,
     Dydsaham 1263 Exon

   Diddesham 1238 *Ass*

   Dyteshamme 1340 *Ass, Dytsham* 1577 Saxton

   Dedishome 1462 Pat, *Detysham* 1465 Pat

   '*Dyddi*'s ham(m).' Cf. Didsbury (PN La 31).

BOSOMZEAL

   Hele 1284 FA, 1396 Exon, (*juxta Didesham*) 1285 *Ass*, (*Payn*)
     1303 FA

   Helbozoun 1368 IpmR, *Helpayne* 1368 IpmR, *Helepayn* 1372
     FF

   Bosumshele 1395–1417 Exon, *Bozon Hele* 1408 Exon, *Bosumys-*
     hale 1482 *MinAcct*

   v. healh. Robert *Bosom* held the manor in 1395 and John *Bozon* in 1408 (Exon), the family, variously spelt *Buzun, Bauzan, Bauceyn, Bozon,* having been associated with the neighbourhood since c. 1170–96 (Totnes). The connexion of the *Payn* family with the manor is not known.

BRUCKTON is *Brockedon* 1298 *Ass* (p), *Brogaton* 1333 *SR* (p), *Brogeton(e)* 1351 *Ass*, 1438 *FF.* 'Badgers' hill,' *v.* brocc, dun.

CAPTON is *Capieton* 1278 *Ass, Capinton* 1285 *Ass, Capyatone* 1330 *SR* (p), *Capeton* 1351 *Ass*, 1475 IpmR. This is clearly a late formation with tun. Cf. Roger *Capia* (1330 *SR*), Will *Capia* (1308 Exon), elsewhere in the county. Cf. Introd. xxxvi.

CHIPTON is *Chypton* 1482 *MinAcct*, cf. Chipley *infra* 465.
COOMBE was the home of Susanna *atte Combe* 1333 *SR*. *v.* cumb.
DOWNTON is *Douneton* 1482 *MinAcct*. 'Hill farm,' *v.* dun, tun.
HALWELL is *Hellewell(e)* 1238 *Ass* (p), 1403 *MinAcct*. HEM-
BOROUGH is *Henneburgh* 1330, 1333 *SR* (p), 1404 *MinAcct*.
Probably 'hen hill,' *v.* beorg. KINGSTON is *Kyngestone* 1438 *FF*.
'King's farm,' but the royal owner is unknown. LAPTHORNE
is *Loppedethorn(n)e* 1347 Cl, 1383 *FF*, *Loppethorne* 1372 IpmR.
'The pollarded thorn tree,' cf. the same name *supra* 170, 281.
LORD'S WOOD (6″) is *Lordswood* in 1735 *Recov*.

Halwell

HALWELL [hɔ·lwel] 145 E 5

> (*to*) *Halganwylle* 10th (12th) Burghal Hidage, *Halgewill(e)*
> c. 1240 Lives, 1310 Inq aqd, 1322 *FF*, *Halgwelle* 1275 Exon,
> *Halgh(e)will(e)* 1330 *SR*, 1368 IpmR
> *Holywille* 1448 *FF*, *Holwell* 1675 Ogilby
> *Hallewell* c. 1400 Exon, *Halewyll* 1476, *-will* 1478 IpmR

'Holy well.' There is a spring just east of the church.

CROCKADON (6″) is *Crocketune* 13th Buckfast, *-t(h)on* 1242 Fees
777, 1303 FA, *Croke-* 1284 FA, 1330, 1333 *SR* (p), *-don* 1368
IpmR. In the earliest reference above there is mention of
William *Crocke de Crocketune*, so presumably the farm took its
name from this man or from one of his near ancestors.

FARMSTONE (6″) is *Farmiston* 1359 BM, *Varmeston* 1361 *FF*,
Fermeston 1394 *Ass*. Possibly '*Farman*'s farm,' *v.* tun. This pers.
name is of Scandinavian origin, but the place-name may be of
late origin and such an Anglo-Scandinavian name would go with
Grimston and Oldstone *supra* 316, and Gripstone *infra* and
Dorsely *infra* 325.

GRIPSTONE (6″) is *Cribeston, Grypeston* 1244 *Ass, Gripiston* 1330
SR (p), 1359 BM, *Gripston* 1333 *SR* (p), 1493 Ipm, *Grypeston*
1356 *Ass* (p). This may well be a late tun formation from a
post-Conquest holder bearing the Anglo-Scandinavian name
Grip.

POULSTON is *Polochestona* 1086 DB, *Pollekest(h)on'* 1242 Fees
765, 776, *Pollokiston* 1341 Ipm, *Pulkeston* 1422 *Ass*, (*oth*.

Pulson) 1740 *Recov.* '*Polloc*'s farm,' *v.* tun. For the pers. name, *v.* PN BedsHu 160. Cf. also Pulsford *infra* 525 and the surname (de) *Pollokesfenne* 1333 *SR* (Newton Ferrers).

RITSON is *Redestan* 1254 *Ass* (p), 1422 IpmR, *-ston* 1281 *Ass* (p), 1372 IpmR, *Rydeston, Reddeston* 1281 *Ass* (p), *Radeston* 1347 Ipm, Cl, 1383 *FF, Retson* 1576 *SR, Ritson* 1700 *Recov.* '(At the) red rock.'

STANBOROUGH HO is *Stanbergh* 1281 *Ass, -burgh(e)* 1285 FA, 1475 IpmR, *Stoneburgh* 1503 Ipm. 'Stone hill,' *v.* beorh. There is an ancient camp here which may have been the site of the Hundred meeting-place, *v. supra* 288.

WASHBOURNE

>*Waseborna* 1086 DB
>*Wasseburn(e)* 1238 FF, 1242 Fees 777, 1284 FA
>*Waysseburn* 1276 Ipm, *Wayssheborn* 1333 *SR* (p), *Westwaisshebourne* 1345 *Ass, Waisschebourne* 1350 Ipm
>*Wassheborn Water, Wassheborn Durant, Wasshborn Bauzan* 1303 FA, *Westwasshebourne* 1340 *Ass,* (*Est*) 1345 Exon
>*Weshbourne, Wesshebourne* 1428 FA

'Sheep-wash stream,' *v.* (ge)wæsc, burna. One manor was held by Richard *Baucan* in 1238 (FF) and 1242 (Fees), another by one *Walter* in 1303 (FA) and the third by the family who held the manor of Dorsely (*infra* 325) in 1242 (Fees 795).

HIGHER BARNE (6″) is *Barne* 1438 *FF.* BICKLEIGH is *Buttelegh, Byttelegh* 1333 *SR* (p), *Bittelegh* 1453 *FF, Bickley* 1576 *SR.* '*Bit(t)a*'s leah.' The *u* in the earliest form may be due to the influence of the *b.* BLACK DOWN is *Blakedoune* 1382 Pat. *v.* blæc, dun. BORESTON is *Boreston* 1244 *Ass* (p), *Boriston* 1359 BM. COLLATON is *Kolethon'* 1242 Fees 776, *Colton* 1284 FA, *Coleton* 1311 *Ass* (p), 1476 IpmR. *v.* Collacott *supra* 50. HONEYWELL WOOD (6″) is *Honewille* 1330 *SR* (p). 'Honey spring,' cf. Honeychurch *supra* 165. KNACKERS KNOWLE (6″) is *Nackershole* 1765 D. *v. s.n.* Crown Hill *supra* 227. It is a 'knowle' rather than a 'hole.' ROWDEN is *Rowedon(e)* n.d. Oliver 172, 1330 *SR* (p), 1427 IpmR. 'Rough hill,' *v.* ruh, dun.

Harberton

HARBERTON 145 C 5

Herburnat' 1108, *Herbernat'* 1109 Sarum
Herburton 1158 Sarum, -*berton(e)* 1220 FF, 1362 Fine
Urberton 1211 RBE, *Hurbertun'* 1212 Fees 98 *et freq* to 1364
   Ass with variant forms -*ton(e)*, *Hurbreton* 1333 Ch
Hurburton 1235 HMC iv, 66, 1253 *St Nicholas*
Hirbirton 1276 Cl
Harberton t. Jas 1 ECP

' Farm by the Harbourne river,' *v. supra* 7.

BEENLEIGH was the home of Isabella de *Bynnelegh* 1330 *SR* (p). Other forms may refer to this place, but are difficult to distinguish from those for Beenleigh *supra* 299. That is an old name and it may be that this place-name is manorial rather than local in origin, the family of Isabella de B. coming from Beenleigh *supra*.

BELSFORD is *Bailleford* 1347 Ipm, *Baillesford* 1383 *FF*, *Bayllisford* 1422 IpmR. Possibly ' *Bǣgel's* ford.' This pers. name is not recorded but would be a regular *l*-derivative of OE *Bǣga*. Cf. Baycliff (W), *Bayleclive* t. Hy 3 BM, *Bayllesclyve* 1316 FA.

CROWDY MILL (6") is *Croude* 1297 Ipm, 1377 HMC xv App. 7, *Crowde* 1437, 1443 IpmR. Possibly a Celtic name corresponding to Co *croudy*, Breton *kraoudi*, 'stable.'

DORSELY

Thurislgh' (sic), *Thuryslegh* 1242 Fees 777, 795, *Thuresle(gh)* 1285 FA, *Thurslegh Durant* 1303 FA
Thor(i)slegh 1345 *Ass*, 1348 Ipm, *Thoureslegh* 1383 *FF*, *Tors(e)ley* 1544 LP
Durseleigh al. Thorseleigh t. Jas 1 ECP, *Dorsley* 1684 *Recov*

' Clearing of *Đur* or *Đuri*,' *v.* leah. For these Anglo-Scandinavian pers. names, *v.* Björkman NP 146, 158, and cf. *đureslege* KCD 784 in the bounds of Ayston (R). ' *Durandus* filius Ricardi ' held part of the manor in 1242 (Fees 777) and his name may have affected the ultimate development. See also Introd. xxxv.

GREAT ENGLEBOURNE is *Engleborna* 1086 DB, -*burne* 1250 Misc, -*borne* 1274 Ipm, *Engeleburne* 1242 Fees 786, 1274 Ipm, *North-*

engleburne juxta Suthengleburne 1317 *Ass*, *Northengleborne juxta Hurberton* 1321 *Ass*, *Yngelbourne* 1428 FA. This name may mean 'bourne or stream of the English,' possibly because at one time it formed the boundary between the British and the invading Anglo-Saxons.

HAZARD

> *Haroldesore* 1086 DB
> *Herewaldeshore* 1242 Fees 790, 1303 FA, *Herewelthsore* 1423 IpmR
> *Herewerdesore juxta Totton* 1296 *Ass*, -*ward*- 1378 IpmR, *Herwarsore* 1493–1500 ECP 3, 520
> *Hawsore al. Hawbersore* t. Mary *CtRequests*, *Harwardsore* 1558–79 ECP 421, *Hazard* 1809 M

'*Herewald*'s bank or slope,' *v.* ora.

HERNAFORD is *Herneford* 1285 FA, 1347 Ipm, *Hurneford* 1244 FF, 1303 FA, 1330 *SR* (p). The first element is OE hyrne, 'corner, angle,' perhaps referring to its position in the south-east corner of the parish. It is not clear what 'ford' is referred to. It may be the ford to the north now called Harbertonford.

EAST and WEST LEIGH are *Lega* 1086 DB, *Legh'* 1242 Fees 765, *Legh omnium sanctorum juxta Hurberton* 1364 *Ass*, *Leigh within the parish of Harberton* t. Eliz ChancP 2. *v.* leah. The third reference looks like Leigh in Churchstow *supra* 296 but that is a long way from Harberton.

ROLSTER, ROLSTER BRIDGE (6″) is *Rostewode* 1308 Oliver 428, *Rostbridge, stone bridge caullid Roste* c. 1550 Leland, *Rostabridge* 1626 *Recov*. This probably contains the OE *hrōst*, 'beam,' the reference being to a bridge made of beams. Cf. Ruston PN NRY 109 and Rossley (Gl), 1333 Ipm *Rosteley*.

DOTTINS (6″), FLETCHER'S COMBE[1] and GILL'S CROSS are probably to be associated with the families of John *Dottin* (1571 *SR*), *Fletcher* or *Flaccher* (15th cent. Totnes), and Roger *Gill* (1571 *SR*).

ASHRIDGE is *Ayssherugg'* 1330 *SR* (p), *Ayshrigge juxta Totton'* 1346 *Ass*. BLAKEMORE is *Blakemor(e)* 1300 Ipm. *v.* blæc, mor. OLD CHOLWELL is *Chollewille* 1372 FF. 'Cold spring,' *v.* cald,

---

[1] *Fletchers Combe* 1677 DA 31.

wielle. DUNDRIDGE is *Donekerigge* 1269 FF. Probably '*Dun(n)e-ca*'s ridge,' or the first element may be ME *dunnok*, 'sparrow.' GOSWORTHY is *Goseworthy* 1504–15 ECP 4, 124. HARBERTON-FORD is *Hurbertonforde* 1571 *SR*, *Harbertonford* 1628 *FF*. 'Ford over the Harbourne river' (*supra* 7). LANGFORD is *Langeforde* 1312 *FF*. 'Long ford.' LUSCOMBE is *Loscombe juxta Hurbertone* 1346 *FF*. 'Pigsty valley,' cf. Luscombe *supra* 310. MON-KEY OAK (6″) is *Monkeneoke* 1626, *Mounkenoake* 1652 *Recov.* 'Monks' oak,' referring to the monks of Buckfast Abbey, who held the manor of Englebourne near by. MOORE FM (6″) is *La More* 1368 IpmR. *v.* mor. SANDWELL is *Sandwill* 1330 *SR* (p), *-well* 1422 IpmR. 'Sandy spring,' *v.* wielle. STANCOMBE is *Stancumb'* 1242 Fees 790, (*Priour*) 1378 IpmR. 'Stony valley,' *v.* cumb. Cf. Stancombe *infra* 329. TRISTFORD Ho is perhaps to be associated with the family of Elizabeth and James *Tryst* or *Trist* of Totnes (1650, 1782 Wills). WHITELEY (6″) is *Whytelegh* 1322 Misc, *la Whyteleye* 1382 Pat. *v.* leah. WINSLAND Ho (6″) is *Wynslonde* 1330 *SR* (p), *Wynneslond juxta Totnes* 1345 *Ass*, *Wynnyslond* 1493 Ipm. '*Wine*'s land.' WOODCOURT (6″) is *La Wode* 1303 FA, *Woodcourt* 1576 *SR*. YEO BRIDGE is *Yeo* 1592 *Deed*, and was the home of Geoffrey de *la Ya* (1238 *Ass*). 'At the water,' *v.* Yeo *supra* 17–18.

South Pool

SOUTH POOL 145 J 5

> *Pola* 1086 DB, *Pole* 1242 Fees 795, 1291 Tax
> *Suthpole* 1284 FA, 1300 *FF*, *Supole* 1284 Exon
> The 'pool' is a tidal arm of Kingsbridge harbour.

COMBE is *Cumba* 1086 DB (Exon), *Comba* (Exch), *Combehalle* 1332 Exon. *v.* cumb.

NORTH POOL is *Pola* 1086 DB, *Northpole* 1238 *Ass*. *v. supra.*

SCOBLE is *Scobbahill* 1284 FA, *Scobehulle* 1330 *SR*, *Scobbehull* 1333 *SR* (all p), *Skoble* 1610 *SR*. '*Sc(e)obba*'s hill.' Cf. Scobchester *supra* 126. For the initial *sc*, *v.* Introd. xxxv, and cf. Stephen *Skobbe* (1377 Exon).

FADICOMBE BARN (6″) is *Vadecombe* 1624 *FF*. HALWELL HO is *Halghewille* 1333 *SR* (p), *Halwyll* 1525 *SR*. 'Holy well.'

WINSLADE is *Wideslade* 1238 *Ass, Wyde-* 1316, 1321 *Ass* (all p).
Cf. Winslade *supra* 107.

East Portlemouth

EAST PORTLEMOUTH 145 J 4

> *Porlamuta* 1086 DB, *-mue* 1219 FF, *Porlemue* 1242 Fees 777,
> 786, 1268–77 Exon
> *Portlemue* 1268–77 Exon, *-mwe* 1291 Tax
> *Porlesmuth* 1270 *Ass, Portlesmuthe* 1317 Exon
> *Portilmuth* 1302 Cl
> *Porthelemuthe* 1308 Exon, *Portelemuwe* 1319 Ipm, *-mouth*
> 1346 FA, *Portelamouthe* 1372 Exon
> *Portesmo(u)th(e)* 1347 Cl, 1368 IpmR
> *Porthlemouthe* 1390 Exon
> *Portlemouth al. Pottlemouth* 1708 *Recov*

The second element is muþa. The first part of the name is
difficult, but it may contain the Old British name of the Kingsbridge estuary, perhaps a compound of *porth*, 'harbour,' and the
word found in Hayle, Helford (Co), which Ekwall (RN 192)
shows to be a derivative with *i*-mutation of *hal*, 'salt.' The
absence of spellings with a diphthong *ai* or *ei* might be due to the
fact that the element occurs in an unstressed syllable. East and
West Portlemouth (*v. supra* 308) are situated on either side of the
narrow entrance to the wide Kingsbridge estuary, a large expanse
consisting of numerous tidal creeks fed by small streams from
the hills above.

GOODSHELTER

> *Godeshalt(e)re* 1203 Cur, 1204 FF, 1244 *Ass* (p), *Godesaltre*
> 1203 Cur, *-heltr'* 1204 Cur, *-halre* 1238 *Ass* (p)
> *Goddyshalter* 1490 Ipm

This is a difficult name. It may mean what it says. Unfortunately the word *shelter* is not recorded before 1590 and its
history is obscure. The earliest form of the word hitherto recorded is *shealter*. Alternatively one might take the second element to be OE *sealtærn*, 'salt-house,' cf. Seasalter (K), DB
Sesaltre, 1316 FA *Sesaltre*, but in that case the persistent *h* offers
difficulties. The first element is equally difficult. If it is the

adjective 'good' we have a place-name of the nickname-type. Goodshelter lies by a sheltered creek of Kingsbridge estuary.

HOLSET is *Holset(e)* 1330, 1333 *SR* (p). The place is in a hollow and is probably a compound of holh and sæte in some sense. WEST PRAWLE is *West Praull* 1303 FA. *v.* Prawle *supra* 319.

Sherford

SHERFORD 145 G 5

> *Scireford* c. 1050 KCD 926, *Sirefort* 1086 DB
> *Shireford(e)* 1281 *Ass,* 1291 Tax, *(Prioris)* 1306 Ipm, *Schireford, Shyrford* 1312 BM

A compound of OE scir, 'clear, bright,' and ford. The manor was held by Plympton priory.

KEYNEDON

> *Chenighedona, Cheninghedona* 1086 DB (Exon), *Chenigedone* (Exch)
> *Kynedon* 1242 Fees 792, 1303 FA
> *Kynydon* 1306 Ipm

'Hill of *Cǣna*'s people,' *v.* ing, dun.

MALSTON

> *Mellestona* 1086 DB
> *Mallestone* 1242 Fees 795, *Maleston(e)* 1244 *Ass* (p), 1284 FA, 1317 Exon (p), *Mauston* 1432 Exon

'*Meall*'s farm,' cf. Malling PN Sx 354 and Mawsley (Nth), *Malesle* DB, *Malleslea* 1181 P, *Meleslai* 1185 P.

STANCOMBE is *Stancoma* 1086 DB, *Stonecumb'* 1242 Fees 777, *Stancumb(e)* 1284 FA, *(juxta Shiraforde)* 1339 *Ass,* *Stancomb(e)* *juxta Stoke in Hammes* 1322 FF, *(Dauney)* 1312 BM, *(Crespyn)* 1303 FA. 'Stony valley,' *v.* cumb. Gilbert *Crespin* held the manor in 1242 and by 1333 it had passed to Nicholas *Dauney* (DA 43, 217). The adjacent manor of Stancombe in Harberton was held by Henry *Prior* in 1242 (Fees 790), *v. supra* 327.

BOWDEN is *Boghedon* 1281 *Ass* (p), 1330 *SR* (p). *v.* Bowden *supra* 37. COMBE is *la Cumbe* 1281 *Ass. v.* cumb. DUNCOMBE is so spelt in 1721 *Recov.* FURSDON is *atte Forssene* 1394 *Ass.*

cf. Fursdon *supra* 278. NETHERTON (6″) is *Nitherton* 1387 Cl, (*juxta Kyngesbrugge*) 1416 *FF*. 'Lower farm.' ODDICOMBE is *Odecumba* 1163 P, *-kumbe* 1219 FF, *-cumbe* 1219, 1294 *Ass*. '*Odda*'s valley,' *v*. cumb. Cf. Odcombe (So). RANSCOMBE is *Rammescumb* 1281 *Ass*, *Raunnescombe* 1312 BM, *Ramescombe* 1316 *Ass* (p). 'Ram's valley,' *v*. cumb. Alternatively *Ram* (OE *ramm*) may here have been a pers. name.

Slapton

SLAPTON 145 G 6

> *Sladona* 1086 DB
> *Slapton(e)* 1244 *Ass et passim*, *Slapetone* t. Ed 1 HMC v, 599, *Slopton* 1339 Cl, *Slepton* 1534 LP
> *Slaplonde* 1270 *Ass*

'Farm by the slippery place,' *v*. slæp, tun. Slapton lies low.

SLAPTON LEY [lei]

> *Laya* 1270 *Ass*
> *le Lay* 1478, (*fishery and stank called*) 1500 Pat
> *Le Leyer* 1506, *pond called Le Leyr* 1508 Pat
> *fresh water called the Lea* 1606 Moulton
> *Le Lay al. Le Lough al. Slapton Lay* 1714 *Deed*

This is the English *lay*, 'lake, pool,' *v*. NED for its history. Slapton Ley is a large freshwater lake separated from the sea by a long pebble bar. The form *Ley(e)r* seems to be an error.

START and TORR were the homes of Mabel de *Sturte* (1333 *SR*) and Richard *atte Torre* (ib.). *v*. steort, torr.

ALSTON is *Alpiston* 1333 *SR* (p), *Albston* 1518 *SR*. Cf. Alston *supra* 225. BLACKLAND is *Blackelande* 1518 *SR*. BUCKLAND is so spelt in 1809 (M). HIGHER COLTSCOMBE is *Colliscomb* 1518 *SR*. DEER BRIDGE (6″) is *Derebrig* 1254 *Ass* (p). *v*. deor. DITTISCOMBE is *Dodescombe* 1330, *Dodiscombe* 1333 *SR* (p), *Duttyscomb* 1518 *SR*. '*Dodd*'s valley,' *v*. cumb. HANSEL is *Handsknowl* 1765 D. LOWORTHY is *Loveworthi* 1282 FF, *Loveworthe* 1333 *SR* (p), *Lyveworthy* 1407 FF. '*Lēofa*'s worþig.' MERRIFIELD is *Miriefeld* 1330 *SR* (p), *Meryfyld* 1525 *SR*. *v*. Merrivale *supra* 247. MINGOES (6″) is to be associated with the family of John and Nicholas *Mingo* (1571 *SR*). POOL is *la Pole* 1366 Exon,

Pole maner' 1370 IpmR. SLAPTON BRIDGE (6″) and SANDS are *Slapton bryge, The Long Sand of Slapton* 1514 LP. WATERGATE (6″) is *Water Gate* 1680 *Recov.*

Stoke Fleming

STOKE FLEMING 145 F 8

Stoc 1086 DB, *Stokes* 1218 FF
Stoke Flandrensis 1261 Exon, *Stokeflemeng* 1270 *Ass, Stokeflemyngg juxta Dertemuwe* 1299 *Ass*

v. stoc(c). The family of *le Flemeng* is first mentioned in connexion with the place in 1218 (FF).

EMBRIDGE (6″) is *Emerigge* 1238 *Ass* (p), *Imerigge* 1249 *Ass, -rugg'* 1330 *SR* (p), *-rigge* 1333 *SR* (p), *Ymerigge* 1311, 1322 *Ass* (p). '*Imma*'s ridge.' For the pers. name, *v.* Redin 67.

ASH is *Asshe* 1270 *Ass.* BLACKPOOL is *Blacke Powle* 1514 LP. BOWDEN is *Boweton* 1392 AD i, *Bogheton(e)* 1333 *SR* (p), 1390 HMC v, 603. 'Farm in or on the curve of land,' *v.* Bowden *supra* 37. BUGFORD is *Bugesford* t. Hy 8 *Ct.* COMBE was the home of Henry *atte Combe* 1333 *SR.* COTTON was the home of Stephen *atte Cotene* 1333 *SR.* This probably represents a ME weak plural of cot(e), cf. Cotton *infra* 415. RIVERSBRIDGE is *Ripperidge al. Rivers Bridge* 1713 *Recov.* THORN is so spelt 1809 M. VENN is *Fenne* 1386 IpmR. *v.* fenn. WHEATLAND is *Whytelond* 1333 *SR* (p). Probably 'white land.' WOODBURY FM is *Wodebury* 1333 *SR* (p). *v.* burh. There is an ancient 'camp' here. WORDEN is *Werledon* 1386 Pat. It is possible that this is for earlier *hwyrfel-dun*, 'circular hill' (cf. Hurlditch *supra* 185).

Stokenham

STOKENHAM [stoukən'hæm] 145 H 6

Stokes 1242 Fees 790, 1258 FF, *Stoke* 1291 Tax
Stok(e) in Hamme 1276 RH *et passim* to 1344 Ipm, *Stokes in Hamme* 1287 Cl, (*in the Hamme*) 1303 FA, (*in Hammes*) 1322 FF, *Stokeinhamme* 1341 Ipm, (*in Hampne*) 1359 *Ass,* (*in le Hame*) 1423 IpmR
Stokenhamton 1402 IpmR

Stawkenham 1576 *SR*
Stockenham al. Stockingham 1714 *Recov*
v. stoc(c), hamm, and South Hams *supra* 264.

CHILLINGTON is *Cedelintona, Cadelintona* 1086 DB, *Chedelington*
1238 *Ass*, 1309 Ch, *-yng-* 1310 Ipm, *Chedlyngton* 1478 BM,
Cheddelington juxta Kingesbregg 1306 *Ass*, *Chidlington al.*
Chillington 1597 *CtRequests.* 'Ceadela's farm,' *v.* ingtun.

COLERIDGE HO
   Colriga 1086 DB, *-rig* 1254 *Ass* (p), *-rigg'* 1310 Ipm, *-rugg'*
   1330 *SR* (p)
   Curigge 1244 FF, *Courigge* 1244 *Ass*
   v. Coleridge *supra* 227.

DUNSTONE is *Dunestantona* 1086 DB, *Dunstaneston* 1228 FF.
'Dūnstān's tun.'

FRITTISCOMBE is *Frettescumb* 1254 *Ass* (p), *Fridescomb* 1330 *SR*
(p), *-coumbe* t. Ric 2 *Rental, Friscombe* 1654 *FF.* The first element
is probably a pers. name *Freði* or *Friði. v.* Redin 122.

HUCKHAM is *Hoccumb, Hokcumbe* 1238 *Ass, Hocumb* 1254 *Ass*
(p), *Hoccoumbe* t. Ric 2 *Rental. v.* cumb. The first element is
probably OE hoc. Cf. Huckham *supra* 56.

KERNBOROUGH is *Kerneberg* 1254 *Ass* (p), *-borghe* t. Ric 2 *Rental.*
This name is a hybrid, the first element being the Celtic *cern*,
'side, hillside,' found according to Ekwall (NoB 16, 68) in Crew-
kerne (So). The second element is OE beorg.

MATTISCOMBE is *Matescumb* 1281 *Ass* (p), *-coumbe* t. Ric 2
Rental. The first element seems to be a pers. name *Mætti*, not on
record but apparently found in Mattishall (Nf), *Mateshala* DB.
It may be a pet-form of an OE *Mǣð*-name. Cf. Martinhoe
supra 65.

START FM and START POINT are *La Sterte* 1310 Ipm, *Stertt* 1514
LP, *a great foreland into the se caullid the Sterte* c. 1550 Leland,
Start point 1586 H. *v.* steort.

TORCROSS is *Tarcross* 1714 *Deed* and is to be associated with the
families of Walter de *la Torre* (1281 *Ass*), Adam de *la Cros* (1316

Ass) and Adam *atte Torre* (1333 *SR*). The 'tor' must have been the hill and promontory to the south of the village, but there is no cross here now, the nearest one being about one mile inland at Mattiscombe.

WIDDICOMBE HO is *Wodiacom(m)a* 1086 DB, *-combe* 1311 Exon (p), *Wydecumb'* 1242 Fees 780, *Wythecumb* 1249 *Ass* (p), *Wydecombe in Stokenham* 1443 *FF*. 'Withy valley,' *v.* wiðig, cumb. The DB and Exon forms, if they refer to this place, must be corrupt.

YARNSCOMBE (lost) is *Arnecumbe* 1204 FF, *Yernecomb* 1303 FA, *Yhernecoumb* 1306 Ipm, *Yarnescombe in Stokenham* t. Eliz ChancP. 'Eagles' valley,' cf. Yarnscombe *supra* 82.

ALLER is *Alre* t. Ric 2 *Rental*. 'At the alder,' *v.* alor. BATTON is *Bateton* 1254 *Ass* (p). '*Bata*'s farm,' *v.* PN Wo 162. BEESANDS is *Base Sande* 1514 LP. It is near Beeson. BEESON is *Bedeston* t. Ric 2 *Rental, Beaston* t. Hy 8 *Ct, Beston* 1616 Wills. Possibly '*Bæde*'s tun.' BICKERTON is *Bekerton* t. Hy 8 *Ct*. The first element may be the OE *bēocere*, 'bee-keeper.' COMBEPARK (6″) · is *Cumbe* t. Ric 2 *Rental. v.* cumb. COTMORE is *Cot(t)emor* 1254 *Ass* (p). '*Cotta*'s mor' or 'mor by the cot(e).' DARNACOMBE is *Dernecomb* 1330 *SR* (p), *-cumbe* t. Ric 2 *Rental, Durnecumbe* 1333 *SR* (p). 'Hidden valley,' *v.* dierne, cumb. DOWN FM is *South Downe* t. Hy 8 *Ct. v.* dun. HALLSANDS is *Hole Sande* 1514 LP, *Helyslands* or *Helysands* 1540 LP. HOLLOWCOMBE HEAD is *Holecombe* t. Ric 2 *Rental. v.* holh, cumb. KELLATON is *Kyleton* t. Ric 2 *Rental, Kyllaton* 1600 *SR*. '*Cylla*'s farm,' *v.* tun. LANNACOMBE BEACH is *Lanacoumbe* t. Ric 2 *Rental. v.* cumb. The first element may be OE *lana*, 'lane.' A long lane ends at the sea here. MIDDLECOMBE is *Middelcomb* t. Ric 2 *Rental.* MOLESCOMBE is *Molscoumbe* t. Ric 2 *Rental.* Perhaps '*Mol(l)*'s valley,' *v.* cumb and cf. Moulsecombe PN Sx 294. MOYSON (6″) is *Mayson* t. Ric 2 *Rental, Moysen* t. Hy 8 *Ct*. MUCKWELL is *Mokewille* t. Ric 2 *Rental*. For the first element cf. Mockham *supra* 61. RIDGE CROSS (6″), cf. *Ruggeparke* t. Hy 8 *Ct*. STOKELEY (6″) is *Stockalegh* t. Ric 2 *Rental* (p). *v.* stoc(c), leah, and Addenda *supra* liii *s.n.* Yardley. WELL (6″) was the home of John *atte Wille* (1330 *SR*). 'At the spring,' *v.* wielle. WIDEWELL is *Widewill* 1238 *Ass* (p), *Wydewell* 1298 *Ass* (p), *Wythewill* t. Ric 2 *Rental*. Probably 'withy spring,' *v.* wiðig, wielle.

Totnes

TOTNES ['tɔtnəs] 145 B 6

Totanæs 979–1016 t. Cnut Coins
(*to*) *Tottanesse* 11th Crawf
Toteneis 1086 DB, c. 1200 Lay, *-eys* 1243 FF, 1249 *Ass*, 1272 Orig, 1284 *Ass*, (*Michell*) 1432–43 ECP 1, 56, *-es*(*se*) 1167 RBE, 1187, 1230 P, 1238, 1244 *Ass*, *-as* c. 1250 Lay, c. 1300 RG, (*Parva*) 1337 *FF*, *-ays* c. 1300 RG, *Lytell Tottneis* 1364 IpmR
Tottenes(*se*) 1233 Bracton, 1286 *Ass*, (*Magna*) 1313 *Ass*, *-eys* 1275 RH, 1285 *Ass*, 1316 FA, *-ays* 1283 *Ass*, *Totnisse* 1501 Seld 16

The second element here is OE næss, referring to the prominent point of land on which the castle stands. The first element is the OE pers. name *Totta*. The OE forms and the numerous later ones with double *t* show that the first element cannot be the word found in the numerous *Tothills* or 'look-out hills.' It appears as *Totton'* in Latinised form in some ME documents.

NOTE. The HIGH STREET is mentioned in 1408 HMC iii. LEECHWELL STREET is the *Lechewelle* 1413, *Lechewille* 1449 HMC iii, perhaps 'leech spring.' WARLAND is *la Werelanda* 1251 *Deed*, *La Worlond* 1286 Exon, *La Werlonde* 1313 *Deed*. The first element may be OE wer. This land is protected by a dam across the outlet of a marshy valley (*ex inf.* Mr H. R. Watkin). Cf. Warcombe *supra* 296.

FOLLATON HO is *Foletona* 1086 DB, *-tuna* 1133–8 Totnes, *-ton* 1244 *Ass* (p). 'Foal farm,' *v.* tun.

BOWDEN HO is *Bowedon juxta Magna Tottenesse* 1313 *Ass*, *Boughedon* 1338 *FF*, *Boghedon* 1417 Exon. 'Bow-shaped hill,' *v. supra* 37. BRIDGETOWN is *Briggeton juxta Berypomeray* 1302 *Ass*, (*juxta Totenesse*) 1318 *Ass*, *Bryggeton Pomeray* 1356 *Ass*. The name would have been applied to the settlement which grew up beyond the bridge over the Dart. BROOMBOROUGH HO is *Brouneberge* n.d., *-burgh* 1414, *Bromburhe* 1276 Totnes. 'Brown hill,' *v.* beorg. GERSTON is *Grestuna* 1133–8 Totnes, *-tonam* n.d. Oliver 241, *Garston* 1535 VE. *v.* gærstun. HARPER'S HILL is *Harperyswylstrete* 1437 BM.